Sound Recording
Practice

Sound Recording Practice

Edited by
JOHN BORWICK

for the Association of
Professional Recording Services

Fourth Edition

OXFORD
UNIVERSITY PRESS

OXFORD
UNIVERSITY PRESS

Great Clarendon Street, Oxford OX2 6DP

Oxford University Press is a department of the University of Oxford.
It furthers the University's objective of excellence in research, scholarship,
and education by publishing worldwide in

Oxford New York

Athens Auckland Bangkok Bogotá Buenos Aires Calcutta
Cape Town Chennai Dar es Salaam Delhi Florence Hong Kong Istanbul
Karachi Kuala Lumpur Madrid Melbourne Mexico City Mumbai
Nairobi Paris São Paulo Singapore Taipei Tokyo Toronto Warsaw

with associated companies in Berlin Ibadan

Oxford is a registered trade mark of Oxford University Press
in the UK and in certain other countries

Published in the United States
by Oxford University Press Inc., New York

© Association of Professional Recording Services, 1994

Third Edition published 1987
Fourth Edition published 1994
New as a paperback 1996

British Library Cataloguing in Publication Data

Data available

Library of Congress Cataloging in Publication Data

Sound recording practice / edited by John Borwick for the Association
of Professional Recording Services.—4th ed.
p. cm.
Includes bibliographical references and index.
1. Sound —Recording and reproducing. 2. Sound recording industry.
3. Magnetic recorders and recording. I. Borwick, John.
II. Association of Professional Recording Services.
TK7881.4.S68   1996   621.389'32—dc20   95-50774

ISBN 0-19-816608-7

5 7 9 10 8 6 4

Printed in Great Britain
on acid-free paper by
Biddles Ltd., Guildford and King's Lynn

Contents

Foreword

It is a pleasure for me to write the foreword for this, the fourth edition of *Sound Recording Practice*. For almost two decades this handbook has uniquely defined the principles and standards of recording studio technicalities. It has remained the favourite manual of every recording industry technical library, and has justifiably become the standard by which other technical books in this field are judged.

The hastening intricacies of technological development in recent years have emphasized that such manuals can rapidly become dated and therefore fail to communicate to the reader the very latest information regarding modern equipment and practices. For this reason the Board of the APRS instructed our knowledgeable and energetic editor John Borwick to update the handbook and to include new chapters written by the most distinguished technical authors. I trust that you will agree that this task has been expertly carried out with the proper degree of hands-on knowledge and precision.

Throughout the last twenty years, the recording industry has expanded in response to the increased software market providing for the many varied new sound carriers demanded by the consumer. Recording studios have responded with improved technical facilities and quality standards, consequently providing greater flexibility to the engineer, producer, and artist. Digital techniques in particular are now rapidly changing the face of the industry. The lower costs of semi-professional equipment capable of matching the performance of high-grade studio equipment has meant that digital multitrack techniques are now readily and economically available to the home-based user. Sampled music of every kind can be used to enhance recordings and create new ones, which can be engineered virtually from the comfort of one's armchair!

The next few years will be extremely critical for the sound recording industry. Studios will need to achieve even higher standards of technical expertise and choose their equipment even more carefully than before. Wise investment and controlled costing will enable the best to progress to a more fruitful future. Poor investment and the lowering of standards may cause others to go to the wall. Investing in this book will at least ensure that the reader is well armed for the battles ahead, with an improved knowledge of the very latest recording techniques. I hope that everyone will derive maximum benefit and enjoyment from reading this book.

DAVID J HARRIES
(Director, Air Studios, Lyndhurst Hall)
Chairman, Association of Professional Recording Services

Editor's preface to the fourth edition

The previous three editions of this book appeared, respectively, in 1976, 1980, and 1987. All reflected current practices and were aimed at the same target readership—everyone interested in the latest technical and practical aspects of professional sound recording. Using a multi-author approach produces a time-scale benefit, since a score of writers working on single chapters in parallel can generate a book much faster than a single author slogging through all the chapters in series. In any case, it is doubtful whether any one 'expert' could be found with a sufficiently detailed 'hands on' knowledge of all the variegated subjects that go to make 'Sound Recording Practice'. So the overriding reason for using a group of contributors becomes clear: it has allowed me to seek out individual practitioners of the recording art for each chapter having a day-to-day involvement in the latest techniques and processes.

Only in this way could a new edition face up to the challenge of today's bewilderingly accelerated rate of change in terms of recording techniques, sophisticated computer-controlled equipment, new digital recording formats, and the proliferation of consumer audio/video media. Thus our fourth edition represents a major overhaul with such key fast-moving topics as mixing consoles, workstations, digital recorders, electronic music, post-production, broadcasting, video, and film completely rewritten. While making every effort to compile a new edition which is up to date and directly relevant to modern sound recording in all its ramifications, we have taken care to make it easy to use. The subjects are grouped in a logical sequence, with mathematics kept to a minimum, and a straightforward style of presentation which should prove accessible for newcomers, old hands, and specialists alike.

JOHN BORWICK
Haslemere, Surrey

Technical Introduction

1

The programme chain

John Borwick

The making and marketing of a successful sound recording is so much a matter of team work that it can almost be likened to a relay race. Each member of a relay team needs to have the right talents, training, and attitudes, and to be on top form on the day. He is solely responsible for his own part of the race but must work hand in hand (almost literally) with his fellow team-mates at the point of handing over the baton. In the same way, the chain of 'runners' who carry a sound recording on its way from the original conception and performance to the consumer must apply a fine balance of skills and experience whilst the recording is in their hands. But they will do a better job—particularly at the hand-over points—if they understand the role of their colleagues throughout the entire programme chain.

To take as an example the now obsolescent vinyl disc case, a disc-cutting engineer has to juggle with various physical limitations of the medium every time he cuts an LP master. This may bring in decisions affecting his choice of average cutting level, the bass roll-off, maximum treble level, and even the relative phase and crosstalk between left and right channels. When the record producer attends the disc-cutting session, these compromise decisions can be discussed and mutually arrived at to ensure that the artistic impact of the music is preserved as much as possible—provided that the producer and engineer understand each other's 'language'. More often the engineer will be working on his own, and will need to use his own judgement, based on experience of the sound quality tastes or aspirations of the given producer or the known needs of the market-place.

It will obviously help if the balance engineer at the original recording and mix-down sessions knows enough about these disc transfer restrictions to anticipate—and avoid—serious problems. He will need to adhere to standard peak levels on the session and master tapes, avoid high amplitudes at extreme bass frequencies, and minimize out-of-phase components.

The stages in record manufacture

Keeping to essentials, let us trace the typical sequence of stages in manufacture of the various disc and tape consumer 'music carriers'. This will introduce the kinds of decisions and skills needed at each stage, though of course a fuller coverage will be found in the relevant specialist chapters which follow.

At the time of writing, the vinyl disc has lost pride of place to the rival analogue tape cassette and the compact disc, not to mention the more recent DCC and MiniDisc formats. Nevertheless it will be convenient, after outlining the stages in manufacture common to all these media, to discuss the differences which apply to vinyl disc, cassette, and CD in that order. Figures 1.1 and 1.2 show the usual sequence of stages.

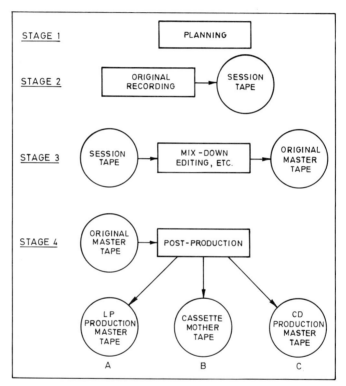

Fig. 1.1. Programme chain: stages 1–4

Stage 1: Planning

While mercenary considerations may be forgotten during the excitement of the music-making and recording sessions, it remains of first importance to recognize that recordings must ultimately make money. The planning stage must therefore work towards this goal and include a close study of all the commercial aspects. The existing recorded repertoire must be surveyed

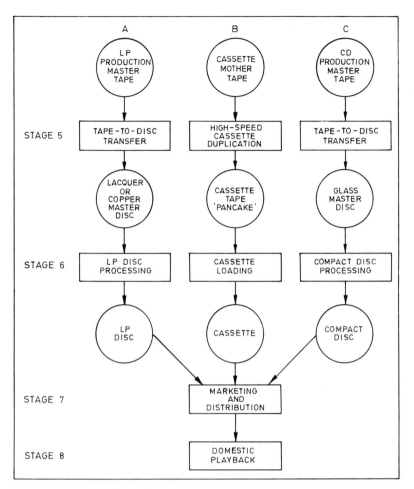

Fig. 1.2. Programme chain: stages 5–8

before any given work is scheduled for recording. However popular the composition is felt to be, its marketability must be coldly assessed in terms of the current record-buying climate, the suitability of the artists available, and even the image of the particular label. Only when a reasonable guarantee of sufficient sales appears likely to make the venture worthwhile can the questions of dates, recording venue, contracts, and detailed costing be considered.

Stage 2: Original recording

As the musicians perform, the acoustic energy radiated by their instruments or voices, modified to some extent by the acoustic characteristics of the hall or studio, is converted into electrical energy by the microphone(s). This electrical signal is then amplified, mixed, and corrected as necessary at the control console. Then, either in analogue form or after conversion to digital encoding, it is passed to the sound recorder (usually a tape machine). Here the electrical energy is converted into magnetic energy for storage and subsequent playback. The usual procedure is to record all takes and retakes (including any multitrack overdubs) so that this Session Tape contains all the programme material, leaving the choice of best takes until later.

Already a number of variations to this basic scheme should be noted. For example, analogue recorders are rapidly being replaced by digital ones with a resulting change in some of the detailed procedures. The former records a magnetic signal which is a close copy (or 'analogue') of the electrical signal waveform leaving the microphone. The latter first converts the electrical waveform into a series of on/off pulses and records these on to the tape. The relative advantages and disadvantages of analogue and digital are discussed in some detail in the Equipment section, as is the possible replacement of magnetic tape by optical disc as a mastering medium.

The best layout of the musicians in the studio calls for a good knowledge of the directional characteristics of each instrument, so that the sometimes conflicting needs of the performers and the microphones can be met. The recording venue will presumably have been chosen because it has sympathetic acoustics. Even so, the amount of reverberation and its tonal quality (all reflecting and absorbing surfaces have an effect on the balance of frequencies in the sound) will need close study. Considerations of extraneous noise may also inhibit the freedom of choice in positioning of microphones.

The choice of microphone types, and their placement, subsequent mixing, frequency correction, and so on, involve techniques which vary considerably with each engineer's creative approach. Some guidelines are given in the Recording Techniques section, though there are so many variable quantities that microphone balance remains more of an art than a science. Control of the dynamic range, proper alignment of the tape machines, and even careful handling of the tapes are all matters which need scrupulous attention if the Session Tape is to maintain optimum quality.

Stage 3: Editing, mix-down, etc.

A perfectly recorded take of a complete musical work is most unusual. Generally the best passages from several takes will be selected and edited together to form the Original Master. Also, particularly in pop recording, the Master may have been built up from several synchronized takes on multitrack tapes and will need to be mixed down or 'reduced' to a two-track version for production purposes.

Whilst most of the value judgements at this stage remain artistic ones, they depend for their realization on expert knowledge of the particular equipment and technical facilities available. The mere act of copying from the Session Tape to an Original Master tape (in the general case where the Session Tape, suitably edited, cannot go forward to production) creates a 'second-generation' recording. Certainly in the case of analogue tapes, the signal-to-noise ratio will have been degraded, though noise reduction systems such as Dolby have done much to remove this potential source of increased noise. On the other hand, copies made in the digital domain largely avoid the problem and provide copies which are to all intents and purposes identical to the original.

It is important for the engineer making the Original Master to strive for optimum sound quality, and minimum noise, at this stage since the recording is now at its peak and all subsequent processes must be expected to downgrade the quality to some degree. Proper regard for the question of phase really begins at the studio session and there is a strong argument against multi-microphone and wide-spaced microphone techniques. The exceptionally clean quality of sound sometimes heard on one-microphone tracks in pop recordings (and coincident-pair stereo recordings) is often remarked upon and can be attributed to the absence of spurious phase effects. Even the restrictions imposed by typical consumer playback equipment should be borne in mind, perhaps by listening to smaller 'nearfield' loudspeakers as an alternative to the full-size studio monitors. If some important ingredient in the musical sounds is missing on the small speakers, perhaps when listening at a reduced level, then correcting action might be advisable.

Stage 4: Post-production

In recent years, refinements in studio equipment and indeed in the results obtainable with advanced multitrack and digital techniques have led to a growth in post-production activities. Original Master tapes are now seen to be capable of further refining or sweetening to optimize the sound quality on the Production Master. In addition, the existence in the market-place of competing consumer formats has made it necessary to provide separate Production Masters for CD, cassette, etc., differing slightly in technical terms and also sometimes in the order and number of musical items or 'tracks' within a given album. The major recording companies can usually accommodate this post-production stage within their own studio complexes, but smaller companies tend to take their Original Master tapes along to a specialist post-production facility, where all the necessary final tweaking and assembly work can be undertaken (as described in Chapter 20) to produce a final Production Master tailored specifically for transfer to LP, CD, cassette, etc.

Vinyl disc manufacture

Stage 5A: Tape-to-disc transfer

For the disc-cutting stage, the Production Master will hopefully have been optimized in terms of side lengths, dynamics, frequency, and phase response, but the cutting engineer will normally play the tape right through and adjust the electronics of his cutting lathe to achieve the best cut he can. Then he will play the tape while the cutter head stylus etches an equivalent (analogue) waveform into the groove on a master disc. This disc is usually called a 'lacquer', since the blank normally consists of a lacquer coating on an aluminium base (the term 'acetate' is occasionally used in error as a hangover from older types of disc coating). There is nowadays another type of blank, having a copper surface for use in the DMM (Direct Metal Mastering) technique, as described in Chapters 21 and 22.

Both types of blank disc require great care in regard to depth and level of cut. Limiting or compression may be necessary, despite attention to this factor at the studio, and such techniques as varigroove will be used to ensure the best compromise between recorded level and maximum duration per side.

Stage 6A: Vinyl disc processing

The lacquer disc is first sprayed with silver, to make it electrically conducting, and then put through a series of electroforming processes to produce successive metal-plated parts as follows:

(a) the Master (a negative, i.e. with ridges in place of grooves);
(b) the Mother (a positive);
(c) the Stamper (a negative) which is the moulding tool to be used in pressing out records from thermoplastic vinyl.

A pair of these metal stampers, one for each side of the record, is placed into the plattens or jaws of an automatic press which, on closing, will mould a 'biscuit' of warmed vinyl material into the final disc, or 'pressing' as it is generally called in the trade. The pressing cycle takes about 20 seconds, though faster processing can be achieved in an alternative injection moulding process commonly used to produce the smaller 175-mm 'single'. Cleanliness is obviously important throughout a pressing plant, as well as a vigilant programme of quality control checks to discover stamper wear or other blemishes before a large number of wasted pressings is produced.

Pre-recorded cassette manufacture

The above sequence has charted the stages in the manufacture of vinyl discs. When it comes to the mass production of pre-recorded cassettes ('musicassettes'), stages 1–4 are broadly the same, but different procedures are followed at stages 5B and 6B, as indicated in the B sequence in Figure 1.2 and described in detail in Chapter 23.

Stage 5B: High-speed cassette duplication

The Production Master supplied from Stage 4 to a tape-duplicating plant differs in several important ways from the straight version supplied to a disc-cutting room for Stage 5A.

It may be described as an Interim Master or Mother tape, and will have been specially equalized if necessary to accommodate the technical limits of the cassette medium, Dolby B encoded, and so on. More particularly, it will consist of a tape suitable for running on a high-speed 'sender' playback machine (at typically 64 times normal speed). On receipt it will be formed into an endless loop and put into a 'loop bin' to be replayed over and over again non-stop. It therefore carries the two pairs of left/right tracks which form sides one and two of the final cassette (one pair recorded in the reverse direction).

The signals from the sender are relayed to a number of slave recorders loaded with large spools or 'pancakes' of cassette tape, enough to record about twenty complete programmes separated by a special low-frequency cue tone. Digital Compact Cassettes (DCC) are duplicated in much the same way, but the tape sender is generally replaced by a digital solid state memory store or 'bin'.

Stage 6B: Cassette loading

The recorded tape pancakes are removed from the slaves and placed on machines known as 'loaders'. These are fully automatic, and continuously splice and spool tape into empty cassette housings called 'C-zeroes'. A sensor identifies the cue tone, stops the tape, and splices it on to the start leader tape before ejecting the loaded cassette. Labelling and packaging processes then follow.

Compact disc manufacture

Since the end of 1982, the record companies have had a third, increasingly popular, 'music carrier' to manufacture—the compact disc. This is potentially a high-quality and low-noise medium, and the Production Master tape generated at Stage 4 should be even more carefully produced for CD than for LP and cassette. It is of course a digital tape (or more recently a digital disc) containing numerous code signals as well as the digital music tracks (see Chapters 20 and 24). The consumer's CD player will scan all this information and display or act upon it as commanded.

Stage 5C: Tape-to-CD master disc transfer

The signals from the digital production master are fed to a special machine which converts the encoding format to the CD standards and passes the resulting train of pulses to a source of laser light. The laser beam is focused on to a precision glass disc coated with a light-sensitive material. The spiralling track (starting at the inner radius rather than the outer edge as on a vinyl disc) therefore consists of an interrupted series of extremely brief exposures to the light, and the disc can be 'developed' in a process similar to that used in ordinary photography. The exposed areas are left as tiny pits in the light-sensitive coating.

Stage 6C: Compact disc processing

In a sequence which bears a superficial resemblance to that used for vinyl discs, the glass disc is vacuum coated with silver or nickel to make it electrically conducting. Several electroforming processes follow, as with vinyl, to produce:

(*a*) the Master (a negative, i.e. with bumps in place of pits);
(*b*) the Mother (a positive);
(*c*) . the Stamper (a negative).

Each stamper can be used to press out several thousand (one-sided) compact discs.

The resulting disc or 'pressing' of clear polycarbonate is still a long way from being a playable object (unlike a vinyl pressing). First the pitted surface has to be overlayed with a very thin reflective layer of aluminium, which will be scanned by the laser beam on a CD player to reproduce the pulse stream by on/off reflection on to a light-sensitive detector. This coating is followed by a further coating process (still under the strictest clean-air conditions) in which a protective layer of clear lacquer is spread over the aluminium surface as a seal against damage or dust. The CD is then suitably labelled, passed through quality control, and packaged. MiniDiscs are processed in much the same way, as are CD-I (CD-Interative), and the various sorts of video disc.

From manufacturer to consumer

Stage 7: Marketing and distribution

Assuming that all the planning details were carried out as described under Stage 1, the record company can now follow this up by proper attention to packaging the product (sleeve design, sleeve-note writing, booklet printing), marketing, distribution, and promotion. Suitable advertising will be necessary, and advance copy discs or cassettes made available to reviewers and broadcasting organizations. Only in this way will a sufficient number of potential customers be alerted to the special attractions of this particular recording—and be persuaded to buy it.

Stage 8: Domestic playback

In the purchaser's home, the record player or hi-fi system reconverts the recorded signals into acoustic energy via the loudspeakers. The sound waves will again be modified by the acoustic properties of the living-room, and there will be other restrictions because of the generally lower listening level, higher ambient noise level, and other domestic circumstances and distractions.

These factors should ideally have been allowed for at all earlier stages in the chain. For example, a slightly drier acoustic than the norm for a particular type of music may be aimed at to allow for the small amount of reverberation added by the listening-room. The full dynamic range of which the studio equipment may be capable will sometimes be compressed deliberately in acknowledgement of the narrower range usually found acceptable in most domestic situations or reproducible on much domestic (or portable) equipment. In fact, the introduction of CD players has provided consumers with a wider dynamic range source than either LPs or analogue cassettes, but the restrictions in terms of domestic ambient noise levels and maximum acceptable loudness still set a limit to what many home listeners would consider ideal.

No operating skills can be assumed on the part of the home user. Equipment and records must therefore be designed to be as foolproof as possible, and, where special instructions are needed, the record companies have a duty to educate users through dealer literature, sleeve notes, leaflets, etc. Even so, the quality of reproduction will vary from poor (with the simplest players) to remarkably good (with a top-flight hi-fi set-up). In the latter case, the domestic listener can indeed enjoy the full impact supplied by today's advanced recording techniques.

What about video?

Rapid advances in the media of television and audio/video have made it impossible for recording studios to plan for sound-only productions without some reference to the parallel video markets. The pop video has become a powerful (and relatively expensive) method of audio disc promotion. Most broadcast companies invest more money, and employ more personnel, in TV than in sound radio. The record companies are having to plan for increased production of video tape albums, not to mention LaserDisc, CD-I, and other videodisc formats.

These trends are likely to accelerate as more and better domestic formats appear in people's homes, and as satellite and cable systems increase the consumer's access to improved-quality entertainment media of all kinds. The Audio Engineering Society, formerly a basically sound-only institution, has added audio/video topics to most of its convention programmes. Figure 1.3 shows, for example, the audio/video chain which it used to schedule the sessions at its May 1986 conference on 'Stereo Audio Technology for Television and Video'. A comparison between this chain and Figures 1.1 and 1.2 is instructive, and explains the many references to video throughout this book—not least in Chapters 26 (television), 27 (video), and 28 (film). The parallel expansion of multimedia formats such as CD-I and computer games was reflected in the 1993 AES Convention in New York, where the theme was 'Audio in the Age of Multimedia'.

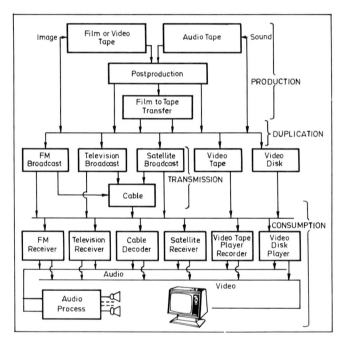

Fig. 1.3. Programme chain for television and video media (courtesy AES)

2   Basic electronics and acoustics

Allen Mornington-West

This chapter attempts to summarize some of the electrical and acoustical terms commonly found in the audio industry. There is not the space to cover any one item in depth, though there should be no great inaccuracy as a consequence.

Units

The basic units and symbols which make up the SI system of units (Système International d'Unités) are given in Appendix 1. The names of the units have often been derived from the names of past scientists and are in internationally agreed use. The wide range of values which these units may have requires an efficient scheme of notation. For example, the range of sound pressure levels (SPL) to which the human ear is sensitive extends to more than one million to one—from the threshold of hearing to the threshold of pain. Although the SPL at the threshold of hearing could be written as 0.000020 Pa, it is more usually written as 20 μ Pa. The μ stands for 'micro' and is a shorthand way of expressing the ratio of a millionth. The range of common multipliers is also given in Appendix 1. It can be seen that they rise in a ratio of a thousand to one.

Voltage, current, resistance, and power

Voltage is an electrical pressure in some ways analogous to the pressure of water, for example in a central heating system. Electrical current is thus analogous to the flow of water in such a system. The flow of electrical current is considered, by convention, to be from a positive voltage to a less positive one. In reality, the current in metal conductors is essentially the flow of small subatomic particles known as electrons. As these particles carry a negative charge, they will be attracted towards the more positive voltage, and thus move in a direction opposite to that in which the current is considered to flow.

Some circuit elements offer a high resistance to the flow of current (rather analogous to the use of thin pipes in a central heating system), whilst other elements will offer very little resistance. Some materials, for example most plastics, have such a high resistance to electrical current that they are referred to as insulators; this can be compared to the way that the pipes make sure that the water stays within them. Examples of good conductors (offering very low resistance) are most metals, the commonest being copper, the best being silver. In between these and the insulators are the materials such as carbon film, various metal oxides, semiconductors, and alloys of some metals (for example, nickel and chrome are used to produce nichrome resistance wire) which can be used to form resistors of a known value. Each of these materials has a range of properties (for example stability with respect to temperature, cost of manufacture, range of practical values) which affect their choice in a given application.

Ohm's Law, resistors in series and parallel

The relationship between voltage, current, and resistance is expressed by Ohm's Law:

$$V = I \times R$$

where V is the voltage (in volts) across the resistance R (in ohms) through which flows the current of I (amperes).

When resistors are placed in series in a circuit, that is to say the same current flows through each resistor (see Figure 2.1a), the total effective resistance is given by adding their resistances together. In the case of resistors in parallel, that is where the current is shared between the resistors (see Figure 2.1b), the effective resistance is given by taking the reciprocal of the sum of their conductances. Conductance (measured in siemens, symbol S) is simply the reciprocal of resistance and is the measure of how easily current flows. The proof of these relationships can be obtained through the use of Ohm's Law, bearing in mind that in the case of series resistors the current flowing through each resistor is the same and in the case of parallel resistors the voltage across each resistor is the same.

As real conductors also exhibit some resistance, albeit small, it follows that the gauge of wire used for any particular purpose needs to be chosen with the current-carrying requirements borne in mind. Doubling the diameter of a conductor divides its resistance by a factor of four, and, for a given current, the voltage across a given length of conductor will fall by the same factor. The amount of resistance offered by different conductors is determined by their specific resistivity.

The resistance of real conductors (and resistors) is dependent additionally on temperature. For elemental metals the rise in resistance with temperature is, to a first approximation, linear: around 4000 parts per million per degree Celsius for copper, for example. Light bulbs, which generally use

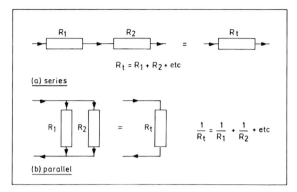

Fig. 2.1. Resistors (*a*) in series, (*b*) in parallel

tungsten filaments, typically exhibit a cold resistance which is one-tenth of the resistance when fully working. Carbon, which is used in many resistor compositions, exhibits a falling resistance with a rise in temperature, typically 300 parts per million, but the value does depend on the process used to form the resistor.

Effects of electric current

There are two effects associated with the flow of electric current which should be noted here. The first is the *heating effect*, and the second is the formation of a *magnetic field*. The heat or power, P, developed in a resistive load of R ohms having a voltage of V volts across it causing a current of I amps to flow is

$$P = V \times I \text{ watts}$$

Using Ohm's Law, this can also be written as

$$P = V^2/R \text{ or } P = I^2 \times R$$

Heat is power, and is the measure of the rate of energy flow measured in joules/second. One joule will heat 0.24 g of water through 1° C. Note further that the power dissipated is independent of the direction of the current through the resistor.

The magnetic field which surrounds any conductor carrying current is used, for example, in moving coil meters where a lightweight coil is suspended in the fixed magnetic field produced from a permanent magnet. The strength of the magnetic field produced by the current flowing in the coil is dependent on the square of the number of turns of wire in the coil and linearly on the amount of current being passed through the coil. Most of the electromechanical meters use this magnetic effect of current. Therefore, when measuring the voltage in a circuit, the meter uses some of the current available from the circuit and thereby affects the reading. Similarly, using the meter to measure current involves a small voltage drop across the coil of the meter itself, and this too can affect the circuit. These are examples of loading effects. The ideal voltage meter would use negligible current for operation and the ideal current meter would cause a negligible voltage drop. If the meter is isolated from the circuit by appropriate buffering, then these ideals can be approached. If the voltage and current in a resistor can be measured, then the value of the resistance can be calculated from Ohm's Law.

Resistor marking

Modern resistors vary greatly in size and shape. Power resistors will usually be sized and constructed such that the heat can be safely dissipated. Nearly all miniature assemblies dissipate low power and it is consequently possible to use miniature resistors. These are normally mounted directly to the surface of the printed circuit substrate. The values of these are sometimes alphanumerically coded on the body and can be read with the aid of an eyeglass. Traditionally sized resistors, rated below say 330 mW, usually have their resistance value and manufacturing accuracy tolerance marked on them using a code of coloured bands (see Figure 2.2). Power and high-tolerance resistors usually have the value printed in numbers directly on the resistor. The colour code used is: 0 black, 1 brown, 2 red, 3 orange, 4 yellow, 5 green, 6 blue, 7 violet, 8 grey, 9 white.

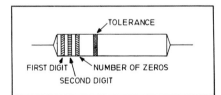

Fig. 2.2. Resistor colour codes

Practical power sources and loading

The currents which have been produced by the voltages referred to so far have been assumed to be unchanging with time. They are referred to as direct current (d.c.). A practical example of such a source of voltage is a battery. However, the battery cannot be taken as a model of a pure voltage generator. A simple model of a battery (see Figure 2.3) must include a small resistance (known as the battery's source resistance) in series with an ideal voltage source whose e.m.f. (electromotive force) is the voltage which

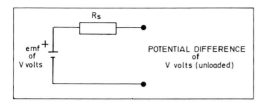

Fig. 2.3. Practical voltage source in which R_S is the source resistance

would be measured by a meter which took no current from the battery during the measurement. The power which this battery can deliver into an external load is a maximum when the value of this load is equal to the source resistance. Half the available power is then dissipated in the external load and the other half heats up the battery. This is not the way that batteries or other power sources are usually operated but the principle is at the heart of what is referred to as impedance-matching.

Alternating currents and voltages

Audio signals consist of voltages and currents which vary with time. The patterns of this variation (alternating currents or a.c.), if plotted against time, would provide a wide variety of waveshapes. Fortunately all waveshapes, however complex, can be considered as built out of sine waves (through the use of the Fourier series). Sine waves are easy to generate and are mathematically simple, and so it is sufficient to describe the response of a circuit to alternating currents by their use. The rate at which a sine waveshape repeats itself is known as its frequency (in cycles per second or Hertz) and the time taken for one complete cycle is its period. Period is simply the reciprocal of frequency.

When an alternating voltage is applied to a resistor, the magnitude of the alternating current can be found using Ohm's Law. Similarly, the rules describing the series and parallel connection of resistors remain valid. In order that the power dissipated in a resistive load by an alternating current can be related to the same power developed by a d.c. source, the root-mean-square (r.m.s.) value is used. The r.m.s. value of a continuous sine wave is the square root of its peak value. Thus the r.m.s. value of a sine wave with a 2 V peak value is $\sqrt{2} = 1.414$ V.

An alternating voltage will not register a sensible reading on the usual electromechanical moving-coil meter, as the meter needle will simply twitch around the zero mark. Meters for direct indication of a.c. voltages do exist, such as moving-iron and thermocouple types. The method most often used involves converting the a.c. voltage into a d.c. one, through the use of a rectifier, and applying it to a conventional d.c. meter (see Figure 2.4). If this is all that is done, the meter indication will be that of the average value of the rectified signal and not the r.m.s. value. Most general-purpose meters

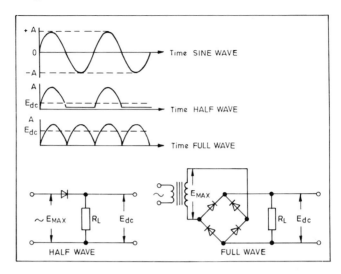

Fig. 2.4. Waveforms and circuit diagrams for half-wave and full-wave rectification of a sine wave

follow this principle and are usually calibrated to read the correct r.m.s. value for a sinusoid whilst responding to its average. For complex waveforms, quite severe errors can arise. Audio signals can be appreciably non-sinusoidal and may have crest factors of up to 10 : 1 (the crest factor is the ratio between the peak value of a signal and its average value). Figure 2.5 shows the relationship between the peak, r.m.s., and average values for a 10 : 1 square wave. The two commonest signal level meters used in audio, namely the volume unit (VU) meter and the peak programme meter (PPM), indicate approximately the average and the peak values of the audio signal respectively.

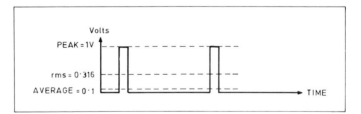

Fig. 2.5. Relationship between peak, r.m.s., and average values for a 10 : 1 square wave

Reactive components, capacitance, and inductance

Both capacitors and inductors can store energy and subsequently release it, capacitance as stress in a dielectric medium and inductance as flux in a permeable medium. At its simplest, a capacitor blocks d.c. whilst an inductor blocks a.c. Each will exhibit an impedance to electrical flow which depends on the frequency of the a.c. voltage applied and on the value of capacitance or inductance.

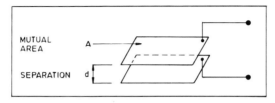

Fig. 2.6. Construction of an elementary capacitor: C is proportional to A/d

A simple capacitor can be thought of as two plates separated by a short distance (see Figure 2.6). The capacitance is dependent on the material between the plates, their area, and their separation. If a source of d.c. is connected to a capacitor value C via a resistor of value R, and the voltage across the capacitor is monitored, it will follow the form shown in Figure 2.7. The waveform of the current flow is the opposite. The current and voltage waveforms are thus not in step and the current is said to *lead* the voltage.

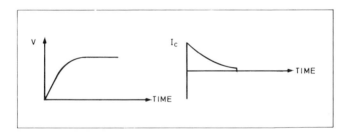

Fig. 2.7. Charging and discharging a capacitor

A similar state of affairs exists for inductors, and the waveform of the growth of current is similar to that for the growth of voltage in the case of capacitance. For an inductance the current *lags* the voltage (see Figure 2.8). A simple inductor can be considered as a coil of wire. The value of inductance is dependent on the square of the number of turns and the size of the coil. The changing magnetic flux caused by a changing current flowing through the coil creates a back e.m.f. in the coil. In a transformer a second coil shares this magnetic flux and thus develops an e.m.f. across its terminals. The magnitude of this secondary e.m.f. depends on the amount of the flux which is shared (the mutual inductance) and the ratio of the turns in the primary and secondary coils.

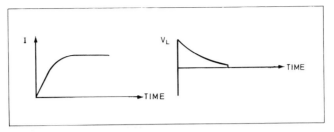

Fig. 2.8. Charging and discharging an inductor

Because the current and voltage waveforms of reactive components are not in phase, care is needed when working out their effective contribution to impedance in circuits. The contribution from a purely reactive element is known as reactance and is given the symbol X. The reactances, in ohms, of a capacitor and an inductor are:

$$X_C = \frac{1}{2\pi f C} \text{ for capacitance and } X_L = 2\pi f L \text{ for inductance.}$$

The expression $2\pi f$, where f is the frequency in Hertz, is commonly replaced by ω (Greek omega).

In the case of a resistor and capacitor in series, it is clear that the same current must flow through both and that it must be in the same phase as the current going through the generator (see Figure 2.9). Therefore, in order that it is 90° ahead of the voltage across it, this voltage must lag that of the generator.

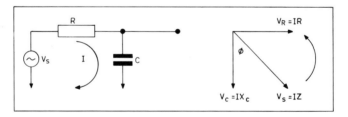

Fig. 2.9. Resistance and capacitance in series

The analysis of an inductance in series with a resistance is similar except that here, as the current in an inductor lags the voltage, and in order that the current through the resistor and the inductor should share the same phase it is necessary for the voltage across the inductor to lead the generator voltage.

Capacitances and inductances in series and parallel

The effect of joining capacitors in parallel is that of increasing the area of the capacitor plates. Thus

$$C_t = C_1 + C_2 + \text{etc.}$$

The net capacitance obtained by joining them in series is

$$\frac{1}{C_t} = \frac{1}{C_1} + \frac{1}{C_2} + \text{etc.}$$

and this can be appreciated by adding together their reactances in the same manner as performed for resistors in parallel. The total inductance obtained when inductors are placed in series is simply their sum:

$$L_t = L_1 + L_2 + \text{etc.}$$

and, in a similar fashion to resistors, the effective total inductance of a parallel connection is given by

$$\frac{1}{L_t} = \frac{1}{L_1} + \frac{1}{L_2} + \text{etc.}$$

When an inductance and a capacitance are placed in series or parallel, they form what is known as a tuned circuit (see Figure 2.10). The resonant frequency is the one where the reactances of the inductance and the capacitance are the same. It is given by

$$f = \frac{1}{2\pi\sqrt{LC}}$$

In the case of a series tuned circuit, the effective impedance at resonance tends to zero, and is limited only by the inevitable resistance involved in the windings of the inductance. A parallel tuned circuit has maximum impedance at resonance. The bandwidth of a tuned circuit is the difference between the upper and lower frequencies at which the peak or dip in the response has varied by 3 dB. The Q factor is approximately given by the value of the centre frequency divided by the 3 dB bandwidth. This should be numerically similar to the ratio between the inductor reactance at centre frequency divided by the sum of any resistance in the tuned circuit. Historically such tuned circuits offered the only way in which analogue equalizers could be designed, though today it is usually more effective to employ active circuit designs to achieve the same responses since this also offers an improvement in overall performance. There are good reasons for retaining so-called LC tuned circuits in some modern audio designs, particularly in passive crossover filters for loudspeakers.

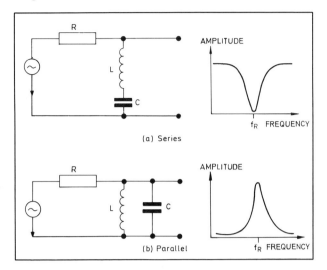

Fig. 2.10. Tuned circuits: (*a*) series, (*b*) parallel

Real components

All real components are in a sense impure. For example, a resistor can be better modelled as an ideal resistor in series with a small amount of inductance (due to the lead-out wires and the usually spiral shape of the resistance element itself), possibly shunted by (that is to say paralleled by) a small amount of stray capacitance. Real inductors are invariably accompanied by some resistance (due to the windings themselves) and by some self-capacitance; real capacitors may well be accompanied by a small amount of stray inductance, due mostly to the manner of manufacture. Just how important these stray effects will be depends on the frequency and accuracy at which the components are being used. Even a straight piece of wire has inductance and capacitance.

In addition, there will be other limitations placed on performance which reflect the materials and manufacturing methods used. Resistors come in a range of sizes and in a range of styles which fundamentally reflect their power-handling ability. Resistors can be considered, within their working range, as behaving linearly, and would seldom be suspected of being the cause of stray magnetic fields or of large amounts of distortion within, say, an amplifier.

Inductors intended to work at low signal powers in the audio band of frequencies (roughly from 20 Hz to 20 kHz) will use high-permeability core materials, such as ferrites and alloys of ferromagnetic metals, whose limit in terms of linear behaviour determines the maximum flux level which can exist in the core. The limit on the amount of power they can handle is in part controlled by the size of the core and the windings around it. A compromise is usually struck between weight and performance. In addition, audio-frequency inductors tend to be sensitive to stray magnetic fields, especially hum fields from mains power transformers. Inductors in passive crossover filters for loudspeakers will often be air cored.

There is a wide variety of materials and techniques used in capacitor manufacture. The maximum working voltage limit of capacitors is set by the ability of the dielectric to withstand the strain (dielectric strength). The dielectric is needed in order to multiply the 'open-air' value of capacitance, but dielectrics can be non-linear in a number of ways. The dielectric constant itself may be a function of the amount of electric stress in the capacitor, which usually varies with frequency. A dielectric material also tends to exhibit losses as the frequency is raised, thus causing the capacitor to increase its effective impedance. Finally, especially in both aluminium and tantalum electrolytic capacitors, the chemical processes employed during manufacture and the physics of the dielectric material itself (usually a metal oxide) can produce very small non-linear effects.

It is worth pointing out that a variety of effects can mar even the production of a satisfactory contact in a connector. Corrosion is the commonest cause of problems, and, although gold itself may be immune from attack by cigarette tar and spilt drinks, the congealed deposition certainly does not aid the process of creating proper electrical contact.

Logs and the decibel

It was pointed out above that the wide range of values which natural signals can take makes the use of a form of compressed notation desirable. A useful method of expressing powers is by the use of logarithms. The logarithm a of a positive real number x, with respect to a base b, can be expressed as $x = b^a$. The commonly used base is ten. The logarithm (abbreviated to log) of 1,000, for example, is 3. Adding logs is identical to multiplying together the two numbers which they represent (it is the principle behind the almost historic slide-rule), and subtracting logs is the same as division. As a negative logarithm represents a number less than one, and a positive logarithm a number greater than one, it can be seen that the log of one is zero, or, in other words, ten to the power of zero is one. Actually, any positive real number raised to the zeroth power is one.

The bel is a unit which expresses the ratio of two powers as a log (the base is assumed to be ten):

$$\text{Bel} = \log \frac{P_2}{P_1}$$

The bel turns out to be too large a unit in practice and so the decibel (dB) is defined as

$$dB = 10 \times \log\left(\frac{P_2}{P_1}\right)$$

Since the power delivered to a load can be expressed as $P = V^2/R$, then provided that the load (or source) resistances are identical the dB can be defined as

$$dB = 20 \times \log\left(\frac{V_2}{V_1}\right)$$

It is fundamentally an expression of the ratio of two power levels. In those environments where both the source and destination impedances are fixed at 600 ohms, the dB will still relate directly to a power ratio. However, since most measurements are performed on equipment and circuits whose output impedance is usually low (less than 100 ohms) and whose input impedance is reasonably high (greater than 10 k-ohms), and as (in addition to the difficulty of measuring power directly) the logarithmic scale is such a useful idea, it is usual within the audio industry to ignore this fact and to use the dB as an expression of voltage ratio. Thus a voltage ratio of $2:1$ would be expressed as 6 dB, and so on. Table 2.1 shows how the first $\pm$ 10 dB relate to ratios. The dB always relates to ratios, and thus if we wish to use decibels to refer to an actual signal level we must agree upon a reference level. The level which is in common use in the audio industry relates to the voltage necessary to develop one milliwatt in a 600 ohm load (the unit is then referred to as dBm). This is 0.7746 volts, and the symbol dBu

Table 2.1. Voltage ratios and the first ±10 dB

+dB	Gain ratio	−dB	Loss ratio
0	1.00	0	1.00
1	1.12	−1	0.89
2	1.26	−2	0.79
3	1.41	−3	0.71
4	1.58	−4	0.63
5	1.78	−5	0.56
6	2.00	−6	0.50
7	2.24	−7	0.45
8	2.51	−8	0.40
9	2.83	−9	0.36
10	3.16	−10	0.32

marks its use as a reference. It is worth commenting that other sections of the electronics industry use other references.

Gain (positive dB values) and attenuation (negative dB values) can now be expressed in decibels, and simple attenuating networks can be designed (see Figure 2.11). The simple resistor and reactance networks referred to above are examples of frequency-sensitive attenuators, and it is useful to bear in mind that, at the frequency at which the reactance is equal to the resistance, the attenuation is 3 dB with respect to the input signal and the phase shift is 45°. These frequency-sensitive attenuators are better known as filters. High-pass filters block low frequencies whilst low-pass filters block high frequencies. Band-pass and band-stop filters can be simply realized by using resonant circuits.

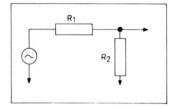

Fig. 2.11. A simple attenuator

It is important to realize that phase is related to the period of the signal and not directly to time. It is thus meaningless, for example, to consider that playing back a 1 kHz tone from a tape recorder one hour later is equivalent to 3.6 million degrees of phase shift! It, and the rest of the audio bandwidth of signals recorded at the same time, have simply been delayed. What might well be audible is the existence of any frequency-dependent non-uniformity in the delay (essentially this is group delay error, which does occur in analogue recordings). However, this error is sometimes expressed in phase terms when the response of complex filters is under discussion. The term 'linear phase response' implies that there is no group delay error within the system being discussed. The term 'minimum phase' refers to the performance of a system in which the phase change of each element is as small as possible. It is thus not the same as linear phase. It is possible to design audio filters which will achieve identical amplitude performance in either linear phase or minimum phase forms, the difference being the excess phase.

More about the transformer

A transformer cannot produce power gain; it merely handles the power available from the source connected to its input (usually referred to as the primary winding) and makes this available to a load connected to its output (the secondary winding). The ratio between the input and output voltages is dependent on the ratio of the turns, so a transformer with a turns ratio of, say, $N:1$ will produce an output voltage which is $1/N$ of the input. It will also reflect the impedance of the load on the secondary back to the primary so that, as far as the source signal is concerned, it sees a load whose value is N^2 times that of the secondary load. This is the property which is used in designing matching transformers, the aim being to make an input or an output impedance appear as a different value to some subsequent circuit or equipment. Any loss (or gain) in signal level can be corrected with an appropriate amplifier (or attenuator).

Transformers offer two other properties. The first is that of isolating the sending circuit from the receiving circuit (sometimes referred to as galvanic isolation). As the transformer primary and secondary circuits are insulated from each other, there is no direct connection between the two; thus there are no parts of the circuits which are common or shared. Most audio signals are referenced to a circuit's zero-volt rail (or its system ground), which is often, in turn, tied to mains earth. Equipments which share the same earth (or zero volt reference) should ideally be located close to each other.

The second property of a transformer is linked with the practice of balanced lines, and is its ability to reject common-mode signals (usually referred to as common-mode rejection ratio, CMRR). The two secondary output terminals can be thought of as providing a signal which is balanced about a centre point. This is sometimes an actual centre tap in the secondary of the transformer, as in a phantom microphone supply transformer, but commonly it is absent and the output signal from the transformer is considered as balanced and floating (floating because there is no connection from the centre tap to either send or receive zero reference). The advantage of operating a sound circuit in a balanced fashion, as distinct from a single-ended fashion (or unbalanced mode), is the much increased freedom from picking up unwanted electromagnetic interference due to stray signals coupling into the cable. This arises because, as any e.m.f. induced into the cable will be induced in the same polarity and magnitude into both of the cable's conductors, there will be no net resulting current in the circuit and thus no signal to be received at the secondary terminals of the receiving transformer. This rejection is not perfect, and it usually worsens with increasing frequency, partly because of capacitance effects within the transformer.

When designing and choosing transformers, it is necessary to bear in mind that the windings have resistance. The effect of this resistance can be taken into account by reflecting it (using the square or the reciprocal of the square of the transformer turns ratio, as appropriate), in order to lump both primary and secondary winding resistances as a single output resistance in series with the output of an ideal transformer. In addition to losses in the winding resistance, there are further losses due to eddy currents and hysteresis in the magnetically permeable core, which tend to increase with frequency.

Active devices

Most of the audio circuitry in use today is designed using semiconductor devices. Certain circuits still require the use of discrete devices, whilst others can utilize some of the many excellently performing integrated circuits (ICs) currently available. Much audio circuit design can be considered as broken down into a series of amplifier units (sometimes referred to as op-amps), and, although a detailed summary of discrete circuit design techniques is out of place here, a comment on the two commonest connections of the op-amp may be helpful (see Figure 2.12). The op-amp is not a universal panacea, because few practical op-amp realizations match the performance required of the ideal op-amp. The ideal is assumed to have infinite open loop gain (the gain when there is no negative feedback in use), infinitely high input impedance, infinitely low output impedance, negligible noise and distortion, and so on. One of the important parameters of an op-amp for handling auto signals is related to its frequency response, and this is its slew rate performance.

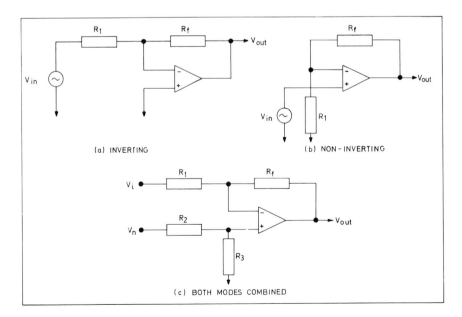

Fig. 2.12. Op-amp connections: (*a*) inverting, (*b*) non-inverting, (*c*) both modes combined

Noise

Any electrical noise present at the input to a mixing console will be amplified along with the required signal, and it is therefore desirable to keep this noise as low as possible. Desk designers usually arrange to place as much initial gain as possible in the first amplifier stage, and thus it is the noise performance of this which sets the limit on the system performance. In practice all the usual real signal sources can be modelled as a combination of a noise voltage generator (in series with an equivalent resistor) and a noise current generator (in parallel with an equivalent resistor). It is the self-noise of the source resistances which sets the lowest noise performance. A good front-end design for a microphone pre-amplifier will increase this noise by only a small amount; a figure less than 1 dB would be considered very good, whilst a figure of up to 3 dB could be considered reasonable. In many practical situations of microphone use, the noise generated at the microphone output by the ambient acoustic noise of the recording environment will greatly exceed the self-noise of the microphone's source resistance. The self-noise of a resistor can be calculated, and is given by

$$E_{n.r.m.s.} = \sqrt{4kTBR}$$

where $E_{n.r.m.s.}$ is the r.m.s. noise voltage, k is Boltzmann's constant (1.38 10^{-23} JK^{-1}), T is the temperature in degrees Kelvin, B is the bandwidth over which the noise is being calculated, R is the resistance in ohms.

For example, a 200 ohm source will have a self-noise of -129.7 dBu over a 20 kHz bandwidth, and this will be gaussian (or equal-energy) white noise. Various weighting curves have been devised in order to relate the spectral characteristics of noise to the way in which the ear perceives it as annoying. Electrical noise measurements are usually carried out using the IEC468 (or CCIR) curve in conjunction with a quasi-peak-indicating metering system. It has been determined empirically that this approach produces a reading some 12.8 dB greater than that of the unweighted r.m.s. measurement. It should be noted that there is a good argument for using the E14 psophometric weighting curve. It has been in existence for some time but it has gained support especially in the realm of digital audio system measurements (see AES Standard on this topic). As a further warning the reader should also note that, where digital audio systems are involved, there exists the possibility for considerable noise shaping and dynamic filtering of noise, and that this will make conventional measurements meaningless. In calculating the noise the bandwidth is assumed to be sharply defined. In practice this is seldom achievable, and it can be shown that, providing the noise has a truly gaussian distribution of amplitudes, the effect of defining the bandwidth with first-order filters only is to increase the noise voltage measured by 1.96 dB.

Introduction to acoustics

Why do we bother with acoustics? The reason is that some characteristics of the sounds we hear are desirable and others are not. Thus we concern ourselves with isolation, room coloration, reverberation, mechanical rattles, and so on. But that's just the room. The study of acoustics also affects the design of the acoustic transducers, the microphones and the loudspeakers and their associated enclosures, their efficiency, their faithfulness, and to a lesser degree their individual foibles and characteristics. In order to appreciate some of the subtleties of the art we need to take a brief look at some of the ideas and terms used in the field of acoustics.

The nature of sound

Surrounding all of us on this earth is an atmosphere, mostly made up of nitrogen and oxygen. Although a gas, it still has mass (its density is approximately 1.18 kg/m³), and under the influence of gravitational pull this mass of air exerts a pressure which at sea level is approximately 100 kPa (15 pounds per square inch). The sounds which we hear are the result of very small variations in this static atmospheric pressure. These sound pressure changes travel through the air and can be referred to as sound waves. Note that it is the wave, or the disturbance in the atmosphere, which travels through the air. The successive compressions and rarefactions which comprise the longitudinal pressure wave essentially leave each particle of air in the same place after its passing. This mode of wave propagation is known as a longitudinal wave, and, by comparison, a wave travelling over the surface of water, as when a stone is dropped in a pond, is known as a transverse wave. We can appreciate this idea better if we consider the compressions and rarefactions found when a simple piston reciprocates in a tube (see Figure 2.13).

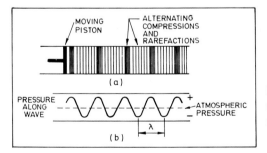

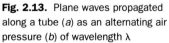

Fig. 2.13. Plane waves propagated along a tube (*a*) as an alternating air pressure (*b*) of wavelength λ

The speed of sound in a gas is dependent on the pressure and density of that gas:

$$c = \frac{\sqrt{1.4P}}{\rho}$$

where P is the atmospheric pressure, ρ is the density of air, c is the velocity in m/s.

Temperature also affects the speed, and, for air, the following relationship holds:

$$c = 332 \sqrt{(1 + T/273)}$$

where T is the temperature in degrees Celsius.

For audio purposes the frequency range of interest is from 20 Hz to 20 kHz, a range of some ten octaves which covers acoustic wavelengths from 17 m to 17 mm. The wavelength, frequency, and velocity of sound are related:

$$c = f\lambda$$

where f is the frequency and λ is the wavelength.

Many a practical sound source can be considered, at least to an acceptable approximation, as a point source, or monopole, producing spherical acoustic waves (see Figure 2.14). The necessary approximation is that the dimensions of the sound source are small with respect to the wavelength of the sound being emitted. The direction of propagation is away from the centre of the sphere, unlike the plane wave of Figure 2.13 which travels in one direction only. The sound intensity from a point source depends on the distance from its centre:

$$I = \frac{W}{4\pi r^2}$$

where I is the intensity in W/m²
     W is the acoustic power of the source
     r is the distance from its centre.

This is known as the Inverse Square Law, since the energy per unit area will decrease inversely as the square of the distance.

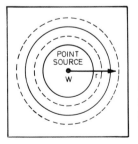

Fig. 2.14. A puslating point source radiates spherical waves whose intensity falls off with distance according to the 'Inverse Square Law'

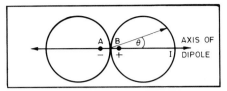

Fig. 2.15. The formation of a dipole source from two spaced monopoles (or point sources) *A* and *B* 180° out of phase. Intensity at any angle θ is *I* cos θ

The combination of two monopoles back to back, but 180° out of phase (an unbaffled or open-backed loudspeaker, for example) gives rise to an acoustic dipole (see Figure 2.15). The dipole illustrates simple acoustic interference effects, as it is clear that, along the axis normal to the line joining the two sources, the soundfield produced by one of the monopole sources is cancelled by that produced by the other. More complex examples of the effect of constructive and destructive interference are its use in acoustic lenses and its presence as an undesirable effect when sound waves are refracted and when discrete reflections cause interference with the direct wanted sounds. The extra complexities are due to the real environment where there are acoustic obstructions which prevent a true free field from existing.

Measuring sound

The easiest descriptor of the intensity of a sound which we can measure is its sound pressure. Other pointers to a sound's intensity, such as the magnitude of particle movement or particle velocity, are best arrived at by measuring the sound pressure. The amplitudes of particle movement for the range of audible sounds is quite small and spans the range from a few mm for loud sounds (which are likely to cause damage to the ear) down to movements of 100 pm (pico-metre), which are associated with sounds at the limit of audibility. We can express the ratio of two sound pressures using the dB, and we can use a dB scale as an absolute scale (thus defining the sound pressure level or SPL) if we first define an acceptable reference. The quietest sounds which can usually be sensed by the average young adult are around 20 μPa, and this sound pressure is used as a reference level, usually expressed as 0 dB SPL. Figure 2.16 gives some idea as to how SPLs are related to some common sound sources.

If we consider SPL to be analogous to voltage and the resultant particle velocity analogous to current, then it is understandable that there will also be acoustic impedance (the impedance of air is around 415 rayls). For any other than a plane progressive wave, this impedance will possess a reactive part, and this also implies that there will be acoustic analogues of inductance and capacitance. This becomes important in loudspeaker design, for example, where full consideration needs to be given to the proper acoustic loading of drive units. This is especially so in the design of horn-loaded enclosures where the high pressure changes (accompanied by small

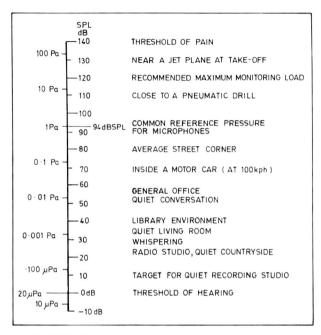

Fig. 2.16. Sound pressure levels for varous typical sources

movements of air) are transformed to small pressure movements (and large movements of air) at the mouth of the horn.

The vented cabinet is a particular application of the Helmholtz resonator, in which the natural resonant frequency of the enclosure is designed to assist the drive unit's efficiency at low frequencies. It has the disadvantage that, at frequencies below this resonance, the drive unit is essentially not loaded and may be prone to damage from very low-frequency signals. In the case of a simple Helmholtz resonator (see Figure 5.9 in Chapter 5) the resonant frequency is given by

$$f = \left(\frac{c}{2\pi} \right) \sqrt{\frac{S}{IV}}$$

where V is the volume of the cavity (m³)
 l is the length of the neck (m)
 S is the cross-sectional area of the neck (m²).

Loudness

Difficulties arise when describing the loudness of a sound. Loudness is a subjective characteristic largely due to the ear's decidedly non-linear response to both level and frequency. Both the phon (a phon is the level numerically equal to the intensity level of a 1,000 Hz tone that is judged equally loud) and the sone (a sone is equal to the loudness of any sound having the loudness level of 40 phons) are encountered in subjective measurements.

Energy

An acoustic wave contains energy (the amount of energy crossing unit area normal to the direction of propagation in unit time is defined as the intensity). As ever, it can be expressed in dB provided that there is a suitable reference level (10^{-12} W/m^2 is used by convention). A large orchestra produces around 10 W and a whisper around 1 nW, and it is not surprising that the 50 MW produced by a Saturn rocket is damaging to the ear! The measurement of sound power is not a simple matter and it requires measurement of both SPL and particle velocity, generally using a special twin-microphone technique.

Acoustic noise measurements

In making measurements of acoustic noise, account is taken of the ear's frequency response by the use of various weighting curves. The curve most in use within the studio environment is the A-weighting curve (see Figure 2.17), whose results are quoted in dB(A). It bears resemblance to the mirror image of the ear's response at around 55 phons and is the most commonly used where a single figure describing noise is acceptable. However, a single-figure result gives no detail as to the frequency composition of the noise, and a more detailed description requires the use of octave or even third-octave

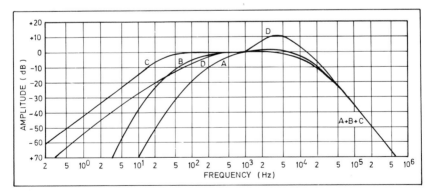

Fig. 2.17. Standard weighting curves for sound level measurements. Curve *A* is the one most used in studio acoustics work

filters in the measurement circuit. Measurements thus obtained may be then compared to particular performance requirements, such as those embodied in noise rating (NR) and noise criterion (NC) curves.

Continual exposure to high SPLs and to high levels of impulsive noise (for example) can give rise to significant hearing impairment, the degree of which depends on the overall exposure. In essence, the damage rises rapidly for exposure to levels above around 90 dB for a significant fraction of a day. To express the exposure, the Leq is defined as the equivalent steady sound level (in dB(A)) which would produce the same A-weighted sound energy over a stated period of time (usually 8 hours) as the time-varying sound. For example, the 90 dB Leq limit would be reached in 4 hours at a SPL of 96 dB, and at 120 dB an exposure of only 15 minutes is needed.

Real rooms

Real rooms contain surfaces which are neither perfect reflectors nor perfect absorbers of sound. Thus the sound from a sound source may bounce around the walls of the room many times before its SPL has died to inaudibility. This is the essence of reverberation. The ear appears to take reflections occurring within the first 30 ms or so of the direct sound as enhancing the level of the source sound, whereas sounds occurring after some 50 ms tend to be discerned as discrete reflections or echoes. The detailed structure of these reflections gives each acoustic environment its particular character.

Reverberation

After the ambient noise level, the reverberation time of a room is perhaps its most important characteristic. Reverberation time (RT) is defined as the time taken for a steady-state sound to die down to one-thousandth (–60 dB) of its initial steady-state SPL when the source energy is cut. The decay is usually linear when plotted using a logarithmic scale for amplitude and a linear one for time. The RT of a room does not necessarily indicate how the room will sound, as there is no simple figure of merit which can be relied on. Of particular significance is the way in which a loudspeaker's varying radiation patterns throughout the frequency range interact with the room's boundaries and any intervening furniture. Amongst the effects of this variation in polar patterns in both horizontal and vertical directions are the isolated shifts in the apparent location of the sound source. This goes a long way towards explaining the need to find a loudspeaker which 'suits' the room and the listener. The traces obtained in making RT measurements do need to be carefully interpreted, and, with the appropriate techniques, many of the room's acoustic mechanisms can be investigated.

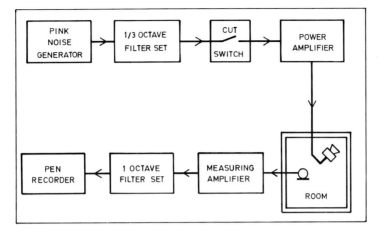

Fig. 2.18. Usual pen plotting arrangement for measuring reverberation time

Conventionally, reverberation time measurements are made by exciting a room with band-limited pink noise (see Figure 2.18). (Pink noise is noise whose energy content is inversely proportional to frequency thus giving rise to a 3 dB/octave or 10 dB/decade slope, whereas white noise is a broad band noise with constant energy per unit of frequency.) The noise is shut off and a high-speed pen plotter used to plot the logarithm of the decay envelope of the sound. A special protractor is used from which the slope of the decay can be read directly as RT. The trouble is that, with isolated pen traces, the consistent patterns in room behaviour are hard to spot and most usually go unnoticed. Methods which average successive traces at each given frequency produce decay traces in which the random elements of room behaviour are averaged out and the dominant patterns become more prominent. Modern measurement tools permit assessment of RT through the use of maximal length pseudo-random noise sequences (MLS) and are more convenient to use.

These techniques allow examination of the clusters of initial reflections which come from the surfaces of various objects, and features of the room close to the path between loudspeaker and listener. Haas showed that reflections of a sound which arrived at the ear within 30 ms (and usually at a similar level) were integrated in the ear and, as a consequence, were perceived as part of one louder sound. On the other hand, reflections which arrived later tended to be perceived as discrete reflections (Haas Effect). Techniques based on MLS and the mathematically related chirp technique used in time delay spectrometry (TDS) allow analysis of such reflections, with the result that it is often possible to identify the group of early reflections which may be causing problems. The room radius, also known as the critical distance, is the distance from the source to where the level of the source (which merges with that from reflections and ambient noise) and the reverberant field (usually obscured by ambient noise) are equal.

The ear

The ear is a remarkable sensor: it can withstand sound pressures above 10 Pa and yet still detect pressures as low as 10 µPa. At such low levels, the movement of the ear drum (in the ear's most sensitive frequency range of 1 kHz to 5 kHz) is around 10^{-11} m, approximately 10 pm (picometer) or around a tenth of the diameter of a hydrogen molecule. However, the ear's frequency response is not flat, and it also varies considerably with SPL. This is usually expressed in the Robinson–Dadson or Fletcher–Munson curves (see Figure 2.19). The biology of the mechanism of human hearing

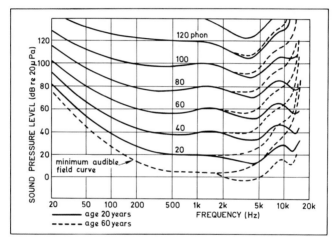

Fig. 2.19. Equal loudness contours for pure tones (Robinson and Dadson)

appears to be very complex, and the models which have been invoked in the many hypotheses do not fully account for all the ear's abilities. The ear is not simply a frequency-selective sensor, and its analytical power appears to be neurologically distributed.

3 Digital theory

Allen Mornington-West

The analogue signal

The sounds which we hear come to the ear as a continuously changing variation in the ambient atmospheric pressure. These small changes are the very ones which we aim to pick up using a microphone. The output of the microphone is an electrical signal (voltage) which is related to the pressure changes which move the microphone diaphragm. This signal is thus an analogue of the originating pressure changes, and hence it is referred to as an analogue (sometimes spelt analog) signal. The principal characteristic of an analogue signal is that it is continuous in time and that there are thus no discontinuities. Indeed, if we use a conventional oscilloscope to trace out the shape of the signal's size or amplitude with respect to time then we might see something such as Figure 3.1. This trace we would refer to as its wave shape. We can contrast this shape with the mathematically much simpler one of a sine wave, as in Figure 3.2.

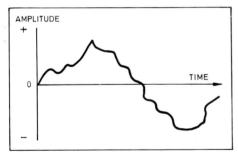

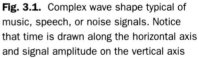

Fig. 3.1. Complex wave shape typical of music, speech, or noise signals. Notice that time is drawn along the horizontal axis and signal amplitude on the vertical axis

It is conventionally and conveniently claimed that the bandwidth of frequencies occupied by analogue audio signals covers the range from 20 Hz to 20 kHz. This range of frequencies might appear to be quite generous, as there are a great many satisfied listeners with medium-wave radio receivers. Yet such receivers rarely have a bandwidth extending beyond 3 kHz, and those with responses 3 dB down at 1 kHz are far from uncommon! It is worth commenting that even modern pop music has progressively less amplitude at higher frequencies (see Figure 3.3).

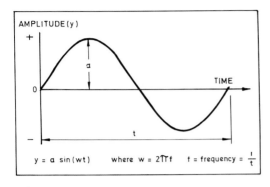

Fig. 3.2. The sine-wave shape typical of a single-frequency electronic oscillator or tuning-fork. The sine function is a repetitive one with a period of $t = 1/f$

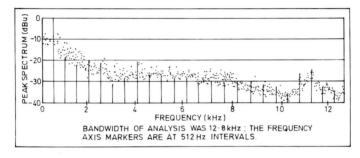

Fig. 3.3. Typical peak spectrum of pop music (first two tracks of the Dire Straits CD *Brothers in Arms*). The peak spectrum is a plot of the maximum amplitude in each of the 12.8 Hz frequency bands

Analogue processing

The simplest control over an analogue signal is probably amplitude control by a fader. A fader acts as a multiplier, and if the value that the fader represents is less than one (less than unity) then the signal at its output will be attenuated. We shall see the consequences of this later when we consider simple digital signal processing. Of course a fader acts on the whole bandwidth of the signal uniformly. If we wish to alter the balance of frequency components in the analogue signal, we must use the reactive components referred to in Chapter 2. For example, a simple low-pass filter (Figure 3.4) clearly has the capacitive element acting as a frequency-dependent attenuator, and it might thus be correctly suspected that we shall again need to use multipliers in order to create filtering action when working on the audio signal in the digital domain.

Whilst we are still in the analogue domain, it is worth noting some typical figures concerning dynamic range and distortion. For studios we can

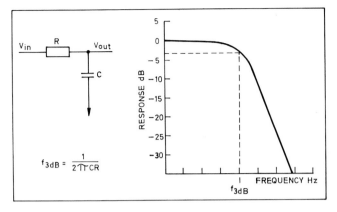

Fig. 3.4. A simple analogue low-pass filter and its response. The −3 dB point is at a frequency of $f = \frac{1}{2}\pi CR$, and the response falls off at a rate of 6 dB per octave (20 dB per decade)

note that current quiet studios can have a background noise characteristic close to NR15 (see Chapter 5). Although it is important to note that the spectrum of the noise is very bass-heavy, the NR15 curve does not imply that the SPL around the 1 kHz octave is about 15 dB. This is quieter than most studio microphone and pre-amplifier combinations, whose output noise (when related to SPL) is around 20–30 dB. This does not set an absolute lower limit of audibility because the human ear has the ability to detect the presence of musical sounds when they are well below the wide-band noise level. By comparison, the loudest sounds encountered in the act of recording might lie at sound levels of 130 dB. If a margin of 20 dB is allowed for future improvements in technology and acoustics, the total acoustic dynamic range is of the order of 120 dB. A professional analogue sound recorder might, under similar considerations, display a dynamic range of some 65 dB prior to the application of noise reduction. The use of noise reduction could add up to 25 dB to this figure, thus producing a total dynamic range of 90 dB. The third major limiting item in the studio environment is the mixing desk. Its dynamic range is greatly determined by the number of channels being summed and their gain: 32 channels set to the same gain can be expected to add at least 15 dB to the noise floor of a mixing desk, if the output gain is left untouched. Should all those channels be active with different signals passing through each, then the output level will also rise by 15 dB. If channels which are not in use are muted (good practice) then the dynamic range of the signal from the desk is independent of the number of channels available and could be around 110 dB.

The digital signal

The digital signal is a representation of the analogue signal by a string of numbers. The numbers will, in their turn, be represented by groups of pulses, and this method of describing a signal is one of the types of pulse code modulation (PCM). Early theoretical work on aspects of PCM dates from the late 1930s, and a comprehensive evaluation, arising from work carried out at Bell Telephone Laboratories, was published in 1948 by Oliver, Pierce, and Shannon.

The essence of the digitizing process is the deriving of the strings of numbers through the twin processes of sampling and quantizing. Sampling is rather like freezing the signal at a moment in time, and is the process which results in what is called the 'discrete signal', because the signal has been caught at a discrete point in time. Quantizing, which is a process applied to this frozen signal, involves measuring the size of the signal to the nearest whole number of measurement units. These processes, of stopping the signal and measuring it, are accompanied by effects and limitations of the practical world, and it will be worth taking a brief look at some of the more important of these.

Sampling

A simplified diagram of a typical sampling circuit is shown in Figure 3.5. The three elements of the sampling circuit are the switch, a capacitor in which to store the sample, and a buffer amplifier. The switch is usually a FET, but a common technique for high-speed sampling uses a diode bridge arrangement. At the instant of sampling, the switch is closed and the value of the input analogue signal is applied to the capacitor. A very short time later, the switch is opened. The capacitor voltage should now be that at the instant of sampling, and the output of the buffer amplifier is a usable copy of it.

The simplest way to reconstruct the signal would be to arrange that the points representing the samples are simply joined up (Figure 3.6). However, should the rate of sampling with respect to the signal frequency be reduced, we shall approach the rate at which the number of samples per input cycle is not enough to describe the input signal adequately. Figure 3.7 shows the situation close to the limit, where the sampling rate (f_s) is a little more than twice the input signal rate. If the samples took place at say the zero crossing of the signal, then there would be no net output.

Figure 3.8a shows the situation when f_s is less than twice the input signal rate. In Figure 3.8b it can be seen how a reconstructed waveform would appear at a different sampling frequency. This illustration of the limit of the sampling rate is the essence of Shannon's sampling theorem. Signal fre-

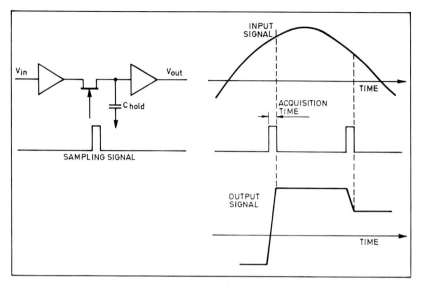

Fig 3.5. Simplified sampling circuit and the associated wave shapes

quencies which are greater than $f_s/2$ will appear folded back into the spectrum occupied by the wanted signal (this is the essence of Nyquist's theorem). These are called aliases, and, once they have been created, they are indistinguishable from the wanted signal and cannot be removed. Thus it is

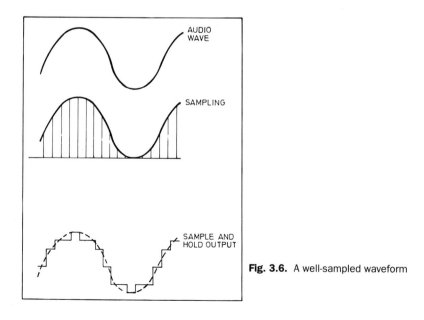

Fig. 3.6. A well-sampled waveform

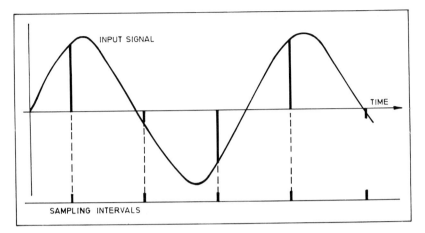

Fig. 3.7. A waveform sampled at just more than twice the input signal frequency

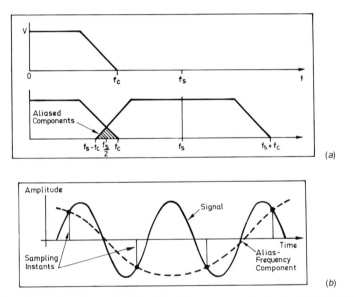

Fig. 3.8. Sampling at less than twice the signal frequency results in aliasing (overlapping of higher-order spectra) and produces a low-frequency sinusoid or alias-frequency component

necessary to removal all frequencies greater than $f_s/2$. Limitations of filter design (principally the difficulty of producing an infinitely fast cut-off rate) dictate that, for practical purposes, the sampling rate is a little more (10–25 per cent) than twice the required bandwidth.

This folding back, or aliasing, can be viewed from another angle. It is necessary to recognize that the ideal sampling waveform has a spectrum which extends to infinity (Figure 3.9). As the process of sampling is similar to multiplying the signal by the sampling waveform, the spectrum of the result (Figure 3.10) will also be repetitive. The requirement for the sampling rate

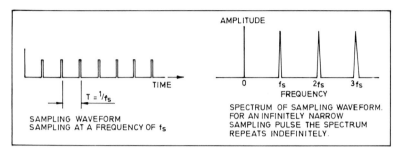

Fig. 3.9. Waveform and spectrum of a sampling signal

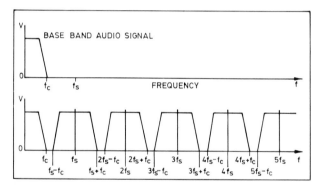

Fig. 3.10. Spectrum of a sampled signal

to be at least twice the signal frequency can be seen as the need to avoid the difference frequency sideband, $f_s–f_c$, from entering the part of the spectrum occupied by the original signal. A more visual example of the creation of aliases is the appearance of backwards-rotating spoked wheels in cinema Westerns, as the stage-coach pulls away.

There is a tight constraint on the length of time (acquisition time) which can be taken in gathering each sample if it is to be considered accurate (shown in Figure 3.11 as total aperture error). An even tighter restriction is placed on the variation in time (aperture uncertainty) between successive sampling points. For a 20 kHz sine wave (arguably representing the worst case of a full amplitude signal at the top of the audio band) the acquisition time will usually be around 1 µs in order not to incur a large aperture loss,

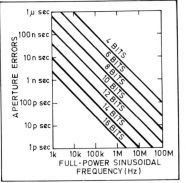

Fig. 3.11. Allowable aperture errors

and the aperture uncertainty less than 80 ps if the signal is to be sampled to an accuracy of one part in 100,000 of the full-scale value. Other sources of error within the sampling process are due to the switching transient, feedthrough of the applied signal, droop of the sampled signal on the storage capacitor after the sampling switch has opened, dielectric storage performance of the storage capacitor, and so on. Variation in aperture error is commonly referred to as jitter. The analysis of jitter is complex. The sampling frequency is analysed as having frequency and/or phase modulated components and these components will usually have a small effect on the signal which is being sampled.

Despite these sources of error, it is not the sampling process which is responsible for the overall noise and distortion performance in high-quality audio systems, as we shall see later. Further, a full-scale signal at the top of the band is an exceedingly rare, and probably unmusical, signal. Plots of the spectrum of musical signals indicate that the level of audio components at around 20 kHz is generally more than 30 dB lower than the level within the first 500 Hz of the audio band (see again Figure 3.3).

To reconstruct the signal, one could present it to a suitable low-pass filter which would remove all of the higher-frequency components. Alternatively, the sampled value can be held in what is called a zero-order hold circuit, until the next sample is supplied, following this stage with an appropriate low-pass filter. The consequence of forming this series of pulses from the samples is that the spectrum of the input signal is modified by a $\sin(x)/x$ shape (Figure 3.12), which effectively causes a linear phase roll-off of the sampled signal of about 4 dB at a frequency of $f_s/2$. The steps in this waveform, and the $\sin(x)/x$ loss, can be dealt with by the low-pass filter. In order to recover the signal fully from the sampled waveform, the ideal response of this filter has an impulse response as shown in Figure 3.13.

However, proper reconstruction will occur only if the input to the filter is a train of impulses of negligible width (and thus infinitesimally small energy). Under these conditions, the succession of impulses from the filter

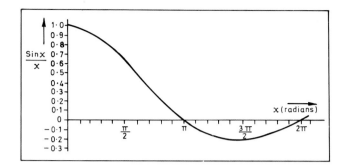

Fig. 3.12. Shape of the sin $(x)/x$ curve

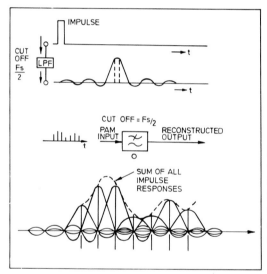

Fig. 3.13. Ideal reconstruction filter impulse response. Each impulse is converted to a sin $(x)/x$ wave and these are added in the filter to produce the continuous output (a sequence of pulse amplitude modulated impulses)

will add up to reconstitute the original waveform. However, real-world samples have finite duration (and finite energy) and are usually lengthened to last for some fraction of the sample period. The result is an aperture loss shown, for some common values of aperture ratio, in Figure 3.14. It is not necessary to make up for sin $(x)/x$ loss by analogue filtering since there is a clever way of doing this digitally, which is used in some Compact Disc players. This is part of the reason why aperture correction for d/a converters is not performed at the encoding stage.

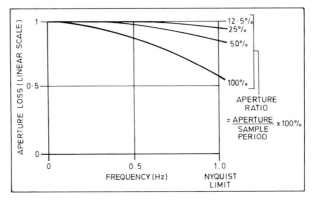

Fig. 3.14. Plots of aperture loss against aperture ratio

Quantizing

Perhaps the easiest way to understand the operation of a quantizer is to apply a linear ramp to a converter and examine the resulting digital output (Figure 3.15). Notice that, as the input rises, the output goes up in steps and so the difference between input and output takes on a saw-tooth shape. This error is referred to as quantization error (also called quantization noise, granular noise, or distortion). The error can be reduced by increasing the fineness of the steps, but there are limits to the fineness of resolution which can be imposed—if not by cost then by technology. The error is really a distortion, as it is correlated, in a complex manner, to the input signal. Figure 3.16 shows the error associated with quantizing a sine wave, and

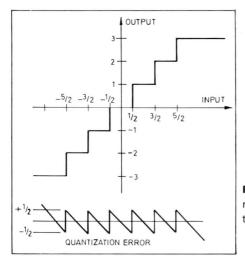

Fig. 3.15. Quantizing: showing a linear ramp's quantized output and its quantization error

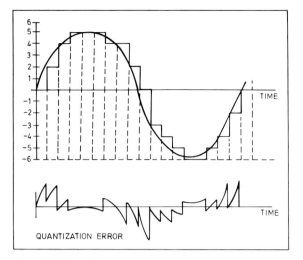

Fig. 3.16. Waveform of the quantization error for a sine wave

it is clear that, at least by eye, the error waveform, though complex, is well related to the originating signal. It is only for complex signals that the correlations in the errors approach a randomness similar to that of noise and the term quantization noise can be properly used.

A particularly annoying instance of high quantization noise occurs when a very low-level signal is just crossing the first quantization level. If the signal were a sine wave, then the output from the quantizer would be a square wave. All the higher harmonics could then be called distortion components. This performance is particularly annoying when low-level, low-frequency tones decay into the noise. They are accompanied at first by noise, and as they decay towards the minimum quantizable level the noise progressively becomes more correlated to the input signal and thus noticeable as distortion. Luckily there is a neat trick which can improve matters without requiring a potentially expensive increase in the quantizer's resolution. It involves the addition of random noise to the signal about to be quantized, at a level such that its peak-to-peak amplitude is approximately one quantizing level. This noise 'dithers' the input signal so that the output is no longer a square wave (Figure 3.17). It has been accepted that the most appropriate form of dithering signal is one referred to as triangular probability density function (TPDF) noise. This is a noise signal which is created by adding the outputs of two uncorrelated long MLSs together. An alternative form which has been used is rectangular probability density function (RPDF) noise. Since an RPDF signal—it is similar to that shown in Figure 3.17—does not have a value greater than +/– one quantizing level, it is clear that the quantizer output will change to silence as the audio signal fades

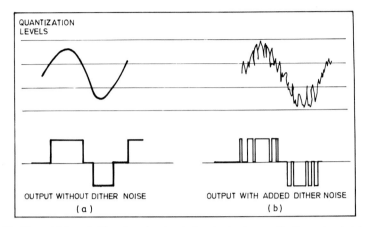

Fig. 3.17. The addition of dither to a low-level signal prior to quantization: showing (*a*) a sine wave around one quantization level in amplitude and its quantized output; (*b*) the same but with dither noise added to the sine wave

out entirely. Although this produces the quietest textbook noise margin, it is considered inelegant to add even this small amount of noise modulation to an otherwise good signal. The TPDF waveform has values which range up to +/– two quantizing levels. Thus, as the audio signal is faded out, there will still be a small but continuous noise and this is considered more benign. Where TPDF dither has been added to the output of a digital process, it is usual to shape the spectrum of the quantizing error noise so that it is placed in an area where the ear is less sensitive. In a digital audio system this approach leads to a loss of some 4 dB in dynamic range, but it does result, paradoxically, in the pleasurable existence of the audio signal below the system noise floor.

So far the quantizers have been assumed to be linear, that is an *n* per cent change in input results, give or take the quantizing error, in an *n* per cent change in output. Non-linear quantizers are in use, particularly in telephony but also in some domestic audio equipment.

Numbering

So far we have considered the quantizing process but without stating what sort of numbers we shall be using. The most useful number scheme to use is undoubtedly a binary one, counting using the base of two. The binary scheme is useful because the two possible digits, 1 and 0, can be represented in many ways. They can also be respectively described as on and off, high and low, true and not true, mark and space, and so on. As there are only two digits, counting up presents very little problem as the rules are simple:

1. Adding two zeros produces a zero
2. Adding a one and a zero produces a one
3. Adding two ones produces a zero and a one to carry into the next column.

Table 3.1 shows the counting sequence for a straight binary count from zero through to 8, and for some of the commoner coding schemes.

Table 3.1. Binary counting codes

(a) Signed decimal	(b) Binary plus sign	(c) Twos complement	(d) Offset binary	(e) Grey code	(f) Unsigned decimal	(g) Hexadecimal notation
7	0111	0111	1111	1000	15	F
6	0110	0110	1110	1001	14	E
5	0101	0101	1101	1011	13	D
4	0100	0100	1100	1010	12	C
3	0011	0011	1011	1110	11	B
2	0010	0010	1010	1111	10	A
1	0001	0001	1001	1101	9	9
0	$\begin{Bmatrix}0000\\1000\end{Bmatrix}$	0000	1000	1100	8	8
−0						
−1	1001	1111	0111	0100	7	7
−2	1010	1110	0110	0101	6	6
−3	1011	1101	0101	0111	5	5
−4	1100	1100	0100	0110	4	4
−5	1101	1011	0011	0010	3	3
−6	1110	1010	0010	0011	2	2
−7	1111	1001	0001	0001	1	1
−8	—	1000	0000	0000	0	0

However, a pure binary count has no provision for negative numbers, and there does need to be some provision because the audio signal, with which we are concerned, can take on values that range from negative through to positive. Thus we need some way of describing a negative number. We could do this by setting a sign bit for negative numbers at the most significant bit (msb) position (Table 3.1(b)), but there will then be two numbers which represent the zero state. Or we could do it by setting the msb for all positive numbers which will make the most negative number in the series zero. This scheme, called 'offset binary' (Table 3.1(d)), has a drawback when it comes to signal processing. For example, adding two negative numbers together could result in a positive number!

The scheme adopted is called 'twos complement' (Table 3.1(c)) and is similar to the offset binary code except that the msb has been inverted. Twos complement code offers a very simple method of performing subtraction by the tidy method of adding the negative of the number to be subtracted. There are many ways of forming the twos complement of a number, but the one which is most used in digital arithmetic is performed by taking the ones complement (inverting each bit in the number) and adding a one to the least significant bit (lsb) position. Interestingly, reconversion to an offset binary number requires the same process.

Another coding scheme which is commonly found in digital audio systems is called the 'Grey code' (Table 3.1(e)). In this code the counting is arranged so that at each count only one of the bit positions changes state. This code finds extensive use in control position sensors and shaft encoders, where it is essential that the inevitable skew of a mechanical assembly is not responsible for any miscounting.

In a linear code, each bit position can be thought of as marking the presence (or absence, if it is a zero) of a power of two. Thus in Table 3.1 column 2 (counting the lsb column as zero) marks the presence of 2^2, that is whether there is a four in the overall binary number. Similarly, column 1 marks the number of 2^1, or two. Finally, the zeroth column marks the presence or not of 2^0, or one. Thus each extra bit position which is used doubles the range of numbers which can be expressed. For an n-bit system the maximum signal-to-noise ratio (r.m.s. signal to r.m.s. noise) is given by:

$$SNR[\text{r.m.s.}]dBu = 6^n + 1.8$$

A 16-bit linear system can thus produce a dynamic range of 97.8 dB, assuming that everything is perfect. For reasons such as the addition of dither and imperfections within the conversion process, a practical value of SNR is of the order of 92 dB. As the use of the CCIR 468 weighting filter worsens noise measurements by about 8.6 dB and the use of a PPM-type meter worsens the noise measurement by around 4.2 dB, the dynamic range (measured weighted using a PPM-type meter) could be quoted as 85 dB. This is comparable to the dynamic range achieved by a high-quality analogue tape system relying on noise reduction systems.

Arithmetic

Figure 3.18 illustrates some simple sums in twos complement binary arithmetic. Note that, because only four bit positions have been defined, any carries have no extra column in which to be placed and have been neglected. There are two rules which need to be recognized in order to avoid an erroneous answer due to overflow or underflow:

1. If, when adding two positive numbers, the msb position is set then the sum has overflowed.
2. If, when adding two negative numbers, there is a carry bit coming from the msb, then the sum has underflowed.

In digital signal processing these conditions need to be trapped, and the output set to the fully negative or positive value, or some very peculiar noises can result. The process of handling overflow and underflow is equivalent to clipping an analogue signal.

Basic addition in $\bar{2}$ is easy:

two positive numbers:

```
    0 1 0 1          +5
    0 0 1 0    +     +2
    0 1 1 1          +7
```

a positive number and a small negative number:

```
      0 1 0 1          +5
    + 1 1 1 0    +     -2
(1) 0 0 1 1          +3
      carry is disregarded.
```

a positive number and a larger negative number:

```
      1 0 0 1          -7
    + 0 0 1 1    +     +3
      1 1 0 0          -4
```

two negative numbers:

```
      1 1 0 1          -3
      1 0 1 1    +     -5
      1 0 0 0          -8
      carry is disregarded.
```

The carry is disregarded, but a change in the sign column occurring when two numbers of the same sign are operated on means overflow or underflow has occurred.

Subtraction in the twos complement system is merely a matter of finding the $\bar{2}$ of the subtrahend (including the sign bit) and then adding it to the minuend:

```
      0 1 0 1        +5
      1 1 0 0    +   -4
(1) 0 0 0 1        +1
    carry is        carry is
    disregarded.    disregarded.
```

Fig. 3.18. Simple sums in twos complement arithmetic

Multiplying binary numbers is also relatively simple (see Figure 3.19). A one times any number will return the same number, whilst a zero times any number returns zero. Also, to multiply a number by two simply

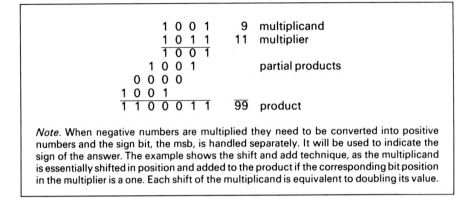

Note. When negative numbers are multiplied they need to be converted into positive numbers and the sign bit, the msb, is handled separately. It will be used to indicate the sign of the answer. The example shows the shift and add technique, as the multiplicand is essentially shifted in position and added to the product if the corresponding bit position in the multiplier is a one. Each shift of the multiplicand is equivalent to doubling its value.

Fig. 3.19. Multiplying two positive numbers

requires a left shift of all of the bits in that number. A zero is placed in the now vacated lsb position. Division by a power of two is similarly a matter of shifting, this time to the right. If the width of the binary number is not adequate, then the lsb will be lost in the division. Note that an n-bit number times an m-bit multiplier can require up to $n + m$ bits to cope with the full precision of the answer.

Although additions can be accomplished at speed, their repetition does lengthen the time needed to perform a multiplication. These processes are mostly carried out inside the heart of dedicated digital signal processing (DSP) chips, which are often rated by the time taken to perform a multiply and accumulate (MAC) step. The division operation is relatively rare in digital signal processing. If division by a constant is called for, it can be thought of as multiplication by a number less than unity; it is then necessary to come to an understanding as to where, within an equipment, the binary point is. It is usual to consider the digitized input signal as filling the range between +1 and –1, and to arrange that all multipliers or coefficients are also within this range. Division by a varying number can, in general, be done only by the time-consuming process of repeated trial subtractions in a manner entirely analogous to the way that longhand division is carried out on ordinary decimal numbers. Multiplication by a figure greater than unity then requires left-shifting of the initial product, and this feature is usually available in digital signal processing (DSP) hardware. Most DSP hardware has to resort to a modification of the straightforward binary representation. The reason is to do with the limitations of the hardware available. Multipliers which handle 16-bit inputs will usually produce a 32-bit answer. In order not to lose the detail in subsequent processing, a greater word width is needed. In digital audio this is often 24 bits; the extra bits can be handled as an exponent. The format is known as 'floating point' by analogy to the decimal system of numbers. Multiplication of numbers in exponent form requires that their exponents are merely added together, along with any change required as a result of the proper multiplication of the mantissa. The exponents could be handled by circuitry extra to the multipliers.

Faders and filters

Just as analogue processing could be seen to depend implicitly on multiplication, so the world of DSP relies explicitly on the power of a multiplier. The elemental outlines of a fader and a simple first-order low-pass filter are shown in Figure 3.20.

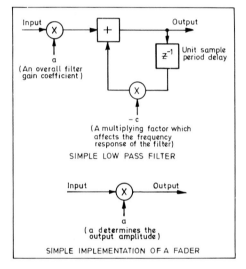

Fig. 3.20. Simple Digital Signal Processing: showing a low-pass filter and a fader

The fader is simply the action of a multiplier on the audio signal. A 16-bit by 16-bit multiply can result in a 32-bit product which will need to be rounded off for practical purposes (rather than truncated), perhaps to a 16-bit output. Rounding off is required whenever the digital representation of the audio signal is effectively requantized. This will occur, for example, when the signal passes from the internal of a DSP chip, where it may be represented as a 56-bit word, to the outside world where it is handled as a 24-bit word. As the signal is being requantized, it is usual to apply TPDF based dither prior to rounding. It is becoming the usual practice to shape the spectrum of the TPDF signal so that the error inevitably created in the requantizing process is moved to a less audible part of the audio spectrum. A similar action is needed for the output of the simple low-pass filter. Note that, just as the spectrum of the input audio signal is periodic as a consequence of sampling, so the filter also has a periodic response and it does not form a precise analogy with the analogue equivalent.

There are two main classes of digital filter, the finite impulse response (FIR) and the infinite impulse response (IIR) types. They also have other names: FIR filters are also known as linear phase and transversal filters, while IIR filters also go by the name of recursive filters. It is more usual to find IIR filters in audio DSP. They are versatile and economical on processing power, but do require accurately calculated coefficients. They key features of a digital filter are the unit delay, the multiplier, and the adder. The unit delay lasts exactly one sample period. Sometimes also written in shorthand as z^{-1}, it is achieved simply by referring to the memory locations where successive samples have been stored. The multiplying and the adding (more usually referred to as a multiplier and accumulator or MAC) functions are the only ones needed to perform digital signal processing.

A more general type of filter is common in digital audio processing (see Figure 3.21). The structure of it does not change when different filter types are required. Characteristics such as shelving cut and boost, low-pass filters, mid-range cut and boost, and so on, are all achieved by operating the same structure but with different coefficients. The subtle difference between them is that in (a) the multipliers are associated with three separate accumulations and two delays, whilst (b) uses only one accumulation but requires four delays. The best filter structure to use depends not only on the characteristics of the hardware in use but, in a more subtle manner, on the performance details of the structure under special conditions of input and coefficient values.

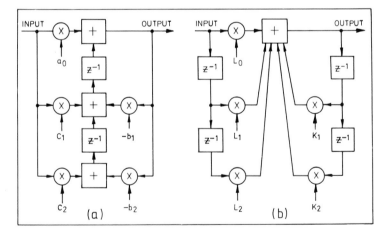

Fig. 3.21. Common second-order filter structures: (a) Direct Form II transpose, (b) Direct Form I. Structure (b) is preferred for its stability and relatively low noise floor

For metering purposes the digital signal needs to be rectified; the negative part of a twos complement number is converted to offset binary by reapplying the twos complement conversion process. Note that the spectrum of the signal has now been doubled and rectified signal components of fundamentals higher than 10 kHz (in a 20 kHz system) will be aliased. In order to create attack and decay characteristics, filtering is needed. The output of the filtering can be applied directly to a suitable digital display or it can be converted to an analogue signal and applied to a conventional meter. The metering law can be defined digitally either by calculation or by use of a look-up table.

Digital reverberation

Digital reverberators can be viewed as collections of very complex filters. One particular architecture splits up the creation of early reflections and subsequent reverberation (see Figure 3.22). The filter-like structure of the early reflection and subsequent reverberation generators is shown in Figure 3.23.

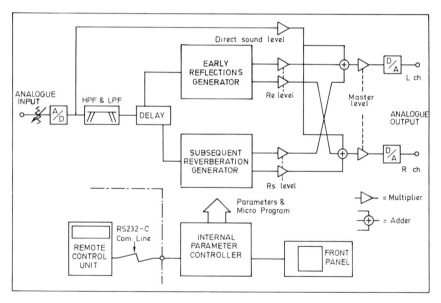

Fig. 3.22. Block diagram of a digital reverberator

The rate at which the digital signal processing computations need to be done is fast, as all of the work must be carried out each time within one sampling period. For a mixing desk channel incorporating a four-band para-

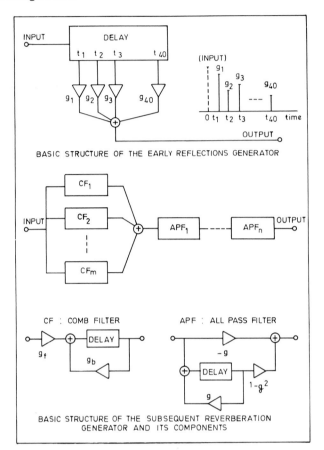

Fig. 3.23. Structures of the early and subsequent reflections generators

metric equalizer in addition to eight auxiliaries, monitor and output fader, and panning, something of the order of 2.3 million computation cycles per second will be needed. This high speed is beyond the ability of ordinary microprocessors, and special processors are required.

Another aspect of DSP that requires mentioning is the need for the retention of as much precision (or word width) as possible. If, for example, we were to truncate the 32-bit output of a calculation to 16 bits then we would lose the detail in the lower 16 bits. This creates a worst-case error nearly equal to the size of the lsb, and makes the result only as good as 15-bit accuracy. The situation is a little better if we round up by adding a one to the 17th bit and then truncating the result at the 16th bit. That process creates only a worst-case error of approximately ½ lsb, and, in general, it has to be done before the final digital output is presented to the output d/a converter. However, if there is more computation needed, then the errors in the output word will accumulate in proportion to the square root of the number of processes involved. Typically, the intermediate results in audio DSP are between 20 and 32 bits long, although 24 bits is usual. Another reason for maintaining the precision of intermediate results is that the complex matter of limit cycle oscillation is more easily avoided. There are other, wider aspects of digital audio which have much to do with the philosophies underlying the way in which audio signals are controlled.

Digital components

All the binary arithmetic described so far requires some hardware to make it happen. Although some of the hardware needed is fairly fearsome in complexity, all of it can be analysed as compositions of three basic functions, AND, OR, and inversion. As the only two states in a binary world can be expressed as 1 or 0, it is clear that the opposite of a one is its inverse, zero. A 'truth table' shows how a gate's output relates to its input (see Figure 3.24).

AND GATE TRUTH TABLE		
A	B	C
0	0	0
0	1	0
1	0	0
1	1	1

OR GATE TRUTH TABLE		
A	B	C
0	0	0
0	1	1
1	0	1
1	1	1

Fig. 3.24. The symbols, truth tables, and Boolean algebraic expressions for AND and OR gates

There is an algebra, called Boolean algebra, which can be used to relate the required output of a logic system to its inputs, and it is a powerful design tool. Rather than trying to design a logic function from truth tables, the algebra can be used to formulate and manipulate statements which define the logical relationship of inputs and outputs. The use of the invert function on the AND and OR functions turns them into NAND and NOR respectively, and their truth tables are shown in Figure 3.25.

There is one final common simple function which is derived from the other functions and is known as an 'exclusive or' (EXOR) gate (see Figure 3.26). It has the useful property of being usable as a controlled inverter; if one input is held high, the output will be the inverse of the other input. In combination with an AND gate it forms a half adder. A full adder is needed in order also to handle a carry as an input. Cumulative delays from previous stages of adders handling a wide word can be lengthy, and a modified form of adder with a look-ahead carry is used.

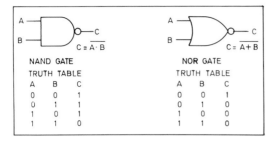

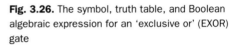

Fig. 3.25. The symbols, truth tables, and Boolean algebraic expressions for NAND and NOR gates

NAND GATE
TRUTH TABLE

A	B	C
0	0	1
0	1	1
1	0	1
1	1	0

NOR GATE
TRUTH TABLE

A	B	C
0	0	1
0	1	0
1	0	0
1	1	0

Fig. 3.26. The symbol, truth table, and Boolean algebraic expression for an 'exclusive or' (EXOR) gate

TRUTH TABLE

A	B	C
0	0	0
0	1	1
1	0	1
1	1	0

EXOR GATE

A simple combination of two NOR gates (two NAND gates can also be used but the sense of the logic will be inverted) will form an elementary one-bit memory or latch. The addition of a further two AND gates will form the JK flip-flop which can be used in most counters, latches, and registers (see Figure 3.27).

Multipliers are not so easily made, and much ingenuity has been expended in trying to achieve both speed and economy. A shift-and-add type of multiplier (an implementation of Booth's algorithm) is too slow for DSP work, and the technique is mostly used within the software in microprocessors, where the slowness of speed can be tolerated. Nowadays multipliers can be implemented as a single chip containing an array of three-bit adders which can perform a 16×16 bit multiply in typically less than 150 ns.

Further advances have led to two interesting developments. The first is the high-speed full arithmetic processor chips which are designed to be used as a co-processor in conjunction with a conventional microprocessor. The second is the emergence of true DSP chips, such as the Texas TMS320 and TMS57000, and Motorola 56000 and 96000 families, which can perform all the processes required in DSP. Like other dedicated DSP chips, they contain their own multiplier, arithmetic logic unit (ALU), program memory, and address sequencer. In due course it is likely that chips designed specifically for digital audio use will be produced and become freely available.

Sampling conversion

Most listeners to music from CD will have little idea that the signals are likely to have spent the formative part of their life as so-called 'studio quality' signals which were recorded using a sample rate of 48 kHz. In order to

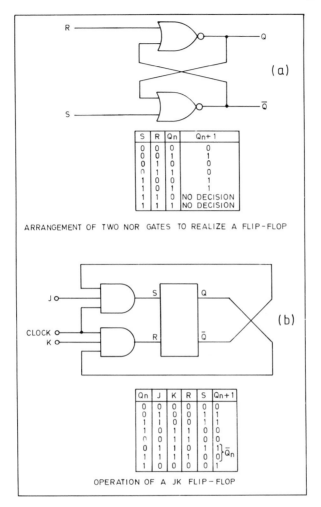

S R Qn | Qn+1

S	R	Qn	Qn+1
0	0	0	0
0	0	1	1
0	1	0	0
0	1	1	0
1	0	0	1
1	0	1	1
1	1	0	NO DECISION
1	1	1	NO DECISION

ARRANGEMENT OF TWO NOR GATES TO REALIZE A FLIP-FLOP

Qn	J	K	R	S	Qn+1
0	0	0	0	0	0
0	1	0	0	1	1
1	1	0	0	1	1
1	0	1	1	0	0
0	0	1	1	0	0
0	1	1	0	1	1
1	1	1	1	0	0
1	0	0	0	0	1

$\left. \begin{array}{c} 1 \\ 0 \end{array} \right\} \bar{Q}_n$

OPERATION OF A JK FLIP-FLOP

Fig. 3.27. (*a*) Cross-coupled NOR gates produce a set/reset (SR) flip-flop, whilst (*b*) the addition of two AND gates yields the JK flip-flop which changes state only when it is clocked

appear on CD, the master copy of these signals will need to be transverted to a sampling frequency of 44.1 kHz. This can be easily achieved by converting the 48 kHz digital signal into the analogue domain and then reconverting to 44.1 kHz, but this process lacks elegance and the result will be watermarked by the response of the converters used. Many CD reviewers, perhaps not aware of this sequence of events, have had subjective reservations about the sound but found them difficult to put into words. However, they may well have a point, since the transversion process has often been far from transparent.

Sampling conversion is a non-trivial highly specific filtering process, and in all the present-day approaches it requires intensive computation. The classic approach, adopted in essence by Stüder, requires something of the order of 7×10^6 multiplications per second per stereo channel, but will convert an input sampled at one frequency into an output at an arbitrary, not necessarily constant, sampling rate. It is not cheap but it does provide a high-quality conversion (the process loses 2 dB of system dynamic range) which is better than could be achieved by converting to analogue and redigitizing.

The detailed manner in which the sampling frequency converter works is quite complex, and a simple analogy will have to suffice here. The input sequence of samples, or the input grid (see Figure 3.28) is digitally resam-

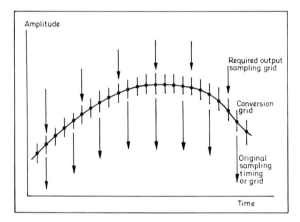

Fig. 3.28. Sampling rate conversion by means of a conversion grid

pled at a new rate, the conversion grid. The output sequence of samples, the output grid, is selected from the conversion grid at a rate which satisfies the required output sample rate. This is a diagram of a conceptual approach; the sampling rate of the conversion grid is around 3.2 GHz! Note that, in this simple model, resampling the signal at a lower rate could lead to the generation of aliases. In order to create the conversion grid to the accuracy required of 16-bit digital audio, the conversion grid needs to be 2^{15} (32,768) times the input sample rate or at around 3.2 GHz. Filters working at this rate are unrealistic and a method is adopted which considerably lightens the computational load. It is as if the only points on the conversion grid which are actually computed are those around which an output sample will be required. As the ratio of input to output sample rate is calculated over some time, there is a finite rate at which the output sequence of samples can keep track of changing sample rates. In other respects there is still the same need for stability of the sampling frequencies, if accuracy is not to be degraded any more than is inherent in the processing. A similar problem occurs when digitized audio signals at the same nominal sampling frequency are required to be processed together. A simpler tactic of sampling rate synchronization can be adopted provided that the difference between the sampling frequencies is no greater than ± 1 part in 10^5. The approach involves collecting incoming samples in a buffer store at the incoming sampling rate and reading them out at the receiving system's sampling rate. If the buffer store should become too full or empty, then the simplest strategy would be to discard or duplicate samples at points where the audio level is low. A more complicated strategy performs a momentary crossfade. Either way the result is an approximation to the ideal. More recently it has become possible to design a high-quality transversion around a single dedicated chip. There are two key problems which have to be solved. The first is to determine to the necessary 16-bit accuracy the exact point at which to take an output sample. The second is to set up coefficients for the filters within the necessary time, and with values determined by the input sampling frequency.

Digital interfaces

Within modern and foreseeable studio practice, there are at least five major types of digital interface. As only one of these caters for digital audio data, the other four are primarily concerned with the transmission of digital control information. They are:

1. The RS group: this includes the venerable RS232C and RS423, and the RS485 group in which is found the RS422.
2. A collection of byte parallel signal interfaces which includes the IEC 625 GP-IB (HPIB or IEE 488), the usual PC parallel port which is able to drive the Centronics port of most printers, and the SCSI (Small Computer Systems Interface) which is increasingly used in digital audio systems.
3. The Musical Instrument Digital Interface (MIDI): discussed in Chapter 18.
4. The AES/EBU digital audio interface, and its multi-channel partner the MADI interface: for serial transmission of linearly represented digital audio data.
5. High speed: based on 100 M-bit/s and 10 M-bit/s ethernet type systems.

A few words on each of these standards is in order (see also Chapters 8 and 12).

The RS group is summarized in Table 3.2. The information is sent in bit serial form, usually in words of seven or eight bits, preceded by synchronization or start bits and followed by parity and stop bits. In this system a mark is a low voltage and a space is a high one. Physical interface to the standard is easy, and there are many sources of the necessary chips. Most equipments using it will be microprocessor-driven. However, hooking up to

Table 3.2. Salient features of the RS type of communication standards

Parameter	RS232	RS423	RS485
Mode of operation	Single-Ended	Single-Ended	Differential
Number of drivers and receivers allowed on line	1 Driver 1 Receiver	1 Driver 10 Receivers	up to 32 drivers 32 Receivers
Maximum cable length (ft)	50	4000	4000
Maximum data rate (Baud)	20 K	100 K	10 M
Maximum common-mode voltage	±25 V	±6 V	±6 V −0.25 V
Driver output signal	±5 V min ±15 V max	±3.6 V min ±6.0 V max	±2 V min
Driver load	3 kΩ–7 kΩ	450 Ω min	100 Ω

Driver slew rate	30 V μs max	* Controlled
		* Determined by
		  cable length &
		  data rate
			N/A

Drive output resistance (high Z state)	Power on N/A Power off 300 Ω	N/A ±100 μA max at = 6 V	N/A ±100 μA max −0.25 V ≤ Vcm ≤ 6 V
Receiver resistance	3 kΩ–7 kΩ	>4 kΩ	>4 kΩ
Receiver sensitivity	±3 V	±200 mV	±200 mV −7 V ≤ Vcm ≤ 7 V

an RS232C port is not always easy because considerable confusion can arise in determining which of the admissible signalling conventions is being used and how it is being implemented. RS485 at the physical level is being considered for bidirectional network control of audio, video, lighting, and musical devices at rates between 100 and 250 kBd.

The byte parallel group is similar in many respects. Eight bits are transmitted on separate lines whilst their validity is signalled by a data ready or strobe signal. Control of the information rate is provided by further handshaking signals, and other signals determine which device is being addressed. Data rates can exceed 1 Mbyte per second with the standard GPIB handling up to sixteen devices and SCSI up to seven. The bus must be correctly terminated and, in order to minimize the risk of interference and crosstalk, it is necessarily limited in length. Typically there can be only one controller or master device.

MIDI: the bus owes its ascendancy to the growth of digitally controlled music synthesizers. Certain studio outboard equipment, such as digital reverberators, can be controlled using the interface. The interface is a derivative of the RS232 serial bus, but it does differ. The baud rate is defined as 31.25 kbaud, which is a non-standard rate. Further, the bus does not support a communications protocol such as the data terminal ready (DTR) or clear to send (CTS) of the RS232C interface. Finally, in order that ground loops can be avoided, the receiving equipment must provide optical isolation. The commands and data are sent as eight-bit words to one of sixteen possible receiving channels. It is widely used in applications other than the original control of music synthesizers, for example in the control of lighting systems and large automated mixing consoles.

The AES/EBU interface (AES 14, IEC958 for the consumer version) defines the physical, electrical, frame and block structure for the serial transmission of periodically sampled and linearly quantized digital audio data from one transmitter to one or more receivers. The driver and receiver technology is similar to the RS422 balanced drive standard except that, in order to satisfy the EBU, the receiver should be transformer-coupled to achieve d.c. isolation. Optical coupling may also be used, and the relevant standard is being ratified at present (1994) within the AES.

The signal format comprises:

- blocks which contain 192 frames,
- frames which contain two subframes, *A* and *B*,
- subframes which contain 32 time slots:
    Four bits of sync which also allow definition of the start of a block (and also the start of subframe *A*) or the start of subframe *A* only or the start of subframe *B*.
    Four bits for auxiliary audio bits or other data.
    Twenty bits for linearly quantized audio data.
    Four data bits named as validity bit, user data bit, channel status bit, parity bit.

Figure 3.29 shows the construction. The 192 frames thus contain 192 bits of channel status and user data per channel. This is transmitted at the same rate as the sampling frequency and constitutes a prodigiously large amount of data. The format of the channel status bit sequence is well defined, whereas that for the user bit is not defined. It is not yet clear which of several possible strategies would be followed should the editing of such audio data be carried out when the edit point does not coincide with a block boundary. A similar problem exists where streams of blocks arrive independently at some equipment interface for further processing. The task may not just be a matter of synchronizing the individual samples but also one of

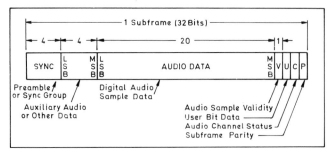

Fig. 3.29. Subframe, frame, and block make-up of the AES/EBU interface

synchronizing blocks and keeping track of the data which is held in the channel status and users bits.

The MADI (Multiple-channel Audio Digital Interface) multiplexes 28 AES channel pairs on to a single coaxial or optical cable. The signalling approach is implemented by FDDI (Fibre Distributed Digital Interface) chips which were developed initially for computer and telecommunications use. Were it not for the need to handle +/– 12 per cent (equivalent to a change of pitch of two semitones either way) of sample rate swing at the professional sampling rate of 48 kHz, the interface could handle 64 individ-ual AES channels. The flexibility has been developed since the standard was first introduced and it is now possible to implement a MADI connec-tion using UTP (Unscreened Twisted Pair) copper cabling in the implemen-tation referred to as CDDI (Copper Distributed Digital Interface).

The ethernet group of interfaces illustrates the convergence of technolo-gies in the field of audio and video. The standard ethernet systems are capa-ble of sending and receiving data at a burst signalling rate of 10 Mbaud whilst the current development focuses on higher rates which are achieved with 100VG (100 Mbaud) ISDN (Integrated Services Digital Network) and ATM (Asynchronous Transfer Mode) technologies. These are derived from the fruits of the convergence of the computing and telecommunication technologies. Indeed, now that audio, and also video, signals are readily available in digital form there is no reason to distinguish between the digi-tal form of such signals and any other data signal. It is the realization of this process which will lead inevitably to consumer equipment for receiving, replaying, and processing entertainment signals being based on the same engine as that used for personal computers.

The key difference between network signals and the simpler serial bus technologies is the possibility for peer-to-peer communication in addition to the conventional master/slave form of operation. These technologies are used to implement digital audio networks in which a number of editing or processing workstations are able to share both the processing and the sig-nals. This implies the embedding of control information within the datastream carrying the audio signal. A key requirement is that the delivery of the audio, or video, signal must be continuous. Networking technologies are also increasingly to be found with audio control systems, where the ability to control and monitor the performance of, for example, a complete installation of power amplifiers can be achieved at one location.

The movement of audio and video in digital form is now closely linked with the generic movement of data from one place to another. Thus it is becoming common for audio signals, particularly where they have been subjected to a bit rate reduction process, to be transmitted within the ISDN system used by telecommunications operations world-wide. For this purpose, audio signals are reduced to fit into the data space offered by 64 kbits^{-1}. One potential problem is that true ISDN working cannot guarantee that two signals will necessarily travel along the same path; only that they will reach their destination in the correct time order. This can be overcome by specifying in advance which paths will be allocated for the signals. An alternative is the use of ATM technology and, in the next few years, it is likely that this technology and the emerging Dark Fibre concepts will come to dominate both the professional and consumer delivery of audio and video signals. This brings with it the realization that there is no reason why the consumer should need to tolerate signals whose quality is any poorer than the professional who formed them. For signals which must be delivered using the scarce resource of cable, terrestrial, or celestial spectrum, there will exist the need to accommodate the signals with some form of bit rate compression (BRC). However, since media costs are always likely to remain low, there is no reason why recorded works should not be disseminated in anything other than full quality.

Analogue-to digital converters

A variety of techniques exist for converting an analogue quantity into digits, and most studios will have equipment, of one sort or another, which incorporates one of the techniques to be described. Some of the techniques simply cannot perform to a 50 kHz sampling rate and 16-bit quantization standard, but that will not have ruled out their use in other applications where the performance criteria are different.

Counter-based techniques

Perhaps amongst the easiest to grasp is that of the kind shown in Figure 3.30. At the start of conversion, the counter is started and an analogue ramp generator starts climbing. The comparator will change state when the ramp has reached the same voltage as the input sampled voltage, and this stops the counter. The size of the count indicates the size of the analogue sample. As a variation, the ramp could be generated digitally, but the principle is

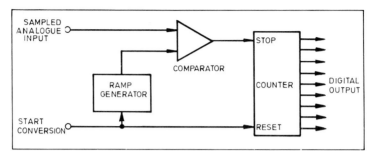

Fig. 3.30. A simple ramp converter

the same. The length of time required for conversion is substantial. For an input equivalent to the maximum count, the counter will have had to count through each of its values. If it were to attempt to reach 16-bit resolution, it would mean counting through 2^{16} (65,536) values, and, if this were required to happen at 50 k samples per second, the clock rate would need to be around 3.3 GHz—which is slightly unrealistic. None the less, it formed the essence of techniques used in early studio delay effects units and in some broadcast sound distribution equipment.

Related to this technique is the dual slope converter which is commonly found in most digital multimeters. Its strong points are its accuracy and cheapness, and its weak point is the slow speed of conversion. Figure 3.31 gives an outline of the converter. The operation cycle starts with S1 closing and S4 opened. The input voltage is integrated for n clock periods, where n is usually the maximum count of the counter. During this time the polarity of the signal can be detected, at the end of the first integration cycle S1 is opened and, depending on the polarity, either S3 or S2 is closed. The counter again counts up from zero but this time it is stopped by the comparator when the integrator output reaches 0 V. The count is then proportional to the input voltage.

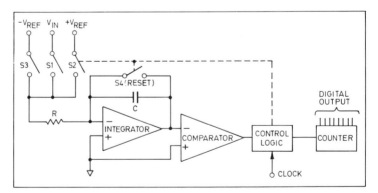

Fig. 3.31. Dual slope converter (the action of the switches is referred to in the text)

The delta modulator method of conversion belongs to a class of integrating-type converters. Figure 3.32 gives a block diagram of a simple delta modulator principle. Note that the output is information regarding the slope of the input signal and not its actual amplitude. Thus to achieve a word which describes the input signal amplitude it is necessary to integrate the output of the modulator. This can readily be done digitally using simple counting techniques.

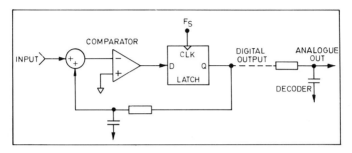

Fig. 3.32. Simple delta modulator and decoder

The analogue input signal is compared to the feedback signal coming from the output of the integrator formed by R and C. The comparator is essentially a one-bit quantizer. The output is converted to a stream of pulses by the D-type flip-flop (acting here as a zero-order hold), which is clocked at some suitable high rate. The output of the flip-flop drives the integrator. The decoder need only consist of a similar integrator. The emergent bit stream can be converted into a more conventional parallel word by counting, over some suitable number of clock periods, the difference between the number of mark periods and space periods at the output of the zero-order hold. This number is used to modify the net number achieved in the previous counting period. There is thus a lot of similarity, in respect of the limitations on the speed of conversion, between this technique and the more blatant counting approaches. However, if some modifications are made to the coding rules, such as transmitting special bits in the serial bit stream in order to indicate that the rate at which the net count is changing, then the system approaches the bounds of usefulness. Developments along similar lines lead to the dbx and Dolby approaches to adaptive delta modulation pulse code modulation (ADPCM).

A two-stage approach is taken in the Sony 16-bit ADC and DACs which are used in the PCM-F1 and CD equipments. The first stage sets the nine more significant bits of the eventual output by counting the time taken for a coarse constant current to charge a capacitor to a voltage just less than the input sampled signal. The second stage sets the seven less significant bits by a similar comparison, using an integrating current which is exactly

$\frac{1}{127}$ the value of the coarse current. The technique has some similarities with the straightforward counting types of converter, with the difference that it involves a two-stage process.

Flash converters

The next obvious approach is to compare the analogue signal to an array of references, each one of which is set to a unique quantization value. The outputs of the comparators are combined to form the required output word. Figure 3.33 shows how simple the block diagram can be. The technique is capable of being very fast but has the disadvantage that an n-bit output requires 2^n comparators. This would be an impractical number for 16-bit conversion but is quite a practical proposition for an eight-bit converter as only 255 comparators are needed. Eight-bit flash converters are extensively used in digitizing video signals. Further, a recent development uses a four-bit flash quantizer in a rather special form of converter which achieves an 18-bit resolution within an audio bandwidth. We shall mention this later.

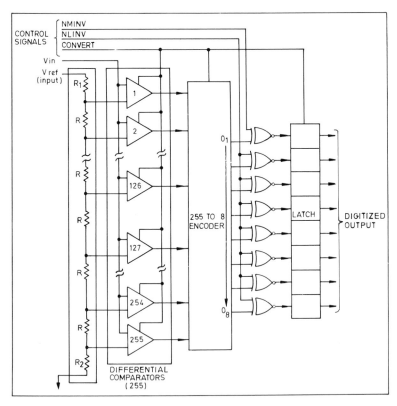

Fig. 3.33. Flash converter diagram

Successive approximation

This is the commonest approach to digitizing audio signals. In Figure 3.34 the general layout of a converter is shown, whilst Figure 3.35 shows the typical waveforms involved, with successive approximation in progress. In the first clock period the most significant bit (msb) of the successive approximation register (SAR) is set. The resulting output of the digital-to-analogue converter (DAC) is compared to the input. If the input is greater, then the msb value is kept. The next clock cycle sets the next most significant bit, and a similar comparison is made. The process is repeated until all the bits have been set and tried.

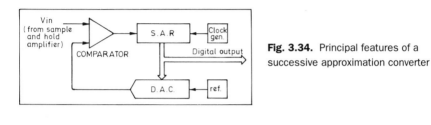

Fig. 3.34. Principal features of a successive approximation converter

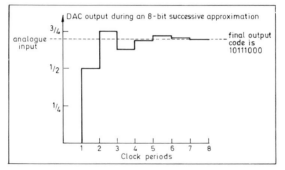

Fig. 3.35. Successive approximation in progress

For an n-bit conversion only n clock cycles are needed; thus a 16-bit conversion at a 50 kHz rate requires an 800 kHz clock rate. This is a practical rate and 16-bit performance can be approached.

Digital-to-analogue conversion

Just as an ADC could be made using counters, so can a DAC. Simply allow an integrator to charge up for a time proportional to the value of the digital word. This method is not much used because it is slow, and the most common technique in use relies on the switching of binary weighted currents.

The R-2R ladder

The approach requires only two resistor values, R and twice R. As Figure 3.36 shows, the $2R$ elements are grounded by the switches either to 0 V or to the virtual earth at the summing junction of the output op-amp. The resistors need to be trimmed to an accuracy better than one part in 2^n (0.0015 per cent for a 16-bit converter). In addition, they need to have matching temperature coefficients and be stable. The operation is based on the binary division of current as it flows down the ladder. The incoming digital data switches the binary weighted currents either to the summing junction, which is a virtual earth, or to ground. An input voltage is needed in order to generate a stable current so that the device can be used as an audio DAC. This is usually a highly stable, very quiet voltage source and is often referred to as a 'voltage reference'. However, there is no reason why some varying signal, such as an audio signal, cannot be used as the voltage source. The output of the DAC would then be a copy of the incoming audio signal but at a level determined by the digital data presented to the DAC. DACs which can be used in this way are called multiplying DACs (MDACs) and can be employed, for example, in digitally controlled faders.

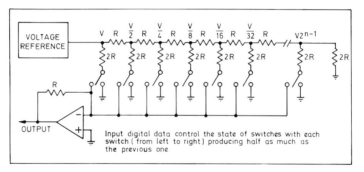

Fig. 3.36. R-2R ladder type of digital-to-analogue converter

A common, and inescapable, problem with parallel-input DACs is the glitch which is produced as the input data word is changed. The causes of the glitch include data bit skew and the different switching times of the individual switches in the DAC itself. As the sizes of the glitches differ for different digital inputs, they cannot be easily filtered out and instead are removed by deglitching. This is usually performed by the zero-order hold circuit, and, as glitch-free switching is very difficult to achieve, most deglitchers essentially replace the varying timing and size of the input glitch for a regular constant-sized one which is more easily filtered out.

The use of an MDAC to control audio level is not without its problems, although the technique is important enough for specially designed logarithmically weighted MDACs to be produced. However, it is not the glitching problem which is mostly responsible for the audible defect, as this is usually well masked by the audio signal itself. The problem is most noticeable when a change in audio level, due to a change in the digital input, occurs at the peak of the audio waveform. A step change in the audio output is created. It is this step which can be heard. Amongst the techniques for reducing its effect is that of arranging for gain changes to occur only at zero crossing-points of the input audio signal.

Not all MDACs can be used successfully in this way as audio attenuators. The alternative approach to generating and switching binary weighted currents is shown in Figure 3.37. The use of an active current source is an advantage in terms of switching speed, and DACs using them are usually found in digital video environments. A mixture of the two approaches to generating binary weighted currents is used in some 16-bit digital audio DACs.

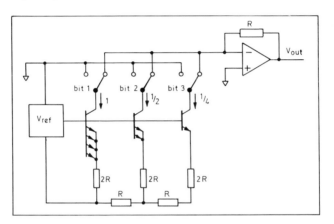

Fig. 3.37. A current-switching DAC (only three bits as shown)

An important variation on the binary weighted current converter was used initially in many of the early CD players. The technique achieves 14-bit linearity without expensive trimming of the current sources integrated on the chip by means of what is referred to as dynamic element matching. The performance is exploited by the oversampling approach to the problems of digital-to-analogue conversion which Philips have pioneered.

Other conversion approaches

Floating-point converters

The floating-point (also called the flying-comma) converter produces an output which is made up of two different parts: the exponent and the mantissa. The exponent part may be thought of as representing the gain applied to the sample prior to quantization by a standard ADC. The output of the ADC becomes the mantissa. Figure 3.38 shows the main elements. Usually the gains are in multiples of 6 dB, so, for example, a three-bit exponent is able to describe a gain range of 42 dB. The conversion of the floating-point word into the commoner fixed-point representation requires the mantissa to be shifted as many spaces to the right as is indicted by the value of the exponent. The technique allows the use of, say, a ten-bit converter with an intrinsic range of approximately 60 dB, to cover a range of over 100 dB. The penalty is that the quantization noise changes with the signal level because the signal level causes changes in the gain of the converter. This results in noise modulation (one of the defects of conventional analogue magnetic tape recording) which produces audible defects if the resolution in the mantissa is inadequate. As a consequence, there exists the need to define the ratio of signal-to-quantization-noise in the presence of the signal (see Figure 3.39).

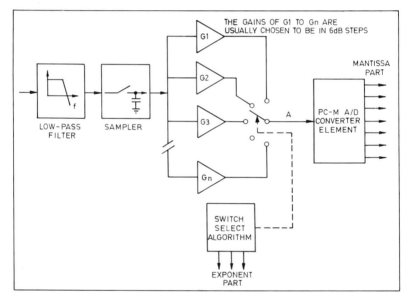

Fig. 3.38. Block diagram of a generalized floating-point conversion system

Floating-point representation is used within many DSP environments in order that the full dynamic range of a calculated result may be retained. The disadvantage of the representation is that for output purposes, including the AES/EBU interface, a conversion must be carried out in order to produce a fixed-point word.

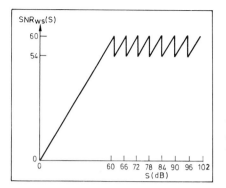

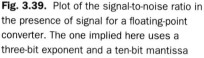

Fig. 3.39. Plot of the signal-to-noise ratio in the presence of signal for a floating-point converter. The one implied here uses a three-bit exponent and a ten-bit mantissa

Because an incoming sample can be validly represented in a combination of exponents and mantissas, and because the converter must be able to change gain across the full range of its capability within the time span of one sample, there exists the need to define the algorithm by which the correct exponent value should be chosen. There are three main ways of doing this: instantaneous, syllabic, and block.

Full accuracy, in terms of monotonicity and linearity, is difficult to achieve if the gain range of the converter is permitted to change at each sample. The stability required of amplifiers, resistor networks, and switches is such that it is probably as easy to design a full-word-width linear converter anyway. In addition, the noise modulation can become objectionable for high-performance audio work, though the technique is used extensively in telephony. The decision as to the correct gain range could also be made over the duration of say 100 to 300 ms. This would be called a syllabic floating-point.

NICAM

In a block-type converter the sampled audio is typically presented to a standard full-range converter which, in the NICAM system used in broadcasting, for example, is 14 bits. A block of samples (typically 32 samples or 1 ms worth of samples in NICAM-3) is scanned, and the largest sample in the block determines the range for the block. The samples within the block are transmitted to ten-bit resolution with respect to the largest word within that block.

Oversampling conversion

Many modern DACs use variations on oversampling techniques. Early CD players from Philips used oversampling and it has since been adapted by a number of semiconductor manufacturers.

The use of a conventional R-2R type ADC places stringent demands on the recovery filter performance. The Philips approach involves resampling the digital audio signal at a frequency four times higher than the original sampling rate. For CD players this is 176.4 kHz and is achieved by a special digital filter chip. The higher sampling rate eases the design constraints on the reconstruction filter but it also allows the output digital word to be rounded off to 14-bit accuracy whilst still maintaining an analogue output with 16-bit resolution. This apparently paradoxical behaviour can be explained by the fact that the quantizing noise is now spread over four times the original audio bandwidth. As only a quarter of this band up to 20 kHz is relevant, the noise power in the audio band is now only a quarter of the total. The signal-to-quantizing-noise ratio is thus 6 dB greater than would be expected from a 14-bit system. A further 7 dB increase in signal-to-noise ratio is achieved by the process called noise-shaping, in which the error created when the output is rounded off to a 14-bit word is fed back to the next sample in such a way that the spectrum of the error signal is moved away from the audio band. The digital output drives a 14-bit ADC but the net performance is that of a 16-bit system. The DAC output is followed by a simple minimum-phase filter in order to remove the sample frequency components from 176.4 kHz upwards.

Similar oversampling and noise-shaping techniques are used, in conjunction with a specialized form of delta-sigma modulator, in an oversampling ADC. A high-speed four-bit flash conversion of the error signal in the delta-sigma modulator is carried out at a 6.14 MHz rate. The digital output is subjected to complex filtering in order to achieve an output at a sampling frequency of 48 kHz with an effective resolution of 18 bits. Incidentally, the process also performs the necessary anti-alias filtering in the digital domain, thus avoiding the imperfections, in both frequency and time response, which accompany analogue anti-alias filtering.

Digital recording

The first aspect of digital audio recording to be noted is the sheer size of the amount of data. For example, the data rate of CD (including formatting and error protection overheads) is 4.3218 Mbits/s, which results in an hour's worth of recording requiring 15.56 gigabits of storage. The requirements of a multi-channel recorder will be proportionally higher. Non-mechanical storage media have been investigated but they are still neither economical nor practical. Random access memory (RAM) sizes are increasing though 256 Mbit RAMs have yet to appear.

Recordable optical disc technology is improving rapidly but, partly because of the difficulty of moving the optical sensor head quickly over the disc surface, such systems are not yet capable of recording more than one fully linearly encoded stereo channel in real time. High-density floppy discs are able to store useful lengths (up to 70s) of BRC processed audio and such machines are finding increasing use as a replacement for the analogue cartridge machines used, for example, for radio station jingles, advertisements, and news items. Magnetic tape is still the preferred medium for multitrack work where long-term storage of the master recording is required. However, magnetic-disc-based systems which can essentially emulate the performance of a short length of multitrack tape are finding use, particularly in post-production areas.

Ideally, there are only two magnetic states recorded on the tape. The record current is simply reversed in direction in order to create the required flux reversals. On replay, these transitions in polarity produce a pulse in the replay head, the size of which is dependent on the rate of change of the flux. It is the timing of successive transitions that is important, and a major feature of a digital data channel is that the signal-to-noise ratio need only lie in the range 21–30 dB—after all, the replay processing has only to decide whether the replayed signal was a one or a zero. The effect of noise is to introduce an error into this decision process, and it is more effective to provide error correction than it is to increase the signal-to-noise ratio (see Figure 3.40).

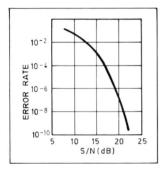

Fig. 3.40. The relationship between error rate and signal-to-random-noise ratio. The signal is assumed peak-to-peak and the noise is r.m.s. measured

The packing density of information on tape is typically around 40,000 bits per inch, and the dominant cause of errors is dropouts. These may be caused by dirt between the tape and the heads or by defects in the tape's magnetic coating. A dropout only 0.5 mm long will cause a burst of errors nearly 800 bits long. The separation of the tape from the replay head causes a loss of signal amplitude at a rate of 55 dB per wavelength of separation, and a fine dust particle only 1 μm in size will cause complete loss of replayed information. There are two main phases in handling errors: first they must be detected, and then they must be concealed or corrected. These stages can be accomplished only by adding more bits to the data already present. These extra bits may increase the number of bits by up to 50 per cent.

The magnetic tape medium has no d.c. response but the raw data (which is in the form of a non-return-to-zero (NRZ) code) does have significant energy around d.c. In order to preserve the timing information and to aid accurate data recovery, it is necessary for the data to be further encoded to match the characteristics of the recording channel. It is also useful if the encoding rule also enables easy recovery of the basic data clock rate during replay, whilst at the same time making economical use of tape. Of the many coding schemes in use, the three commoner ones in the digital audio arena are the HDM-1 scheme used in DASH format recorders, the EFM scheme used in the CD system, and MFM (also known as modified frequency modulation and self-clocking Manchester coding), which is common in floppy and hard magnetic discs. The AES/EBU digital audio interface uses the similar but simpler FM channel coding. The replay signal is fed to a data separator which produces both the clock and the data outputs.

The two main types of recording format in use are stationary-head and rotary-head. Originally rotary head recorders were based on available video recorder transports, since these could achieve the high head-to-tape speed required at the same time as requiring relatively slow linear tape speed. Thus the organization of the data on to tape has been dictated by the details of television standards. Indeed, the choice of sampling frequency for CD is related to the constraints imposed by television. Stationary head recorders employ multiple tracks in order to maximize the use of tape area, and currently are the only way of achieving 24- and 32-track recorders. Modern editors provide greater flexibility than was possible with cut-and-paste editing of analogue tapes. Thus audio editing has arrived at much the same state that video editing reached some time before.

Magnetic disc systems are emerging as a viable alternative to tape, offering up to one hour of stereo on a single disc. Advances are being made in both magnetic and optical recording technology, and are discussed throughout this book, for example in Chapters 12 and 28. Current emphasis on optical techniques is providing the relatively low cost magneto-optical (MO) drives which are available within the computer industry.

Error detection

The choice of an error protection scheme needs to be made after consideration of the error-generating characteristics of the recording medium. Most errors in magnetic recording will arise in bursts, and so schemes which can handle bursts of corrupted data are preferred over those which can handle isolated randomly spaced errors.

The simplest scheme used to detect errors is called 'parity'. The data word to be protected is scanned, an extra bit is added on to the word, and it is set to a one or zero in order that the number of ones in the whole word is

	data	even parity	
Input A	10110101	1	} correct
Input B	01011010	0	
	↓		
Output A	10010101	1	} incorrect, parity check fails
Output B	01011110	0	
	↑		

Fig. 3.41. The principle behind simple parity checking

an even number (called even parity); see Figure 3.41. Parity can only indicate when an odd number of errors has occurred and it cannot indicate which bit is in error. Failure of a parity check is thus an indication that some further action should be taken.

A more complex detection technique is the cyclic redundancy check (CRC), in which a checkword is added to the data word in order to make it an integral multiple of a known divisor. This has enough power to detect all errors whose burst length, in bits, does not exceed the checkword length. Developments of CRC techniques permit the location of the error to be determined. As in any one-bit position there can be only one of two states, so that knowledge of the position of the error automatically indicates the correct setting at that bit position.

The most common codes in digital use, however, are developments of the CRC approach to detection applied to whole words, and are known as Reed–Solomon codes. These are a class of block codes which have been devised to handle burst errors and their correction efficiently. Further improvement in the robustness comes about through interleaving the code words. The effectiveness of the technique relies on distributing a long-burst error over a longer length of data, such that it appears as an apparently random sprinkling of much smaller-burst errors each of which can be easily detected and corrected (see Figure 3.42). The process is refined in the cross-interleave Reed–Solomon coding used in CD. The Xs mark the location of words assumed to have been corrupted. After de-interleave, the errors are distributed throughout the sequence of words.

The DASH format, however, uses a similar cross-interleave method but employs a development of the simple parity technique in which two sets of parity code words are created. The first, known as P code, is formed before the interleaving process, and the second, known as Q code, is formed after the process.

Having detected that a particular word is in error, it is necessary to decide what to do about it. if the correct value of the word can be deduced then it

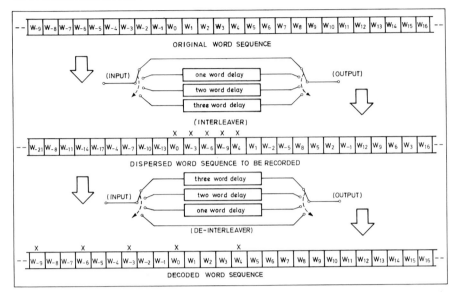

Fig. 3.42. Interleave and de-interleave

can be fully corrected. It will then appear at the output of the digital audio system as if it had never suffered any deprivation. Where the correct value of the word cannot be deduced, but is known to be in error, it can be replaced either by the last known good word or by the average of two good words on either side of it. This latter process is known as interpolation and is a form of error concealment. Other forms of interpolation (another example of digital filtering) involving many previous correct samples are not much in use at present. If the severity of the burst of errors is such that no suitable samples exist in order to perform interpolation, then the commonest strategy adopted is to mute the output. This will usually take the form of a rapid fadeout to silence until a correctable sequence of samples is again available.

The correction power of these codes is fairly formidable. For three of the common digital audio formats they are as shown in Table 3.3.

Table 3.3. Typical correction powers

Format type	Full correction	Concealment	
		Good	Marginal
EIAJ	rotary head	4,096 bits	8,192
DASH	stationary head	8,640 bits	33,982	83,232
CD	optical disc	3,874 bits	13,282	15,495

The random error correctability of various coding techniques is shown in Figure 3.43.

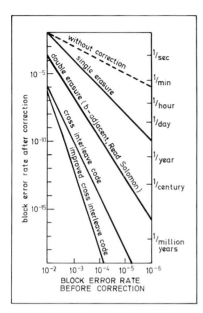

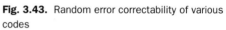

Fig. 3.43. Random error correctability of various codes

Digital terminology

Analogue (or analog)	A continuous signal representing the variation of some physical event with the passage of time.
Bit	Short for binary digit.
Baud	The number of bits per second used to transmit a digital signal. It includes the signalling information such as the stop and start bits, and so the number of data bits actually sent per second is less than the baud rate.
Byte	A digital word comprising eight bits.
Nybble (*sic*)	A digital word comprising four bits.
Word	A digital word the size of which is dependent on the processor handling capacity. In digital audio processing this is commonly 24 bits.
Digital	Represented by a number.
Digital signal	A group of digital words which represent an analogue signal.
DSP	Digital Signal Processing; processing a digital signal using digital computing techniques.

Quantizing	Measurement of a signal amplitude to the nearest whole number of quantizing intervals or steps.
Quantizing noise	The ineluctable error resulting from the act of quantizing. The difference between the original signal and its quantized equivalent is unwanted noise or distortion.

For example, for a signal quantized by a perfect n-bit converter the peak value of the maximum signal will be $2^{(n-1)} \times Q$ and the maximum sine wave signal that could be passed is thus $Q \times 2^{(n-1)} \sqrt{2}$. We can estimate the quantization error energy by taking the energy for a given error X and multiplying it by the probability of this energy occurring $Pr(x)dX$. The integral between $\pm Q/2$ of $X^2 Pr(X)dX$ for all possible values of error gives the error energy. This, when transformed into a voltage, works out to the 'known' equation SNR[dBu] = 6.02 $\times n + 1.76$.

Dither	A low-level random signal, added to the analogue signal prior to sampling and quantizing, which acts as if to spread the highly correlated quantization noise across the audio spectrum. It results in low-level signals being quantized more linearly. Low-level signals can thus be encoded below the apparent noise floor of the system.

A very important need for dither arises at the output of a DSP unit when the output word is required to be rounded down to 16 bits. A small pseudo-random binary number is added to the full-range digital audio word at bit positions 17 downwards and the top 16 bits of the digital word are output. Forming a 16-bit result from a longer word (usually called *truncation*), by simply taking the top 16 bits without even rounding up, is a process identical to quantizing an already sampled signal and is thus subject to the same limitation when the signal is represented by the bits at the lsb end of the 16-bit word. Adding a pseudo-random number, with a peak value equal to half an lsb (in this case up to and including the 17th bit), is analogous to the addition of random noise to the sampled signal during the original digitizing process.

Binary	A signal represented as one of two possible states.
Gate	A basic item of logic hardware. There are really only two gates, AND and OR. With the addition of the negation or inversion operation, all the other types of gate can be formed. These include NAND, NOR, EXCLUSIVE OR types.
ADC	Analogue-to-digital converter.
DAC	Digital-to-analogue converter.
Interface	A catch-all word for describing the way items of equipment need to talk to each other. An interface can be implemented in either software or hardware or a combination of both.

Hardware	The physical nuts and bolts, gates and connectors, transformers and chips, which comprise equipment.
Chip	A plentiful component of impoverished deserts (the silicon in sand) which is processed in order to enhance its semiconductor nature and thus provide transistors, microprocessors, and so on.
Microprocessor	A chip which is capable of executing a program.
Software	A program written for a microprocessor or other computing device. Sometimes used to refer to the recorded music.
Firmware	A program for a computing device which is resident within the equipment. It is not usually modifiable and forms part of what is known as the operating system. It may be held (stored) in ROM (usually an EPROM) or on a magnetic disc.
EPROM	Erasable Programmable Read Only Memory. Usually erased by short-wavelength UV light; other types include EEPROMs which are erasable electrically. Their main characteristic is that they can be read from many times faster than they can be written to. PROMs may be programmed only once, by the chip manufacturer in what is often referred to as a silicon foundry.
RAM	Random Access Memory. There are two main types—static and dynamic.
Flip-flop	A general term for a circuit which can be configured to behave as a latch, a counter, or a register. Sometimes loosely called a *bistable*.
Monostable	Related to a bistable, but produces an output which, when triggered, is present only for some definable time.
Alias	Sideband created when an analogue signal is sampled. If the sampling frequency is not more than twice the highest frequency component of the signal, then the alias will appear within the bandwidth of the signal.
Sampling	Freezing or capturing the amplitude of a signal at some constant rate.
Anti-alias filter	A filter which will ideally remove from a signal all components above some critical frequency. These filters are difficult to design as they must provide a high cut-off rate with minimal group delay distortion.
Parity	The primeval error detection technique. The number of ones in a word are added up. The answer will be either odd or even. The parity bit is an extra bit which is appended to the word in order to make the sum of all the bits either even (even parity) or odd (odd parity). This simple process can detect the existence of any odd number of errors but it cannot point to where the error is and thus cannot correct it.

Domain	Often heard in phrases such as the digital domain, the analogue domain, and so on. It is simply a way of stating what aspect of a signal is of fundamental interest.
Monotonicity	When the input to a converter (a/d or d/a) is increased, then the output should also increase. This is known as monotonic performance, and for 16-bit audio quality converters it is difficult to achieve.
Dynamic range	This is the ratio, in dB, between the peak level of a signal (at, say, the level of 3 per cent distortion) and the noise floor associated with it (measured here as the quasi-peak CCIR weighted noise unless otherwise mentioned).
Discrete	A signal is described as discrete when it has been sampled and quantized. It is a single, discrete point, whereas, by comparison, the analogue signal is continuous.
Recursive filters	Also known as IIR response filters, they are a common form of filter in audio DSP because of their speed. It typically takes only five MAC operations to perform a DSP equivalent of the analogue state variable filter. However, IIR filters are sensitive to the values of the coefficients used and can produce limit cycle oscillations with certain combinations of filter structure and values of coefficients.
FIR filters	Also known as transversal filters, they form the other main class of digital filter (there is a third class, a hybrid, called lattice filters). FIR filters can produce linear phase response (low or zero group delay error), unlike IIR filters. They do delay the signal more because of the larger number of stages involved, and this severely limits the rate at which groups of samples can be handled by a processor. Filters used in oversampling converters are usually FIR types.
Limit cycles	An affliction of IIR filter types; certain structures are more prone to the problem. It is a condition in which the output of a filter is an oscillation, often at a low amplitude, which is caused by a particular circumstance of the input sample sequence and the coefficient values. Sometimes the problem arises through not being able to implement sufficient precision in the coefficients.
Port	A term used in electronic engineering to indicate a terminal or point from which a signal can be received (output port) or to which it can be sent (input port). Clearly there can also be bidirectional ports. The port might consist of several points (or lines) in parallel. Port is also used as a verb, and it then refers to the preparation and subsequent debugging of software which has been written on one system and is required to work on a different system.

COPAS

Computer for Processing Audio Signals. An interesting development pioneered by G. McNally at the BBC. The Mk 2 system underpins the development of the Neve DSP desk system.

Deglitcher

As the input code to a DAC is increased or decreased by small changes, it passes through what are known as major and minor transitions. The most major transition occurs at half scale (around zero volts for an audio signal) and is the point at which all bits change state. If, at major transitions, the switches of the DAC differ in the switching rates, then, for a short time, the DAC output will be a very different value. These short-term spikes or glitches are very difficult to remove by filtering. A deglitcher is a device which either removes them or at least makes them all the same. It usually comprises a fast sample-and-hold circuit which holds the output constant until the DAC switches have settled. The function is usually combined with the DAC output zero-order hold function.

A law and μ law

Descriptions of the quantizing law used in two similar non-linear ADCs. Fundamentally suited to telecomms use, the A law is in use in Europe and the μ law is used in the USA. The encoding performance yields a dynamic range of a twelve-bit linear encoder but uses only eight bits. The encoding law is part of the intrinsic chip design but is also describable mathematically. Manufacturers' data books will reveal more.

Shannon and Nyquist

Shannon's paper, 'Communication in the Presence of Noise', Proc IRE vol. 37 January 1947, comes long after Nyquist's 'Certain Topics in Telegraph Transmission', Trans AIEE April 1928. Both papers can be related to sampling. Shannon said that a signal can be completely defined if sampled at more than twice the required signal bandwidth. Nyquist said that so long as this is so there will be no aliasing.

Complement

Two forms of complement are used here:
Ones complement is another way of saying that each bit in a digital word is inverted. Thus a one becomes a zero and a zero becomes a one.

Twos complement of a number is formed by taking its ones complement and adding 1 to the lsb. For example: to form the twos complement of 0110, first take the one complement 1001, and then add a one to the lsb 0001, which gives the result 1010.

You can play with complements using ordinary decimal numbers: nines complement is the equivalent of the binary ones complement and tens complement is the equivalent of twos complement.

Cyclic redundancy   A form of error detection. It words by adding, to a digital word, a number known as the checkword which will make the total an integral multiple of some dividing factor. In decoding, the replay information is divided by that factor, and, if there is no error, there will be no remainder and the original digital word will be able to be produced by subtracting the checkword. If an m-bit cyclic redundancy checkword (CRC) is added to a k-bit long data word, the code word formed will be $n = m + k$ bits long.

The technique can detect all burst errors of m-bits or less, and the misdetection of a burst error longer than m-bits is $2^{(m+1)}$. Clearly the longer the checkword the greater the detection ability, but the redundancy overhead is also increased. The division by the polynomial factor is achieved using a shift register with feedback.

4

Studio planning and installation

Andy Munro

Studio planning encompasses many disciplines, including some not immediately associated with the business and operation of recording studios. Installation is simply the execution of the planned schedule of works, and success or failure is almost entirely a result of the technical competence and experience of the studio 'designer'.

The word 'studio' is taken generally to mean any area associated with the technical or artistic procedures involved in the recording process. It may be argued that, to some clients, the quality of a studio's facilities in terms of catering and recreation are just as important as the quality of the studio acoustics or mixing console. However, a successful studio design is invariably the result of interpreting the exact requirements of the client, who presumably (but by no means always) has an equal understanding of his own (and his customers') recording and business philosophy.

The first step in the planning procedure is always the client's brief, assuming that there exists a normal client–designer relationship. Should a studio owner decide to perform the role of designer or utilize the expertise of his own staff, then the procedure remains essentially the same, although there will be many decisions which will necessitate outside help, if only for reasons of legality. The decision to appoint a studio designer and, with more difficulty, which type of designer to choose, does not lie within the scope of this chapter. However, it is hoped that the reader placed in such a position will be better able to judge his requirements for a particular project through awareness of the various disciplines involved.

The design brief

The brief for the design of a new studio can be broken into four main areas for the purposes of initial planning:

1. Establishing the studio format

Apart from the obvious requirements regarding format, it should be established that the studio is intended to provide a particular technical facility and that any present or future needs are fully understood. For example, the requirement may be a 24-track room suitable for recording mainly electronic music but with the need for overdubbing vocals and single acoustic instruments. There may be additional requirements for synthesizer programming and other 'off line' activities as well as for copy and duplication facilities. This description of a fairly typical contemporary studio could conceivably materialize into a 50 m² home 'workshop' or a complex electronic music and mix-down facility covering 250 m² and costing £1 million. The format, therefore, must include a detailed analysis of the type of equipment envisaged, the precise nature of the material intended for production, and an analysis of the requirements of clients, engineers, and producers.

2. Outline budget

No studio facility can be successfully designed without a thorough understanding of the capital cost requirements in relation to the intended use and revenue of the business. There are relatively few situations where studios are not subject to some form of fiscal analysis and it is essential to work within precise cost constraints from the outset. Costs can be divided into three distinct categories:

1. Building and fixed plant
2. Equipment and facilities
3. Operational costs and overheads.

At the feasibility stage of any project, the designer should present the client with such information as will enable both capital and running costs to be established. The client should also make the designer fully aware of all cost constraints from the beginning, so that all upper limits can be agreed.

It is the responsibility of the designer to set out the benefits and aesthetic requirements of various levels of expenditure, giving as much value for money as possible and a scale of expenditure priorities. An example of poor design would be where the reception desk cost more than the chairs for the engineer and producer.

3. Building requirements

Having established the format and budget, the requirements for a suitable building are logical in terms of space and cost. Additional factors must be considered, and these fall into five categories:

(a) Geographical location: may be important for many reasons including proximity of clients (e.g. Soho for film work); by contrast, a rural location might be chosen for peace and tranquillity.

(b) Environmental considerations: studios are invariably places which function in isolation from their immediate environment. It is therefore important that the outside world should not impose itself on the studio in terms of noise, pollution, or interference. It would not be advisable to build a studio under a railway arch, or next to a glue factory or a first-division football ground. The fact that people sometimes do is testimony to the unfailing optimism of the music industry!

(c) Aesthetic appeal: is sadly neglected in the planning of most studios. Cost is the usual excuse for this, but in reality it is often simply a lack of imagination and design. The successful conversion of derelict dockside warehouses in London and Liverpool is a perfect example of industrial renovation and architectural enterprise.

(d) Planning restrictions: take many forms and are intended to prevent an individual or company from establishing an entity or activity which will detract from the balance and well-being of the locality and its occupants. The fact that a well-planned studio makes virtually no impact at all on its environment is a source of constant amazement to planning officers who invariably expect to contend with noise, heavy traffic, and undesirable aliens disguised as musicians. This having been said, do not expect to turn a Victorian listed church into a multi-studio and business complex without a considerable amount of persuasion, often involving meetings in draughty community halls trying to convince local pensioners that they have less to fear from a recording centre than from almost any other commercial activity. One factor which can cause considerable problems is that of an hours-of-use restriction. In residential areas it is common for commercial activity to be prohibited at night.

As in all matters relating to planning, no approach should be made without consulting a local surveyor or architect with a view to identifying possible pitfalls.

(e) Building regulations: often overlap various planning requirements and are basically related to public safety. Areas of particular concern to studio planning are:

• Fire regulations and means of escape
• Floor loading and structural safety
• Suitability of materials and building methods.

In all but the most basic of studio projects, it is necessary to appoint a qualified structural engineer in order to satisfy by calculation any local statutory regulations.

Having satisfied all the preceding requirements, the preliminary feasibility work can be started, assuming that a suitable building is available or proposed. It is at this stage that a direct relationship can be established between the area and expenditure in terms of unit cost per square metre. The final costing should reflect the decisions and approach taken at this stage, and will make the difference between satisfactory completion and a project that simply runs out of money.

4. Market research

There has been an explosion in the audio recording industry in recent years, prompted by an increased demand in almost every market sector. The complex interaction between the record, broadcasting, and cinematograph industries has fuelled the growth in specialist facilities and studios capable of providing a wide range of technical expertise in addition to the traditional concept of music album production.

In any growing industry it is difficult to predict precise market trends but it should be an essential step in any proposed new venture to analyse and examine the degree of commercial viability of the project. One thing is certain: assuming a static demand, for every new and technically advanced facility which is brought into service there must be a pruning of existing outdated studios in order to maintain equilibrium. For this reason, established successful studios are constantly updating and improving their facilities in order to avoid what is best described as the 'leap-frog effect'.

Feasibility study

If we can assume that the project has passed through the initial critical analysis contained in the briefing stage, it then becomes necessary to carry out a detailed feasibility study. Assuming that a suitable building space has been found, a full survey should be carried out and drawings produced at 1: 50 scale. From these the designer and/or client should prepare accurate presentations of the studio areas at 1: 50 in order to establish the suitability of the space. By way of example, Figure 4.1 shows an effective plan for a corner location.

At this point the designer will have initial discussions with various consultants concerning primarily the acoustic performance, structural requirements, services such as ventilation and electrics, and possibly interior design. The degree of involvement of specialists in any of these areas will depend on the complexity of the project and the existence of particularly difficult design situations.

It must be said that in most cases the acoustic requirements will take precedence in the decision-making process, although if such decisions are taken in isolation the results will invariably be aesthetically disappointing. Following agreement of a basic scheme, full costing should be carried out from a set of 1:100 drawings together with sufficient information as deemed necessary by the various consultants. It is the acceptance of this costing which marks the transition of the project from feasibility to full appointment and contract.

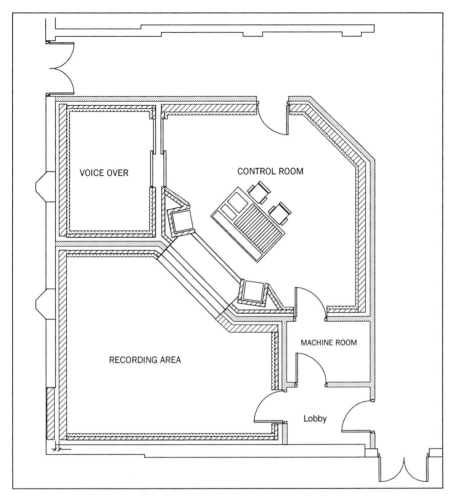

Fig. 4.1. Outline plan for a corner location. The cross-hatching indicates different wall constructions and acoustic treatments

Appointments and contracts

It is now necessary to agree on the following appointments, again allowing for the actual scale of the project:

(*a*) Architect and/or project manager
(*b*) Structural and services consultants
(*c*) Acoustic designer/consultant

(d) Quantity surveyor

(e) Interior designer.

Some or all of these functions may overlap or be dispensed with by agreement with the client. Most specialist studio design companies offer a degree of rationalization of the individual roles, based on a thorough knowledge of their craft. When a studio owner attempts to fulfil some of these roles himself, this invariably ends in less than satisfactory results with little, or even a negative, cost advantage.

However, the client will probably have a reasonable idea of the required studio performance in terms of existing, comparable facilities, together with a firm opinion on what is right or wrong with such operations. A strongly expressed desire for such things as natural lighting or a feeling of openness (or possibly intimacy) will indicate to the designer a sense of the direction in which to proceed.

Acoustic requirements must be defined very precisely, as there is no area of discussion more open to ambiguity and evasive definitions. There is a precedent for acoustic design being enveloped in marketing concepts, much as in the way 'designer' clothes are packaged. The advantages of this are difficult to see, except to clients who literally have no sense of uniqueness or individuality, and to whom the concept of a packaged product offers some sense of safety.

Unfortunately, the laws of acoustics are such that even relatively standardized design systems can lead to widely differing results. It is equally gratifying, frustrating, and stimulating to find that it seems impossible to quantify the acoustic performance of rooms. The first concerted efforts to do just this were made by Beranek in the USA, by relating precise acoustic measurements in concert halls to the subjective appraisal of performances given in the same auditoria. Although several basic design criteria were established, subsequent projects proved that there were undoubtedly several 'missing links' to providing the 'perfect acoustic environment'.

There is, without doubt, a growing awareness of the possible improvements that are being made in acoustic design through an understanding of the complex relationship between time, energy, and frequency as perceived by the musical observer. Works carried out by such brilliant individuals as R.C. Heyser, M. Schroeder, and V. Pentz all concentrate on the overriding importance of the time domain in the qualitative assessment of acoustic performance. Several aspects of acoustic specification will be defined later in this chapter.

The completion of the feasibility stage of design will have several immediate effects. First, all specialists will either be given full appointment, or retention will cease. There are important legal considerations to take into account, all of which should be explored by the architect or designer. Full legal responsibility can be established only through precise procedures, and it is important that any client makes himself aware of the protection or lack of it afforded by professional liability and indemnity. It is equally important that the designer satisfies himself of the integrity and solvency of the client, as in many ways the designer carries the greater risk.

In law any contract which is deemed to be valid must satisfy these simple criteria:

- Agreement: definition and evidence of terms
- Certainty: evidence of acceptance by both parties
- Consideration: evidence of benefit to both parties
- Capacity: an invalidation due to age or insanity
- Consent: both parties must freely consent
- Legality of objects: the contract must not constitute an illegal act
- Object: the object of the contract must be possible
- Formality: sometimes a contract must be written to be valid.

When one has presented the full feasibility study and obtained consent to proceed, after making all necessary amendments and adjustments, the following information will be required:

(a) Full production drawings at 1 : 20. These will be distributed to all consultants with instructions regarding the information required.

(b) Full instructions to the quantity surveyor in order to verify and establish the project budget. Any cost variations not anticipated at the feasibility stage must be referred to the client, excepting of course minor 'swings and roundabouts' fluctuations.

(c) Statutory consents must be obtained from all relevant authorities such as planning, fire, pollution, offices, building, and electrical supply. Outline approvals, obtained at the feasibility stage, should ensure that this stage will be a formality unless significant design changes occur.

(d) Agreement of professional fees. It is standard architectural practice to base all professional design fees on the RIBA percentage scale. In the event that a complete design–build package has been negotiated in advance, this will be irrelevant. It is hard to imagine any other industry where the client agrees to pay for something to be built before it has been designed, but this does sometimes occur in the recording industry.

It is the purpose of architectural design to ensure that the client will receive the most appropriate service for every aspect of his building. Whenever possible, competitive tender will be sought for each phase of the work involved, and payment will ensue only upon satisfactory completion of the work. The design–build approach often involves advance payment for work, which in all legal senses is extremely risky. Ultimately, the client should satisfy himself of the risk and exposure to which he is committed, but there can be little double than an independent designer–client relationship, with separate appointment of contractors, offers the greatest degree of protection to all concerned.

Design fees should be paid in stages according to the contracts finalized at this stage of the project. Any cost adjustments resulting from savings during the main contract will be adjusted on completion.

As production information flows into the design office, it is important to establish a formal series of drawings issues. This prevents specialists working with outdated information as the design progresses. For example, a decision to move technical ducting may require the repositioning of air-conditioning ducts, which may interfere with acoustic treatment. Such breakdowns in information exchange can turn a site during contract into an extremely unpleasant environment, where nobody trusts the information available. It is the function of the designer to provide fully co-ordinated information to all concerned. This is one of the two most important, even crucial, aspects of any project. The other is the appointment of the building main contractor.

Whereas the feasibility stage of a project must satisfy client, backers, investors, and bankers, the production stage of the design must produce sufficiently accurate information for persons totally uninvolved in the design process to comprehend fully and appreciate exactly what is required and expected. There will be aspects of the work which are so specialized that nominated subcontractors must be appointed. Typical areas for this approach will be computer installations, specialist acoustic materials supply, and monitor systems. In these cases, negotiations and appointment will be discussed with the client and negotiated directly with the individuals concerned.

The appointment of the main contractor would always ideally be the subject of competitive tender, but, for the following reasons, this may not be the case:

(a) The client may wish to negotiate with a single known contractor
(b) Time may prevent a full tender procedure
(c) Design cost constraints may not allow full production of tender information
(d) A geographical constraint may dictate a properly managed package format.

Where full tender procedure is used, every care must be exercised to ensure that the contractors invited to quote are sufficiently equipped and experienced to carry out the work. It has been said that there is no such thing as a specialist acoustic builder, just good builders and bad builders. It is true!

Following successful tender, the appointed builder must agree to the standard form of contract chosen for the purpose. This will include discussions on damages in the event that the contract is not completed according to schedule. Considering the high cost of delays to opening a studio, the builder must be fully satisfied that he can meet the completion date specified.

Prior to appointment of the contractor, a detailed briefing should be given to the client in order to agree formal acceptance. It should also be pointed out to the client that, on appointment, the architect must act as mediator and arbitrator to both sides. This is particularly important in the matter of issuing stage payment certificates.

Prior to commencing the contract, the appointed contractor must submit a schedule of works. This will enable all specialists to plan site visits and their own time slots as required. Regular site meetings are an essential part of all building programmes, and they make possible an exchange of information with the minimum of paperwork. Minutes of site meetings should be distributed to all present, with actionable items highlighted for the individuals concerned. At each subsequent meeting, previous minutes should be discussed and results measured. Failure to take action on the agreed procedures may invoke penalties and ultimately lead to the dismissal of the persons responsible.

A standard form of building contract in use in this country is published by the Joint Contracts Tribunal (JCT) and is accepted by all professional bodies, including chartered surveyors, engineers, and architects. There are nineteen standard documents published by JCT, covering everything from minor works to multi-million-pound developments. Contract law outside the UK will inevitably differ and interested parties should consult with a local architect.

When working outside the protection of a formal contract, both parties should adhere to the law of simple contract as previously discussed. No contract can be expected to run perfectly from start to finish, and some provision must be made for variations. Technical revisions, unforeseen site difficulties, and changes of mind may all cause prolongation or increased quantities and costs. Extensions and additional instructions should be issued in written form, with agreement obtained from both client and contractor.

Stages of completion are subject to inspection, and, following discussions regarding defects and remedial action, certificates are issued to authorize payment in full. It is usual to negotiate a retention by the client for a fixed period, in order to ensure rapid attention to defects occurring in the initial period of occupation.

Aspects of the project

Having covered the broad scope of the design and contract procedure, it is advisable to discuss in detail some specific aspects of each part of the project. A complete list is beyond the scope of this chapter, but the most important aspects are outlined below.

1. Acoustic isolation

There is a great deal of misunderstanding about isolation in studios, but there are really only three requirements.

(a) Isolation from the outside environment: the traditionally accepted ambient noise level inside recording areas is NC15, and within monitoring areas NC20–5 is often specified (see Chapter 5). In practice these levels can be achieved in central city areas only by elaborate floating structures designed to give isolation down to 25 Hz.

The efficiency of a resiliently mounted structure is frequency-dependent and defined thus:

$$\text{Efficiency } (\%) = 100 \times \left(1 - \frac{1}{(R^2 - 1)} \right)$$

where R is the ratio of the forcing frequency and the natural frequency.

The natural frequency of a resilient mount under load is given by:

$$\text{Fn} = \frac{16}{\sqrt{d}}$$

where d is the static deflection under load in mm.

It can be seen that without additional damping such resilient systems can become unstable if the forcing frequency is equal to the natural frequency. It is therefore imperative that such systems are both damped and have a natural frequency of at least half the lowest significant exciting frequency.

(b) Isolation between rooms inside the studio complex: can be defined simply at the design stage by predicting sound levels in one area and the required background noise in another. For example, if the monitor system in the control room generates boundary levels of 120 dB, and a small adjacent studio is required to record speech with a noise floor of 20 dB, the required isolation would be approaching 100 dB.

Such a situation would represent poor design in that 100 dB of isolation would involve extremely expensive structures, whereas a simple planning decision could relocate the voice studio to another part of the complex. The creation of buffer zones and sound locks is far cheaper than lead-lined double-skin structural shells. Acoustic doors and windows are expensive items and should be minimized through similar zoning.

To emphasize the difficulty of achieving isolation to the order of 100 dB, the requirement by Mass Law alone (see Chapter 5) would be for three sheets of 15 mm float glass, each independently mounted, with no direct air coupling between them. This is not impossible, but is certainly at the limits of technical achievement.

(c) Reduction of noise generated inside the complex: internally generated noise consists of services such as ventilation, equipment with mechanical movement, and fan cooling systems. With the advent of digital recording, there is a tendency to place tape recorders in separate clean-air environments, with the added advantage of reducing noise in the control room. Similarly, amplifiers and computer racks should be installed in a separate technical area (machine room).

Noise transmitted through air-conditioning ducts must be attenuated before it enters critical areas. Low-velocity air supply will eliminate noise caused by turbulence, but this will increase the cross-sectional area requirements for ductwork and grilles. Typical design figures are 1 m/sec for grille velocity and ten changes of air per hour for medium-sized rooms. Air-conditioning contractors should give written performance specifications for every room, based on a brief provided by the designer.

2. Room acoustics

As this subject is dealt with in the next chapter, it is only necessary to elaborate here on aspects relating to planning and execution.

The acoustics of both recording rooms and control rooms must be discussed at great length in order to establish a final specification. Control room designs, as previously mentioned, have often been shrouded in marketing jargon rather than involving specific criteria.

The simple requirements are as follows:

(a) Control room: (i) There should be sufficient area at the mixing console for engineer and producer to hear a faithful representation of the material replayed through the monitor system (see Figure 4.2).

(ii) The monitor system should deliver a faithful representation of the signal applied to it in terms of level, frequency and phase response, harmonic distortion, and impulse response. Should the system require equalization to perform correctly, there should be true minimum-phase correlation between the amplitude and phase response.

(iii) The ratio between direct and reflected energy in the room should be sufficient to maintain accurate stereo imaging and tracking of the sound balance. At this point it should be noted that the D/R ratio will be affected by the acoustic Q of the monitor system, with higher values of Q increasing D/R.

(iv) The total decay time of the room should not be so long as to prevent distinct perception of reverberation and time delay applied to the recorded signal itself. The exact value as measured by the traditional RT60 method should be between 0.2 and 0.3 sec at middle and high frequencies, rising gradually below the 125–150 Hz band.

(v) Standing waves in the room should be sufficiently damped and distributed as uniformly as possible across the audio spectrum. Tuned narrowband absorption may be introduced to reduce particular modes.

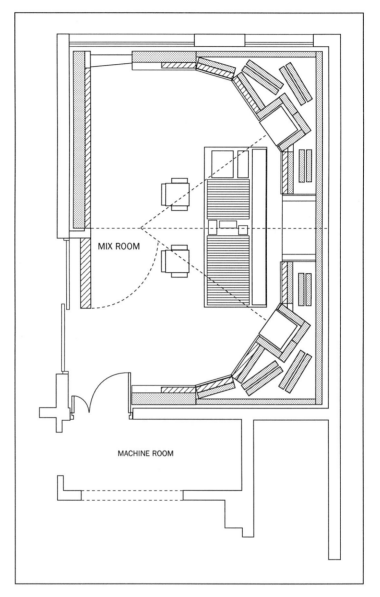

Fig. 4.2. Plan view of a typical mixing suite

(vi) The reflections making up the reverberant soundfield should be as diffuse as possible in order to eliminate 'hot spots'. This is particularly important in large control rooms where the rear of the room is used by musicians, the object being to extend the area over which accurate monitoring is maintained.

(*b*) Studio: Whereas the control room environment should be designed to give neutral listening conditions, the studio is very much part of the performance being recorded. It affects not only the direct sound quality but also the way in which the musicians deliver their performance and their attitude to it. It therefore follows that the studio acoustics should optimize the feel and musicality of the instruments being recorded.

For orchestral work this involves recreating the atmosphere of the concert platform. A room of 400 m² and a minimum height of 6 m would be required to provide the best reverberant conditions. For pop, rock, and jazz recording there is a distinct trend to use acoustics as a form of enhancement, making drums and guitars sound particularly bright and expansive. There is also the requirement for a completely dry sound to which signal processing can be added at a later stage.

The fashion of designing large studios, made small again by large areas of absorbent trapping, seems largely out of favour. The advantages of inverse square-law sound propagation in such rooms is largely outweighed by the oppressive, unnatural feeling imparted to the musicians and their instruments.

3. Acoustic construction

Attention to detail is the main consideration in studio building. Every aspect of good isolation goes against the grain of traditional building practice, in the sense that most structures need to be held apart rather than together. This said, it is quality of workmanship which matters in the end, and building contractors should always be chosen for this reason above all.

The main elements of the building programme will be contained in the schedule of works, an example of which is shown in Figure 4.3. It can be seen that many operations must take place in sequence, which requires precise timing if delays or congestion are to be avoided. Off-site fabrication of woodwork, finishing panels, and audio looms is essential if projects are to be completed within the kind of time-scales shown even for small to medium-sized studios.

4. Air-conditioning

One aspect of studio design frequently underestimated is the cooling requirements of men and machines in a sealed enclosure. For all but the smallest studio, a three-phase supply is required, providing anything up to 100 amps per phase, even for an average-sized complex.

The precise cooling load for a control room depends largely on the equipment power consumption and the rate of airflow into the room for a given outside air temperature. The standard of thermal insulation in studios is usually very high and therefore the only way of maintaining normal room temperature is by controlled cooling. As previously mentioned, the

STUDIO A	WEEK									
	1	2	3	4	5	6	7	8	9	10
SITE PREPARATION	▓									
FOOTINGS AND GROUND WORKS	▓	▓								
SHELLWORK AND SLABS			▓	▓						
1st FIX TIMBER WORK				▓	▓					
2nd FIX TIMBER WORK						▓				
DOORS AND DECORATION							▓			
ELECTRICAL			▓	▓		▓				
HVAC			▓	▓		▓				
AUDIO WIRING					▓			▓		
EQUIPMENT									▓	▓

Fig. 4.3. Example of a schedule of works

air-conditioning contractor should be briefed as to the required operating conditions, and asked to provide limits of such operation under adverse environment conditions. It is not unusual for the HVAC cost to represent up to 25 per cent of the total building budget.

5. Other services

(a) Electrical installation: This represents a relatively straightforward part of the design and installation programme, although timing is often critical. Wiring should always be designed with future requirements in mind, allowing easy access to ducts and junction boxes. Several important points should be noted, such as the total power requirement per phase. Single-phase systems should be configured so that air-conditioning is supplied via a separate 'head'. Distribution of phases should avoid potential high-voltage links.

Provision of a high-conductivity technical earth is often desirable, but is by no means essential in areas with normal electricity supply. The practice of removing the mains earth from equipment is not advisable—in fact in most cases it is probably illegal.

Lighting requirements for studios fall into both technical and aesthetic areas, but it will be the job of the chosen electrical contractor to carry out the installation. Typical allocations for electrical wiring would be 5–10 per cent of the building budget, provided that an existing supply is adjacent to the studio.

(b) Audio installation: The subject of audio, and possibly video, systems could easily fill another chapter, but several basic rules will prevent the wiring of the studio equipment becoming a nightmare.

(i) Plan the wiring in advance with every termination numbered, and number every cable during installation.

(ii) Decide and maintain a shielding convention. Do not confuse shielding with earthing—they perform different functions.

(iii) Use suitable grades of connector and cable for permanent and demountable interfacing, with optimum matching of pin numbers.

(iv) Always provide suitable trunking and cable access with ample room for replacement and updating. The minimum trunking cross-section for interfacing a modern multitrack console is 400 cm².

(v) Avoid parallel runs of audio and electrical wiring. A suitable convention is to supply electrical wiring from high level vertically, and to run audio at low level horizontally.

(vi) Allow ample 'Christmas tree' terminations inside fixed racks to provide easy installation of outboard equipment.

(vii) Provide termination on all studio panels for MIDI, foldback, and ties. When establishing a formal tender procedure for the audio installation, it is important to establish the exact method proposed by each company—the cheapest is rarely the best.

Typical wiring budgets form 10 per cent of the main contract. Some companies quote installation based on 10 per cent of the equipment budget, but this method is not accurate enough for budgets in excess of £100,000.

Final installation

On completion of all contractual work, the equipment is finally installed in its normal working position. Some equipment must be terminated *in situ* and therefore the wiring team will remain on site during this phase.

Some equipment will be installed by the manufacturer, although this is unusual. Responsibility for acoustic measurements and system testing must remain with the designer and his technical associates. The following is a typical check-list for a control room:

- Test absolute polarity of all signal paths.
- Test noise and hum levels through main signal paths.
- Check patch-bay for correct identification.
- Check all systems for RF interference.
- Test monitor systems for correct operation under standard conditions (1 W at 1 m). Check impedance.
- Test absolute system frequency response from microphone input to monitor output, together with phase and distortion.

The precise method of verifying the acoustic performance in the control room and studio will vary with the test equipment available and the chosen methods of the acoustician. The following represents the minimum list of acoustic measurements which should be taken:

- Nearfield monitor response, left and right, using pink noise and third-octave real-time analysis.
- Monitor response at the mixing console, left and right, then summed.
- The sum level of noise should increase by between 3 and 6 dB depending on the symmetry of the reverberant soundfield and the value of the direct/reflected energy ratio.
- Any decrease in level must represent a phase problem and should be investigated.
- If suitable equipment is available, a full set of measurements utilizing time delay spectrometry should be taken with particular emphasis on the following: Energy–Time curves (ETC), Energy–Frequency curves (EFC), Phase–Frequency curves (PFC), Frequency–Time curves (FTC).

TDS as a standard method of measurement has been limited in the past to relatively cumbersome and expensive hardware and has therefore been slow in gaining wide acceptance. This situation has improved in recent years thanks to the introduction of compact microprocessor-driven analysers with friendly software. Examples of TDS measurements are given in Figures 4.4–4.7.

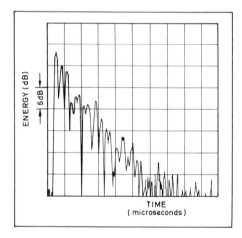

Fig. 4.4. Typical TDS measurement of energy–time response

Recent developments

The past few years have seen a contraction in the number of traditional, general purpose studios and a large increase in the number of home-based 'project' studios. In contrast, the television industry has woken up to sound in a big way and there are many more dubbing and post-production facili-

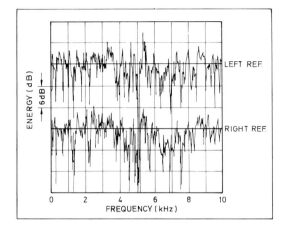

Fig. 4.5. Typical TDS measurement of energy–frequency response

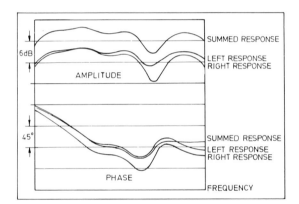

Fig. 4.6. Typical TDS measurement of amplitude and phase response

ties than ever before, especially in countries opening up their media markets through independent satellite and cable broadcasting.

Many changes have been brought about by digital technology, enabling many tasks previously requiring multitrack consoles to be broken down into a series of events which can be stored as data and assembled into a master at the final mixing stage. The planning implication of this is that, for every large master control room, there are usually two or three preparation or programming rooms where composition and compiling take place. This means that the machine room often becomes an elaborate transfer room, where digital programme material is coded, synchronized, and trans-

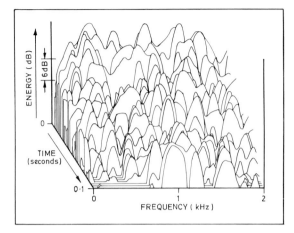

Fig. 4.7. Typical TDS three-dimensional plot of time–energy–frequency response

ferred from one format to another in order to ascend the evolutionary scale from domestic level to fully professional. More and more space is being allocated to computers, although their size is diminishing almost as quickly as their power increases, and so it is unlikely that facilities designed today will prove inadequate in the future.

Most facilities now make less use of the actual recording area or studio than before. Many well-known names in the recording world hardly know how to use a microphone, except for vocals, which are often recorded in a room too small to accommodate even a kit of drums. However, the prospect for real recordings is not bleak and the demand for live music is showing signs of overcoming the supermarket mentality of some people in the pop industry.

Surround sound monitoring

There is a rapidly growing demand for the so-called 'home theatre' effect which recreates the spatial imaging familiar to cinema-goers in recent years. For this reason many television and music producers are tempted to make their products future-proof by encoding the final mix in Dolby Surround format (see Chapter 28). On the face of it this would not appear to present many problems and many studios have simply set up a small speaker on top of their video monitor, balanced a couple of redundant nearfield speakers on a shelf at the back of the room, and then claimed to offer the latest in post-production sound. Needless to say, this approach inevitably fails to satisfy anybody.

For instance, most video programme material is actually received and watched in mono as well as stereo, and any balancing anomalies in the studio mix tend to cause a considerable difference to the dialogue level, relative to music and effects: often the background music drowns low-level voices and special effects are either too loud or almost disappear.

The key to the whole issue of mix encoding is the monitor system, and the accuracy of each channel in relation to the prescribed levels and spectrum. Logically the most important channel is the front centre, which is totally alien to most recording studio engineers. This provides the anchor for the mix, and all levels, phase, and time delay must be referenced to it, as must the sub-woofer channel if used. Therefore the centre speaker must be of the highest quality and it should be mounted to provide a strong direct signal with a minimum of reflected and diffracted interference.

The listening distance should be chosen in deference to the above and if possible should be more than three times the screen width. This poses problems in small video post-production facilities, giving a tiny listening area confined to one operator. Rule No. 1 is to buy a good projector and think big. If surround sound is to blend and integrate properly, the environment should be as close as possible to that of a small theatre. The centre (dialogue) speaker must have a wide bandwidth and an absolute minimum of coloration, directivity problems, etc. as speech is one signal source which almost anyone can judge objectively. The BBC have recognized this fact and have, for many years, designed their own monitoring systems.

Having established a centre speaker reference, the left and right channels should be identical. That means if either is summed with the centre, the sound level at the mix position will increase by 6 dB at all frequencies. This is not easy to achieve but it can be approached if the speakers are matched to 1 dB and the room acoustics and positioning are geometrically correct.

Some equalization is permitted but take care: EQ means phase shift and corrected levels may result in imaging problems. Any serious professional system must be set up using a maximum-length-sequence (MLS) based or equivalent analyser which can measure time, energy, and frequency simultaneously.

The rear channel(s) are not so phase critical but the correct level and spectrum, relative to the main channels, is just as important. Good low-frequency reproduction is desirable in order to minimize distortion caused by loud sound effects such as explosions. Although space is often at a premium, the surround speakers should match the main system in overall character, albeit at lower power levels.

The rear channel is used to create off-screen ambience and special effects like front-to-back panning. The rear sound should therefore be as non-directional as possible. This is achievable in three ways:

1. Reducing direct sound by aiming speakers away from the listener, and using reflecting or even diffusing surfaces to scramble directional clues.
2. Increasing the number of loudspeakers from two to four or more. Stereo rear channels will require more in larger theatres, to maintain stereo in all seats.
3. Time delay in the rear channels gives precedence to the front channels. An adjustable delay of 15–30 ms is required in typical control rooms.

The total power of the surround speaker array should match the centre channel, and therefore a large number of small speakers is acceptable. The sub-bass channel in most Dolby systems can be used to reduce the size requirement of main speakers, but sub-bass is not used as a discrete ingredient except in some digital surround formats. The Dynaudio Acoustics Surround System uses a summing sub-bass system and can be employed where space is restricted.

Summary

It may appear from the preceding pages that planning and installation have more to do with contracts and paperwork than designing. Although this may be largely the case, the scope for imaginative, progressive thought is still what makes the difference between the mundane and the exceptional. Also, there can be no better test of a studio than the sound it creates and the finished recorded product; the most important tools of the studio designer are ears and imagination.

5 Studio acoustics

Alex Burd

The aim of sound recording practice as described throughout this book is to enable the practitioners of the commonly used techniques to create a more or less permanent record of sound—which may or may not exist as an entity.

If the studio is the first link in the chain, which of course it will not be in the case of location recording, then the environment must assist the performers or the engineers (or both) to create the desired final product. While location recording can provide an environment which is unrivalled in the stimulation it brings to the performer, few locations these days can provide the quiet uninterrupted conditions which are necessary for economic recording. This chapter aims to describe the principles of acoustic design, together with the audible consequences of the design decisions that are taken. Various classes of studio, control room, and other technical rooms may need to be created to satisfy the manifold demands of clients. No one type of room can be expected to be suitable for all programme material, but certain fundamental considerations remain constant for all types.

Principles

In order to understand more clearly the interactions of sound with the structure which forms the studio, it is worth looking briefly at certain aspects of the generation and propagation of the sound. Sound is a pressure wave (see Figure 5.1) which is generated naturally by the movement of surfaces—strings or skins, amongst others—or the variation of airflow in a

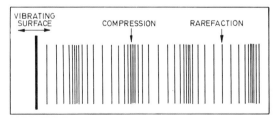

Fig. 5.1. Generation and propagation of plane sound waves by a vibrating surface

tube past an obstruction—as in woodwind, brass, or vocals. These are the natural sources of sound, for which a studio and its acoustics will be important. Of course, the ever-growing family of synthesizers and electronic keyboards have no audible existence until the loudspeaker converts them into sound, and in these cases what used to be known as the control room may become the hub of all activities.

The sound waves cover the entire audible frequency spectrum from 20 to 20,000 Hz, and a corresponding range of wavelengths from those of the low frequencies which are comparable with the dimensions of entire buildings (17 m) down to 17 mm for the highest frequencies (see Chapter 2). This large range leads to fundamental differences in the type of interaction between the sound and the physical parts of the studio. The loudness of sounds is related to the amplitude of the pressure variations in the air and the corresponding amplitudes of vibration set up in the ear. The effect varies with frequency, the ear being at its most sensitive at frequencies around 1.4 kHz, where a practical limit to the useful increase of sensitivity is set by the random molecular motion of air particles.

Most musical sounds have their origins in a simple harmonic motion—a single frequency with harmonic overtones; the particular overtones selected and their relative intensities are the governing factors of the quality of sound. Starting transients and cut-offs also influence our judgement as to the instrument producing the sounds.

When the sound waves strike the boundaries of the studio, part of their energy is converted into vibration of the surface, while the remainder is reflected back into the studio. Of the vibrational energy in the structure, i.e. that which is not reflected, a part may be dissipated as heat (absorbed), while the remainder is transmitted through the material and re-radiated on the far side.

The amount of sound which is reflected is a function of the impedance mismatch at the boundary. Heavy materials have a large mass reactance, and only a small part of the acoustic energy is converted into vibrational energy. The impedance of the surface increases both with increase of the mass of the surface and with higher frequencies, and this gives rise to the so-called 'Mass Law' for sound insulating materials which will be referred to later. The simple Mass Law behaviour is found in most materials over a frequency range which is bounded by resonances of various types; at the resonance frequencies, the impedance of the material changes radically, and therefore related characteristics, such as sound insulation, will also be seen to show large variations.

If the reflected sound inside the studio is examined in more detail, it may be seen that under some conditions—flat surfaces whose dimensions are large compared with the wavelength of sound, for instance—specular reflection of the source waves will result. A limited number of discrete images will thus be found, and the resulting soundfield will show large variations from position to position. At the opposite extreme, rough surfaces having proturberances which are comparable with the wavelength will give rise to a large number of reflected waves scattered randomly in all directions, a condition which is known as a diffuse soundfield.

Porous or fibrous materials represent a special case, in which little sound will be reflected from the surface and large amounts of energy may be dissipated within the structure of the material by viscous flow in the interstices. These types of material will be seen to be particularly useful as acoustic absorbing materials. If no solid skin exists, then a large part of the incident energy will pass straight through such materials.

Background noise

The single most important design decision which has to be taken relates to the background noise levels which are necessary for each category of recording. This decision will have consequences on the acceptability of the site chosen for the premises and on the type of structure that is needed to exclude or contain the noise (although these first two considerations are related and interact with each other), and the implications for the building services can also be extremely expensive (as discussed in Chapter 4).

While noise levels can be described by single-figure descriptors (dB(A), NR, or PNC levels, etc.), it is essential for design purposes to look at the entire spectrum of noise—possibly even extended beyond the frequency range which is generally considered in architectural or environmental acoustics; architects may consider only a range from 100 to 3,150 Hz; environmental considerations will typically extend from 31.5 Hz to 10 kHz.

Noise spectra are most commonly expressed these days as Noise Rating criterion curves, as shown in Figure 5.2. These curves are the standardized form approved by the International Organisation for Standardisation as a derivative of many other families which have existed in the past. The curves relate octave-band sound pressure levels to the centre frequencies of the bands; note that if one-third octave sound levels are used the entire curve will be shifted 5 dB downwards. Each curve is given a numerical value corresponding to the octave-band level at 1 kHz.

The shape of the curve bears some resemblance to the ear's equal loudness response (see Fig. 2.19, page 36). The human hearing system is generally less sensitive at low frequencies. The curves do not follow the ear's response in detail, and a sound whose spectrum follows an NR contour accurately will actually sound hissy. The shape of the curves varies at different sound levels—the higher the sound levels the flatter the curve—and in this respect also the curves follow the behaviour of the human ear.

Studio noise levels used to lie in the region NR 15–NR 25, depending on

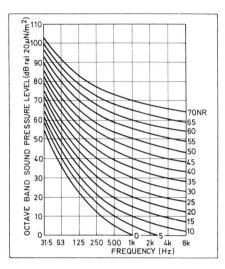

Fig. 5.2. Noise rating (NR) curves

the requirements of different types of programme. Such sound levels were audible on many types of programme and required a certain discipline on the part of the programme originators. In recent years there has been a steady improvement in the recording techniques available and in the quality of equipment available even on the domestic market. The growth of the market in compact discs and the advent of Digital Audio Broadcasting are perhaps the major factors in this respect. Studio background noise levels for the more critical types of programme have had to respond to these requirements, and NR 10 may be taken as the current norm for the best-quality recording studios equipped with digital recording machines, and therefore having the potential to achieve signal-to-(recording) noise levels 80 dB or greater. Some specialized studios may achieve even lower levels than NR 10, but this is uncommon in UK practice where costs remain a major consideration.

Sound levels are usually determined with a precision sound-level meter, with which a time and a spatial averaging of the noise level will be carried out. Where more than one noise level exists, the total sound level may be the quantity to be specified; any tonal or intermittent characteristics in the noise render it more obtrusive, and if such characteristics exist they must be at a level 5–10 dB lower than the continuous noise. An alternative approach specifies the continuous sound level—probably arising from the ventilation system—and uses this level to mask other intrusive noises. These have to be attenuated to a lower level than the specified continuous level in order that they will be inaudable and not raise the measured level by more than 1 dB. (As will be seen later, this approach may give savings in expensive areas of design.)

The design of a ventilation system to achieve such low levels requires great attention to detail: efficient anti-vibration measures to isolate all moving or vibrating parts; duct silencers at critical points; reduction of air velocities through the system, together with many other similar precautions.

Noise arising external to the building (traffic, aircraft, trains, etc.) or from other parts of the building (offices, other studios) have to be measured or estimated, and the steps necessary to attenuate these are described in the next section.

Sound insulation

The prevention of external noises penetrating into our quiet studio depends on a combined use of sound insulation techniques together with structural isolation measures.

As was seen above, the ability of a wall to reflect, that is not to transmit, energy is largely related to its surface density (mass per unit area in kg/m²); see Figure 5.3. Within the so-called Mass Law region, the insulating proper-

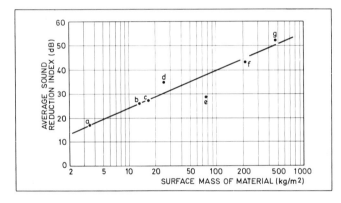

Fig. 5.3. Average Sound Reduction Index of various materials as a function of their surface mass. The materials are: (a) 6 mm plywood, (b) 18 mm chipboard, (c) 6 mm glass, (d) 11 mm plywood with lead bonded (absence of resonances improves SRI), (e) 50 mm wood wool with 2 × 12 mm plaster (serious resonances degrade SRI), (f) 112 mm brick with 12 mm plaster, (g) 225 mm brick with 2 × 12 mm plaster

ties of the surface increase by a theoretical 6 dB per octave (i.e. each doubling of the frequency); equally, at a given frequency, the insulation properties will increase by a further 6 dB for each doubling of the surface density. The extent of the Mass Law region is restricted by many resonances in the partition governed by the various stiffnesses associated with the material (see Figure 5.4). At resonance, the severity of the reduction in

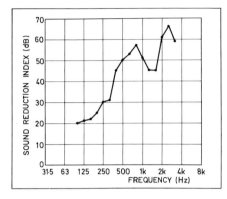

Fig. 5.4. Resonance (coincidence effect) in glass with low internal damping

the sound insulation will depend on the damping present; this damping may be the internal damping of the material or it may be added externally. The effect of the resonances is to reduce the theoretical 6 dB/octave variation to a practical 5 dB/octave.

Various single-figure derivatives of the measured sound insulation values can be calculated, the simplest being the mean of the one-third octave values between 100 and 3,150 Hz. This corresponds to the normal range of interest for domestic situations but may be inadequate in many studio applications if the resonances are designed to occur just above or below the defined frequency range in order to optimize the single-figure value.

Simple Mass Law constructions are usable up to mean sound reduction indices of 50–55 dB; above this value, the mass becomes excessive and leads to a cumulative thickening of all walls and foundations. Multiple-leaf constructions are necessary for higher values, the spacing between the leaves governing the frequency range within which a useful increase occurs. Where the spacing between the leaves is a fraction of a wavelength, the two leaves will behave as a single Mass Law partition. With rising frequency, a progressive improvement is found which depends on the spacing, and on the acoustic absorption within the cavity, until at high frequencies the SRI may increase at 10 dB/octave, indicating that the two leaves are acting independently. The presence of more than one panel introduces additional resonances, the most important of which occurs when the two panels move in anti-phase.

For the higher values of sound insulation at which multiple skins are required, flanking of the designed structure by any continuous walls or floor slabs can became a serious problem. It will frequently be necessary to introduce isolation joints in ground slabs, elastomeric pads beneath walls, and, in the limit, the isolated 'box-in-box' construction shown in Figure 5.5. Where the lowest internal noise levels are required, and high levels of external vibration exist on the site, often arising from underground trains, it may

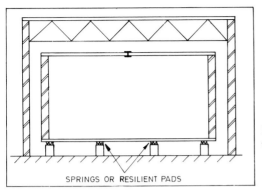

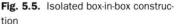

SPRINGS OR RESILIENT PADS

Fig. 5.5. Isolated box-in-box construction

be necessary to isolate an entire building by constructing it on rubber bearing pads.

In certain cases it has proved advantageous to use a combination of massive structures, which may be in the load-bearing elements of the building, and construct the isolated rooms of lighter framed construction. In such cases it is necessary to take account of the sound absorption which will result from the lightweight panels.

This is not the place to enter into details of sound insulation, but a few representative examples may serve to show the wide range of values required and to indicate the types of construction that are used.

In a typical studio centre, the roof may be required to exclude aircraft noise, and an average sound level difference of 70 dB may be specified. A structure to achieve such a value could be an inner roof of 150 mm reinforced concrete, supporting on resilient pads a second, lighter skin of wood wool slabs with suitable waterproofing and weather protection.

Walls to exclude traffic noise will have to achieve at least 65 dB average sound level difference. One possible construction is a cavity wall having two leaves of 225 mm brickwork and a cavity of 100 mm minimum. Some degree of structural isolation will be necessary to minimize flanking transmission through the ground slab.

Control room windows, to achieve compatible results, must be of heavy glass, and an air-space of minimum depth 200 mm with absorptive reveals is necessary. It is essential that the two glasses are of different thicknesses—say 8 mm and 12 mm—to ensure different resonance frequencies.

Where ventilation ducts or other services pass through a sound insulating partition, it is of course necessary to ensure that the sound level difference by that path does not degrade the overall insulation. The use of attenuators, commonly called 'crosstalk silencers', is the answer in the case of ventilation ductwork, while other cable ducts can be packed with sandbags or bags filled with mineral wool.

Acoustic quality

Having constructed the shell of a studio which is not subject to interference by noise from either external or internal sources, it is now necessary to ensure that it sounds 'right' to those who use it—both artists and engineers. The sound that is heard live in a studio, or at a microphone output before processing, is a combination of the direct sound from the source together with a multiplicity of reflections from the surfaces of the studio and from the furnishings and fittings.

When a short sharp sound is produced in the studio, it is possible to display electronically the pattern of reflections which results; this display is known as the impulse response. In the early part of such a display, shown in Figure 5.6, the first signal, which has travelled direct from source to

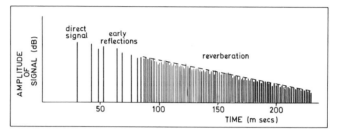

Fig. 5.6. Impulse response of an auditorium

microphone, can be seen, followed by several discrete reflections from floor, ceiling, walls, and furniture which are spaced apart by time intervals of a few milliseconds. After a time which will be a function of the size of the studio, the reflections are seen to arrive so close together that it is impossible to separate them. These later signals arise from multiple reflections within the studio, and, since energy will be lost from the sound wave each time it is reflected by a surface, the sound amplitude will gradually die away. This region, known as the reverberation, was the first part of the characteristic of sound in an enclosure to be systematically studied. It probably remains the most important single feature of the soundfield, although current research in concert halls is demonstrating the importance of the early sound, both in the aural judgement of the size of a room and also in defining subjective characteristics of the soundfield.

Within a room there exist regular series of standing waves arising from the reflection of sound by the major surfaces of the room; these are known as the natural modes or eigentones of the room. Figure 5.7 shows the three lowest modes which can exist between a pair of plane-parallel surfaces. The modes arising from the three pairs of opposing surfaces in a rectangular room comprise what are known as the axial modes of the room. The other

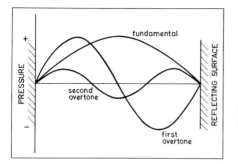

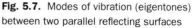

Fig. 5.7. Modes of vibration (eigentones) between two parallel reflecting surfaces

series are the tangential modes, in which two pairs of surfaces contribute, and the oblique modes, which involve all three pairs of surfaces. The axial modes have been shown to be the most significant by virtue of the energy they carry and the longer duration of their decay.

An undue concentration of modes in one frequency region will often be heard as an accentuation of sounds around that region. By analogy with optical terminology, in which light of a particular colour arises from an electromagnetic vibration of a particular frequency, such an emphasis is called coloration. Coloration of the sound in a room results when modes are widely spaced, typically when one mode or one group of modes is separated by about 20 Hz from the adjacent modes, and when that frequency region is excited by a source of sound. This effect therefore tends to be associated with small rooms, where the lower-order modes are in the audible frequency range.

If two (or more) dimensions of a room are the same, or a simple multiple of each other, then their axial mode series will be the same or will have many common terms. The chances of coloration being audible are therefore increased and the acoustic designer's aim of a uniform distribution of sound is made more difficult to achieve.

In small rooms, the lowest frequencies in the axial modal series lie in the speech frequency region and are spaced well apart in frequency. The twenty lowest modes calculated for an echo room whose dimensions were adjusted to distribute the modes are shown in Table 5.1. For comparison, the modal frequencies of a well-known and highly coloured speech enclosure—a telephone booth—are also shown.

At first sight it might appear that these problems would be resolved by constructing non-rectangular rooms, a solution which has often been proposed. In practice, however, the room still has its eigentones and audible acoustic effects still result.

One important example of a standing wave is the regular series of reflections set up between a pair of plane-parallel reflecting surfaces. This is known as a flutter echo. This type of response is particularly apparent in an otherwise dead room, and can result from comparatively small areas such

Table 5.1. Modal frequencies of two rooms

Room 1 (echo room)[a]				Room 2 (telephone booth)[b]			
n_x	n_y	n_z	Frequency (Hz)	n_x	n_y	n_z	Frequency (Hz)
1	0	0	34.02	0	0	1	76.22
0	1	0	43.20	0	0	2	152.44
1	1	0	54.99	0	1	0	201.77
0	0	1	56.15	1	0	0	211.73
1	0	1	65.65	0	1	1	215.68
2	0	0	68.08	1	0	1	225.03
0	1	1	70.85	0	0	3	228.67
1	1	1	78.59	0	1	2	252.88
2	1	0	80.63	1	0	2	260.90
0	2	0	86.44	1	1	0	292.47
2	0	1	88.25	1	1	1	302.24
1	2	0	92.89	0	0	4	304.89
2	1	1	98.25	0	1	3	304.96
3	0	0	102.00	1	0	3	311.64
0	2	1	103.08	1	1	2	329.81
1	2	1	108.54	0	1	4	365.60
2	2	0	110.03	1	0	4	371.20
0	0	2	112.30	1	1	3	371.25
1	0	2	117.34	0	0	5	381.11
0	1	2	120.32				

Note: a Length (x) 5.03 m; Breadth (y) 3.96 m; Height (z) 3.05 m.
      b Length (x) 0.81 m; Breadth (y) 0.85 m; Height (z) 2.25 m.

as control room windows or doors. The cure for a flutter echo may be to add more absorption, to make the surface diffusing, or to angle one of the surfaces relative to the other.

The decay of the soundfield in a room was studied by Sabine in the early part of this century. He noted that the reverberation time was a function of the volume of the room and of the total amount of absorption that it contained. He derived the relationship

$$T = \frac{0.161\ V}{\bar{\alpha}S}$$

where T is the reverberation time, RT (sec)
       V is the volume of the room (m³)

S is the surface area of the room (m²)
$\bar{\alpha}$ is the average absorption coefficient.

The reverberation time is defined as the time taken for the sound to die away to one-millionth of its original energy (60 dB), although, of course, measurements are seldom possible over such a wide range. The average absorption coefficient is obtained by adding together all the individual items of absorption and dividing by the total area:

$$\bar{\alpha} = \frac{1}{S}\{\alpha_1 S_1 + \alpha_2 S_2 + \ldots\}$$

where S_1 is the area of material of absorption α_1, etc. The above formula assumes a continuous absorption of sound, whereas with the exception of air absorption, the removal of energy is a discontinuous process occurring each time a wavefront is reflected from a surface.

Modifications to the formula have been made by later researchers, the most successful being that by Eyring in 1930 which allows for the discontinuous absorption and gives a greatly improved agreement with measured values at low reverberation times (high absorption coefficients):

$$T = \frac{0.161\ V}{-S\ \log_e (1 - \bar{\alpha}) + 4\ mV}$$

The 4mV factor accounts for air absorption, which is significant at high frequencies and in rooms of large volume.

As was mentioned earlier, physical roughness of a wall surface will cause diffuse reflections of a sound wave; the size of the roughness determines the frequency at which the effect becomes noticeable, and it will be necessary to introduce projections of 200–300 mm in order to be effective for low frequencies. It has been shown that varying the absorbing characteristics of the surface can be equally effective in creating diffuse reflections, and it is therefore usual in studio design to distribute and intersperse the different types of acoustic absorbing material.

In addition to control of the general reverberant conditions, it may be necessary to eliminate strong reflections of sound from hard surfaces which can interfere with the direct sound at the microphone and cause a comb-filter distortion. The most common example of this effect is found in speech studios where interference results between the direct sound and that reflected from the table and/or script. A similar audible effect results when a free-standing loudspeaker is placed near to a reflecting wall or corner. The reflecting surface may also create difficulties in otherwise dead studios where pick-up by a microphone can lead to unwanted broadening of the stereo image.

Acoustic absorbers

It is necessary to adjust the absorbing characteristics of all studios in order to achieve the correct acoustic conditions. To this end, materials which absorb sound in particular frequency ranges have to be selected in the correct amounts and installed in the optimum positions. Acoustic absorbers operate by dissipating energy as heat, either in internal losses in vibrating materials or as viscous losses due to air movement in porous materials. The main categories of acoustic absorbers are described here.

1. Panel or 'membrane' absorbers

When a panel or membrane of a mechanically lossy material is excited into vibration by sound waves, energy will be dissipated. If such a panel comprises the exposed face of a closed box, a low-frequency resonator is formed; the resonance frequency is controlled by the mass of the panel and the combined stiffness of the material itself and the enclosed volume of air. Thus variation of the weight of the material, or of the volume of the air-space, will adjust the frequency at which maximum absorption occurs. In most cases it will be necessary to introduce additional damping into the box in the form of porous material; this must be mounted directly behind the membrane, since this is the position at which the particle velocity is at its greatest.

An extremely efficient form of membrane absorber developed in the BBC Research Department used bituminous roofing felt as the membrane. This material has a low inherent stiffness, and a considerable variation of resonance frequency results from alteration to the depth of the air-space. Results for this type of absorber are shown in Figure 5.8. Most other thin panel materials will act in the same fashion, but usually without achieving comparable bandwidths of absorption or allowing adjustment over a comparable frequency range.

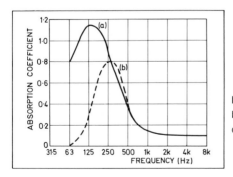

Fig. 5.8. Absorption coefficients of membrane absorbers with various air-space depths: (*a*) 300 mm, (*b*) 25 mm

2. Helmholtz resonators

An alternative resonant absorber for use at low frequencies is formed when an enclosed volume of air is coupled to the studio through a 'neck'. This form of resonator is well known to anyone who has blown over the neck of a bottle (see Figure 5.9). The resonance results from the movement of the mass of air contained in the neck, controlled by the stiffness of the enclosed volume of air. The frequency is governed by the volume of air and by the size of the neck, so that tuning can be accomplished by changing one or the other. It will always be necessary to add a resistive material to the neck, to ensure absorption of energy over a useful bandwidth. Such absorbers have been used on occasions to damp out particular low-frequency modes in small rooms.

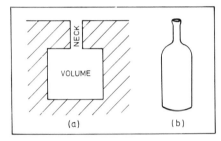

Fig. 5.9. Helmholtz resonator: (*a*) theoretical, (*b*) practical

3. Porous absorbers

The greatest range of absorbing materials lies within this general classification; mineral wools and hanging curtains, wood wool slabs, and unplastered blockwork walls all dissipate energy by viscous loss in their pores. Provided the material is sufficiently dense, efficient absorption will result at high frequencies. As the thickness of the material is increased, the absorption will extend to lower frequencies; to some extent the same effect results from increasing the density of the material, but this may lead to increased surface reflection at higher frequencies.

The first maximum in the absorption occurs at a frequency for which the thickness of the material is about one-eighth of a wavelength; doubling the thickness will lower this frequency by one octave. Progressive doubling of the thickness of absorbing material becomes expensive, and it useful to note that there is not a great loss of efficiency if a layer of porous material is backed by an air-space to give the same total depth. Results typical of the behaviour of such porous absorbers are shown in Figure 5.10.

The absorbing characteristics of this type of absorber can be modified by the use of a perforated facing material. Perforation providing a distributed

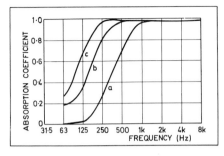

Fig. 5.10. Absorption coefficients of porous absorbers: (*a*) 25 mm layer, (*b*) 50 mm layer, (*c*) 25 mm absorber plus 175 mm air

open area of 25 per cent or greater will not significantly modify the absorber characteristic within the normal audio-frequency range. Reduction of the open area will cause a progressive cut-off of high-frequency absorption. When low-percentage perforations are reached (say 5 per cent or less) the behaviour is more like that of a surface containing a large number of Helmholtz resonators in which the perforation acts as the neck and the appropriate part of the space behind each perforation acts as the enclosed volume. Resonance absorption characteristics in the range 70–1,000 Hz can be produced by selecting the appropriate perforation and depth of air-space; typical results for absorbers which have been produced as a range of manufactured modular absorbers are shown in Figure 5.11.

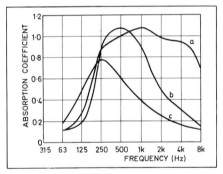

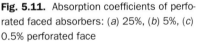

Fig. 5.11. Absorption coefficients of perforated faced absorbers: (*a*) 25%, (*b*) 5%, (*c*) 0.5% perforated face

Acoustic design: studios

The principles, and their practical implications, can now be applied to the design of the infinite variety of studios, control rooms, mix-down rooms, edit rooms, etc., which can exist. Only a few examples can be described, but these may be used as the models for many more similar rooms.

Music studios

A limited number of studios are still built to accommodate the activities of groups of classical musicians. This term is used, for want of a better one, to describe a conventionally balanced group—a symphony orchestra, a chamber orchestra, or a string quartet, for example. The music created by such a group is already internally balanced and can be recorded on a single microphone (or stereo pair) without the addition of any spot microphones.

For such a musical group, the performing space constitutes an important part of the performance. The size and shape of the studio must allow the musicians to hear one another clearly in order that they may maintain an ensemble and adjust their balance one to another. Beyond this point, the acoustic characteristics of the studio should complement the sounds of the instruments to allow the individual sounds to blend and build up a warm, full tone. These and similar aspects of the studio design are important if the musicians are to give of their best, although to some extent modern technology can overcome the deficiencies of a less than perfect studio in the quality of the final output.

These requirements have implications for the dimensions of the studio as well as its purely acoustic characteristics. Orchestral musicians require a minimum of 2–3 m^2 of floor-space each, but it is also desirable that the walls of the studio should not be unduly close. The ceiling height has also been shown to be important for the larger orchestral groups, with an optimum of 9–10 m above floor level to give reflections over the whole orchestra after a suitable time delay. Given these requirements, it is generally found that studios range from 10,000 m^3 for symphonic studios to 1,000m^3 for small recital studios.

Having determined the volume to accommodate the required number of musicians, an estimate of the required reverberation time can be obtained from published information such as that in Figure 5.12. However, although the size of the studio is clearly related to the anticipated use through the given numbers of musicians, some additional account may need to be taken of the type of music, if this is specific; thus romantic-style symphonic music will benefit from a longer reverberation time of 2.0–2.5 seconds, whilst chamber music, which developed in more intimate surroundings with closely textured scoring, can be better suited to a shorter reverberation time.

Opinions differ to some extent on the shape of the reverberation time/frequency characteristic. UK practice has generally favoured a flat curve, but others feel that a rise at low frequencies—such as is normal in concert halls—can give added warmth. Only limited areas of designed absorption will be required to achieve the desired reverberation characteristics, though additional measures may have to be taken to increase the diffusion by shaping the surfaces appropriately.

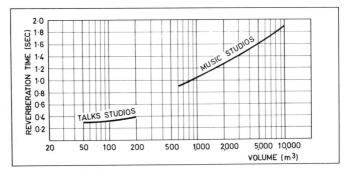

Fig. 5.12. Recommended reverberation times for broadcasting studios (courtesy BBC)

Light music studios

The radio orchestra was undoubtedly the first step in the development of multi-microphone techniques; correct internal balance of the orchestra is no longer automatically necessary, the balance being achieved by the engineer in the control room rather than by the conductor, and the final recorded sound may be quite different from the real sound in the studio.

Under these conditions, the natural acoustics of the studio are no longer so directly relevant, and the aim has become that of ensuring good separation between the various instrumental groups. The reverberation time of the studio can be reduced to a reasonably low value which musicians still find acceptable; in addition, the widespread use of screens, partly absorbing and partly visually transparent, can help to provide the necessary separation.

Pop music studios

Pop music studios are the logical extension of the light music studios mentioned above. The studios are made as dead as possible and microphones are brought as close as practicable to the individual instruments. When all the musicians play at one time, it becomes necessary to strive for separation between the individual microphones. However, in the now popular technique of split-session recordings with overdubbing, it has become possible to record in an environment which suits the individual instruments without any necessity to deaden the space artificially. The use of gating circuits to limit the duration of the pickup from percussive instruments gives a comparative freedom from the traditional necessity for excessively dead drum booths (see Plate 1).

Acoustic design in pop studios has become a more creative subject and a wide variation in the acoustic characteristics can be seen in recent designs.

Plate 1. A modern isolation booth with drum kit and microphones in position, showing the acoustic wall panels: Air Studios, Lyndhurst Hall, London (Photo: Paul Burgess)

Small studios (talks, DJ, demo)

The acoustic design of small studios has to make allowance for the widely distributed modal standing waves pattern. A fairly dead acoustic response is normally desirable, and the use of large amounts of acoustic absorbing material gives the possibility of damping the more troublesome modes adequately. Problems can occur if the treatment is not well distributed, and a design aim which ensures that the average absorption coefficients of each pair of surfaces are similar (difference not greater than a factor of 1.4) has been found to be adequate. Control of the low-frequency reverberation is the greatest problem, and some increase of RT below 200 Hz has been found to be compatible with many types of material.

Television studios

Television studios are designed to be acoustically dead, as this is the condition which can be compatible with the widest range of programme requirements, the most critical of which may be the simulation of outdoor conditions. All the available surfaces are therefore treated with broad-band absorbing finishes of mineral fibre over a 200 mm air-space, which usually houses additional low-frequency panel absorption over an area of up to one-third of the total amount of treatment.

A recent design incorporated 100 mm screeded wood wool planks, as both the exposed acoustic absorbing face and an isolated sound-attenuating inner lining. The larger (600 m²) production studio in this development is designed with music in mind and includes an electroacoustic artificial reverberation system. With this system—the Multi-channel Reverberation (MCR) system by Philips—the reverberation time can be varied between 0.8 and 1.4 seconds. The studio has proved successful for music productions but has also used the electroacoustic enhancement for a variety of other programme types.

Control rooms, monitoring, mix-down, etc.

The acoustic design of control rooms has, over the years, produced innumerable variations, each based on a new philosophy. However, there are some points of agreement between many of the designers.

Traditionally, control rooms were small and had the potential to introduce audible colorations. This, together with the knowledge that more critical judgements could be made in non-reverberant conditions, led to the inclusion of a reasonable amount of sound-absorbing material. Rooms have grown larger over the years because of the increase in the physical size of mixing consoles, the proliferation of ancillary equipment, and, recently, the translation of much of the keyboard and synthesizer activity into the control room for direct injection (see Plate 2).

Reverberation time may not be the prime variable, but it is usual to find that the amount of acoustical absorbing material present reduces the RT to less than 0.2 seconds; such dead conditions can lead to rooms which are extremely oppressive to work in. Any lack of left/right symmetry—either physical or acoustical—can upset the stereo balance, and this requirement will often dictate the relative positions of studio window and mixing console.

Beyond this point design philosophies vary. In broadcasting it is usual to find that the acoustic absorption is distributed within the room in order to create diffuse conditions which give a greater uniformity within the room. This approach is followed by the EBU Technical Recommendation on 'Acoustical Properties of Control Rooms and Listening Rooms for the Assessment of Broadcast Programmes'. Recent work by R. Walker at the BBC Engineering Research Department has led to a shaping of the source end of the room such that all reflections arriving within 20 ms of the direct sound (and with a strength greater than −20 dB relative to the direct sound) are excluded from a zone surrounding the monitoring position. This has allowed reverberation times to be increased to 0.35 seconds or greater thus giving more pleasant working conditions.

There are two current approaches to the idea of a live-end, dead-end design. In one the sound originates from the live end of the room and is

Plate 2. The main control room at Air Studios, Lyndhurst Hall, London, showing the acoustic wall and ceiling panels (Photo: Paul Burgess)

completely absorbed at the rear of the room after a single pass by the head of the engineer.

In the alternative approach, the reflective end of the room is behind the engineer and the pattern of reflections is designed to complement the early impulse response of the origination.

The Equipment

6 Microphones

John Borwick

The programme chain as described in Chapter 1 begins with one or more microphones and ends with one or more loudspeakers (the usual number is two, suitably spaced to produce the stereo effect of musicians arranged more or less naturally across an arc). Microphones and loudspeakers belong to the large family of 'transducers', that is devices whose job it is to convert energy from one form to another.

The microphone converts acoustical energy into electrical energy, whilst the loudspeaker, interestingly enough, does the same job in reverse, converting electrical energy (supplied as an electric current) back into acoustical energy (radiated as sound waves). Other examples of reciprocal transducing devices are to be found in the recording/reproducing chain. A tape recording head, for example, converts electrical energy into magnetic energy, whilst a tape playback head does the reverse. (Indeed, a single head is used on the majority of cheaper domestic type machines, simply switched according to which function is required at the time.) A disc cutter converts electrical energy into mechanical vibration of the stylus, and leaves a 'record' of the sound waves etched into a groove in the master disc surface; the gramophone pickup stylus retraces this waveform, and its vibrations are used to generate an electric current. Again, the laser source which 'cuts' a track of digital pits on the photo-resist surface of a Compact Disc master converts electrical energy into light energy, whilst the light-sensitive device in a CD player, which receives the reflected laser beam, reverses the transducing process and converts light energy into a usable electric current.

The transducing action in a microphone can be seen as comprising two stages, though of course they happen simultaneously:

(a) the changes in air pressure due to sound waves set a light diaphragm into mechanical motion,
(b) the vibrations of the diaphragm are used to generate an alternating voltage.

The acoustical/mechanical conversion

For the first stage, two basic methods can be used to produce mechanical vibration from the action of sound waves. The most simple method is

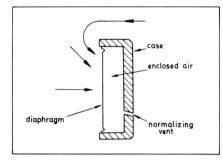

Fig. 6.1. Typical construction of a pressure-operated microphone

called *pressure operation* and has the diaphragm open to the air on one side only, with its back effectively enclosed (Figure 6.1). The diaphragm will then tend to move inwards and outwards as the instantaneous air pressure alternates above and below the normal atmospheric value.

Such a pressure-operated microphone is theoretically non-directional (the preferred term is 'omnidirectional'), since pressure is a scalar rather than a vector quantity; the tendency for diaphragm movement will be the same regardless of the direction from which the sound waves are coming. The graph (polar diagram) of the microphone's output voltage for a given level of acoustic pressure variation in a given plane will therefore be a circle (and a three-dimensional plot would yield a sphere with the microphone at the centre).

In practice, however, the physical size of the microphone causes it to act as an obstacle to sound waves at higher frequencies (shorter wavelengths). The waves then tend to be reflected, with a boosting effect for front incident sounds and attenuation of sounds arriving at the back and sides. The family of directivity patterns for different frequencies therefore looks like the example in Figure 6.2, with the circular, omnidirectional pick-up pattern for low frequencies progressively narrowing and becoming front-biased as the frequency is increased.

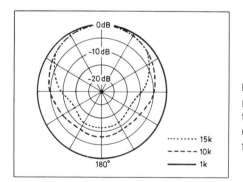

Fig. 6.2. Family of polar diagrams for a pressure-operated (nominally omnidirectional) microphone, showing the progressive narrowing of the response at higher frequencies

This changing frequency response at oblique angles has obvious practical consequences. Knowing that an omnidirectional microphone has its maximum high-frequency response on axis enables a user to tilt or offset the microphone angle in situations where a slight softening of the treble is desirable. Note that the family of curves is related solely to the ratio D/λ, where D is the microphone diameter and λ is the wavelength. Reducing the size of the microphone and mounting the diaphragm at the end of a narrow cylindrical case, for example, will raise the frequency limit for omnidirectional response.

The second method used to produce mechanical vibrations in response to the acoustical energy in sound waves is called *pressure-gradient* (or sometimes *velocity*) operation. In this method, the diaphragm is open to the air on both sides do that the force acting on it at any instant is due to the pressure difference or gradient at the two faces. As is shown in Figure 6.3a, this will be a maximum for normal incidence on the axis at 0° and 180°, when the extra path length for sounds to reach the back of the diaphragm is a maximum D. It will diminish at increasing off-axis angles, falling to a theoretical zero at 90° and 270°. Plotting such a response over the full 360° produces the familiar figure-of-eight graph shown in Figure 6.4. In mathematical terms, this is a graph of the expression $Y = X\cos\theta$, where Y is the sensitivity (response) at a given angle θ and X is the maximum sensitivity on axis. In practice, X is proportional to the distance which a sound incident at 0° must travel around the mounting or case to reach the remote face of the diaphragm (shown as D in Figure 6.3b), which explains why the voltage output from a pressure-gradient microphone is in effect proportional to sound particle velocity.

Many modern microphones are designed to combine the pressure and

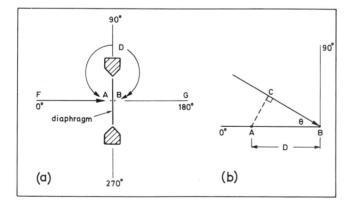

Fig. 6.3. Pressure-gradient operation: (a) front and back of diaphragm are effectively distance D apart, (b) distance reduces according to D cos θ for oblique incidence

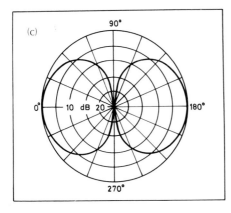

Fig. 6.4. Figure-of-eight polar diagram for pressure-gradient microphone

pressure-gradient principles of operation in specific proportions to provide directivity patterns intermediate between the circle (omnidirectional) and the figure-of-eight (bidirectional). The sensitivity at any angle will then be given by the expression $Y = Z + X\cos\theta$, where Z is the sensitivity of the pressure-operated element and $X\cos\theta$ represents the contribution of the pressure-gradient element as before.

In the special case where $Z = X$, i.e. the pressure and PG elements are of equal axial sensitivity, the directivity pattern is heart-shaped and therefore referred to as a *cardioid*. The derivation of a cardioid pattern by simple addition of circle and figure-of-eight patterns having the same maximum sensitivity is illustrated in Figure 6.5.

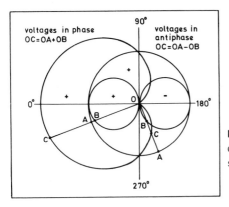

Fig. 6.5. Derivation of cardioid by combining a circle and a figure-of-eight of the same sensitivity

By choosing different relative values for Z and X, it is possible to derive other patterns which in effect look like unsymmetrical figures-of-eight. The two most common are shown in Figure 6.6. The *hypercardioid* results from values $Z = 0.25$ and $X = 0.75$; the *supercardioid* has $Z = 0.375$ and $X = 0.625$. It will be seen that these patterns give better attenuation of sounds at 90°

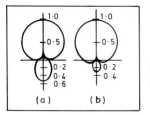

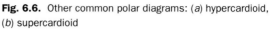

Fig. 6.6. Other common polar diagrams: (*a*) hypercardioid, (*b*) supercardioid

than the cardioid, which is the best choice, however, when rejection of sounds from behind the microphone (at 180°) is a main requirement. The attenuations in dB at 90° and 180° for the five directivity patterns so far mentioned are summarized in Figure 6.7.

CHARACTERISTIC	OMNI-DIRECTIONAL	CARDIOID	SUPER-CARDIOID	HYPER-CARDIOID	BI-DIRECTIONAL
POLAR RESPONSE PATTERN					
POLAR EQUATION	1	$\cdot 5 + \cdot 5 \cos\theta$	$\cdot 375 + \cdot 625 \cos\theta$	$\cdot 25 + \cdot 75 \cos\theta$	$\cos\theta$
RELATIVE OUTPUT AT 90° (dB)	0	−6	−8·6	−12	−∞
RELATIVE OUTPUT AT 180° (dB)	0	−∞	−11·7	−6	0
ANGLE AT WHICH OUTPUT = 0	—	180°	126°	110°	90°
DISTANCE FACTOR (DF)	1	1·7	1·9	2	1·7

Fig. 6.7. A comparison of the five most common directivity patterns

There is also a useful differentiation in practical terms of the total amount of the soundfield picked up by these different microphone types. The omnidirectional microphone picks up all the ambient sound (direct sound plus reverberation), whereas the figure-of-eight and cardioid pick up only one-third. This means that these can be positioned 1.7 times further from the musicians for a given balance of direct-to-reverberant sound (see Figure 6.8). The supercardioid and hypercardioid can be set back even further, at 1.9 and 2.0 times respectively. It should be borne in mind that these diagrams and distance values are the theoretical ones. In general, there is the same tendency for values to change at high frequencies due to microphone case dimensions as was mentioned in the case of the omni microphone.

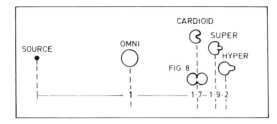

Fig. 6.8. Distance factors for different microphone types, giving the same ratio of direct-to-reverberant sounds

Effects of distance on frequency response

The distance between the microphone and the sound source has a number of important effects on the frequence response, particularly in the case of PG-operated microphones.

At short distances where the sound radiation may still be regarded as consisting of spherical waves (say at one-wavelength distance or less) the low-frequency response becomes severely accentuated. This is called the *proximity effect* and is illustrated in Figure 6.9. There is practically no such bass tip-up with omni microphones, which partly explains why these are favoured for close working, except that some vocalists (from Bing Crosby onwards) have found that some bass boost gives an added warmth to their sound. Of course, bass equalization can be applied to diminish any undesirable effects when PG microphones have to be used at short distances (such as in BBC talk studios).

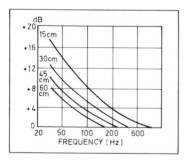

Fig. 6.9. Proximity effect: showing the bass tip-up to be expected at various close distances from a pressure-gradient-operated microphone

Another effect comes into play when large distances are used in a hall or studio. At all distances, the total output of a microphone is not due simply to the direct sound arriving on axis. It is made up of the sum of the direct sound (for which the axial *free-field* frequency response curve applies) and the numerous reflected sounds which arrive, after various time delays, more or less equally from all directions. A microphone's response to this reflected off-axis sound is called its *diffuse-field* response. Ideally this should run parallel to the free-field response curve, simply being at a lower signal level due to the attenuation with distance. Changing the microphone distance will then give the balance engineer a means of altering the apparent balance between direct and reverberant sound without materially affecting the balance of frequencies. This result is achieved in the better-quality PG microphones.

In pressure (omni) microphones, however, the diffuse-field response curve always shows a distinct falling off in treble response compared with the axial free-field response (due to the narrowing directivity illustrated in Figure 6.2). Some designers face up to this need for compromise by giving the axial response a degree of top lift; others go for a flat frontal response and leave it to the balance engineer to introduce some treble EQ on distant balances where necessary. The Brüel and Kjaer omni microphones are supplied with alternative front grilles for close and distant working (see Figure 6.10).

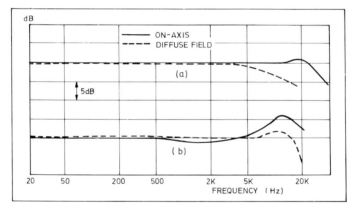

Fig. 6.10. Use of a special grille to optimize response of an omni microphone, either (*a*) for close working or (*b*) distant working in the diffuse field (courtesy Brüel and Kjaer)

Microphones for stereo

Ever since the launch of stereo records around 1958, the vast majority of music recordings have been made in two-channel stereo using a variety of microphone techniques where the directivity pattern is a vital factor. Some of these may be summarized as follows.

Coincident pair (Blumlein)

This technique uses a pair of identical directional microphones placed as nearly as possible in the same point in space. There is therefore minimum time-of-arrival difference at the two capsules, and the whole of the directional (stereo) information relies on the controlled intensity difference between the two microphone outputs. The method appeals to purists, because it avoids phasing problems and gives a more or less ideal spread over the standard 60° listening arc. It also has the benefit of historical respectability, since it was described in detail by A. D. Blumlein, who pioneered stereophonic recording in his famous Patent No. 394325 as long ago as 1931.

If the two microphones are set at 90° to each other (the usual arrangement), various acceptance angles—which will be reduced to the listening 60° arc on replay—are achieved depending on which directivity pattern is in use. Blumlein described the effect of using crossed figures-of-eight, which give a 90° acceptance angle, and this arrangement remains a favourite, but Figure 6.11 also shows the acceptance angle for two other patterns, hypercardioid and cardioid.

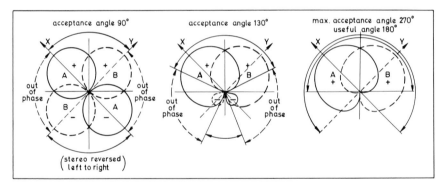

Fig. 6.11. Polar characteristics and acceptance angles for coincident pairs of figure-of-eight, hypercardioid, and cardioid microphones set at a mutual angle of 90°

MS stereo

This technique again uses coincident microphones, one of which is a Middle component microphone (usually cardioid or omni) pointing straight ahead. The other is a figure-of-eight Side component microphone arranged laterally (see Figure 6.12). The microphone outputs are processed by a sum-and-difference network to produce conventional left and right signals, making use of the fact that the two lobes of the figure-of-eight are in opposite phase.

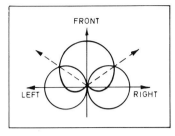

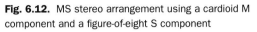

Fig. 6.12. MS stereo arrangement using a cardioid M component and a figure-of-eight S component

Many variations are possible, the MS system being particularly attractive to broadcasters because it gives ideal compatibility with mono transmissions—simple addition of the left/right signals gives the M signal alone:

$$(M + S) + (M - S) = 2M.$$

Near coincident pair

Several systems have been evolved with the microphone pair spaced a short distance apart, with or without a physical baffle between them. These include the ORTF method of the French Broadcasting Organization, and various binaural recording systems using a real or stylized dummy head as the baffle. The latter technique of course succeeds best on headphone listening, when uncanny directional realism can sometimes be reproduced in all planes.

Spaced pair

A widely spaced pair of omni or other type of microphones (1–5 m apart) gives well-differentiated stereo but needs care if odd phase cancellations and a 'hole in the middle' effect are to be avoided, the latter caused by the lack of any microphone aimed directly at the centre stage (where soloists are often located). A solution often employed is to add a third microphone at the centre to control the apparent width and give improved focus on the centre image.

Multi-microphone stereo

It is also common practice to mix together a number of (mono or stereo) microphones, either recording them all at a single take or one or two at a time during a number of overdub multitrack sessions. Then the engineer has the responsibility of panning each source to that part of the stereo arc which seems to give the most artistic result. In pop recording there are no hard-and-fast rules, but for the classical repertoire it is usually best to employ a basic stereo pair out front and then pan each spot microphone until the spotlighted instrument appears in the same position across the stereo stage as it does in the overall stereo pair balance.

The mechanical/electrical conversion

A vibrating diaphragm can be made to generate a proportionate voltage using a number of transducer principles. These include piezo-electric (crystal and ceramic), contact resistance (carbon), thermal, ionic, magnetic (moving-coil and ribbon), and electrostatic (condenser and electret). Only the magnetic and electrostatic types are found in professional sound recording studios, and so the others will be left out of this discussion.

Magnetic or 'dynamic' microphones rely on the electromagnetic interaction between the field of a powerful permanent magnet and a moving conductor. In the moving-coil type, a coil of wire is fixed to the back of the diaphragm and is free to move in the circular gap of an annular magnet/polepiece assembly (see Figure 6.13a). Diaphragm motion results in the coil cutting through the magnetic field so that an electric current is induced in the coil. Impedance is low and therefore a step-up transformer may be built into the microphone. Even so, the sensitivity (voltage out for a given acoustic pressure level) is relatively low, but this is not a serious limitation in the applications for which moving-coils are commonly used, namely hand-held for vocals or interviews, lavalier types, and close balance of percussion instruments. They are well suited to this kind of application because their main resonance is mid-frequency and well damped, making them fairly impervious to wind and mechanical interference. Most moving-coils are pressure-operated and therefore omnidirectional, but more sophisticated cardioid or unidirectional models are also common.

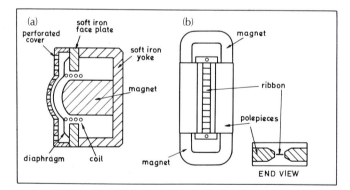

Fig. 6.13. Typical construction of (*a*) moving-coil and (*b*) ribbon microphones

Ribbon microphones use the same principle as moving-coils but have a thin strip (usually of aluminium leaf) doing double duty as diaphragm and conductor. The ribbon is only a few μm thick by 2–4 mm wide and is corrugated and held under light tension in the gap between specially shaped magnetic polepieces (see Figure 6.13*b*). The impedance is very low and so a built-in transformer is essential. Weighing only about 0.2 mg, the ribbon has an excellent transient response and a smooth frequency coverage, but it is very sensitive to wind noise and external vibrations, which restricts the situations in which it can be used. The open construction means that ribbon microphones are normally pressure-gradient-operated to give the classic figure-of-eight directivity pattern, but a few designs partially enclose one face of the ribbon or introduce an acoustical delay network (as in some condenser microphones) to produce cardioid or similar patterns.

Electrostatic microphones (otherwise called 'capacitor' or 'condenser') are now the type most commonly used in professional recording. This has come about despite the fact that they are difficult, and therefore expensive, to make and often need care in handling, storage and exposure to climatic extremes.

The thin, 1–10 µm, diaphragm is made of metal or metallized plastic film and supported around its rim at a small distance (5–50 µm) from the thicker metal backplate (see Figure 6.14). The thin diaphragm and fixed backplate

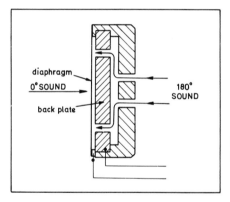

Fig. 6.14. Typical construction of a condenser microphone

therefore form the two electrodes of a simple capacitor and are oppositely charged by the application of a polarizing voltage. Vibrations of the diaphragm in response to the changing air pressure due to sound waves cause the spacing and therefore the capacitance of the two-plate condenser to alternate about its mean value, and this is used to generate the required output voltage. The very high (capacitative) impedance of the microphone capsule makes it impracticable to use a direct cable feed. A built-in head amplifier very close to the capsule is therefore essential, as much for impedance matching as for voltage gain. However, as an amplifier is obligatory, the output sensitivity and impedance can be optimized to suit the standard circuits used in professional applications. Early head amplifiers were naturally based on thermionic valves, then replaced by more compact, and quieter, solid-state components. In recent years a nostalgic return to valves has taken place, where a subjectively more 'natural' vocal quality is sought. Some older microphone designs have taken on a new lease of life, and a few new valve models have appeared.

The output of a condenser microphone is proportional to the d.c. polarizing voltage applied, and so simple switching of the value of this voltage can be used to give a range of directivity patterns from a single microphone (see Plate 3). In Figure 6.15a, for example, the microphone consists in effect of two cardioid capsules back to back. The polarizing voltage to one of the diaphragms (on the right in the diagram) is fixed at +60 V with respect to the common backplate to give a forward-facing cardioid response. The voltage to the second diaphragm can be switched from −60 V through 0 V to +60 V, and, since the a.c. signal outputs of the two capsules are connected in parallel through capacitor C, the five polar diagrams of Figure 6.15b can be obtained. In the centre position 3, for example, the rear diaphragm is at 0 V and contributes no signal, leaving the forward cardioid in operation. In position 1, the two contributions are equal but in opposite phase to give a figure-of-eight response, and so on. Remote-controlled switching is of course perfectly possible, with a greater number of switch positions or a continuously variable potentiometer if required.

Plate 3. Electrostatic microphone showing switching for four directivity patterns (left), sensitivity and bass roll-off (right) (Photo: AKG)

It is clearly a disadvantage that the condenser microphone requires a separate source of d.c. power both to polarize the plates and energize the built-
in amplifier (though a 'phantom power' system usually supplies the
required voltage along the signal cable). This situation has been met in part
in recent years by the development of *electret microphones*, in which the
diaphragm or back plate is made from a permanently polarized electret
material. This has reduced the cost of manufacture and somewhat extended
the freedom of application, since electret microphones can be very light and
small in size. A low-voltage (battery) supply is still needed for the amplifier
but the high-voltage polarizing source is eliminated. Note, however, that
this also removes the possibility of variable-directivity switching with electret microphones.

Microphone sensitivity

The electrical output from a microphone for a given sound pressure level
(defined as the sensitivity) should clearly be as high as possible, to provide a
high signal-to-noise ratio (even more important now that digital recording

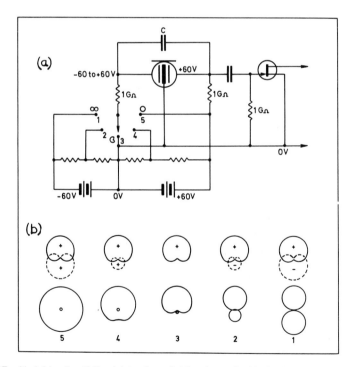

Fig. 6.15. Variable directivity: (*a*) basic switching for a double-diaphragm condenser microphone, (*b*) the polar diagrams for the five switch positions

and the Compact Disc have greatly reduced other sources of inherent background noise). The word 'noise' is used here to mean electrical noise, interference, mechanical handling, cable rubbing, and indeed all the unwelcome accompaniments to the desired signal before it reaches the microphone input sockets on the control console.

In practice, the microphones used in professional recording vary widely in sensitivity, and it does not help that several different ways are used to specify this parameter in manufacturers' specifications. The IEC and British Standards method is to specify the voltage output per pascal (a sound pressure unit equal to 10 microbars) measured under open circuit conditions: a typical value would be 8.0 mV/Pa. The generally accepted threshold of hearing at 1,000 Hz corresponds to a pressure of 20×10^{-4} Pa, and Sound Pressure Level (SPL) in dB with reference to this threshold is frequently used instead of pressure in Pa. On the SPL scale, 1 Pa = 94 dB SPL, which corresponds to quite a loud sound. In a commonly used method of specifying sensitivity, the reference SPL is 74 dB, which is about the level of speech at 20 cm (and equals 0.1 Pa or 1 microbar); the sensitivity is given in terms of the voltage output level (in dB ref. 1 V, or sometimes 0.775 V).

Some manufacturers also quote an overload or *maximum SPL* for which the total harmonic distortion from the microphone reaches a stated value (say 0.5 per cent). As an indication of the microphone's *inherent noise*, the rated equivalent SPL which would give the same output voltage as the inherent noise is often quoted, and this can be either unweighted (measured via a meter flat from 20 Hz to 20 kHz) or weighted to the IEC A curve and given as a dBA value. Subtracting the equivalent noise level from the maximum SPL gives the microphone's total dynamic range. For example, if noise SPL is 14 dB and overload SPL is 134 dB (both very good values) the dynamic range is 120 dB.

Special microphones

A whole range of microphones designed to meet the needs of special applications has evolved over the years, and some of these will be described briefly.

Ultradirectional microphones

The need for higher directivity than can be got from cardioid or supercardioid microphones arises in such long-distance recording situations as sport, bird-song, and environments with high ambient noise, as in some television situations where the microphone must be kept away from the scene in shot. An early approach to this problem was to construct a parabolic reflector of say 0.5 or 1.0 m diameter and mount the microphone at the focal point. This effectively concentrates the parallel rays of sound arriving on axis and discriminates against sounds from other directions. It is unwieldy, however, and ceases to be effective for low-frequency sounds where the wavelength is equal to or greater than the reflector diameter.

A more versatile solution is the line or 'shot-gun' microphone, in which the microphone capsule is mounted at the end of a thin pipe having holes spaced along its length. Acoustic delay elements ensure that only the sounds arriving on the gun axis reach the capsule in phase and therefore add together to produce the desired narrow-angle response.

Boundary effect or PZM microphones

A more recent development seeks to avoid the interference effect when sounds are reflected on to a microphone from a nearby surface, producing the well-known comb-filter type of distortion, as cancellation nulls appear at the frequency for which the spacing is ¼ wavelength and its harmonics. Provided that the microphone diaphragm can be mounted very close to a primary reflecting surface, the incident and reflected waves will be in phase and reinforce each other.

The boundary layer or pressure zone microphones (PZM) based on this idea have a small pressure-operated capsule mounted into a flat plate which can be laid on the floor or taped to a wall or lectern. The capsule receives the direct and reflected wave simultaneously and can have a consistently smooth frequency response over a whole hemisphere. Cardioid versions also exist.

Direction-sensing microphones

An extension of the boundary microphone idea has led to the production of direction-sensing microphones. These have two cardioid capsules back to back feeding a special mixer unit. This senses the ratio of sound from the two capsules and gates 'on' the appropriate signal for which the talker is within ±60° of the axis.

Contact microphones

Transducer elements which can convert the physical vibrations of an instrument string or body directly to an electrical signal have been in use for many years in electronic guitars, keyboards, and other instruments. A more recent move has been towards the use of a contact capacity trans-ducer in the form of a very thin (1 mm) tape supplied in various lengths. This can be applied to the curved surface of a double base or drum casing, and gives a very high ratio of instrument pick-up to ambient sounds.

Wireless microphones

Where complete freedom from the trailing microphone cable is needed, in complicated stage or TV shows for example, a radio microphone can provide the answer. This employs a conventional hand-held or (concealed) tie-pin/lavalier microphone attached to a miniature radio transmitter worn by the user. A special receiver is tuned to the transmitter frequency and produces an audio output signal suitable for feeding into the normal line input of the control console. Several radio microphones may be used at once, tuned to different radio frequencies. There are also 'diversity reception' systems in which the microphone signal is picked up by more than one receiver and automatic switching reduces the risks of fading as the artist moves around.

Soundfield microphone

Whilst the four-channel quadraphonic recordings promoted in the 1970s failed to secure a wide public following—due partly to the confusing parallel promotion of several competing non-compatible encoding systems and partly to the poor sound imaging which resulted—a small band of researchers continues to search for a commercially viable surround sound system. Very acceptable results can be demonstrated using the Ambisonics system, and a by-product of this research has been the Soundfield microphone. This consists of four microphone capsules arranged in a regular tetrahedron inside a single casing and orientated in such a way as to capture all the directional information needed to reproduce (through a suitable array of four or more loudspeakers) the full 360° three-dimensional soundfield.

This surround-sound application has still failed to attract a substantial show of interest from the major record companies or broadcasters, though film and video producers are now producing three-dimensional soundtracks for playback through appropriate arrays of loudspeakers. However, the Soundfield microphone has proved to be extremely versatile as a tool in two-channel stereo recording. The remote-control unit allows the engineer to steer the microphone's directivity and alter the stereo width and such other parameters as direct-to-reverberant sound balance, apparent height, and so on.

7 Mixing consoles: Analogue

Richard Swettenham

In order to cover all the features likely to be met in consoles for recording use, this chapter will describe the units and systems found in a typical console for multitrack recording, considered mainly from the operational rather than the engineering design point of view. By way of illustration, Figures 7.1 and 7.2 show the controls layout and block schematic diagrams for a console having extensive computer-assisted mixing facilities. Plate 4 shows the same console in a 36 channel version.

Microphone inputs

The main factors of importance here are: source and input impedances, noise in relation to gain, and gain range and headroom. The majority of studio microphones have nominal impedances in the range of 150–300 ohms, and for practical purposes may be regarded as 200 ohms. Almost all capacitor microphones fall into this group, though some have provision for internal connection for 50 ohms. This gives half the output voltage, which is sometimes useful to avoid overloading the input of equipment basically intended for use with low-level dynamic microphones. With the average studio console it is not useful or desirable.

Some dynamic microphones are still supplied in the 30–60 ohms impedance range. Hence some older consoles had a '50–200 ohm' input switch which varied the input transformer ratio to give extra step-up, with the intention of improving signal-to-noise ratio. However, with most input amplifier designs the noise at high gain will be related to the source impedance presented to the input (seen after the transformer, if there is one). So, though the transformer appears to give 'free gain' the advantage in fact may be small. Current practice is simply to regard the lower-impedance microphones as less sensitive types.

The impedance seen by the microphone is also important, because a dynamic microphone is not a pure resistive source and its impedance, particularly at high frequencies, may be somewhat higher than the stated value. If it were noticeably loaded, this might well degrade the frequency response. Hence microphones of all types are intended to be used as unloaded voltage generators and their published response curves are taken

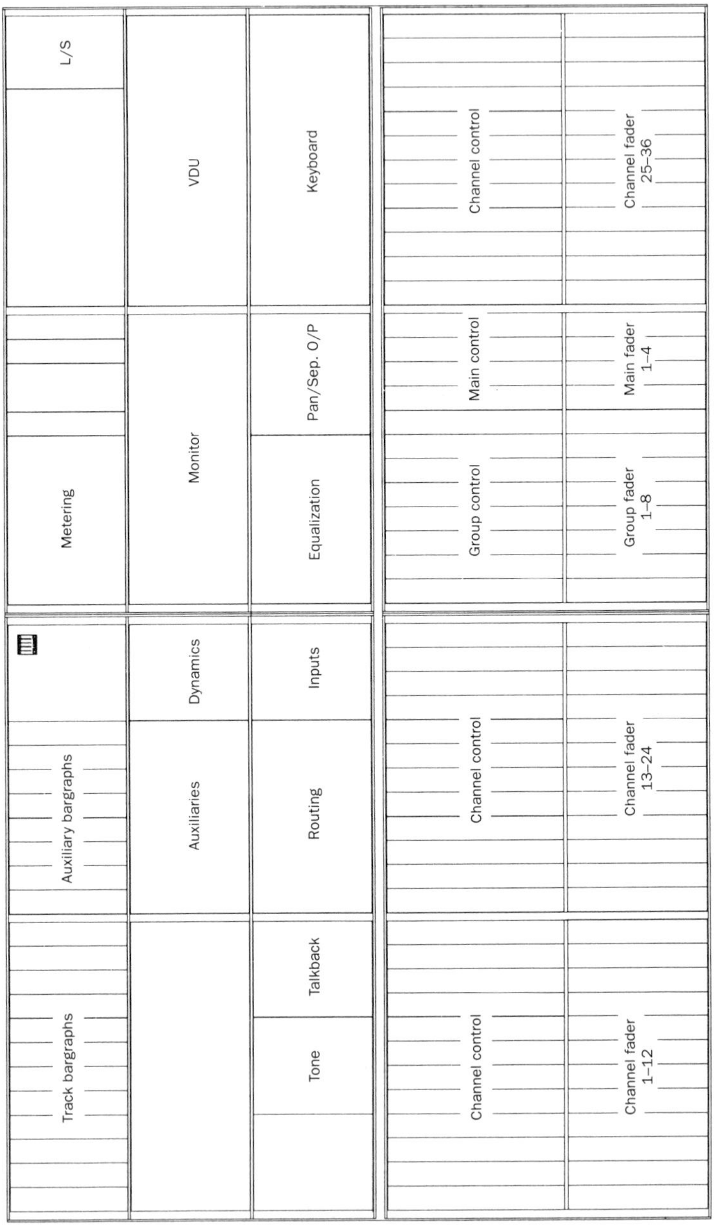

Fig. 7.1. Controls layout of the mixing console shown in Plate 4

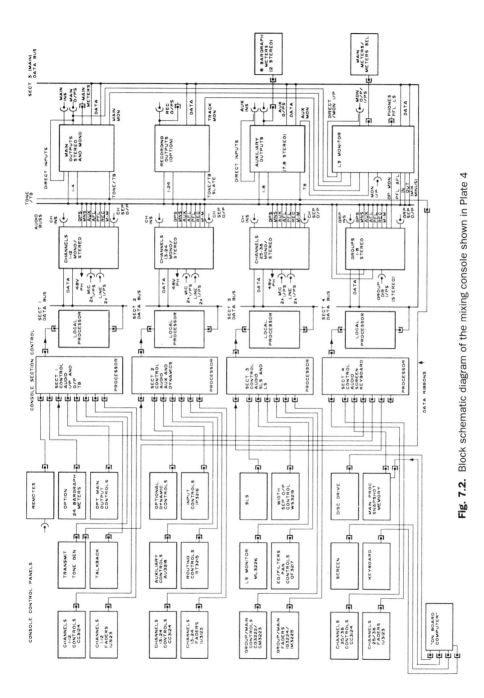

Fig. 7.2. Block schematic diagram of the mixing console shown in Plate 4

Plate 4. Typical modular analogue console having extensive digitally controlled mixing facilities (Calrec T Series)

in this way. Standard recommended practice, therefore, is for the impedance looking into the microphone input of the console to be at least five times that of the microphone, that is 1 k ohms or higher over the whole frequency range, and this value must also be unaffected by any feedback gain change or the introduction of input pads.

Noise

In comparing manufacturers' specifications, it is essential to compare the stated test conditions and regard with caution any figures which do not state them clearly. Noise is normally specified at maximum gain, and is stated either as 'equivalent input noise' or 'noise figure'. Equivalent input noise is the noise measured at the amplifier output in dBu (dB relative to 0.775 V) plus the amplifier and transformer voltage gain in dB when the input is terminated with a resistor of the normal microphone value (usually 200 ohms). Note that a 600 ohm source, sometimes specified, will produce an apparently worse figure, and a 30 ohm source (sometimes not mentioned) an apparently better figure.

Example: Noise measured −57 dBu, gain 70 dB,
Equivalent Input Noise = −127 dB.

The Noise Figure is the amount by which the Equivalent Input Noise is higher than the thermal noise of a 200 ohm (or other specified) resistor. Here the source value is part of the calculation, so the above ambiguity is avoided. It is also necessary to state the bandwidth of measurement, or the weighting network used, and the type of voltage-measuring instrument. A nominal 'r.m.s.' microvoltmeter will give a lower reading on noise than a peak instrument such as a PPM.

The above figures give a measure of the quietness of a microphone amplifier at highest gain. As the gain is reduced, the noise will reduce at first in proportion to the gain, but then tend to level off towards a certain minimum noise at low gains (Figure 7.3). The Noise Figure in top-class designs has been very close to theoretical limits for some years, but the general improvement in amplifier devices has meant that the noise/gain relationship can now be maintained down to much lower gains.

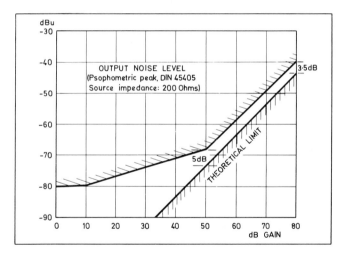

Fig. 7.3. Noise level limits for microphone amplifiers (Nordic Broadcasting Authorities' recommendations)

Input gain range

The microphone circuit requires the widest range of gain adjustment in the whole audio system. On the one hand a ribbon microphone over a clavichord may call for all possible gain; on the other, a capacitor in front of a bass drum may well deliver 0 dBu or more to the console. In the past, many strategies combining negative feedback with attentuation, and even the switching in and out of amplifier blocks, have been used to cover the whole range. An available input gain of 80 dB used to be considered necessary in broadcasting consoles, but when it is realised that this means a peak signal-to-noise ratio of worse than 55 dB it becomes obvious that this is hardly usable in modern recording. General practice seems to have settled on a gain range of 20–70 dB, with a balanced pad at the input giving a further loss of 20 dB.

Overload margin

The maximum voltage output available from a microphone amplifier will depend simply on the supply voltages, as in all other amplifiers in the console. Yet the designer has to consider whether extra headroom should be provided for unexpected high-level input peaks by arranging the gain structure to give a lower 'normal' output level from the first amplifier and making it up later in the system after a level control. Some broadcasting specifications demand this, having in mind the unrehearsed live programme situation, but in the music studio it is less of a problem. In the case of a microphone amplifier with transformer input, when the gain is low and input level high (as with close miking of loud instruments with capacitor microphones), harmonic distortion may appear, due to saturation of the transformer, particularly at low frequencies, though the output level is normal. This may be avoided by switching in the resistive pad mentioned above (which is always in front of the transformer). Sometimes it may be desirable to put in a pad and then put back a few steps of gain.

Transformerless (electronically balanced) microphone amplifiers are now in general use though they took some years to equal the noise figure of transformer types. They can provide virtually perfect wideband and transient response. Yet there remains a case, here if nowhere else in the console, for the retention of the transformer as an isolating device. The all-electronic circuit has to be carefully trimmed to reject any common-mode (audio pair to earth) signals from being amplified, and protected against excessive voltages damaging the input circuit. Large electrolytic capacitors are also required to isolate the phantom power supplies for capacitor microphones.

Phantom power supply

Phantom-operated capacitor microphones (as mentioned in Chapter 6) fall into two groups: those which utilise about 48 V d.c. directly for polarisation and head amplifier powering, and those which generate operating voltages by an oscillator–rectifier arrangement from any available supply from 9 V upwards, with phantom splitting resistors chosen according to supply voltage. Since a console may have to supply microphones of both types, the built-in supply will be 48 V and the resistor value chosen for the microphone type which draws the greatest current. The 'true 48 V' types draw very little current, so there is minimal voltage drop.

Gain settings

The key to the correct setting of microphone amplifier gain, with respect both to noise and overload margin, is to keep the channel fader at the intended 'normal' setting (e.g. 10 dB from maximum) when the channel is contributing a signal to the mix that produces a peak-level indication. This assumes of course that the group master fader is also at normal.

A useful approach to the correct situation is to set all faders to normal on rehearsal and attempt to produce a plausible balance on the microphone gain controls. It should be realized that any downward movement of the fader from this position, other than to reduce the amount of that channel heard in the mix, is eating into the available headroom. If restoring any fader to the reference mark causes the level meter to go over peak, then microphone gain must be reduced. An LED overload warning light is commonly found in input channels, and desirably these should respond to preset warning levels detected both before and after the equalizer.

Filters and phase reversal

A phase-reversal switch, operating on both microphone and line inputs, and a low-frequency cut-off filter are normally found in each channel. High-frequency filters are common, but not universal. The filters have a slope of 12 or 18 dB per octave from the turnover frequency, and are usually switched into circuit only when required.

The LF cut-off filter has considerable use since the normal response specification of 20 Hz to 20 kHz is usable only under ideal conditions. More often it is necessary to curtail the response below the lowest fundamental note of an instrument to cut off air-conditioning rumble, vibration of microphone stands, and hum from guitar amplifiers. High-frequency filtering is less necessary in live recording, but may be useful to cut off overspill, say from cymbals picked up on a microphone covering a bass instrument whose harmonics do not come far up the frequency range. Typically, switched LF filters will operate at 40, 80, 120, and 180 Hz, and HF filters at 12, 8, 6, and 4 kHz. Filters with 'sliding' turnover frequency are now available in many consoles; these can be moved up from about 15 Hz to say 350 Hz, and from 25 kHz down to say 3 kHz (see Figure 7.4).

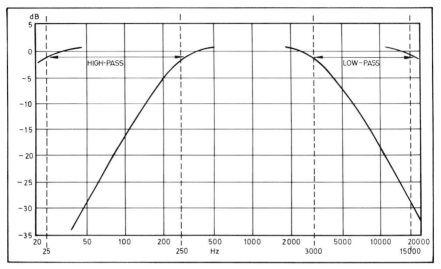

Fig. 7.4. Variable high-pass and low-pass filters

Equalizers

The very simplest equalizers found in mixing consoles provide high and low-frequency shelving curves similar to the treble and bass controls of domestic equipment (Figures 7.5 and 7.6), plus a mid-range lift or cut at various switchable frequencies from about 500 Hz to 6 kHz (Figure 7.7). This is often called a 'presence' control as its effect is to make the signal affected stand out in the balance, as if closer to the microphone. If applied in an exaggerated way, it will give a hard metallic effect which destroys realism. The mid-frequency dip, called in European terminology 'absence', has the contrary effect. It is used to reduce those parts of the range of an instrument which 'stick out' too prominently in a mix, or to counteract in remixing the excessive use of 'presence' in the original recording.

It will be obvious that a normal shelving bass lift, which levels off and continues at a raised level down to the bottom end of the frequency range (Figure 7.6), will exaggerate any hum or rumble present in the input, which will in turn call for a low cut-off filter. For this reason, there is a strong case for bass boost to take the form of a fairly broad resonant curve (Figure 7.8), so that if the 200–300 Hz region, say, is lifted to 'warm up' a male voice or a cello the response will have returned to flat by about 60 Hz, and need not then be curtailed. Likewise, high-frequency shelf lift (Figure 7.5) should be used very sparingly, to avoid exaggeration of mechanical noises from close-miked instruments or the lifting of microphone amplifier hiss.

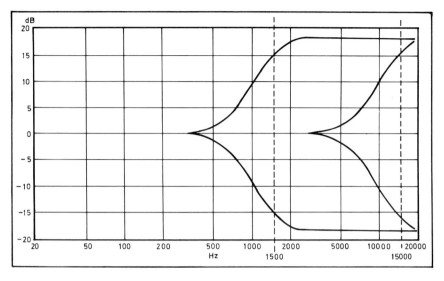

Fig. 7.5. Shelving treble EQ at −3 dB frequencies of 1.5 and 15 kHz

For many years, equalizer controls had precisely calibrated steps of both level and frequency in the interest of returning to repeatable settings, and because circuit design with inductors etc., required it. But engineers came to prefer continuously variable adjustment, and the most common preference today is for the so-called parametric equalizer (see Figure 7.9). In these

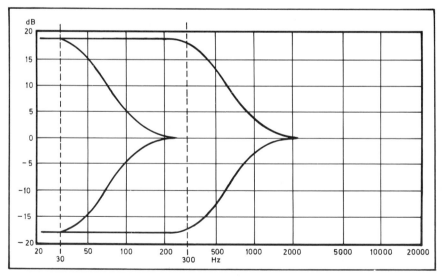

Fig. 7.6. Shelving bass EQ at −3 dB frequencies of 30 and 300 Hz (approx.)

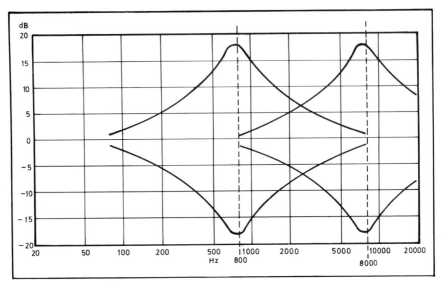

Fig. 7.7. Mid-range EQ at centre frequencies of 800 and 8,000 Hz (approx.)

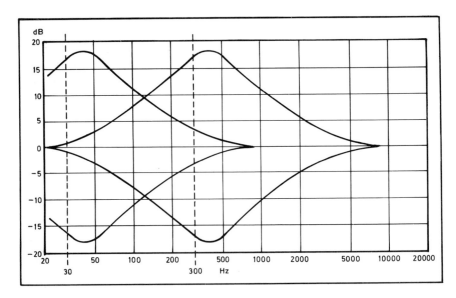

Fig. 7.8. Bass EQ using a broad peak at 30 and 300 Hz (approx.)

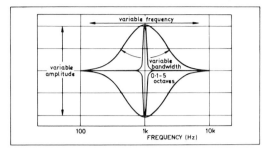

Fig. 7.9. Range of control in one section of a parametric equalizer

units the frequency spectrum is usually divided into four regions. The frequency of peak or trough in each region is continuously tuneable by a potentiometer. The amplitude of the peak is also continuously variable, and lastly the sharpness or bandwidth of the peak (known as 'Q') may be varied in steps or even continuously. The frequency regions may overlap, any one region having a ratio of highest to lowest frequency of say 20 : 1, though even wider is possible. The highest and lowest regions may be switched from a peak to a shelf form. All this can require up to twelve knobs per channel, consuming a great deal of panel space. With such equalizers it is possible to produce very strange and exaggerated effects, and it is important to bear in mind exactly what one is trying to achieve and proceed very logically in setting the controls.

An equalizer is designed to have the same maximum output level as the other amplifiers in the console. With its controls at flat, it will not overload sooner than the microphone amplifier. But with any considerable amount of boost applied to a region where full level is coming from the source, more of the headroom at the equalizer output will be taken up. It will naturally 'sound louder', and one will tend to pull down the fader. However, since the fader comes after the EQ, it may be better to reduce the input gain instead.

Insert points

Break-in points are customarily provided in each channel before and after the equalizer (and sometimes also after the fader), at which an outboard processing element can be inserted. The signal path may simply be led out via normalled jacks, but it is commoner today to have a switch in the channel for each insert point so that the effect of the inserted device can be compared with that of 'straight through', or the device can be switched in and out on cue. To reduce the number of jacks in a large console, the switch may be arranged to select one of the possible break-in positions and bring it out through a single pair of jacks. Wherever possible, levels are arranged so that all the insert points through a console are at standard line level.

PFL, AFL, and Solo

The pre-fade listen (PFL) circuit provides a means to check (a) that the correct signal is present at the correct level, before opening a fader, and (b) to verify the technical quality of an input signal at a standard listening level without disturbing the recording balance. This signal from one or more channels may either appear on a small speaker in the console or be substituted for the main monitor signal, which is momentarily muted.

The after-fader listen (AFL) circuit is exactly the same, but takes its signal from the output of the fader, and is therefore heard at a level proportional to its level in the mix. Either PFL or AFL will enable the operator to judge how much 'overspill' from other instruments is entering any studio microphone. In American terminology, AFL is sometimes called Solo or Audition, and the solo as usually referred to was earlier called 'Solo-in-Place'. In AFL, the selected signal is heard by itself, usually in mono, and without the echo return which may be associated with it. Solo operates by muting all channels whose solo buttons are not pressed, so that those soloed are still heard at their proper levels and stereo positions in the mix, and with their proper echo, if the echo returns are excepted from being muted. Use of Solo during recording would destroy the mix, so provision is usually made to disable Solo or convert it to AFL when recording, though the Solo enable/disable switch is sometimes used as a means of muting and unmuting a group of channels during a take.

Auxiliary sends from channel

A signal may be taken off before or after the channel fader via switches and level controls to feed echo and effects and foldback ('cue' or artist headphone) mixes. Foldback is normally taken before the fader so that it is unaffected by balance changes. Echo send usually follows the fader, though a pre–post fader switch is often provided. In consoles for general-purpose broadcasting or recording use, no distinction is generally made between echo and foldback, and each auxiliary feed will have a pre-fade, off, post-fade switch. A channel direct output jack may also be provided after the fader to access individual channels. A broadcast-type console, where only occasional multitrack recording is required, may have an output taken from before the fader via a level trim control and buffer amplifier.

Stereo panning

In the early days of stereo, a relationship was established between the proportion of signal level fed to two loudspeakers and the apparent position of the sound source (Figure 7.10). If the levels to left and right are controlled

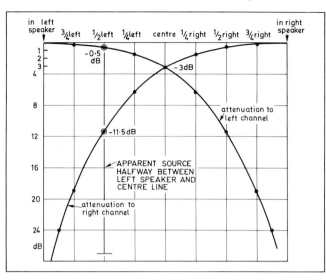

Fig. 7.10. Pan-pot law: the attenuator will give constant loudness for a single source panned across a pair of loudspeakers

according to these curves, the sum of the power outputs from the two speakers will remain constant, so that when a source is panned from one speaker to the other the loudness will not vary. To produce the exact curves, a double-stud potentiometer was originally used with precision resistors on as many steps as practicable. An acceptable approximation is made nowadays with linear continuous pots and fixed resistors.

While the 3 dB loss in the centre produces constant acoustic level from a pair of loudspeakers, if the two identical −3 dB signals are added electrically further on in the system to produce a mono output the voltage will be doubled, and the mono will therefore be 3 dB higher with the pan-pot central than with the pot to one side. (The same will happen if the stereo recording is combined to mono in a playback system.) A 6 dB loss at the mid-point would remove this effect, but produce an apparent level dip in the centre on stereo. Where mono results are still considered important, as in broadcasting, a compromise value of 4.5 dB at the mid-point may be adopted.

Various provisions were made in console design for the short-lived requirements of quadraphony. These are mostly redundant, except that one useful by-product, the 'front–back' pan-pot, has found a new use. If the 'back' outputs, left and right, are regarded as 'stereo output no. 2', and the front–back pots are initially set to half-way, two stereo mixes are obtained, which can be separately recorded. Initially they are the same, but by altering the 'front–back' ratio one may be given, say, a touch more of vocal, solo instrument, or echo return, or have one channel, say commentary voice-over, turned off altogether. Mixing on the faders then proceeds normally, listening to stereo no. 1, and the versions are compared afterwards. There is also a modern use for the 'joystick' in preparing tracks for cinema surround-sound, directing the signal to left, centre, right, and surround.

Channel routing to groups

For multitrack recording, the ability to send any input channel to any tape track is essential. Basically this is a simple matter of switching, but care in design is necessary to minimize crosstalk between tracks, assure reliability, and to give a self-evident presentation of routing in the minimum space.

Initially, rotary switches selected the channel output to any one of the available groups. If it was desired to record stereo pairs of signals on adjacent tracks, the switching in of the pan-pot also connected a second switch-bank to the next higher-numbered group, that is selection of '1' plus 'Pan in' gave panning between groups 1 and 2, and so on. Sometimes two switches were provided, leading to odd- and even-numbered groups.

Early in the development of multitrack recording it was felt necessary to be able to route an input simultaneously to any or all tracks. The standard way of doing this is by latching push-buttons, often with illuminated caps. The pan-pot, if inserted, operates between two sets of buttons, again leading to odd- and even-numbered groups. The push-button system was excellent for up to 16 tracks, with numbered button caps, but with 24 or more outputs it consumes a great deal of panel space. Hence buttons have been reduced to the minimum possible size, with LED indication. In some lower-priced consoles the number of buttons is halved and labelled '1–2', etc., with further 'odd–even' switches.

Besides occupying space, this vast number of buttons had been a serious cost element in large consoles and a source of worry about contact reliability in polluted atmospheres. Until recently there has not been an economic alternative, due to the cost per cross-point of any other method. Technical problems with solid-state switching elements have also taken time to overcome. Logic-operated systems are now prevalent, in which numbers representing the channel and the destination are keyed in to latch reed relays or solid-state switches, at the same time giving a visual indication of the routing established. This also gives the possibility of memorizing and recalling complete sets of console assignments. The addressing arrangements must include secure latching against accidental alteration of routing by power supply disturbances, and memory is commonly preserved by battery backup against power interruption.

Voltage-controlled amplifier grouping

Group fader control was made very much more flexible by the availability of the voltage-controlled amplifier. In spite of some initial weaknesses, VCAs have for some years offered fully acceptable quality standards for top-class consoles. The VCA takes the place of the audio fader in the input channel, and its gain is controlled by a sum of d.c. voltages derived from channel and 'grouper' faders. Switches select which grouper has control of each channel. In some cases the grouper is a separate dedicated fader, while in others the fader of one channel controls its own gain and that of others selected to the same control bus. Groupers can further be placed under control of other groupers, or of an overall master fader. It is now no longer necessary for the audio groups to tracks to have group faders, though level trim pots are usually provided. Any channels requiring to be controlled as a group are simply switched to any available grouper. There is a further

Plate 5. Motorized faders on computer-assisted mixing console (Photo: AMS Neve)

splendid advantage not previously achievable: channels routed to different tracks may now be controlled with the same fader, easing problems of physical reach and simultaneous operation. The VCA was also the sole key to the introduction of fader automation for some years before the motorized fader (illustrated in Plate 5) became a viable alternative.

The channel fader

For many years, the straight-line slide fader has been almost universal in studio consoles, except for a small percentage of quadrant lever types which are basically the same internally. The stud construction with precision resistors once used has been replaced by continuous tracks of conductive plastic. At first there was concern about lack of accuracy of calibration or stereo matching, but trimming techniques have now been established to control the law as closely as desired.

Considerations in the choice of a fader are smooth physical feel, freedom from electrical noise, minimum breakthrough of signal with the fader fully closed, and susceptibility to damage by dust and liquids spilt on the console. A switch may be fitted at the 'off' position to start remote machines, mute loudspeakers, or illuminate signal lights. A further switch known as 'overpress' is sometimes fitted, which is operated by pressing the knob past the 'off' position. This can turn on the pre-fade listen circuit, or possibly change over the channel input between two sources.

The moving fader

In fader automation systems using VCAs or digital attenuators, the level in the Read mode is set by the value returned from the automation data. In order to modify the level on any part of a track in a mix which is otherwise acceptable, i.e. Update, the fader position must match the value read from automation. In the earliest systems a small meter was provided in the fader top plate to do this. This was soon superseded by 'up and down' LEDs showing which way the knob should be moved. On correct matching, the light went out. Having made the desired change, the fader could be brought back to the point where it matched the previously existing data, after which one could leave the update mode. An alternative method was to ignore where the fader settings were 'supposed to be' and set the faders of any tracks to be updated to the zero mark. After entering the change, the knob is returned to zero.

In the moving fader, a small motor is provided which physically moves the fader knob up and down according to automation signals. On taking hold of the knob, the motor drive may be declutched completely and the fader stays under manual control until brought back to a matching setting.

Alternatively it may be set to 'leap back' (or glide back) to the Read value when the knob is released.

Probably the first motivation for the moving fader development came from users who wanted the memory facility of automated mix-down but who were suspicious of the possible effects of VCAs or their equivalent on sound quality. They wanted the audio to pass only through physical resistive tracks. Hence the fader contained an audio (semi-log) track and a servo track matching a DC voltage, representing the knob position, with a control signal. The automation system could be regarded as a 'system for moving levers' rather than manipulating audio. The other motivation came from the 'instinctive' feeling given by seeing the fader knobs exactly reproduce a manual mix and its changes, and being able to intervene manually without switches. The ergonomic benefit of moving faders is now very widely accepted, cost being the only problem. But, as the objections to 'VCA sound' are overcome and the huge advantages of multiple control voltages operating on one VCA in each channel are realized, we come to the use of moving faders controlling VCAs. In the simplest form, a single linear track could be used, so the control and servo voltage are the same.

However, in an ideal situation, provision should be made (both in moving and manual faders) for the following: a VCA gives linear dB per volt attenuation, right down to its maximum attenuation. With a linear resistance track, we will therefore get linear dBs per millimetre of knob movement. But looking at a conventional audio fader we see that the scale is more open at the top end, and the dB markings get closer together at the bottom as we approach the fade-out region. Operationally this is the most desirable configuration. Therefore, to produce this with a VCA, a track is used with a special law which modifies the control voltage to produce the same scale as the audio fader. Alternatively the actual voltages from the faders may be modified in a computer using a 'look-up table' procedure on the way to the VCAs.

The rolling track fader

In digitally controlled consoles (discussed later) which are a logical extension of automated mixing techniques in which the audio signal does not pass through control surface components, it is often desirable to have a fader with no fixed top and bottom end stops. It then becomes an incremental device which simply gives 'more' or 'less', with respect to a starting point. The physical realization of this is by a continuous band pushed up and down by the fingertip, rotating a disc with a conductive or optical pattern, producing count-up or count-down pulses convertible to, say, VCA control voltage. If you roll it down below 'zero' as determined by the device being controlled, nothing further happens, but the moment it is moved upwards again the level increases from zero. At the top end it may permit you to reach for a value 'higher than maximum' if the circuitry will allow. Also the 'dB per millimetre movement' sensitivity can be varied.

Mixing circuits

After the microphone amplifier, the actual method of mixing the signals from channels is the next most critical area of design from the point of view of good signal-to-noise ratio. There are two main approaches, 'passive' and 'active' mixing. Passive mixing is possible in a small to medium-sized mixer, with each channel always feeding to the main output and a series resistor connecting each channel to a common point. The voltage produced at the common point is the source voltage divided by the number of sources. The mix point feeds into a voltage amplifier which restores the loss. The noise is naturally proportional to the amount of gain needed, which follows from the number of sources. When amplifier noise was not as good as it is today, a step-up transformer was sometimes used to improve the situation, exactly like a microphone input. But when sources are being switched on and off, as in the multitrack case, each source switched off must be substituted by a dummy resistance or short circuit, or else the mixing loss, and the level, will vary. So the noise is always 'worst-case'.

In the 'active' alternative, the mixing amplifier is an inverting type, with feedback returned to the input mixing point through the same value resistor as the inputs. This produces a current summing point which has almost zero impedance. The voltage gain from any source to the mix amplifier output is normally zero, though some gain can be produced if required. Sources may be connected and disconnected with negligible change of level. The noise produced by such a circuit varies with the number of sources connected and is minimum with only one source, though with a number of sources it will be the same as in the passive case. Hence its almost universal use despite some well-known design problems.

Group outputs

Following the track mix amplifier will often be found a further insert point with a switch, and a group overall level control before the line amplifier feeding the recorder. In the days of eight and sixteen tracks, these group controls were often main faders, though they tended to get little use. With 24 and more tracks, they have mainly become rotary trim pots. Some faders may be retained for their usefulness as subgroups in mix-down, odds and evens being again combined on to groups 1 and 2 and used as the main stereo mix, unless a separate stereo bus is provided. Auxiliary sends from groups may be provided in exactly the same way as from channels, feeding to the same auxiliary mixes. The line output will normally go to the recorders via a patch-bay (jackfield) and the record signal returning to the monitor input selection will be taken after the jacks, so that what is heard is always what is actually arriving to that track of the machine.

The mixing and output arrangements for an auxiliary output, echo, or foldback will be basically similar to that which feeds a tape track. An overall rotary level control will be provided (and in many cases a simple equalizer and insertion point) and in the case of a dedicated echo send a second insert point for tape or digital time delay.

Where there are several foldback mixes from channels and from tracks, there may additionally be a further combining matrix of rows of buttons, whereby different outputs to studio headphone feeds may each consist of a different combination of sources plus echo returns, external signals such as click-tracks, and very often a basic feed of the main stereo mix. Talkback can be superimposed on each headphone feed, usually reducing the level of foldback while it is in use.

The multitrack monitor system

During the recording of a multitrack tape, it must be possible to monitor the input or recorded signal on all tracks, and present this as a reasonable approximation to the final stereo balance on the monitor speakers. So for each track the following controls are provided:

(a) *Track level.* Usually a short-throw slide fader; sometimes a full-length fader if space permits.

(b) *Pan-pot.* This affects monitoring only.

(c) *Solo and cut switches.* These operate as described for the input channel. Solo here has no effect on recording, so may be operated at any time.

(d) *Monitor echo send.* A level control and selector switch enables echo to be sent from a track round one of the echo systems and returned (via further return switches and level pots) into the monitor system only.

(e) *Sync switch.* Depending on the remote controls provided with the multitrack recorder, this may or may not exist as part of the console. It enables the operator to decide whether he will hear the already recorded signal coming back from the machine's record head, or the input signal to the track. Automatic switching will transfer monitor back to input when the machine is put into record on that track.

(f) *Foldback send pots* (one or more per track). These feed the machine sync signal and/or the live input to the track to the artist headphones mix. When the machine drops into record, the sync signal disappears and the artist hears the live signal instead, if he was not already doing so. An output of the track monitor mix is taken before the main monitor volume control to a stereo recorder to permit a simultaneous reference recording.

Console main monitoring

A series of buttons is usually provided to select the input to the main monitor system between multitrack monitor mix, main stereo output, returns from each stereo recorder, cassette, disc player, and the like. There may also be positions to check each echo send and return, foldback sends, and externals signals at the patchbay, such as from another studio. This selection leads to the master control of listening level, which may be a fader but is preferably a detented rotary control, so that the choice, or alteration, of reference listening level is a deliberate decision. A dim key with trim control is provided so that listening level may be brought down a pre-set amount to check balance at low level, or when using talkback or conversing in the control room, and then restored to standard level. Monitor mute is also provided, which is actuated when speaking idents on to tape ('slate'). Further buttons are usual to monitor stereo as mono, to mute one speaker, and to invert phase momentarily to one speaker if a phase error is suspected.

Switching is often provided to substitute alternative sets of monitor speakers for the principal ones. A pair of fairly small units is often placed on top of the console. These are high-quality 'nearfield' monitors; smaller speakers built into the console may provide a further choice, to simulate portable radios and to serve for intercom between control rooms.

Studio playback is provided for by a similar set of source selector buttons and overall volume control. Precautions are taken to prevent microphone signals being accidentally returned into a studio speaker.

Talkback

Talkback arrangements will vary widely in complexity, but one is likely to find provisions for:

- Talk to studio on loudspeaker
- Talk to each headphone circuit separately or all together
- Talk to conductor's stand or another control room
- Speaking identification on tape (slate).

In large music studios, provision will also be made for a conductor to speak to the control room, or to address the orchestra through the studio talkback speaker.

Metering

Level meters used in recording consoles are basically of two types, VU (Volume Unit) meters and PPM (Peak Programme Meters). The VU meter is an a.c. rectifier voltmeter, whose instrument has a specified ballistic (i.e. rise time and overshoot) behaviour when it is connected to the signal source through a specified value resistor. Its performance is defined by an American Standard specification, and it is important to realize that only meters conforming to this specification, and fed through the correct resistance, give readings that can be meaningfully compared on programme material. Not every meter having the usual VU scale does conform, particularly in semi-professional equipment, though all such meters will normally give consistent readings for 0 VU on continuous sine wave tone.

The normal sensitivity of a VU meter with its resistor (3.6 kilohms) is +4 dBu (1.23 V r.m.s.) for a reading of 0 VU. Standard line level for studio equipment is normally +8 dBu for peak recording level. The difference relates to the fact that the VU meter, due to its mechanical inertia, gives a lower reading on average programme material than on steady tone. Opinions vary as to the amount of 'lead' which should be allowed between tone and programme, from the above 4 dB to 6, 10, or even more. In fact, in relation to VU readings there is really no such thing as 'average programme material', and the permissible VU readings for different kinds of sound are something which is learned only by experience. Analogue magnetic tape is fairly forgiving as to the subjective effect of overload, but digital media are not, which strengthens the case for the peak meter. If a VU meter with resistor is connected across a 600 ohm source, it is possible to measure a small increase in distortion due to its presence. For this reason, and to permit setting of sensitivity to a desired value, VU meters are now commonly fitted with small buffer amplifiers.

The PPM (see also Chapter 25) has a drive amplifier and rectifier circuit which detects and applies to the instrument the momentary peak values reached by the audio voltage. It holds this value by charging up a capacitor, which then discharges through a high resistance. Thus the peak value of a short transient will be held long enough for the meter movement to reach the correct scale reading, and then fall back slowly, so that the eye can register the value reached without being confused by very rapid pointer movement.

A PPM (particularly of the all-electronic type) can be designed with virtually instantaneous rise time, but as certain transients are so short that if their full amplitude was registered they would produce a tendency either to under-record average levels or to disbelieve the meter, the charging time is deliberately slowed. In the BBC programme meter circuit this charge time is 2.5 milliseconds. PPMs are semi-logarithmic, that is the scale is more or less linear in dB (whereas the Vu meter is basically a voltmeter). There are various PPM circuits in use in different countries, which vary as to the rise and fall times and the number of dB on the scale length.

In Europe for many years the standard precision programme meter was the so-called light spot meter, but these were too large and expensive for multitrack use. They have been superseded by 'bar graph' displays using either high voltage neon (plasma) columns or rows of very small LEDs. Backlit liquid crystal units are also popular. A 'peak hold' facility is easily added, allowing the highest value reached momentarily to be held for a few seconds, or to be held during a whole item until released. Column meters are also provided with Peak/VU switching, where the VU ballistics are electrically simulated, or even both indications displayed side by side. For digital recording, an indication of the absolute instantaneous peak level is essential and so the bar graph displays have zero rise time and/or peak hold.

Current practice is often to have some kind of column indicator for each track, with the main stereo output, or selected monitor signal, shown both on a high-quality column and on large conventional VU meters.

Console layout and ergonomics

Having reviewed the features required in a large console and indicated the very large number of manual controls called for, it will be evident that the layout and physical location of these controls require a great deal of intelligent thought. It is of little use to provide every possible flexibility of adjustment if this leads to a situation in which the operator can hardly reach controls which he needs to operate simultaneously, or if the number and layout of these controls cause operator confusion and mistakes when working under stress. Thus the art of panel layout may well be described as the intelligent choice of what to leave out, and the organization of what remains in the most comprehensible form.

Large music-recording consoles started out in a straight, long-table form organized in a more or less left-to-right way: first, all the input channels, then the groups with group master faders, then the track monitoring, then ancillaries. As more and more channels and groups were called for, operators had to roll their chairs up and down. For stereo listening, this was obviously a bad thing. So, first of all, the track monitoring and things like foldback were turned through 90° on one side. This also generated a useful space in the corner section to contain master monitor controls and auxiliaries such as compressors.

For ideal stereo monitoring, it was desirable for the engineer to sit centrally with the controls organized symmetrically on either side of him. Those controls requiring constant visual attention should be in the centre, those constantly being adjusted falling under his hands, and those requiring occasional adjustment should still be within arm's reach. This was the motivation for the development of the wrap-round console which had its greatest popularity through the 1970s and offered what was in many ways an optimum solution. But, though the angle sections of wrap-round designs generated even more usable space within arm reach, the demand for more input channels made the central straight section grow again. Wrap-round consoles were all custom-built, and the domination of the market even for large music consoles by quantity-produced 'straight' designs has forced users to forgo the ergonomic advantages. Automation has also reduced the need for large numbers of rapid 'live mixing' control moves. But the general ergonomic principles governing operators at control desks remain valid and must be remembered in any new designs.

The arrangement of meters and visual displays is a further area in which ergonomics seemed to suffer a temporary defeat. A strong case can be made for the arrangement of multiple meters of the conventional kind in some sort of rectangular block, so that they can be observed as a group with a minimum of head-turning. This was a viable tactic up to 16 tracks. For 24 tracks, one option was 12 meters selectable between tracks 1–13, 2–14, etc. on the basis that in the studio tracks are filled up sequentially. Alternatively, an 8 × 3 meter layout was possible, but in too many cases the worst choice—a single line of 24—was adopted. The coming of the vertical column meter has at least reduced this to the width of 24 channels, and given the additional possibility to provide the subsidiary display of a frequency spectrum or VCA fader settings rather than track levels, but the optimum display of many track levels, plus other information, has for a long time been the video screen, and at increasingly reasonable cost.

The 'in-line' console

The vast majority of current production multitrack consoles follow what might be called the accepted compromise solution to the ergonomic problems mentioned above. This line of development, which was introduced as a space and cost saver, has brought in some useful by-products of its own in the organization of the system. Perhaps its main drawback has been the exchange of console depth for console length (though more recently extreme length has returned as well!). The placing of the monitor controls in line with the channel inevitably called for some extension of reach, but the manufacturing convenience of construction of channels in one straight module at a very shallow angle has produced another 'worst-case' situation which users have come to accept. In most current layouts, it is possible to reach the input gain, and some equalizer controls, only at extreme arm reach or by standing up.

The significant features of the in-line channel strip have now become established more or less as follows: there are two parallel signal paths, usually known as 'channel' and 'monitor', corresponding to the separate modules described earlier. The 'channel' side is fed with microphone amplifier output, echo/effects device return, or tape return in mix-down. 'Monitor' receives tape track record, sync, or play signal, according to the machine switching. There may or may not be 'console master mode' switches which force the inputs into preselected states, unless overridden by local switches. The output of the 'channel' side goes to the selection switching to tracks, and possibly a separate stereo output, with an optional pan-pot between odd and even tracks. The track (group) mixing and line output amplifiers for track no. 1 reside physically in channel strip no. 1, and so on; the back wiring provides that each mix amplifier picks up the right signal from the track select switching. Instead of 'group faders', rarely needed, there is a 'group level trim' pot to enable the overall level to track after mixing to be adjusted. This will normally be left at maximum unless many inputs to a track cause a build-up which might overload the tape.

The output of the monitor side goes directly via the 'main' pan-pot, close to the operator, to the stereo mix, which is also the feed to the main stereo recorder for simultaneous recording and for mix-down. There is a 'large' fader (the normal channel fader) which is driven by the automation system when in use, and a 'small' fader with shorter travel lever. When laying down tracks, the operator may choose which one will be in the input channel, the other controlling the monitor mix. In mix-down, the large fader will be used. If a large number of effects devices are in use and channels are used up, these signals may be brought back into the monitor side, through the 'small' fader, and added to the stereo mix, thus doubling the number of inputs. This is just the same as adding the monitor mix to the main mix in a separate-monitoring console. Each fader has its own solo and mute buttons.

Switching is provided so that the filters, equalizer, dynamics (compression/expansion/noise-gating—often provided at least optionally in each channel) can each be 'flipped' across the channel to monitor side as required. Also, as the demand for effects and foldback sends has steadily increased, as many knobs as can be physically accommodated are provided, with switches to allow each signal to be picked up before or after the fader in the channel or monitor side. The auxiliary mixes from the channels may be further subdivided on the way to the outputs, to give a maximum of separate sends.

Dynamics in the channel

Several designs now offer a compressor and expander or noise gate in each input channel, with a flexibility comparable to a sophisticated rack-mounted unit. Switching also allows the filters or equalizer of the channel to be separated and placed in the side chain of the dynamics. A further option now offered is for a digital delay in the channel.

Because the group mix and output stages are in the channel strip, two other useful provisions are easily made. When 'one source to one track' recording is being done (a very common case) there is no point in routing the signal through unnecessary wiring and circuitry. A 'Direct' switch can take the channel signal from the fader straight to the output stage. And, if it is desired to have a fader in audio control of a track, or to re-equalize or compress the whole feed to that track, a 'Group' switch will substitute the normal channel input by the group mix signal, which will then pass through all the facilities of the channel (including the possibility of deriving auxiliary sends from this group) and then emerge from the track record output.

If the console, as is very commonly the case, has say 32 channel selection but only 24 tracks feeding to a recorder, a group of channels may be routed to, say, mix no. 30; channel 30 can then be put in the 'group' mode, and its output sent to, say, track 20.

Central system control

For many years, tape machine control boxes were built into any available space in consoles. With the number of remote switches and indicators increasing, this became impractical, and the mixing engineer tended to become surrounded by trolleys, with other boxes being placed on top of any faders or modules not actually in use. It is now becoming generally accepted that the console must contain all the essentials for running a sometimes very complicated session. So a central area is being designated for machine and automation management and log-keeping. As all these are related to the same time reference, normally a time-code on one of the tapes, it makes sense that one and the same electronic system, a smart computer, should deal with them all, and with an increasing amount of the housekeeping of large audio consoles.

Developing trends

As mentioned above, size, number of controls, component density, and heat output are the constant design problems as consoles have kept up with more demanding operational requirements. More ability to store and recall set-up and mix information in short and long term appears the main desire of the near future. At one point is seemed that the quantum leap to provide all these things, and incidentally eliminate many electronic design problems, was to digitize all audio at the earliest possible stage, and let the mixing console become one very fast, very clever computer in which the 'block diagram', and every kind of signal processing, became a matter of software algorithms. Such consoles are now available, but are definitely not the only, and certainly not the easiest, way forward. It has given rise to the term 'the virtual console', which is now being loosely applied to any kind of system in which the audio no longer flows through pots and switches behind a front panel.

Digitally controlled analogue mixing consoles

History

At about the same time as consoles based on digital signal processing were being projected, research also started into designs in which digital commands were used to control elements of familiar analogue circuitry, possibly physically removed from the control position. The digital school of thought believed that it was only feasible to achieve satisfactory indirect control of functions such as fading, equalization, and the like in the digital domain. Thus began the family of consoles of which the Neve DSP was the pioneer. The other school felt that, despite certain known problem areas, digital was very much the hard way to do it, fraught with many unsuspected pitfalls. Digital tape recording had been hard enough. So they proceeded from the state of the art in fader and mute automation as applied to conventional consoles, and extended this technique to the control of all console functions. Both approaches very quickly demonstrated heavy development costs.

Great credit is due to the BBC, and later to Thames Television, for encouraging and funding development at a time when cost limits were not established, and greatly above what it appeared the commercial market would contemplate. The units delivered to these two organizations and later to Turner Television in USA firmly established the validity of the concepts, and the reliability of the equipment under live broadcast conditions. The fear of 'computer crash' was shown to be illusory—and after all any fully digital mixing system is itself a large computer.

Technically the designers were waiting for the computer power at low cost, which has now arrived, to realize equipment for which the recording industry was prepared to pay. It did seem by 1985 that product would soon appear from several sources, but only two designs were launched, and they cannot be said to have succeeded commercially. However, both of them were constructed in the 'Big Impressive Console' style, with all the electronics in the console itself. They took no advantage of the space savings possible and, by comparison with the well-proven conventional industry standards at the high end of the market, may not have shown the benefits clearly, and may have seemed 'gimmicky' to established record engineers. Product is now appearing which takes full advantage both of the technology and the familiarity of today's engineers with computer assisted equipment. An example is illustrated in Plate 4 and Figures 7.1 and 7.2.

Concept

The control surface, made up of faders, pots, switches etc. no longer has any physical connection with the audio circuit elements. It now consists of 'actuators' which may retain the appearance of familiar controls but, when scanned, send out digital values which operate switches and pots in familiar audio circuitry. Also, all or part of these control signals may be memorized and recalled (as in the Play mode of fader automation) and further modified on their passage through a control computer.

Benefits

The benefits derive from two main areas: the ergonomic, technical, and maintenance advantages of divorcing the circuitry from the panel controls, and the ability to store and recall every element of a mix and modify it as desired. These benefits are:

1. The control surface does not contain anything but digital signals, so it is not susceptible to hum, radio frequency interference, 'dirty contacts', or other disturbance to the audio signals.
2. The control signals are sent from console to rack in a manner long proven in the computer industry to be reliable and interference free.
3. Assignable panels, e.g. for equalizers and dynamics, save panel space, bring controls under the operator's hands, and permit generous sized knobs and markings without crowding. Layout of panels is not constrained by size or shape of components behind the panel.
4. The control codes are independent of the arrangement and circuitry of the control panels, or of the audio cards, so that whatever device (fader, rotary encoder, push-buttons) emits a command and whatever piece of audio circuitry it is finally applied to the practical result is exactly the same. Further, the control computer may perform calculations on and insert look-up table values into control data, using software which can be updated at any time.
5. All changes may be made either by manual action, or related to timecode locked to an existing sound track or television picture so that, having been set, they happen precisely on time.
6. The operation of one control may be arranged to make many pre-programmed things happen simultaneously.
7. Every control move, manual or pre-programmed, is remembered by the computer and repeated accurately until changed, and may be archived to hard or floppy disk.
8. Status of controls is displayed on the panel and/or VDU, or other graphics.
9. It is an economic proposition to supply custom panel layouts according to intended use, or for applications where space is restricted.
10. It is feasible to modify or replace the control surface during the life of a system at acceptable cost.

11. Nothing under the control surface need generate any serious heat, and the whole unit may be of light weight, and no larger than dictated by the actual area of panels.

12. Channel cards in audio racks are designed for technically optimum layout, with no controls brought out to front panels. Layout provides for optimum isolation of digital and audio tracks. Screening and cooling are optimized.

13. All cards in the audio racks may be instantly changed in case of fault, often without stopping work. Cards with improved (or modified) performance may be introduced as plug-in exchange items. Servicing practice is familiar.

14. If real advantages are offered by digitized-audio signal handling, it may be retrofitted by exchange of cards or whole racks without any change to control surface, data transmission, or methods of working.

Control surface

Very many limitations disappear as soon as the panel controls are no longer connected to commercially available pots, rotary switches, etc. All the familiar forms of control may be retained, with others added, indeed anything that makes sense to an operator. Whereas in the case of digital workstations operators have had to adapt to new controls as well as displays imported both from video editing and computing, the digitally controlled console may be built with an appearance as familiar as a conventional audio design. But to duplicate all the controls per channel, besides being costly, would be to throw away much of the advantage of the technique. A free choice is now possible between those functions which it is felt must exist on a per-channel basis, and those which can be made assignable, i.e. presented on central panels and accessed by the channels. Till now it has been the general rule that there must be a physical fader for each audio channel which, as it were, holds the identity of that signal, and can be moved at any time without touching anything else first. One may also choose to have permanently associated with the fader one or more 'soft' knobs whose function can be selected as pan, aux send, or whatever. Beyond this we are in an area of compromise between 'a knob for everything' and access by a channel button to central control and display areas.

The term assignable means that, on touching an access button above a fader, the controls in the central panels address the routing, equalization, dynamics, aux sends, etc. of that channel, and its current status appears on the panel displays and/or VDU. On touching the access button of another channel, the central area displays and takes control of that channel. If it is desired to retain manual control of the equalizers of two channels during an item, the panels may be duplicated, and the buttons arranged to access them alternately. One compromise which has been tried is to have a reduced number of knobs per channel whose function can be switched. But it is then necessary to look at an indicator before touching a knob to verify what it is controlling at that moment, and the danger of mistakes is considerable.

Control elements

So far, the rotary knob has been retained as the most 'instinctive' control element, along with the slide fader. Users accept that turning something clockwise produces 'more' of the value controlled: increase of level, higher frequency, and so on. And a knob may be turned fast or slowly. The first alternative is a pair of 'up-down' buttons. As the value desired is in any case being quantized in digital steps, this would appear the most logical controller. But it introduces the element of time; the button must be held while the right number of steps are counted and the desired value displayed, and released at a precise moment. If the count is set too fast, you may overshoot and have to come back; if too slow you feel you are waiting for it to catch up. Either way it is a distraction. This is probably why an early design which eliminated knobs altogether did not gain acceptance.

It is very important not to let technology derived from computing compel operators to do things in sequence (set, then execute) rather than 'grab it and do it'. We speak here of the primary requirements of live sound recording and broadcasting. However, one may distinguish between set-up controls and those likely to be moved during a mix; it is less critical to have instant and instinctive control of those things which will be set up for a session or an item and not accessed thereafter. Off-line mixing of recorded tracks is again less critical in time; many things may be taken to a workstation and assembled bit by bit.

A system which calls up the control of any channel into a set of knobs, and resets it to values returned from automation, implies that a knob must be ready to vary each parameter from 'where-it-is-now', and there must be an indication of where it is. Mechanical servos turning the knobs in the same way as moving faders would introduce too much time delay, so we must have a rotary control which has no inherent position, but emits up or down count pulses as it is turned. This is called a rotary incremental encoder, and is available commercially in varying degrees of precision. This is probably the most essential device in building assignable control surfaces. In order to know the present status of the control in the actual audio channel, we may read the last control value and show it on a circle of LEDs representing the dial pointer of a conventional pot. Alternatively vertical and horizontal LED columns may be used. In addition, displays of all channel functions on a VDU are helpful.

Having made substantial reductions in the area of the active control surface by using assignable control panels, we may reconsider the need for a fader for every signal source. In current practice the number of signal sources still increases, though probably less of them will be live microphones. But the number of faders one operator can span is fixed, as is the number which can be moved at once. One fader placed above another is a solution to the total span, and this is now available. But let us study the case if we have a limited number of input faders, say 12, and make them assignable. Assuming live performers in a studio, we route the inputs to channels, channels to tracks, VCA grouping if desired, and bring up the first 12 channels on faders as on a conventional desk (using routing buttons). Having set a reasonable balance of these channels and applied EQ and compression from the assignable panels, we can now release control of these channels, which remain exactly as they are (but can be controlled by VCA groups if we wish) and call the next 12 into the faders. And so on until we have a conventional studio mix—though only the last 12 channels selected are actually under our hands. Releasing these, we can call back any channels we have second thoughts about. By now it will be clear which individual channels are likely to need 'gain riding' in the course of the take, and these will now be set out on some of the 12 faders, remembering we still have the VCA groupers in control of the rest. This assumes the most difficult case, when the whole item is to be recorded in one pass of the tape, and all the above is done before anything has been recorded. After an acceptable take, we have the full automation to assist us with overdubs and mixing.

The Access buttons over a full run of faders are replaced by a block of channel access buttons, plus a button over each of the reduced number of input faders. Touching a channel and an input button together puts that fader in control of that channel. Electronic labels may be provided above the faders, and these can change at prearranged time points, letting go of one channel and accessing another, with unchanged level until the fader is moved.

Displays

There is virtually no limit to the graphical and numerical displays which can be generated to assist the operator and draw his attention to important things, using software now familiar in the personal computer world. The only temptation to designers is to devise screens cluttered with too much changing information, which may end up causing distraction. From the above it follows that there is a vast area of options for the co-operation of designers and sound engineers to realize control surfaces for different applications. These can be simple to build, representing a relatively small part of the cost of a complete system, and can be connected via standard data transfer systems to audio racks of varying degrees of complexity.

Control systems

The collection of information from the fader and mute area of the control surface, and the return of fader matching lights in automation read mode is exactly as in any standard fader automation system, and whether it is sent along its own data channel or combined with other data is a matter of convenience. The passing of fader move and mute data requires the fastest transfer rate; everything else can be slower. Set-up information is slower still, and it may be convenient to lock out any changes to set-up during an audio item.

On powering up, all the panel controls are 'saying nothing' to the audio racks. Initial default settings may be read from a standard preset status memory, or from the set-up of the last item worked on. The audio rack assumes these settings, and they appear on the LEDs of the assignable panels. The first stage of data capture is to scan all the panel controls serially at whatever clock rate has been decided, and note any changes as controls are touched. From one clock to the next, status is compared and anything reading 'no change' is ignored. Change information is forwarded to the output interface of the assignable panels. At this point the system only knows 'Button 7 touched' or 'Knob 3, up 4 steps' but not what this means in instructions to the audio. So the electronics under the control surface are relatively simple, presenting the list of changes to Interface Connector No. 1. Likewise display instructions will come back as 'LED column 1, turn on Nos. 1–12'. Simple stuff.

Connector 1 leads to a box, which at the time of writing may conveniently be a dedicated plug-in fitted into a personal computer with as much memory as we need, so that we can make the general purpose processing do as much of the work as possible. This package of box plus computer plus specialized software works out the answers to questions like:

- Which channel are we addressing ?
- Which switch in the channel card must be actuated by Button 7?
- What digital value is to be added to the current value driving the control element in this channel represented by Knob 3?

It can also do many other things by reference to look-up tables, such as altering the law of faders and pan pots, meter scales, and the like. It will take care of the extra switching necessary if a reduced number of faders is used, as above, and the generation of label displays for faders and meters. Finally it can generate all kinds of VDU displays from the information passing through it.

Normally the software will be written to conform to the specific arrangement of the control surface but, as has been said, there may be many alternative layouts, and a change of panels is possible at reasonable cost. In this case a new issue of software will take care of the changes. There is also a case for moving some at least of the 'translation' intelligence back into the console prior to interface No. 1. Then everything between Connectors Nos. 1 and 2 could have a totally standard specification, with the possibility of an industry standard data exchange system between 'front ends' and audio racks from different manufacturers.

A command data stream representing the total of updated instructions to all channels emerges from Interface Connector No. 2 and goes to the audio rack. At the same time it is being written into RAM in the computer, referenced to timecode so that it may all be recalled in the Read mode of automation. Automation data may be periodically archived to the computer's hard disc, and floppy discs may be downloaded for work in progress.

Application of instructions to audio circuitry

At the audio rack, the incoming data stream will be applied to a converter card which feeds it to a parallel bus to all channel and group output cards. At the card there is decoding circuitry which first recognizes the card address, then decodes the instruction burst and applies it through latches to all the elements in the audio circuit which require logic or digital value inputs. The cards are so laid out that the danger of any digital 'fizz' breaking into audio circuits is minimized. Unless the address code for a channel is recognized, no digital pulses pass into that channel card.

The instruction words for a channel arrive at a regular clock speed but, if executed instantly, there is a possibility of the audio waveform being 'chopped' by a change of level, resulting in an audible click. Therefore the new value is held by a latch and released when a 'zero crossing detector' circuit determines that the audio waveform in that channel is passing through zero. Switching functions on an audio card are usually provided by FET (field effect transistor) switches specifically designed to handle analogue waveforms with low distortion. If the circuit arrangement follows sensible rules, this is quite satisfactory in practice.

For the application of level changes to the audio signal, whether as a fader, elements of an equalizer, or compression/expansion, there are two main kinds of device, the voltage controlled amplifier (VCA), and the multiplying digital-to-analogue converter (MDAC). Despite many claims by manufacturers that the VCA is outdated by their 'new proprietary gain control element'—which turns out to be some form of MDAC circuit—top-quality VCAs continue to be the basis of many excellent designs. The control value arriving in digital form is converted by a simple DAC to a DC voltage, which can be smoothed before application to the control port of the VCA, further reducing the perception of any step changes. VCAs are inherently logarithmic (dB per volt), so the number of control steps need not be great and can be preshaped by the computer. The principle of the MDAC is that a number in binary form is applied to an n-bit parallel input, and the output is a voltage, multiplied by a factor represented by a voltage applied to an analogue input. If this voltage is unity and constant, the output is an analogue representation of the binary input, i.e. a simple digital-to-analogue conversion. But for our purpose we look at it the opposite way round. If we make the analogue input an audio signal, the output is now audio multiplied by the value of the binary (control) signal, and if we vary this we get attenuation of the audio.

If the binary input is 8 bits (256 steps) and all bits are high, the multiplication is by 1, and the audio passes through with no attenuation. When the digital value is equivalent to 128 decimal, the input is multiplied by $^{128}\!/_{256}$ or $\frac{1}{2}$, and the output is −6 dB. If the control value has only the first bit turned on, the signal is multiplied by $\frac{1}{256}$ or 0.0039, which equals −48 dB. Now these attenuation values may do for steps of an equalizer or pan-pot, but not for a fader, because they are nothing like linear in dB, and do not go down far enough. For this purpose one may resort to a 12-bit MDAC, which is fortunately available, but the system must now deliver 12-bit values for faders, though 8-bit may be adequate for everything else.

Having implemented suitable elements to take the place of pots and faders in the audio cards, and the necessary logic to address them from the decoded instructions, the design of audio rack cards follows well-established console technique, but with the considerable advantage that printed circuit layout is not constrained by the size of modules or position of manual controls, and optimum solutions can be chosen for short paths and minimum crosstalk.

Future prospects

The commercial battle between digitized-audio and digitally controlled analogue mixing is by no means won, and does not need to be won. It has been shown that many mixing techniques which appeared to demand digital audio were always equally achievable without it, given the full exploration of control technique and the assistance of computers now available at very acceptable cost. What is contained in the audio processing rack is becoming relatively less important. There is a vast area for choice and new design in control surfaces common to both techniques; room for common standards in the console-to-rack path which can save a lot of reinventing of wheels, enabling analogue and digital engineers to return their attention to the audio rack, and address again the question, 'Can we make it sound any better?'

8 Digital mixing

Paul S. Lidbetter

Digital audio systems have come a long way in recent years. There have been major advances in audio performance, the use of software control systems, and economic effectiveness, all of which have resulted in the appearance of increasing numbers of digital audio consoles and systems for both music recording and post-production applications. The driving force is, as always, higher integration on silicon and higher storage densities. One such example is the use of interactive graphics technology which has evolved on the wave of the PC-based Windows environment and is continuing to evolve as technology gears up for multimedia applications. Another is the ever-increasing computer processing power that is available from embedded systems along with trends towards the ease of interprocessor communications through networks.

It remains a fact that analogue consoles are still the mainstay of the recording and broadcast industry but the situation is beginning to change. Even current analogue systems have had to turn towards digital and software control systems to be able to meet the increasing functional needs of users, such as automation and recall of more than just faders and mutes (see Chapter 7). There is no doubt that it is the digital control approach, along with assignable concepts and graphics, which have made the most impact on users and studios. Smaller control surfaces can be used, even though the number of channels and functionality has increased. Many functions made possible by the use of digital control techniques cannot be provided by analogue means.

Against this background the use of Digital Signal Processing (DSP) to process the audio has probably been of less concern to the average user. This is because it is the functionality that brings in clients, and the fact that a console or system may employ DSP is not necessarily an important issue. However, as more studio equipment employs digital techniques and more information is carried and stored digitally, this view is rapidly changing. The need for DSP is growing in order to maintain audio quality throughout the signal chain, by keeping signals in the digital domain, and to reduce costs by using efficient digital transmission and storage methods such as low bit rate encoding and other compression techniques.

The digital chain is becoming an everyday reality as Digital Audio

Broadcasting (DAB) looms closer and other digital audio applications gain a hold in the consumer market with products such as DCC and MiniDisc. Video applications are also driving digital audio, with digital video recorders carrying 4 channels of 20-bit audio, and other applications such as CD-I (CD Interactive) with full motion video having digital audio as part of the compressed data package.

This chapter looks at professional digital audio systems using both digital control and digital signal processing from the user's point of view. The digital console surface will be discussed first and illustrated by some current successful examples, along with the use of graphics systems. The topic of automation in digital systems is briefly covered, followed by a discussion on DSP considerations from a systems point of view, which naturally leads on to the topic of interfacing and synchronization.

The digital control surface

When assignable control was first considered, it was thought by some people that one assignable channel strip would be able to control a large console. The industry has come a long way since then, with the realization that there is room for different amounts and methods of assignability, depending upon the application. For example hard/optical disc editors, or Digital Audio Workstations (DAWS) as they have come to be known, have used assignability very well for non-real-time applications such as sweetening and editing audio for picture. Here the use of graphics with mouse or trackball is now commonplace. Such an approach has allowed the amount of hardware to be reduced to a minimum, whilst improving functional flexibility through software, as well as providing functions which cannot be obtained by using analogue techniques. It is the latter point which has perhaps increased the acceptance of assignability and digital processing, with the economic opportunities that such new equipment can offer a studio.

At the other end of the spectrum, large mixing consoles have developed over about twenty-five years to become very similar in overall presentation and architectures. Users are very familiar with their operation and the methods of achieving good performance. It may be difficult for some operators to change to a new technology and the associated methods of operation. However, there are users who have made the change, knowing that new methods and systems will inevitably come to the industry, and the quicker they get to grips with these new ideas, and indeed help to shape the changes, the quicker they will become leading experts once again.

Console surface layout

As with analogue systems, the control surface of a digital console or the front panel of an effects system must be designed with the user and the applications in mind. Just because digital technology is being employed does not give the designers a right to develop products which do not fulfil the basic criteria:

Ease of use: The system should be intuitive to operate allowing even the novice user to pick up the basics quickly without recourse to a 700-page operational manual. Once confidence has been gained, then the more complex features can be explored as desired.

Speed of use: For many applications the speed of use is critical, and can be impaired by poor accessibility, whether through graphics menus or through layered control on a physical surface.

Feedback and clarity: It is essential that the system provide clear status information to the user as to the system set-up, errors, and of course important operational criteria such as levels, overloads, etc.

Size: The control surface should be of a size that will satisfy the above points. The level of assignability for a given system will increase as the surface size falls.

Installation/upgrades: The requirements for installation must also be considered. A console surface is basically a large remote-control unit, and must be interconnected with the control/audio processing system, talkback, and machine control systems as well as to mains power. How upgradable is the system once installed? Can the surface be increased or decreased in size with more or fewer faders, for example?

Clearly for many, if not all, applications there will be a conflict of these criteria, but the priorities and compromises which need to be made must be carefully considered by the user.

Typical digital console surfaces

The surface of the AMS/Neve Capricorn console will be described in some detail, followed by two other surface concepts, namely the AMS/Neve Logic 1 and Sony DMX-S6000 consoles, for comparison.

AMS/Neve Capricorn

Plate 6 shows the AMS/NEVE Capricorn console, which is aimed at music recording, mix-down, and post-production applications. This console system has been designed to take over from the Neve V Series analogue console, but offers many more functions than are found in analogue systems, including total dynamic automation. The Capricorn surface is made up from three types of section modules. These are the Assignable Facilities Unit (AFU), the Main Monitor section, and the Strip section. Each section is self-contained and can be placed on the console frame at any location before and after installation.

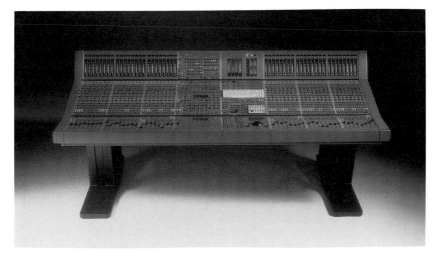

Plate 6. The AMS/Neve Capricorn console

Strip detail

Each Strip section contains 24 faders and their associated channel strip controls. Up to five Strip sections can be fitted providing a maximum fit of 120 faders. This concept allows sections to be placed in any order along the console length and indeed additional Strip sections can be added or subtracted as required, even after installation. The basic concept is to provide all the major controls such as microphone gain, trim levels, track send/return switching, overdub, pan, mute, meters, automation and aux levels in the fader strip along with a high degree of status information such as path configuration indication, and gain reduction metering.

In order to reduce the depth of the channel strip there are four FAC (function assignable controls) present (see Plate 7), the function of which is defined by the global selection keys on the AFU. The top FAC is allocated to gain control and source selection. The FAC can be selected to provide microphone gain, line level gain, offset trim, and input balance as well as being used to select the input source for the strip and the aux contribution. The next two FACs are allocated to aux contribution levels, which can be assigned from the AFU. If stereo, the upper FAC will be gain and the lower FAC will become the aux pan. The final FAC defaults to pan, but can be assigned to width or balance from the AFU. In addition there is an EQ key on the AFU which will allocate the four FACs to operate as an EQ, with the top FAC controlling the selection of the band, the next FAC controlling gain, the next frequency, and the lowest Q. This provides a strip EQ function allowing multiple adjustment across the surface if required. This is not

Plate 7. The FAC (Function Assignable Controls) showing the peripheral circular bargraphs

the main method for EQ adjustment but is an option more in tune with non-assignable surfaces allowing simultaneous adjustment of a number of EQs.

Meters are an important feature and those adopted on Capricorn use a Vacuum Fluorescent technology allowing the display to be treated as a pixel map on which any text or graphics can be presented as a function of the drive software. It is this flexibility which allows the meter displays to be used for a number of purposes. First the display area can be used for metering information or as a general purpose display for path configuration data, etc. In the meter mode the display is split, with small meters in the lower quarter and the remaining area used for the main signal path bargraph meters and path label.

The lower quarter of the meter display supports four small bar meters, of which two are allocated for stereo input path metering, plus a further two for the dynamics control voltage meters. The top three-quarters of the display supports the main stereo or mono meters depending on the path configuration and signal path labels. The small meters are always assigned to the path controlled by the fader, whereas in addition the main meter bars can be switched for track send and/or return monitor modes, as well as for a graphics mode in which path configuration information can be displayed. The main bargraphs support peak characteristics with peak hold and peak riding options. The meter scale can also be changed as a function of the drive software.

AFU detail

Moving on to the AFU, it contains all those controls associated with a strip, including a duplicate fader, along with 4-band EQ, filters, dynamics, and a key routing matrix. In addition there are 16 aux contribution level controls available which can be configured as mono or stereo sends. Thus aux sends are available directly from the AFU for the accessed paths or can be operated from the strip FACs.

The AFU is assigned to a fader channel strip by pressing one of two fader 'access' keys. For example, if fader 1 is accessed, all the controls on the AFU are now assigned to fader 1 and operate on the accessed path. The concept is to provide only one level of access to all the major channel controls for real-time music recording applications. For instance, if the AFU is currently assigned to a path on fader 2 and the EQ gain must be adjusted on a path allocated to fader 4, the operations are (a) access the path on fader 4 and then (b) adjust the required EQ controls directly on the AFU. There are no further levels of assignment necessary. In music recording there is little time to look for controls which may be hidden in lower levels of assignment, or in menus on a graphics system. As the controls for only one channel are present on the AFU, they can be well spaced out for ease of use and good visibility.

When sitting in front of the AFU, it is possible to access any channel via the specific strip fader access key(s) or to scroll across the whole desk by using simple up/down keys on the AFU. This brings us back to the idea of controlling a large number of channels with only one assignable fader and channel strip: the AFU. Indeed the console could be used in that way, but the scroll feature has been designed to allow the operator to remain in one position while accessing channels during the session setting-up period and/or during operation.

All console rotary controls have circular LED bargraphs (see Plate 7) to indicate the relative parameter values. However, absolute values may be indicated in several ways when a rotary control is touched. Of the four rows of FAC controls on the Strip section, three have alphanumeric displays which will show absolute gain and/or aux levels, and also EQ parameters if the EQ option is selected. For those rotary controls on the AFU a further feature is available which uses a vacuum fluorescent panel to display channel information, the channel currently accessed, the control in touch, the path name, processing configuration, and numeric settings. This also covers absolute frequency, gain, Q, thresholds, attack times, etc. of all controls operative on that channel when any one of the controls in a control group (e.g. EQ, filter, limiter, etc.) is touched. For instance, if any EQ control is touched, the display will go to the EQ settings, but will change to indicate limiter parameters if any limiter control is touched.

Any audio path, i.e. input/output/monitor/aux/group, etc. can be assigned to any of the physical faders present on the surface. This allows ease of operation, for the frequently required channels can be located on faders close to the AFU providing a central operating area. Note that the faders can be assigned to mono or stereo paths with all associated controls on the strip and AFU (when accessed) also becoming mono or stereo. Thus a 24-fader console can control 24 mono, 24 stereo, or any mixture of paths. Up to 12 fader banks are provided each of which represents an assignment across the console surface. So, for example, a 24-fader console could control up to 12×24 (288 audio paths). As more faders are added to the system, the number of total audio paths that can be controlled does not increase but the level of assignability falls until the point is reached where there can be one physical fader per audio signal, or the maximum of 120 faders is reached. The level of fader assignability is therefore up to the user.

Two rows of access keys (primary and secondary) and associated alphanumeric displays are provided for each fader. Any of the 12 fader banks can be assigned to the primary and secondary access key rows. Such an arrangement allows the operator to select instantly from twice the number of displayed paths as he has faders, without the need to change the fader bank. A good example of use is to assign the input paths on one bank, and the track return paths on another. If both these banks are assigned to the faders then, by selecting one access key or the other on each fader, the operator can switch between input and monitor return on the one fader as on an in-line console. There are of course many other such examples of use.

Audio signals can be assigned to paths which can be an input, track return, cue master, aux master, or group, for example. These paths are digital processing routes which can be assigned to faders and hence to fader banks without restriction. This allows signals to be placed on adjacent faders or within defined fader groups, and/or in specific fader banks if required. Thus bank 1 could be strings, bank 2 could be vocals, and so on. Due to the flexibility of this approach, the console can be configured with bank 1 as inputs and bank 2 as track returns, thereby creating an in-line console architecture in which the global switching between send and return paths is performed by the bank switch, or individual paths may be switched by use of the fader access keys. As faders can be assigned to more than one bank, it is possible to have important signals such as outputs always present on the surface, and on the same faders, regardless of the bank selected. The faders and indeed all control types can be linked together or ganged. This very powerful feature provides for ease of operation when several controls of the same type must track each other with or without an offset. For instance, the EQ across a number of inputs may be required to track, or the panning must track but with spatial offsets which are already defined. The number of controls in a link, and the number of links, is not limited.

Path routing is a key element in any system set-up and is addressed by keys on the AFU. There are groups of keys arranged to represent the specific bus types. Thus there are 48 track send keys for track routing, 24 keys for sub-group routing, eight keys for main output routing along with four film keys. Routing is straightforward and can be instigated in a number of ways, which cannot all be covered here. The fundamental concept is to allow the operator to route forwards or in reverse by using surface keys or graphics. In reverse routing the user selects the reverse routing key and the key/bus to which he wishes to route; say group 4. After selecting group 4 any access key(s) then selected will route those accessed paths to group 4. Each access key LED will remain on to indicate what has been routed. Once the reverse key is deselected the routing will be executed. This reverse method allows the destination to be defined and then all sources selected, which can be the best way to allocate routing to a destination with multiple sources. For forward routing the path to be routed is accessed on a fader and the destination routing key selected on the AFU. This allows a source to be easily routed to multiple destinations, for instance an input path to several group paths, or outputs.

The four film keys each provide film routing over eight track sends. If film key 1 is selected, the track sends 1–8 become allocated to film busses across which mono sources can be three-way panned and routed, as well as stereo and mono sources. These film busses can be used for any multi-channel format from the standard Dolby Stereo to discrete channels up to a maximum of eight. It is therefore possible to record five-channel discrete plus other tracks for foreign languages, etc.

Monitor detail

The Monitor section of the console contains the controls associated with features such as control room/headphone and SLS (studio loudspeaker) monitor selection, machine control, track arming, talkback keys, along with global controls for automation, overdub modes, and main output/aux/cue metering. The Monitor section also contains a trackball for use with the high resolution interactive graphics system. This is a powerful feature through which the operator can control many off-line system functions. The key ones are: system data file handling and storage for automation and system configurations/snapshots, etc.; assignment of paths to faders to bank; the allocation and order of processing functions in each path; the assignment of digital output word length for each output port available, etc. through to small trial adjustments such as the brightness of the meters, the trackerball gearing, cut solo levels, and so on. The main point is that through the intelligent use of graphics the user can have access to a great deal of very useful functionality which can be packaged in a small area. Other functions are: master cue and aux controls which provide aux/cue master level along with a cue feed selection matrix; machine control through assignable display and track arming matrix, along with transport keys.

A Vacuum Fluorescent meter display is provided as in the AFU section, but is used in this application for machine control and timecode selections via soft keys. Such an approach allows the addition of future features through software upgrades.

Further examples of surfaces

By way of comparison, two other surface designs will be described briefly.

AMS Logic 1

The AMS Logic Series of consoles have been developed primarily for audio editing in video post-production applications, and are often found in conjunction with workstations. Plate 8 shows a Logic 1 in which the surface can be seen to be very different from that of Capricorn, even after allowing for the central Audiofile control surface. This product reduces surface size through assignability and by allowing each fader and its strip logicators (a logicator module has four channels per module) to control up to a maximum of four signals. There are no fader banks and so the number of faders grows as the number of paths increases. The path assignment is selected from one of the four access keys per fader. This preserves more of the traditional control surface ideas whilst allowing a maximum of four channels to be stacked below each fader. A joystick module is also available for multichannel applications, giving very flexible assignable panning control.

Plate 8. The AMS/Neve Logic 1 console

For applications with workstations and in small studios specifically designed for audio-for-video, the Logic 1 provides a high level of assignably for the control of processing functions. For example, to operate an EQ parameter, the operator accesses the required path, then an EQ, and then the EQ parameter required before adjustment. In a real-time situation this may not be acceptable, but for non-real-time situations, this increased level of assignability has the benefit of a much reduced console surface size.

The Logic series of consoles supports direct interface to the Audiofile hard-disc systems, and can include the Audiofile system within the surface design. Thus for editing applications the surface combines both the mixing functions as well as those of the hard-disc system and machine control.

Sony DMX-S6000

One further example is the Sony DMX-S6000 series console, shown in Plate 9, which is available in several sizes. The surface concept uses channel strips which are in line, allowing selection between two paths of processing functions and routing. Each strip has dedicated controls for mute, solos, and pan. Thus the assignabilty is very low with respect to channel strips and faders. Each fader strip has access to separate assignable control panels for the major controls such as EQ, filters, dynamics, signal routing, and aux contributions. This approach, as used on the Capricorn console, gives fast access to processing functions. As the console size is directly proportional to the number of faders, the design allows for several sets of assignable panels for ease of access across a large console surface. A central monitor sec-

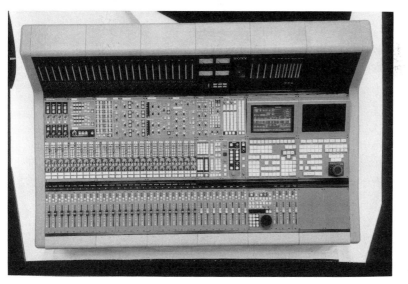

Plate 9. The Sony DMX-S6000 console, 24-track version

tion provides global control of tape machines, the automation system, and functions such as monitor selection, talkback, etc.

Clearly this design uses assignability in a different way compared with the two previous examples, although it is closer to the Capricorn than the Logic. The use of assignable processing functions, aux contributions, and routing has allowed the depth of the surface to be reduced, and the use of assignable panels has provided clear and easy-to-use controls. The use of an in-line architecture certainly provides the operator with a familiar layout but does limit the system flexibility and, along with the fader per pair of paths approach, results in a console width which expands proportionately as more channels are required. The design is a kind of halfway house that some will adapt to straightaway, due to the similarity to an analogue in-line system, but with just enough assignabilty to improve operation. Two other console designs are illustrated in Plates 10 and 11.

Graphics

Graphics plays a part in all of the above examples. Most studio systems now support some form of graphics, whether PC based or embedded within a system. Graphics offers a very powerful tool for several reasons. First, the visual representation of information can be very efficient, detailed, and effective, especially when colour is used correctly. Second, graphics systems can provide a very high degree of functionality within a small space, which can easily be updated and/or modified for specific applications. Such flexibility increases the lifetime of the product for new applications. Plate 12 shows the graphics screen of Capricorn in which the two columns of icons can be seen on the right side of the screen, with the selected application running in the centre section. The lower portion of the screen displays status information such as running time, code automation, storage details, etc.

There is also a negative aspect to graphics. This is the temptation for product designers to put as many features as possible into the graphics system without regard for the priorities, real-time issues, and ergonomics of such a move. Designing a good graphics system is one thing, but designing the graphics information and interaction to be logical and easy to use is another.

Menu-driven systems are used extensively especially when the console is based on a Windows environment. This can be slow if several levels of selection are required, but is a widely known concept which is easy to customize. Another graphics approach is to use icons, i.e. small pictures to represent the function or feature to be selected. Such an approach provides a more intuitive feel, whilst allowing a high degree of customization for different applications.

Plate 10. The Solid State Logic Scenaria digital post-production mixing system

Automation

Automation systems have developed to very sophisticated levels and are very software intensive. Initial analogue-based systems offered only fader VCA and mute automation to SMPTE timecode, with some subsequently moving on to include important key switch information such as processing in/outs. With the advent of digital control, full console automation across all control types has become a reality with many such systems running on separate PC platforms with graphic packages for the user interface. However only with digitally controlled digital processing does the automation system begin to evolve once more. Gone is the VCA and its associated performance limitations; with DSP so much more can be achieved in terms of the manipulation of audio parameters with timecode and efficient storage.

The AMS/Neve Flying Fader system (see Plate 5 on page 157) is fitted to many analogue consoles throughout the world and has been emulated with varying degrees of success by others. The Capricorn automation system, although it is based on the philosophy of Flying Faders, has extended automation to all controls (except microphone gain) and includes the ability to have different automation modes on different controls, across the surface, and even within one channel strip. For instance the fader may be in Play, whilst the EQ is in Touch Record, and Mute is in Record. Other systems such as DAWS have also evolved automation systems for use directly with audio/video editing applications in which the automation data can be tagged against a parameter which is then automatically moved with any timebase shifts.

Whatever automation system is used, there are certain key factors which must be addressed by the designer and user in selecting the requirements. First the automation system must have sufficient real-time control processing to allow the storage and recall of all the system parameters in real time.

Plate 11. A pair of Yamaha DMC 1000 digital mixing consoles in use on a classical music recording (Photo: Deutsche Grammophon)

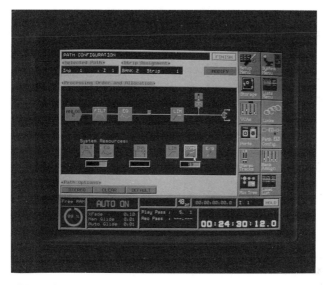

Plate 12. The graphics screen of the AMS/Neve Capricorn console

This means within a SMPTE frame or better. Such performance demands high control bandwidths, and processing power to read information, store it, process it, and finally replay it. The necessary processing power may be supplied by an automation processor and associated memory, or by a distributed system in which the data is stored locally with the DSP parameters and processing to reduce transfer real-time data bandwidths and delays to a minimum. Both concepts have advantages and disadvantages but the performance of automation systems is crucial to the ease of operation and success of a system as more importance is placed on automated features within a console and studio, which will usually include MIDI.

The Capricorn automation system follows on from Flying Faders in using a mix-tree approach. This represents the storage of data as passes within mixes. From the root of the mix-tree each pass creates a new play pass store, thereby creating a sequence of in-line passes which are shown numbered and linked on the graphics screen. By using the trackball, the operator can go back to any previous pass and start a new tree branch or even a new mix. All this interconnectivity is shown graphically, allowing even large mix-trees to be easily manipulated.

Digital Signal Processing

Systems

Digital Signal Processing (DSP) usually conjures up thoughts of complex algorithms involving digital filters along with talk of coefficient quantization, limit cycles effects, Z planes, etc. This is certainly one aspect of audio DSP, but there is a lot more to digital audio systems than just digital filtering. Systems also need to contain some or all of the following: signal routing, level control, ramping of parameters, coefficient generation, data storage, and analogue/digital conversion. Also the control of such systems takes on a much more crucial role in the current trends of increasing demands on system functionality.

The challenge for designers and users is to create products that operate as coherent systems. This implies an ability to provide operational features and audio performance which are both acceptable for the application, and an ability to interface correctly with other audio equipment. It is this ability to provide an overall economic and competent package which is the key to a satisfied operator and studio.

Figure 8.1 shows the principal parts of a digital system. Clearly analogue to digital converters (ADCs) and digital to analogue converters (DACs) are necessary, along with other building blocks such as various types of digital interfaces, central digital signal processing, data storage, and control systems. The amount and performance of each function will vary between applications, but there are several key factors to be considered by the user and designer alike in any digital audio system.

The type of technology employed in a system is of little interest to the user as long as the performance, functionality, cost factors, and sonic standards are met. However, issues such as upgradability should not be ignored. For instance, can the user upgrade the system at a later date with more processing, add more/improved converters, more hard-disc storage for audio or automation data, etc?

The technical performance of a system is governed by many design factors. Yet it is necessary as a potential user or owner of a system to measure and listen to the system, and not be convinced that the system must be good because a specific processor or type of DAC is used, etc. Clearly such factors are important but it is the performance of the overall system that matters, and this will be only as good as the weakest link. One example is the use of 32-bit IEEE floating point processors and the assumption that, because they can provide approximately 1,500 dB of dynamic range, the system must be good. There is no doubt that floating point processors can provide very good performance when used correctly, but the fact that they can support a dynamic range of 1,500 dB is not a key factor for audio; seismology perhaps,

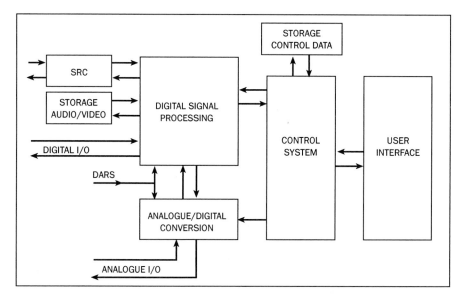

Fig. 8.1. Main components of a digital system

but not audio. It is how the technology is used that counts rather than the technology itself.

Converters

ADCs and DACs now come in many shapes and sizes (see Chapter 3) offering a wide choice of possible implementations and performances. Conversion techniques have also evolved. The multibit converter using successive approximation techniques is still widely used, but has been adapted in many applications with mild oversampling (up to 8 times) to reduce anti-image and anti-alias filter complexity. The oversampling process creates a lower noise floor in the audio pass-band as the overall noise power is distributed over the bandwidth defined by the higher sample rate; noise shaping can improve the noise performance further. In order to operate the converters at the higher sample rate, digital filters must be used to interpolate up and decimate down from the system sample rate. Also converter designs with high rates of oversampling are now available which operate as data stream or 1-bit conversion systems. Such Delta Sigma conversion techniques have reduced manufacturing costs and chip count, and improved consistency. Hybrid designs are also emerging which use both multibit and bitstream ideas to try and obtain the best of both worlds!

Early Delta Sigma designs required an analogue sampling device and a separate digital filter. However, as technology has evolved, such converters are now available as one-package solutions, although it is still true to say that the best designs require two packages and/or optimized post-filtering in the case of DACs.

Oversampling ratios of 64, 128, or even 256 times the baseband sample rate are common. The converter therefore operates at MHz frequencies and in fact may be only a 1-bit system. In the case of the ADC it is necessary to decimate the 1-bit converter output down via a digital filter. In the DAC, a digital filter is used to interpolate the sample rate up to MHz prior to the output analogue filter. One-bit converters have not been without their problems, but the deviation between quantization steps is avoided, which gives very good linearity.

So what makes a good converter? The number of bits in a converter defines the performance, or does it? As with many digital products, more bits are assumed to offer better performance but this is not necessarily the case. The number of usable bits will potentially define the dynamic range of the signal being handled (this is not to be confused with the number of bits provided via the device pins), but what of the linearity of the converter, e.g. the distortion at high and low operating levels, or at different frequencies, signal/noise modulation effects, the nature of the quantization noise, the effects of jitter, the signal path delay, the change of parameters with age, the type of dither applied, and so on? It is therefore important not to judge a converter on the type of technology employed or the buzz words associated with it, but actually to measure and listen to it. Also it must be remembered that the performance of a stand-alone converter may not represent the performance and/or sonic quality of such a converter once designed into a system. The added noise, clock jitter, and power supply issues found in a systems environment may degrade the performance.

The choice of converter depends on the application and the trade-offs involved with technical performance, and sonic quality against size and cost. Clearly, in a music recording console, the microphone inputs demand a high dynamic range ADC with low distortion. However, if the ADC is for an editing system operating on say 16-bit data, then a 16-bit converter with good linearity is clearly acceptable. The other extreme is in applications aimed at multimedia for the PC or other volume consumer products such as games, in which a 16-bit or less converter can be used with only reasonable linearity and performance, but which is small and low in cost.

DACs are used in all types of equipment to convert the final digital audio back to analogue for monitoring. Whether the monitoring is in the home on a hi-fi system, on a PC soundboard, or at the output of a high-performance recording console, the choice between performance and cost is there. Highly oversampled DACs have a built-in signal path delay caused by the need to perform the considerable digital filtering, which for applications requiring minimal path delay, such as cue feeds, may be a problem.

DSP engines

The DSP engine in a product may vary from a simple one-chip solution for a stereo effects box up to a multi-processor, multi-PCB system offering GFLOPS (10^9 floating point operations per second) of processing power along with associated control systems for coefficient calculations, parameter updates, routing, and interfacing; i.e. a large-scale digital console. DSP has therefore a huge range of applications, interpretations, and implementations which mean different things to different people. DSP is therefore not just a chip. In the context of this chapter it is a system designed to provide varying degrees of functionality and performance.

Such a system must be designed to have an architecture that will support the number and type of processing functions required, as well as the necessary data I/O bandwidth for interfacing to the number of digital and analogue external interfaces necessary. Thus the number of bits used and the processing power may vary throughout the system.

A signal processing system can be made using a variety and mixture of technologies to implement the required functionality and performance. The designer can turn to discrete components, but these days DSP chips provide a varied off-the-shelf solution which, if still not suitable in functions, performance, or cost for the application, may be satisfied by using custom silicon. Designing a DSP system is not only a matter of selecting a DSP device or devices. The major design issues are the ability to interconnect the DSP devices to provide the number of signal paths required, the processing functions necessary, and the interconnection of functions, all at the performance and cost required. It is often the case that a DSP engine can perform efficient signal processing, but the architecture may not support the number of inputs, interprocessor signals, control signals, and outputs required; i.e. there is not enough I/O bandwidth in the system design.

Some systems have adopted the pool of processing approach in which, as processing functions are allocated by the operator, they are taken from a pool of processing power. Once the pool runs dry, processing functions must be de-allocated back to the pool or the pool size increased by purchasing more hardware. As processing is not required in all paths at the same time, this approach results in lower hardware costs, but more software to run the processing allocation algorithms. Within the pool concept there are variants. The Capricorn system provides all routing, gain, and mixing processing for all hardware channels present and is therefore not limited by the size of the pool. However processing functions such as EQ, DRC (dynamic range control), etc. are allocated from a pool in which sub-pools of EQ power, DRC power, etc. are provided.

The Logic range of consoles operate a pool from which all functions are allocated, thereby potentially decreasing the amount of hardware needed, but requiring the hardware to be general purpose and capable of performing all the functions. In contrast the Sony DMX-S6000 console has dedicated processing for each input/monitor pair of paths. This approach has been avoided in the past due to the increased cost of having dedicated hardware that will not all be used in most circumstances. However, software complexity is much reduced, and the architecture of the console follows that of an analogue system.

There are therefore many trade-offs in a DSP system design including the control aspects. A DSP system needs to be controlled from the control surface of a console, or the front panel of a piece of rack-mounted equipment. In the case of a console, the ability to read thousands of controls, convert the control updates into DSP language, and then send the correct updates to the correct DSP functions, which of course may be moving about in the actual hardware depending upon the allocation, in real time is not a trivial task. In addition the severe processing demands of automation means that systems need as much real-time computing power and software as that required for the audio DSP.

One factor which falls between audio processing and the interfacing of a system is that of dither (see also Chapter 3). Why do we need dither, and what is it? In any system, the word lengths adopted may vary, and indeed it will certainly be the case that any filtering will adopt greater word lengths than are required at the output. An ADC creates quantization distortion and the fewer bits of resolution the worse the error becomes. Quantization also takes place in the digital domain. When a signal is reduced in size/resolution, severe problems may result especially within recursive structures (e.g. filters) such as limits cycles and other effects. However, consider the simple case of the output of signal processing system which has a 24-bit fixed point format and actually has 24-bit resolution available. How can this be interfaced with a 16-bit DAC, or say a 20-bit hard disc system? Clearly the unwanted LSBs (least significant bits) can be chopped off or truncated, which will result in loss of resolution, but will provide the number of bits required. One approach is to round up or down the truncation process to try and average the error. However this process will still result in quantization, which we know will cause signal distortion.

Dither is an effective solution to this as it randomizes these errors in such a way that the quantization process will become increasingly linear. In the early days of digital audio no dither was applied, or it was simply a white noise signal added to the new LSB. Such practice has a lot to do with the poor quality of early digital audio. However, much more work has been done on dither, with many options now available, the most favoured of which is triangular probability density function (TPDF) dither as discussed in Chapter 3.

Note that in multitrack systems the dither should not be coherent across

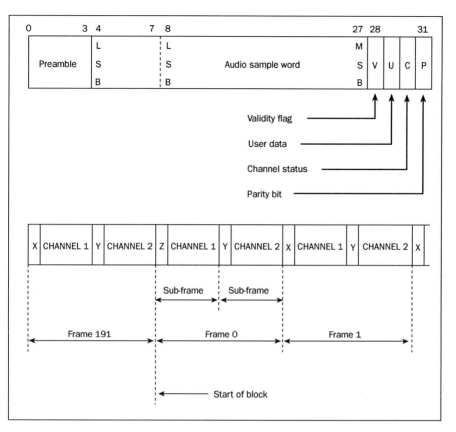

Fig. 8.2. The AES/EBU format

all outputs, to avoid any coherent noise build-up in the subsequent mix-down stages. Once a signal has been truncated, the resulting quantization error cannot be removed by subsequent processing and so dithering tends to be performed on system outputs rather than inputs. DSP systems must be carefully designed to avoid internal quantization effects which are more severe than the final interface quantization, unless dither is to be applied after each quantization stage throughout the system rather than just at the final stage.

Interfacing

Digital audio has certainly had its fair share of interfacing problems over the last few years due to a mixture of actual incompatibility issues as well as general misunderstandings of digital technology, the interfaces, and their methods of interconnection. There are two main factors involved in any interface, the electrical characteristics and the data format itself. The first is the way in which the data is packed, encoded, etc. and the second is the physical way in which the data is carried, e.g. on twisted pair cable of 110 ohms impedance. These key factors work together to ensure that the data is transferred and received without degradation. However, even when an interface is understood, problems may still arise because, although the data format is correct, the electrical characteristics are in error, e.g. the incorrect voltage swing, wrong cable impedance, etc. has been used.

In any interface there is a need to re-clock the incoming data at the receiver. One option is to send the bit clock with the data, in parallel, but this will work only if the delay skews are small, which limits such interfaces to short distances and relatively low clock frequencies. Another option is to use an interface in which the data is transmitted serially, but this will also require a synchronized bit clock at the receiver. Clearly the bit clock can be sent separate from the data, but this method will still suffer from some skew problems. The answer is to embed the bit clock frequency within the data stream such that it can be recovered at the receiver, and used to clock the serial data in without error. There are many such encoding schemes but one of the most common is bi-phase encoding which doubles the data bandwidth required over the interface, but does allow the bit clock to be easily recovered, has virtually no d.c. content, and is polarity independent.

Initially some manufacturers developed their own interface methods such as Sony with SDIF-2, Mitsubishi with MELCO, etc. The AES/EBU interface (AES3–1985) was the first general digital audio interface to be defined and was aimed at twin channel applications. This interface is described in Chapter 3 and several publications, but an outline of the basics will be given here before moving on to other interfaces that support the AES/EBU data format.

The AES/EBU interface provides two channels of digital audio data along with four other bits which carry V, U, C, and P information and a preamble code. The format is shown in Figure 8.2 in which the sub-frame format, frame, and channel status block are indicated. Each sub-frame contains audio data, up to 24 bits of linearly encoded 2's complement data of which the least significant 4 bits may be used for other associated applications such as talkback channels, etc., the V, U, C, P bits, and a preamble.

P: Parity bit is set to a zero or a one on transmission to make the number of binary ones in the sub-frame even. An odd number detected at the receiver would flag a possible transmission error.

U: User bit is a single bit per sub-frame which can carry user data; one such application is currently defined for carrying labels and is covered by AES standard AES17–1991.

V: Valid bit defines if the signal is valid.

C: Channel Status bit carries a repeating series of 192 bits known as the channel status block. The 192 bits are defined in 24 bytes of data which can carry information about the signal such as sample rate, stereo/mono modes, sample address timecodes, time of day code, source/destination addresses, etc.

Note that the preamble is a code which violates the bi-phase data encoding system used. Thus a receiver can detect the start of the serial data for each frame. In fact three preambles are used: X, Y, and Z. Of these, X and Y allow the start of the A and B sub-frames to be defined, whilst Z indicates that an A sub-frame is also the start of a block. These preambles can be used to obtain a recovered sample clock from the interface receiver.

It is the C data which historically caused most problems, as different manufacturers implemented different amounts or sections of the channel status data. For instance, if one manufacturer implements a CRC check on an equipment's AES/EBU input port and another does not bother to transmit correct CRC, then the receiver will flag an error, even if the audio is correctly received. It is due to this type of problem that the AES/EBU interface specification has been updated to AES3–1992 in which many minor changes and clarifications have taken place, one of which is to define clearly three levels of implementation of the channel status data, to be used by manufacturers. Of the three implementations defined, the 'Standard' is the best compromise as it supports the first three bytes of the 24-byte series, and also byte 24 the CRC check code. Thus the basic static information such as sample rate, stereo/mono modes, emphasis, etc. is supported, but not the dynamic information such as timecodes or source and destination labels, without going to the 3rd level of implementation.

The AES/EBU interface has been adopted by many manufacturers and, after some problems resulting from poor implementations and misunderstandings, the interface has become a real standard as well as a paper one. This situation has been possible through the development of AES/EBU interfaces on silicon, from such companies as the BBC, Crystal Semiconductors, Motorola, Yamaha, and others. These devices have brought the cost and complexity of interface implementation down whilst increasing consistency.

MADI

MADI (Multi-channel Audio Digital Interface) is also described in Chapter 3 and is an interface for multi-channel applications such as interconnection of multitrack recorders and digital consoles. The interface was conceived by four manufacturers; Mitsubishi, Neve, SSL, and Sony, who worked together to define the format and electrical specification. Once the interface had been defined it was discussed with various bodies, including the AES and after some minor changes became AES10–1992.

MADI supports up to 56 channels of digital audio data. It is transparent to AES/EBU signals in that the data and flags are maintained across a MADI interface. The MADI format is shown in Figure 8.3 in which the 56 channels can be seen to support the 24 bits of audio data along with the C, U, V, and P bits for each channel. Note that the MADI interface does not employ bi-phase encoding as this would push the data rate up from 125 Mbit/s to 250 Mbit/s, and would have been non-economic and unnecessary, as at these bandwidths other transmission systems are available. The one selected is adopted from the communication industry and provides silicon implementations of the encoder and decoder that will support data rates of 125 Mbit/s including the 4/5B encoding method adopted and the necessary clock recovery systems. MADI is available on multi-channel products and has also been successfully implemented using fibre optic technology for long distances and harsh environments. In fact MADI has been used by the BBC as a feed format for experiments on high data rate, fibre optic data highways for interstudio communications. Serial formats for audio/video are a likely future development.

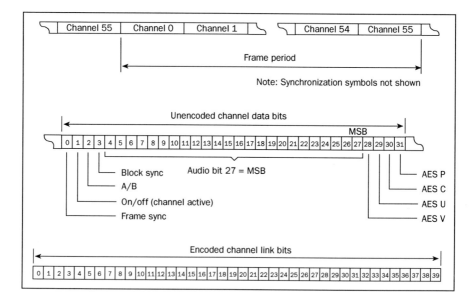

Fig. 8.3. The MADI structure

Synchronization

Many of the problems encountered in early digital systems resulted from poor installation and synchronization methods. Digital audio is discrete in that data is handled at specific moments in time, i.e. at every sample clock throughout the system. Each piece of equipment must have the same sample rate clock, and a stationary phase relationship, to be defined as synchronous. If the phase relationship is changing, then the sample rates are not exactly the same and a sample rate converter or synchronizer buffer must be used. Even when equipments share the same sample rate clock, problems can occur. For example in systems in which equipment is connected serially, the phase of the audio signal between one piece of equipment and another can vary due to cable delays, jitter, and equipment propagation times. These phase errors may accumulate until a complete sample period is repeated or lost, or at worst a signal being fed back to an earlier piece of

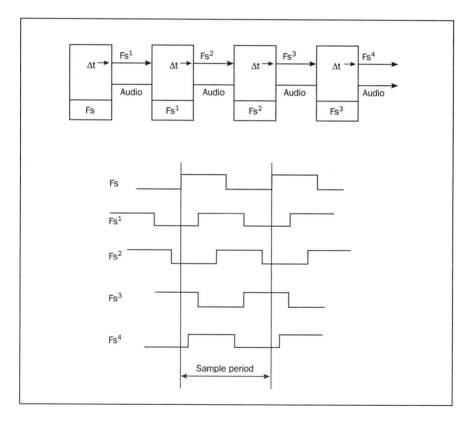

Fig. 8.4. Serial connection

equipment in the chain has lost time alignment. Such a situation may result in an audio 'splat' and is shown in Figure 8.4.

It was due to problems of this type, where a system would work fine until one more piece of equipment was added and then, for what seemed to be an unknown reason, the audio started splatting, etc., that a recommendation for installing equipment was considered by the AES. As a result of much work AES11–1991 was developed in which a method of synchronization is defined along with the associated definitions. Basically AES11–1991 recommends that the synchronization signal (the sample rate clock) should be common to all equipment from a master source. Such a signal is called a DARS (Digital Audio Reference Signal) and is an AES3–1992 signal distributed to other equipment as shown in Figure 8.5. This avoids the accumulation of signal

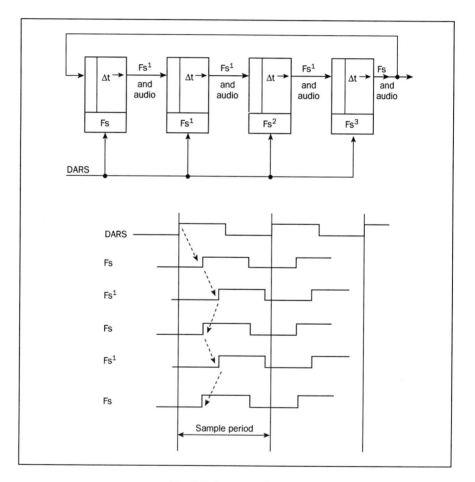

Fig. 8.5. Common reference

phase delays because each piece of equipment retimes the received audio and also transmits audio with reference to the DARS. The accuracy of the DARS signal is therefore important and is specified in AES11, along with phase limits for the receiver and transmitter to be defined as synchronous which are:

1. An AES transmitter shall transmit AES/EBU signal to be within ±5% of the DARS reference signal.
2. An AES receiver shall receive an AES/EBU signal within ±25% of the DARS reference signal.

These tolerances are to cater for practical designs, along with cable delays and the inclusion of one or two serially interconnected pieces of equipment (necessary as not all equipment possesses a DARS synchronization port). Signals within this tolerance are defined to be synchronous and should be handled correctly by the equipment designed to meet AES11.

Further issues for synchronization surround the use of video with audio. First, several sample rates may be used, especially in the USA, where drop frame operation is employed. Also for television the standard sample rate is 48 kHz, which does not match well with the NTSC system in which an integral number of audio samples only fits into a repeat pattern of 5 video frames. For PAL there is no real problem as there is an integer number of samples in each PAL frame. So the video and audio worlds need to be locked together and several devices are available to generate a DARS signal from the video reference. However, there needs to be a way of defining the video and audio references such that a known phase relationship will exist between them in a studio. This will allow audio machines to be locked to a video reference and still be synchronous with other machines locked to a DARS.

Jitter is often associated with interfacing and synchronization, and it can markedly affect a system's performance. Jitter is the time uncertainty associated with a sample point and is usually measured in terms of time. For example, a signal may have ±14 ns of jitter which implies that the signal may vary within ±14 ns of the timing point. Jitter also has a frequency component, i.e. the period of the jitter. Clock jitter is a serious problem as it causes additional quantization noise to be generated due to the movement of the sampling point, and hence increases the conversion error. Severe jitter may affect digital interface operation by causing data to be misclocked.

Sample rate conversion

If a system must handle signals at different sample rates then a sample rate converter (SRC) must be used. This basically interpolates the input signal to a theoretically very high sample rate from which the required output samples, at the new sample rate, can be identified. In practice, sample rate converters do not interpolate to the common factor, which for 48 kHz/44.1 kHz would be in the order of 2.1 GHz. Digital audio electronics do not operate at these frequencies. Instead tricks are used to calculate the required samples. The first commercially available SRC was developed by Stüder, and was a stereo device housed in a small 19-inch rack unit. The SRC of today can be purchased as a single silicon chip for a fraction of the cost. Thus sample rate conversion is no longer a major technical or implementation issue, but should still be avoided by running all the components of a system at the same sample rate where possible.

Networks

After many years using communication systems which covered the globe via terrestrial networks and gateways, the ever-growing computer industry has also adopted networks such as Ethernet, which is now commonplace in small and large businesses alike. The same ideas have started to hit digital audio. One common problem is how to move around data that may no longer be on a digital tape. Using hard-disc/optical-drive storage with fast networks could improve this situation. Also the need to share information such as that found in sound libraries, or even audio data within a single studio, is increasing the need for audio networks. Storage devices now offer Gbytes of storage, and even a small optical 3.5-inch drive offers upwards of 128 Mbytes. There are two major areas of interest at present:

(a) creation of efficient transmission methods for digital audio over existing transmission formats such as ISDN, and further on to satellite systems for inclusion in TV and Digital Audio Broadcasting (DAB);

(b) development of audio networks to carry the raw data from system to system or to share common data storage pools.

Transmission

Such applications have led to the development of low bit-rate encoding/decoding algorithms as the necessary gateway to cost-effective transmission solutions. MPEG (Motion Picture Expert Group) has created a number of low bit-rate encoded audio gateways or layers. Each layer has a broad outline of data rate, etc. but the actual algorithm used for compression may vary from manufacturer to manufacturer, and application to application.

Shared data

The network idea has progressed and several companies now offer audio networked DAWS using Ethernet and higher bandwidth systems such as FDDI. SSL, Sonic Solutions, and others offer networked systems and the trend is towards more such systems and the need to provide a standard method of interchange if possible. Indeed OMFI (Open Media Format Interchange) is an organization which has started to work on a common interface standard for the interchange of information, and has recruited many members including audio- and computer-based companies.

9 Sound processing

Richard Elen

'Sound Processing' is an excellent catch-all phrase. Once the signal has entered the recording chain, and before it reaches the final medium—the Compact Disc, record, cassette, or whatever—virtually everything that happens to it can be described as 'sound processing'. Even level control is a form of processing. But, fundamentally, we are concerned here with techniques of altering the sound's *character*. This can be done in a number of ways, and the primary techniques to consider are those involving the frequency spectrum, dynamics and time and spatial localization.

Mixing consoles often contain a fair number of signal processing facilities, notably equalization, one of the most obvious forms of processing as discussed in Chapters 7 and 8. Some also offer control of dynamics, and some, by providing programmable time delays, offer some control of the time domain. The common-or-garden pan-pot offers basic control of spatial parameters. However, the more comprehensive forms of processing often require some kind of outboard equipment, generally rack-mounted. This, of course, gives the recording engineer a great deal of choice as far as signal processing is concerned. With so many possibilities available, this chapter can do no more than give a general overview of the techniques, without going into too much detail.

Equalization

Equalizers are designed to manipulate the frequency spectrum of a signal, giving prominence to certain frequencies or frequency bands, and reducing the amplitude of the signal in others. So why the term 'equalization'? Simply because, in the early days of signal transmission and recording, manipulating the spectrum of a signal simply for effect was frowned upon: the idea was to provide an essentially 'flat' frequency curve—why mess around with it? The equalizer arose as a means of correcting deficiencies in the frequency response—caused, for example, by imperfect microphones, transmission lines and recording equipment—to achieve this goal: to 'equalize' a signal to flat. This concept still exists in the way we refer to the adjustment of a tape machine to one of a number of recording 'equalization' standards—the idea is to get back from the machine what you put in.

Today, things are different. The equalizer, like many other areas of sound processing, has become completely integrated—in the minds of most recording engineers—with the idea of manipulating the sound for effect, to achieve a creatively more pleasing result. The original idea of 'capturing' a sound in the most accurate way possible has disappeared from many areas of recording, especially the recording of popular music, where the use of close-miking techniques and multitrack recording is an integral part of the creative process, and the concept of an 'original sound' waiting there to be captured is meaningless. In modern multitrack recording the 'original sound' can only be said to be what emerges from the speakers in the control room.

It is possible, however, even in the case of multitrack work, to break the use of equalization into two distinct areas. In the first, an equalizer is used to compensate for deficiencies in the signal arriving from the input to the console, particularly as a result of microphone placement. In the second, we find the resulting sound transformed by equalization to something that did not exist before. The areas, of course, completely run into each other, but they are worth examining separately.

The modern recording studio bears little or no relationship to an auditorium or concert hall with acoustics specifically designed to carry musical sounds to an audience. Together with multitrack techniques has developed the art of studio design, and in many ways both have fed off each other to direct the course of recording techniques in general. In the search for improved separation in the studio, acoustics have by and large become more controlled, and more 'dead'. This has required the use of microphones closer to the instruments they are capturing, often too close to allow the microphone to capture the subtlety of tone which would be present in a more 'open' recording environment. So when the sound from a close-miked instrument arrives at the console, it may not bear much resemblance to the sound that is actually going on in the room outside. Alteration of the frequency spectrum picked up by the microphone—and also of the dynamics—may be necessary to render a reasonable representation of what the instrument actually sounds like. Equalization can help in this situation, and generally the console equalizer will be sufficient to do the job.

On an orchestral session, this kind of manipulation may be quite sufficient as far as equalization is concerned (allowing for the idea that there is a need in many classical engineers' minds to compensate for the fact that the listener to a record will not 'be there' by making the sound just a little more exciting than the 'real thing'). On a pop or rock session, this is just the beginning. The engineer in such a situation will make a transition from using the equalizer to compensate for conditions to using it for creative effect—without even thinking about it.

Such modifications are, of course, entirely up to the production team at the time. But, in passing, it is worth making a few comments about the use of equalizers. In recording, just as in any other field, you seldom get something for nothing. The more extreme any signal processing the more the sound will—in some way, subtle or horribly not so—be degraded. An equalizer will emphasize noise in frequency areas that are boosted as well as the signal you want. It may affect the transients and other aspects of the 'clarity' of the sound, if only simply because the audio path has been extended by going through yet another set of electronics (and, in the case of a piece of ancillary equipment, no doubt a jackfield, a set of cables, and a few other odd bits).

There is thus a great incentive, despite the requirements for microphone technique imposed by a modern studio, to get the sound as right as possible before it ever gets to the console. It *is* worth experimenting with microphone technique. It *is* worth getting the right sound on the instrument 'out there', if it has the flexibility to do so, as do many modern instruments, especially synthesizers. All that work minimizes the 'traditional' role of the equalizer (or any other processing system, for that matter), that of getting the sound right at the console before you start messing with it, leaving you more room to use outboard devices *creatively* rather than simply to correct something you got wrong elsewhere.

Types of equalizer

Equalizers come in a great number of shapes and sizes, but in essence they all do the same thing: they allow the manipulation of the amplitude of selected parts of the frequency spectrum of a sound.

At its most basic level, an equalizer offers a pair of controls: one to select the operating frequency and one to adjust the gain (and/or attenuation: some units, more commonly referred to as filters, offer only the latter). In such devices the unit will operate on a band of frequencies around the selected one, depending on the 'Q' of the tuned circuit employed. At the extremes of frequency, and in filters, it is most common for the frequency characteristics affected by the gain control to extend up (at high frequencies) or down (at low frequencies). This type of response is referred to as 'shelving' and is shown in Figures 7.5 and 7.6 (page 151). At other frequencies, a 'peaking' response is more usual, where the effect of the gain control is centred on the set frequency (Figures 7.7 and 7.8).

Originally, due to the complexity of the circuitry then required, it was most common to find a *switchable* frequency control, allowing selection of one of several frequencies. Today it is much more common to find 'sweep' equalizers in which the centre frequency of each band is infinitely variable between upper and lower limits. Often the bands overlap, and the combination of variable frequency and boost/cut makes this type of equalizer very flexible indeed.

Sweep equalizers are often erroneously called 'parametric' equalizers. These—in which all the parameters are available for modification—exist, of course, but they offer more than a simple sweep EQ unit. Most importantly, they allow control of the 'tightness' or Q of the response curve, often with a multi-position switch or infinitely variable knob. At the extremes of the range, the Q can be adjusted to act on one narrow frequency band—tight enough, for example, to 'notch' out hum—or wide enough to have a very broad effect over a range of frequencies. This added facility offered by parametric units makes them exceptionally flexible, but equally they are most difficult to use effectively in haste, under the pressure of a session.

A particularly sophisticated type of parametric exists in which a computer is used to set up a complete full-range frequency response characteristic by allowing the engineer to 'draw', with a joystick control, the response curve required. The computer then generates the nearest approach to this curve by controlling a multi-band parametric EQ unit.

An alternative form of multi-band equalizer has been produced by one or two manufacturers in which the bands are deliberately allowed to interact, rather than remaining separate as on conventional units. The result is that both Q and overall frequency response can be modified with a remarkably small number of operator controls. These are very uncommon, however.

One of the most familiar of multi-band equalizers is the so-called 'graphic equalizer' (Figure 9.1). Here, a number of frequencies are available with amplitude sliders, enabling the engineer to set up an entire frequency curve, with the sliders displaying the approximate shape of the curve. The number of sliders—and thus the number of centre frequencies available—varies from half a dozen to as many as twenty-eight. The centre frequencies are standardized according to ISO recommendations. Graphics are somewhat of a double-edged sword, however. Although both easy to use and flexible, the large number of frequency bands controlled by such a unit can cause signal degradation especially as regards phase response. It is possible to design EQ units of all types with minimal phase errors, but this is not always seen in practice. The degree to which such effects are audible, however, depends on a large number of factors, notably the perception of the listener.

Time-domain processing

There is no simple name for this kind of signal processing. But time-domain effects are today a central part of the recording art, whether the effect be time delays, reverberation, flanging, or one of the more esoteric effects now available. Before modern digital delay processing systems came along there were tape machines to offer delay facilities—and, of course, real room reverberation is a time-domain effect.

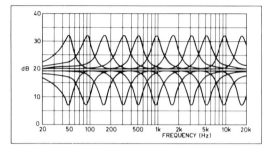

Fig. 9.1. Range of controls on a typical graphic equalizer

Central to all these effects is the ability to take a sound and delay it, reproducing the sound—often at varying levels—once or a number of times. Heard with or without the original signal, the effect is exceptionally valuable.

Basic time-delay effects

At the bottom of all these effects is the simple time delay, and digital (or occasionally analogue) delay lines—which offer this facility flexibly and with great ease—are commonplace in the studio. At delay times of a few tens of milliseconds, delays can be used to 'double' a sound, creating an effect generally referred to as 'ADT' or 'Automatic Double Tracking'. This does not give quite the same effect as getting a musician to play or sing the same part twice, but it is very useful. Modern delay lines generally offer the facility to vary the delay with a low-frequency oscillator, adding a certain degree of 'detune' and time slippage which can liven up an effect that might otherwise sound somewhat mechanical. A delay of this order can also be used to split a mono sound into pseudo-stereo, and is the basis of a number of stereo synthesis devices and techniques.

Longer delays give the possibility of a 'slapback' echo-repeat (echo as distinct from reverberation) when heard with the original signal, as found on rock'n'roll records. Add a touch of regeneration—feeding a portion of the output back to the input—and the repeats can be made to last for some time. Some more sophisticated delay systems allow the length of the delay (and thus the time between repeats) to be controlled by an external signal— say a click-track or bass drum—so that repeats can be made to occur after a pre-determined number of beats. Some devices allow various 'taps' to be taken off the delay to allow multiple repeats (in the old days it was tape loops and a number of replay heads).

Make the delay shorter, and interesting things happen if the delay is heard along with the original sound: as the delay time falls within the lengths of time associated with audio waveforms, various cancellation and summing interference effects will be heard between the original and the delayed signal. We are now looking more at phase-related effects than separate repeats. Other things happen, too.

Phasing and flanging

At longer delay times, if the original and the delayed signal are split in stereo, our brains tell us that the sound source is in the direction of the original rather than the delayed sound (which is why the delayed signal in an ADT split left and right must be louder than the original to 'balance' left and right in apparent level). We interpret the delay as exactly that—the kind of time delay that happens because of sound reflections in the real world. As the delay increases, however, the phase effects take over. If the delay between left and right is zero, we are listening in effect to two-channel mono. So the result of decreasing the delay to zero is that the sound pans across from one side (where the original is located) to the centre—phase-shift panning. If instead of using the original sound and a delayed sound split into stereo you used a sound delayed by a fixed amount on one side, and by a variable amount on the other, enabling you to sweep one delay *past* the other, the sound would pan wildly from one side to the other as the variable delay passed the setting of the fixed one. Listening to the same effect in mono, we have a very well-known effect born of the phase cancellations caused by the delay: 'phasing' where small time differences produce a sweeping sound, or 'flanging' where longer delay is used to give a more coloured effect.

Exactly how this effect was discovered one can only guess. *When* it was discovered, and by whom, is similarly uncertain. The earliest well-known instance is the theme music to the film *The Big Hurt*, made in the mid-1950s. But there may be at least one example from the late 1940s. The familiar 'swooshing' effect was then rediscovered by more or less everybody in the 1960s: perhaps by Steve Reich in the United States: by Ken Townsend at Abbey Road with the Beatles; or by George Chkiantz for the Small Faces' 'Itchycoo Park'. The last example, however, is almost certainly the first time the effect was used under control.

In those days, phasing or flanging (the origin of the latter term is disputed, too) was done with tape machines. Later, devices based on notch filters were used to produce elements of the same effect. But it was with the development of delay lines that the effect became easily available with true repeatability in the studio. Today, it is a standard effect, and studio equipment can generally allow the effect to be controlled manually, by means of a low-frequency oscillator, or sometimes by the amplitude of the input signal. Generally, time-domain processing devices offer some or all of these effects.

Pitch-shifting and time-squeezing

In a digital delay system, the input signal is digitized and stored in memory. A short time later it is clocked out again and reconverted to analogue (unless you are working entirely digitally, of course, and are very lucky). The output will be a delayed version of the input if the rate at which it is clocked into memory is the same as the rate it is clocked *out*. Otherwise the pitch will be altered. Clock it out slower than it went in and the pitch will drop; faster and the pitch will rise. Chop up the contents of memory into slices and loop them, so that the signal lasts the same time whatever the clock rate, and you have a pitch-shifting device. In the old days, this was done with special tape machines, of which the Tempophon was the best-known. These had rotating heads on a drum which could run backwards or forwards with respect to the tape, at a wide range of speeds. The tape itself could also be speed-controlled, producing a range of effects, including speed change without pitch shift and vice versa. Today this can be performed with digital-delay-based systems, with or without the linking of the delay system to tape varispeed.

Reverberation

The most complex time-domain effect is that of reverberation. Natural reverberation is caused by the interrelation of a large number of reflections produced in an acoustic environment. After the original signal, there will be a pause followed by a number of distinct reflections: the sound being reflected, off the walls for example, and being picked up directly. Later, a complex series of multiple reflections will arrive at the listener, produced by sound having bounced off a number of surfaces first.

Figure 9.2 shows the kind of reflections (heavily simplified, of course) which produce reverberation effects. These can be simulated with a large number of delays (and delay taps) or via sophisticated algorithms involving memory storage. They can also be simulated by large sheets of metal fitted with transducers, as in the EMT echoplate and its successors; by springs fitted similarly with transducers; and, of course, by rooms and chambers of various sizes, which is how it was originally done. There is no doubt that modern sophisticated digital devices can simulate rooms very well—along with a large number of other effects—and it is the advent of microprocessor-controlled digital signal processors which has brought artificial reverberation down in size. Modern units are also quite affordable.

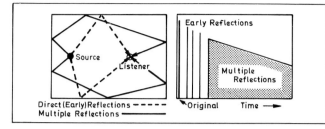

Fig. 9.2. Showing how reverberation is made up of direct (early) and multiple reflections

In addition to imitations of natural reverb, many of the more recent units can produce reverb effects, for example 'gated reverb', a sound fashionable in the early to mid-1980s (and now fully integrated into the overall reper-toire of signal-processing effects), in which the reverb is cut off after a pre-determined time.

Control of dynamics

The dynamic range of a recording system is simply defined as the ratio between the noise level at one end and the onset of distortion at the other. Almost all recording and transmission media have limits placed on their dynamic range by the technology, and several musical instruments and other sound sources encountered in the course of everyday studio life are capable of dynamics which exceed these limits to a greater or lesser extent. Even with digital systems—typically 16-bit in most studio applications—there are occasions when it is necessary to modify the dynamic range of a signal being recorded, though systems with higher bit rates now provide wider dynamic capability.

In addition, it must be remembered that many of the media via which the finished recording will be heard possess considerably less dynamic range than can be recorded on the master tape. AM radio, for example, has the smallest dynamic range of any of the mass means of audio signal distribu-tion, yet it is also one of the most important, certainly as far as popular music is concerned. FM radio has limitations, as do vinyl pressings. Cassette tapes—particularly the pre-recorded variety—do not even get that far. Of all the current media, only Compact Disc, DAT, DCC, and MiniDisc offer the same dynamic range—potentially at least—as a digital master tape.

As a result, dynamic range control in the studio is a vital part of the recording process. Studio applications can be divided into three main areas: control of dynamics to enable 'difficult' material to be recorded or to sur-vive the final medium; dynamics control for effect; and analogue tape noise reduction systems (the intention here, of course, being to increase the dynamic range of the medium).

Sitting on a fader, pulling it down during the loud passages and pushing it up during the quiet sections, is one of the most fundamental methods of dynamics control, and still one of the most effective. Manufacturers of compressor/limiters have spent many years developing equipment to do the job of fitting wide dynamic range material into a smaller space as well as a trained balance engineer can do on a complex live broadcast, for example. Here, the art is to anticipate changes in overall programme level and adjust the level gently so as to preserve the contrast between musical events. So-called 'gain riding' is still a very useful method—indeed, in the multitrack environment it may well have increased in importance with the introduction of fader memory or 'console automation' systems which enable gain manipulation on the faders to be repeated until it is right, the system then remembering it for the rest of the mix.

Automatic gain control systems—compressors, limiters, and expanders—are some of the key tools in any studio, even where classical music is concerned. However, one of their primary uses is in the contemporary music field for effect purposes: to tighten up an errant bass drum or bass guitar, for example, or to enable a vocal to maintain energy and stay out in front however lacking in power the voice may be in certain registers.

The most common gain control element utilized in such devices today is the voltage-controlled amplifier (VCA) placed in the audio path, whose gain can be adjusted by a d.c. control signal derived from the input signal or, optionally in some units, from an external programme source (for example another track on the tape machine).

On the face of it, automatic gain control devices are pretty straightforward. Limiters and compressors reduce the gain in the audio path as the level rises above a pre-set threshold level; expanders reduce the gain as the input level falls. A limiter does not allow the output level to rise above a pre-set point. Simple, isn't it? But in practice automatic gain control devices are some of the most complex studio ancillary units for the novice recording engineer to operate successfully. There are a number of reasons for this.

Compression and limiting

Figure 9.3 shows a pair of compression characteristics. The gentler of the two, the 2 : 1 slope, shows that above the threshold setting (0 dBm in this case), an increase of 2 dB on the input results in only a 1 dB increase in the output level. The threshold setting for the 'infinity' slope—limiting, in other words—is +10 dBm. After this level is reached at the input, however much the input level rises, the output increases not at all. Typical compressor/limiters (often the two functions, which are essentially similar, as can be

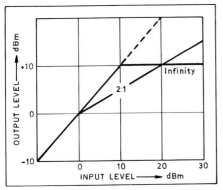

Fig. 9.3. Compressor/limiter characteristics

seen, are combined in one unit) usually offer a range of compression ratios. There will generally be an indicator or meter showing the difference between the input and output levels—the 'gain reduction'. A typical unit will have input and output controls as well as a compression ratio control. The threshold setting may well be fixed on simpler units—the effective threshold therefore being set by the input level—or it may be a separate control.

It should be noted from the graph that there is a point where the two lines intersect. Here, the gain reduction is the same, but at this particular input level the gain reduction has been achieved in two quite different-sounding ways. No real audio signal is constant, and the difference in sound between the two curves is dramatic. The softer compression retains much of the original dynamic range (half of it, to be precise), whilst the limiting characteristic simply squashes the dynamics altogether when the level at the input rises above a certain amount.

For this reason, limiters are often used to stop a signal dead, for example to avoid major distortion or even—in the case of disc-cutting applications—damage to the equipment. The threshold is generally set up 'out of the way' to catch wayward transients without affecting the normal course of musical events.

In compressor and limiter applications, it is important to determine the rate at which compression or limiting occurs, particularly when it comes to limiting. Often the attack and release times of the system are variable. To 'catch' transients with a limiter, it is important that the attack time is fast—to avoid too much overshoot—and that the gain is recovered rapidly after the transient has passed. In compression applications, however, for example 'tightening up' a bass guitar, a slow attack is often a good idea, as the deliberate overshoot at the front of the sound can add punch to the notes. Some units have an optional programme-controlled attack/release characteristic which allows the unit to set its own parameters according to the characteristics of the potential overload.

214 / Richard Elen

It is interesting to note one effects application of compressor/limiter systems, known as 'overlimiting'. It is often difficult to achieve on modern units, but the effect can sometimes be useful. In an overlimiting condition, the output level is squashed so hard by the limiting action that it drops below the threshold level: in other words, loud input signals (above the threshold) emerge at a lower level than quieter (below-threshold) signals. The result can be interesting.

The release time is also important. With a long release (or 'recovery') time, the signal level after a transient will take time to return to its original value. Quiet passages after a loud transient will be quieter than they would otherwise have been, thus reducing the overall average level. This should be watched, as it is the average level which determines the overall apparent loudness of the signal. Yet rapid attack and release times combined with a large amount of compression can sound quite horrifying, as various undesirable side-effects begin to creep in with fast gain changes. This is particularly noticeable on bass-end signals, where the compressor can begin to follow the excursions of the actual audio waveform, flattening it out. The result sounds like a form of distortion, which of course it is. But with some pop material it is surprising how much you can get away with before it becomes noticeable. If you wish to subscribe to the school of thought which forbids the peak level to vary beyond 5 dB for the duration of the song, this is the direction to head in: a careful compromise between gain reduction and rapidity of attack/release. The end result can, with care, sound much louder than it really is.

There are other undesirable side-effects of the compression process. It is very easy, for example, when one is compressing an entire mix, to end up with one dominant signal in the track (typically bass drum and/or bass guitar) pushing the rest of the track down when it plays. This can be uncomfortable on playback, but it is often difficult to know that it is happening when you lay down the mix, especially if you are listening at high monitoring levels and the ears are doing compression of their own. In circumstances like this, it is as well to listen briefly at a markedly lower level (or, if the producer objects, put your fingers in your ears) and watch for tell-tale signs. One of the most obvious is that changing the level of parts of the rhythm section by a very small amount appears to affect the overall balance dramatically.

Not only can a loud instrument in a full balance 'modulate' the rest of a track; a solo instrument out on its own can modulate the total system noise, especially if the compressor is right on the end of the chain. This shows itself as a 'breathing' or 'pumping' effect and is quite distasteful. As noise is particularly noticeable in the upper frequency ranges, solo bass instruments are the most likely to cause problems. There are a couple of ways round it: use a band-splitting compressor (in which separate gain control elements handle different parts of the frequency spectrum); or use a compressor where you can access the side-chain, the signal path in the unit that derives the gain-changing control voltage. Insert an equalizer in the side-chain and roll off the bottom end, thus ensuring that bass signals produce a minimal change in gain. Then, if possible and necessary, compress the solo instrument on its own.

Similar solutions are required in disc cutting where excessive high-frequency energy—in sibilants, for example—can cause problems. Here the traditional approach was to equalize the side-chain so that a compressor/limiter reacted only to high-frequency information. Again, the problem here is that the whole track is turned down to remove sibilance. An alternative approach used increasingly today is the band-splitting comp/limiter, which can treat the upper end of the frequency range separately without affecting other parts of the spectrum.

Comprehensive band-splitting compressor/limiter systems have wide potential applications for both of the instances described above, and they will no doubt become more common in the studio—as opposed to the specialist areas like disc cutting and broadcasting—as time goes by.

Expanders and noise gates

Expanders and noise gates are, in simple terms, the inverse of compressors and limiters respectively. As can be seen from Figure 9.4, the effect of an expander is to *increase* the dynamic range by attenuating the output signal when the input level drops below a pre-set threshold. The attenuation is usually set by a control ranging from no attenuation to 'off'—infinity. A gentle characteristic will gradually increase the attenuation as the level falls; a harsh ratio—or infinity, as in a noise gate—will simply reduce the output at a stroke the moment the input level drops below threshold (at a rate depending on the attack characteristic).

While expanders are quite difficult devices to use effectively, noise gates are a very common and effective way of reducing the apparent noise level on multitrack, simply by turning tracks more or less 'off' when they are not playing. To do this effectively, of course, the gate must operate very fast, preferably in microseconds rather than milliseconds—otherwise transients will be cut off dramatically. Modern noise gates, in fact, have tended to become more and more like basic synthesizer envelope generators: one very common unit has, in addition to input, output, and threshold controls, three further adjustments, labelled 'attack', 'hold', and 'release'. The time taken for each stage is independently adjustable, leading to a great deal of flexibility. The same unit allows optional access to the side chain (a 'key' input—very common in gating systems—to enable the opening and closing of the gate to be controlled by a *separate* signal, for example to tighten up a

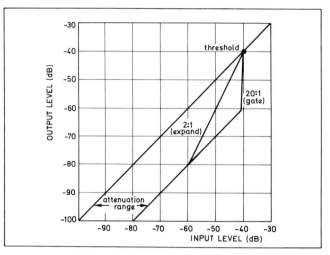

Fig. 9.4. Typical expander/gate characteristics

bass guitar by keying it with the bass drum) and has adjustable low-pass and high-pass filters in the side-chain to allow the keying signal to be tailored exactly to requirements. This is exceptionally useful, as it enables a complex signal, say part of a drum track with a lot of spillage, to be filtered so that only the desired components of the sound are used to control another signal. It is thus possible to separate parts of a track and treat them as separate entities: the snare, for example, can be isolated and given its own EQ and reverberation without affecting the rest of the drum tracks.

The selection of 'gating' and 'ducking' is also possible on several units, the latter allowing the keying signal to *turn down* the main audio path when a keying signal is present, thus allowing, for example, music programme to be attenuated automatically in broadcast applications when the presenter is speaking.

Noise reduction systems

Compressors and expanders are occasionally used together. It is a difficult business, as one tends to counteract the other, but there is one application where that is exactly what you want—as long as there is a tape path in between the two—and that is in noise reduction for analogue tape machines.

There have been several approaches to noise reduction over the past two decades, and it is interesting that Ray Dolby, whose Dolby A system was introduced in 1966, exactly twenty years later announced a new system—'Spectral Recording'—at just the moment when many people in the industry were predicting the final eclipse of analogue tape recording systems by digital ones.

There were of course attempts at noise reduction before Dolby. The simplest—which relied on the fact that noise is more noticeable at the top end than in the bass—was a simple static pre-emphasis/de-emphasis system. You boost high frequencies on record, and cut them by the same amount on replay. This 'poor man's Dolby B', as one friend of mine once called it, does work (it has been used on FM radio for many years), but it has disadvantages when it comes to tape, which is at its most sensitive to overload at the high-frequency end. Static equalization curves were not the long-term answer.

One approach was to use a compressor on the record side, with an exactly complementary expander on replay. Such approaches are utilized in telephone systems to maximize the signal-to-noise ratio, but there they have the advantage that a control channel can be sent along with the audio (for example outside the audio bandwidth) to supply control data, ensuring that the input and output sides track successfully, because any error is doubly audible. This is impractical in current analogue recording applications.

The idea still sounds good, but there are other problems. One is that of overshoot on transients on the record side: in such cases the signal is *not* being effectively controlled by the compressor, and, however accurate the control information fed to the expander at the other end, it will be wrong. Then there is the question of modulation of one part of the signal by another, and the effects caused by throwing a single compansion system across the whole audio band.

Today, Ray Dolby's solution may seem obvious, but it is still a very clever approach to the problems presented by the analogue tape system. Dolby A is based around three primary factors:

1. Treating only the low-level signals in which noise is not masked;
2. Splitting the audio spectrum into four bands and treating them separately to avoid modulation effects;
3. Deriving a signal component which can be added to the direct signal on encode and subtracted from the signal on playback to maintain the integrity of the control signal, and enabling the same circuit components to be used for decode as for encode.

The system also includes circuitry to limit transient overshoot in the compression stages.

Dolby A operates only on low-level signals: signal manipulation occurs below −40 dB. Above this level, the processing action is gradually removed and by −10 dB it is non-existent. The presence of a processing threshold, however, does mean that the system is sensitive to the input level. As a result, it is vital that a reference level is established on a tape-to-tape basis

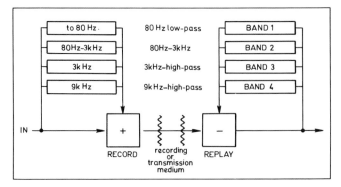

Fig. 9.5. Signal path in the Dolby A noise reduction system

to ensure that encoding procedures carried out during recording are exactly undone in the playback stage. The later, consumer development of the Dolby system—Dolby B, which operates only on the upper frequency band, where noise is the most noticeable—also requires levels to be precisely correct, and this factor is one of the primary difficulties with the system.

In professional applications a 'Dolby level' must be established, and a Dolby reference tone must be included on the tape to permit alignment for subsequent deprocessing. In the early days, as Dolby rapidly became an international standard, there was a great deal of confusion as to how the Dolby reference level should be set, and this still continues to a lesser extent today. You were recommended to set operating levels in one of three ways: standard record level with Dolby level at 0 VU; elevated operating level with Dolby level at standard reference level; or elevated operating level *and* Dolby level. Over the past twenty years, tape technology has changed and so have normal operating levels, so it is always important to know what the Dolby level is on a tape, especially on an old recording, otherwise unpredictable results can occur.

Despite its noise reduction benefit—10 dB of noise reduction over the range 30 Hz–5 kHz and up to 15 dB at 15 kHz—and the fact that copies of encoded tapes could be made without decoding, producing an encoded copy with minimal additional noise compared to the master, many engineers were suspicious of Dolby A. There was a widely held belief—still existing today, to some extent—that Dolby 'changes the sound'. Some of this feeling could well have been the result of incorrect alignment in the early days; in other cases it may well have been that the reduction in noise level revealed faults in the recording that would previously have been masked. It is also possible for internal settings related to the processing bands in a Dolby processor to get out of alignment—a factor which cannot be corrected by the operator or even by a studio maintenance engineer—but this is unusual.

It may be that some aspects of transient handling in the system, for example the overshoot protection circuitry, are capable of producing audible artefacts. But no firm conclusions have ever been reached, and as a result the alleged 'sound change' of Dolby A must be left to the individual engineer to judge.

While Dolby A continues as the primary noise reduction system in the studio to the present day, refinements were made to the consumer system. Dolby B operates on frequencies above approximately 500 Hz and offers around 10 dB of noise reduction. The later Dolby C system gives almost twice as much. A later addition to the procedure—Dolby HX (for 'headroom expansion')—controls record bias and EQ according to the HF information, giving improved HF response, among other things.

In the professional field, other approaches were made to the problem of analogue tape noise. Some systems appeared and disappeared, like the Burwen 'Noise Eliminator', while at least one stayed around and still performs well under the right circumstances: the dbx system. This was developed by David Blackner and appeared on the market some time after Dolby. It suffered as a result of the fact that Dolby had already taken off—and also as a result of some inherent features.

The system utilizes a simple 2 : 1 compansion system coupled with pre- and de-emphasis (which is placed *before* the compression on record and *after* the expander on playback). This relieves some of the noticeable fluctuations in background noise which would otherwise occur in a wide-band compansion system. Figure 9.6 shows the basic features of the system. Another notable feature of the system is the use of true RMS level-sensing, rather than peak or averaging systems. This has the great benefit of representing the sum of all the signal components, irrespective of phase.

The dbx system provides up to 30 dB of noise reduction, but this is not achieved without a price. 'Pumping' and 'breathing' effects are not entirely eliminated, making it unsuitable for some kinds of programme material (although it is quite happy in many cases). In addition, when handling stereo programme, the two compansion channels cannot be linked. (This would upset the encode/decode process, as the system would operate on one channel under the control of signals in the other which may not be present in the same relationship on both channels.) The result is that the stereo image can 'wander' according to programme content. In many multi-track applications, however, it is entirely satisfactory. In addition, the simple compression characteristic adds headroom on tape to a useful degree.

The telcom c4 system, developed by AEG–Telefunken and later handled by ANT, came along late in the day and therefore benefited from hindsight as far as noise reduction system development is concerned. It can offer in excess of 25 dB of noise reduction, basically by combining the best elements of both Dolby and dbx. The spectrum is divided into four overlap-

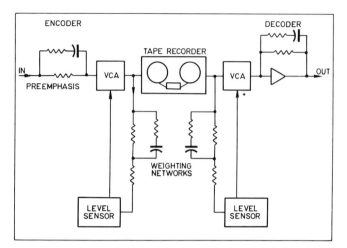

Fig. 9.6. Block diagram of the dbx noise reduction system

ping frequency bands whose sum produces a flat response, resembling Dolby in some ways. Each band, however, is treated by a simple 1.5 : 1 compansion characteristic, not unlike dbx, but with a gentler slope. The combination avoids a reference level—as dbx—but minimizes frequency-related modulation effects by means of the band-splitting (and the gentler slope).

One problem with band-splitting systems, however, can be the interaction of adjacent bands. In telcom c4 the bands overlap, potentially even more of a problem. It is important to derive a control signal on record which can be duplicated on playback. The telcom system handles this in an ingenious fashion. While the band-splitting in the audio path is generated by 6 dB/octave filtering, the control signal is generated using 12 dB/octave filters with the same centre frequency. The result is a control signal which does not suffer interference from adjacent bands, yet retains a smooth band overlap in the audio path. The combination is a good one, and while telcom c4 has suffered from arriving late it has gained a good following.

Perhaps the last word in analogue noise reduction, Dolby Spectral Recording (or 'SR' for short) has enabled some studios to put off the fateful decision between competing digital systems more or less indefinitely. Dolby SR claims to offer a level of performance on current analogue recording machines which is audibly equal to, or better than, 16-bit digital. Owing something to the Dolby C consumer system, SR, rather than dealing simply with the activity below a certain level in a number of bands, instead develops a three-dimensional 'gain surface' which is a function of time, frequency, and the changing spectral properties of the signal. Figure 9.7 (courtesy Dolby Laboratories) shows the basic structure of the system.

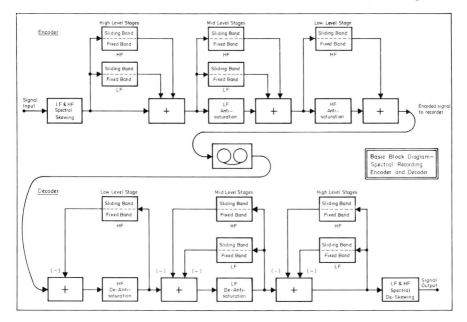

Fig. 9.7. Basic block diagram of the Dolby Spectral Recording (SR) encoder and decoder

The circuitry is mounted in a Cat 280 card, physically similar to the original Cat 22 Dolby A cards and capable of fitting into the same rack (both telcom and dbx units are also available in this format). In the record mode, the main activity of the system is to add gain to those areas in the frequency spectrum of a signal which contain low- and medium-level components. On playback, exactly complementary degrees of attenuation are applied to these areas.

The input signal is first passed through a low- and high-frequency spectral skewing system which reduces the problems caused by signal components at the extremes edges of the frequency spectrum, where tape machine response can be uncertain. This is compensated for in the decode stage. There then follow three separate side-chains, dealing with high-, medium-, and low-level signals, the output of each being summed into the main path. In each side-chain, the signal is split into LF and HF processing areas (with the exception of low-level signals, which are dealt with only at HF). Each subpath has sliding and fixed-band dynamic control, whichever is the most effective being used at any one time—a process which Dolby refer to as 'Action Substitution'.

There are three thresholds, −30, −48, and −62 dB. As the signal level drops below each of these, a separate gain control stage is brought into play, called 'Action Staggering' by Dolby. Behind the entire process is the fundamental idea of leaving the signal alone unless it needs treatment, and minimizing the treatment to exactly what is necessary. There is a related domestic system called Dolby S-type.

There are other kinds of noise reduction which are worth a brief mention here. One type—exemplified by the MicMix 'Dynafex' unit—is a single-ended noise-reduction system: it acts on replay only. While basically an expander-based system, it is also frequency sensitive.

One problem with expanders is that they can be unpredictable, and can produce side-effects. The entire signal level can ramp up and down at around the threshold level in a non-linear and disturbing fashion. Yet the principle is useful. Another approach to noise reduction—as utilized on some early cassette records by Philips, and referred to as 'DNL', or 'Dynamic Noise Limiting'—involved sensing the maximum frequency present in a signal above a pre-set threshold and generating a control signal used to adjust the 'knee' frequency of a low-pass filter, thus effectively 'turning down' the level above the maximum significant frequency. This can produce a dramatic apparent lowering of the noise-floor (the majority of noticeable noise being in the upper-frequency region), but it too suffers from problems. The apparent noise level can wander up and down according to the presence or absence of an upper-register solo instrument, for example. But the system is useful, and is available in some professional devices.

In the Dynafex, these characteristics—expander and frequency-sensitive HF roll-off—are combined in such a way that their side-effects tend to cancel out, or at least ameliorate, each other. The result is a unit with a simple threshold-setting control, the ability to gang channels for stereo, and a useful noise reduction capability when no other means are available. As it is sensitive to frequency and level, however, there can be some unwanted attenuation of low-level signals present in isolation, for example reverb decays, and this should be borne in mind.

All the systems so far discussed were designed to operate on the analogue tape path. There have, however, been a couple of attempts to tackle the problem of noise on vinyl discs. Here, the noise problem is more frequency-dependent than on tape, and there is a case for treating the problem in a slightly different way.

One approach to disc noise reduction is to try and reduce the audibility of clicks and pops on vinyl pressings. Such systems were at one time available in the consumer market-place, but professional systems of the type are often used to rejuvenate classic archive recordings for reissue. The technique is in fact a time-domain processing approach, but it is included here along with other types of noise reduction. In essence, the system relies on putting the signal through a short delay, slightly longer than the average click or pop. A sudden transient click is sensed by a time and level-dependent circuit (often with frequency-sensitivity as well) which is theoretically capable of discriminating between clicks and musical transients. When a click is sensed, the delay is either dumped completely (thus 'editing out' the click) and gradually restored, or a substitution is made with an immediately previous section of programme without the click. In both cases, the amount 'edited out' is very short, and as a result minimal side-effects are heard. The problem is in sensing pops and clicks accurately.

Spatial localization processing

Since the first days of stereo, engineers have been concerned with positioning signals in a sound-stage of one sort or another. Monophonic recordings, of course, have no spatial localization information available. But stereo and modern multi-dimensional systems offer at the very least the capability of placing a sound source along a straight line between the speakers.

In a true stereo system, for example a recording made with a Blumlein or cross-cardioid microphone pair, the localization of sound sources is dependent on the original material. In this sense, stereo is simply a more realistic method of capturing what is going on. The same applies to dummy head or 'binaural' records where, to varying degrees, attempts are made to emulate the human hearing system. Binaural techniques recur every few years and are hailed every time as if they were something new; then they go away again. Some major advances in this field have been made in recent years, both in binaural recording, in the shape of Hugo Zuccarelli's controversial 'Holophonic' system, and in coincident microphone systems, like the 'Soundfield' microphone. They are not really 'sound processing' techniques as such, and will not be discussed further here.

The majority of current 'non-monophonic' recordings, however, whether made direct to two-track or via multitrack procedures, use a mixing console and multiple inputs. In this situation, it is necessary to position essentially mono sources in a sound-stage, usually a stereo environment created via two speakers, fed from two channels of information. This type of spatial manipulation is more accurately referred to as 'pan-potted mono' than as true stereophony, as the standard method of achieving localization is to control the relative levels of a given source between the two channels. A signal present only on the left channel will appear left; a signal present equally on both channels will appear centre-stage; on the right channel only it will appear hard right; and various combinations in between. The standard device to achieve this is the humble console pan-pot.

Localization by level

Pan-pot design is a surprisingly complex area, primarily because it is traditional—and necessary—to consider not only the stereo listener but also the listener equipped with mono listening systems. As a result, a pan-pot must produce both a respectable stereo effect and a minimal effect in mono—so-called 'mono compatibility'. A number of approaches are current in this area, and they differ in the 'law' by which the pan-pot acts in dividing the mono input signal between the two output channels across its travel, and whether the sum of the two channels is constant across the travel of the pot or not. The two basic laws are 'constant power' and 'constant voltage', and are discussed in Chapter 7.

A development of the basic pan-pot occurs in the form of the autopanner, in which VCA devices are used to control the relative levels of the two output channels, the control voltage being derived from a number of sources. Often these devices can handle two input channels, and the outputs behave in opposition to each other (so, for example, as one sound moves right, the other moves left). Autopanner control signals may be derived from a low-frequency oscillator, allowing a number of wild dynamic effects, from a push-button trigger, initiating a time-controllable pan from one side to the other, or in many cases from a pulse counter which can be fed with a clock-track or other rhythmic signal to cause the pan effect to occur at musical intervals. Generally, the panning width can be defined on the front panel.

Sum-and-difference and phase-shift panning

An interesting development of level-based panning has now rather unde-servedly fallen out of use, that of sum-and-difference panning. It can produce extremely exciting dynamic effects, including that of placing a sound beyond the width of the speakers, but its compatibility with mono is severely limited, to say the least. It relies on having available a sum-and-difference matrix encoder and decoder, and in these post-Blumlein days such things are hard to come by. The basic set-up is shown in Figure 9.8. A two-channel signal is fed into the encoder, and two signals, sum and difference, are supplied by the output. These are fed into console channels and level-controlled. They are also capable of being panned, but not directly to the stereo output; instead they are fed to a pair of groups (for example) which are fed into the decoder input. This would normally yield the original left and right signals, but in this case the left–right and level relationships between the sum-and-difference pair may well have been scrambled, resulting in the feeding of variable proportions of anti-phase signals from one side into the other. The effect is very useful, and is found in some consumer portable stereo systems (in a pre-set fashion) to generate a 'wide stereo' effect.

The generation of anti-phase signals is just the start of a whole load of other possibilities. Level is only one of the ways in which our brains determine the direction of a sound source in real life. As a stereo localization

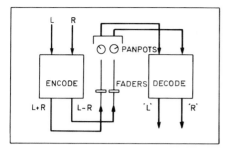

Fig. 9.8. Outline arrangement for sum-and-difference panning

system in recording, it suffers severe drawbacks, notably the fact that a sound can appear to move about in the sound-stage as you move between the speakers, on account of the fact that the relative level of a sound in the two channels is all that defines where it appears to be. Move to the left, for example, and the source will follow you, dramatically.

In real life, we use at least three systems to determine localization. Level is certainly one, but arrival time and phase are two other important considerations. Arrival time localization—or 'Haas Effect'—is noticeable when we ADT signals and split them left and right, as discussed above. The earlier sound will be the one we use to determine position, our brains interpreting the delayed signal as a reflection off some imaginary surface. In recording, this is less a localization system and more a nuisance, as in stereo ADT splits we need to enhance the delayed signal level to make it sound as loud as the direct: the 'spatial balance' and the level balance can differ significantly.

But, as was also discussed in the time-domain processing section, as the delay time is reduced, localization effects occur as the delay becomes measurable in terms of phase rather than gross time delay. Around the point where the two signals are nearly in phase, extremely dramatic panning can occur, extending beyond the speakers. Under control, this can be used to advantage, and at least one effects unit on the market uses phase-shift panning to create stereo effects. Once again, however, they are limited in their mono compatibility.

If level and phase are combined under control, we have a system which can emulate in the studio many of the characteristics of natural sound localization. Also, as a combination of level and phase cues can uniquely 'tag' the localization of a sound source virtually anywhere around the listener, we have the basis of a very powerful surround-sound system with good stereo and mono compatibility. Those cues can be used equally by the listener directly, or by a decoding system capable of deriving interrelated loudspeaker outputs to project the sound from the intended places.

Surround sound

Surround sound has had a chequered history. It was entirely natural to attempt to extend the 60° stereo sound-stage right around the listener, but it was difficult to do in practice. In the early 1970s, such attempts revolved around the idea that you could take four speakers instead of two and place them in a square around the listener, treating each side of the square as a stereo layout.

Unfortunately, such attempts had only limited success. 'Quadraphony', as it was called, relied on generating four individual signals, rather than the two associated with stereo. There were several problems with this approach. First, in the natural world it is only vaguely acceptable to reduce a soundfield impinging on the listener to four sources. Second, stereo operates successfully with the speakers placed so as to subtend an angle of 60° to the listener, not 90° as is the case with quadraphony. The result was a tendency towards 'holes' in the image between the speakers, although in some cases so-called 'discrete quad' was very impressive. Third, there were no four-channel transmission media available at the time (although some were developed, notably those using subcarriers and employing sum-and-difference encoding—as in FM stereo radio—on each channel of a stereo disc). So there was a need—to maintain compatibility with stereo and even mono once again—to develop matrixing systems to encode the four quad channels into two for stereo transmission and recover them at the other end ('4-2-4' systems). Regrettably, this is mathematically impossible.

However, matrix quadraphonic systems have survived in the film industry, in the form of Dolby Surround, a development of the more common original systems. They are capable of impressive effects in the cinema, though they are not at their best when trying to reproduce natural soundfields. Commercial consumer decoders are now available for this system, to decode home video releases derived from surround-encoded movie soundtracks.

Another fundamental problem with traditional quadraphonic techniques was that, particularly when quadraphonic mixes were being performed in the studio, the only method of synthesizing spatial localization was to use level-based localization only, generally with quad pan-pots. The disadvantages of level-only localization have already been discussed as regards the listening position in stereo; in quadraphony they are at least four times worse, and the listener is confined to a central position in the middle of the loudspeaker layout.

We have already seen that phase has a part to play in localization. Some recording systems—notably coincident-pair techniques—preserve many aspects of the soundfield, including both level and phase data, and the difference is easily heard in any situation in which coincident stereo pairs are combined with mono spot mics. If an orchestra, for example, is recorded with a coincident pair, it will be noted that the image is not only very stable as the listener moves about between the speakers, it is also capable of reproducing distance from the listener. A spot mic added into the balance to enhance a soloist, say, does not have these benefits, and will move about in a straight line between the speakers when the listener moves, in contrast to the orchestra.

This fact was used as the basis of a current surround-sound system developed in the UK in the 1970s. Called Ambisonics, it was originally designed to capture the natural soundfield and replay it—in three dimensions, with height if necessary—in an ordinary listening environment. Sound processing devices based on this principle are now available for mix-down applications, allowing the engineer to synthesize a soundfield in the studio, either for eventual surround-sound decoding by the listener, or simply as a means of creating stereo recordings with greater depth and image stability than is possible with conventional level-only localization techniques.

The basis of the Ambisonic system was derived directly from Blumlein's work in the 1930s on stereo recording. He used a pair of microphones, one an omnidirectional unit deriving the sum of left and right, and the other with a figure-of-eight characteristic, pointing left, and therefore deriving a difference signal. This sum-and-difference pair was then fed to a matrix decoder to derive left and right feeds. Ambisonics extends this technique into three dimensions, as shown in Figure 9.9. These signals can be generated by a 'Soundfield' microphone or can be synthesized from mono or stereo sources in a mix by a set of signal-processing devices. The signal is referred to as 'B-Format', and its four channels contain all the data required to pinpoint a sound source in three-dimensional space.

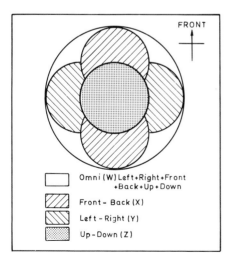

Fig. 9.9. Composition of the Ambisonics B Format signal

Of course this four-channel signal cannot be transmitted easily with currently available media. In addition, sum-and-difference signals are not in common use. So once again a matrixing system was developed to transmit as much data as possible via the channels available, while offering mono/stereo compatibility. The matrixing system is referred to a 'UHJ', and is a hierarchy of signal formats, each one being compatible with the one below it. Thus four-channel UHJ encodes all the spatial information, including height. Take away the fourth channel and you have three-channel UHJ, capable of high-definition horizontal (or 'planar') surround. Take away the third channel and you have two-channel UHJ, the normal format for commercial applications.

Future developments in sound processing

The processing systems described in this chapter are increasingly being handled digitally, either inside or outside the console environment. With the inevitable coming of all-digital recording systems, it will be possible to remove the conversion processes that often precede and follow such processors, especially as regards time-domain processors. Digital equalizers are already a reality, as are digital dynamic control systems. The tendency to digitalization means that signal processing in all its forms is increasingly a matter of number-crunching and computer power. Outboard processors already exist which offer a wide range of software-generated effects, and can be updated merely by inserting new ROMs or diskettes. This development will continue.

Control systems for signal processors are also increasingly available for computer access, either via RS232/422 serial data interfaces or via the high-speed MIDI (Musical Instrument Digital Interface) standard used in the vast majority of modern music synthesizers. This is inevitably leading, along with the development of 'tapeless' digital recording systems, to the integration of certain aspects of the music-making, recording, and signal processing chain in the modern recording studio. Already, signal processors can be interfaced both with music sequencers and with console automation systems.

Microphones will probably be the final link to be digitized, but once digital microphones are perfected there will be no need for the highly financed studio to use analogue techniques in any major form. Such an all-digital studio will not be cheap, however, and analogue techniques will not die out for some time. Neither will the need for outboard signal processors disappear overnight, for the great advantage of individual units—whether they are centrally controlled or not—is that the user is not tied down to one manufacturer's signal-processing techniques, but instead can call on the unique sound-manipulating ingenuity of a wide range of manufacturers all over the world.

Until there is a single software-based system which does everything, and there is agreement on the basic input/output and control parameters required of signal-processing software for such a system—both rather unlikely at this point—engineers in studios the world over will continue to be surrounded by black boxes of one sort or another.

The new technology of signal processing has added to the repertoire of sounds available in the studio, and has made effects that were difficult to obtain now relatively easy. We are always looking for new sounds, and today's signal processors—and no doubt tomorrow's—indeed offer that. The technology of sound processing opens up even more creative potential.

10 Loudspeakers and monitoring

Edward Veale

Studio monitoring is very subjective and emotive. What we hear is the result of the process of hearing, and this is based upon our individual learning and experiences of different sounds and sound patterns. Because no two people are likely to have had precisely the same experiences, we all tend to interpret sound in different ways. For these reasons, it is difficult to gauge what another person is hearing or interpreting from a pattern of sound. Also, the response, texture, and quality of the sound reproduced by a loudspeaker is affected by the construction of the drive units, the enclosure within which the units are mounted, and the room or space within which the reproduction is heard. With so many personal and physical variations, it is little wonder that recorded sounds are given different interpretations by different people and, furthermore, that they actually sound different from one room to another. In fact, one may marvel that any similarity is achieved at all.

Since their humble beginnings, recording studios have moved from simple stereophonic and four-track systems to 46 tracks or more, analogue and digital. This rapid growth in techniques over recent years has placed increasing demands upon monitoring systems. Single-source dual-concentric loudspeaker systems were once extremely popular, and, to some extent, they remain so. To satisfy the demands of the late 1960s (for ear-melting sound levels) twin-bass driver systems were introduced. About the same time, systems emerged which employed an efficient compression driver for the mid-range frequencies.

With the passage of years, measuring instruments have become more effective and better understood. The development of the microprocessor has enabled equipment to be designed and built which can, almost simultaneously, discriminate between the amplitude, phase, and time domain. This process is called Time Delay Spectrometry, or TDS (see also Chapter 4). In more recent times, with increases in the dynamic range of recordings, the benefits of advanced technology in console design, digital signal processing, and digital recording, the demands on studio monitoring systems have again changed, the latest requirement being a consistency of sound perspective over the full range of sound intensity. This latest demand, coupled with higher standards for definition in the stereo placement of sounds, has resulted in two developments coming to the fore: the nearfield monitor and the multiple-element soft dome monitor system.

The passage of time has also brought a better understanding of the behaviour of loudspeakers and how systems work when several drivers are housed in a single cabinet. The low-frequency output of systems can be improved by incorporating the enclosure into the building structure, though this may introduce transmission problems unless care is taken. Improvements in the transparency of the middle and high frequencies have been achieved by co-ordinating the acoustical centres of the drivers, thus minimizing phase shift, or time delay, between adjacent crossover frequency bands.

The demands which are placed upon monitoring systems by different sections of the industry also vary. Sound broadcasting, television, film, and video all have their particular needs. Sound broadcasting studios are most particular and selective about the monitors they use, and it is in this field that significant advances have often been made, particularly by the British Broadcasting Corporation. Within the other fields, the film industry is probably better organized, with standards and frequency tailoring introduced to allow for the acoustic needs of the cinema auditorium and the optical transfer process, as for example in the Dolby Stereo and THX Theatre systems. The particular demands placed on a recording studio monitoring system are greatest of all, in that it is required to reproduce sound in a manner which can be related to any other environment or reproductive system.

History of the loudspeaker

The loudspeaker can be traced back to 1925, when the first direct radiator dynamic device was developed by Chester Rice and E. W. Kellog. The theory of the direct radiator loudspeaker was first established in 1877 and discussed by Lord Rayleigh in his *Theory of Sound*, Volume Two, published in that year. The mathematics of a direct radiator in an infinite baffle are presented in that book, but it was some forty-six years later before the first dynamic loudspeaker was actually developed.

In 1931 the first two-way system, described as a 'divided range' system, was demonstrated by Frederick of the Bell Telephone Laboratories. Coaxial loudspeakers were developed to extend the frequency range of the single magnet/coil assembly. To overcome the problem of diminishing high-frequency response in the larger cone device, a smaller cone was introduced in the centre. The addition of this smaller cone improved the performance at the higher frequencies, and the introduction of a mechanical crossover arrangement enabled this to be effective from about 2 to 15 kHz.

The compression driver was later developed for public address work. The process of using a small diaphragm acoustically coupled to, and loaded by, a horn device produced a very efficient loudspeaker. There are two inherent problems with this device, distortion at the higher frequencies and physical limitations on low-frequency reproduction. To overcome these problems, the compression driver was integrated into systems employing traditional bass drivers and high-frequency units to extend their useful frequency range and maximize their efficiency.

Dual-concentric devices were made popular by Tannoy and Altec in the 1950s. These comprised a cone loudspeaker for the bass frequencies, with a compression driver mounted at the back and feeding through a horn in the centre of the magnet to emerge in the middle of the cone. These were compact, wide-range systems and offered great flexibility. They were much liked because the reproduced sound emerged from a single point; they are still produced and are to be found, for example, in current studio systems marketed by Tannoy and JBL under the UREI name.

The first purpose-built studio monitor was marketed by Cadac in 1970. This was a bi-amplified three-way system. It used the Altec 604 dual-concentric driver and a separate high-frequency array. The crossover was passive and designed to correct misalignment of the acoustic centres within the driver components. The design of the system also recognized the benefits of having short interconnecting leads between the amplifiers and speaker components, and later versions had the amplifiers mounted in the base of the enclosures.

The electrostatic loudspeaker provides a presentation of sound unequalled by conventional moving-coil devices. Many systems were developed, including one by Leak, but that by the Acoustical Manufacturing Company, under the 'Quad' banner, was the only one to become popular. Unfortunately, the electrostatic system cannot achieve the high sound levels demanded by most studio users, and so it has never made much progress in the studio market, except for some classical music monitoring. A number of hybrid systems using cone-type bass drivers were developed, but these have not been taken up by the recording industry. However, there can be little doubt that the electrostatic loudspeaker has created standards by which the conventional system has to be assessed.

Since the mid-1970s there has been a significant growth in the number of studios engaged in professional sound recording, and it has become worthwhile for small, specialist firms to produce purpose-designed monitors; this is reflected in current product ranges and available systems. Since the early 1980s there have been many significant developments. Purpose-designed drivers have been produced for studio use and cabinet designs have advanced. A great deal of work has been done to overcome the problems associated with inefficiency, phase or time delay, frequency response, power handling, and distortion.

As well as a new breed of main monitor loudspeaker systems employing soft-dome drivers, smaller 'nearfield' systems were introduced to the market. Major advances in main monitor systems have been made. Many companies have introduce tri-amplified systems employing conventional and soft-dome drivers. Others have introduced nearfield monitors which dispense with compression drivers and are adaptable to a variety of applications.

Monitor uses

As already mentioned, the demands placed upon monitoring systems by different sections of the industry vary considerably, as do the acoustical qualities of the listening rooms. Broadcasters tend to favour small to medium-sized systems and build control rooms with the monitors placed to approximate a typical domestic environment. Film sound studios have their dubbing theatres designed to emulate the typical cinema. The recording studio is the most varied, and control rooms frequently sport three different monitor systems, selectable at the press of a button (see later reference to nearfield monitors).

Broadcasting within the United Kingdom has been largely guided by the activities of the British Broadcasting Corporation, and many of their design practices have been embodied within a Code of Practice for the control of Independent Local Radio. This Code of Practice document produced by the late IBA has become widely used and recognized as a reference for studio design and installation. It covers the requirements for the electrical systems and the studio acoustics.

The film industry has sought to improve the quality of film soundtracks by many new techniques. One has been to simulate, within the dubbing theatre, the environment experienced by the cinema audience, so that sound is mixed and equalized to optimize for such conditions. Electrical filters are provided to simulate the effect (or degradation) of the transfer of the soundtrack from magnetic to optical media. A great deal of work has been done by Dolby Laboratories to improve the quality of film soundtracks. This work extends to reducing background noise, increasing the dynamic range, and producing a stereophonic effect within the space available on the 35-mm optical soundtrack (see also Chapter 28). Their work continues with surround sound, digital recording of sound between the film sprocket holes, and many more ideas. As a result of efforts to standardize the listening conditions in both the cinema and the dubbing theatre, the American National Standards Institute, together with the Society of Motion Picture and Television Engineers, produced a standard audio reproduction characteristic which was published in 1984 as ANSI/SMPTE214M. This stipulates the curve to which cinema auditoria and dubbing theatres are to be equalized (Figure 10.1).

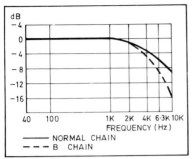

Fig. 10.1. ANSI equalization curves for cinemas and dubbing theatres

The sound recording studio, on the other hand, strives to attain excellence with no particular standards to guide those engaged in their design or operation. Because the recording industry is comparatively small, major advances tend to develop as a result of efforts by entrepreneurs or engineers who happen to design something which is appreciated by the studio users. As a result, trends in equipment and control room design advance in definite phases which are more readily apparent than elsewhere.

It is because the recording industry is so small that, historically, most advances have occurred as spin-offs from other sectors, and this is particularly true for monitoring systems. Only in recent years have loudspeaker drive units been specifically designed for studio systems and complete studio systems been developed uniquely for this application.

Studio monitors

To define the requirements of loudspeakers for studio monitoring, it is necessary to understand design practice, the placement, use, and characteristics of the systems available, and also the working needs of the studio. The monitor loudspeaker is the link between the electrical information, which represents the recording, and the listener. The loudspeaker performs the opposite function to that of the microphone by turning variations in electrical signals into variations in air pressure which our ears can perceive.

The environments in which we listen to sound vary considerably in range and quality: from home to office, discothèque to theatre, motor car to concert hall, headphones (for personal listening) to piped music in hotels, and so on. All of these have different acoustical qualities which influence the sound that we hear from either live or reproduced music.

With the advent of electronic music synthesizers and keyboard equipment, developments in the electronic world, digital recording, and other advances which have been introduced to the recording chain, the demands placed upon the modern control room have grown considerably. Particularly with this in mind, we should not overlook the length of time that is devoted to making individual recordings and then refining and mixing these to produce the final master. Engineers and producers can spend many days concentrating on a single recording to obtain perfection. The overall environment and the quality of the facilities in the control room can either help or hinder this work.

The performance and the sound quality perceived from the monitoring system can be described in many ways. Many expressions are used by engineers or producers to describe sound quality, including such vague terms as transparency, harshness, definition, transience, darkness, lightness, and aggressiveness. However, such terms often have different meanings for different people, and engineers involved with the technical design and manufacture of loudspeakers continue to strive for methods of measurement which will demonstrate a direct relationship between the subjective and the measured results.

These problems are further compounded by digital recordings which demand higher definition over the entire amplitude and frequency range, coupled with a wider dynamic range. This puts a greater strain, not only upon the power-handling capacity of the loudspeaker, but also on the design of the power amplifiers driving the loudspeaker, the crossover system, and every other link in the monitor chain.

Advances in measuring equipment have produced benefits for those engaged in product development by making available FFT (Fast Fourier Transform) analysers and TDS (Time Delay Spectrometry) systems. Such techniques now enable the measurement procedure to separate the loudspeaker from the room without the need for anechoic chambers, and to investigate these separately. Thus the actual response of the loudspeaker can be investigated in terms of frequency/amplitude/phase/time without the need for removal to laboratory conditions. Likewise the events within the room, either separately or in combination, can be investigated in greater depth. This has advanced our understanding of the behaviour of sound within the controlled environment and encouraged a better approach to design.

Whilst such equipment enables more investigations to be made in greater depth, the level of sophistication creates other problems: more information is produced and the control parameters of the measuring equipment have been enhanced to such a level that errors are easier to make and less easy to detect. Notwithstanding such advancements, it should not be forgotten that current measuring practices use a single microphone to receive information, which limits the amount of information that can be either received or processed. We, as mere mortals, have been given two ears which, coupled with the brain, perform analysis functions beyond the capability of even the finest equipment or latest measurement practices.

A considerable amount of information about the electroacoustic performance of loudspeaker systems is usually available from the manufacturer. Such information includes frequency/amplitude response, power-handling capacity, impedance characteristics, distortion values, dispersion or directivity in terms of Q factors or polar plots, and, for complete systems, phase coherence (often referred to as time alignment). There is no standard method of expressing all such factors, although there are ANSI (American National Standards Institute), BSI (British Standards Institute), and IEC (International Electrotechnical Commission) standards which apply to some of them.

For these reasons the qualities of loudspeaker systems are difficult to quantify, and this leads to personal assessments and preferences. Bodies such as the Independent Broadcasting Authority have set up panels of listeners to assess loudspeakers, and, from their judgements, lists of acceptable products can be made. This demonstrates the problems that individual consultants and users may experience when asked to recommend a monitor system.

A further influence on the sound perceived from a monitor is the surrounding environment (room acoustics). There are varying ideas as to what constitutes a good room: these range from very dead to moderately live, with live-end: dead-end, and other special constructions to add variety. Add to this the effect that the building materials can have (especially on the low end) and the effect of the equipment (console, tape recorders, equipment racks, keyboards, etc.) on early reflections and diffusion, and the resultant effects are seen to be compounded and very complex.

It may now be realized how it is that some engineers and producers prefer certain types of monitor, and why it is that the same monitor can sound quite different between one location or studio and another.

One may be forgiven for thinking that there is a common standard for design in present-day studios, but this is not the case. For example, the designers of sound recording studios go to great lengths to ensure that the information delivered by the monitor loudspeakers is presented to the listener in the most efficient way possible and with the least amount of modification or room influence. This includes such techniques as mounting the monitors in such a way as to avoid energy radiated from the sides and back of the enclosure being reflected by the front and side walls and arriving at the listener at significantly different times. Such reflection problems do not appear to worry broadcasters, because their monitor loudspeakers are often intentionally placed at distances of one metre or more from all wall surfaces, and indeed this suggested placement is set out in European Broadcast Union Technical Recommendation R22-1985.

It must always be borne in mind that the recordings will ultimately be listened to in a variety of situations where the listening conditions may be very different. Popular music, for example, could be heard on loudspeakers or headphones, from a hi-fi system, in a discothèque, in a car, on television, or on a small personal radio. The engineer and producer need to be satisfied that the 'mix' will still be effective when listened to in any of these situations. To achieve this, it is common practice to have at least one or more alternative speaker systems on which the recording can be replayed. These range from the main installed monitor system to good domestic speakers and very small speakers representative of lower-grade systems. These small speakers are often referred to as 'nearfield' speakers, because they are usually positioned very near to the listener. A range of nearfield monitors has emerged to satisfy this demand, created by engineers and producers who listened to their mixes on good-quality smaller speakers placed on the console meter bridge to eliminate room acoustics. Current models offer a choice of two- or three-way systems which are compact and provide a good frequency range.

The attitudes of recording engineers towards monitors also vary. There are those who will work exclusively on the main monitors and make only occasional checks on the alternative speakers, and there are those who will do most of their work listening to a good-quality pair of hi-fi or nearfield speakers, occasionally turning to the main monitors to hear how the mix sounds at very high level, or to impress visitors. There are also a few engineers who appear to have no difficulty in relating to the sound they hear from any monitor or speaker system, and who work with whatever system seems satisfactory to others on the session.

Most recording engineers will probably agree that listening to the mix on the main monitors at a moderate level enables the perspective of the sound to be most accurately assessed. Listening to the small 'nearfield' systems (often perched on top of the console meter housing) has the effect of reducing any room effects and creating a system response more compatible with in-car and other domestic listening environments.

Monitor positioning

The positioning and mounting of monitor systems is an important consideration. Obviously, they must be securely fixed to the main structure, and large obstructions are unwanted because they can affect the overall performance of the system and the quality of the sound presented to the listener.

In recording studios, the preservation of the stereophonic picture is of primary importance. Additional speakers are installed in control rooms where film work is done, to provide centre and surround-sound information, but these are secondary. The traditional equilateral triangle is always a good position from which to start, with the two loudspeakers subtending an angle of 60° to the listener (Figure 10.2). However, modern control rooms often dictate that a different approach is necessary. In the larger control

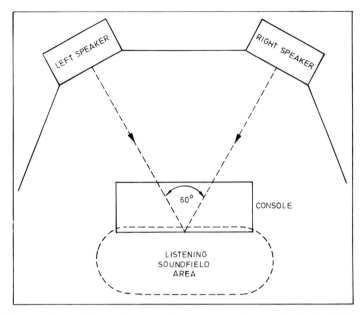

Fig. 10.2. Traditional 60° speaker layout for stereo monitoring, showing the listening sound-field area

room, this traditional approach often reduces the designer's task but caution has to be exercised to ensure that the console position and the volume of space between the speakers and the console do not contribute to a poor bass response.

Whatever is done, whatever loudspeaker location is chosen, whatever the system, one thing is paramount: the quality of the sound presented to the listener in the main working area. This area is generally described as being equal to the width of the control console and extending from the seated position at the console to about two metres back. The height within which this area has to apply should be from about one metre to two metres above floor level. For convenience, this region is often referred to as the soundfield. The quality and texture of the sound presented to the listener within the soundfield will be affected by the type of monitor system selected, its location in the room, and the acoustics of the room including the presence of unwanted standing waves.

Many control room designs are now created where the console is moved forward to the edge of, and sometimes into, the nearfield response of the main loudspeakers. The demand for space between the speakers to accommodate television monitors, etc., whilst still meeting the same needs for a suitable coverage angle, has meant that the traditional approach to layout has often to be abandoned or greatly modified. In other situations as we have said, a separate pair of small monitor speakers may be placed on top of the console itself (to simulate domestic playback conditions). This will generally produce a reduced listening soundfield area (Figure 10.3).

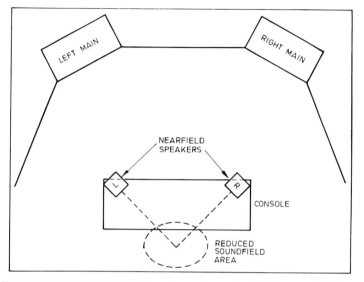

Fig. 10.3. Using small nearfield speakers reduces the listening soundfield area

A further influence on the effect of the soundfield is the elevation at which the monitors are mounted. This can be anything from the horizontal listening plane to an elevated position above, for example, a vision window. Thus the position selected for the monitor system will often be the result of a compromise between the space available, the coverage area required, and the type of system specified. To optimize the results within the soundfield, the designer normally contours the surfaces of the room and carefully selects and positions the acoustical treatments.

It is always a good design policy to reduce compromise wherever possible. In this regard, the monitor loudspeaker system can be selected to have characteristics which are complementary to the design needs. In this context, the coverage angles are important. These related to the dispersion angles of the speakers and are often tailored by the designer of the system to direct the radiated energy into the desired space. This makes the system more efficient and can reduce room boundary effects.

In room designs which require the console to be close to the monitors, the required horizontal angle of coverage is greatly enlarged. Additionally, the ratio of distance between the loudspeaker and the nearest and furthest listening position is considerably increased. This creates a demand for monitor systems which have an exceptionally smooth frequency response and wide angle of coverage. The soft dome radiators used in the latest breed of monitor systems are proving most suitable for these conditions.

With this interest in both monitor directivity and the listening soundfield, the dispersion characteristics of loudspeaker systems become significant in any calculations. This information is best obtained from a series of polar plots (see Figure 10.4) and to obtain sufficient information these plots should be made in one-octave increments in both the horizontal and vertical planes. Should any unexpected variations be observed in the horizontal or vertical results, then plots at a 45° angle should be performed; such plots will reveal any elliptical element within the dispersion field: this could cause a different sound to be presented at the extremities of the soundfield. Armed with an analysis of the prescribed speaker system directional performance, the required position and angle of the monitor system to the soundfield can be determined in relationship to the required soundfield.

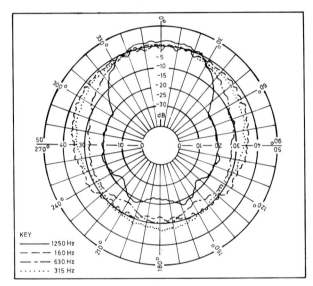

Fig. 10.4. Typical polar plot of a loudspeaker

Of great importance is the centre image, and this can be seriously affected when the distance between the two monitors exceeds the distance from the monitors to the listener (see Figure 10.5). Plots of the dispersion characteristics enable the angles at which the monitors are set to be adjusted so that any deficiency of the centre image is largely corrected. The sound intensity at the listening centre should remain constant when a signal is panned from left to right through the centre position. If variations exist, then the perspective and possibly the position of individual sounds within the stereo picture will change when reproduced on another system.

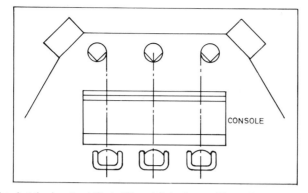

Fig. 10.5. Showing the image shift at different listening positions along the console. The characteristics and angle of the loudspeakers should be chosen to minimize this displacement effect

At frequencies below 400 Hz and particularly around 60 Hz, most speaker systems become omnidirectional, and energy is wasted by being radiated outside the area of interest. The design of some monitor systems has been adjusted to compensate for this reduction in on-axis amplitude at low frequencies by some form of low-frequency enhancement, and this may have to be catered for in choosing positions and layout.

A method which is often employed by designers to correct the effect of low-frequency fall-off is to recess the enclosure into the front surface of the room. This has the effect of increasing the area of the enclosure's front baffle and so preventing the low-frequency information being lost around the sides. This technique has the added benefit of eliminating any variations in frequency response which may occur in the listening area due to energy radiated from the rear of the enclosure being reflected by the front wall. These naturally arrive some time behind the original sound and give rise to phase errors which can cause cancellations and additions to the sound pressure at frequency-related distances.

Whilst building monitor systems into the front wall of the room can provide benefits in performance, care must be taken to prevent the construction materials from behaving as an extension of the enclosure. To induce vibrations into the air, the drive units vibrate mechanically, and some of this energy is induced into the enclosure or cabinet. If the cabinet is directly connected to the structure, then these mechanical vibrations can be transmitted into the structure, and this must be avoided as far as possible.

Sound is conducted through building materials at higher speeds than in air, and a responsive surface elsewhere in the room can easily be excited and act like a speaker in its own right. Such effects often occur over quite narrow frequency bands and, when they do, the information within the soundfield is blurred by the arrival of information which is different from the fundamental. These wavefronts may even arrive in advance of the direct sound and have a more confusing effect than normal acoustic reflections.

Isolation of the enclosures from the main structure is therefore very important (see Figure 10.6) and, for optimum performance, should be equal in all directions. It is of little benefit to use a suspension system which is soft or damped in one plane but rigid in another. Vibration from the enclosure will be transmitted into the structure in the more rigid plane and unwanted excitation of structural members will probably result. Free-standing monitors should be equipped with suitable stands. These should be as rigid as possible, to restrain movement, and be free of resonances. The manufacturer's recommendations for mounting should always be consulted.

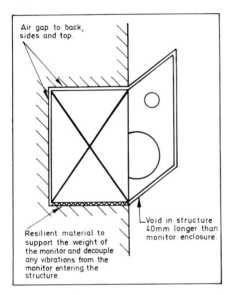

Air gap to back, sides and top.

Resilient material to support the weight of the monitor and decouple any vibrations from the monitor entering the structure.

Void in structure 40mm longer than monitor enclosure.

Fig. 10.6. The building-in of monitor loudspeakers to minimize transmission of sound energy into the main structure

Setting up monitors

The procedure for commissioning, checking, or setting up a monitor system should follow a standard pattern. A suitable procedure would be to check that each drive unit is working correctly and in the correct phase relationship to the other units, that the output of each section is adjusted for optimum performance, that crossover points are correct, and, finally, that optimum adjustment is made to any built-in frequency-tailoring facilities which may be available.

In relationship to monitor speakers and frequency tailoring, there is a myth that should be dispelled: that monitor equalizers are a cure for all ills. They are not. In fact, if equalizers are wrongly used they can make the situation a great deal worse. During the mid-1970s it became the fashion to install equalizers on most systems, and it was not long before this became referred to as 'room equalization'. The fact is that rooms cannot be equalized by adjusting the electrical response of the monitor system. If acoustical problems exist, their character and effect will vary according to the listening position. Electrical equalization may appear to produce an improvement at one point, but the effects at other points may be exacerbated.

There is no doubt that equalizers have their place, and correctly used they can be of significant benefit. Few monitor systems are perfect, and a number of electrical problems can be greatly reduced, if not eliminated, by careful adjustment of the equipment. Electrical equalization of loudspeaker systems was first introduced in the late 1960s and made popular by the Altec Acoustavoice system. This was first designed for public address installations and was developed as a convenient way to reduce feedback and improve acoustic gain and thus intelligibility within existing and new sound systems. It was not long before these equalizers found their way into the recording studio and were installed into monitor systems. With the growth in popularity, additional types of equalizers were produced by a variety of manufacturers. A wide range of equalizers is available, but those which meet the particular needs of monitor systems divide the frequency spectrum into one-third octave bands.

Adjustment of monitor equalizers needs to be approached with caution. There is considerable interaction between adjacent frequency band controls. For example, adjustment of three adjacent bands by the same amount of movement on each control will produce a result whereby the upper band will be affected to a greater degree than the lower. Also, the two bands immediately above the upper band will be affected. Adjustment should not be attempted without suitable checking equipment and some prior experience.

The following sequence, for which a real-time analyser should be used in conjunction with a pink noise source, may be followed:

1. Ensure that all the drivers are working.
2. Check that all the drive units within each system are in phase with each other and that both systems are in phase overall. If in doubt, reverse the phase of a suspect unit or system and compare the results, perhaps using sweep tones.
3. Check and observe the sound pressure response of each monitor system in the nearfield and at several points within the listening soundfield. Note any significant deviations.

4. Select a microphone position on the centre line between the two monitors, and at a distance along the centre line where a reasonable average of the various observed patterns is found. If there are any peaks or troughs which are clearly the result of acoustic effects, ignore them and choose a microphone location that takes a mean.

5. Adjust the controls provided on the monitor systems, power amplifiers, and crossover units to obtain the best balance and smoothest response possible.

6. Replay a known musical recording over the monitor system and listen for any obvious defects. Note these defects and estimate the frequency bands in which they occur.

7. Return to the pink noise source and analyser and observe the response within the frequency bands noted. There may be peaks or troughs which need adjustment, and it is possible that an acoustical effect has masked the result of excessive adjustments carried out in step 5; should this be the case, then return the controls to a normal setting.

8. Repeat step 6.

9. If equalizers are installed, return to the analyser and pink noise source and further refine the response with the aid of the equalizers, taking care not to compensate wrongly for any acoustical effect.

10. Repeat steps 6 and 9 until optimum results are achieved.

11. Check compatibility and summation. This needs to be done by feeding the signal at a fixed level to both the left- and right-hand monitors and switching the monitors on and off in turn. Note the mean response of the left-hand side and compare it to that of the right. Should there be any significant difference, adjust the overall gain until they are identical. Switch on both monitors and note the increase in sound level. A well-matched system in a reasonable acoustic environment will produce a rise of around 5 dB across the frequency spectrum. Should this not be the case, then phase errors within or between the systems should be suspected. With satisfactory results so far, a check should be made of the stereo picture. This is done by feeding the noise source to the monitors via a pan-pot and panning the signal from left to right; the spectrum and the sound pressure level indicated on the real-time analyser should remain constant. This condition will occur only when the whole system is correctly matched; this includes the pan-pot, monitor systems, monitor angles and positions, as well as the room acoustics.

Remember that what we hear is not always the same as what we see on an analyser. This is because the adjustments affect the phase of components as well as their amplitude. So proceed with caution. It is a good policy to check the performance of monitor systems periodically. Drive units do change their response with age and use. Systems used consistently for high-level monitoring will deteriorate much faster than those used for more moderate work. The time intervals between checks will need to be judged according to use. The monitoring system deserves to be as well maintained as any other piece of equipment within the recording chain, if best and truly consistent results are to be achieved.

11 Tape recorders: Analogue

Hugh Ford
(Revised by Keith Spencer-Allen)

The structure of magnetic tape

Magnetic tape is constructed using a base film to support the magnetic layer, or coating. This magnetic coating is applied on one side of the base film, whilst an additional non-magnetic coating is frequently applied to the reverse side. Modern magnetic tapes use polyester as the base film, marketed under a number of trade names such as Mylar from Du Pont or Melinex from ICI. Various grades of polyester, or more properly polyethylene terephthalate, are available from the manufacturers and have widely differing mechanical properties.

Figure 11.1 shows the typical dimensions of the cross-section of a standard-play studio recording tape, where the overall thickness is typically 55 µm, allowing 730 m to be wound on to a standard 267 mm NAB reel. In the long-play version, and other extended-play versions, it is common to reduce both the base film thickness and the coating thickness.

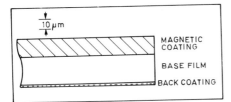

Fig. 11.1. Cross-section of a Standard Play tape with back coating

Studio recording tapes generally employ gamma ferric oxide (Fe_2O_3) as the main magnetic material, whilst recorders which operate at short wavelengths, such as video recorders and cassette machines, commonly employ alternative magnetic materials such as chromium dioxide (CrO_2) or pure metal pigments.

In practice the magnetic coating cannot consist of the magnetic material alone, because, for one thing, it would not adhere to the base film. Furthermore, the surface properties have to be controlled so that the coating does not adhere to the recorder's heads and the tape does not deposit debris on the heads. A further factor is that the tape must not accumulate static electricity, not only because this might cause arcing, but also because static electricity interferes with the fast-winding performance of the tape. The requirements of these and other factors mean that the 'dope' used to coat the base film is a combination of a number of materials in addition to the magnetic material. Such additives include a wetting agent to assist with the dispersion of the magnetic material, a binder to secure the coating to the base film, anti-static agents, abrasives to keep the heads clean, lubricants to avoid sticking—all a rather complex piece of chemistry.

Other than surface properties and conductivity of the coating, the properties of the back of the tape have a considerable influence on the winding performance, with a smooth untreated back to the base film giving poor winding. Thus the base film may be designed to have different properties on its two sides, or a thin coating (2–3 μm thick) may be applied to control the surface characteristics and conductivity of the rear of the tape.

The mechanical properties

The basic mechanical properties of recording tapes are the tape width, thickness, and length. Whilst the length for a given size of reel is up to the manufacturer, the common lengths for a given reel size and type of standard-play tape are shown in Table 11.1.

Table 11.1. Typical standard-play tapes

Reel type	Reel size		Typical length	Tape time at 15 ips (38 cm/s)
	(inches)	(cm)		(minutes)
AEG	11½	29	3280 ft/1000 m	43
NAB	14	35.5	4800 ft/1463 m	64
NAB	10½	26.7	2400 ft/732 m	32
CINE	7	17.8	1200 ft/366 m	16
CINE	5¾	19.6	900 ft/274 m	12
CINE	5	12.7	600 ft/183 m	8

The maximum tape thickness and the standard widths are defined in the International Electrotechnical Commission IEC Standard 94-1, as shown in Table 11.2.

Under operational conditions in professional audio recorders, the tape tension is a compromise between good head-to-tape contact, good tape winding, power consumption, and other factors. As a general guide, a tension of 70 g (2.5 oz) for 6.3 mm (quarter-inch) standard-play tape is ideal, with the tension being increased in proportion to the tape width.

Table 11.2. Standard tape widths and thicknesses

Tape width		Tape thickness	
(inches)	**(mm)**	**(inches)**	**(mm max.)**
2.000 +0/ −0.0024	50.80 +0/ −0.06	0.0022	0.055
1.000 +0/ −0.0024	25.40 +0/ −0.06	0.0022	0.055
0.500 +0/ −0.0024	12.70 +0/ −0.06	0.0022	0.055
0.248 +0/ −0.0024	6.30 +0/ −0.06	0.0022	0.055
0.150 +0/ −0.0020	3.81 +0/ −0.05	0.0008	0.020

The magnetic properties

The basic magnetic properties of recording tape are measured by plotting the applied magnetic field (H) against the magnetization (B), which provides a hysteresis loop as shown in Figure 11.2. Proceeding from a state of zero magnetization marked 'O', as the field H is increased (X axis) the magnetization (Y axis) increases to point A, beyond which the application of a larger field does not increase the magnetization. The magnetization at this point is known as the saturation flux (B_S). Decreasing the field to zero from point 'A' leaves a remnant magnetization called the remanence (B_R). As the applied field is reversed, the magnetization eventually falls to zero, at which point the applied field defines the coercivity (H_C).

Magnetic tape specifications commonly specify the coercivity H_C, the remanence B_R, and the squareness ratio, which is B_R/B_S and relates to the

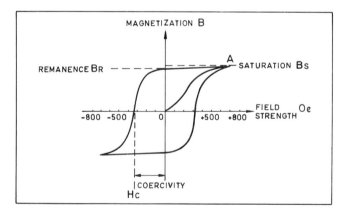

Fig. 11.2. The hysteresis loop

efficiency of the recording medium. Clearly, the coercivity (specified in oersteds or amperes/metre, where 1 Oe = 79.58 A/m) relates to the ease of erasing a recording. This extends to the self-erasure in the recording process, which is a phenomenon that erases short wavelengths (high frequencies) more than long wavelengths (low frequencies) during the recording process. Thus there is a compromise in coercivity, as a high coercivity is desirable for good high-frequency performance, but too high a coercivity makes it very difficult to erase a tape.

Typical coercivities for professional recording tape are in the range 20–8 kA/m, whilst for compact cassette recorders operating at 4.76 cm/s (1⅞ ips), where the recorded wavelength is very short, there are four types of tape which have been standardized by IEC, as shown in Table 11.3.

Table 11.3. IEC cassette tape categories

IEC type	Tape construction	Typical coercivity (kA/m)
I	Single-layer iron oxide	24–32
II	Single-layer chromium dioxide and pseudo-chrome	34–57
III	Double-layer or doped	No requirements
IV	Metal pigment	72–96

It is logical that the remnant flux should relate to the maximum output available from a magnetic tape, and this is indeed the case at long wavelengths if the construction of the record head allows the full thickness of the magnetic coating to be penetrated. However, at shorter wavelengths the full depth of the coating is not penetrated and this relation does not hold.

Whilst the remanence is specified in milli-maxwells/millimetre (mM/mm), which multiplied by ten becomes nano-webers/metre (nWb/m) and represents the fluxivity per unit tape length, the retentivity cannot be directly compared. The latter is measured in gauss or milli-tesla, where 10 G = 10 mT.

The electroacoustic parameters

The parameters of interest to the tape user and their effect upon the record/replay process may be summarized as follows:

Sensitivity. This relates the input to the recorder to the output for a stated input frequency. Figures quoted may refer to a specified reference tape.

Distortion. Three per cent harmonic distortion at 1 kHz (or 5 per cent at 315 Hz for low-speed machines) is related to a given recorded fluxivity as determined from a calibration tape. At high frequencies the tape saturation (the input level at which an increase of input does not produce an increase in output) is also related to a given recorded fluxivity.

It is also common to measure the third harmonic distortion at a specified recorded fluxivity and frequency of 320 nWb/m at 1 kHz or 250 nWb/m at 315 Hz.

Bias noise. The noise produced by a tape which has been recorded in the presence of bias without any audio input is referred either to the distortion as determined above at mid-frequencies or to a reference fluxivity.

Noise is weighted, that is the frequency response of the measurement is modified to correspond to the subjective effect of noise. Two weightings are in common use, 'A' weighting or CCIR Recommendation 468-3 weighting. The results of the two methods cannot be directly compared.

Direct current noise. Direct current noise is measured by the same method as bias noise, but with a d.c. current applied to the record head, and sometimes a different weighting is used. Direct current noise gives an indication of modulation noise, that is noise which is programme-related and not present in the absence of an audio signal input.

Print-through. Print-through, the layer-to-layer transfer of signals during storage, relates the recorded signal level at a given frequency to the level of the first pre-echo after storage at a specified temperature for a specified time.

All these parameters depend upon the tape speed, and they also vary according to the types of head used on the recorder. However, standard measurement conditions do exist. Another variable is the level of the high-frequency bias applied to the record head, which has little effect upon bias noise or print-through. It does, however, have a significant effect upon all the other parameters above.

The measured performance of a tape depends upon the frequency response of the record and replay amplifiers. Tape performance is normally measured using a constant record current. The equalization of the replay amplifier, that is the relation between the recorded fluxivity on tape, frequency and output voltage, is set to one of a number of standards which will be discussed later.

These effects are shown in Figure 11.3, where the top curves indicate the maximum output level (MOL) for 3 per cent third harmonic distortion at 1 kHz and the saturation at 14 kHz, versus bias. Increasing bias tends to increase the MOL, whilst reducing the high-frequency saturation. Thus a compromise is needed for satisfactory recorder performance. Lower down in Figure 11.3 it can be seen from the sensitivity curves that the frequency response of a recorder will also depend upon bias, because the relation

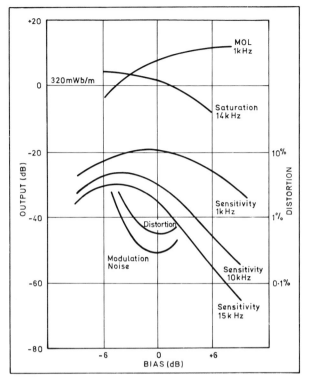

Fig. 11.3. Bias-related tape characteristics

between bias and sensitivity is not the same at all frequencies. This means that the frequency response of the record electronics must be equalized for a given type of tape at the operating bias current.

Even more critical is the relation between distortion at a fluxivity of 320 nWb/m and the modulation noise, versus bias. These parameters have a distinct optimum bias, occurring at 0 dB in the diagram. When aligning a recorder for optimum performance, it is desirable to set the bias to this operating point, but most users do not have the equipment necessary to measure distortion or modulation noise. Instead, it is far simpler to record a tone whilst monitoring the reply output level and changing the bias level. This is the common method of setting the bias level.

Recorder manufacturers (and some tape manufacturers) often recommend a degree of over-bias: the basis is slowly increased until the peak of the output voltage is found and then further increased until the output voltage has fallen by a specified number of decibels.

In the past a 1 kHz tone was commonly specified, but, as can be seen in Figure 11.3, this part of the sensitivity/bias curve is rather flat, making the optimum bias point at about 1 dB over-bias very difficult to determine accurately. If a higher-frequency tone is used, such as 10 kHz, the curve at the optimum bias is much steeper, making accurate adjustment far easier. It is now common to adjust recorders to around 3 dB over-bias, using tones of 20 kHz at a speed of 30 ips, 10 kHz at 15 ips, or 5 kHz at 7½ ips. However, it is wise to consult the recommendations of the tape manufacturer as over-bias settings can vary considerably depending on the type of tape and the record head gap, particularly when using high-level formulations.

Equalization and calibration tapes

Equalization is the process of modifying the frequency response of the replay amplifier, with a corresponding alteration of the frequency response of the record amplifier, to obtain a flat overall frequency response. The purposes of equalization are twofold, first to match the frequency distribution of the recorded signal to the capabilities of the recording medium, and second to obtain the maximum signal-to-noise ratio.

Because the MOL, high-frequency saturation characteristics, and the noise spectrum are related to tape speed, different tape speeds are optimized by different equalization characteristics. In all cases, high frequencies are attenuated in the record process, so that the recorded fluxivity decreases with increasing frequency. In the replay process, high frequencies are boosted to compensate, the cut/boost effect being introduced at lower frequencies for lower tape speeds.

In addition, some systems boost low frequencies during the record process and cut them in the replay process, in order to reduce power-line hum problems during replay.

To enable pre-recorded tapes to be replayed with a flat frequency response, it has been essential to standardize the replay equalization for any given tape speed. Unfortunately, more than one standard is in common use for some tape speeds. The equalization is expressed in terms of a time constant given by the expression

$$t = \frac{1}{2\pi f}$$

where t = time constant in seconds, and f = the 3 dB transition frequency in Hz.

Table 11.4 and Figure 11.4 illustrate the standard replay time constants in common use for each tape speed.

In order to simplify the adjustment of the replay chain of a recorder to any desired standard, calibration tapes for each standard are available. Such

Table 11.4. Standard replay time constants

Tape speed (ips)	Time constant (µs)	Standard
30	17.5	AES, IEC 2
30	35	IEC 1
15	35	IEC 1, CCIR, DIN
15	50 + 3180	IEC 2, NAB
7½	70	IEC 1, CCIR, DIN studio
7½	50 + 3180	IEC 2, NAB, DIN home
7½	50	NAB cartridge
3¾	90 + 3180	IEC, NAB, DIN
1⅞	90 + 3180	IEC, NAB, DIN
1⅞	120 + 3180	Cassette (ferric oxide)
1⅞	70 + 3180	Cassette (chrome & metal)

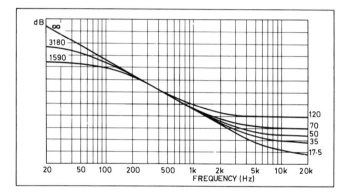

Fig. 11.4. Replay characteristics for some of the standards in use

tapes contain recordings of a series of tones at a constant level for adjusting the replay chain to a flat frequency response. The frequencies of these tones are typically 31.5 Hz, 40 Hz, 63 Hz, 125 Hz, 250 Hz, 500 Hz, 1 kHz, 2 kHz, 4 kHz, 6.3 kHz, 8 kHz, 10 kHz, 12.5 kHz, 14 kHz, 16 kHz, 18 kHz, and 20 kHz for professional recorders.

In addition to these tones, calibration tapes have a standard reference level section and an azimuth alignment section. The standard-level section contains a mid-frequency recording at a specified fluxivity for aligning the metering on recorders and setting Dolby level where a Dolby noise reduction system is to be used. In European calibration tapes, the level section is a 1 kHz tone at a fluxivity of 320 nWb/m as measured by the open-circuit method, whilst American calibration tapes commonly contain a level section of 400 Hz, 700 Hz, or 1 kHz tone, typically at a flexivity of 185 nWb/m as measured by the short-circuit method.

This fluxivity is also known as 'Ampex Operating Level' and 'Dolby Level', and corresponds to 200 nWb/m when measured by the European open-circuit method. Other fluxivities may be encountered, and the most common of these are listed in Table 11.5.

Table 11.5. Common tape fluxivities

European fluxivity	USA fluxivity	Notes
510 nWb/m	470 nWb/m	Stereo format
320 nWb/m	295 nWb/m	30, 15, & 7½ ips
280 nWb/m	260 nWb/m	Elevated operating level
250 nWb/m	230 nWb/m	3¾, 1⅞ ips, & cassette
200 nWb/m	185 nWb/m	Dolby/Ampex level
160 nWb/m	150 nWb/m	Cassette

The purpose of the azimuth alignment section is to set the vertical gap in the replay head at precisely 90° to the edge of the tape. Reference to Figure 11.5 shows that an azimuth error loss takes the form of a (sin x)/x plot, having a series of peaks at high frequencies. As azimuth alignment is carried out by moving the head to obtain maximum output, it would be easy to align a recorder accidentally to one of these peaks instead of to the correct optimum. This difficulty is overcome by the fact that the azimuth

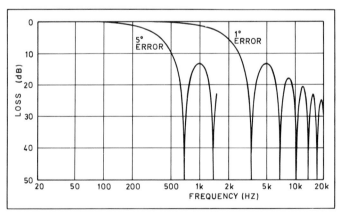

Fig. 11.5. Azimuth error for a 15 ips full-track tape

alignment section has a period of medium-frequency tone followed by a period of high-frequency tone. The recorder is first aligned using the medium-frequency, where severe azimuth errors are readily visible, and then by using the high-frequency section.

Tape recorder mechanics

At first sight, the recorder has only a small number of simple tasks to perform: to unwind the tape from a supply reel, pass it over the heads at constant speed with good alignment and head-to-tape contact, and then rewind the tape on to a second 'take-up' reel. Unfortunately, tape has a will of its own. Rather like one of those flexible steel tape-measures, if it is bent through an angle it tries to go in all sorts of odd directions. Furthermore, the tape is elastic and is easily stretched; wind it too loose on the reel and it forms concertina sections, wind it too tight and it permanently distorts.

As a consequence, the recorder has to provide accurate and consistent tension control at all tape speeds—which immediately implies difficulties in moving the tape at a constant speed. The fact that tape is unwilling to travel in a straight horizontal line while being led round bends means that the edges of the tape must be guided, particularly near the heads, where azimuth errors must be minimal.

Figure 11.6 shows the typical layout of a reel-to-reel machine. The tape is pulled continuously from the left-hand supply reel and passes over a spring-loaded arm before travelling to a roller, which may be a rotating guide having an inset slot of just over the maximum permitted tape width. To the right of the machine, a similar arrangement is used prior to the take-up reel, whilst the erase, record, and replay heads are grouped at the centre. This

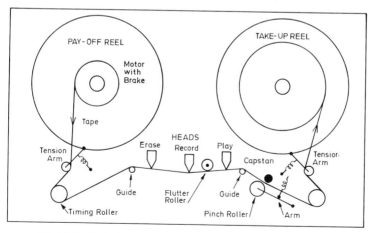

Fig. 11.6. Typical mechanical layout of a reel-to-reel tape recorder

area commonly incorporates further tape-edge guides, which may be fixed steel posts with slots, again of just over the maximum permitted tape width.

The reels are usually driven directly by motors with solenoid-operated band brakes fitted to the motor shafts, the brakes being operational only when the tape motion has stopped. In less expensive machines, the motors may be a.c. driven so that they operate at constant torque rather than at constant tension. In this case the spring-loaded arms simply damp tape movement during acceleration and deceleration. More advanced machines use servo-controlled reel motors, with the spring-loaded arms fitted with tape tension sensors, and thus run at constant tape tension (see Plate 13). A further advantage of the use of servo control is that the tape tension is much better controlled during fast winding. Also, the fast winding speed can be held constant throughout a reel.

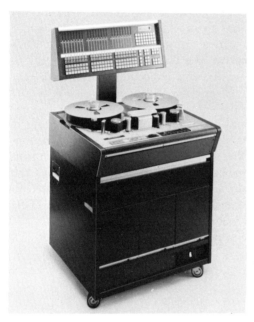

Plate 13. 24-track analogue tape recorder (Photo: Stüder)

In simple machines the roller guides may act solely as guides, or possibly drive a tachometer disc to activate the tape time counter. However, more sophisticated machines have a separate roller guide which monitors the tape velocity and relays this information to the servo control microprocessor, which may also be fed with spool rotational speed to derive control information. This information may be used to activate regenerative braking of the reel motors during auto-locate functions, control tape tension during acceleration, and so on.

Most machines control tape movement in the record and replay modes by means of a capstan against which the tape is held by a pinch roller which is itself mounted on a solenoid-operated arm. The capstan forms part of the capstan motor shaft, and may be made from steel or ceramic. A ceramic capstan has the advantage that it does not wear, but it can be more readily broken than a steel capstan.

Capstan motors in inexpensive machines are a.c. driven and are locked to the power line frequency, but more expensive machines frequently use d.c. servo motors fitted with a tachometer. These motors are phase-locked to a crystal-controlled reference frequency and may thus be driven at very accurate speeds irrespective of the power line frequency. In addition, such systems may be phase-locked to an external reference, permitting several machines to be accurately synchronized with each other.

Pinch rollers are typically made from an elastic material mounted on a metal core within which is a self-aligning ball-bearing which fits on to a spigot at one end of the pinch roller arm. High-quality machines use a cast-alloy arm hinged on a sleeve-bearing near its centre. At the far end of the arm, the pinch roller pressure is controlled by an adjustable spring which is tensioned by the pinch roller solenoid. The solenoid is engaged by passing a high current through its coil, the current being reduced once the roller has locked into its operating position to reduce heat dissipation in the solenoid coil.

Within the head area, the heads and guides may take the form of a plug-in subassembly (see Plate 36, page 462) or may be mounted directly on the recorder's chassis. In either case the heads should be firmly mounted whilst having provision for three mechanical adjustments: height, zenith, and azimuth. The zenith is adjusted so that the front surface of the heads is at 90° to the tape transport surface, the height so that the tape passes correctly in relation to the head pole-pieces, and the azimuth so that the tape edge passes at 90° to the vertical head gaps. The head pole-pieces may be manufactured from metal or from ferrite. The latter is more expensive but is almost immune from wear caused by the abrasive nature of the tape—iron oxide is used by jewellers for polishing in the form of jeweller's rouge!

Some machines also have a free roller just touching the tape in the head area. This is known as a flutter roller, and its function is to damp longitudinal vibrations set up in the tape because of its elastic nature.

The accurate passage of the tape over the heads relies on a mechanically stable tape transport. Therefore the more sophisticated recorders are based on a ribbed alloy casting, and not bent sheet metal as in cheaper machines. Such a casting can be precision-machined with reference faces to ensure accurate alignment to all the tape transport components, thus providing an extremely accurate and stable tape transport overall.

Whilst long-term tape speed variations depend upon the stability of the capstan motor, short-term fluctuations in the form of wow and flutter also depend upon accurate tape tension control and the precision of all rotating components in the tape path.

Tape recorder electronics

The electronics of any analogue recorder can be divided into three separate sections: the record amplifier, the replay amplifier, and the bias/erase oscillator. In multitrack machines, the record and replay electronics will be duplicated for each extra track, but there will usually be a single bias/erase oscillator, both for economy and to avoid frequency-beating between separate oscillators.

Figure 11.7 shows the block diagram of a simple professional recorder's audio section. The audio signal input is typically balanced with respect to earth to minimize the introduction of mains or radio frequency interference in the input cables. The signal circuit is then unbalanced and may be fed to some form of low-pass filtering to reduce the risks of radio frequency interference even further. A variable gain control is then included, allowing the input level to the recorder to be adjusted to match the output level for the given tape.

The signal is then subjected to equalization, as already discussed. The

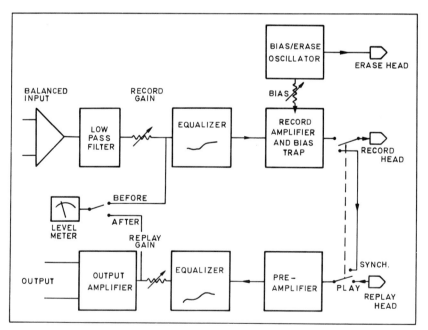

Fig. 11.7. Block diagram of the electronics in a typical recorder

equalizer section will have a high-frequency control to set the required high-frequency boost and may also, in the case of NAB equalization where a low-frequency time constant is used, have a low-frequency equalizer control. More sophisticated recorders include further equalizer networks operating at high to mid-frequencies to obtain an extremely flat frequency response, and may also include a control to compensate for phase shift in the record amplifier.

After equalization, the audio signal is mixed with the pre-set variable level of high-frequency bias before it is fed at constant current to the record head. Within this 'mixing' section is a bias trap to prevent the high-frequency bias from being fed back into the record electronics. This bias trap usually takes the form of an adjustable tuned circuit. The bias oscillator performs two functions. It generates the high-frequency bias signal, of course, but it also provides a high-frequency signal to drive the erase head(s). Multi-channel machines will often have separate amplifiers and tuning controls for each track. An important features of the bias/erase oscillator is that it must have minimal even-order harmonic distortion, because even harmonics magnetize the record head and increase tape noise. Also, to avoid problems with beating, the bias frequency should be at least five times the highest audio frequency.

Within the replay chain, the low-level signal from the replay head is fed to a pre-amplifier. This may be separate from the main audio electronics so that short leads can be used from the heads to avoid pick-up of interference. There follows the high and low-frequency replay equalization, which normally involves two adjustments with a further control allowing the replay gain to be set.

The final audio output may be balanced or unbalanced. Level metering is switchable between the input (after gain adjustment) and the output. Such switching may be manual or automatic, whereby the input is automatically monitored in the record mode and the output in the replay mode.

In multitrack machines it must be possible to monitor the signal from the tape at the same physical position as the record head, so that a new track may be laid in precise synchronization with any tracks already recorded. For instance, a vocal track may be laid in sync with a backing track. This mode of recorder operation is known as the sync mode and clearly requires that individual tracks of the record head can be switched to act as replay heads. On older machines this used to produce a degraded replay signal because record heads usually have wider gaps than replay heads (less high-frequency resolution) and the head design is different. Furthermore, in many machines the heads were simply switched to the standard replay electronics so that no special equalization was provided for the sync mode. In modern machines, however, there is frequently only a small difference in quality between the sync and standard replay signals.

With separate sync level and EQ almost universally provided, any signal difference can be almost ignored.

Machine alignment

The alignment of recorders may be discussed under two headings, the mechanical alignment and the alignment of the record/replay electronics. The mechanical aspects must always be properly attended to before any attempt is made to perform the audio signal alignment.

First the machine must be thoroughly cleaned, paying particular attention to the heads and the tape guides. Deposits of the magnetic tape coating can usually be removed safely using cotton buds dampened with isopropyl alcohol, or products designed for computer disc maintenance. The use of other types of solvent may cause damage to the recorder or leave undesirable deposits; therefore the recorder manufacturer's recommendations should be strictly followed.

The next action is to demagnetize all metal components in the tape path, because magnetized surfaces will introduce excessive tape noise and possibly damage existing recordings. This demagnetizing should be done with a unit specifically designed for the purpose. Many of these have metal tips which should be wrapped in a soft covering such as adhesive tape before use, so that they do not create damage if they are brought into direct contact with the tape heads.

The demagnetizer should be switched on while it is a metre or so away from the recorder, and then passed slowly across all metal parts in the tape path before being slowly removed from the recorder and then switched off. Occasionally it may be very difficult to demagnetize ferrite heads. If the head block is removable, then the heads can be properly demagnetized by using a bulk eraser.

Following this demagnetizing procedure, the machine should be loaded with an unused tape and run in the play and fast-wind modes, while one is carefully observing the tape at the reels and guides. If the tape touches the surface of the reels or is seen to ripple at the heads or guides, it is probable that mechanical alignment is needed. Similarly, if starting or stopping gives erratic tape movement, the reel brakes or pinch roller may need adjustment; the recorder manufacturer's instructions should be followed in detail. If higher than usual wow and flutter figures are observed, this will also reveal the need to adjust the pinch roller mechanism.

Where the reel motors are electronically controlled, or the capstan is servo-controlled, adjustment of the controls in the electronics may be necessary. Again the recorder manufacturer's instructions should be followed, as the procedures vary widely from one recorder to another. Whilst some manufacturers suggest the use of spring scales for measuring tape tension, this is not a very satisfactory method and dynamic measurement using a Tentelometer™ is to be preferred.

Once satisfied that the mechanical performance is in order, the machine should be set to its lowest operating speed (or the speed to be used if time is short) and a suitable calibration tape loaded for alignment of the azimuth of the replay head. Accurate alignment in multitrack machines requires the use of a dual-trace oscilloscope or a phase meter to observe the alignment of the waveforms from the tracks at the two tape edges. The mid-frequency azimuth section of the calibration tape is first replayed, and the replay head azimuth adjusted for maximum output or exact phase alignment of the two output signals. This procedure is then repeated for the high-frequency alignment section of the tape.

Following this azimuth adjustment, the reference level section of the calibration tape is replayed and the replay gain control set for the desired output level. At this stage the metering in the replay mode should also be adjusted for correct indication of the desired setting. In the case of VU meters, the zero VU indication should normally be set to correspond to between 8 and 10 dB below the 3 per cent third harmonic distortion point for the tape type in use. In the case of peak indicating meters, such as the BBC-type PPM (peak programme meter), the peak indication (PPM 6) should correspond to the 3 per cent distortion point. Some organizations have their own internal standard for metering, to preserve compatibility between the levels of different tapes, but the above settings allow the maximum capabilities of particular tape types to be used.

Normally the next band on the calibration tape is the frequency response section, starting with a mid-frequency section of tone at the prescribed level and followed by short sections at other frequencies starting at the low frequency end. These tones are usually at 10 dB or more below the reference level to keep clear of saturation risks at the boosted end of the equalization curve.

Most calibration tapes are recorded across the full width of the tape. This will lead to quite large errors in apparent frequency response at low frequencies due to fringing at the replay head pole-pieces, but only minor errors at mid-frequencies (less than 1 dB at 1 kHz), which may generally be ignored. These errors depend upon the recorded wavelength and are therefore larger at high tape speeds. Furthermore, the errors depend upon the particular pole-piece design of the head and the contour effect, which gives ripples in the low-frequency response.

Unless one is familiar with these errors, or has access to a calibration tape pre-recorded for the track format in use, it is better to align the low-frequency replay equalizer using the record/replay process. An alternative is to use a flux loop, which is a wire loop placed in contact with the replay head and driven by an oscillator; but such devices are not commonly used in studios.

Having noted the machine's output level for the mid-frequency tone (often 1 kHz), the high-frequency sections of the calibration tape are then replayed and the high-frequency equalizer(s) adjusted for optimum frequency response. These procedures are repeated for all tracks at all the available tape speeds (or the speed about to be used) before setting about the record channel(s) alignment. As has been explained, the high-frequency bias level affects many parameters, so this is the first adjustment to be made. Bias is set while recording and replaying a high-frequency tone at a level well below tape saturation (and also well above tape and machine noise to avoid spurious bias pick-up in the outputs). A level 20 dB below the reference level is normally suitable. (Where separate sync replay amplifiers are fitted, they are aligned using the calibration tape in the same manner as for the normal replay chain.)

Whilst recording and replaying the desired high-frequency audio signal, the output of the replay channel is monitored on the meter and the bias is gradually increased from some low value until the output reaches a peak and begins to fall. The bias is then decreased until the peak output again falls, and is finally set to the desired amount of over-bias. This will typically be about 3 dB under the conditions listed in Table 11.6.

Table 11.6. Common conditions for 3 dB over-bias

Tape speed (ips)	Frequency (kHz)
30	20
15	10
7½	5

After the bias has been set for all channels at all tape speeds, the record equalization is adjusted for the optimum frequency response by sweeping the frequency of an oscillator applied to the input. Low-frequency record equalizers are not usually fitted, but the low-frequency equalizer in the replay channels may be set for optimum low-frequency response at this stage, whilst the record high-frequency equalizers are adjusted for the optimum high-frequency response.

The final adjustments in the record channels are to set the record gain controls so that the input levels match the output levels, and to set the metering so that the indication when monitoring the inputs to the recorder matches the indication when monitoring the outputs.

Digital control: increased options

When treated with care and properly maintained, a tape recorder can continue to work to its original specification for many years. However, significant changes have taken place in analogue tape recorder design in recent years to improve the performance in all operational aspects, possibly spurred on by the increasing practical competition from digital recording systems (as discussed in the next chapter). Some modern machines have developed far beyond the basic principles described earlier in this chapter.

The use of microprocessors has extended digital control over a wide range of tape recorder functions, from the relatively simple control of direction, speed, and varying tape tension to the optimization of transport control to allow very fast tape handling but with increased care for the tape. For example considerable stress can be placed upon the tape when play is selected and the rotating capstan comes into contact with a stationary tape/pinch wheel and is dragged up to play speed. Microprocessor control can allow the capstan to be brought into contact with the tape only after the reel motors have taken the tape up to the required play speed. However, so as not to increase the time taken to reach a stable play speed, the microprocessor will temporarily modify the power supplied to the reel motors on the play command to achieve the required acceleration ramp to reach full speed quickly but without overshooting it.

Many machines now offer user programmable transport controls and although these are frequently manufacturer specific, features such as reverse play, varispeed selection in musical semitones or percentage change, and user-settable function sequences are available to help the tape machine adjust to the intended application.

Multiple tape position location points can be selected and memorized, and specific instructions given as to machine functions at those points. Aside from simple shuttling between sections of a tape during the mixing process, some machines allow automation of the process of replacing part of a recorded track. Traditionally this has been performed manually by entering (dropping in) the record mode on the intended track at the correct time and then 'dropping out' of record at the end of the insert. However if the drop-in and drop-out points are very close to recorded material on the same track that needs to be kept, there is a strong chance that during repeated attempts (for artistic reasons) a timing error may be made by the operator, causing damage to the already existing recording. Under microprocessor control, the tape recorder can be programmed to perform this operation automatically, even with the addition of a rehearse mode.

However, perhaps the greatest advantage of microprocessor control has been the automation of the electronics alignment procedures. One industry source calculated that a 24-track tape recorder needing alignment of four tape speeds, two equalizations, two tape formulations, and the noise reduction interface will require nearly 2,500 adjustments. In its simplest form the tape machine has an alignment panel with blocks of key buttons and an LCD display. The operator then sets the required control parameters—many may be copied from track to track—until the alignment is complete. The resultant settings from this process are stored in the machine's memory and the appropriate values loaded as required. A change in the type of recording tape to be used requires just a simple master button selection to install the correct set of alignment parameters. While the initial set-up procedure may be almost as long as the manual process, subsequent operations are far quicker.

Even more convenient is the fully automated alignment system. In this case the operator enters the desired values for the range of parameters and loads the replay alignment tape, and the machine takes over and automatically aligns itself to the set parameter values.

Interfaces

The use of microprocessors and digital control has allowed the control of the tape machine to become far more integrated into the total studio system. At one level this may mean that the recorder is operated under the machine control system of the mixing console. This means that the operator can begin to think of the studio as more of a single entity for the purpose of his work rather than separate machines.

Many tape machines are now fitted with both parallel (for remote control) and serial interface (RS232/422) ports to allow this type of interfacing to take place. One immediate benefit is the greater ease with which tape recorders may now be synchronized to one another, to a master system, or, with the increasing demand for better-quality audio in film and television production, to a video tape recorder. In the pressured business of video post-production many audio tape recorders can be equipped so that they may be operated under the control of the video editor through the video control system. To achieve this the tape recorder has to act like a video recorder through the use of an emulation system. In many of the more sophisticated tape recorders operating under programmable software control, the limits of the future application of these interfaces has been left purposely open-ended with the manufacturers suggesting that they will adjust the internal software to meet industry needs.

Formats

Improvements in tape, head design, and noise reduction systems has led to a profusion of analogue tape formats in recent years. Much of the professional recording industry remains standardized on the 24-track/2-inch format. Greater track requirements have been met by running a pair of 24-track machines in synchronization to achieve 46-track capability, one track on each machine being sacrificed for the SMPTE timecode required by the synchronizer.

At the less expensive end of the range, formats have been developed based on very narrow track widths, achieving up to 8 tracks on a single ¼-inch width tape. Audio quality is maintained only through the use of a built-in noise reduction system such as dbx or Dolby C. Such narrow tracks also preclude the use of some multitrack recording techniques which are standard on larger track widths. While not meeting professional standards in quality, the end result of material recorded on such machines can be quite acceptable in skilled hands provided that the limitations of the format are kept in mind.

In situations where quality is important but the user cannot justify the cost of fully professional standard tape recorders, machines based around 8 tracks per ½ inch of tape width (8 on ½ and 16 on 1 inch) can produce excellent results. However, the user should make certain that the normally lighter construction of such machines will be robust enough to meet the nature of the work load intended. That said, these machines, together with a 24-track/1-inch format using Dolby S noise reduction, have proved satisfactory in professional applications. Table 11.7 lists the main track formats found in professional sound recording.

The digital competition

It is inevitable that, at some point in the future, digital will be the standard form of recording. Significant advances have helped analogue tape recording maintain a strong position, even in the very area where digital can excel—low noise. The introduction of the Spectral Recording process (SR) by Dolby Laboratories (see Chapter 9) has led to substantial improvements in achievable dynamic range using standard analogue tape recorders and tape—arguably in excess of the abilities of 16-bit PCM digital encoding.

For users who prefer to work without noise reduction systems of any type, the development of a new generation of recording tapes has removed many of the earlier limitations. While these new tapes show improvements in most physical parameters, it is the level handling ability gained from the use of new ferric oxide formulations that is of most benefit. Operating levels such as +9 dB with reference to 320 nWb/m are possible, thereby reducing any tape noise to very low levels. Alternatively the user may opt to maintain the standard operating level and enjoy the benefits of more headroom.

With analogue recording still showing an ability to develop higher perfor-

Table 11.7. Track formats used for professional audio recording over the past ten years

(Does not include cassette systems, magnetic film stock, or obsolete formats)

Tape width	Tracks	Notes
0.25 inch	1	Full-track using the complete width of the tape
	2	May be either two independent channels or stereo—some machines with differing track widths
	2 + TC	Standard twin-channel format but with addition of third cue track between audio tracks, normally used for SMPTE timecode signal
	4	Four independent parallel tacks
	8	Eight independent parallel tracks—early machines used a pair of offset four-track heads
0.5 inch	2	Normally a stereo mastering format
	2 + TC	Standard twin-channel format but with addition of third cue track between audio tracks, normally used for SMPTE timecode signal
	4	Four independent parallel tracks
	8	Eight independent parallel tracks
	16	Sixteen independent parallel tracks
1 inch	8	Eight independent parallel tracks
	16	Sixteen independent parallel tracks
	24	Twenty-four independent parallel tracks
2 inch	16	Sixteen independent parallel tracks
	24	Twenty-four independent parallel tracks
	32	Thirty-two independent parallel tracks
	40	Forty independent parallel tracks—US manufacturer's proprietary standard

mance standards and greater flexibility of operation, it is difficult to say just how much longer there will be a thriving analogue presence in professional recording. As long as there is a need for a simple recording system which produces good results, it seems logical to suggest that it may be the next century before digital recording will show a clear advantage over analogue in every professional audio application.

12 Digital Recorders

Keith Spencer-Allen

One of the accepted benefits of analogue recording has been the stability and universality of the recording formats and standards. It is possible to find compatible machines for the mainstream formats anywhere in the world. Further, those same formats have changed very little over the last twenty years in the case of multitrack recording and far longer in the case of stereo. Even if the format is not a precise match, there is every likelihood that, provided the tape width is the same, something audible can be extracted from the recorded information.

Digital recording is not like that. There have been more formats in the fifteen years since digital recording products have been commercially available than in nearly sixty years of analogue tape recording. Once sound is converted into numbers there are hundreds of ways that those numbers can be arranged to be stored on tape. The tape can be open-reel or cassette type; the recording system stationary or rotary head. However, even if the physical format is the same, unless every other parameter is also matching, playing digital tape A on player B will result in little more than silence.

With a technology that is developing so fast, it is inevitable that there will be new ways of storing digital audio. Not just new but cheaper, faster, smaller, easier, and there is no reason for this progression to cease. So there is little chance of ever seeing the kind of standardization we had with analogue; but that may not be a bad thing as digital systems may become far better tailored for individual tasks than analogue could have been.

Early systems

In the cut and thrust of commercial marketing the word 'digital' is often purposely linked with anything from washing machines to cars in order to create an aura of perfection, of accuracy, and tomorrow's technology sneakily here today. While such practices may be exaggerations in the world of household goods, professional audio has lived with these terms in practice as digital technology evolved around it. While digital recording has now become a core technology in professional circles, early systems did not generate much empathy for those expressions—perfection (it is not), accurate (it may be, but I don't like the sound of it), and tomorrow's technology (it's not working yet!).

It is hardly surprising that the use of digital technology for audio in those early days gave rise to difficulties. There was little awareness of some of the technical and practical problems that the new technology was to pose for the designers and impose on the potential user. It was recognized that audio was very demanding of certain digital performance parameters and that, in several areas, it was pushing at the limits of what was then feasible in digital processing. Early systems were a compromise between cost and availability. First, the audio analogue-to-digital converters were limited in the number of digital bits that they could reliably output, though 16-bit was seen as a realistic target to aim for. Following Nyquist Theory the sampling rate needs to be greater than twice the highest audio frequency to be handled by the converter, but there were no standards. Assuming a sampling rate of 44 kHz, the necessary bandwidth required to store this data is greater than 700 kbit/s per channel and that is without error correction bits. So to store a stereo signal requires a medium on which it is possible to record and retrieve approximately two Megabits per second.

In the early digital systems therefore the recording medium was not one of choice but necessity. Computer hard-disc systems were a possibility; they could handle the data rate but did not then have the storage capacity needed for a suitable audio recording medium. Tape was also a possibility but the technology of the tape and heads then available could not deliver a sufficiently high recording density to handle the required data rate in a practical manner. The only way to achieve the high data rate would have been to run the tape at very high speeds, which is clearly impractical for many reasons.

However, the rotary helical scan tape system used in video recorders provided a possible solution. In these mechanisms both the heads and tape move. The heads are mounted on a drum and the tape is held wrapped around at least 180° of the perimeter. The drum then rotates at high speed, recording long diagonal tracks while the tape moves relatively slowly. In this way the head-to-tape speed is sufficient to achieve the necessary data rate for recording digital audio. Many of the first digital recording systems were therefore based around video recorders of varying types. Recording digital data on to a video recorder requires formatting the digital data into a signal resembling a video waveform, where the binary aspect of the data translates into black or white information. This is then recorded by the VTR as if it were a standard video signal.

It would appear that the first public demonstration of digital audio recording used a system developed by the NHK Technical Research Institute, Tokyo in 1967. The digital processing was 12-bit companded with a 30 kHz sampling frequency and the recording medium a one-inch, two-head helical scan VTR. The results were apparently much appreciated by those present but reports say that it was considered impractical to develop into a product at that time.

The next organizations working with digital recording were record companies who had the resources to build and develop their own systems. In 1972 Nippon Columbia (Denon) were using a digital recording system based around the NHK research (again recording on a VTR) in sessions intended for commercial release. Decca developed a recording system that used a variation upon VTR use. They bypassed the video section of an IVC one-inch helical scan deck, using its transport but designing their own electronics and editing system. Interestingly this allowed off-tape monitoring, or confidence monitoring as it is known in digital parlance, a feature which was not to appear in digital VTR-based systems until the four-head Sony DMR-4000 U-matic VTR appeared many years later, designed specifically for digital audio applications.

Commercially available systems started to appear in 1978. Sony launched the PCM-1 and PCM-1600 digital processors intended to be used with consumer and broadcast VTRs respectively. In the same year twelve major Japanese electronics companies agreed a format for PCM (Pulse Code Modulation) adaptors intended for use with domestic VTRs and this became known as the Electronics Industry Association of Japan (EIAJ) standard. All PCM adaptors for the consumer market that followed claimed allegiance to that standard but ranged from the essentially 12-bit PCM-1 to 14-bit systems from Japanese manufacturers such as Sharp, Technics, Sansui, Alpine, Akai, Pioneer, JVC, and Sony with varying degrees of sophistication.

Improved professional systems appeared in the form of the Sony PCM-1610 and JVC VP-900, all 16-bit and offering sampling rates of 44.1 kHz and 44.056 kHz. Both offered editing systems and were part of the intended mastering system for compact disc. The systems were not compatible and with CD manufacturing plants then specifying that masters should be in PCM-1610 format for acceptance into the mastering process, the Sony system became the format of choice (see Plate 14).

It was the arrival of the PCM-F1 (Plate 15) that brought the first 16-bit processing capability at a cost low enough for everyone interested to get a first experience of digital recording. Developed by Sony as a consumer product, it bypassed that market completely and, when partnered with the SLF1 portable Betamax VTR, it had a great effect on the location recording market. Some suggested that it sounded better than the PCM-1610 but such debates ended when Sony launched the PCM-1630 processor which, when used with a U-matic VTR, has generally remained the recommended standard for CD mastering.

While the use of PCM processors recording on VTRs worked well for

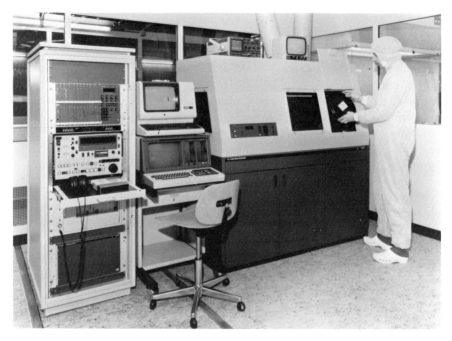

Plate 14. Digital mastering installation for compact disc tape-to-disc transfer stage, showing Sony 1610 digital audio recorder and U-matic tape unit on rack at left (Photo: Polygram)

Plate 15. PCM-F1 portable digital audio processor with AC power unit (Photo: Sony)

stereo recording, it was clearly not suitable for any form of multitrack recording. If finding storage capacity for stereo had been difficult, then a 24-track machine requiring data storage at 24 Mbit/s ruled out existing solutions. What was needed was something closer to a digital version of an analogue multitrack, where processing could happen on a track-by-track basis. And so, following developments in tape, heads, and electronics, 3M launched the Digital Mastering System (DMS) which comprised a 32-track/1-inch multitrack and 4-track/½-inch mastering machine. Whilst this was a significant achievement, it lacked the robustness of a proven technology and early users frequently paid a high price in frustration and down time until the basic machine problems were overcome. That having been completed, some are still in use today with a good sonic reputation.

Along with the digital learning process, and only a gradual move towards an agreement on standards, the early years have left a legacy of incompatible tapes. Few of these early systems are still in use today but it is worth considering the range of possibilities should you need to identify and replay a video based digital recording. Aside from the processors already mentioned, we should add the dbx 700, By The Numbers Collossus, and Denon; then the possible videotape formats, U-matic, Betamax, VHS, and 8 mm, all in either PAL or NTSC video format; a vast array of possible combinations.

Current systems overview

In a still rapidly evolving technology the term *current* can mean little more than 'at this moment in time'. Preferences and applications resulting from practical recording experience have now begun to shape the new generations of products. Although there is a tendency to look at digital recording as just a better replacement for analogue, in the longer term far more can be expected. This is happening already, with the emergence of digital storage formats other than tape.

In digital systems there is an irony. The most important component is the choice of storage medium, because that determines the capabilities of the recording system, yet that same choice has virtually no effect on sound quality provided it meets required technical parameters. Quality factors are determined elsewhere in the signal chain. Digital systems are therefore best looked at in terms of the storage medium used as, despite having different implementations, key elements in operation remain fixed.

Tape is still the predominant storage medium. Both rotary and stationary head systems are well established and have developed their own specific application areas. Large multitrack recorders are all stationary head whilst smaller multitracks, under 12-track, are largely rotary head. Stereo mastering recorders are either fixed or rotary head, although cost factors have led to a domination of the latter.

Disc systems are the most recent addition to the list of digital recording media. Almost all available disc systems were developed for the computer industry and storage capacities have increased to the point where they can be seriously considered as a digital audio recording medium. The most suited is the Winchester hard-disc drive, offering fast and reliable access to data recorded upon it. Recording times depend on disc capacity, with maximum current sizes allowing approximately three hours of mono audio. Stereo would reduce the recording time by 50% and four channels by a further 50%. Depending on the control systems used, four tracks is about the maximum that a single disc drive can be expected to handle without compromise in performance; so, for long record times and multiple tracks, several disc drives are required. Unlike tape, a disc drive does not record silence and therefore, if nothing is input on a particular track, no storage capacity is used and that storage is available for use elsewhere, giving a greater recording time than calculations might suggest.

While the problems of multitrack disc systems have largely been overcome by increased disc capacity and the use of multiple parallel drives, there still remains the up and down loading of data to the discs. A tape-based recording system allows the change of a reel or cassette within seconds, but the time taken to copy off and reload a full hour's worth of 24-channel audio on disc could be quite considerable, even with the fastest back-up media. The strength of hard disc systems is not as a simple recording system but using the non-linear storage medium to allow near-instant random access to any section of the audio; also the ability to edit non-destructively and, perhaps most important, to remove the concept of linear tracks and work in terms of outputs and audio events in time—all quite impossible on tape media. While disc has a role as a recording medium, it would be undervaluing its developing capabilities to view it as simply that.

Optical disc formats have also appeared and these come in a variety of formats mainly having either WORM or Magneto-Optical drives. The Write Once Read Many (WORM) disc has application where data is to be permanently stored, unchanged. Additional audio may be recorded until the disc is full but no erasure is possible. Suggested applications would be for the recording of incidental music tracks or sound effects where repeated access might be needed. The Magneto-Optical Disc (MOD) is closer in operation to the Winchester drive allowing repeated record and erase of digital data. It has the advantage of being mounted in a removable cartridge format so that loading and unloading is quick. The MOD drive does not possess the operating speed of a Winchester drive, and any system based around MOD has to accept certain operating limitations which vary according to the manufacturer's control system. A number of MOD systems have been introduced and they are largely being used for short-term recording/editing rather than as a dedicated recording system.

It would seem logical that in the longer term disc-based recording systems will become the norm, provided that the need for swift up and down load of multitrack audio programme can be solved, together with some form of agreed file exchange format so that editing and DSP abilities can be moved between systems of different make. It should be noted, however, that there are estimated to be over a hundred separate manufacturers in this field and moves towards co-operation even at simple levels are very slow.

Finally, when comparing tape and disc formats, we should note the main advantage of tape, its high storage capacity. A 48-track digital tape with a playing time of 60 minutes contains about 15,000 MBytes of data. This is well beyond a practical disc system and may remain so unless a different operational technique comes along. A few solid state Random Access Memory (RAM) recorders have appeared but the high cost of RAM chips has kept recording capacity down to minutes rather than hours. Such systems boast very fast operation and are more suited to editing applications, while their vulnerability to losing data in the case of mains power failure requires the addition of special power supplies and hard disc drives for back-up.

The arrival of the recordable compact disc provides another competing medium (Plate 16). CD-R is a 'record once' format on a blank 'pre-grooved' CD which uses a CD recorder to store two tracks of standard format CD audio. The recorded CD meets the 'Red Book' CD standard and can be played in any standard CD player. Record time depends upon the blank disc used but can be as much as 73 minutes. Some systems allow the writing of a temporary Table of Contents so that audio may be recorded in different sessions until the disc is full, rather than just in a single pass. Applications are varied but as some CD manufacturing plants have expressed a willingness to accept CD-R as a master for CD preparation, it may achieve wider use.

Plate 16. The CD Printer is a recordable CD unit forming part of a computer controlled CD mastering system (Photo: Sonic Solutions)

The tape formats

Despite the increasing number of digital tape formats, there has been a degree of rationalization. It is not possible to look at such developments without considering the impact of commercial pressures. Development of digital products is expensive and manufacturers are therefore keen to look for partners to assist in development and marketing. From the user's point of view, if you are investing a large sum of money on a digital product, you have more confidence when compatible systems are available from more than one manufacturer.

A number of such multi-vendor formats have appeared and, although the products are compatible, the various manufacturers within a format have tried hard to differentiate their own products by adding special features. So, although it is possible to look at formats in broad terms, there are often variations within those formats that are manufacturer dependent.

Stationary head formats

The characteristics of stationary head storage systems include:

1. Longer playing times as most systems use open-reel rather than cassette.
2. Cut-and-splice editing is frequently supported, although rarely used.
3. Generally bigger, heavier machines.
4. Design suits larger track formats.
5. Off-tape monitoring is easier to implement

There are three systems in current use (1994).

DASH: Digital Audio Stationary Head, a format developed primarily by Sony but supported by a large number of signatories (Plate 17). There is a complete family of possible machines within the proposals although only three are available: 2, 24, and 48 track. All machines use open-reel tape transports running ¼-inch tape on the 2-track and ½-inch on 24/48 machines, and are 16-bit with switchable sampling rates of 44.056, 44.1, and 48 kHz. On the multitracks, record time varies a small amount with the selected sampling rate but a 14-inch reel running at 44.1 kHz sampling rate gives 65 minutes. The 2-track runs at 15 in/s offering 1.5 hours recording time (the Sony PCM-3402 also has a DASH-S 7.5 in/s mode which translates into 208 minutes with a 12.5-inch reel at 44.1 kHz). Operationally DASH allows cut-and-splice editing, ±12.5% varispeed, two analogue tracks, and timecode track. While not part of the standard, most of the multitracks also carry RAM memory for sampling, editing, and moving sections of audio in time.

The DASH format was set up in the early 1980s and, aside from a revision in the 2-track format (to produce Double DASH, a more robust

Plate 17. 24/48-track DASH recorder (Photo: Stüder)

15 in/s standard meeting requirements for cut/splice editing using what was originally designated as a 4-track format), it has remained constant. One of the benefits of an integrated format is shown by the ability of the 48-track to take a recorded 24-track tape and not only replay it in full but also add a further 24 tracks.

Sony did experiment with a variation on their PCM-3402 2-track machine to allow 20-bit recording, by spreading the increased data over tracks previously used for error correction, to support cut-and-splice editing. Known as DASH-X, it is now used only for Sony's own record company work. DASH machines are produced by Sony (2, 24, and 48 track), Stüder (2, 24, and 48 track) and Teac (24 track).

ProDigi: Also known as Professional Digital or PD, is a family of proposed machines ranging from 2-track to 64-track. Prime developer was Mitsubishi who had introduced a 2-track (X-80) open-reel mastering machine in the early 1980s (not PD compatible) before developing the ProDigi format. Digital format is 16-bit with switchable sampling rates of 44.1/48 kHz applied as 2-track on ¼ inch (15 in/s), 16-track on ½ inch, and 32-track on 1-inch (30 in/s). A number of variations were developed on the X-86 2-track to allow playback of original X-80 tapes (X-86C), to allow 7.5 in/s operation for extended record time—up to 4 hours on a 14-inch reel (X-86LT), and the X-86HS, a standard X-86 with optional sampling rates of 96/88.2 kHz. This enabled a 30-kHz frequency bandwidth to be recorded on tape, with other claimed benefits.

The PD format supports cut-and-splice editing, two analogue tracks, timecode, and ±10% varispeed. Introduced in the mid-1980s, PD gained from the increasing interest in recording greater numbers of bits than 16, and allowed for up to 20-bit per recorded sample in the X-86 tape format. Although the machine is supplied only with 16-bit converters, external 18/20-bit systems enable recording of higher resolution to be made. Supporters of the PD format were Mitsubishi (2, 16, and 32 tracks), AEG-Telefunken (badged Mitsubishi) and Otari (32-track). However, the exact status of the format is at present unclear as Mitsubishi withdrew from manufacture of the machines in 1992, leaving Otari as the sole producer. There are significant numbers of the multitracks in use and continuation of the format seems likely.

Yamaha: In 1990 Yamaha launched an 8-track stationary head recording system using a proprietary cassette to house the tape. The format allowed sampling rates of 48, 44.1, and 32 kHz with corresponding changes in tape speed—at 48 kHz the tape has a running time of 20 minutes. Digital signals are stored on tape as 20-bit samples, which was unique in a multitrack format at that time. Varispeed capability was ±10% but there were no means of editing the tape and the recordings are not compatible with any other machine. The system is supplied in two forms—as part of a combined mixer/recorder (DRM8) and as a stand-alone unit. The format supports two analogue tracks and timecode making it possible to synchronize several of these units for larger track requirements.

Rotary head formats

The characteristics of rotary head storage systems are:

1. Systems can be more compact.
2. Tape is normally in cassette form and therefore more protected.
3. Record times are restricted by available cassette format.
4. May require more frequent mechanical alignment than stationary head.
5. May be less costly for the same number of tracks.
6. Requires electronic editing.
7. Stereo formats often cannot be used as two independent tracks—this is true for all systems recording on to video formats, and most R-DAT machines.

Sony PCM-1630: Although 'elderly' in digital terms, the 1630 is still recommended as the standard processor for CD mastering. It requires the use of a U-matic VTR as a storage medium and is normally partnered by digital audio optimized U-matic designs such as the DMR-2000 or DMR-4000. The basic format is 16-bit with switchable sampling rates of 44.1/44.056 kHz and record time is limited by the length of the U-matic cassette used. Editing requires the use of the Sony DAE-3000 digital editor. There is no room in the format for expanding beyond 16-bit and this will probably be the last tape-based CD mastering system available. Sony are looking at disc-based systems for this role in the future.

Akai DR1200: The first of the low-cost digital multitracks using Akai's ADAM 12-track recording format. The recording medium is a standard Video-8 cassette with a digital specification of 16-bit running at 44.1 or 48 kHz sampling rate. Recording time is limited to 17 minutes by the playing time of the cassette. There are no editing capabilities, nor is the system compatible with anything else. It is, however, easy to run two DR1200 units in sync under a single remote control.

ADAT: A format developed by Alesis recording 8 tracks on a standard S-VHS video cassette. Digital format is 16-bit with 48 kHz sampling rate, but may be varied by the user between 40.36 kHz and 50.85 kHz. Maximum playing time is 40 minutes. Encoded within the format is an Alesis synchronization interface allowing up to 16 ADAT systems to be run together. However, full control requires the use of the BRC control system, which also allows external equipment to address the ADAT system with standard SMPTE timecode. Editing capability is limited to assembly editing under the control of the BRC. Fostex have recently licensed ADAT technology and will be producing compatible systems, although with a different professional emphasis.

Teac Tascam DA-88: A format which shares much in concept with the ADAT system. DA-88 is an 8-track on a Hi-8 Video-8 cassette with switchable sample rates of 44.1/48 kHz. Record time is dependent upon the cassette used but a maximum of 114 minutes is available. Up to sixteen units may be synchronized by interconnection, although timecode has to be addressed through the remote controller. Editing is limited to assembly type editing. At present Teac are the only producers of this format.

Nagra D: A hybrid format which uses rotary heads but with an open-reel transport designed principally for film and TV production sound recording. Sampling rates can be 32, 44.1, or 48 kHz, while two or four tracks can be selected for recording on ¼-inch tape whose speed doubles when recording four tracks. Maximum record time is four hours with a 7-inch reel, 2-track. Uniquely the Nagra D format can record a 24-bit sample on tape and the format also supports analogue cue and timecode tracks.

DAT (sometimes called R-DAT): The shortened name commonly used for 'Rotary Head—Digital Audio Tape', a standard agreed upon as a consumer format in the late 1980s by a large number of manufacturers (Plate 18). It uses a very small rotary head and a DAT format 3.81 mm wide cassette tape which has a linear speed of 8.15 mm/s. The DAT standard has two manda-

Plate 18. Professional portable DAT recorder (Photo: Technics)

tory modes—16-bit record/playback at 44.1 and 48 kHz—and a further three optional modes, one of which is a four-channel format with 32 kHz sampling rate. Record time is up to 120 minutes depending on the cassette length used.

Early DAT machines intended for the consumer market were not able to record at 44.1 kHz, with the idea that this would prevent the consumer from making direct digital copies from a compact disc (also 44.1 kHz, 16-bit), which was something that concerned the record industry. Professional machines (or consumer machines with the 44.1 kHz inhibit defeated) were not limited in this manner. Subsequently this policy was changed and a system known as SCMS (Serial Copying Management System) was introduced. In this system the DAT recorder identifies a copyright flag in the data stream from the CD player digital output. The DAT recorder can make a recording of the digital signal with the copyright flag included but, should there then be an attempt to make a digital copy of the DAT copy, the recording DAT's SCMS system will identify the incoming copyright flag and refuse to enter record. The intention of SCMS is to allow the consumer to make a single digital copy of a CD but not to duplicate the copy. A machine intended for professional applications should not have SCMS as this will severely restrict its usefulness.

While being a relative failure in the consumer market, DAT was adopted with enthusiasm by many professional users. It was small, cheap, and of good enough quality for most applications. After the early use of modified consumer machines, there are now dedicated professional systems and machines with specific design applications. Most machines include methods of writing cues and other data in the subcode, while an increasing number also include SMPTE timecode. While limited to assembly editing for the first years of its existence, DAT now includes full editing systems which allow crossfades and greater control of edit points.

There is also an increasing use of DAT as a mastering format and this still raises some controversy. Some users have reservations about the format in terms of its robustness, longevity, and absolute quality capabilities. There were undoubtedly some problems in the early days and these were frequently tape related. Professionals now tend to fall into the pro or anti lobby—those who have found that DAT meets all their operational needs, perhaps with a second backup machine, and those who have had some catastrophic experience or find the format too limiting in quality terms. Whatever the majority feeling, DAT is now the accepted medium of digital audio exchange in so many areas that its continuation as a professional format is assured for years to come.

Advantages of digital recording

Digital recording (minimum 16-bit) offers significant advantages over analogue systems in many areas. The most obvious is the very low noise floor, there being no tape noise or other modulation effects. The dynamic range available is greater than in most analogue recording situations (although the use of Dolby SR processing can challenge that) with wow and flutter non-existent. Distortion is lower, provided the correct recording levels are observed. The frequency response is flatter than analogue, although the total bandwidth may or may not exceed that of analogue depending on the sampling rate used. Copies are theoretically identical to the original and there is no degradation.

There are disadvantages but these are generally correctable. Digital systems have an absolute upper level and exceeding that can create an unpleasant sound unlike the soft tape saturation of analogue. Higher resolution A/D converters are required to match analogue performance in all respects. The very short recorded wavelength can make digital tape far more susceptible to damage than analogue and tape editing is generally not so easy as with analogue. On balance, while there may be shortcomings in digital recording systems, they do offer advantages over analogue recording and this differential will surely increase as the technology develops.

Digital improvements

There is a general recognition that more bits is the important quality consideration at present. Manufacturers of stand-alone analogue-to-digital convertors are pushing at the upper limit of current technology which is probably about 19-bits despite wilder claims. A long-term aim is 24-bits, with an acceptance that this is probably as far as will ever be needed. Media capable of recording samples up to 24-bit are available although it will be many years before those capabilities are fully implemented.

Meanwhile there are considerable improvements to be made in existing products. Are those 16-bit converters really 16-bit output? Are there improvements to be made in digital filters? Can jitter (small timing errors) be reduced to allow better defined data and so reduce noise? Are there efficiency improvements to be made in digital design to allow improvement in the recording time possible on portable digital systems? The direction for progress is well established.

Interconnection

While it is quite possible to connect most digital devices via their analogue inputs and outputs, this should be avoided if possible. Connection in the analogue domain requires the digital signal to pass through a digital-to-analogue converter in the first device, into the analogue input of the second device and then through an analogue-to-digital converter to return to digital. The quality of converters used in most digital equipment has improved considerably in recent years but there will be an element of degradation and this will be increasingly more obvious with each conversion.

The back panel of most pieces of digital equipment will contain at least one digital interface connector. In some cases this might be to a proprietary standard such as used by Yamaha, Sony, and Mitsubishi for connection between some of their digital products. In cases such as this, the manufacturers can often supply interface systems which convert their format into a more widely available standard. The cost of such interfaces should be factored into the cost of any digital recording system. Some of these manufacturer standards (e.g. Sony) have found application on other producers' equipment and these may aid interconnection but, as with all interfaces, they should be checked before relying on them. Different *interpretations* of standards abound.

There are some universal, non-manufacturer standards whose use is to be encouraged (see also Chapters 3 and 8):

AES/EBU: A two-channel interface which can carry up to 20-bit audio data with sync and other information within the sub-frame format. Typical connector is a 3-pin XLR-type socket and interconnection can be standard twin screened, such as microphone cable. Cable lengths of up to 100 metres are acceptable for standard operation. There is a consumer version of this interface, SPDI-2 (Sony Philips Digital Interface) which has slight differences; some of the data format is used to indicate what product type the unit is, i.e. CD, DAT, PCM adaptor. The interface connection is normally an RCA phono socket and is unbalanced, restricting interconnect length. In some cases it may be possible to connect directly between AES/EBU and SPDI-2 although recommended practice is to use a converter.

MADI: In the late 1980s a group of interested manufacturers—Sony, Mitsubishi, Neve, and Solid State Logic—formed a committee to propose a standard for the interfacing of large numbers of digital channels. The resulting MADI (Multi-channel Audio Digital Interface) standard is now finding greater acceptance. MADI allows up to 56 channels of audio data to be transmitted down a single cable—co-axial or fibre optic. The digital format is similar to the AES/EBU and allows for 20- or 24-bit audio data in addition to the status bits and other data.

SDIF: A Sony interface (Sony Digital Interface) which has found wider use. There are several variations on the electrical interface and connectors used but the most common, SDIF-2, requires the use of a single cable per audio channel and can accept up to 20-bits.

A number of specific interface systems have also been developed such as Hilton Sound's PDASH which allow copying between DASH and PD format digital recorders, but it would seem logical that MADI will supersede the need for these.

Practical digital

Digital recording makes certain demands on the user. Since the medium is quieter than analogue tape, the removal of the masking effect of tape noise reveals problems that were not audible before. The rustle of clothing, creaky chairs, noisy air conditioning, and the mechanical noise of musical instruments becomes far more prominent. The choice of microphones may also change. Types that worked well with analogue sometimes just don't sound right when recording in digital. A resurgence in the use of ribbon types has taken place as many users have found them well suited to digital recording. Noise can also become more apparent from consoles and outboard gear. It is a gradual learning process which teaches the user to look at familiar equipment in a new way.

There are no specifications that need to be adhered to for monitoring digital audio, other than a clear understanding that monitoring requirements increase. Digital recording adds a complete usable octave below the frequency limits of analogue tape and, while you may not choose to use it, there is a need to be aware of what 'sonic garbage' there might be down there. Since the introduction of the compact disc, professionals have slowly realized that the listener at home may frequently be able to hear aspects of the recording not audible in the studio control room. The designers of earlier studio monitoring systems were perhaps too single-minded and the shortfall can be only too obvious. Much better monitors are now available but there is always a need to consider the possibility that the monitoring environment may not tell the complete truth.

One of the key benefits of digital recording equipment is the small amount of attention that it requires. The regular line-up procedures of analogue machines are no longer needed. Most manufacturers will make recommendations about servicing schedules but these require considerable resources and are probably best left to the manufacturer. Mechanical alignment of rotary head systems may be required with greater frequency to maintain performance but manufacturer guidance is again recommended. However, cleanliness of the machine is vital as the short recorded wavelengths make the tape very vulnerable to dirt, possibly causing severe dropouts. Many machines require the recording tape to be formatted prior to recording—both the timecode and control tracks. On some systems this can be done during the record process but only if the tape is to be run from beginning to end continuously.

Multitrack recorders are also easy to synchronize with each other, normally needing little more than the addition of a few cables. One point that should be noted is that digital systems frequently require a sample rate clock in addition to SMPTE timecode information. In a large system, as with a digital console, there should be a master clock with all connected systems locked to it. Such details are beyond the scope of this chapter and manufacturer recommended practice should be followed.

For all digital recording it is wise to consider the end application, when choosing the sampling rate. If recording music, then 44.1 kHz may be the wisest choice as this lines up with the CD standard. If the recording is to be used in a broadcast environment, then 48 kHz is to be preferred. The correct decision at this point can remove the need for subsequent sampling rate standards conversion which, while not a difficult process, is best avoided.

New recording techniques become possible with digital multitracks. With many DASH machines there is now onboard RAM—up to 40 seconds full resolution on some machines with the ability to divide it into one, two, or four channels. Signals can be loaded in from the tape with timecode data or from external analogue or digital sources. Once in memory, the signal can be edited and then laid back on tape manually where wanted, against timecode values, or from an external trigger, a switch or an audio sample such as a snare drum. The modular digital formats such as ADAT allow the user to select individual offsets between tracks and then additional offsets between synchronized machines.

There is increased freedom in the placement of tracks that would not have been possible in analogue. Stereo pairs can be placed anywhere on a machine without the potential for azimuth errors causing phase cancellation. With digital sample locked machines it is even possible to spread stereo over both machines and still have a totally stable phase coherent stereo image! There are no concerns about print-through or leakage from adjacent tracks and the edge tracks are just as usable as the centre tracks. However, any edge damage to the tape is far more critical than with analogue and so greater care has to be taken in tape handling with open-reel formats.

Some aspects of recording do need a new approach. The use of analogue tape saturation to create certain effects is of course lost and new recording techniques have to be devised. A major concern for those new to digital is the question of maximum recording levels. Unlike analogue there is a definite maximum record level and, although exceeding that level does not always produce the unpleasant effect we might expect, it is not recommended. Unfortunately there is no way of knowing what maximum level may be encountered in a live recording. It is therefore necessary to leave some headroom, but how much? This has to depend on the circumstances and one's experience with the equipment. Leaving too large a margin reduces the dynamic range available, as fewer of the available bits are utilized. Too little headroom and there is a danger of running out of bits.

Future developments

Two new consumer digital recording formats have appeared and, although there are no immediate professional applications for either, their technology does have some points in common with future professional directions. Both the Philips Digital Compact Cassette (DCC) and the Sony MiniDisc (see Plate 19) use data compression techniques to reduce the storage requirements. Put simply, data compression reduces the bit requirement for encoding the signal. Techniques for achieving this vary according to the system used but all involve some degree of psychoacoustic masking. The benefits can be a reduction in storage requirements of four times or more. The debate as to their audibility continues but some of the better systems seem to have potential for use in professional recording. Several hard disc systems are beginning to employ these techniques and this can dramatically increase the storage capacity.

However, there are grounds for concern about the use of data compression in recording formats which should by their nature be used to provide optimum quality. For broadcasting and data transmission, such techniques would appear to offer great advantages.

At the other end of the quality scale, there is a requirement for a new

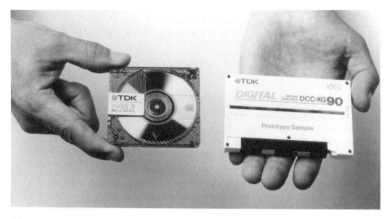

Plate 19. Comparing the MiniDisc (left) and the DCC cassette, two consumer digital formats launched in 1992 using data compression techniques (Photo: TDK Electronics)

mastering format to replace the ageing PCM-1630 system. DAT is sometimes used for CD mastering but, with increasing interest in greater resolution, there is a need for a format which can handle 20-bit samples. Neither DAT nor 1630 can accommodate this and Sony have introduced an optical disc-based machine known as the PCM-9000 (see Plate 26 in Chapter 20). This will store up to 80 minutes stereo at 20-bit/44.1 kHz and longer durations for 16-bit. There is also room within the format to meet future 24-bit requirements.

Developments within digital audio recording continue at a rapid pace and it will probably always be so. Just as there have been immense changes since the previous edition of this book, we may expect the same degree of change before the next.

13

Mobile recording units

John McErlean
(Revised by Malcolm Johnson)

The purpose of an integrated mobile recording unit fitted with all major items of sound control and recording equipment is to provide a comfortable, pleasing on-the-road version of a static control room. The main problem is to maximize facilities in a restricted space.

Mobiles range from simple panel van conversions, incorporating straight-to-stereo tape and/or line equipment, to purpose-designed high-specification articulated semi-trailers incorporating acoustic treatment, built-in multitrack and stereo recorders, computer-assisted control desk, and a host of peripheral equipment. Before commencing on esoteric and costly designs it is obvious that customer needs and aspirations, as well as the size of his budget, have to be evaluated.

The old carry-in idea with lots of portable units crammed into a panel van, manhandled into a venue, and connected together in a boxy backroom is still the cheapest method of providing mobile recording. However, this lacks not only creature comfort but also a repeatable defined environment, and is rarely satisfactory from an acoustic point of view.

Panel vans

Conversions of panel vans offer sensible solutions to the customer who does not require multitrack, environmental control, or lots of built-in equipment, but there is little that can be done to control the acoustic properties of the finished vehicle apart from some of the suggestions made here.

Vehicle shapes are subject to personal choice, but the choice of basic van should first be made on its physical dimensions, particularly the internal width and height. Few such vans have perpendicular sides, and a vehicle which has a maximum width dimension at control desk height has an obvious advantage in maximizing the size of the desk that can be installed. Internal height dimensions are critical for operating crew comfort; a vehicle in which a normal person cannot stand upright, at least in the central section, will be the source of constant frustration. It is recommended that an internal height of 2.2/2.3 m in an unmodified van will produce an adequate floor-to-ceiling dimension of 2.1 m in the central area of the fitted vehicle. Achieving this means obviously a high-top van with a metal rather than a fibre-glass roof to provide for strength, electrical screening, and the mounting of external fittings. Other factors which should influence the choice of vehicle are as follows.

Access doors

For safety, personnel access to the mixing area should be from the nearside or the rear of the van. The choice between a sliding or normal hinged door on the nearside depends on the vehicle manufacturer's options, but passing pedestrians may be somewhat surprised by a hinged door opening without warning. Door widths need to be great enough to allow installation of the control desk and other equipment.

Floor height

To allow easy ingress and egress, a low floor height is sensible, although the addition of a fold-down step in the vehicle skirt is usually straightforward for a reputable coachbuilder.

Spare wheel

Whilst the provision of a spare wheel is both normal and essential, the siting of the wheel can be a problem. It should ideally be stored externally, either under the floor or secured to a rear door to leave maximum internal space.

Van layout

The vehicle layout is dependent on its purpose, and by way of example only a stereo recording/broadcast van will be described (see Figure 13.1).

Although van dimensions preclude ideal stereo monitoring, placing the control desk either behind the front seats facing forwards or over the rear axle facing the rear can be satisfactory. Experience shows that the latter solution produces the best results. The control desk weight is borne by the rear suspension, providing a stable ride, and any vehicle wheel-arches can be 'lost' under the sides of the desk. The desk can be installed through the rear doors for ease of servicing. The area between the desk and the rear door can be covered with ribbed aluminium sheet for durability and to provide waterproof storage of cable drums and an undercover termination point for signal and power cables.

To increase the usable space in the van, the front seats can be changed to a rotating type which is lockable either in the normal driving position or facing into the vehicle. These seats can now provide work stations for producer and secretary. The remaining area of the vehicle can be used solely for technical furniture and personnel. Furniture built into the sides of the vehicle can house tape recorders, power control system, desk power supply,

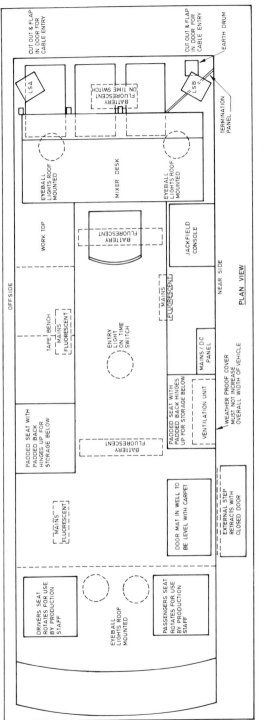

Fig. 13.1. Layout of a stereo recording/broadcasting panel van

technical battery and charger (if required), and other associated equipment. Although technical a.c. and d.c. power systems are covered later, it may be noted that any technical batteries included in the vehicle should be installed outside, and a sliding ventilated battery locker can be built into the vehicle skirt by a reputable coachbuilder.

Construction details

Before any furniture or wiring fitments are installed, various measures need to be taken to improve the basic van. The steel panels used to form the vehicle will resonate at low frequencies (this can be shown by striking the van walls with a clenched fist). All panels, including the roof and door as well as the walls, need to be damped with purpose-made self-adhesive sound deadening material. This material should be affixed off panel centre lines to avoid frequency-doubling effects. Although space inside the van is limited, it is suggested that a flat wall surface is produced, because the vehicle-structured ribs are never ideally positioned for attaching fitments.

After any additional structural members necessary to support heavy items have been welded on, the vehicle walls should be lined with 6–10 mm plywood, with the void between this and the vehicle skin filled with mineral wool (rockwool) to improve sound isolation. Once the required fixed cupboards and equipment bays are complete, the walls need a hard-wearing decorative finish; carpet is suggested for this, as its acoustic properties and type specification (which are covered later) offer benefits. Further trimming details for the ceiling can be a matter of taste, but an open-weave fabric over mineral wool will provide a resilient surface.

Purpose-designed vehicles

These fall into two categories, rigid and articulated. A 'rigid' vehicle is one where the driving cab, engine transmission, and payload area are all mounted on a single chassis. An 'articulated' vehicle is signified where a prime-mover, or tractor, draws a trailer either by a drawbar or by the well-known 'fifth wheel' close coupling used by normal heavy transport vehicles. Drawbar trailers are capable of being moved on their built-in axles, whilst a close-coupled trailer has axles at the rear only and is supported at the front by the tractor rear axle or, when uncoupled, by a pair of landing legs. This latter type is known as a semi-trailer and is most commonly used by the heavy transport industry. Each type has distinct features, and thought needs to be given to the choice.

In the UK, government regulations (particularly the Motor Vehicle (Construction and Use) Regulations) control and restrict the vehicle designer. For example, all vehicles are limited to a width of 2.5 m, rigid vehicles to a length of 11m, and articulated semi-trailers to a length of 16.5m including the tractor. These dimensions are maxima and include all bumpers, rub rails, clips, etc. It cannot be emphasized strongly enough that ignorance of the regulations could prove disastrous and that a copy should be obtained from Her Majesty's Stationery Office before the design commences.

Rigid vehicles are based on commercial truck or coach chassis, and bodybuilders' drawings, which give dimensional weight information, are available from the various vehicle manufacturers. These show the designer which parts of the vehicle need to be accessible for maintenance and help to identify areas which cannot be utilized without penalizing the access. Truck chassis, for instance, often have a tilt cab, which folds forward to give access to the engine and gearbox. The bodybuilders' drawings will show an arc of tilt which should not be obstructed.

Coach chassis, apart from having awkwardly placed mid or rear engines, have restricted axle weights which can easily be exceeded with the type of technical equipment and vehicle techniques described here. Apart from this, coach chassis can offer a low chassis height and softer suspension, which may prove advantageous. The solution to the low axle weight capability is, at the design stage, to calculate the axle loadings and to have an extra axle added (common practice at the rear, but an additional steering axle at the front is a specialist matter).

Articulated vehicles have several advantages which will become apparent later, but the main one is that the vehicle can be longer and heavier in terms of the UK Road Traffic Act. Also, once the standard dimensions for fifth-wheel coupling are taken into account, much greater freedom is available from the trailer format.

Weight calculation

As an aside, weight calculation is amongst the most important design routines. An overweight vehicle is both illegal and unsafe, whilst an insufficiently laden vehicle will transfer the suspension 'bounce' to the equipment within. The method of calculation used successfully by the writer is as follows, and is equally valid for all types of vehicle.

The vehicle manufacturer's data will show the gross vehicle weight, maximum permitted axle loadings, the unladen vehicle weight, and its axle distribution. The proposed vehicle body-weight should be calculated from the wall, roof, and floor areas and the density of each area. This weight can be considered borne equally by each axle (unless very obviously different) and added to the basic vehicle axle loadings.

The remainder obtained by deducting this sum from the gross weight of both the vehicle and each axle will show how much *maximum* payload is available. Great care must now be taken to compile a list of all items to be carried on the vehicle; not just the control desk and tape machines but also technical batteries, air-conditioning plant, furniture, cable reels, etc. (A cable reel with 50 m of multi-pair cable can weight 50 kg and ten of these amount to half a tonne!) By comparing items on this list and their respective positions to each axle, applied mathematics can be used to calculate moments about each axle, multiplying the distance from the axle by the item weight. It may be noted that an item located behind the rear axle will have a positive moment (i.e. loading) on the rear axle but a negative one (i.e. lifting) about the forward axle.

This mathematical process is rather tedious, and greatly aided by a microcomputer programme, but will highlight any glaring errors in axle and vehicle loading and will aid the basic vehicle chassis choice. However, if all the calculations show a gross vehicle weight of say 10 tonnes, do not be tempted to buy a 12-tonne GVW chassis, but instead choose a 14/16-tonne GVW one. This will provide not only a margin for error and some 'spare' capacity for future additions, but also ensure that the vehicle is not under-powered. Remember, few transport vehicles operate at 100 per cent gross vehicle weight for 100 per cent of their life. Unlike technical vehicles, they run empty occasionally; also remember the times you've cursed a struggling underpowered truck on a mild gradient.

Now, armed with an idea of how much things weigh and their effects—and having made a choice of favoured control desk, tape machines, and other technical equipment—the designer is ready to combine these and other vehicle-related systems into the desired finished mobile. Before considering the finer points of layout and finishes, vehicle-related systems must be considered. It is very important that the vehicle should 'sound' right, particularly at the mixing engineer and producer seating positions, and that everybody should feel comfortable within the vehicle no matter what the ambient conditions are outside. Also, power systems, termination panels, and storage areas need to be thought about. Accordingly, acoustic properties, air-conditioning, a.c. and d.c. power systems, and the provision of storage will now be discussed, in that order.

Acoustic design

Many learned papers have been written on acoustics relating to buildings but few have been specific on vehicles. The same principles can be applied, however, with attention to related detail on the two facets, insulation and response.

Insulation

Sound insulation, particularly at low frequencies, always presents a problem in vehicle design as the vehicle is subject to size and corresponding weight restrictions. As can be deduced from the above with regard to vehicle weights, the heavier the basic vehicle the less the payload that can be carried.

Sound insulation is dependent on wall surface density (mass per unit area), and, although a restriction of wall surface density increases the vehicle's payload, it also reduces the degree of sound insulation which can be achieved; also, the need to restrict wall thickness, thereby increasing the internal volume, precludes the use of a double-leaf construction. (The term 'wall' implies all vehicle surfaces including roof and floor.)

Wall construction

The wall construction chosen for a recent series of sound vehicles (see Figure 13.2) offers substantial improvements over previous vehicles. The construction is in a 'sandwich' form. The outer surface is 15 mm-thick glass-reinforced plastic-faced plywood followed by a 25 mm layer of mineral wool infill, a layer of heavy flexible material-loaded plastic on a fabric backing (barrier mat), a further 25 mm layer of mineral wool, and a 15 mm internal plywood wall. The internal wall is faced with sound absorbers and carpet. Structural strength is provided by horizontal and vertical aluminium 'top-hat' sections built into the sandwich.

The choice of mineral wool rather than rigid foam avoids the disadvantage of a dip in insulation which may occur in the mid-frequency range due to combined material resonance. The barrier mat provides a useful increase in mass per unit area without substantially adding to the wall thickness. This type of construction needs to be continuous around the operational area and any air-conditioning ductwork or air-handling unit situated outside the operational area.

Doors

External personnel doors are a particular problem, giving sound leakage paths which assume greater significance with the improved sound insulation given by the vehicle's wall construction. Double, or preferably triple, seals under moderate compression are necessary over the entire door perimeter. Door catches and locks should be chosen so that they do not interrupt or damage the seals.

Windows

Windows should be avoided, as not only do they take up valuable wall space and present a hard reflecting surface, but they are difficult to install while providing the necessary isolation. A small window in the door(s) is, however, a good idea for safety. This window (150 × 300 mm) can be constructed with a proprietary sealed double-glazed unit on the outside and an additional single-glazed pane flush with the inside face of the door.

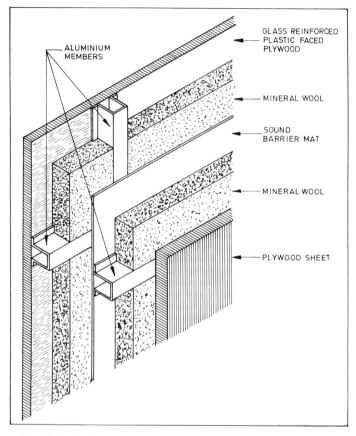

Fig. 13.2. Sandwich form of construction for a recording vehicle wall

To complete the sound insulation measures it should be ensured that vehicle skirt panels and any vehicle sub-panels are braced and adequately damped to prevent sympathetic vibrations from being conducted into the vehicle structure and thus into the interior. Also, any cable ducts should be adequately pugged with linen bags containing dry sand, other cables or pipes filled with mastic or similar material. As with static installations, the places where the acoustic skin is perforated should be minimized and chosen carefully. These combined measures have been used on recent high-specification vehicles and produce isolation figures of greater than 42 dB averaged between 100 Hz and 2.5 kHz.

Acoustic performance

For a mobile recording vehicle to be successful, the perceived sound inside, especially near the control desk where the mixing engineer and producer sit, must be closely controlled and designed to emulate the best that static control rooms can offer.

The physical dimensions inside even the largest mobile are very limited; the internal height is limited by the maximum overall height desired for the vehicle and the height of the chassis from the ground; the overall legal limit of width to 2.5 m reduces, with the acoustic isolation measures outlined above, to approximately 2.3 m; length is determined by which type of vehicle is chosen (rigid or articulated) and the chosen vehicle layout. This small enclosure size produces problems, particularly in the lower frequency ranges. Firstly, there is the effect of room modes (eigentones) which are more widely spaced than in larger static control rooms. The result is to make an overall acceptable characteristic difficult to achieve, due to variations in sound quality and reverberation time from place to place. Secondly, the space restrictions preclude the use of bulky low-frequency absorbers which would be effective in low-frequency control.

Another problem is that the monitoring loudspeakers are closer to the walls than in a static control room, and acoustic irregularities are caused by reflections from wall-mounted enclosures, such as cupboards, bays, and benches. Some of the problems can be minimized by placing a dividing wall across the operating area, effectively separating the interior into control and recording areas, and by expanding the width of the control area on site. These measures were taken some years ago in the design of the BBC's Digital Control Vehicle (see Plates 20 and 21), providing an amazing transformation of listening conditions compared with other vehicles in service at the time.

Also, extensive acoustic treatment on the walls and built into the ceiling will help control the listening conditions. Design reverberation times of 0.3 sec from 250 Hz upwards have been used for recent large mobiles. The acoustic treatment used has taken the form of low-frequency and all-band studio-style modular absorbers sited on the side and end walls (as well as on the ceiling) to control the eigentones effectively. The ceiling absorbers are unobtrusive, as they form part of an integrated design with air-conditioning ducts and grilles and electrical modules containing fluorescent and incandescent eyeball-type down-lights.

Wall-mounted absorbers have to be placed carefully, as reflections from the hard front panel can produce edgy or tinny sound quality. In a vehicle where walls and ceiling may be within one metre of the sound control position, it is necessary to place the absorbers where they will not cause specular reflections from the loudspeakers. Surfaces within the vehicle from

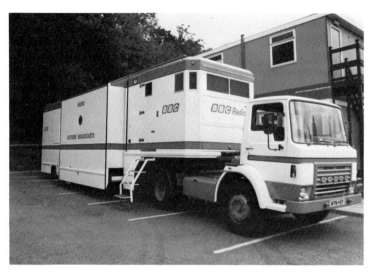

Plate 20. Digital recording vehicle, showing the expanding wall sections in the extended position (Photo: BBC)

Plate 21. Neve DSP digital console in the BBC vehicle shown in Plate 20 (Photo: BBC)

which troublesome specular reflection would occur need to be covered with a material having sound-absorbing characteristics which do not rely on 'averaging' between areas of high and low absorption. Conventional all-wool (or at least 80 per cent wool) Wilton carpet, without underlay, is used for this and has the advantages of being visually attractive and hard-wearing.

To mitigate the high-frequency reflections from the control desk, the ceiling area immediately over the desk should be covered with a long-haired shag-pile carpet. The floor needs to be covered with a hard-wearing robust covering, for obvious reasons, and a haircord carpet will suit whilst ensuring that the high-frequency response of the vehicle will not be too damped.

Following even this type of treatment, it has been found that the control area can still sound bass-heavy and that some limited monitor equalization is necessary. This appears best set up by ear initially using graphic equalizers, before a permanent equalizer is installed. A simple bass roll-off of 10 dB at 50 Hz on a 6 dB/octave curve, with two or three shallow notches at higher frequencies to reduce any sound colorations caused by specular reflections, is all that is usually required.

Monitoring loudspeakers are a matter of much argument and personal taste. The only point to be recommended is that, to achieve a stereo image which is good and stable, the speakers and listening position should form the classic equilateral triangle as far as possible. The loudspeakers should be placed close to the side walls (accepting the other problems of doing this). Special trapezoidal-shaped cabinets assist in this, and a version of the BBC-designed LS5/8 bi-amped loudspeaker was formulated especially for sound Outside Broadcast vehicles. Independent commercial loudspeaker designs have been similarly adapted.

Vehicle choice

Rigid vehicle chassis, even the specially designed ones used for fire-engines and the like, can still be restrictive. Articulated semi-trailers can overcome some of these limitations. One of the problems in use of a rigid vehicle is mechanical breakdown. If the tractor of an articulated unit fails, then, at least temporarily, another can be hired. Also, a replacement tractor can be used when the normal unit is in for maintenance.

In large organizations, with their own transport as well as electronic maintenance engineers, almost inevitably the transport engineers have the mobile placed over a pit before the electronic engineers arrive, on the rare occasions when the vehicle touches base. This often leads to the electronic equipment on a rigid vehicle leaving for its next show without equipment faults being rectified, whereas an artic can be simultaneously maintained.

Other advantages of the artic mentioned earlier, increased length and weight, can be significant in the provision of storage and creature comfort areas as well as permitting the weight penalties of acoustic isolation construction. Figures 13.3, 4, and 5 show layouts of mobiles based on truck, coach, and articulated trailer chassis respectively. The truck layout is of a workhorse mobile without multitrack, whereas the coach and artic both offer the concept of large automation-assisted consoles, multitrack, and stereo tape machines.

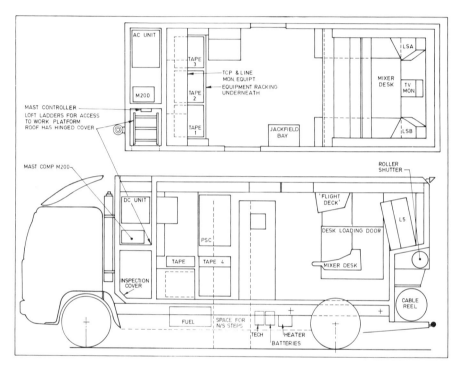

Fig. 13.3. Layout of a truck for sound recording

Figure 13.6 also shows an articulated vehicle, but a very special one, the BBC Digital Control Vehicle (see Plate 20). This vehicle houses a Neve DSP digital control desk (Plate 21), digital multitrack and stereo tape machines, and a BBC NICAM digital distribution system. This unique vehicle has a number of points of interest apart from the digital system. To provide an ideal working environment for the assessment of digital audio, the normal control room dimensions of a mobile were judged unsatisfactory in terms of volume. A novel system was evolved where the sides of the vehicle in the control room area were made to expand by 600 mm on each side (see Figure

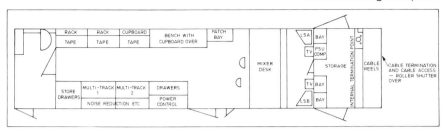

Fig. 13.4. Layout for a coach for sound recording

13.7) increasing the volume of the control area from 20 m³ to 30 m³. This was achieved on each side with a pair of hydraulic rams moving the complete side section, which was supported on seven slide mechanisms. Two continuous compression seals around each side, in both the retracted and expanded modes, ensured acoustic isolation. Figure 13.8 is a side view of the Digital Control Vehicle showing an acoustic separate area, constructed as a cab where all the processing equipment is housed, with only a pugged cable duct connecting into the control area. An isolation average of 62 dBA exists between the two areas. The same principle was used a few years later in the design of the BBC TV Master Sound Control Vehicle, where a separate isolated room was constructed to house the processing racks for the AMS Calrec assignable system used in that mobile.

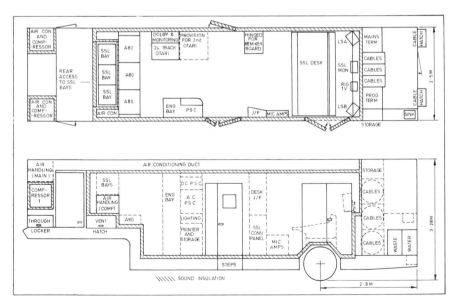

Fig. 13.5. Layout of an articulated trailer housing an automation-assisted control desk, multi-track recorders, etc.

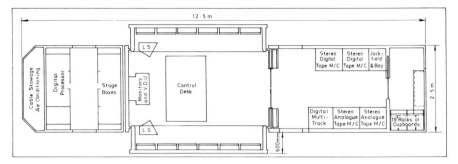

Fig. 13.6. The BBC's first all-digital control vehicle

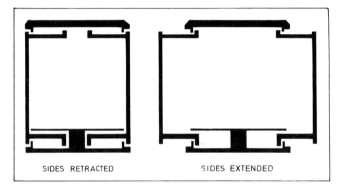

SIDES RETRACTED   SIDES EXTENDED

Fig. 13.7. Section through BBC digital vehicle, showing how the sides can be extended on location

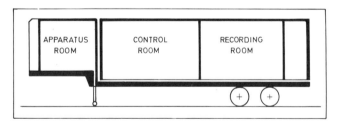

Fig. 13.8. Side view of BBC digital vehicle, showing how two separate acoustic areas have been built

Suspension

Technical equipment finds it difficult to survive the hard life of mobile recording, even when permanently installed in a vehicle. The vehicle suspension system is critical in providing a good 'ride', and it is recommended that an air suspension system is provided for the rear axle(s), particularly if the control desk is situated above. In fact, deliberately siting the control desk over an air-suspended rear axle is a good policy; the weight of the desk is borne by the suspension, where there is always the greatest load-carrying capacity, and a soft ride is provided. Tape machines are best installed so that accelerative shocks to the motors are taken vertically, not laterally, by the motor bearings. Also, the machines themselves need to be securely bolted or strapped in place, as do all items carried in the operational area. The damage caused to finishes and equipment by a loose microphone stand, let alone a multitrack machine, has to be seen to be believed.

Another advantage of air suspension, particularly on a trailer (where compressed air is provided by the tractor via a flexible hose) is that it can be evacuated on site; the suspension will then sit on its bump stops providing stabilization. For levelling, a trailer can be uncoupled from its tractor, the suspension evacuated, and the front end lowered on the landing legs until the vehicle is level. A word of warning though—do not allow the driver to couple tractor to trailer by reversing at speed (a common 'transport' trick). This will not succeed due to the difference in height between tractor and lowered trailer, and damage will result.

Levelling

On the subject of levelling and stabilization, the addition of simple mechanical jacks at each corner is useful to stop the vehicle rocking on site. This will relieve distracting motion when somebody enters or moves around in the vehicle. On-site convenience will be aided if these jacks have several coarse adjustment slots, with a screw section attached to a broad foot piece for fine adjustment.

Storage and creature comforts

Storage space on vehicles is always at a premium. Inside, small and large cupboards for the storage of tapes, instruction manuals, paperwork, tools, spares, and similar should be carefully planned around an ergonomic equipment layout with the intention of providing as many cupboards as possible. The customer needs to be consulted as to any specific requirements and the size of internal divisions. The catches on the cupboards need to be simple in operation, strong, and not prone to opening in transit and allowing the contents to fly out.

Outside storage also needs to be comprehensive. Apart from lockers housing stabilizing jacks, technical batteries, air-conditioning compressors, and similar vehicle system hardware, unallocated space needs to be provided for all sorts, shapes, and sizes of equipment. Large areas with full-size doors, big enough for a person to stand in, will hold PA speakers, large stands, extra cable drums, equipment transportation trolley, and the like. Smaller lockers built into available spaces will have a variety of uses, and, if possible, a through locker arranged across the vehicle will house a ladder for access to venue cable entries and for slinging cables. Locker doors should clip back close to the vehicle body for public safety and ease of access, with gas struts aiding the raising/lowering of horizontally hinged doors.

Since many cable drums (multi-pair signal, single XLR-XLR, CCTV camera, and mains power) are needed to cover even the simplest show, storage and ease of use must be considered. Other than multi-pair cables and high-current mains cables, most cable drums are reasonably small, so that skirt lockers can be arranged to house them. The two former cable types require purpose-built storage as they are both large and heavy. Several multi-way cables will be needed to service the long runs of multi-mic set-ups, so easy-to-use storage is necessary. A useful mechanism has been devised, by one of the leading UK sound vehicle coachbuilders, which mounts each multi-way drum on a frame supported on a pair of sliders. This frame can be latched into a recessed locker or slid out and locked in position, enabling the cable either to be unreeled *in situ* or the complete drum removed and transported to a remote point.

Mains cables can be similarly treated, or, for space saving and ease of rewind, a d.c. motor-powered reel can be built in. A type of reel used successfully recently was developed by a proprietary manufacturer from one of his fire-engine hose reels! Alternative locations for this large cable drum storage can be seen in Figures 13.4 and 5. Both locations are similar in that cables are reached via the rear of the vehicle. This allows safe access wherever the vehicle is parked.

Cables slung across a roadway, and maintenance of any roof-mounted aerials or aerial bases, will require climbing on the vehicle roof. A loose ladder placed against the vehicle side is likely to be unsafe on uneven or sloping terrain. A fixed ladder attached to the vehicle solves this problem, but, to comply with the UK's Health and Safety at Work Act, the ladder should fold close to the vehicle when not in use, and some means of preventing unauthorized climbing should be provided.

If space and finance permit, as shown in Figures 13.4 and 5, consideration can be given to some creature comforts. Apart from air-conditioning (covered elsewhere in this chapter), these include a sink with hot and cold water, for freshening up and removing the inevitable grime of cable running, and a water boiler (which can also provide the hot washing water) to make tea or coffee, a refrigerator, and somewhere to hang wet clothes and muddy boots.

The provision of a water system requires some comment regarding health safety. The storage of fresh and waste water is fraught with difficulty, and the simplest solution is to use two equal-volume plastic jerrycan containers, clearly marked and not interchangeable, so that as the fresh water container empties the waste container fills; the two containers thus have to be serviced together. Water can be sucked from the fresh water container by a suction-valve-operated electric pump, and delivered either to the cold tap or to the water boiler. A small caravan-style stainless steel sink with appropriate plumbing connected to the waste container will complete the system.

Air-conditioning

One consequence of good sound isolation is that it prevents natural air-flow through the vehicle. This, with the heat gain deriving from equipment and people, means that some environmental control is necessary. Solar gain is small due to the high U value of the wall build-up, and, although calculable, can be almost ignored.

An air-conditioning system needs to be capable of providing stable comfortable working conditions for the number of people expected to work in the mobile, as well as coping with the power dissipation of the technical equipment and the lighting. The modes of operation necessary are 'cooling', 'heating', and 'ventilation', with thermostat and humidistat control. It is essential that the air-conditioning plant is properly planned, normally by a specialist working in conjunction with the coachbuilder. Obviously, the specialist will need all details of power dissipation, occupancy, and problem areas to provide a good system.

A reasonable basic specification for a system in the UK is for the 'cooling' mode to provide reduction in average air temperature inside the vehicle body to 21°C dry bulb at 45 per cent relative humidity, when all the technical equipment is switched on, the vehicle is exposed to summer sunshine on a windless day, and the external shade temperature is 30°C. A differential of at least 9°C should be maintained up to an external shade temperature of 40°C. To avoid draughts, the temperature of the air leaving the ducts should be no more than 5.5°C cooler than the average air temperature inside the vehicle. Filters, 95 per cent efficient at 5μm and easily removed for servicing, should be fitted. Also, as a draught precaution, air pressure in the vehicle with all doors closed should be slightly higher than external air pressure. A 10 per cent bleed of fresh air should be introduced to prevent stale odours and stuffiness.

The 'heating' mode is similar to the 'cooling' except that the system should now be capable of maintaining 21°C dry bulb, 45 per cent relative humidity when the external temperature is −5°C, 100 per cent relative humidity. Electric heater batteries in the supply air-flow achieve the necessary climatic effect. The 'ventilation' mode is useful where limited mains power is available. In this mode, the compressor and heater batteries are disabled and the air-handling unit is used purely as a fan for moving air through the vehicle. For the 'cooling' and 'heating' modes to work correctly, the vehicle doors need to be closed, and continual opening and closing of doors will cause shortcomings in system control.

The silencing of the plant is of prime importance, and care should be taken in mounting the air-handling unit and the compressor, with anti-vibration mounts used where necessary. Silencers should be installed in the supply and return air paths, to prevent motor and fan noise being coupled into the duct system. A noise-level specification should be agreed, noting that possible beneficial masking effects of air-conditioning noise in a building do not apply in the much smaller environment of a vehicle. Compressors and fans should be mounted outside the acoustically isolated operational area, and, apart from anti-vibration mounts, the coolant pipework should have flexible sections inserted at both ends to prevent noise transmission into the body. It is important that liquid coolant does not enter the compressor, and a sump heater with delayed start-up may be necessary.

On the basis that continued noise is less noticeable than intermittent noise, and to prevent the start-up surges on the mains supply which will upset some technical equipment, the compressor must run continuously. To achieve this, the compressor needs to be fitted with a hot gas bypass system or preferably a secondary evaporator and diverting control valve. The latter system provides a more constant load to the compressor, prolonging its life, but its mode of operation and the control gear requirements are quite complex and outside the scope of this book.

Safety devices such as high and low-pressure cutouts and de-icing thermostats should be fitted. The evaporation condensate should collect in drip trays which self-drain to the outside. These drip trays need to be of sufficient volume that condensate does not leak into the vehicle when it is parked off-level.

The air ducts must be adequate in cross-section, avoiding sharp turns and restrictions which cause turbulence and noise and reduce the air-flow. The ducts should be as long as possible and, for maximum noise attenuation, lined with underfelt formed in a corrugated fashion. Simpler lining, such as fire-retardant foam, may be used on longer ducts, but, on fire safety grounds, foam should be avoided wherever possible. A lined duct presents a fairly high impedance to the air-flow, and care should be taken that internal panelling is positioned so that air is prevented from taking low-impedance paths and bypassing the system.

Supply grilles need to be of a low-noise flush-fitting type with volume control dampers, and consideration should be given to air extraction from the main body and also directly above any particular heat-producing equipment. All grilles should be checked for sympathetic vibration and acoustic damping. The ideal place for control gear is with the power control switchgear described in the next section.

Before leaving the subject of air-conditioning, other items of environmental comfort need mentioning. The first is a diesel-fuel-fired coach heater. This simple device is useful as a source of heat, both in vehicles with and without air-conditioning or electric heating, but for different reasons. The reason for a source of heat in the former is straightforward, but in the latter it may seem superfluous. The use of a diesel-fired coach heater in an air-conditioned vehicle is to keep moisture out overnight, or to provide some warmth in the vehicle before the power supply is connected. Incidentally, the unit is best fed from its own tank, as, although fuel demand is low, it could be embarrassing to run the engine fuel tank dry; also, the heater can be run on rebated (i.e. cheap domestic fuel oil) rather than diesel road vehicle fuel.

The second useful item is the ventilator fan. In vehicles, such as panel vans, without air-conditioning a ventilator fan can be useful to clear stale air. Unfortunately, most of these units tend to be noisy and are therefore not really compatible with sound control mobiles. Recently, the author discovered a variant on the ventilator fan theme. This unit, made by a Japanese company, incorporates a heat exchanger coil whereby the exhaust air pre-warms ingoing air, supplying this by a two-speed fan motor. The unit has two ports, one for input and the other for output, and is impressively quiet in operation. When mounted resiliently on the vehicle and two separate 600 mm ducts formed, each lined with corrugated underfelt, the system is very quiet and certainly satisfactory for a budget mobile.

Second air-conditioning system

A second system with 'cooling' and 'ventilation' modes can become necessary where technical equipment power supplies or an automation system computer produce high heat loads, or have integral noisy cooling fans leading to the necessity of an acoustically isolated enclosure to house them. The basic ideas expressed above for a personnel area system still apply, although the noise criteria can be relaxed provided that sound isolation from the equipment housing to the main area is good. Fresh air bleed is not necessary; a recirculating air-flow is adequate. The 'cooling' mode still requires a continuously run compressor, for the reasons outlined above, but care should be taken with the system specification to avoid 'hot-spots' in the equipment, and also overcooling, which could cause condensation inside the equipment.

The 'ventilation' mode is for use in minimum power situations where the computer is bypassed and switched off along with other unnecessary equipment. In this mode the compressor is unpowered, and the recirculating system ducts are converted to 'total loss', with flaps allowing fresh air to be sucked in by the air-handling unit fan through an outside grille, passed over the equipment, and exhausted directly back to the outside.

Power systems and lighting

Both d.c. and a.c. systems are necessary on sound recording mobiles and will be discussed in that order.

Direct current systems and lighting

Direct current power is required to operate battery lighting, rigging lights, alarm systems, control and ignition of diesel coach heater, powered cable drums, and standby power for technical equipment having a low voltage input as well as a pneumatic mast compressor (if fitted). Internal battery lights will be useful in the absence of power on first arrival at side, or on derig, and also to produce minimum power demand at limited venues. For this application, experience has shown that fluorescent-type lamps are most suitably powered on an automatic changeover circuit, from technical batteries to a d.c. power supply powered by a.c. mains. This arrangement allows a single on–off switching arrangement adjacent to entry doors, and neatly avoids duplication of d.c. and a.c. switchgear, chokes, and the like associated with fluorescent lighting. Also, d.c. fluorescents radiate less radio-frequency interference than their a.c. counterparts.

Rigging lights, mounted so that they shine on termination panel areas, entry doors, storage lockers, and around the perimeter of the vehicle, will provide safety and security. Many types of lamp unit are available, but none are designed for the purpose, and consequently they are not entirely satisfactory. Recent vehicles have been fitted with reversing lamps set on an angled bracket within the dimensions of the vehicle cant rail. These lamps have been the most satisfactory, requiring no adjustment on site and providing a very good light coverage down the side of the vehicle and a few feet out from the side. Additionally, a powerful rotatable work lamp adjacent to the fixed ladder is useful for shining along the roof and up at buildings or highlighting a required area.

Alarm systems, warning of doors or hatches opening in transit, over-temperature of equipment, fire, or unauthorized persons, are sensible precautions. Door warning and intruder alarm can both be achieved with micro switches. Mechanical switches are difficult to align in view of vehicle movement and they also suffer from corrosion. However, magnetic feed switches are quite satisfactory, being tolerant of line-up, robust, and corrosion-proof. The use of magnetic switches does require care in mounting, avoiding close proximity to steel-work which will reduce the effectiveness of, or even defeat, the switch. An alarm indication panel visible from the outside of the vehicle, with a composite mutable audio and visual indicator in the driver's cab, will provide useful identification of a problem. Over-temperature alarms for equipment are fairly self-explanatory, and fire detectors, or, more accurately, ionization-chamber smoke detectors, are straightforward domestic types installed in all compartments where fire, due to electrical or human failing, can start.

Diesel coach heater manufacturers supply the necessary data with their products, as do other equipment manufacturers, to design these control systems. In budget mobiles, the technical equipment can have the option of battery input. This can be especially useful at venues where no a.c. power is available; of course, battery tape machines are then also needed, and monitoring may have to be done on headphones! Installation and component specification details are similar to a.c. systems and are covered below.

Batteries and charger

The source of supply for the d.c. power system will be battery. A pair of series-connected lead-acid 12 V 100 AH batteries with an associated charging system is all that is required. The batteries themselves need to be superior to ordinary automotive units, as the charge/discharge cycle is a series of deep discharge and heavy charge. A semi-traction battery has been found to survive the experience due to its construction comprising greater amounts of lead.

The batteries must be installed in a ventilated enclosure to disperse charging gases; siting them in a vehicle skirt compartment open to the outside air will be satisfactory. The compartment should allow for easy maintenance and be painted with an acid-resisting paint in case of spillage. The batteries need to be charged, when the vehicle is powered, by a mains-powered automatically regulated charger. The charger should have an output of at least 10 amps and must not overcharge the batteries when switched on for long periods.

It will also be useful if the technical batteries are charged from the vehicle alternator when the vehicle is in motion. If the vehicle alternator is of insufficient output, or a different voltage to the technical batteries, then it may be possible to fit a second engine-driven alternator. An automatic changeover system should be provided to prevent the batteries being charged from two sources.

Alternating current power systems and lighting

The a.c. power requirements of a sound recording mobile are varied and complex. A simple low-budget mobile will run on a single 13 amp input, whilst a fully equipped high-specification mobile will need approximately 50 amps. (The previously mentioned Digital Control Vehicle was originally calculated, based on manufacturers' maximum data, as requiring 180 amps or approximately 50 KW.) The measures to be taken to cover safety, diversity, and the ability to run basic facilities on minimum power require considerable thought.

The prime consideration is the safety of people operating and associated with the mobile. In the field, power earths can be questionable and only large venues may have a low-impedance earth available. At large, regularly visited venues negotiation with the owners or management company should lead to the provision of a supply point of sufficient capacity with low-impedance earth; often direct connection to the supply bus bars will be possible. The power control system needs to incorporate an earth loop impedance tester, for checking the incoming supply before connection to the mobile, and built-in sensors for deviation in 'earth' potential.

On the basis that saving lives is more important than saving a recording or broadcast, devices which are now known as Residual Current Circuit Breakers (RCCB), previously called Earth Leakage Circuit Breakers (ELCB), should be connected in series with each power input to the vehicle and with any power takeoff provided for use with external equipment. This device monitors the current in live and neutral conductors; any imbalance of more than 30 mA integrated over a 30 msec period will cause the device to trip and disconnect the supply. If calculations show that a normal standing earth current of 30 mA or more will be set up by equipment (for example, switching mode power supplies in the control desk), then an RCCB will not be satisfactory. Additionally, experience shows that RCCBs have a tendency to trip with 'spikes' on the supply. If this is not acceptable, a bypass switch could be used during actual recording, but this removes any safety precautions.

An alternative system to the RCCB is a proprietary system with current transformers in the live and neutral lines, and a processing circuit which provides an aural and visual alarm when a pre-set limit has been exceeded. This system has been used successfully in several recent mobiles and provides an excellent indication on an ammeter of standing current deviation, with a lamp and mutable buzzer giving the alarm at the pre-set limit. The system requires a closely defined power and earthing system, which is necessary anyway to avoid circulating currents, common impedances, and a generally 'clean' earth for the technical equipment.

Mobile generator power supplies

Recent experience has revealed examples of poor Automatic Voltage Regulator design on some modern generator sets, giving rise to large spikes on the neutral rail. While these systems may be quite satisfactory for lighting rigs, buzz problems have proved difficult to overcome when powering sound vehicles and TV OB units. When considering the use of mobile generating sets for use with today's mobiles, having a high proportion of switched mode power supplies on board, good AVR design on the generator is essential.

Earthing

Earth connections are needed to all exposed metal surfaces (except those trim plates and fittings screwed to the wooden body with no possibility of power connecting to them), conduits, boxes, and mounting racks. Also, earths are required to vehicle chassis (best connected where any vehicle battery is joined to the chassis), technical battery negative terminal, incoming mains connectors, and technical equipment earth system. All these earths should be flexible, of the correct cross-sectional area, and individually connected to a single point. This must be the only point where earths join, and is known as a 'star' system. Sub-branches from each star leg are acceptable provided no loops are formed.

Additionally, for use where a venue has no supply earth or where the earth is not low-impedance, an earth spike should be supplied and connected to the central point of the star earthing system. This spike can be driven into the ground and kept moist to provide a reasonable earth, the longer and broader the better, but practicalities often limit the spike to a 1 m long 25 × 25 mm section passivated steel rod.

Power distribution and systems

The total load of all equipment installed in the vehicle must be calculated, with an allowance for extras. Ignoring apparently insignificant small loads will be regretted in service.

The loads should be listed and split into distributions such as technical, general services, and air-conditioning. Careful planning and switching of these distributions will allow for a high current input powering all systems and changeover switching to less current inputs powering reduced facilities at low-power venues. For example, if the 'ventilation' mode of the air-conditioning is run from the 'technical' or 'general services' distribution and high-demand technical equipment (such as a multitrack recorder) run from the 'air-conditioning' distribution, then, at a low-power venue, switching off the 'air-conditioning' distribution will allow the mobile to function, albeit in a limited form.

Each mains input should be fed through waterproof connectors and flexible cable. Phase indication to guard against live/neutral reversal should be installed. A pair of series neons, one green connected to the live and one red connected to the neutral with the common point connected to earth, will show an inversion. Voltmeters and ammeters are also useful to show supply and load parameters.

The use of more than one supply phase is not recommended, but, providing the loads are kept separate and adequate monitoring provided with safety in mind, there is no reason why a system cannot be devised. The BBC's Digital Control Vehicle has three power inputs, each capable of a 60 amp load, to cope with the high demands. The power system has been designed so that the vehicle can run on one, two, or three phases, dependent on available supply.

Miniature circuit-breakers (MCB) of the magnetic type are recommended as the fuse element in each distribution, for two reasons. Firstly, they repeatedly trip on overload currents at defined points and do not suffer the metal fatigue failures which seem to affect wired fuse links subject to vehicle motion. Secondly, MCBs double as switches for deliberately isolating circuits for load shedding or servicing.

The circuit configuration recommended is a double-pole MCB feeding each distribution, with single-pole MCB feeding individual subcircuits or items of equipment. The type of MCB should reflect the fusing adversity, ensuring that a subcircuit MCB fails before its distribution MCB, and also the type of load. Various delay curves, to cope with inrush currents and motor start characteristics, are available and need to be chosen to suit manufacturer's data.

MCBs are also available, and are recommended similarly, for d.c. power control systems. A power control cabinet housing all the ammeters, voltmeters, RCCBs, MCBs, alarm devices, etc., with d.c. systems separated by a metal barrier from a.c., is recommended for a tidy installation. An electrical engineer or specialist company will be able to advise, design, and construct such a control cabinet.

However, in view of the vibration caused by vehicle motion which all the wiring and fittings will be subject to, suitable precautions need to be taken to ensure that connections do not work loose, and a few pointers are necessary in component choice and installation. Where possible, crimped stud and spade terminals should be used, particularly on power control cabinet components; screw terminals and soldered joints should be avoided. If screw terminals have to be used, say on socket outlet plates, then some form of anaerobic liquid should be used to 'lock' the threads. Metal conduit or trunking should be used, with any sharp edges over which cables pass protected by grommets or plastic edging strip. Ducts should be formed for multiple cable runs with a.c. and d.c. power separated by a metal barrier, and all circuits should be run as 'pairs', that is line and neutrals must be run together; common neutrals are not acceptable. If the mains supply sub-circuits are run as on the ring main principle, the earth conductor must not be included in a ring. These two latter points will help avoid hum loops being generated inside the vehicle.

Obviously, adequate power outlets should be available where needed to avoid trailing cables inside the vehicle.

Lighting

As mentioned under 'Direct current systems and lighting', it is recommended that switchable fluorescent light be designated on a changeover supply from d.c. to a.c. These fittings can be used in all compartments, except the small lockers, to provide general high light levels.

For more intimate operational light, eyeball fittings recessed into the ceiling around the acoustic treatment will provide light sources which can be aimed at specific areas, such as tape machines, engineering bay, and the like. Over the central desk similar fittings or spotlights can be used. Incandescent lighting is recommended for operational purposes, because, although its power consumption is higher than fluorescent, dimmers can easily be provided. Dimmer types should be chosen for minimum radiation of radio-frequency interference.

Technical equipment and systems

The heart of a mobile is its technical equipment, which must be capable of coping with all the production demands made of it. The vehicle must be as flexibly and fully equipped as possible, with spare space for the addition of equipment on a temporary basis neatly and well engineered. Attention must be paid to the provision of as many permanent facilities as possible. The more basic facilities like equalization and dynamics which are built into the control desk the better, as valuable space would be taken up with these common requirements on outboard racks.

Also, narrower desk modules will allow more of them to be fitted inside the restricted width of the vehicle (see Plate 22). As noted before, the internal width with acoustic isolation build-up will be approximately 2.3 m; this will house 56 60-mm modules or 64 35-mm modules, allowing for desk framework. The useful desk width can be maximized by omitting end cheeks, or the wall build-up can be relieved in the desk area, though this of course will provide lower isolation.

All equipment should be examined for robust construction, tidy well-supported cable forms, and retention of components and subassemblies. Good-quality connectors must be used, gold-plated if possible. Poorly located boards with edge connectors tend to 'saw' their way through the mating

Plate 22. Mobile recording vehicle, showing control and monitoring area (Photo: BBC)

connector in transit and should be avoided. For a simple mobile, a 25-8-2 desk is likely to be satisfactory, whereas in a large mobile a 48-32-4 desk could prove limiting. One solution to this problem is to provide a fixed sub-mixer adjacent to the main desk to cope with the overspill.

Mobiles are often co-sited with TV or PA companies using a common mic rig, and it becomes necessary to decide who supplies phantom power and has the primary signal and who has split feeds. It is wise to arrange that the mobile control desk has individually switched phantom power per channel, with some form of indicator of the presence, or absence, of phantom power, no matter what the source. Mic signal splitting is occasionally the source of argument over who has the primary feed; it is not wise just to parallel feeds, as a fault on one will reflect directly on to all the others, apart from the obvious impedance mismatch. A system with a straight through route for the primary feed and a transformer coupled with resistor buffers for the other routes (normally two will be sufficient) works well. The transformer will not pass phantom power and therefore the primary route supplies it. The transformer needs to be selected with the source and load impedances and the dynamic range of signal levels in mind. A splitter must work equally well on the least sensitive dynamic microphone, through capacitor microphones, to the high-level output of synthesizers. Also, the breakdown of flash-over voltage between primary and secondary windings of the transformer with associated wiring and connectors needs to be considered. Some safety regulations insist on the complete unit surviving a 4,500 V flash test! This could be critically important in a mobile operating under adverse weather conditions or near power installations. A recent large mobile includes this type of splitter permanently installed on all seventy incoming mic lines, as well as a number of portable units for additional or alternative on-stage splits.

Signal cables from the performance area to the mobile need to be robust mechanically and electrically. Multi-core microphone cables terminating in a converter box will save much time and frustration compared with single-pair cables. Specially developed multi-way cables with a thick plastic outer sheath and an internal overall electrical screen enclosing individually screened 'quad'-type inner cores are strongly recommended for use in the hazardous environment met by mobiles. Braided, or at least lapped, screens should be chosen in place of foil to minimize handling noise. A 'quad'-type inner array, wired as a pair, very effectively reduces the thyristor dimmer noise that plagues a mobile operating near lighting rigs. The multi-pin connectors used also need to be similarly robust. Military specification types with gold-plated contacts and positive cable clamp and lock mechanisms are expensive but are worth while in minimizing contact problems and maximizing cable survival. Obviously, multi-way connectors are not suitable for all circuits, and a number of single-pair and screen connectors of both gender for miscellaneous circuits will be useful. Recent developments in the use of fibre optic cables can now offer an efficient alternative to traditional copper-cored multi-way cables. As digital multiplex techniques are further applied to audio, so the days of the conventional 'copper multi's' from stage box to mobile termination panel will become a thing of the past, replaced by smaller lighter high-capacity fibre optic systems.

The mobile ends of the cables need to connect to an easily accessible 'termination panel' close to the main cable storage. If a number of cables can be run from the vehicle simultaneously, rigging time will be greatly reduced. It is recommended that this panel be on the rear face of the vehicle, protected by a door or weather-proof roller shutter against road dirt. The rear of a vehicle in motion is a low-pressure area, and road dirt will be sucked against the vehicle and permeate all but a well-sealed compartment. Recent large mobiles have had all or part of the termination panel installed in a walk-in storage area to protect the connections still further, and also to provide an undercover plugging area for the technical staff. Vehicle internal wiring connecting the termination panel to the desk patch-bay (jackfield) through a properly planned and accessible cable duct can have a lower specification than the external cables. The internal wiring must be flexible to cope with vehicle motion, but individual or multi-way foil-screened cables will be satisfactory.

Even on small mobiles the desk patch-bay is the interconnection point for incoming and outgoing circuits, internal tie-lines for tapes, reverberation, flanging, and similar units and a host of desk input, output, insert circuits. As space is limited, especially as the patch-bay needs to be close to the control desk operator, using normal 6.3 mm B-gauge telephone-type jacks means that either the patch-bay is reduced in size and facilities or it has to be divided. The latter is usually unsatisfactory and so a method of achieving the former must be found. Fortunately, mini or bantam 4.4 mm jacks solve both problems. Patch rows with 48 or even 56 bantam jacks can be fitted on a standard 19-inch panel.

It is recommended that as much normalling (innering) as possible is included on the patch-bay to avoid trailing cords and movement noise on low-level circuits. For earthing reasons, circuits leaving the patch-bay should be wired as three-wire with the screens interconnected only at one point, usually at the patch-bay itself. Great care needs to be taken to avoid earth loops and spurious earths, particularly on low-signal-level (less than -20 dBV) circuits. Jacks themselves need to be mounted on insulating material to break earth continuity between individual jacks and the frame, except where the desk manufacturer advises otherwise.

Many control desks have the option of transformer or electronically balanced inputs/outputs. At the risk of fuelling controversy, the author recommends that microphone inputs are transformer-coupled, with longitudinal stop filters, as even with special cables high common-mode voltages can be generated in the cables of a mobile rig. It is almost impossible to predict the electrical/magnetic conditions which will be met at each and every possible mobile venue. Some manufacturers have produced very impressive figures, supported by 'golden ears' judgement, for their electronically balanced inputs, but the risk factor for a mobile desk is too great. Internal, and therefore predictable, circuits to tapes and other equipment are ideal candidates for transformerless techniques, but the transformer coupling should be repeated for any circuit that supplies signal outside the vehicle, including all line-send amplifiers for any output sent by PTT line. In the UK, British Telecom is very strict about connection to any part of its network, so any intended line-send amplifier should be checked for compliance with BT's regulations. The distribution amplifiers can usefully be employed as common buffers for all equipment requiring a feed of desk output, such as stereo tape, audition cassettes, and external monitoring.

The type of tape machine is again a matter of preference, as most modern types are independent of supply voltage and frequency, both of which can be unsure at remote sites. If any video or simulcast work is envisaged, then centre-track time-code is necessary. Any multitrack recorder and associated noise reduction system needs to be selected bearing in mind size, weight, and compatibility with relevant automation and synchronizer systems as well as capacity to handle large-diameter spools to give longer recording times. Larger mobiles will carry two multitracks for continuous recording or to provide a greater number of tracks by synchronizing the two machines (see Plate 23). A synchronizer with a time-code generator will be useful for pre-striping the tape without tying up the automation computer to generate time-code. Now that digital multitrack recorders are achieving prominence in mobile as well as fixed studio set-ups, it is important to provide appropriate synchronization information for these machines. Timecode generators must be referenced to the digital clocks within the tape machines and, if work is undertaken with a TV unit, a video reference such as 'black and colour burst' must be applied so that any subsequent combined TV and audio post-production work maintains perfect synchronization.

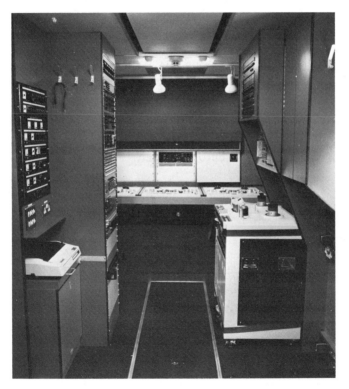

Plate 23. Mobile recording vehicle, showing 2-track and 24-track recording area (Photo: BBC)

Reverberation and other modern digital signal processors have already been mentioned in terms of patch-bay space, but the siting of these units can present problems. Either they can be installed in an engineering bay with all the distribution and line-send racks and myriad remote controls wired to the desk, or the units can be housed in an operationally more satis-factory position. Small racks can be accommodated under the control desk edges, providing you have not craftily hidden the wheel-arches there. Alternatively, a 'flight deck' arrangement placed over the control desk and built as part of the ceiling can be used. This is quite useful as it is close to the operator and safe from accidental damage and inadvertent reset, although a bleed of air may be necessary for cooling.

Comprehensive monitoring and direct tape-to-tape dubbing systems which are completely independent of the control desk are great savers of time and aggravation. A stereo tape system needs to be arranged so that each tape machine can be lined up independent of whatever the other machines or the control desk are doing. A similar system for the multi-track(s), without the dubbing facility, will also be useful. The system designed for some recent mobiles incorporates a microprocessor-controlled switching system with miniature relays as the signal-switching element. This has proved very successful, as hard wiring is minimized and reduced to printed circuit board/connector wiring only. The oscillator used for tape line-up must have a very low output impedance capable of supplying a con-stant voltage to a low-impedance load—two 32-track tape machines, with all tracks paralleled, may present a load as low as 160 ohms.

A sound mobile intended to work with TV or video companies will need a video system to interface with them. Also, a CCTV system, enabling the vehicle operator and producer to see the artists, is almost essential and need not cost a lot.

Basic video facilities needed include tie-lines from the termination panel, video patch-rows, distribution amplifiers with integral equalizers, and a simple switcher for routing to a colour monitor. This colour monitor can be the same one as for CCTV, and if a TV tuner is required this can be a sepa-rate device routed as a source to the switcher. A video cassette recorder, suitable for professional cassettes (if possible, capable of acting as master to a synchronizer), will complete the system.

Communications are also vital, not only between the mobile and artists, but also to stage technical personnel and PA/TV companies. Control desks developed for studio work usually incorporate sufficient talkback to cues and studio loudspeaker circuits to cope with artist communication, but extras will be needed for other functions. A radio talkback system (beware problems of frequency allocation and power output) will be useful in com-municating with mobile personnel on stage or around the venue, with switched talkback input from the desk microphone(s) and 'back contact' input for cue purposes.

Additional talkback circuits, fed as above but pluggable on the patch-bay to termination panel tie-lines for onward connection as necessary, should be adequate for most requirements. If a customer requires anything more complex, then a purpose-designed communications system will be necessary.

Reverse talkback into the mobile is also needed. This can be achieved using existing control desk provisions or via additional low-quality self-powered loudspeakers. A simple multi-input talkback mixer can be useful to avoid too many small loudspeakers cluttering up and confusing the operational area, although some people prefer a number of RTB loudspeakers to provide directional coding of talkback source.

In a short chapter, it is impossible to cover all aspects of mobile recording vehicles, let alone their use and inherent problems. In closing, the author would like to thank his colleagues who have assisted him with work on mobiles, in particular E. W. Taylor of BBC Research Department for his work on acoustic design and related problems. The author would also like to thank the Director of Engineering, British Broadcasting Corporation, for permission to publish.

Reference

Taylor, E. W., *The Acoustic Design of Outside Broadcast Vehicles*, BBC Research Department Report Number RD 1984/3.

14 Maintenance

Malcolm Atkin

As the audio industry has matured, there has been a great increase in the number of small manufacturing companies producing an ever-wider range of equipment for studio use. This in turn has meant a changing role for the maintenance engineer. He may no longer be asked to build an in-house mixing console, but he will be expected to have wide experience ranging from antique musical instruments to the merits of the latest software updates. He will also be the person whom everyone calls upon when things go wrong.

A professional studio should have a fully qualified technical engineer available at any time that a session is in progress. Whilst breakdown cover can be provided by mobile service engineers, this should not be a substitute. A true recording studio is always being modified and re-equipped as tastes and methods change, and a full-time engineer who has intimate knowledge of the installation and operation of all the equipment in the studio is a tremendous asset to the company.

Basic requirements

All studios require a separate service area, preferably with natural light and on the same level as the studio to allow free movement of machinery. Adequate deep-bench area at waist height will be required for each engineer, with plenty of power outlets and patch access through the more common connector systems of the studio to central music sources, oscillators, monitor systems and the like. If space permits, specialized service areas for items like tape machines are very useful and a good monitor system is essential for checking out equipment. All workshops will require some metalwork facilities, and if possible these should be sited in a separate area with a solid bench and vice. A good selection of tools will be required for panel and box manufacture. If more ambitious projects are envisaged, a pillar drill, fly press, small grinder, and a selection of hand power-tools will prove invaluable.

Up-to-date manuals should be maintained for all equipment. All modifications should be noted at the relevant point. Where more than one manual of the same type exists, master copies should be clearly marked.

Diagrams or sections which are used frequently should be copied and filed separately so that the originals are kept in good condition.

Trade magazines are a valuable information source and should be filed and continuously updated. Modern reference and text-books will also be very useful.

The spares holding in any studio will be subject to many considerations. The first of these is obviously financial, since heavy investment here will have to be at the expense of something else in the studio. A fine balance has to be struck between availability and accessibility from manufacturers' stock and the omnipresent danger of excessive down-time. Even the best maintenance team cannot be expected to report faulty assemblies immediately, so the spares holding in many areas is quite obvious. Experience is the best guide as to what should be kept. A careful log of all faults will soon help to show which areas need most careful attention to stock levels.

General electronic spares are best kept in wall-mounted storage systems. Specialized items for specific equipment are best stored separately, so that the spares kit can be carried to the equipment if required.

Electronic test equipment

The test gear required for a studio workshop would consist of most of the following items:

1. *Audio function generator.*
2. *Counter timer.*
3. *RMS voltmeter*—a good-quality high-impedance meter calibrated in dB is a useful reference item.
4. *General-purpose multimeter*—some modern meters incorporate dB scaling, and hand-held counter versions are invaluable for circuit board check-out.
5. *Oscilloscope*—to cope with modern digital equipment; a minimum bandwidth of 50 MHz is required.
6. *Bench power supply*—capable of supplying ±30 volts.
7. *Spectrum analyser*—an accurate analyser is an expensive item but very useful in many areas, especially for checking loudspeakers and microphones. A pink-noise source will be needed.
8. *Audio analyser*—an expensive bench item which can feature many of the above. Whilst very useful, it should not be provided to the exclusion of single-feature test equipment.
9. *Distortion analyser*—again a fairly expensive item, probably not as useful as most of the above, and may be featured in other analysers.

A well-equipped workshop will also contain most of the following items:

1. *Test tapes*, essential to the line-up of analogue tape machines; should cover all equalization standards, speeds, and tape widths. These tapes are

expensive and should be used only as a reference. Before running a test tape on a machine, the heads should be de-magnetized and the tape path cleaned. Each project should have tone runs made from these tapes for daily checks. With care, multiple-tone tapes can be made for use in copy rooms and the like to reduce the use of master tapes. Test tapes should be stored in a cool secure place well away from stray magnetic fields.

Computer software on floppy disc systems should all have back-up copies made and be stored as above. Working copies of these programs should be generated at regular intervals to minimize failures. Software in EPROM form should also have back-ups available.

2. Complex console strips will require the use of *custom electronic test jigs* for testing or repair without recourse to the console facilities. An example is shown in Plate 24.

3. *A microphone test jig*, consisting of a speaker inside an anechoic box, with fixed connections for all types of microphone, will enable comparative response tests to be made in conjunction with a spectrum analyser. To this end, the frequency response of all microphones should be logged when purchased.

4. *A variable mains transformer* can be very useful in the repair of old equipment. Sometimes a fault condition can be noticed and corrected before full power is applied.

5. *Accurate spring gauges* are required for setting tape tension. Some transports require the use of a Tentelometer, a proprietary mechanical meter. If hand lapping of heads is carried out, lapping blocks and realignment jigs will be needed.

6. Some manufacturers supply *extender cards* for their equipment. These are essential in many cases to access card assemblies whilst still in circuit. Extenders should be obtained for all relevant studio equipment.

7. *A vacuum de-soldering station* is a useful addition. Repair of high-density digital boards requires very careful handling to prevent damage to components and board pads. LSI circuits directly soldered to the circuit board are almost impossible to remove by any other method.

8. In order to connect test equipment to all other studio systems, *interconnecting leads* of all types are required. As most test gear uses BNC connectors, this problem is considerably reduced. A lead rack holding test leads of a uniform length on a convenient wall space will prove both tidy and time-saving.

Hand-tools

Every technical engineer requires a comprehensive set of hand-tools. These tools are often personal property and are usually best selected by each engineer, as individual preferences vary widely. As well as a good selection of

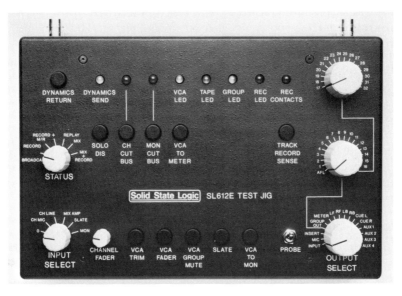

Plate 24. Solid State Logic test jig allowing bench testing of all logic and audio functions of individual modules (Photo: SSL)

general tools, a studio engineer will also require specialized cabling tools and a basic set of metal-work tools.

A good tool kit will contain most of the following items: sets of flat-blade, cross-point, and jewellers' screwdrivers; temperature-controlled soldering iron; set of BA and metric spanners and Allen keys; wire cutters—several sizes; pliers—general and long-nose; wire-strippers; sleeve-strippers; sleeve-expanders; internal and external circlip pliers; small torch; inspection mirror; small hacksaw; steel ruler; set square; scriber; files—various; small hammer; centre punch.

Communication

As in all businesses, good communication is essential if a studio is to provide an effective service to its clients. A studio maintenance department is no exception to this rule and must therefore have well-established methods of communication within the department and to the other areas of the studio operation. Since technical engineers are not primarily employed for their business skills, these procedures are best kept as simple as possible. As many studios operate shift systems, a diary is an invaluable method of logging session requirements and problems. An order book is also very useful for logging spares deficiencies as they arise, so that re-ordering can be a routine function not requiring a stock control meeting!

Control-room log-books are also an invaluable method of communication. The log-book should be constantly used by both the balance engineer and the technical staff to note faults, modifications, and routine line-ups. As a diary, it should note any special requirements of the day, and a constant dialogue should be encouraged.

Routine procedures

Most of the following procedures can be performed by an assistant engineer, since they consist largely of aural and visual checks. A few minutes checking before the start of a session can save a lot of aggravation later, since a known problem can often be bypassed until a repair can be effected.

Tape machines

As the prime function of the studio is to record, the performance of the tape machines is paramount and should be checked first. Obviously at the start of any set of sessions the analogue tape machines should be subjected to a rigorous line-up procedure using a tone reel containing tones at 1 kHz, 10 kHz, 100 Hz and a record pad. Usually the studio will have been left set up from the previous day's work, and the following checks should be sufficient to spot most problems. (Checks should be performed only after the equipment has been allowed to warm up.)

Analogue. 1. Carefully clean all audio head assemblies and guides with pure isopropyl alcohol or a recommended head-cleaning fluid. Care must be taken to prevent excess fluid getting into bearings, etc.

2. Play the tone reel and observe the level at 1 kHz at the machine meters, noise reduction systems (if used), and console meters from both the playback and sync heads of the machine. If possible set up a roughly equal mono mix from all tracks and note the level.

3. Observe the tape carefully in the play mode. It should show no tendency to 'ride' on to any of the guide systems. Special attention should be paid to the travel over the head assemblies.

4. Play the high-frequency tone from the tape and again check levels. The mix set up at the 1 kHz tone will still read approximately the same level if the azimuth is correct. Note that EQ and effects returns in the system will distort this check.

5. Ensure that all the cue sends are cut and noise reduction systems bypassed, then set the desk oscillator to 1 kHz at the standard operating level and route to all multitrack sends. Observe the meter level on all console sends.

6. Set the multitrack to read input and again observe the level on all recorder input meters.

7. Set up the record pad (a sample of tape from the same batch as the master tapes) on the tape machine, zero the machine clock, and record 1 kHz tone on all tracks for at least one minute. Observe the level returning from tape on the machine meters.

8. Leave the machine in record mode, set the oscillator to 10 kHz, and carefully observe the level returning to the desk. In analogue machines some transport problems become very apparent at this stage.

9. Set the desk oscillator to 100 Hz or lower and again observe the returning level at the console. Secondary gap effects on analogue machines may prevent an exact level match unless the send frequency has been carefully selected, and so this should be used only as a guide.

10. Finally, return to the beginning of the record pad and deselect the desk oscillator. Initiate record on all tracks to erase the previously recorded 1 kHz tone and listen carefully to each track individually at a high monitoring level, remembering to lower the volume between each track select. Many problems related to erasure, biasing, tracking, and system noise will quickly become apparent. Even if no other checks are made before a recording session, a test similar to this should be performed. Any noise reduction systems should now be switched back in and checked.

Digital. On digital storage media, cleanliness is even more important. A very small amount of dirt can cause an uncorrectable error. As with analogue machines, heads and guides should be cleaned at the start of the session and at convenient times during the session. Cotton gloves should be worn if the tape needs to be handled, as perspiration can cause problems.

Machine performance can be simply checked at the start of a session by recording pink noise on all tracks and observing the error correction indicators on playback. These indicators should be checked constantly during the session, as excessive correction will eventually lead to muting. Recordings should be copied immediately if a problem is detected.

Other areas

1. Check control room diary/fault book.
2. Check desk power-supply/indicators if fitted.
3. Check amplifier and computer installations for signs of overheating.
4. Check headphones and monitor systems with music. Fresh ears will sometimes hear substandard reproduction not noticed at the end of a long day.

Periodic procedures

As well as the daily performance checks outlined above, the whole control room and studio should be subjected to regular service procedures. In a busy studio these will have to be fitted around the booked sessions. A good manager will ensure that preventative maintenance is not allowed to be left for too long and that adequate time is allocated for it.

Tape machines

The easiest solution is to carry a spare machine. Since this will be invaluable for editing, copying, slaving, and extra tracks, as well as providing a very quick method of fault-finding, there is a strong case for its inclusion in every professional studio. Servicing is then a matter of finding suitable periods when the spare machine is not required and removing it to the service area. Periodic checks should be performed as follows:

(a) *Head assemblies.* On analogue machines, a constant visual check should be maintained for signs of uneven wear due to wrap or zenith problems and gap breakup on ferrite heads. If a bad wear pattern is allowed to persist, a very expensive head will need to be replaced long before its rated life. Heads should also be checked regularly for high-frequency spacing loss and lapped when a problem is detected. Note that manufacturers' alignment jigs are essential when refitting heads. Some assemblies also feature flutter idlers. As their name suggest, these idlers can induce flutter if bearings are not maintained.

Most head assemblies will gradually become magnetized if left unchecked, with a resultant loss of high frequencies due to erasure. It is therefore essential that all head assemblies are demagnetized on a very regular basis. Care must be taken to move the degausser slowly at all times in the vicinity of the heads, or the head could end up being more magnetized due to a sharp movement. All master tapes and test tapes should be moved well out of the way before using one of these tools, and the tape machine must be switched off to prevent the replay electronics being damaged.

Head assemblies on digital machines should not be touched, as they are set to a much finer tolerance and can be set up only by the manufacturer. Degaussing of these heads is not normally required.

(b) *Transport.* Many transports have pinch roller systems which push the tape against a capstan motor to control absolute speed. These assemblies need regular inspection and cleaning to ensure that they do not cause tape tracking problems. Tape tension should also be checked regularly since a small drift can have dramatic consequences on the sound reproduction. Digital tape, being thinner and more fragile, requires greater tension control from the transport. Hence even greater care must be exercised when setting up these machines.

(c) *Electronics.* The alignment of the tape machine electronics is necessary to compensate for variations in manufacture of the magnetic tape used on the machine, as well as the more usual processes of wear and ageing. Thus the electronics are subject to far more routine adjustment than other items.

As well as the rudimentary checks mentioned above, there is a strong case for checking sensitivity and bias on a regular basis, especially if tapes from different batches are being used on the same set of sessions. As the heads wear, the resonant circuit on the erase head will change, and realignment for optimum erase depth is required on an occasional basis. If the master bias oscillator frequency is adjusted for any reason, then all bias trap circuits must be checked. Digital machines also require regular checks in many areas to ensure a standard performance, and these should be performed in accordance with the manufacturer's specification.

Monitor systems

Being the acoustic interface between the electronics and the human ear, the control room monitor systems are exposed to constant subjective analysis by all present. A modern studio monitor usually requires multiple power amplifiers, both passive and electronic crossovers, and nowadays many studios also utilize ⅓ octave equalizers for further control. The loudspeaker itself is a very fragile item and can be damaged by even moderate abuse. This can be further aggravated by a badly set-up system. Adjustment should be attempted only with a clear understanding of the strengths and weaknesses of the whole monitor chain. An accurate spectrum analyser is an essential item for setting up the system but should be used only in conjunction with critical listening tests on known material.

Consoles

The modern music recording console is a very complex system containing several hundred front panel controls and switches. It is therefore inevitable that faults may occasionally be present for some time before they are noticed. For this reason, the whole console should be periodically tested in an orderly fashion and every function and indicator exercised. In addition the following checks should be made:

1. Noise measurements from every strip should be checked against the specification.
2. Meters and gain structure should be checked against an external reference.
3. Faders should be checked for smooth operation and visually inspected for the ingression of various solids and liquids.
4. Power supplies should be checked for correct voltage and trip operation. A console's performance can be severely compromised and damage can occur through incorrect power rails.
5. Computers for automation and general data storage are now commonplace and complete digital systems a reality. If the computer is maintained in a prop-

erly air-conditioned and dust-free environment, then these systems can be extremely reliable. Floppy-disc storage systems should be regularly cleaned and the whole system occasionally checked by running diagnostics programs.

Microphones

Microphones are at the boundary between the recording system and the sound source, and as such are subject to the same vagaries as loudspeakers. A microphone can be rejected for no other reason than that it does not sound right. Microphones are extremely fragile devices and should be treated with great care. Capacitor microphones are very sensitive to dust and spittle, which can give rise to a severe loss in level. This type of microphone should be regularly inspected and the capsule occasionally cleaned with distilled water, exercising extreme care. Any wrinkling or rupture on the capsule surface will probably compromise its performance and can be repaired only by the manufacturer.

Ribbon microphones contain a large permanent magnet and again are very fragile. Do not carry two in the same hand or leave near magnetic tapes. Storage should be in separate compartments. Repair of some types can be effected but ribbon replacement is again best performed by the manufacturer.

The third main category is dynamic microphones. These are probably the most robust and are very popular in high-risk areas. Consequently most problems are due to physical damage. Apart from reassembling the pieces, capsule replacement by the manufacturer is usually the only answer.

Leads

Connecting leads are one of the mainstays of any studio. They are used in all areas to customize the whole set-up to the session's requirements. Since leads are in essence very simple pieces of equipment, there can be few problems more frustrating on a session than having to cope with faulty leads and connections. All microphone leads, machine looms, and ancillary looms should be visually checked at frequent intervals for signs of damage, and connector clamps securely tightened. Regular testing for continuity on leads in high-risk areas, such as microphone leads, should be performed. A simple test facility in the studio will prove very useful. Console patch bays usually utilize GPO or bantam jack systems. Due to the high insertion force and contact method, the patch jacks used in these fields are usually made from unplated brass. Regular cleaning is therefore essential to maintain these cords in a usable state.

As well as the standard looms and leads, every studio soon collects a myriad of interconnecting leads to cope with different clients' personal equipment. Storage of these can be a problem since some will be only rarely used. Whenever possible these leads should be made a standard short length to enable them to be hung straight on a cable rack.

Custom equipment

One of the more interesting tasks for the technical engineer is the construction of specialized equipment for the studio. Today manufacturers provide a very wide range of equipment for the audio industry. However, a manufacturer can only respond to a sizeable demand, and a creative studio environment will soon discover the need for something not available commercially. Projects of this nature can provide very worthwhile innovations; however, careful consideration should be given at an early stage to the cost, time required, and eventual usefulness.

Another inevitable consequence of the wide choice of manufacturers is a lack of common standards. This means that the studio is many cases has to provide the interface. This is a more common area for custom-made equipment and can provide the technical engineer with ample scope to exercise his talents.

Reliability

Since the repair of unserviceable items is one of the main tasks performed by a technical engineer, a clear understanding of the main causes of failure is essential. Reliability is the subject of many textbooks and is a major consideration during the design of any equipment. The problems facing a technical engineer are of a different nature. Until all else fails, he must normally assume that the design engineer has done his job correctly; previous experience is usually the greatest asset when identifying the causes of malfunction. Most components follow what is colloquially referred to as the 'bath tub' law (see Figure 14.1). Failures usually occur in the first few hours, or after a number of years. In the interval between, the equipment is usually very reliable, as indicated in the diagram.

Active electronic components

Curiously enough, if the design of the electronics is good and the equipment is thoroughly soak-tested by its maker, then this is one of the more reliable areas. Unfortunately, it is also the area which can cause the most problems, as failures can be quite subtle, often not appearing until the equipment has warmed up for hours, and then sounding faulty to only the most fastidious ears.

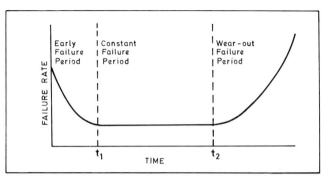

Fig. 14.1. The 'bath tub' curve, showing the periods when maximum failure rate may be expected

Passive components

Again this is usually a very reliable area, with the notable exception of capacitors. These have a definite shelf-life, after which they should be discarded. Capacitors in old equipment which has been left switched off for a long period will also be highly unreliable. Equipment in such a state should be gradually brought up to full power by using a variable transformer on the mains input.

Electromechanical components

Switches, connectors, relays, loudspeakers, disc drives, and the like all come under this heading by virtue of the fact that they all have moving parts. Problems due to wear, contact corrosion, metal fatigue, arcing, and so on are a major cause of failure and can occur at any time due to use or abuse. Troubleshooting is usually quite easy although repair can sometimes be very awkward.

Solder

In common with most metals, solder is prone to fatigue. Its widespread use in the field of electronics is due to its low melting-point and good conductivity. However, it is mechanically very weak, and every joint must be supported, usually by the use of a printed circuit board or support pillar. Excessive vibration (plenty of that in the average studio), loose nuts on switches, and similar problems will very quickly cause failure of solder joints.

The other main problem with solder is the phenomenon known as the 'dry joint'. This is due to oxidization of the surface of the component pin and/or board prior to soldering, or lack of flux during soldering. This gives rise to a solder joint where surface tension prevents a true weld.

Unfortunately, this can sometimes give rise to a joint which initially looks and performs perfectly. Progressive oxidization can then cause a high resistance and fault condition long afterwards.

The third problem is one of temperature. A low-temperature soldering iron will cause the flux to burn off prematurely, giving rise to all the problems mentioned above. When the solder does finally melt, it will make a very crystalline joint, and there is a very real danger that the component will have been damaged.

Other facilities

As well as the actual recording systems, every studio requires a complex electrical and air-conditioning system. Whilst the audio technical engineer should not be expected to undertake installation and full maintenance of these systems, he should have a clear understanding of their operation.

Electrical

All electrical systems should be installed and tested by a qualified electrician. Insurance cover may well be invalid if current regulations are not strictly adhered to. These regulations now require that all exposed metal surfaces are locally bonded to earth. This can sometimes be at odds with the audio requirement to have only one earth connection, to prevent induced hum loops. Great care must be taken at all times that both these requirements are fully met. Most professional studios have a separate technical earth rather than relying on the supply authority's connection. A high-impedance earth can be the root cause of many studio technical problems and should occasionally be checked. There is also a legal requirement to provide an emergency lighting system, adequate fire alarm system, and fire extinguishers. These should be regularly checked and logged. If any filming or video shoots are envisaged, there will be a heavy power requirement for lighting. Suitable outlets at an accessible point would be very useful.

There is a tendency amongst lighting design engineers to install banks of thyristor dimmers. Whilst these can be successfully installed in a studio and can look extremely decorative, great care should be exercised in the siting of all such cable runs, which must be installed in earthed steel conduit or mineral cable.

Most mains-borne interference can usually be removed by an isolating transformer on the main control-room power feed in conjunction with a radio frequency filter. Mains voltage regulation should not normally be necessary, with the possible exception of location work. If heavy voltage fluctuation is a problem, there is probably a good case for a generator.

Air-conditioning

An effective air-conditioning system is expensive to install, maintain, and run. Since a failure in this area will quickly bring a studio to its knees, the technical engineer should have a working knowledge of its operation and protection systems. Much money can be wasted in a system which has been incorrectly designed, operated, or maintained.

One of the acoustical requirements of a studio control room is a very quiet environment, isolated from external noise sources. This is usually achieved by the use of heavy lagging, isolated structures, and sealant, all of which give rise to a room perfectly sealed against heat dissipation. Coupled with 10 kW of heat from machinery and lighting, this calls for an air-conditioning design which needs to work irrespective of the external temperature. A system with spare capacity will soon pay dividends.

Any plant room should be visited daily to ensure that no pumps or compressors have tripped. The water or air send and return temperatures should be noted, together with pressure readings from compressors etc. Standby systems such as pumps need to be rotated regularly and filters cleaned or renewed.

Recording Techniques

15 The spoken word

Derek Taylor (revised by Peter Wisbey)

At the outset it should be said that all microphone balancing is an art or a technique, not a science. It is impossible to lay down hard-and-fast rules. If you say something must always (or never) be done, the next day some combination of programme requirement/studio acoustic/equipment characteristic will prove that the only practical solution is the exact opposite. The only criterion is: will it sound right to the listener? The only way of being sure is to try something and listen. This may take time, and this chapter is designed to help to obtain the desired result more quickly by using well-tried methods and avoiding some of the pitfalls. In practice the method adopted will be controlled to a large extent by the facilities and time (that is to say money) available.

A single voice

The simplest form of programme likely to be encountered is a single voice, as in a talk or story reading. The object should be to produce an accurate representation of the person's voice, not iron out all voices to a standard 'good quality'. The best plan with a new speaker is to go into the studio and have a short conversation to put him at his ease, and listen to the character of his voice.

The studio should have a reverberation time in the order of 0.25 to 0.4 sec at all frequencies, with an even decay. Also, it should not be too large, something about the size of an average living-room. A large studio, even if it is dead enough, sounds wrong. The impression of size is given by the timing of the first reflections; the longer these are delayed the larger the studio sounds. Acoustic screens can help in such a case. Arranged round the microphone, they may not have any significant effect on the total reverberation time but they will provide an earlier first reflection.

The microphone type is not critical provided it has a smooth frequency response. Avoid bright-sounding microphones as they often have resonances in the upper-middle and top registers which emphasize sibilance. Some microphones which sound good on orchestral strings are very unpleasant for speech. At the same time, working too close to a pressure-gradient microphone (i.e. a ribbon or any microphone with a figure-of-eight polar diagram) will produce bass tip-up which can alter the character of a voice and reduce clarity. This bass tip-up effect is much reduced with cardioid microphones and absent from omnidirectional microphones, as explained in Chapter 6.

As far as microphone mounting is concerned, the choice is either a table stand or suspension from the ceiling or a boom. If a table stand is favoured, strict precautions must be taken against mechanically transmitted bumps and rumble. Movements of the speaker may produce very little airborne noise but considerable mechanical interference. Also, structure-borne noise, such as footsteps in another part of the building, traffic, or tube trains, can be a problem. The stand should be as solid as possible to provide inertia and there should be no loose joints or spigots to cause clicks and rattles. There should also be effective mechanical decoupling between the stand and the microphone. Flexible swan-necks are quite effective for lightweight microphones. In studios rigged permanently for speech, such as news studios, a more elaborate set-up is often used, with the swan-necks mounted via shock absorbers on to a low steel frame bolted to the floor. They then protrude through a hole in the table without touching it. It is probably simpler to avoid these problems by suspending the microphone over the table from a boom with elastic cables.

The type of table and accessories, such as script racks, can have a significant influence on the sound quality and ruin an otherwise good studio. Any hard objects can reflect sound up into the microphone, but they will reflect only sounds whose wavelengths are shorter than the dimensions of the reflecting surface. Thus the bass frequencies are not affected, but the higher frequencies are reinforced with a slight delay, or phase shift, and often produce a harsh quality.

Tables should be as acoustically transparent as possible; a satisfactory construction has proved to be a wooden frame covered on top with perforated steel (approximately ¼-inch holes closely spaced) covered with loudspeaker cloth (Figure 15.1). An ⅛-inch thick layer of felt or plastic foam under the cloth can increase its stability; the cloth must be fixed only at the edges, as any movement on the steel may cause rustling noises.

Script racks or lecterns should also be acoustically transparent, but they are a doubtful asset. It is important that the speaker should speak directly into the microphone, and a rack may help him to keep his head up and not read into the table, but the script can also cause HF reflections, and the angle of the rack may direct the reflections into the microphone. It is better to encourage the speaker to hold the script up at the side of the microphone so that he can speak directly into it and simply divert his eyes to the side to read.

The main factors in the balance of a single voice are perspective and volume, and both are a function of the distance from the microphone. The perspective is the ratio of direct-to-indirect sound being picked up—the further

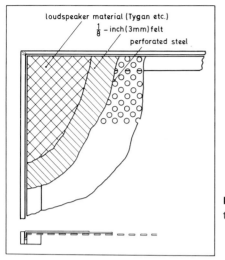

loudspeaker material (Tygan etc.)
$\frac{1}{8}$ – inch (3mm) felt
perforated steel

Fig. 15.1. Construction of an acoustically transparent talks table

away the more indirect sound is received. However, this is also a function of the polar diagram of the microphone (see Chapter 6). A figure-of-eight will pick up less reflections from the studio walls, ceiling, and so on than an omnidirectional microphone, as it is live on only two faces. Thus the ribbon will sound closer.

Very close working for speech should be avoided (except for special effects in drama). The technique of modern singers who handle microphones like ice-cream cones should be actively discouraged. A good working distance is about 45–60 cm, and even this is too close for a ribbon microphone unless the bass tip-up is countered by a filter to roll off the bass. Any close working tends to emphasize the mechanical processes of speaking giving rise to teeth clicks and lip-smacking; also, the sheer weight of breath can cause blasting and popping of the microphone, especially on the explosives—Ps, Bs, etc. A windshield can help with the latter. If the speaker has a weak voice, it is generally better to increase the microphone gain than to allow him to sit too close to the microphone.

Electronic frequency correction is best kept to a minimum. As mentioned, a high-pass filter may be essential when using a ribbon microphone, but, with a very woolly voice the addition of a presence hump can improve clarity; conversely, some reduction of the higher frequencies, such as a presence dip, can help a very sibilant speaker, but discretion must be used.

Interviews and discussions

The term 'balance' is more applicable where two or more voices are involved. For interviews it is more natural for the two people to be facing one another, and if their voices are of similar volume and have no unusual characteristics a ribbon microphone placed between them will serve very well (Figure 15.2). The figure-of-eight polar diagram will accommodate the two speakers whilst being dead to the rest of the studio, and will therefore reduce any ambient noise. If the volumes of the voices are not well matched, however, the microphone can be placed nearer to one speaker than the other, but there is a limit to how far this can be done as there is the danger of excessive bass on one voice. Also the perspectives will change. In this situation two cardioid microphones arranged back to back are more satisfactory. The perspectives will be better maintained, as the microphones can be placed at the same distance from each speaker, any bass tip-up is greatly reduced, and the compensation for volume is done electrically.

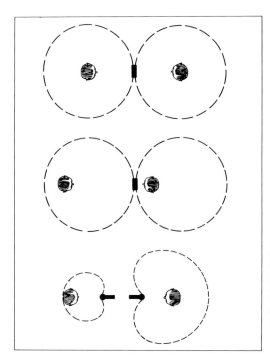

Fig. 15.2. Two evenly balanced voices can use a single bidirectional microphone (top). If one voice is louder, the distance can be adjusted (centre) or separate cardioids can be used (bottom)

A cardioid microphone can be used for round-table discussions. It can either be hung with the dead side upwards, which will reduce ventilation noise from the ceiling, or stood on the table. It is even better in a well in the centre of the table, which will reduce problems like script rustles, but of course it may then be subject to bumps if the table is knocked or kicked. A word of warning regarding cardioid microphones may not be out of place here: many microphones described as cardioid are only so over a restricted frequency range. They are frequency omni in the bass and single-sided in the top, getting narrower as the frequency increases. Therefore, if you are going to work around a cardioid, as distinct from into the front, it is better to arrange the microphone either a little above mouth level, if hanging, or below if table-mounted. This avoids working in the areas where the level is likely to vary with frequency.

As with two-voiced programmes, a single microphone works well for larger groups if all voices are of similar volume or if all speakers are experienced broadcasters; if not, then a multi-microphone set-up is needed. One cardioid microphone per person is often used. Some news studios have a large D-shaped table with room for a presenter and news-reader on the straight side and up to six contributors round the curve, each with his own microphone. This is a rather elaborate solution, and having a large number of microphones open together in a small studio can cause problems of increased ambient noise, and also phasing due to a voice being picked up by more than one microphone.

Whenever more than one microphone is used at a time, great care must be taken to ensure that they are in phase, otherwise the voice will take on a thin and distant quality. This can cause complications if mixed polar diagrams are involved, as the two sides of a figure-of-eight or a hypercardioid are in opposite phase. Therefore, for example, if a cardioid microphone is placed in the field of the back of a ribbon both microphones may pick up the same voice, but out of phase.

Panel games and quizzes before an audience present problems of their own. The main possibilities are either a long or horseshoe-shaped table with the question-master in the middle and the team split equally either side, or two tables facing each other on either side of the stage with the question-master on one and the team on the other. This is useful if there is a guest artiste who appears for only part of the show, as he/she can share the question-master's table. For the team, one microphone between every two artistes is a practical alternative to everyone having their own. Picking up questions from the audience is best done with a hand microphone on a trailing cable, or a radio microphone passed to the questioner by an assistant. Attempting to pick out one person in an audience with a rifle microphone is often unsatisfactory.

Actuality interviews using portable gear are best conducted by holding a cardioid microphone vertically at about chest level between the interviewer and the interviewee, somewhat nearer to the latter. The habit of some interviewers of holding the microphone first to their own mouth and then thrusting it in the face of their victim for the reply, is disturbing to the person concerned and usually produces a lot of handling noises from the microphone. This sort of technique should be adopted only in cases where the background noise (traffic, machinery, etc.) is excessive and it is not practical to move to a quieter venue.

As stereo portable tape recorders are now common, two tie-back/lapel microphones can be used, one on each track, and then the interview balanced later in the studio. The two tracks can either be mixed to mono or, if it is going into a stereo programme, the two tracks panned a little way left and right of centre. An interview full left and right would sound too wide apart.

Drama

The balance engineer's job in drama is to provide the actors with a suitable environment which will convey to the listener the impression that the action is taking place in the locations indicated by the plot. This aural scenery is created partly by the acoustics and partly by effects, and within this setting the actors must be able to make convincing moves.

The most important factors in the acoustics of the settings are the reverberation time and the size of the location. To cope with all types of dramatic productions, the studio needs to be fairly large—around 850 cubic metres—and the acoustic treatment varied to give different reverberation times in different areas, with curtains to shut an area off if required. A separate very dead or anechoic room leading off the main studio is very useful for outdoor scenes but must be fairly large. Typical reverberation times are 0.2–0.3 sec for the dead end, 0.5 sec for the normal part, and 0.7–0.8 sec for the live end. It is a great advantage if the live end has a carpet which can be rolled back for lives scenes or laid to deaden it down and give a bigger normal area. Portable acoustic screens with one reflecting and one absorbing side can be used to modify the studio acoustics and give a larger number of different sets.

Some productions have been recorded partially or completely on location, but this can be very costly, especially in time, and in cash terms if the cast is large. The results can be very good, but finding locations without unwanted extraneous sounds is very difficult. In addition, monitoring conditions are likely to be rather primitive, and if faults are found during the subsequent editing session, repeats may be difficult or even impossible to arrange. Much of television is recorded on location, but in radio drama the entire story has to be conveyed to the audience in sound terms. In television most of the information is in the picture, and unfortunately sound quality has sometimes to be sacrificed. Location pictures may end up with studio sound.

Mono drama

In mono drama the most useful microphone is a ribbon. Its figure-of-eight polar diagram means that actors can face each other, which is more natural and comfortable for them than standing side by side. Also, having two dead sides means that the studio can be made to give the impression of much greater size than its physical dimensions dictate. The reason for this is that our judgement of distance is determined by the ratio of direct-to-indirect sound; the more indirect the further away the source appears. Thus anyone standing close to the microphone in the dead field will not be picked up except by reflections from the studio walls, and consequently will sound very distant. If he then backs away from the microphone and circles round on to the live side, he will appear to have made a long straight approach. To produce the same effect on an omnidirectional microphone would require three or four times the studio space. For normal speech, the actors should not work closer than about arm's length from the microphone, and should step back or turn off slightly when using a very loud voice. However, for very intimate scenes or 'thought-voices' they may work much closer, down to three or four inches. In this case it is essential to work across the microphone instead of straight on to it, to avoid popping and blasting. It may well be worth while rigging a cardioid with a windshield close by for the actor to turn to for thought-voices.

A cardioid microphone suspended with the dead side upwards is often used for scenes involving a large number of actors, especially in fairly live acoustics such as courtrooms. This gives much more room to work, and very long approaches and recedes are not usually required.

Artificial reverberation or 'echo' is often required. The traditional 'echo room' has gone out of fashion, but echo plates are still used. Digital reverberation/delay devices provide a much more elegant solution, and in theory almost any acoustic can be synthesized. As has been mentioned, the aural impression of room size is largely determined by the timing of the first reflection; it is therefore desirable to delay the start of the reverberation signal when simulating a large location. Adding straight reverberation may work for a small prison cell, but for a convincing church ambience, some delay is required.

It may be thought that, using such a versatile digital device, a dead studio and a single microphone is all that is required. However, this is not likely to produce the best results from the cast: experienced actors make their moves and project their voices to suit the acoustic, and they need their acting area to be defined. This may mean only a few hard screens round the microphone in the dead part of the studio for a drawing-room, and another microphone in the live part, using the whole area, for a church; much of the engineer's job of dynamic control will then be done for him.

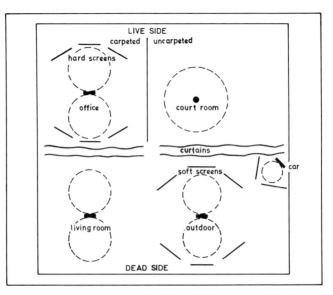

Fig. 15.3. Typical layout for mono drama in a live end/dead end studio with movable screens

A typical set-up is shown in Figure 15.3. The requirements of the script are: living-room, outdoor, car interior, office, and courtroom. For this a figure-of-eight microphone on the dead side will suffice for the living-room. The outdoor must be as dead as possible, and is therefore on the same side of the studio but surrounded by soft screens for more absorption. There is no need to use screens on the dead sides of the microphone, and those on the live sides must be angled so that any reflections from them are dissipated into the dead studio and not back at the microphone. No two screens must be parallel, otherwise standing waves will be set up.

The car interior must sound small and boxy, so there must be a reflecting surface very near to the microphone. A good plan is to screen off a corner of the studio and place a ribbon microphone with one live side close to the wall (but not quite parallel to it), with the actors sitting side by side on the other face. The office would be on the live side of the studio with hard screens to reduce the size of the location. If this proves to be over-bright then soft screens should be used.

The courtroom could be the majority of the live side with a suspended cardioid microphone. If this is not bright enough, artificial reverberation can be added, but for a long scene this may be tiring to listen to. It may be better to rig another cardioid or omni microphone high up for atmosphere and crowd reaction and add any necessary reverberation to that. The reverberation times achieved will almost certainly not be those found in real locations, but they should provide suitable contrasts to give the right impressions to the listener.

Sound effects

The addition of background effects will heighten these impressions, especially on outdoor scenes. However, too much reliance must not be put on them. The technique of using only one acoustic and just adding different backgrounds is very unconvincing and distracts from the action of the play.

Effects are divided into two groups, recorded or spot. Spot effects are those performed in the studio during the action of the scene, such as doors, crockery, pouring drinks, telephones, and so on. Recorded effects are backgrounds and sounds which cannot conveniently be accommodated in the studio, such as express trains. At one time, spot effects were used to simulate all the sounds that could not be got into the studio, like lead shot on a drum for sea-wash, the thunder sheet, wind machine, and the like, but with the reduction in size and weight of mobile recording gear there is less necessity to fake effects, and with the improvements in transmission and reception it is more difficult to pass them off on the listener.

There may be a temptation to record all effects and play them in from tape, or dub them in afterwards, but it is much better for the actors and much easier to get the perspectives right if spot effects are used when appropriate. The timing of an effect is vital and can turn high drama into farce if mistimed. A good spot effects operator works with the actor and positions himself either alongside or in the same perspective on the opposite side of the microphone, and the scene is acted out naturally. A separate spot microphone should be avoided if possible, as it tends to alter the studio acoustic and distort perspectives when it is faded up; it also divorces the spot operator from the action.

Doors are difficult to make sound convincing. If they are built into the wall for the sake of solidness, they are nearly always in the wrong perspective and sound wrong anyway as there is no room beyond them. Portable doors, on the other hand, are much more convenient and easier to get into the correct perspective but tend to sound flimsy.

Choosing the best source for recorded effects and the most appropriate system of recording depends largely on the time and resources available. Given access to a good library of recorded effects, and only a limited time to complete the programme, the choice is obvious. However, if the effects can be recorded specially for a particular programme, the end result is likely to be better. The arrival of the compact disc has greatly improved the storage and speed of access of recorded effects. Gone are the vinyl discs with their surface noise and limited life. The CD allows rapid access to as much as two hours of material on each disc; quiet backgrounds really are quiet. DAT is another useful medium both for field recording and playing-in of special effects. Access is less speedy than on CD, but is certainly superior to reel-to-reel tape.

Whichever system is employed, it must be flexible and fast enough to enable the effects to keep pace with the action. It is no good having all the effects in rigid order and duration, with the cast having to wait for cues to allow the effects to happen, for the whole flow of the play will be lost.

Gunshots are very difficult to balance; they either overpeak or, if held back, sound very flat and lacking in dramatic impact. It is probably better to pre-record them. The microphone gain can be set at normal level and the gun fired about three metres from the microphone. This will overpeak and distort but the tape will saturate and act as a limiter. When the tape is replayed, it will not need to be held back so far and will give a longer sound with more impact. Some artificial reverberation can also help. Of course a limiter can be used, but this will require experimentation with cutback and recovery times to get the most convincing result.

The usual method of cueing the actors is by cue-light but, where very quick reaction to an effect is required, as with a shot or a series of reactions, it may be easier to use foldback and let the actor react naturally. If the fold-back loudspeaker is situated on the dead side of the microphone, and the level kept fairly low, it will not affect the microphone balance. Foldback is also useful for telephone calls where one actor is on the main microphone and the other on a distorted microphone in another part of the studio. In this case it may be better to put foldback on to single headphone earpieces.

Stereo drama

Much of what has been said about mono drama also applies to stereo, but stereo does bring its own problems. Most of these are in production rather than technicalities, especially when the programme must be mono/stereo compatible. This compatibility is very important in broadcasting as it must be assumed that a significant proportion of the audience will be listening in mono. Many will be listening on portable transistor receivers or car radios, and only a small proportion of them will be sitting centrally between two stereo loudspeakers giving their full attention to the play. Thus, although directional information will heighten the enjoyment of the production, it must not be essential to the understanding of a situation. Also, stereo gives the listener greater powers of discrimination than mono (the 'cocktail party effect'), and dialogue which is perfectly audible in stereo may be drowned by effects or studio crowd in mono.

The transmission system in use is compatible from the point of view that the stereo listener hears two channels (A—left and B—right) and the mono listener hears one carrying both sets of information (A + B). This is achieved in simple terms by modulating the main carrier with A + B, or M as it is usually called, and a subcarrier with A − B (or S). If a sound is central in the stereo picture it will be equal in both channels and thus, when they are added, will form M (in practice 3 dB up); when they are subtracted, they will cancel completely and produce no S signal. A sound fully left or fully right will produce equal M and S signals. On the other hand, an out-of-phase signal will not produce any M and will be inaudible to the mono listener. Thus the system is compatible, but the programme material may not be, as any phase shifts will tend to cancel. This explains one of the reasons for the preference for coincident microphones rather than spaced pairs in broadcasting. The spaced pair relies largely on phase shift for its effect. With the coincident pair all sounds arrive at the same time (in the horizontal plane anyway) and the stereo effect is produced purely by volume differences, and is therefore potentially more compatible.

The acceptance angles for coincident microphones of different polar diagrams are shown in Chapter 6 (Figure 6.11). It will be seen that a pair of crossed figures-of-eight gives an acceptance angle of 90°. A sound on the X axis will be picked up only on the A microphone, as it is on the dead side of the B microphone, and vice versa on the Y axis. A sound in the centre is picked up equally on both, or in other positions more on one microphone than the other. However, if the sound source is moved round to one side beyond the 90° arc, it will be picked up on the front of one microphone and the back of the other, and so be out of phase. Normal stereo will be produced in the back 90° arc but the left and right directions will be reversed. Working in the out-of-phase angles must be avoided as this will produce cancellations in mono and unpredictable location in stereo.

Crossed cardioids have no back lobes, and therefore there is no out-of-phase area. The useful angle is shown as 180°. This is the full extent of the stereo picture from one loudspeaker to the other. Using the greater angle of approximately 270° will give perfectly acceptable quality but no more width; the level will fall off the further round you go. The area at the back will give a very distant perspective, and the sound is liable to jump from one side of the picture to the other rather suddenly. Hypercardioids give an angle between figure-of-eight and cardioid, about 130°.

The different acceptance angles can be very useful, so variable polar diagram capacitor microphones with two capsules in one case are favoured. However, two mono microphones mounted with their capsules as close together as possible with their axes at 90° are perfectly satisfactory. The fact that the stereo effect is dependent on the polar response means that the two capsules must be very accurately matched at all frequencies. This of course makes the microphones expensive, and even with good microphones the angles should not be taken on trust but should be checked in the studio, as the dead sides are often not true to the theoretical shape and reflections from the studio walls etc. can modify the angles and give a lop-sided work-ing area. In drama the crossed cardioid is the configuration most often used, as it gives the maximum working area. The main thing the actor has to remember is that to move in a straight line across the stage he has to walk in a semi-circle.

Coincident pairs must always be lined up, whether they are in one case or two. To ensure that the gains are equal, the microphone axes must be turned in line, and while an assistant is talking in front of the microphones the engineer listens to the S signal (i.e. both outputs on one loudspeaker but out of phase with each other) and adjusts the gains of the two channels for the null point. The monitoring should then be restored to stereo (in phase), and, with the microphones still facing the same direction, the assistant should walk slowly round the microphones talking continuously. His voice should stay in the centre of the stereo picture. It will become more distant as he passes the dead side (S), but if it moves from side to side the polar dia-grams of the two microphones do not match.

With the microphone axes reset to 90°, it is as well to check at which points the voice becomes fully in each loudspeaker. The angle found on crossed cardioids may well be greater than the theoretical 180°, due to inac-curacies in the cardioid pattern. This does not matter as long as the actors are aware of the limits of their stage. Alternatively, with variable polar dia-gram microphones, the angle can be narrowed by setting them towards the hypercardioid condition.

Working in stereo is more demanding in terms of the studio itself. Much more room is required for approaches and recedes as the dead side cannot be used as in mono. It is very difficult to get a good open-air sound as the stereo microphone reproduces the studio acoustic much more accurately, and thus very large, very dead studios with no ventilation or outside noises are required. Such a studio is unlikely to be found in practice and the best has to be made with what is available. The actors can help a lot with dis-tance by pitching their voices as if projecting, but not using much actual volume. Turning away from the microphone and talking into a soft surface can also help.

Great care must be taken with spot effects to ensure that they are in the same position and perspective as the associated voice. Footsteps may prove difficult, as coincident microphones are usually mounted one above the other, so the sounds from the floor reach the bottom capsule before the top one. This produces a time delay which gives the footsteps a slight off-set. Generally speaking, the greater discrimination given to the listener by stereo means greater realism is needed for spot effects; faked effects become all too obvious.

Recorded effects should of course be recorded in stereo, but these may not always be available. There are methods and devices whereby mono recordings can be used and produce a reasonably convincing result. With crowds, good results can be obtained by pre-recording and taking several copies of the same crowd, starting them from different points in the duration of the effect, and panning them to different places across the sound stage. There are electronic 'stereoizing' devices which rely on introducing some degree of phase shift. These work quite well on some types of effect but not on others, and it is a matter of trial and error, always bearing in mind the need for mono compatibility.

With any stereo effects, care must be taken to get the width in correct scale with the perspective. For example, a horse and cart passing in the far distance would be a point source, and a mono effect panned across would be quite appropriate. However, in the foreground the horse has two pairs of feet and the cart two sets of wheels and would take up most or all of the sound stage. Thus with stereo effects used in a different perspective to the original recording, width and off-set controls are required on the stereo channel to enable the effect to be narrowed and moved. Of course, if two ganged mono channels are used, the width and movement will be controlled on the pan-pots. In fact an effect can start distant and narrow on one side, come closer and wider in the centre, and narrow down and fade out on the other side, but this does require more than the usual complement of hands, so some pre-recording would be indicated.

At one time nearly all radio drama was performed live, and the studio techniques were developed to this end. With the introduction of tape recording and editing, and the added complexity of stereo, there was a move towards rehearsing and recording each scene, not necessarily in sequence, and compiling the production in the editing room as with film. However, with the stress on economical use of facilities and time, there is now a move back to the continuous performance with perhaps the more difficult sections pre-recorded and played in.

Binaural stereo

In recent years there has been renewed interest in dummy head recording brought about by experiments in Germany to produce a standard artificial listener for evaluating auditorium acoustics. The idea of placing two microphones in a dummy head has been used on and off since the 1920s or even earlier, but only as a source of loudspeaker stereo. During the German experiments, however, some startlingly realistic all-round sound was obtained on headphones, especially those of the open type.

Coincident microphone stereo depends for its effect on a difference in level between the two channels, derived either from the polar response of the two microphones or a mono source electrically divided between the channels. In binaural stereo, two omnidirectional microphones are placed ear-distance apart, separated by a suitable baffle to give the correct time difference. When reproduced via headphones, each ear receives the sound with a time difference which varies with the angle of the sound source, and only a very small volume difference. Thus the basis of binaural stereo is much nearer to natural hearing and produces a very realistic sound.

However, although side location and perspective are good, frontal perspective is poor for many people. The usual complaint is that the frontal image either collapses into the listener's head or even moves round behind. A minority of people do get full 360° soundfield and in tests can accurately plot the moves made by the actors in the studio. From statistics taken from listeners' letters received following BBC transmissions of binaural programmes, it seems that although only 26 per cent reported an all-round effect (62 per cent had a front hole or rear bias, 12 per cent did not mention direction), 80 per cent enjoyed the binaural effect and only 0.7 per cent were distressed by it.

The reasons for the differences in directional perception between individuals are not clear. Any sounds on the centre line will have equal time of arrival at the ears, and therefore confusion will result unless other factors can be brought in to resolve it. If it cannot be resolved, the brain puts the sound inside the head towards the back, as with mono on headphones. What these factors are seems to vary from individual to individual, and they probably have their origins in the learning processes from infancy. Sight undoubtedly plays a significant part: most people have difficulty locating sounds in fog or in a wood at night, for example. It is probable that slight head movements are used in normal locating to modify the arrival times in a sort of scanning action, but as the microphones are fixed this facility is lost.

Very accurate models of the head and ears have been made for microphone mounting, but the directional information has not proved significantly better than two microphones spaced by a simple baffle, and the quality and frequency response is degraded. Using a live human head and lodging small microphones in the outer ears may give better quality but no improvement in direction. Interestingly, experiments using extremely small microphones placed in the ear canals right up against the drums produced better results for the person involved but not for others.

One microphone set-up often adopted uses a 10-inch diameter Perspex disc with a rod through it, a little off-centre, and two electret lapel microphones mounted ear-distance apart on the rod on either side of the disc. This gives a simple, light, and unobtrusive arrangement which in practice gives at least as good results as the more elaborate and scientific designs.

Effects and music must also be recorded in binaural. If mono is used, the sound is in the middle of the listener's head; even stereo effects, although they may have some width, can only move a short distance beyond the ears and are confined to a band across the head. Binaural effects perspectives can stretch into the far distance.

Edits tend to show up much more than usual, as an angled cut interrupts the background ambience in one ear before the other and can cause a sudden sideways jump and back again, so vertical cuts must be used. Therefore mixing or dub-editing is often employed instead, although the less equipment the signal has to go through the better the quality. From the broadcasting point of view, if the binaural system could be improved in the frontal area it would be ideal, as it would produce all-round sound which could be transmitted over a stereo network without modification.

16 Classical music

Adrian Revill

The techniques involved in recording classical music are different from those used to record other types of music, and this is largely because the philosophy behind the production of the recordings is different. The record industry uses the term 'classical music' to encompass many types of music, not just the strictly classical works of Mozart or Haydn but also Romantic works by composers like Tchaikovsky and Wagner, twentieth-century music, and a growing catalogue of early music. The styles and the sound of this repertoire are very diverse but the philosophy common to the recording production is to capture a perfect performance and give the listener the impression of hearing it from a perfect seat in the concert hall. The producer and engineer keep this ideal in mind even when hundreds of takes need splicing together from sessions recorded in a venue with non-ideal acoustics. The purist approach is to use a single microphone (or stereo pair) and record the music in long continuous takes with no editing; indeed for some people this is the only valid approach. However, it must be said that the majority of classical recordings are not made in this way. Many different microphone techniques are used and, to understand how these have evolved, it is necessary to consider the parameters which contribute to the sound of a classical recording.

Sound characteristics

Figure 16.1 shows a straightforward orchestral layout with the simplest microphone technique: one coincident pair in the position shown. Listening carefully to the playback of a recording made in this way will reveal a number of characteristics which contribute to the overall sound. Perhaps the most obvious one will be perspective. Is the overall effect that the orchestra appears too close and too dry, or too distant and indistinct? Is it all in the same perspective or are some sections of the orchestra closer than others? The next feature to be noticed will probably be the width or spread of the sound. Are the violins cramped up in the centre of the picture or so widely separated from the double basses that the notorious 'hole in the middle' is apparent? The music might include a passage where the woodwind is playing a musically important part but is not heard clearly

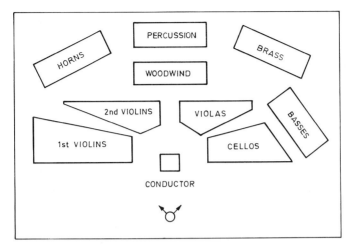

Fig. 16.1. Normal orchestral layout, showing the use of a coincident pair of microphones

because the strings are too prominent, or the strings may be drowned by the brass in the climaxes: these are problems of balance. Throughout the playback, the listener will consciously or unconsciously register the overall sound quality. Is the bass full and firm, do the top strings sound harsh or edgy? Could the sound be described as boxy, or coloured, or smooth? All these characteristics, *perspective, spread, balance*, and *quality* are interrelated yet it is possible to make a fine recording which has small deficiencies in one or other of them. In classical music recording, quality is the most important parameter and it will be considered first.

Quality

When discussing recording quality today, we can assume that most of the technical deficiencies of the medium which were once inevitable are now largely absent. For most of the history of classical music recording, technical shortcomings dominated the techniques used. The music has a wide dynamic range and this introduced distortion at high levels and noise, particularly from analogue tape, at low levels. The human voice and instruments like the pianoforte revealed electronic deficiencies very clearly and there was a constant search not only for better equipment, but for techniques to give the impression of greater realism. The availability of digital systems now offers the prospect of recordings which are for practical purposes free from obvious technical blemishes. Care is still needed and placing the analogue-to-digital converters as close to the microphones as possible, for example, is one way to ensure that the signals enter the digital domain at the earliest point. High-bit processing, at say 20 bits, produces master recordings suitable not only for transfer to current 16-bit media such as the compact disc, but for improved consumer formats in the future. Such recording equipment will have a flat frequency response and wide dynamic range. The cables and connectors will be chosen with care and the monitoring equipment will be sufficiently analytical to enable the recording engineer to hear any technical defects.

However, the factors which most influence recorded quality are not so amenable to engineering solutions. The single most important contribution is probably made by the acoustics of the recording venue. With the exception of the Abbey Road studio of EMI, very few purpose-built studios are currently used for classical music, whilst buildings intended for quite different purposes have proved successful. In London there are meeting-halls such as those in Brent and Walthamstow, churches such as All Saints' Tooting, and former places of worship like St John's Smith Square and the Henry Wood Hall. Excellent recording acoustics can be found in unlikely places, but generally the venue should be a large building which might be considered a little too reverberant for public concerts, and not built of concrete and glass. It is necessary to choose an acoustic appropriate for the music. A live acoustic which is ideal for Wagner, for example, might pose problems when recording a chamber orchestra. It is also very important that external noise is minimal. The location and construction of many otherwise suitable buildings, combined with a long reverberation time, means that noise from road traffic or aircraft makes them unusable: there are many examples of audible traffic rumble on disc.

The other most important factor affecting recording quality is the performing standards of the musicians themselves, since only a great orchestra will produce the quality of sound required to produce a really fine orchestral recording. On many occasions, the engineer and producer may worry about the microphones, fuss about their position, and make many adjustments at the start of a session, only to notice that the quality improves as the musicians warm up; the playing becomes more secure and the actual recorded sound quality starts to improve. On the other hand the experience of working with different orchestras in the same venue on successive days shows that microphone positions set up for one will not produce the best results for another, and the quality of the strings in particular may change.

Certain technical deficiencies will adversely affect quality, of course. Microphones in particular should not only possess a smooth on-axis frequency response but also uniform response off-axis, since the reverberant soundfield contributes much to the overall effect. High-quality omnidirectional microphones have always played a prominent part in achieving the sound quality desired for classical music. Some equalization of microphone channels may be used, but it is usually minimal, whereas microphone positioning must be very precise if accurate reproduction of instrumental tone is to be achieved.

Perspective

In the simple recording envisaged earlier, we may have been concerned that the orchestra sounded too close. Opinions differ about perspective, but generally classical recordings are made with a reasonable amount of reverberation. If this is overdone, orchestral detail may be blurred and the impact lost, but the very dry recordings produced in the early days of the industry reduced the scale of the performance, making the orchestra sound small and reducing the apparent dynamic range. The recording venue plays an important part here too. For example, large concert halls may have long reverberation periods but sound relatively dead in the stage area, so that microphones placed close to the stage will produce a dry unreverberant sound, whilst the loudest musical passages excite the main reverberation of the hall, causing the perspective to shift. It is frequently necessary to rig 'space' or reverberation microphones towards the back of the hall, and there are several possible configurations (see Figure 16.2). Any of the normal stereo types can be used, including a backward-facing coincident pair, spaced cardioids, omnis, or pressure zone microphones. The space microphones should in themselves produce a balanced sound, and should not be too distant, or time-delay effects will make satisfactory blending into the mix difficult.

As important as the overall perspective are relative perspectives, and the general aim with an orchestral recording will be a realistic gradation of perspective with, for example, the woodwind sounding rather more distant than the strings. The single microphone pair used in the first example (Figure 16.1) can therefore be moved backwards or forwards to produce the desired effect; moving further back will produce a more reverberant result,

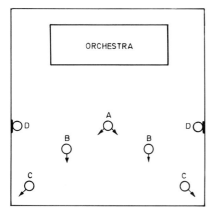

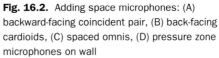

Fig. 16.2. Adding space microphones: (A) backward-facing coincident pair, (B) back-facing cardioids, (C) spaced omnis, (D) pressure zone microphones on wall

with more uniform perspectives. The dangers of moving the microphone too close are that, whilst the strings may be brought into the correct perspective, the instruments towards the rear of the orchestra will sound disproportionately distant.

Spread

As the single coincident microphone is moved backwards and forwards, the apparent width of the orchestra will change. The usual aim is to fill the sound stage with an even spread of orchestral sound, whilst the positioning of instruments and groups of instruments is unambiguous and credible. Using the single microphone pair, the spread, perspective, and balance are closely related, and they all depend on the position of the microphones and the polar diagram selected. Usually a compromise position has to be sought.

Balance

Although balance can become the predominant concern of the producer and engineer, it is not necessarily the most important parameter contributing to the sound of a classical music recording. Nor is a satisfactory balance particularly difficult to achieve when recording a straightforward orchestral work with a good orchestra and conductor. Indeed if only a single coincident pair of microphones is to be used, as in the example considered in Figure 16.1, there is little scope for modifying the musical balance. If the microphones are placed too close, then the nearer instruments will be too prominent relative to the more distant ones: the mistake most frequently made by the inexperienced. Recordings of violin-heavy orchestras with indistinct woodwind are quite common. If the balance cannot be improved to the satisfaction of producer and engineer by microphone positioning, then it will be necessary for the musicians to move or to change their internal balance, and the conductor will be involved in any decisions of this nature. This is where the notion of 'natural' balance comes in, although it is a term to be viewed with suspicion. Recording balance may not be 'natural', in the sense that techniques are adopted to change the balance which would be heard by a listener seated in front of the orchestra. Very often the acoustics of the recording venue will influence this. The recorded balance should sound realistic and give the correct musical prominence to orchestral sections or soloists. It is always worth checking by listening in the studio, if serious adjustments seem to be demanded, but it is certainly not the experience of the record industry that placing one microphone in the 'best seat in the house' necessarily produces the best recordings.

The most obvious case of the difference between recorded balance and natural balance is that of songs with orchestral accompaniment. In the concert hall, the vocal part may often be covered by the accompaniment to the extent that at times the voice is inaudible or the words unintelligible. To reproduce this balance on record would be unacceptable and, since recordings began, techniques have been adopted to give unnatural prominence to the soloist. In the early days, recordings almost obliterated the accompaniment, but they were sold on the name of the prima donna rather than the composer. To some extent the tradition lingers on, although the famous Decca recordings of Wagner's *Ring* made by John Culshaw in the 1960s were characterized by a full orchestral sound supporting the vocal lines, which resulted in recordings that sounded exciting, satisfying, and also natural and which perhaps influenced taste away from over-dominant soloists.

Recorded balance is a major preoccupation of the engineer and producer, and the following sections will describe techniques which have been evolved to control balance, but which at the same time affect all the other parameters which make up the sound of classical recording.

Single microphone pair

Once the decision is made to employ a single coincident-pair microphone technique, the only decisions remaining are the choice of polar diagram, the mutual angle, and the distance from the sound source. As the polar patterns are switched from cardioid to figure-of-eight, for example, the stereophonic image widens and the amount of reverberation, picked up on the back of the microphones, increases. As the microphone pair is moved away from the source, the stereophonic image narrows, the amount of reverberation increases, and the perspective of the whole recording will change. Very often a suitable compromise position and setting of the polar responses can be found. The height of the microphone pair can also be chosen to optimize the balance. Normally a height of 3–7 m is typical, with the intention of reducing differences in perspective between the rear and forward sections of an orchestra by increasing the height. However, an improvement in balance can adversely affect quality, since, for example, violins do not sound their best from directly above and a warmer tone can be picked up from a height nearer to that of the instrument. Thus it can be seen that all the parameters of the recording, perspective, spread, balance, and quality are interrelated, and that they should all be considered when any alteration is made in the microphone's position or polar response.

It can also be seen that certain deficiencies cannot be corrected with this technique, and the use of additional microphones is often required. Before these are considered, mention should be made of non-coincident microphone techniques.

Spaced pairs

Although some recordings are produced with non-coincident pairs of micro-phones, spaced a few centimetres or sometimes a couple of metres apart, the approach will be similar to the coincident technique described above. A different approach, using much wider spacing, is shown in Figure 16.3.

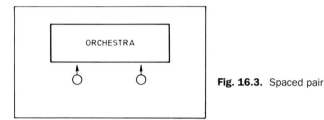

Fig. 16.3. Spaced pair

One of the earliest methods of producing stereophonic recordings of clas-sical music used a widely spaced pair of microphones. This is still the basis for more complex layouts, but in itself it rarely produces satisfactory results. The stereo imaging is imprecise and frequently the effect is of no definition in the centre of the sound stage, giving a 'hole in the middle'. The advantage of the technique, however, is the presence and attack cou-pled with width, which makes the recording superficially more impressive and glossy than coincident microphone techniques. Indeed, unless consider-able care is taken, a single coincident pair can produce a recording of the normal orchestral layout which favours the middle of the orchestra in bal-ance, spread, and tonal range. The spaced-pair technique produces record-ings of almost exactly opposite character, which verge on an extreme reproduction of width and tonal balance with undue prominence given to the back desks of the string sections (not usually the best players in the orchestra).

A more commonly employed layout uses three microphones, where the centre one fills in the 'hole' and acts as a pivot for the main pair. In this lay-out it is common to use omnidirectional microphones for all three, or sometimes cardioid microphones for the outer ones with an omni for the centre. It is worth noting that the centre microphone has to be very care-fully mixed into the picture, otherwise it can reduce the width by an unac-ceptable amount.

Hybrid techniques

Starting with a single coincident pair, it is a natural step to add one or more 'spot' microphones to enhance soloists or important orchestral sections; it is a short step from this to a technique which attempts to cover all the important sections of the orchestra with individual microphones in addition to the main coincident pair. Figure 16.4 shows a typical microphone layout for a large-scale performance.

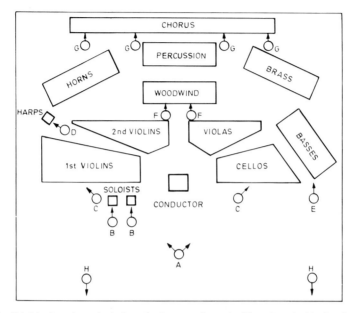

Fig. 16.4. Hybrid microphone technique for large-scale work: (A) main coincident pair, (B) solo microphones, (C) string reinforcement, (D), (E) examples of spot microphones, (F) spaced pair on woodwind, (G) chorus microphones, (H) space microphones

In producing a balanced result, the engineer will often use the coincident pair as a kind of camera to suggest the orchestral positions. The outputs of the mono spot microphones are then panned to the same positions in the picture, and their levels increased until their contribution is just audible. With care, this technique can produce recordings with very clear spatial definition and very accurate control over the balance. Perspectives need to be carefully checked, to avoid giving too much prominence to less important sections, but the recording quality, although open to criticism on theoretical grounds, can also be superior to that produced by single microphone techniques.

Concern is often expressed that such an approach can give tonal distortion, due to the phase cancellation between different microphones which are picking up the same source. In practice this rarely seems apparent, probably because not only are the sources separated by a large number of wavelengths' distance but the reverberant soundfield is extremely complex, so much so that a mathematical analysis is impossible. Quality can suffer, however, by injudicious choice of microphones, and it is necessary to choose types which have a very good off-axis frequency response.

Critics of multi-microphone techniques can point to a body of evidence: recordings spoilt by crude mixing, faulty balance, and distorted perspectives. Certainly, considerable skill is required of the engineer, but the technique is extremely flexible and capable of instant control from the sound mixing desk. For this reason it is very commonly employed for live radio and TV broadcasts as well as for specially mounted studio recordings. In its favour it can be said that many of the best recordings of classical music issued in the last two decades use the above technique or a similar one derived from spaced microphones—and therefore a truly multi-microphone approach.

Multi-microphone technique

In the layout shown in Figure 16.5, no main pair or cluster is used, the sound being built up from a number of mono microphones positioned over sections of the orchestra. Coverage depends on the layout, and is most effective when engineer and producer have full control over the seating arrangements, so that closed-circuit recording sessions are often engineered in this way. The sound picture is built up by careful balancing of the microphones on each section according to musical requirements, and the spatial balance is achieved by the addition of spaced pairs or trios. The two parameters interact, however, and care should be taken to ensure that microphones are at similar distances from the sections with similar microphone amplifier gains. Typical heights will be between 2 and 3 m above the musi-

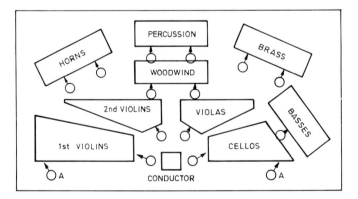

Fig. 16.5. Multi-microphone technique: note that the microphones all face outwards, and the wing microphones (A) are often omni

cians, and once again omnidirectional microphones are frequently used, especially for the string sections.

It is possible to cover straightforward orchestral recording with about a dozen microphones, but the technique is capable of considerable expansion. The CBS quadraphonic recordings produced in the 1970s used up to eleven microphones on the woodwind alone. Nevertheless, it is impossible to mike up each individual pair of musicians, as one might in a TV or light music studio, and less than twenty microphones is the norm. The technique has been evolved for classical orchestral music, is very usable for operatic and choral recordings, and can be adapted for modern symphonic music. The remainder of this chapter will look into different categories of classical music and suggest microphone techniques which are appropriate.

Orchestral music

As seen above, a coincident technique, a hybrid technique, or a multi-microphone technique are all capable of producing highly satisfactory results. The music to be recorded remains the most popular section of the record catalogue—from Mozart and Beethoven through to Stravinsky—and the aim will be to produce the effect of large forces smoothly blended. The control of dynamic range will have to be undertaken carefully, but on the whole this is not the most difficult type of music to record.

Chamber music

From string trios to wind octets, this category of music is in itself wide. A typical challenge can be the recording of a piano quintet (piano, 2 violins, viola, and cello), as shown in Figure 16.6. Despite the small forces involved, such a combination can produce very difficult problems of balance and perspective for the engineer. Chamber music in general is not easy to record, since deficiencies of balance are immediately and glaringly obvious, variations in perspective are very apparent, and the positioning needs to be accurate and convincing. A simple coincident microphone technique should be tried if possible, but it is frequently not totally effective. It must be said that the presence of a grand piano in any combination of chamber music proportions usually presents a problem, since much of the repertoire was conceived for instruments producing less volume than those used today. The piano is frequently both too loud and too distant, and a hybrid or multi-microphone technique is frequently needed to achieve a satisfactory result. Thus Figure 16.6 shows a main coincident pair *A*, in combination with possible spot microphones *B* and *C*.

The position of the musicians is extremely critical. They will have spent long hours practising together, and for the producer or engineer to move

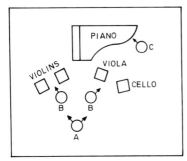

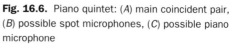

Fig. 16.6. Piano quintet: (*A*) main coincident pair, (*B*) possible spot microphones, (*C*) possible piano microphone

them around to suit the microphones will simply result in an inferior performance. It is essential that the musicians are seated so that they are comfortable, have good lines of visual and aural communication, and can produce the standard of performance which is the basis of the record.

Pianoforte

As mentioned above, it is not always easy to record a grand piano. In Figure 16.7 position *A*, the tail balance, is frequently the most effective approach, giving a good tonal balance from an instrument with the lid open. Coincident microphones in position *D* can also produce good results, and sometimes a combination of mono microphones at *B* and *C* with a coincident pair at *D* is effective. It is often necessary to use such a set-up to minimize the distortion of perspective which can occur where the top two octaves of the instrument sound more remote, more reverberant, than the middle and bass.

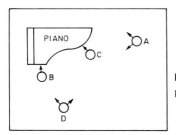

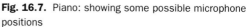

Fig. 16.7. Piano: showing some possible microphone positions

Voice and piano

Figure 16.8 shows a typical layout for recording a singer accompanied by piano. It is usually necessary to introduce a solo microphone *B* and to balance this against the main pair at *A*. For certain passages, piano microphones at *C* and *D* may also be needed. The problem with these layouts is

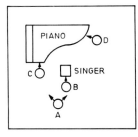

Fig. 16.8. Piano and voice: (A) coincident pair, (B) solo spot microphone, (C) and (D) possible piano microphones

one of separation, which is sometimes not helped by a soloist who does not wish to see any microphones nearby, or who moves backwards at times to lean on the piano.

Early music

The move towards 'authentic' performances of early music solves certain problems for the recording engineer and producer. Early music was probably not intended to produce the same smooth blend to which we have grown accustomed with nineteenth-century composers. It may have been that the different tonal qualities of the instruments were exploited for dramatic effect, or to clarify the part writing. Authentic performances will use instruments with gut strings played with lighter bows, which sound different from the more frequently encountered modern variety. Also baroque wind instruments sound very different from their modern counterparts, so that the engineer should approach the recording with an open mind. However, the forces employed will have been chosen so as to eliminate problems of balance, and this may suggest that a more simple microphone technique can be employed. Yet the recording should not be too distant or else the clarity and articulation of the performance could be lost, and the distinctive character of the sound might not be fully reproduced. A hybrid or multi-microphone technique has produced many very effective recordings of baroque music in recent years. For recordings of earlier Renaissance music, a similar approach may be required, with the very unusual and distinctive qualities of the instruments contributing their own balance problems.

Modern music

There is a considerable catalogue of modern orchestral music now on record. Recording techniques need to be sophisticated for the venture to be successful, and the engineer and producer require an open mind since the tonal effects intended by the composer are very often unusual and extreme. The dynamic range is also often very difficult to control, and can be made more difficult by the large size and ungainly nature of the score. It is helpful when the composer can contribute to the discussions of balance—the only category of 'classical' music where such help is usually available!

General considerations

Dynamic range

The wide dynamic range of classical music poses particular problems for the recording engineer, for although modern digital media can record and reproduce the full range encountered, satisfactory records for home listening will not usually be produced without some restrictions. The aim is to give the effect of a wide range, without either the pianissimo passages being inaudible behind domestic noise or the fortissimo passages causing distress or offence. In the past, engineers were taught to control the range using a carefully marked-up score which, from rehearsal or a previous take, had settings noted to accommodate the loudest passages. The main fader setting was then carefully reduced in the bars leading up to the climax so that, without further alteration, the peaks just reached maximum permissible level. This does not often produce the most convincing results, and more experienced balancers will adapt the technique to incorporate 'potting the peaks', that is acting like a musical compressor by reducing gains actually during the loudest passages.

Live performances

The recording, or radio or TV broadcasting, of live classical music performances places a number of constraints on the techniques adopted. There is usually no possible control of seating or orchestral layout, and microphones need to be unobtrusive (or, for opera, invisible). Microphone booms are rarely acceptable, so that vertical microphone stands and slung microphones are normal. Because of its foolproof nature, the single coincident-pair technique is often a good start, and a hybrid technique based on this is that most commonly employed. Space microphones need very careful positioning if they are to capture reverberation without audience noise. Since retakes are impossible, it is frequently necessary to use multitrack recording to cover balance problems caused by accidents, or by the changes in acoustic when an audience is present. At rehearsal, when the concert hall is empty, the mix will be different in many respects from that needed for the actual event. For instance, considerably more reverberation, natural or artificial, is almost always required.

Mixing classical music

Whatever technique is employed, the actual process of mixing classical music for a satisfactory result is not the same as that used for other types of music. Even when a microphone is carefully positioned, and labelled on the mixing desk channel '1st violins', listening to that channel on its own will reveal that it has most of the orchestra on it as well—often with other sections louder than the violins. Mixing is a process of carefully balancing the outputs of several such channels which inevitably have poor separation, and it is only when pairs or groups of channels are balanced across the stereo sound stage that the complete picture is built up. Equalization and special effects are seldom used, except that artificial reverberation may help close microphones to be blended in without distorting the perspective, and time delay can be used for the same purpose. Even recordings made in such reverberant acoustics as the Royal Albert Hall or St Paul's Cathedral have incorporated artificial echo.

Microphone placing

The secret of recording classical music is to put the microphones in the right place. The preceding paragraphs have outlined the general principles but no rules can be laid down, and the optimum positions have to be found by trial and error. Experienced recording teams try to minimize the errors by carefully noting the position and height of the microphones for every session. They may use the same venue year after year, and often the same microphones. Without building up this kind of documented experience, it is easy to spoil a recording by placing microphones too close, but at least this misjudgement can be corrected later by adding reverberation. On the other hand, too distant a balance is usually impossible to put right. It is unfortunate that subtleties of perspective can be difficult to judge at many recording venues, where listening conditions are rarely up to studio standards. Throughout the recording the musical score should be guiding the eye and ear, and all adjustments to microphones and channel settings should be made with careful attention to the interaction of balance, perspective, spread, and overall recorded quality: a very demanding business.

17 Popular music

Mike Ross-Trevor

This chapter describes the basic guidelines for recording live music in the recording studio. This falls into two main categories: (*a*) orchestral music with rhythm section as used for easy listening albums, musicals, TV background music, and commercials; (*b*) small ensemble rock and pop groups aimed at the popular music charts. These guidelines can in no way be described as definitive, as the methods and ideas of today's producers and engineers vary considerably. We shall concentrate on the recording of live musical instruments as opposed to the computer and MIDI-based areas of recording. The approach can of course be modified to suit individual situations and requirements.

Setting up the recording session

The engineer should have some knowledge or contact with the producer or composer, and in some cases the musicians, before the start of the session, to assess the type of music to be recorded and the approach required. Most producers have a preconceived idea of how they would like the finished recording to sound, and they will try to impart these ideas to the engineer to enable him to set up the studio and equipment accordingly. The engineer should also establish how many tracks the producer wishes to use during the initial recording stages. In most cases where every section of the orchestra is recorded at the same time, all the tracks can be used because overdubbing will not be necessary. However, it may be wise to keep at least one track free for any last-minute overdubbing. In analogue recording, Track 24 is normally used for recording a timecode for use with mixing console automation or synchronizing slave machines and music computers. Digital multitrack recorders have dedicated timecode tracks, allowing the option of using all the available tracks for music recording.

When working with pop singers or rock bands, only a few tracks are used during the initial stages, as much overdubbing of electronic keyboards, extra instruments, and vocals will take place later on. Therefore the more tracks left open for subsequent overdubbing the better. This will make the engineer's job easier at the mix-down stage, avoiding the need for sharing tracks, which could result in several sounds on the same track requiring different amounts of equalization, echo, or effects.

The engineer should also establish with the producer what kind of equipment should be made available. The three methods of multitrack recording commonly used today are:

(a) 24-track analogue running at 30 ips, using Dolby A noise reduction (though many engineers prefer to record without Dolby A using a higher recording level to reduce tape noise);

(b) 24-track analogue running at 15 ips, using Dolby SR;

(c) 24/32/48-track digital, using a sampling frequency of 44.1 kHz without high-frequency emphasis.

In the case of a 24-track recording with multiple overdubs, it soon becomes apparent that more tracks are needed, so a second 24-track recorder is synchronized with the original using timecode recorded on Track 24 of both machines, which are now treated as master and slave respectively. Timecode is then read by a synchronizer such as a Lynx or Adam-Smith module. To avoid running both machines during overdubbing, and waiting for the machines to lock up together, a two-track monitor mix of the main tracks from the master machine can be recorded on the slave machine, and the performers can then overdub to this.

If a second multitrack has to be avoided for the sake of time or expense, a second option known as 'track bouncing' is available. Two or more recorded tracks can be mixed together by replaying them from the sync heads through the mixing console, adding EQ if necessary, and re-recording on to a spare track on the same machine. The original tracks can then be erased and used again for overdubbing. It should be noted that this process can result in a generation loss in sound quality, so signals of wide dynamic range should not be bounced in this way for fear of high-frequency losses and increased tape noise. The most common use of this technique is for recording vocalists who perhaps need to record with double or triple tracking. Once all the parts have been recorded, using as many as nine tracks, these can then be bounced down to two tracks in a stereo picture, leaving nine tracks available for further overdubbing.

Digital multitrack recording makes many of the problems associated with analogue equipment obsolete, such as tape noise and tape saturation. There is also greater track availability in digital 48-track recorders, and the option of track bouncing in the digital domain without any degradation in the process. Also sounds can be moved around the tracks for grouping or inserting musical corrections from one track to another.

All this equipment information should be confirmed with the producer, ideally several days ahead, so as to allow time for things to be set up. On the day of the session, everything should be well prepared, as time wasted is money spent, especially when working with professional musicians booked on a set fee for a three-hour session. Correct preparation in advance helps to create an easy and relaxed environment for the session itself.

Studio layout

In an effort to obtain separation between the sections of the orchestra, and each instrument in the rhythm section, it is frequently necessary to adopt a multi-microphone technique, using directional microphones, with each microphone or group of microphones fed to its own track on the tape. The orchestra used for popular or light music consists of four main sections: strings, woodwind, brass, and rhythm (made up of drums, bass guitar, electric guitar, piano, electronic keyboard, and percussion). It is important for musical and recording purposes that members of each main section are seated together in their own separate parts of the studio, and that everybody can see the conductor clearly.

The main problem with recording large orchestras is excessive leakage between instruments/microphones. Brass, drums, and percussion cause the most serious problems, due to their wide dynamics, leaking into the microphones above the strings, for example, and therefore sounding 'distant' or lacking in definition. For this reason the drums are often set up in an isolation booth (see Plate 1 in Chapter 5). The drummer will then wear headphones or 'cans' so as to hear the rest of the orchestra. A talkback system should be organized for communication between the control room, conductor, and drummer. The brass section can also be separated from the rest of the orchestra by high acoustic screens. It is not possible to isolate the brass completely as they need to retain a certain open acoustic quality, not always possible in isolation booths. It should also be noted that, with the drums in the isolation booth, the other players and the conductor may need separate foldback/headphones to hear the drums properly.

Figure 17.1 shows a typical seating plan for a light music orchestral session in a modern recording studio. It will be seen that the string section is set out in the live area. Although artifical reverberation can be added at the mix-down stage, it is much more satisfactory to capture the live room acoustically, and results in a much larger string sound from a minimum of players. Of course it should be remembered that a certain lack of control is experienced when working this way, so finer points of balance and sound quality should be settled at the time of recording, and not left to the mix-down. The conductor can be of great help here in adjusting dynamics, asking soloists to play louder, or the accompanying musicians to play quieter.

Brass, as mentioned earlier, is often separated from the string section by high acoustic screens. French horns can sometimes benefit from being placed in the live part of the studio, bearing in mind that leakage on to the

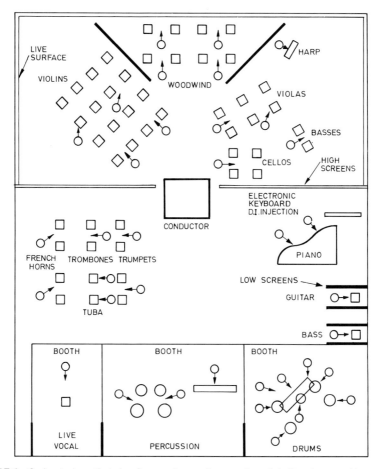

Fig. 17.1. Orchestral seating plan for popular music recording of rhythm, brass, strings, etc.

strings microphones will occur. A look at the musical score should establish if this is permissible.

The woodwind section can be set up behind the strings, as their dynamics do not cause any great leakage concern. Also, by using the live area, it is possible to position the microphones high above the players, avoiding the breathy or edgy tone, and key noise, so often heard in close-mic recordings.

Live rooms or areas are always helpful in that microphones can be placed at a reasonable distance, compared with the close technique and dry acoustics required when maximum clarity and separation are demanded. No recording studio is perfect, and in fact complete separation is possible only if the various sections of the orchestra are recorded individually. If time allows, it may be decided, for example, to overdub the strings separately. The brass and rhythm sections can take a recording break, while the string players record listening to the previously recorded brass and rhythm on headphones. Obviously this string overdub could take place at a later date.

The rock band

The favoured drum sound, as heard on many successful recordings, usually has a live quality which cannot be achieved in the usual isolation booth. A number of studios now use live booths made of tiled and mirrored walls and ceilings, with hard reflective materials on the floor. The live area in a normal studio can also be used for the drums when only a few other instruments are being recorded. The engineer can use ambience microphones as well as the close microphones, and carefully balance these to produce a large live drum sound. It should also be noted that each element of a drum kit will usually have its own microphone and be recorded on to a separate track. Remixing can take place later, adding echo, EQ, compression, and noise gating as necessary.

In Figure 17.2 it can be seen that acoustic screens or isolation booths are often used for the bass guitar and electric guitar, as well as the keyboard amplifier/speaker, to prevent leakage into the ambience microphones at the live end. A guide vocal is often recorded at the same time as the basic track. The vocalist(s) will have to be placed in an isolation booth to avoid leakage on to the instrument tracks. This vocal will usually be erased and re-recorded later. With the musicians separated into different parts of the studio, they need a headphone feed from the console of vocal and rhythm. Up to four different headphone mixes may be needed on separate cue systems.

Figure 17.3 shows the layout for a small ensemble where clarity is of the utmost importance. Each instrument plays into its own microphone, positioned very close. A dry sound will result but echo and effects can be added at the mix. This method does permit a greater degree of separation, and is normally favoured by small rhythm groups or for recording advertising jingles where some instruments may be deleted at mix-down, making absolute separation essential.

Rigging for the recording session

All rigging is usually carried out several hours ahead of the session, either the day before or in the early morning. Choosing microphones for particular instruments or sections is a matter of personal preference, but certain types of microphone have become popular choices through experience. As a general rule dynamic microphones are used on drum kits and electric guitars,

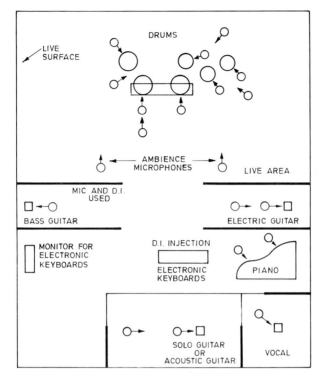

Fig. 17.2. Rock group studio set-up, showing live recording of drum kit, and isolation of electric guitar in case re-recording is needed at a later date

and capacitor microphones on acoustic instruments such as strings, woodwind, brass, acoustic guitars, piano, etc. Electronic keyboards and bass guitar are normally direct-injected into the recording console using a DI transformer box. A pair of ambience microphones may be used if the drum kit is set up in the live area. The following is a list of microphones commonly used for drum kit recording:

Bass drum	Electrovoice RE20
	AKG D12E or 20E
Tom-toms	Shure SM57 or SM58
	Sennheiser MD421U
Snare drum	Shure SM57 or SM58
	AKG 414 ULS
	Neumann KM84
Overhead cymbals	AKG 414 ULS
	Coles 4038
	Neumann U87

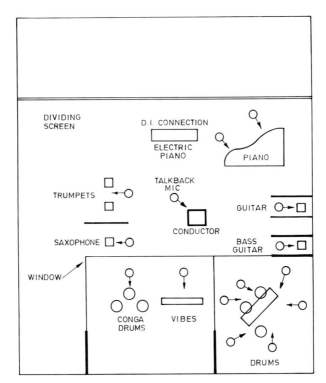

Fig. 17.3. Small ensemble studio set-up when a dry controllable sound is needed

Hi-hat	AKG 414 ULS
	Neumann KM84
Ambience	B&K 4006
	AKG 414 ULS
	Neumann KM83

There are two methods of recording an electric guitar. For the guitar which is playing a basic rhythm pattern as part of the musical arrangement, a good-quality dynamic microphone can be placed 30 cm in front of the guitar amplifier, with the guitarist making his own adjustments for loudness, EQ, etc. This results in a very satisfactory guitar sound for the basic rhythm section approach. When working with rock bands where the guitar sound is an integral part of the song, a much more spectacular sound needs to be found. This requires a double or triple microphone balance, miking the loudspeaker cone very close with a dynamic microphone and then, some 3 or 4 metres away, using a pair of capacitor microphones, such as Neumann U87 or U67, as a room pickup. The microphone angles and distances can be adjusted to produce the required sound; microphone polar patterns can also be changed to alter the room ambience.

Recording the bass guitar requires direct injection, but some engineers prefer to record the amplifier as well, and mix the direct and amplified sounds; bass players like their bass to be direct injected, using their amplifier to monitor the sound live, but mixing the two can give very good results if the amplifier is of sufficient quality. Due to the wide dynamic range of the bass guitar, it is sometimes necessary to use compression on the original recording to avoid overloading.

Now we come to the easiest instrument to record, the electronic keyboard, with the sound self-contained within the instrument and good-quality output terminals for direct injection. In many overdubbing situations the keyboards can be set up inside the control room. This has the advantage of giving the player a very good monitor mix, and good communication with the producer and engineer. Sections of the music can be discussed and recorded at the same time. There will also be occasions when the keyboards must be set up in the studio, perhaps for better communication with the other musicians. Then the keyboards are direct injected into the recording console and, if the player has difficulty in hearing his instrument, a small amplifier can be provided for monitoring. The volume of this amplifier should be kept low, as any leakage into other microphones might prevent re-recording at a later stage.

Recording the piano usually requires two microphones, one near the low strings at the tail end, and the other at the top end close to the right-hand high strings. These microphones can be as close as 15 cm above the strings, with the lid open on the half-stick. This produces a very sharp transient sound which is suitable for today's rock music. It is important, however, to ensure that all notes sound in the same perspective; careful positioning of the microphones can achieve this. If a percussive effect is required, the microphones should be moved close to the hammers and, if a warmer sound is wanted, they can be moved towards the tail end. Care should also be taken to avoid picking up too much damper and pedal noise.

For a natural piano sound, the lid should be fully opened and a pair of microphones placed in a semi-arc some 1 or 2 metres away. By carefully moving the mcirophones along the arc, and changing their facing angles to pick up more or less reflections from the lid, the required sound can be found. As a general rule, placing the microphones at the top end will produce a bright sound, whilst a position near the tail will give a warmer quality. Microphones commonly used for piano include Neumann U87, U47, KM83, and AKG 414 ULS. A pair of good quality ribbon microphones can also prove effective.

The players in the string sections traditionally sit in pairs or 'desks', arranged in ranks one behind the other. An average string section consists of ten first violins, eight second violins, six violas, four cellos, and two double basses. The section will be arranged in a semicircle facing the conductor, with the highest instruments on his left and the lowest strings on his right.

A system of using two microphones per section should be employed. The first microphone is set up directly over the first violin or leader seated on the first chair, at a minimum height of about 2 metres above the instrument; this will be suitable for any solos and will also be sufficiently close to pick up the first two or three desks. A second microphone is placed above the fourth desk to pick up the rest of the section. A similar method applies to the second violins, violas, and cellos. The double bass microphones will be positioned about 50 cm away from the bridge, and will be carefully mixed to achieve definition, as most of the bass resonance can be produced by the ambience microphones placed high above the conductor.

Good-quality capacitor microphones are always used for strings, such as Neumann U87, KM84 or U89, AKG C12 or 414 ULS, and Schoeps MK5 where a bright sound is required. Popular ambience or overall microphones are the B&K 4006, Neumann M50, TLM50, or KM83, and the Schoeps MK2S.

A typical brass section for popular music has four trumpets, two tenor trombones, one bass trombone, tuba, and four french horns. A close balance on trumpets and trombones is difficult to control, but it will help if the players are prepared to co-operate by leaning into the microphone on muted or quiet passages and moving back for loud passages. Without this co-operation, the engineer will need to make drastic changes of level during the recording, and possibly resort to heavy compression. One microphone is used for each pair of instruments plus one each for tuba and bass trombone. French horns should be recorded from behind but, if there are wall or screen reflections, a microphone at the front may be better. Microphones often used are Neumann U67, U87, TLM170, or U47, and Coles 3048.

Woodwind players also sit in pairs as a rule. A typical section would consist of two each flutes, oboes, clarinets, and bassoons, given a separate microphone for each pair. They usually sit in two rows, flutes and oboes in front, clarinets and bassoons behind. Woodwind players often change to a second instrument (piccolo, bass clarinet, etc.) and the engineer should know about this possibility in advance. It is important not to place the microphones too close to avoid key noise, breathing, etc. Typical microphones are Neumann KM86 or KM84, and Schoeps MK5.

Once all chairs, music stands, and microphones are placed in position, the engineer must check that each fader is correctly assigned to the intended microphone. Each microphone should be checked with audio, either speech from an assistant or an audible click generated by a digital metronome or computer and fed to a loudspeaker in the studio. It is very important to check that all microphones are wired in the same phase; if microphones are used out of phase, cancellation problems will arise when mixing to mono or using pairs in stereo. Mono collapse can also occur when mixing film music for 'Dolby Stereo'.

If a microphone is found to be out of phase, the wiring should be reversed or, more usually, there will be a phase reverse switch on the mixer console. A simple method for phase checking is to choose one microphone as having the 'correct phase' and then get an assistant to hold this microphone close to all the others in turn while he speaks equally into both. Listening in mono, any out-of-phase microphone will be identified by the thin hollow sound produced.

All communication circuits should be checked and headphones aurally tested. Talkback facilities between engineer, producer, and conductor must be tested as well as foldback to the drums isolation booth, etc. Before each session begins, all new tape should have timecode recorded on track 24 for future synchronizing with other machines and for console automation. For digital recording, all new tape will need to be formatted or striped with control code from the relevant digital tape machine, and timecode should also be recorded on the machine's dedicated timecode tracks. All tape machines should be realigned to the correct recording standards and tape heads, rollers, and guides cleaned with the correct cleaning solution.

The recording session

In the case of a multitrack recording session, the balance engineer will adopt a scheme of allocating instruments and voices to various tracks. A typical track arrangement for an orchestral session is shown in Table 17.1. When recording a live rock band, the track split will use up more tracks for the drum kit, and many tracks will need to be left open for future overdubbing. A typical scheme for a rock band is shown in Table 17.2.

The engineer or assistant must keep the track sheets up to date as the session progresses, to avoid erasing wanted tracks and to keep the producer informed of track availability. The first priority is to work on the drum sound and balance as quickly as possible because, with the drummer in an isolation booth, a balanced mix must be available on headphones for the rest of the musicians from the outset. Sometimes the drums are set up before the session, enabling the engineer to get a balance before the others arrive.

Once a drum sound has been achieved, the musicians can begin running through the music, while the engineer listens and balances the remainder of the orchestra. With the drum sound already established, the bass guitar, electric guitar, various electronic keyboards, and percussion will be added to provide a complete rhythm mix to be sent to all the headphones in the

Table 17.1. Track arrangement for orchestral session

Track 1	Bass guitar
Track 2	Bass drum
Track 3	Snare drum
Track 4	Hi-hat
Tracks 5 & 6	Stereo mix of tom-toms & overhead cymbals
Track 7	Electric guitar
Tracks 8 & 9	Stereo piano or electronic keyboard
Tracks 10 & 11	Stereo woodwind mix
Track 12	First violins
Track 13	Second violins
Track 14	Violas
Track 15	Cellos
Track 16	Basses
Track 17	Trumpets
Track 18	Trombones & tuba
Track 19	French horns
Track 20	Harp
Track 21	Percussion
Track 22	Guide vocal
Track 23	Spare
Track 24	Timecode

Table 17.2. Track arrangement for rock band session

Track 1	Bass guitar DI
Track 2	Bass guitar amplifier
Track 3	Bass drum
Track 4	Snare drum
Tracks 5 & 6	Stereo mix of tom-toms
Tracks 7 & 8	Stereo mix of overhead cymbals
Track 9	Hi-hat
Tracks 10 & 11	Stereo drum ambience
Track 12	Electric guitar
Tracks 13 & 14	Stereo electronic keyboards
Tracks 15–22	Open for vocal overdubs, guitars, or keyboards
Track 23	Guide vocal
Track 24	Timecode for sync to a second machine if more tracks are needed later

studio. The drummer will need a separate headphone mix containing the orchestra as well as the rhythm.

The other sections of the orchestra are now added to the rhythm mix, starting with the brass, woodwind, french horns, and finally strings and harp. As the various parts of the rhythm and orchestral sections are being recorded on to separate tracks, the finer points of balance can be carried out at the later mixing stage, so a good monitor mix is the main priority. Echo will be added to this to enable the producer to judge how the final result will sound. The monitor echo will not be recorded to the multitrack machine but the producer may ask for this monitor mix to be recorded on a cassette or DAT machine for reference after the session has been completed. Once a satisfactory balance and echo setting has been achieved, the only thing left is to go for a perfect musical performance, leaving the engineer to keep an eye on the recording levels to prevent any overloading. Some pre-mixing is undertaken during this initial recording stage, and it is important to watch the brass section, where levels may swing by as much as 10 dB.

When orchestral sections are sharing microphones or tracks, as in the case of brass, it may be necessary to ask them to play a few notes separately to ensure that the microphone is picking up all instruments evenly. The engineer can, for example, ask the brass to play a built-up chord. Then he can quickly detect if any player is blowing away from the microphone or too close; and a slight adjustment of seating can usually put things right. It is also important that the players remember their positions.

As mentioned earlier, doubling of instruments occurs, particularly in the woodwind section, and quite large changes in level can result. The percussion section also needs careful watching. Tympani, vibraphone, xylophone, and various Latin American instruments require constant changes of microphone position and fader setting. The producer or arranger can help the engineer by giving musical cues for these.

As well as being concerned with these complexities, it is one of the engineer's duties to ensure that a good headphone mix is always available. In most cases the control room monitor mix sent through the headphone circuits will be sufficient, but the musicians will often ask for an entirely different balance, usually a lot of bass and drums.

The engineer must also look after the headphone levels of the 'Tempo click track'. This click provides a fixed tempo in beats per minute and can be set to any tempo required to help the musicians keep in time. This system of following the click is particularly useful during film soundtrack recording, where a section of music has to fit into a predetermined number of picture frames on the film. A constant problem is the need to ensure that leakage does not occur from the headphones to the microphones. The engineer may have to raise the click level during the loud passages and lower it again for quiet music.

All this of course applies to the typical three-hour recording session using paid session musicians. When working with rock bands, the atmosphere is much more relaxed as there is no time limit on starting or finishing. Sessions very often go on well into the night with much experimentation and musical ideas constantly being recorded and re-recorded.

Equalization on the recording session

It should be emphasized that EQ should not be used without first trying to achieve the desired result by moving the microphone or changing to a more suitable type. Certain microphones have peaks in their response, and careful selection of the best type for various instruments reduces the need for excessive EQ. The main purpose for EQ during live recording is to remove unwanted frequencies which are above or below the required bandwidth for the instrument in question. A low-frequency cut-off on the strings microphone is often needed to remove low-frequency leakage from the bass guitar and piano. Close-miking the strings to prevent such leakage can introduce mid-range harshness. A slight rolling-off at mid-frequencies can eliminate this problem and produce the same result as raising the microphones without experiencing the extra leakage that this would cause. Again, a slight high-frequency boost will add brilliance to the string sound. Lower-mid EQ is sometimes added to the violas and cellos to give more body or richness. Brass often benefits from a slight mid-lift, somewhere in the region of 5–7 kHz. EQ is always a matter of personal taste so definite rules are impossible.

Certainly there are no hard-and-fast rules for recording drum kits. The most important points are to make sure that the kit is properly tuned, and that all loose fittings have been tightened. The front skin of the bass drum is nearly always removed, and the inside of the drum filled with a blanket or cushion pushed up against the back skin, and the microphone placed just inside the drum, towards one side. This sometimes results in 'bass tip-up', the low-frequency boost that occurs with cardioid or figure-of-eight microphones placed very close to the sound source. This can be compensated for with suitable bass cut and lifting the recording level to make the bass drum sound tighter and firmer. Lower mid-frequencies can then be raised to create power and definition; some compression may also be needed.

Tom-toms and snare drums are recorded with the microphones positioned very close to the edge of the skin, working at a minimum distance of 5 cm. These instruments often 'ring' when close-miked in this way, and small pieces of masking or gaffer tape should be applied to the skin to reduce the effect. Some compression on tom-toms will help to reduce the dynamic range and make them easier to record with a powerful sound. Some drummers also remove the bottom skins of the tom-toms, so the microphone can be placed inside from underneath. The same problem of bass tip-up sometimes occurs, and bass-cut will make the sound brighter and firmer.

Snare drums often benefit from a lift in the high or middle frequencies. Tuning of the snare drum is the secret to creating a good sound, and the drummer's co-operation will be needed. If the cymbals and hi-hat are of good quality, no special EQ is necessary though some bass cut may help, as well as a slight boost in the upper frequencies. When working with professional session musicians, these problems do not often occur as their kits have been specially tuned and treated for recording purposes. The problem mainly arises with rock drummers whose kits are tuned for live stage work.

When recording live, problems are often experienced with the acoustic guitar. Because of the quiet nature of the instrument, the microphone gain is set to a relatively high level and leakage from the surrounding instruments will become audible. Acoustic guitars are therefore usually placed in isolation booths, with a microphone like the AKG 414 set about 15 cm away from the main hole of the instrument, where the strings cross; sometimes two microphones can be used as a stereo pair. However, bass tip-up may occur with close-miking and a reduction of frequencies below 200 Hz will be essential to reduce any booming effect.

When recording vocals, there can again be no set rules since the human voice is so variable. If the artist has a good voice, all that is needed is a good-quality capacitor microphone with no EQ or compression; just a slight lifting or reduction of the odd word or phrase. Good microphones favoured for vocals include the Neumann U87 and AKG 414. Many engineers now use valve microphones, such as the old Neumann U67, U48, and U49, and modern valve designs have appeared including the AKG Tube and Sony C800, and C800G. Sibilance, an exaggeration of the letter s, is sometimes a problem, and also popping on the letters p and b. One way round the sibilance problem is to ask the singer not to over-pronounce the letter s, and to sing across the microphone instead of straight into it. This reduces some of the extreme high frequencies but is not always practicable as the singer has many other things to think about.

A de-esser device is available to the engineer for eliminating unwanted sibilance, but care should be taken not to cut off all the treble and give the singer a lisp. A pop shield can be used on the microphone to protect the diaphragm from puffs of air generated by the letters p and b. Many types exist, the most effective being a circular frame of nylon placed between the singer and the microphone, which does not reduce the vocal presence.

Compression will have to be used for a singer with a wide dynamic range, though care should be taken not to reduce the dynamics to such an extent that the singer sounds 'squashed'. It is also important not to ask for too many repeat takes. It is usual to keep all the takes on separate tracks, and then, when four or five takes have been recorded, these can be played back for the producer to mark the best parts of each. The best sections can then be bounced down to a new track to build up the final performance.

Overdubbing

The most favoured technique of pop music recording is overdubbing. Here the engineer can experiment with different types of microphone, position, and ambience. With only one or two musicians to worry about, there is plenty of time to get things just right. Ambience and a feeling of depth are very important parts of a recording, giving the listener the feeling of actually being at the performance. What most engineers are striving for is the natural live sound. Strings are definitely at an advantage when overdubbed as the engineer can move the microphones as far away as necessary to achieve a large string sound without the close-mike harshness. Sometimes, when working in extremely good acoustics, only a single stereo microphone or pair of spaced omnidirectional microphones may be necessary, thus giving a natural sound which might be impossible to achieve when recording the whole orchestra together. Brass too can benefit from overdubbing, as microphones are taken further away to reduce valve or air noises. Of course experiments with distancing microphones can be carried out only when working in a live acoustic. A dead room will almost certainly muffle the sound, but reflective panels can often help. Today there is an increasing trend towards building a live area in studios, and some major studios are now completely live.

In an overdubbing situation, the musical passages can be recorded in sections. The first eight bars might be recorded first; then this is played back to the musicians, the record button is pressed at the start of the ninth bar, and the musicians will start playing from this point until a musical error or other problem arises. This process of 'dropping in' or 'punching in' will continue until a perfect performance has been recorded. When all recording and overdubbing has taken place, the multitrack tape is ready for mixing down to a single two-track stereo mix.

The mix-down

This is another area of recording where no strict rules apply; the final sound is down to the taste of the engineer, producer, and artist. Many hours or even days can be consumed on this task. Before attempting the mix-down, the engineer has to establish what special effects are required: will the vocals need harmonizing, how many digital delays are needed, are there any special effects? Finally, is the mix-down to be analogue or digital? The most popular methods are:

(a) analogue half-inch 30 ips non-Dolby or Dolby SR;
(b) Sony PCM-1630 digital, recording on U-Matic cassette;
(c) an outboard digital processor, recording on U-Matic.

There are many digital processors available, and it is a matter of taste which will suit a given project. With an outboard processor, many engineers now use DAT and transfer to an editing system when mastering and compiling the various recordings.

Today's multitrack recordings are so musically complex that manual mixing has become a thing of the past, except in cases where a live recording is being made direct to stereo, and the musical arrangement predicts the mix which should not be changed. Manual mixing of a rock band, by moving the faders at predetermined points to alter dynamics or emphasize some point in the music, can be a very complicated task, the engineer having to remember perhaps thirty or forty different moves during three minutes of music.

All modern recording consoles have automated mix-down facilities which have taken over from the old-fashioned manual approach. The electronic applications of automation will not be discussed here but it is important to know that the console automation is run from the timecode recorded on Track 24. The fader, mute, EQ, and mix information will be stored on to a hard-disc computer, with a software program designed for that particular console. Most of today's console manufacturers include a floppy disc mix recall system; simply inserting the disc will recall all relevant information. Remember that fader control will not be activated until the original timecode from the multitrack is read by the computer. This recall system enables the engineer to make small changes at any time without having to mix the entire piece of music again. It should be remembered too that any outboard equipment information used for the mix-down will not be stored in the recall system. Therefore careful notes of effects units and settings should be made on outboard recall sheets, and stored with the floppy discs and multitrack tapes.

An important tip about automation is not to mix and EQ each track one at a time, and then put all the tracks together. As fader gains and EQ are always related to other tracks, a more convenient starting point is to make all necessary mutes of unwanted sections and tracks before starting to balance a rough working mix. This mix will give the artist and producer an overall picture of how the final mix should be. Once this rough mix is established, and everyone is happy with the degrees of echo and EQ on the various instruments, the delicate art of balancing the finer points can be undertaken. This rough mix can now be 'written in' by running the automation system; all mix information will now be stored on the hard disc and can be recalled at any time. Once completed, this mix can be read back and any new moves will be stored into this new 'pass' and assigned a number. Each new pass is similarly treated and so, if any mistakes are made, an earlier pass can be recalled.

Each section can be treated individually. Perhaps the bass guitar needs to be boosted in certain areas of a song, or a guitar solo needs lifting. The producer may decide to accent the brass in places to make the arrangement more punchy. He may wish to simplify the arrangement by omitting the strings until the second chorus is established, thus building the song as it progresses. Most important, the vocal may need to be raised in certain sections where words are being lost. This process can take hours as the engineer and producer are trying to come up with something that sounds exciting and different which could possibly make or break the recording.

Many up-dates are made, and time can be saved by locating the tape to the area that needs changing, without running the complete song from the beginning. It should be remembered that during up-dates only fader and mute information is stored, not the EQ and echo settings. Therefore, before leaving the studio, a final console 'recall store' should be made and transferred to the floppy disc.

Sampling

Another important aspect of mix-down is sampling. This simply means locking a musical sound from another source, like a snare drum beat or bass drum pattern, into a digital memory or sampling unit. This memory can then be edited to play only for the duration of the locked-in signal required. It can be triggered by the original unwanted recording made during the session, started by hand at a predetermined point or by triggering the sampling device from the timecode on the multitrack.

A complete new drum sound can be built up in this way. Many engineers and producers have their own library of samples stored on floppy discs. This sampling procedure is often carried out during the recording session itself, with good snare and bass drum samples triggered by the live drum sounds. It does ensure that the desired drum sound is maintained during the session, and this can save time provided the required samples are chosen before the session begins. Many modern sampling devices are very versatile, enabling the user to change the speed, pitch, and frequency response of the chosen sample, as well as its duration.

'Spinning in', as it is known, is another technique which can save time and trouble. Providing the sampling device has a long enough memory, the vocals from the first chorus of a song can be sampled and stored. Then, by switching on the first chorus sample at the appropriate time, it can be sent to the multitrack at the start of each later chorus section. This allows the singer to concentrate on perfecting the performance just once for the sample. Sampling and spinning in can be used for virtually any sound or instrument.

In cases where the sampling memory is not long enough, or a suitable device is not available, sounds or vocals can be recorded on reel-to-reel tape and 'spun in' by pressing the replay button at the right moment.

Echo and effects

Using echo during mix-down has now become extremely complicated, with as many as five or six different echo units employed at the same time. The engineer could have at his disposal several digital reverb units, including the versatile Lexicon 480L or 224X, and also up to six digital delay units for signal delay, harmonizing, or repeat echo effects, as well as a large array of compressors and limiters, noise gates, and equalizers. The reason behind using such a complex set-up is that most modern recordings rely on over-dubbing, with each sound recorded in isolation with a minimum of ambience.

To give the audible impression that all the musicians are playing together, an ambience has to be created by artificial means and adding simple echo does not achieve this effect. Stereo harmonizing on vocals and guitar solos can be very effective. A slight change in pitch can add a three-dimensional effect in the stereo mix. When mixing down drum sounds, it is often necessary to use noise gates, which should open when a loud signal is received and close again when the signal stops. This allows only the desired sounds to be recorded, without leakage from the other elements in the kit, resulting in an extremely tight and clean drum sound.

Noise gates can also be used on electric guitars to eliminate amplifier hiss and hum when the guitar is not being played, or even between notes in a quiet passage. On brass, they can clip the decay at an earlier point, thus creating a very tight and percussive sound. Noise gates are often used on room ambience microphones and echo returns, to give the effect of hearing the echo only at the point of impact. This puts the instrument into a large acoustic without the problem of the echo decay overlapping into the next portion of the music.

Equalizing is almost always carried out at the mixing stage, although there are two schools of thought on whether there should be a good deal of EQ performed at the original session or none at all. Of course either method has its own advantages. EQ at the recording gives the option of changing microphones or positions to avoid excessive use of EQ. Recording everything flat allows decisions to be delayed, but might mean that a sound only obtainable via a microphone change has been missed.

The positioning of the various tracks across the stereo picture is another mix-down decision for the engineer and producer. It is normal practice to place the bass guitar and bass drum in the centre, with stereo drums panned left and right. Rock band stereo positioning can change from song to song, as most of the important sounds are played on guitars and keyboards with positioning dictated by the musical arrangement.

Orchestral positioning follows a standard orchestra pattern, with the high strings on the left and low strings on the right. French horns appear on the left, brass on the right, and woodwind at the centre. This is not a completely strict rule, and the producer may place things differently. However, when the orchestra has been recorded live in a particular layout, this has to be maintained during the final mix-down. Panning an instrument from left to right, for example, can cause problems since leakage from this instrument will remain on the left and possibly confuse the listener.

People often ask, 'How do you start mixing down?' The most popular method is to start by building up the rhythm section, and then add the vocal. Then the brass and strings can be mixed into the picture and echo adjustments made. One of the most serious problems is running out of gain from the multitrack. This is caused by constantly raising fader settings, on the old maxim, 'let's have more of that, and more of this'. Sometimes it will be much easier, and better, to take something down in order to hear something else 'louder'. It must be realized that boosting certain frequencies will also raise overall level, and fader settings may have to be adjusted to compensate.

Another point to remember is that most of the record-buying public are not listening to the recording on expensive monitoring systems. It is therefore important to monitor the mix on domestic loudspeakers at low levels at some stage. It will then be noticed that the bass end is much reduced and high frequencies are changed in quality. This can be corrected by the engineer to provide a more ideal mix for domestic consumption.

When the mix is finally completed to everyone's satisfaction, DAT or cassette copies can be made for the producer, artist, and engineer to take home and check, again on domestic speakers. A remix may often be needed, especially if the mix was made late at night when the ears and mind were not so fresh. In fact it is often advisable to allow a two- or three-day break between recording and mix-down, to avoid the unnecessary expense of a remix sesson. However, if a remix is necessary, the recall disc makes it easy to select a particular passage for update.

Tape presentation

Finally, the engineer and assistant must label all master tapes correctly. Technical information should be clearly marked, together with song titles, locate timings, artists, producer, client, etc. The tape should carry a set of reference tones, all recorded at the operating levels relevant at the time of the mix-down. This will enable the mastering engineer to realign the mastering machine to play back the tapes in exactly the same way as in the recording studio without any loss in quality. The multitrack tapes should be stored with the relevant track split information, recall sheets, and recall discs. This question of presentation and many other practical matters are discussed in *The Master Tape Book*, published by the APRS and The British Record Producers Guild.

18 Electronic music

Jonathan Gibbs (Revised by Peter Howell)

Since the tentative beginning of electronic music at the turn of the century it has been hoped that the electronic manipulation of sound might, in theory, offer the composer the most glorious opportunities to explore new forms of musical expression. But there have been major stumbling-blocks. The penalties have been the long hours spent slaving over a tape editing block, turning crude physics-laboratory waveforms into pleasing sounds, programming sluggish computers in low-level languages to perform tasks they were not designed to do. For the professional composer of electronic music those long hours have been a significant barrier, because, unlike the composer for conventional instruments, he has to be intimately concerned not only with the music the instruments will play but also with the very design of the instruments themselves. Too often that has meant a struggle, and if it takes him a day to create one really good note it is inevitable that integrity must suffer.

But within the last twelve years or so the technology of electronic music has exploded, and it is now expanding so fast that it is quite impossible to stop and say, 'This is the state of the art'. What is a problem today will be solved tomorrow, only to bring up a new set of problems. We now have cheap synthesizers and controllers which can, with care, begin to realize some of the dreams of electronic music—to create any sound imaginable or unimaginable, to make that sound worth listening to, and, most important in the professional environment, to do it quickly. The lead time between conception and realization of a sound is reduced to insignificance. That is good news not only for the accountants but also for the talented composer, because he need not waste time on an approach that is not going to work, but can go for the approach that will.

The technological explosion has brought machines which are not only cheaper, more flexible, and easier to use, but which also offer a much greater variety of sounds. In addition to the subtractive-synthesis family, in which voltage-controlled oscillators generate raw waveforms such as square and saw-tooth which are then filtered and shaped, there are also sampling devices, which make digital recordings of live sounds and then play them back through the keyboard; frequency-modulation devices, in which sine-wave oscillators are arranged to frequency-modulate each other; additive synthesis, in which the amplitude envelopes of harmonics can be individually adjusted; and wavetable synthesis, in which the initial waveforms of subtractive synthesis are more elaborate and can be changed through time. And there are even large computer systems which combine all these processes in one machine.

The sounds not only have greater variety, but they can also be more attractive. In the small-scale environment of individual notes, the ear is bored quickly and needs continuous changes of pitch, volume, and timbre to find those notes interesting. This can easily be proved by making a single-cycle loop in a sample of, say, an oboe, and then comparing that loop with the sound of the real thing. The sampling synthesizer may be giving a perfect copy of one cycle of oboe tone, but the minute changes in quality which the oboist naturally makes give his note far more interest than that unvarying electronic loop. But greater control of a synthesizer's parameters, using bend-wheels, key pressure, and the like, coupled with more complex note envelopes, means that synthesized sounds can now be much richer than before. More significantly, they can break away from the limited ideals of perfectly imitating well-designed instruments of the orchestra into much more progressive ideals of developing new instruments.

MIDI: advantages and disadvantages

The most significant development has been the ability to link together this considerable armoury of synthesizers with the Musical Instrument Digital Interface, or 'MIDI'. This is the internationally accepted set of protocols for communication between synthesizers and peripheral devices, based on a serial communication line operating at 31.25 Kbaud. It is virtually *de rigueur* on all new electronic instruments, and there are even kits to transform grand pianos into generators. At its simplest level, it means that playing a note on one MIDI synthesizer will send out three eight-bit bytes from the 'MIDI out' socket on the back of the machine, which may be routed to the 'MIDI in' socket on another machine and so tell it to play the same note at the same velocity, that is hit with the same force. When the note is released, another three bytes are sent, to tell the second machine to release its note.

While this in itself may not seem all that significant—after all, organists have been linking Great and Swell manuals for years—the real power of MIDI becomes evident when that 'note on, note off' information (and a whole lot more besides) can be stored in a sequencer. Once that raw data is available in the sequencer, it may be edited and modified, new material may be generated by manipulation within the sequencer itself, and whole pieces may be built, not as fixed individual acoustic tracks on a multitrack recorder but as files of data on a computer disc, so that every performance is first-generation, and there are infinite possibilities of changing and improving that performance.

The MIDI standard means that machines from different manufacturers can talk to each other. Also built into the specification are 'System Exclusive' protocols for individual machines from the same manufacturer to store and communicate data about, for example, the make-up of a particular voice, or a rhythm sequence, or a particular sample. So, in theory, the musician can go to a studio, which is equipped with the right synthesizers and sequencers, carrying just a box of floppy discs or, more and more likely these days, one or two magneto-optical discs, which contain both the music and the sounds.

It is not only synthesizers which respond to MIDI. There is a whole generation of treatment devices—reverberation, harmonizing, delay, and all the other peripheral 'black boxes'—which can be made to change their parameters according to standard MIDI instructions. There are even mixers which respond to MIDI, although the speed restrictions of that 31.25 Kbaud make full automated control of substantial numbers of mixer channels a highly complex proposition. However, it is certainly possible to control the peripherals from that floppy disc, as well as the synthesizers.

It would be wrong, though, to suggest that MIDI is the answer to every prayer. When it can be so successful at controlling music synthesizers, there is a temptation to run absolutely everything with MIDI. Although the speed as originally specified is quite adequate for musical performance (and initial gloomy prophecies about propagation delays have largely proved false), it is pushing it to the limits to expect it to adjust many fine controls at once such as melodic lines with very dense pitch bend information or dense MIDI data travelling down the same cable. This is simply because MIDI is very slow when transmitting continuous control movements. MIDI information can be recorded only in a digital storage system, such as a sequencer, because the frequency is too high for analogue multitrack tape. Therefore, when MIDI data for electronic instruments is being recorded alongside analogue tracks of live instruments, the sequencer must rely on control tracks on the multitrack (either timecode or dedicated pulse trains) to run in sync, and those control tracks may be extremely vulnerable. In particular, a few pulses missed through dropout in a dedicated pulse train will throw out the sync from that point on. These days it is becoming more and more prevalent in MIDI music studios for the multitrack facility to be magneto-optical or hard disc based, in which case *it* is controlled by the sequencer and not the other way round; previously it had always been a case of 'the tail wagging the dog'.

MIDI has been developed for the world of conventional chromatic music based on the keyboard, and anyone wishing to work with more adventurous ideas of microtonal or macrotonal music will find it sadly lacking, because the smallest pitch change definable on most MIDI synthesizers is one semi-tone. Increasingly, however, synthesizers are being developed with custom designable tuning scales, and sequencers with custom nameable notes.

Despite these drawbacks, MIDI has the huge advantage that it is a recognized standard, and there are thousands of devices on the market which adhere to that standard. Even if MIDI itself is superseded (and no doubt it will be), those machines will be around for some time. Also, with such commercial pressure behind it, the drive to make MIDI a universal recording studio data transfer language is huge.

MIDI in practice

MIDI devices are usually fitted with three five-pin DIN sockets, labelled MIDI IN, MIDI OUT, and MIDI THRU (see Figure 18.1). MIDI IN is the input, and goes straight to the sound generation or modification circuits of the device; MIDI THRU sends out a perfect copy of what comes into MIDI IN, buffered with an opto-isolator, so that further devices may be daisy-chained; MIDI OUT sends out MIDI information which has been generated locally by the device itself, from its keyboard for example. Note, therefore, that MIDI OUT does not normally carry the data coming into MIDI IN; it is

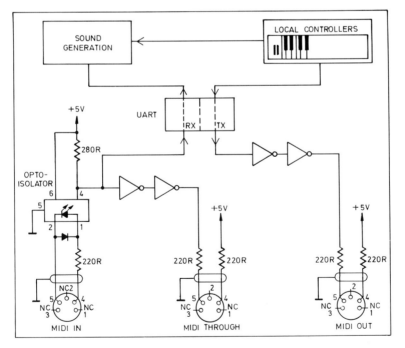

Fig. 18.1. Basic MIDI connections

not a 'mix' of input data and locally generated data. it is inadvisable to make very long daisy-chains of instruments using THRU connections (say more than three), because the opto-isolators used may cause cumulative rise-and-fall time errors in the data. Cables connecting standard MIDI devices should not run longer than 15 m without a repeater. If the device does not have any means of local generation—a synthesizer without a keyboard, or a peripheral such as a reverberation unit—then it may not need the MIDI OUT socket. Some devices do not implement MIDI THRU.

The MIDI system allows for 16 channels. This means that data intended for several different devices may be sent down the same cable to all those devices in a daisy-chain, or in parallel, but only those which are set to respond to the correct channel will hear the data meant for them. However, with the latest multi-timbral channel-hungry synths (many are themselves 16-channel capable) ways of multiplying available channels were eagerly sought. The result was better than any of the users could predict. By coding the MIDI data as it leaves the controlling sequencer software, at the point at which it is running much faster, and redesigning the interface with 16 ins and outs, the manufacturers have achieved a remarkable 236 available MIDI channels. The coded information is descrambled at the interface and sent (16 channels at a time) to the countless MIDI devices. As a point of reference, the number of MIDI channels used in an extremely well-equipped studio with MIDI mixing and routing is currently only 110; so there is plenty of scope to accommodate future demands.

MIDI messages

MIDI messages are of two basic types: *channel messages*, which will be heard only by devices set up to receive that channel (or to receive all channels, in omni mode) and which include the fundamental 'note on, note off' messages; and *system messages*, heard by all receivers regardless, which include data such as synchronization clocks. (System messages will be explained later, in connection with sequencers.) If a receiver has no use for the incoming data it will ignore it. Synchronization clocks, for example, mean nothing to a synthesizer, but may be relevant for a sequencer or drum machine. It is clearly important that, if channels are being used, the right devices are set to the right channels. The specification states that on power-up a receiver should default to omni on/poly on mode, that is to say it will hear all incoming channels and play polyphonically. However, it is expedient for some devices (such as racked modular banks of synthesizers) to default to specific channels.

The MIDI data itself is divided into two groups, *status bytes* and *data bytes*: a receiving device will know the difference because status bytes have bit 7 set, i.e. are greater than 127. A complete listing is given in Table 18.1

at the end of this chapter. When a receiver hears a particular status byte, it can make decisions about whether to act on it—is this data on my channel? Is it relevant to me?—and, if necessary, listen out for further data bytes before acting. So, for example, if a synthesizer on channel 1 hears a status byte which says 'Note start on channel 1' (i.e. hexadecimal number $90, decimal 144), it will listen out for two further data bytes, which will define the key number and the key velocity.

There are eight principal categories of channel information. These are *note off* and *note on*, which may also define a velocity (that is how fast the note on the keyboard is depressed or released). Such velocity information can be used by the receiving synthesizer to control level, for example, or harmonic 'brightness'. *Polyphonic key pressure* and *channel pressure* send information about how hard the note is being pressed after it has reached the bottom of its travel (after touch); polyphonic key pressure deals with individual notes, channel pressure with the whole keyboard as one. *Program change* messages call up different voices (pre-set sounds) in the receiver; in peripherals such as reverberation units, they may call up different pre-set settings. *Pitch bend change* messages echo the movement of bend wheels or levers used to shift the tuning of the whole instrument, although different synthesizers may impose different scalings on that data. *Control change* messages carry changes in controllers such as pedals, wheels, and switches. Each controller has a number, and certain numbers have been generally accepted as linked to certain common controllers. A list is given in Table 18.2 at the end of this chapter.

The last category of channel information is *mode change*. In practice it may be tricky to use, because transmitters cannot know what state a receiver is in, but in theory it allows a transmitter to control how the receiver will respond to its transmission data. In *omni on* mode, the receiver hears all channels; in *omni off*, only one specific channel. In *poly on* mode, it distributes incoming notes polyphonically up to the limit of how many voices it can play at once. In *poly off* mode it either plays one note at a time regardless (omni on), or it assigns incoming channels monophonically to individual voices (omni off). In practice, most contemporary synthesizers are polyphonic, and there should be few problems about mode. One additional command in this category is the *local control on/off* command, which controls whether or not the receiving synthesizer's local keyboard can talk to its sound-making circuits, or relinquish control entirely to incoming MIDI. In some cases performance will be reliable if the local processor does not have to waste time paying attention to its local keyboard.

Clearly, a good knowledge of how MIDI works, and what it can and cannot do, is as essential to the electronic music studio engineer as is his knowledge of signal paths in a mixing desk. But what of the synthesizers themselves?

Analogue synthesis

'Analogue' has come to be a generic term applied to all synthesizers which make sounds in a similar way to Robert Moog's classic first voltage-controlled synthesizer, using the basic tools of oscillators, filters, amplifiers, and envelope shapers. In fact, of course, current versions incorporate digital technology both for control and sound generation, and there is plenty of cross-fertilization between 'analogue' functions such as filtering and digital functions such as sampling; however, the terminology of analogue synthesis has become the universal language in the field.

The older machines need a 'CV' (control voltage) from a keyboard to define pitch, and most take a logarithmic scale of 1 V/octave. This voltage is (notionally) applied to a voltage-controlled oscillator, VCO, which produces one of several waveforms—usually square, saw-tooth, pulse (in which the mark-to-space ratio may often be voltage-controlled), triangle, or sine. Some machines allow greater control over this initial waveform. The user may create his own waveform, or even use a succession of different waveforms which course through as the note sustains.

This waveform is then filtered in a voltage-controlled filter, VCF. The principal controls here will be *cut-off frequency, Q,* or *resonance* (which gives a variable peak at the filter cut-off frequency and may even drive it into oscillation), and *envelope* parameters. Envelope generators have at least four elements: *attack time,* the time it takes to reach the initial attack level; *decay time,* the time it takes to decay to a holding sustain level; the *sustain level* itself; and *release time,* during which the envelope dies away after the note is released (hence 'ADSR'). An envelope is active as long as a gate voltage is present, which will usually be taken from the keyboard, and it enters the release phase once the gate voltage drops. More modern envelope generators may have more than these four elements, with perhaps two or more initial decay sequences.

After filtering, the signal passes to a voltage-controlled amplifier, VCA, in which another envelope generator defines the overall amplitude shape of a note. The other principal components of an analogue system are low-frequency oscillators or LFOs, which generate sub-audio waveforms to introduce effects such as vibrato and tremolo; noise generators, for white or pink noise; ring modulators, which combine two input frequencies to produce a sum-and-difference output frequency; and sample and hold generators, which take a sample of an incoming voltage and then hold that level until the next clock pulse arrives, so producing stepped voltage changes. All these classic terms may be conveniently applied to most synthesizers.

Early analogue synthesizers allowed all the elements to be interconnected with patch cords, and a specific arrangement was called a patch.

More modern equivalents allow all parameters and routings to be stored digitally as a voice number, and later recalled and edited.

This type of analogue synthesis is basically subtractive—the harmonics in a rich waveform are filtered out to varying degrees. With *additive synthesis* sounds are built by giving harmonics individual envelopes, rather than by filtering. To work usefully, however, the phase relationship between harmonics has to be controllable as well as their relative levels, and this facility is uncommon. Additive synthesis may give interesting results when a Fourier Analysis is made of a sampled sound, and the results used to 'rebuild' the sound using oscillators. Such facilities are naturally to be found only on the more expensive computer synthesizers.

FM synthesis

When the output of an LFO is applied to the control voltage input of a VCO, the result is vibrato. If the frequency of that vibrato is increased, so that it is comparable with that of the VCO carrier itself, and if the deviation of the carrier frequency is also increased, then sideband frequencies are produced, including 'negative frequencies' which are perceived as positive frequencies with reverse phase; the result is a dramatic change of tone colour. If, further, the modulation frequency and the deviation are varied dynamically, then remarkably 'unsynthesized' sounds occur. These principles were developed in the late 1960s by Professor John Chowning of Stanford University, and he subsequently took his ideas to Yamaha of Japan. The outcome was the Yamaha DX range of synthesizers, one of the most significant steps forward in easily accessible electronic music. For those interested in imitative synthesis, it is possible to produce extraordinarily lifelike sounds, especially with bells and brass.

The DX synthesizers allow six sine-wave oscillators (termed 'operators') to be interconnected on one of thirty-two different algorithms, such that cascades of modulator–carrier relationships may be formed, or arrangements where operators are simply mixed. Each operator has its own envelope generator, and may give a frequency which is either fixed or which tracks the keyboard. There are several methods of controlling the output level of each operator, and thus the deviation of any carrier it is acting upon, in addition to its envelope generator: the level may be made sensitive to key velocity, to aftertouch, to various controllers, to an LFO, or to the position of the key on the keyboard. Pitch control is more limited, to the bend-wheel, LFO, or a master pitch envelope.

There are a great number of parameters to be adjusted in a DX synthesizer, and they are accessed by the now common method of selecting the parameter to be edited with a push-button, and then using a data-entry slider or up/down buttons. By using Systems Exclusive MIDI commands these operations can be done remotely, and there are several 'DX editor' software packages available for microcomputers fitted with MIDI interfaces to make the job easier, with graphic representation of envelopes and so on. These may be useful, since processes such as softening a sound, which is easy on an analogue synthesizer (just reduce the filter frequency), can involve adjustments to several operators. Indeed, developing sounds with an FM system is often a more challenging affair than with an analogue system, because there may be several ways of approaching the same problem, and predicting the result of a change is not easy.

Sampling

A sampling synthesizer is one which makes a digital recording of a sound and then replays it at appropriate pitches on triggers from an input source, such as a keyboard or incoming MIDI. From digital recording theory it is clear that the higher the sampling rate, and the greater the resolution (the 'number of bits'), the better the sample. The first sampling synthesizers, such as the Fairlight Mks. I and II, used eight-bit resolution and sample rates up to about 33 kHz; later machines use twelve- or sixteen-bit resolution, helped by compansion, and sample rates which reflect those in the parallel technology of straight digital recording. Improvements in this area are directly dependent on developments in memory technology.

Samples of simple percussive events are fairly easy to use, because the incoming trigger (from keyboard or MIDI) just 'fires' the sample at the appropriate pitch, which then plays through to its conclusion. But, for sustained notes, the sample must be able to continue playing as long as the note is held down. This means making a 'loop' in the sample, whereby a defined section of the sample will be played repeatedly as long as the note is held. To avoid hiatuses, the end of the loop must be at the same instantaneous level as the beginning, and the loop must be long enough not to be uncomfortably recognizable. In an effort to make loops less noticeable, some machines offer 'backwards–forwards' looping, where instead of shuttling from the end of the loop to the beginning the looped section is played backwards to the beginning, then forwards again. Other options include automatic looping, where the machine itself selects suitable zero crossing points to define the loop.

The simplest sampling synthesizers offer merely the ability to make digital recordings and define loops. More advanced machines give the user the opportunity to modify the samples, and to mix or edit together different samples. It is here that the opportunities exist to create innovative new sounds from natural sources, and develop the concepts of *musique concrète* outside the limitations of classic tape manipulation. Techniques borrowed from analogue synthesis, such as filtering and envelope shaping, or even from word processing, such as 'cut and paste', are currently being applied to sampling.

Digital recording is a memory-intensive business, and the cheaper machines which rely on floppy-disc storage have limited sample lengths. Unlike a digital recorder, a sampling synthesizer needs effectively instantaneous random access to the recording. But bigger synthesizers which use hard-disc storage can offer very long sample lengths, so that the conceptual division between a 'sample' and a 'finished recording' is merely semantic. Here the worlds of synthesis and digital recording begun to blur, and a sample may in effect be a whole piece.

One specialized division of the sampling family is the drum machine. While older versions used analogue resonant circuits and noise generators to simulate percussion sounds, modern drum machines employ samples of real instruments which have been carefully recorded using all the best studio tricks.

Sequencers

Sequencers bridge the gap between music as it is notated, with bar lines, note lengths, and expression marks, and music as it is played, with LSI chips. They store and replay not sounds but the instructions required to make those sounds, in a form which makes sense to the musician. In addition, they may be able to print out a score in standard musical notation.

The data is put in to a sequencer in one of two ways: real-time recording and step-time recording. With real-time the composer sets the sequencer running, probably with a click to give the timing, and plays a MIDI keyboard; and MIDI data is then recorded 'live'. It may subsequently be edited, to clean up mistakes, or even quantized, to bring fudged notes into correct timing. With step-time recording the notes, note values, and other parameters are entered by hand, directly into the sequencer itself.

For certain kinds of repetitive work, such as rhythm sequences, it is easier to build individual bars and then assemble those bars into complete pieces. This philosophy is usually found in drum machine sequencers. Here a bar or number of bars will be repeatedly played, and the composer can keep adding new material to the loop until it is complete. That 'subsequence' is then compiled with other sub-sequences to form the final track.

Most serious MIDI sequencers borrow the 'tracks' concept from multitrack tape machines and allow several different tracks to be recorded in parallel. The MIDI data for each track may then be sent out from physically separate MIDI OUT sockets or mixed on one socket, with different MIDI channels assigned to each track. It is also possible to drive more than one sequencer in synchronization using special MIDI messages. So, for example, a rhythm sequence can be built with a drum machine, which is then slaved to a master sequencer which provides the rest of the music. The *system common* MIDI messages are used here: synchronization clocks, which are prescribed at 24 clocks per quarter-note (crotchet); the *start* message, which makes the slave play its sequence from the top as soon as it receives clocks; the *continue* message, which makes is resume playing from wherever it happens to be, again on receipt of clocks; and the *stop* message. *Song select* MIDI messages allow different sequences to be selected, and *song pointer* messages direct the slave to a particular start point in the sequencer. The data number which is transmitted after a song pointer status byte is the number of elapsed clocks since the beginning of the sequence, divided by 6. So, to point to the second bar of a sequence in 4/4, for example, the song pointer number would be $(24 \times 4)/6 = 16$; that is 4 crotchet beats elapsed at 24 clocks per crotchet, divided by 6.

MIDI sequencers are locked rather strongly into the concept of bars (or measures, as they are often called). This is fine for straightforward songs, but for a composer of incidental music for TV or film it is highly unlikely that the 'hit points' he wants to use as the skeleton for the cue will fit nicely on to a regular 4/4 beat. He is therefore faced with the prospect of either disregarding bar lines completely—which will create a havoc of unreadable tied notes if the music is to be printed out—or building in tempo changes in the sequence to 'pull' the bars into the skeleton. Some sequencer packages now offer a valuable facility. Music that has been played 'on the fly' with complete disregard for the sequence tempo or the bar lines (it could for instance have been played looking at action on a video) can be automatically realigned against bar lines by means of inserted tempo changes. As far as the ear is concerned, the original speed and performance are retained whilst visually the sequencer has laid it out neatly across bar lines. Literally the best of both worlds.

Sequencers offer software designers ample opportunity to show off their talents at graphic presentation. The more basic dedicated machines just give numbers on an LCD display to show note pitch, duration, start time, and velocity; others use VDU displays either to show the music in proportional representation (with blocked-out lines on a musical stave, the length of which shows the duration), or in full musical notation, including all the Italian marks. The latter are clearly limited by the resolution of standard VDUs, and need movable 'windows' on the score.

The merging of music's natural flow with the strict time requirements of a film or TV programme has always been a tricky area. Most sequencers now feature 'locked markers', named cue points which lock to certain SMPTE times, around which the MIDI music can flow freely until a satisfactory result is obtained. There is always, however, slight competition between the pure rock music user and the film composer as to which features they would most like to see in the next update. So, as in all things, software never pleases all the people all the time.

Music computers

Virtually all modern synthesizers incorporate microprocessors and could therefore be called dedicated 'computers', but certain larger systems reserve the title Music Computer because they set out to offer complete music systems. They give complete studios in a box, needing only loudspeakers, and offer all types of synthesis together with sequencing, synchronization, and even final digital mastering. The music computers in use at the research establishments such as IRCAM, Stanford, and MIT have not yet made an impact on commercial electronic music, though this may well change. The IRCAM 4X, for example, allows the composer to build systems using software modules rather than hardware. Such ideas are already penetrating the mass-production market. There is already one sequence package on the market designed by the originator of the IRCAM system which deals with composition in an object-orientated way; most suitable for modern music and sound pieces.

At the other end of the scale, the personal computer market has taken a very great interest in electronic music, not only for editing DX sounds but also for sequencing and data storage. More sophisticated programs are available for machines such as IBM and IBM compatible PCs and the Apple Macintosh range which offer complete MIDI control systems, together with score print-outs. When linked with dedicated MIDI synthesizers, however, such systems may be very powerful indeed. One outcome of this market development has been that more and more people are able to afford to set up small 'bedroom studios' where material can be prepared, ready to be given the final gloss in the professional recording studio. As a result, the boundaries between what is 'professional' equipment and what is not are increasingly blurred: while there is a clear difference in performance between a studio tape machine and a domestic one, a MIDI sequencer package for a home computer may well be more useful to a composer than a dedicated machine with a much higher price-tag. Good software is good software, no matter what it runs on.

Music technology: the future

Recent developments in the music market-place have been characterized by two distinct sorts of product: those which break new ground in computer-linked real-time audio recording for use alongside MIDI-generated music (thereby allowing session played instruments to be synchronized with a

MIDI studio), and those which further explore MIDI technology and synthe-sizer design.

1. Digital audio recording

It may now be said with conviction that analogue tape is on its way out. Centre stage are the new audio recording products which will not only monitor the sound but will perform complex editing tasks thereafter. As ever there are top-end professional systems at enormous cost, but also an increasing number of smaller units which perform very well, and can easily challenge the professional market. They also have the enormous advantage of being part of MIDI sequencer packages which allow the recording of live music and MIDI music to coexist, and be edited at the same time.

The modern digital recording facility will offer the user 'on board' non-destructive editing, EQ, time-stretch, variable pitch, compression, and no doubt eventually all the facilities to be found in the post-production envi-ronment. There still remains, however, a choice as to how the data is stored.

Users fall into two camps: those who favour storing data on large hard discs associated with computers (PCs and Apple Mac systems are often used) and using computers to supply them with the processing power, and a friendly interface through which to perform all the editing tasks; and those who value dedicated machines provided with removable storage media such as magneto-optical discs. The latter have the advantage of no downloading initially and remastering thereafter, and of being a piece of equipment solely devoted to the digital recording and editing of sound, rather than the 'Do-It-All' PC which may be a jack-of-all-trades but is at times master of none. The trade-off is in the usability, where the sort of display and screen size of the PC or Mac is preferable.

However, a new hybrid has recently appeared, which uses the reliability of the stand-alone device with the front end being controlled by the com-puter. The advantage here is that all the heavy computation is done by a box devoted to the task, and all the aesthetic feedback is provided by the user-friendly environment on the Mac or PC. The magneto-optical discs have slower read/write times, meaning that more than two stereo tracks cannot be read from the same drive at any one time. However, multiplexing of units will allow multitrack work controlled by a sophisticated central remote. But tapeless digital systems are not yet able to challenge the reel-to-reel 48 (or more) track machines used in pop music studios for sheer bulk, although with storage media becoming cheaper, no doubt it will not be long before such a challenge is met.

2. MIDI devices

MIDI can be regarded as one of the few examples of successful co-operation between rival companies. The universal application of a common interface language across many different devices has revolutionized and facilitated work in the modern studio. Inevitably though, the limitations of the medium have started to show; notably the speed of MIDI data is unable to deal with simultaneous complex operations, but more importantly the resolution of 128 steps per controller is inadequate for fine adjustments. MIDI has been used by many firms to control their mixers (and, for 'passive' style setting up of session mixes and recalling them later, the system is perfect) but for active fine control of audio level, EQ, etc., MIDI will cause an unwanted stepping effect as sound is raised or lowered. (For those of us old enough to remember, it is very reminiscent of the jumps in level experienced on the BBC's rotary stud faders.) A method of combining two controller numbers, indexing one with the other, was introduced but has not really been taken up as yet.

In the early days of experimentation in electronic sound, because activity in the area was comparatively small, users could rightly say that although music technology was very expensive, it was designed particularly for their use; and indeed they could in many ways affect the way it progressed. Such days have long since passed. Most devices have become very much cheaper but are designed for the mass market. Whether rightly or wrongly, the manufacturers have decided that the 'middle of the road/semi-professional/rock music composer-performer' forms the largest share of their market. Although his needs may overlap with those of the applied music composer (with film, TV, or multimedia work to do), it is the mass market that wins the day. Obviously the revenue from that market allows the design of the equipment in the first place, so one must not be too critical.

For many years we have all become used to the ubiquitous '1U' rack-mounted box, containing anything from EQ and synthesizers to echo and FX devices. The manufacturers have encouraged it, not really because of an altruistic desire to save space, but mainly because of the saving they make on knobs and switches. This has led to an enormous increase in what can only be described as 'brain fag'. The visual feedback given to the user when he moves a knob or switch and can gauge his action by seeing an overview of all the other knobs and switches, is enormous. To deny this overview is to dissuade a user from experimenting; and it is not surprising that we are in an age of easy-access ready-made sounds, when creating our own is made so difficult. Yamaha acknowledge that over 90% of their DX7s returned for servicing still had the factory presets in them, unaltered; so why bother with the front end? Many expander boxes now simply contain presets (albeit hundreds of them).

In fact the complexity of creating new sounds and samples has spawned a new profession, that of the 'Sound Creator'. His time is so taken up with making the sounds that he has no time to use them; instead he earns his living by selling them. However, help with the creation of new sounds may be at hand. There are already desk-mounted banks of MIDI controllers on the market whose sole job is to MIDI-control other devices, providing a much needed tactile front end. They are still in their infancy (with insufficient real-time display of labelling on faders and switches) but in the future, especially with the further development of large flat screens to act as video working 'desks', we may at last be able to regain a much needed overview.

There is now also a new outlet for applied music: multimedia. Well-crafted music in an interactive CD (CD-I), for example, will greatly improve the product and may, especially when the virtual reality boom takes off, encourage music-makers to experiment again, and encourage the manufacturers to give them the facilities to do so.

Table 18.1. MIDI messages

Status byte	followed by data bytes	Description
Channel messages—for specific MIDI channel reception		
1000 nnnn	key number key velocity	Note off event (nnnn = channel number 21) Middle C = key number 60
1001 nnnn	key number key velocity	Note on event Velocity 0 = note off
1010 nnnn	key number pressure value	Polyphonic key pressure/after touch
1011 nnnn	control number control value	Control change (see notes)
1100 nnnn	program number	Program change
1101 nnnn	pressure value	Channel pressure/after touch
1110 nnnn	LSB MSB	Pitch wheel change
System Common messages		
11110000	none	Start of System Exclusive message
11110010	LSB MSB	Song position pointer number of MIDI beats into song, where MIDI beat = 6 MIDI clocks
11110011	song number	Song select
11110110	none	Tune request
11110111	none	End of System Exclusive message

Table 18.1. (*continued*)

Status byte	followed by data bytes	Description
System Real-time messages		
11111000		Timing clock
11111010		Sequence start
11111011		Sequence continue
11111100		Sequence stop
11111110		Active sensing
11111111		System reset

Table 18.2. MIDI control numbers

Control number	Function	Control number	Function
0	Undefined	66	Sostenuto
1	Modulation wheel or lever	67	Soft pedal
2	Breath controller	68–95	Undefined
3	Undefined	96	Data increment
4	Foot controller	97	Data decrement
5	Portamento time	98–121	Undefined
6	Data entry	122	Local control on/off
7	Main volume	123	All notes off
8–31	Undefined	124	Omni mode off (all notes off)
32–63	LSB for controllers 0 to 31	125	Omni mode on (all notes off)
64	Damper pedal (sustain)	126	Mono mode on (poly mode off)
65	Portamento	127	Poly mode on (mono mode off)

Notes on Controllers: Control numbers 0–63 are for up to 32 continuous controllers, such as wheels or sliders. The MSB values are given after control numbers 0–31; corresponding LSB values, if required, are given after control numbers 32–63. Controls 64–95 are for switches. Controls 122–7 are reserved for Mode messages.

19 The role of the producer

Phil Wainman

For many years, when a problem has arisen in the studio, I have often wished I could refer to an imaginary 'Producer's Handbook' which had the answers to everything from machine breakdowns to people with similar ailments. Thus I see my chapter in this book as being perhaps more along the lines of a 'Dr Spock of Record Production', something that reflects my own experiences through the years, rather than a tome on the dos and don'ts of recording, mixing and cutting.

A painting analogy is probably apt as, like an artist with his raw materials—paint, oils, brushes, and canvas—the record producer begins with a song, a piece of music, someone to sing it, someone to play it, and some studio time, in the same way as a painter would begin with a blank canvas. The challenge is to produce work interesting enough to attract an audience.

The dictionary definition of 'produce' is 'to bring forward or show for examination', and of 'producer' it says 'a person producing articles of consumption or manufacture'. I have heard the role of a producer in the record industry being likened to that of a director in the film world, and I suppose that is true in at a record producer has to be creative, efficient, and something of a psychologist (as does a director), but I would add other elements. After all, a producer is working within the framework of a song which leaves room for interpretation, whilst a film director has to work more closely with his original material in the form of a script.

What a producer needs

First I would say that a record producer has to have infinite patience. He has to have discipline (definitely an asset with some bands) and responsibility, and the ability to pick a good song, together with the ability to add an element of surprise to that song (when he gets into the arrangement and production of it) in order to end up with a record which stands out from the hundreds of others.

Production is a very human part of the music business. It's very personal, and the producer should be able to contribute artistically to the end-product. Record production is all about people and working together, and I think you can actually tell when a record has been put together by people who all enjoyed the process. Conversely, you can hear if there has been friction, musically.

If you can get all these elements together, including of course a hit song, you should be in pretty good shape. It all sounds great, doesn't it, but there is a minus side which you should think about carefully if producing is your professional aim.

You will have almost no social life! So, if your social life is important to you, perhaps you should reconsider your career. You have to be prepared to give up so much in the way of a personal life that you sometimes wonder why you're doing it. If you have a family, they will need to take second place to your work, at least until you are a track-record producer and have the luxury of being able to pick your projects. It is not uncommon to work 16-hour days which leave you feeling jet-lagged and completely out of sync with what is going on in the outside world. Music is one thing and the 'normal', conventional way of living is another. So you have a choice—either you continue with your social life, friends, family, or whatever, or you become a record producer!

I began producing in the 1970s, and I was lucky to get a start then, because the music business was a very different animal from the one it has become in the 1990s. Also, I was fortunate to be around when so much was happening musically. The Beatles were strong influences and from America had come Motown. Those records and sounds are still being emulated today. I was beginning to get noticed as a writer and player, having come off the road touring as a drummer in France, Germany, and Scandinavia, to join The Paramounts (who were later to become Procol Harum).

As a writer, I had been demo-ing my own songs for some time and had begun the laborious business of trekking around the record companies trying to get my songs recorded by bands who already had record deals. I had been doing some session work too, which helped to get me in the door to the A. & R. departments.

A. & R. (Artists and Repertoire) men are basically the people who sign talent to record companies, whether it be in the form of finished masters or new bands needing development. Some young artists are quite often signed to a music publisher simply because the writers have shown some potential. A good music publisher plays an active role in the development of young talent. He can help structure the act and subsequently open doors to the relevant A. & R. department.

In the 1970s, production was all about the strongest-willed person; it was whoever shouted the loudest. I think it was that, coupled with my reputation in the studio for coming up with ideas for sounds, arrangements, and song structures, that really gave me my first production break.

The song was 'My Au Pair', and was a rewrite of 'Little Games', a title of mine which the Yardbirds cut when Jeff Beck and Jimmy Page were in the line-up. It was a minor American hit for the band; I really liked the melody, so I decided to change it a bit and go in with an orchestra and take a very different approach. Obviously the costs of working with an orchestra were and are much higher, and I needed the talents of an arranger. I knew what I wanted to end up with musically, and I could hum the parts, but, as I said, an orchestra is expensive and you must have a written arrangement for the musicians to be sure of getting all the orchestral parts down in one session. However, I still needed a budget in order to get into the studio in the first place.

Luck plays a large part in this business and I had a nice slice of it handed to me at just the right time. I met a man who wanted to get into the music business and he agreed to finance my project—as long as I would produce a particular girl singer on the same session.

We agreed to work together, and I went ahead and cut both my song and his. Both titles were released and although they did not make the charts they gave me a working introduction to the record companies. As I mentioned, I had worked for a lot of them as a session player, but now they saw how enthusiastic I was about getting into production and I began to get regular work as a producer.

Getting started

In some ways it is much easier to get a start today. Home recording set-ups are relatively easy to put together, both from a technical and a cost point of view, and many writer-producers start in a domestic situation working with their own portastudios, guitars, synthesizers, and songs.

These songs may then be heard by A. & R. departments, who may say, 'OK, we believe you've got something here; the ideas are great but the technical quality is not good enough.' In these circumstances the record company will probably let the writer-producer loose at a professional level in a proper studio with good equipment, state-of-the-art desks, monitors, effects, etc. Before you know where you are, you are on your way to producing; remember that hits can be created in your home set-up too. In fact, going back to the 1950s and 1960s, although recording was far less sophisticated then, a spate of 'garage band' hits came out, mainly from America, and here in Britain too there have been chart records that started life as home-recorded tracks. Thomas Dolby and Dave Stewart certainly came up the portastudio route, as did many others, because it is a way for germinal writer-producers to express themselves with little capital investment.

The other road to record production is via a professional studio, beginning as a tea boy and working up through tape copier, tape operator, assistant engineer, to engineer. Provided you have the other qualities I mentioned earlier, you should soon start contributing creatively to the sessions you are working on. Then, if you are lucky, you will get to work with a particular act as co-producer, maybe working on the B-side of the next single. If the record company likes what you have done with the track, you might be offered a band to produce by yourself.

I think the engineer-producer probably has it easier than the writer-producer in these early stages, as the engineer has already got all the tools to hand. He just needs to prove himself by growing up in a professional environment.

I can appreciate both types of producer and I believe the differences add colour to the chart. I am primarily a musician and a writer, and therefore I like getting involved in the material itself, working closely on the arrangements with the band. I tend to rewrite lines sometimes, put in key changes and breaks, and generally work as another writer within the band to develop their songs. Of course I will take a look at the technical side too. I like to look at it objectively, through the ears of a potential record buyer, but I think that an engineer-producer sees a different picture. He thinks mainly about creating different colours with sound and may not look at the musical details of the songs as much. Providing there is somebody in the band who is a good writer, the engineer-producer can complement him and that can work very well.

Hits and budgets

The only way record companies can survive is to have hit records. That is of course stating the obvious, but it is very unlikely that a record company would sign an act just because it loved the music. A band or a singer must also look good; the image is very important. Above all else the record companies are looking for hits, and they have to feel that any act they sign has all the ingredients. The choice of the right producer for a new signing is very important, and he is expected to become part of the team and deliver that potential.

Second only to the material, the main concern for a producer is the budget. Record sales fluctuate from year to year; budgets do the same, and the recording is only a part of the whole process of making an act successful. Once the recording is completed, the company has to invest heavily in marketing. For instance, a video to promote the record on television can often cost far more than the recording itself.

If you are asked by an A. & R. department whether you think you can bring a particular single or album in for a certain budget amount, and you say that you can, you have to stick rigidly to that figure. Otherwise you will find that you lose credibility as a producer (and in some cases money) no matter how wonderfully creative you may be in the studio.

So it is important to evaluate exactly what you have got to work with before committing yourself. How much are you going to need for recording time and for mixing time? Is the band going to need additional musicians, booked on a session basis? Can they handle their own backing vocals, or do you feel you might like to add, say, a girl vocalist to the voices you've got, to change or brighten the sound? Are you going to need to hire in specialist players, synth programmers, and the like? What about an arranger?

All these different things have to be looked at, and it may be an idea to budget each area separately. Whether you actually use or need them or not, you are developing your credibility with the company.

Remember, there are ways to save money too. A lot of the work can actually be done before going into the studio. Working out the routine of the song is very important, because you can usually tell early on whether you have got it right; it is also cheaper to work things out in a rehearsal room rather than in high-cost studios. If you find the band can handle their own backing vocals, it might be worth spending some time working out what everyone sings, so that, when you are in the studio, you can do all your back-up vocals in the shortest time possible. Routining outside the studio also gives you a chance to get to know the people you are going to be spending a lot of time with; you can also find out how temperaments interact and whether there are musical weaknesses in the band which need covering by session players.

I can recall working for the first time with a certain group in Edinburgh. I had gone up there to cut some exploratory tracks and to get to know them, when I became aware that they were in fact checking me out. The leader seemed to keep coming up with the silliest questions, but I knew my time to turn the tables on him would come.

When it came to his vocal overdub, his tuning left plenty to be desired—either he was very flat or the track was very sharp! I told him that there was a well-established technique I often used to overcome this problem. We would record him whilst he was standing on a chair, and this would help him to hit the high notes. We did a take, and then I told him that he was now singing too sharp, but that if he bent his knees a little, it would be about right. He really fell for it, by which time the rest of us were in hysterics. This evened the score and certainly helped to break the ice. After that, of course, we became firm friends and subsequently worked together for some years.

Another way to cut costs if you have agreed a tight budget, is to work in less expensive studios to record, and then work in more upmarket ones when it comes to mixing. It is a question of how much you have to spend.

In any case, you will not be expected to come with a budget at the first meeting when you are called in to discuss the project. A. & R. men are used to producers taking time to evaluate the situation before committing themselves; but when you have, you must be responsible for the recording from start to finish. It is not just a question of going in there and being one of the boys having fun making records. You have got to remember the money side and be as cost-conscious as possible.

Once you have delivered the record and perhaps remixed it because the A. & R. man does not think you have got quite enough voice in one spot (or there is not quite enough bass throughout), the marketing machine takes over. Marketing includes press coverage, sales, and promotion. The record company will aim to get the record higher on the chart than the competition. This means air-play and television exposure, and their ability to achieve this is also part of your responsibility. You should have taken care to avoid any reasons for air-play not being forthcoming—bad language, say, or plagiarism, or out-of-date references.

The recording session

Let us look a the recording process in more detail. If you are working with a straight rock band, the best way is to start with the rhythm section; alternatively, with today's electronic techniques, you may start right from scratch and lay down a timecode which will govern your timing. I personally prefer to work with the musicians, as I think that ideas will come from the rhythm section as they actually begin playing. It also means there is a basic element of feel to the track. The bass player may come up with something to complement what the drummer is doing. (The producer can also have his input, and soon the pattern will begin to emerge.) The chemistry between the musicians and the producer during the actual session improves things to my mind. It is certainly more human and less mechanical. However, having said that, there is a lot to be gained from tracking individual instruments in certain situations. It is part of the producer's responsibilities to work out which is the best method for any given situation.

It is a good idea, too, to lay a guide vocal at the same time as you are putting down the rhythm track, as the musicians get a feel for the song. Certainly, once you have got the basics, you must include a guide vocal, as it is around this that you are going to build all the other musical lines towards the finished production. Next you should look at the backing voices, if any. Use as many tracks as you need, then bounce them down to stereo pairs in order to retain as many tracks as possible for other overdubs, synths, guitars, brass, or whatever. Finally, lay the lead vocal—the icing on the cake.

During the sessions you may find that the band are coming up with ideas for arrangements, instrumentation, or interpretation, and of course their ideas should be discussed and tried. You will get situations where you completely disagree with each other, and then it is a question of knowing where to stop, which is where psychology comes into play. You have to know how strongly the band feel about their ideas and whether you can use them, elaborate on them, or adapt them, or whether you have to insist on taking your own route; but remember that time is money. It is sometimes a fine line you have to tread when dealing with this kind of situation. Diplomacy comes with experience, as does dealing with a temperamental artist.

It is your responsibility to get the best vocal performance from an artist, again knowing where to stop. It is pointless continuing if the singer's voice is strained after two or three hours working on the same title. It might be that you just take a break from that and do some other overdubs, coming back to the lead vocal at another time. However, if you are very close to the right sound, then you should continue and capture the performance at that moment. The trick is knowing when you have it. You have to know when enough is enough, and say, 'We've got it. I'm very happy with that one.'

The best way of working with a band depends on what sort of band it is. If there are one or two writers in the line-up, they may feel that they need constantly to bounce their ideas off someone else. This someone else could be another member of the band, which would make them pretty self-contained, but it is more usual for that other person to be more objective about the whole unit—and then it is important for them to record with a producer at the helm.

A producer's role with a solo recording artist is somewhat different in that there are only two people to make the decisions. The song is the key here, as its direction and feel will dictate what type of track you are going to be looking at recording. You will certainly need a rhythm section, but you may be looking at a piece of work which cries out for orchestral backing, so you have to plan your sessions accordingly. You may decide to use a rhythm section which is an integral unit, either a band in their own right or a nucleus of musicians who regularly work together in recording studios or backing solo singers on live gigs. There your approach will probably be similar to that used in recording a group line-up. However, if you are thinking in terms of an orchestra, you may wish to hand-pick your rhythm section for certain individuals, to make up the total picture you have in mind. In any event, you will need to lay down a guide vocal early on and plan your overdubs around that, be they brass stabs, guitar solos, or a fully arranged orchestral session featuring string, brass, percussion, etc.

Sometimes fate can take a hand, turning something bad into something good. On one occasion, my multitrack tape was at one studio, whilst my forty-piece string section and I were at another. I had asked the studio holding the tape to have it biked over to me, but, for one reason or another, the multitrack arrived one hour after the musicians had left. In the meantime, however, I did have a 7½-in copy of the track with me and so I played that to the string section and recorded their parts straight to quarter-inch stereo. Then, when the multitrack finally arrived, I spun the strings into spare tracks. There was a bonus is that the strings phased with the original track, giving it a unique overall sound which I would not have got otherwise.

With a solo artist, too many people tend to look 'middle of the road' and play safe. Of course you have to get into the songs, to see what you have to work with, but then you should go to the extreme and try to be different. Try to create something which will stand out from the rest of the current chart releases. It is often worth trying something really weird and wonderful if your budget will run to it. But do remember that you and the artist are both in there to come up with a hit record, and you have to consider what he is trying to bring out in his material. If you push him or her too hard, you may find yourself with a difficult artist on your hands. You will then be better off taking five minutes or so to cool off and talk—always outside the studio, and never in front of the other musicians or studio staff.

The tack to take in this situation is to say, 'It's in both our interests to come up with a recording and a performance that is better than average, and that is the reason why I am pushing you.' You may even have a word privately about the singer's interpretation or diction.

Finally, let us look at the self-contained artist or one-man band. If you have a writer who sings and plays guitar or synths, he will be able to programme his own machines. In this situation you would definitely begin with a timecode or click-track, from which you would develop a drum pattern. Against this you would track all the other instruments, laying them one on top of the other. It has become fashionable to work this way, and it is certainly cost-effective. For myself, I still prefer to work with a band, as I find there is a tremendous amount they can give me. I then become part of a team, rather than a producer working in a purely mechanical fashion where most of my input would be at the mixing stage.

Live albums

Live recording is another area you need to understand in order to be a successful producer. As an artist's recording career progresses, he will inevitably want at some time to record his material in concert. I would say that the main thing you have to remember is that you are not going to be able to stop the band in mid-set, in order to re-record something you could not get right first time. The most important thing is to make sure that all the microphones are working and conveniently placed for the band, so that nothing handicaps the live performance, and leads are not going to be pulled out or anything knocked over by accident.

You, as the producer, are usually stuck in a vehicle outside the venue, and once the show starts your only method of seeing what is going on is via a TV monitor; the rest of it is very much an aural exercise. I remember, when making a live album with Sweet, that I got myself out of trouble by ensuring that I had plenty of ambient mics around. On that particular date I ended up with some mics not working, and the ambient mics really saved the day. Of course, if it is necessary, you can add a little sound sweetening in a remix room later.

The engineer

When it comes down to it, the producer has to be the final arbiter, either in the studio or on a live recording date, but someone equally important to the project is the engineer. I have one rule I always try to adhere to. Do not get in his way. Of course you are directing the session, but once you have established what it is you are looking for let the engineer get on with his work. The producer has to look at things objectively, remembering the potential buyer's ear. If something sticks out as being really wrong, then you have to do something about it. Other than that, you should give the engineer his head and let him contribute, rather than suppress him. If there is a particular sound you want or, for instance, you need more tracks and think the solution is to bounce down (which of course it very often is), listen to him, be guided by him; that is what he is there for.

At the moment we are looking at two different trends in engineering. There are those from the old school who are able to handle a complete line-up of musicians, though they are getting fewer and fewer. A lot of the younger engineers are very contemporary in their approach to modern-day recording, in that they are used to synthesizers for everything, and you virtually never see a live musician playing an acoustic instrument on their sessions. Everything is plugged in, and, with a lot of engineers today, if you say 'We have a live drummer today', they may have a problem in knowing how to mike up a real kit. Choose your engineer according to the type of session you are producing. If you have an orchestral session, look for an engineer who can handle that, and conversely, if you have an electronic set-up, look for an engineer who is used to working with that format.

Some of the larger studios do get large line-ups, more particularly for film music, and these studios are able to train youngsters accordingly. However, line-ups are generally getting smaller, due to budget limitations, and those smaller line-ups are often used in conjunction with synthesizers.

I personally do not think that the industry is doing enough to address this problem, but, with costs escalating for live line-ups, the only alternative is to use synths, and this seems to be the route many are taking.

The mixing session

Never say, 'We'll sort it out in the mix.' If it's wrong, it's wrong; and it's going to take twice as long to do it later. So do make sure you have everything you need on the tracks before you finish your actual recording. When you feel you've got to the point where you have everything on the tracks, it's time to begin your mix.

Mixing, again, is all about personal taste, and you can mix in thousands of different combinations. First decide on the vocal interpretation you want. You might decide to use a chorus from one track, a verse from another, and a second chorus from yet another. There are really no dos and don'ts in mixing, but basically the vocal track has to have first consideration as you need to be able to hear the voice to determine what the song is actually all about. Apart from that, you need a bottom end, a top, and various degrees of middle. If you bear in mind our painting analogy when you are mixing, you are actually painting a sound picture. When you look at your picture it must have perspectives, and this is important to understand. You may be sitting between a pair of speakers, listening to the detail: the detail is important, certainly, but you have to remember that you must make the overall sound of the record as interesting as possible.

At this stage, you may decide to use some ancillary equipment to enhance a particular sound on a vocal or instrumental line. You are trying to deliver three minutes or so of excitement, and this sometimes means taking a chance to try something wild. Provided you have got it right on the basic tracks, you can afford some experimental trickery with the new digital equipment available.

Finally, your work as a producer on any given project is not finished until you have delivered the master in the formats that enable the record companies to produce the sound carriers to be sold to the buyers. At one time this meant only cutting the master on to lacquers for black vinyl production, but you now have to consider CD and cassette production, possibly video too.

With CD you must first prepare a production master on a digital format. You must make sure that the production master for vinyl is not used for this, as there are compromises made for vinyl production, which are not necessary for Compact Discs. For instance, there can be a loss of top in the vinyl production process which you have to compensate for in the cutting. This does not happen with CD, where the digital production master and the subsequent disc will sound identical to the finished mix. Take care too, when deciding the running order for an album, that the general level from title to title is the same. With cassettes, the running order may differ from the album version so that the two sides are equally balanced in terms of running time.

Nowadays most of these decisions are finalized in a post-production suite. You should make friends with the engineer there and use his experience and knowledge of the pressing plant requirements to achieve best transfer to CD, etc.

And there you have it: a potted guide to production. Of course there is much more that I have not talked about. It would be impossible to cover every eventuality; every artist and every session is different; each recording studio has its own little quirks; every A. & R. man his own ears. If you have decided to make record production your career, grab every chance you can to talk to people with experience and a love of their craft. At the end of the day, you will only learn by your out-takes and by making the most of every opportunity that comes your way. See you in the charts.

The Consumer Product

20 Post-production

Ben Turner

Before the advent of the compact disc in 1982, and indeed the introduction of digital recorders from a few years earlier, recording studios mixed down to analogue stereo masters, which would then be edited into the correct running order. This tape was then taken into a cutting-room, where level changes and equalization would usually be applied at the time of transfer to lacquer disc. A simultaneous tape copy, reflecting any changes made to the original programme, could also be made. This copy was used as a 'production master' from which further copies could be taken. The arrival of the compact disc along with the Sony digital 1610 U-matic format, and later the F1 Betamax format, meant that digital editing, digital EQ, and final PQ encoding of the CD master could take place only at specialized and relatively expensive facilities houses.

A further revolution has since taken place, the result of which is that most studios and many private individuals can mix to DAT and, with the aid of computer workstations, carry out their own resequencing, equalization, and fades; in fact, do their own post-production work. As we shall see, they can even go some way towards making tapes ready for use as the production master for consumer formats. Thus in a short time the black-magic 'art' of analogue has been almost wholly replaced by the seeming ease and simplicity of playing DATs, of getting computers to carry out intricate procedures at the touch of a button, and of transferring the result back to some digital medium.

However, some problems will always remain, and the new 'simple' digital era has thrown up entirely new problems, almost all of which are technologically more difficult to solve, and are more expensive in terms of time if nothing else. Consider one small example. In the brave new digital post-production studio a completed album lies waiting to be delivered to the client. The computer workstation's hard discs lie empty, waiting for the next day's work to be transferred. A late evening phone call: 'Change track 4 to the extended version'. The entire album is re-recorded to hard disc, the new track is transferred on to disc and edited in, and the whole is recorded back to DAT. In essence this is a simple operation, but it will require at least the patience necessary to play through the album twice, plus the editing time. In a classical editing studio the ramifications are even more unpalatable—a similar amount of work might be needed to change just one join.

Given that CDs are now the pre-eminent consumer format, reference is generally made below to 'CD mastering', but most of what follows is relevant to all formats. The terms 'mastering engineer' and 'post-production engineer' are somewhat interchangeable, and they can refer to anybody who is responsible for the action of performing final changes to a studio master tape. Such changes may include equalization, level adjustments, editing, and so on. Similarly, the 'post-production studio' can now encompass any room where these changes are undertaken, be it the latest high-tech studio, or the kitchen table with a DAT machine and hard-disc editor. Professionals may balk at the latter proposition but, given the low price of much professional and semi-professional equipment these days, it is in this direction that much work is headed. We can begin by looking at some of the general categories of specialist post-production work.

Equalization

To be frank, the best location for equalizing stereo masters is in the recording studio or mixing-room where individual EQ on discrete tracks can be performed: not in the post-production studio. However, it may be necessary at the post-production stage to refine the sound: that is, make up for a general deficiency, such as adding an overall 'brightness' to a mix, or compensating for a poor recording environment.

It is not possible after the mixing stage to add 'edge', for example, to one element of a stereo mix without affecting those other elements which share the same frequencies. If one accepts this, then in all cases the judgement should depend on whether a change can be made which at best does not seriously upset these other elements. Consider, as one example, adding high-frequency content to 'brighten up' string tone. This action may have the desired effect of brightening the tone, but does the resulting lift in the cymbals make the track sound like a hi-hat concerto? To make matters more difficult, one needs to judge the effect not only on the area being EQ'd but also to consider possible repercussions at the opposite end of the frequency spectrum, which in this case may have the effect of diminishing the amount of bass perceived. This addition may also highlight previously buried high-frequency whistles from synthezisers or television equipment. Adding bass may give a firm foundation to a sound, but may bring up unacceptable rumble. It may also lead to an increase in level on the meters forcing, in turn, reduction of the overall gain, or the use of compression. What might this do to the overall sound? In other circumstances, subtraction of bass to reduce rumble will necessarily decrease the bass from instruments: is this a desirable consequence? What is the least objectionable option; the original rumble or the effect that reducing it brings?

Finally, one must also make a judgement about whether the use of equalization could severely 'corrupt' the sound of a recording. To take a specific example: old dance-band records played on modern studio speakers can sound very piercing, and a lot of time might be spent in trying to 'tune out' this 'defect'. Our audio forefathers were not deaf or unskilled—they had different listening conditions and balanced the sound accordingly. If one listens to the originals at low volume and from a single speaker, the 'problem' vanishes. Should the mastering engineer alter a sound to 'adapt' it to suit present-day listening standards? Taking a slightly different view, what should be done, for instance, with older material which sounds 'dull'? Is this dullness an original facet of the recording, or has it been caused by multi-generation copying? If one adds high-frequency EQ, should one worry about residual hiss being unduly emphasized? Experience is really the only basis upon which one can rely to answer these questions.

As will become clear, the mastering engineer has complex decisions to make, all made more difficult because there is rarely a right or wrong answer—any decision will be a matter of personal taste, and no two persons' tastes are identical.

Level

The signal level generated on to a CD master tape is effectively the level at which the CD will sound when played back by the consumer. Thus a CD master with low level will result in CDs which sound softer compared to the general run of CDs. Fortunately, there is no modern counterpart to the days of cramming on as much level as possible when cutting vinyl records. The benefit of this may be that balance-engineers can afford to let their individual sound translate to the consumer format in a more natural way. The widespread 'mono-ing' and perhaps compression of bass, once the order of the day in some cutting-rooms, led inevitably to a certain similarity of sound. On CD, a large amount of throbbing bass may in fact lead to a perceived reduction in overall level, but this could be a price well worth paying for the individuality given to the sound.

The technical reasons for recording via A–D converters at as high a level as possible are discussed elsewhere in this book. If a mastering engineer receives a tape with seriously low level, the damage has already been done. Indeed, raising the level may make matters worse. The mastering engineer may have to make his own decision—either leave the level where it is, and risk the wrath of the client, or raise the level and again risk the wrath of the client. If a rule of thumb is required, then it may be said that most CD masters should peak to leave no headroom at some time during the programme and that, if more than a few dB of headroom is left, some increase may be necessary in order to 'standardize' the level as discussed above. Some solo instrumental records may prove to be an exception. For instance, harpsichord or acoustic guitar recordings will appear to be very 'loud' if they peak to zero headroom, and this may force a mad dash for the volume control in the consumer's living-room. However, this is not the end of the level problem. A more insidious difficulty occurs when one is presented with recordings with too much level. It may be asked how is this possible, when digital recorders peak to 'zero' and then stop?

A brief explanation of 'over-level' must necessarily follow here. Strictly speaking there is no such thing once audio signals are in the digital domain; a better phrase might be 'maximum level'. An input may be 'trying' to feed a digital device with ever-increasing level but, once all the available bits have been used, no level increase is possible. When an 'over-level' indication is given, it means that a number of samples in succession have been encoded at the maximum number of bits. There is no set 'standard' for how many of these samples constitute 'over-level'. On some equipment there is a user-friendly option for defining this number. Again as a rule of thumb, if we take 'over-level' to mean about four samples in succession, we may perhaps allow an occasional occurrence, providing that clipping cannot be heard—remembering that constant high level may put the analogue circuitry of consumer equipment under some strain.

The unfortunate effect of continuously battering at the brick wall of maximum bits is either severe distortion or, more insidiously, audio limiting. It is surprising that some 'state-of-the-art' converters give no indication of potential overload, thus the unwary may allow peaks of as much as 6 dB 'too high' into such a converter, without noticing that unfortunate effects might be taking place: distortion at worst, or else a recording that sounds very loud when compared with another peaking to just within zero headroom. For the mastering engineer working with two sources, one 'over-recorded', the other not, it takes a great act of will to trust his ears, ignore all meters, and reduce the level of the faulty recording to match that of the other.

One standard trick to get round a recording which has too many over-level indications for comfort (providing that a lower-level version is unobtainable) is to reduce the gain by, say, 0.1 dB on transfer. As far as a digital system is concerned, the previous material at '0' headroom and 'above' will peak to 0.1 dB of headroom and everything will appear to be in order. However, this is purely an illusion, for distortion will obviously not disappear as a result (note the remarks on 'dither' below).

At the opposite extreme, the audio industry has perhaps failed to pay enough attention to the problems of allowing a dynamic range which is too wide for normal consumer comfort. This is particularly relevant to classical music recording where the recording engineer should perhaps take an active role in deciding some of the limits that should be set. However, even in the field of pop music, the engineer must be careful, for instance, not to make fades so long that, in a domestic environment, the music seems to have excessively long gaps between tracks.

Editing

Digital editing techniques have evolved in two main ways (ignoring the seldom-used 'razor-blade compatible' digital reel-to-reel formats).

The first type is the 'assembly' system whereby a master is constructed by copying from session tapes on to a new master tape. A typical editor of this type is the Sony DAE-3000 (Plate 25), and there are also DAT-only variants of this. The 3000 editor can handle U-matic, DAT, and DASH tapes as the source, and generally records on to U-matic tape. Thus at the end of the editing process, with appropriate checking and PQ-encoding, no further transfer is necessary before CD replication can be made. Editing is accurate to within one sample; gain changes can be made during transfer and, with appropriate ancillary equipment, signal processing can be carried out during the copying process. If one takes an extreme example, one could edit from a 48 kHz DAT tape, via a sampling-frequency converter, apply reverberation and EQ as desired, make all necessary fades, and so on—all in one single pass from the session tapes. No other present-day digital system comes

Plate 25. The DAE-3000 Digital Audio Editor (Photo: Sony)

close to this in sheer efficiency of time. The obvious drawback is that changes to a finalized master, which involve changes in duration, cannot be made without another complete copying pass. However, the 'insert' capabilities of this editor—down to a sample if necessary—are very comprehensive. If a single track, or a short portion of it, needs amendment, making the change need not be a complicated process.

The virtues of this system have been overshadowed by hard-disc editing on computer workstations. In these systems it is generally necessary to transfer material on to large disc drives, perform editing and other tasks, and then transfer the result on to a permanent medium—be it DAT, U-matic, CD-R, or Exabyte. The advantages of hard-disc systems are many. The first is, generally speaking, that such a system is much cheaper than a fully configured 3000 system. Secondly, there are many ways in which the use of hard discs and computer technology have opened up new ways of working with music. There is nearly instantaneous access to any material; a variety of crossfade types for edits is normally provided—varying the duration of the fade, its shape, and so on; instantaneous gain and EQ manipulation on whole sections of material is possible, as is moving sections using 'cut and paste' techniques. In addition, these changes are usually reversible. If, for example, a different running order is required, only a moment's work is required to come up with a new sequence ready for audition.

It may be heresy, but it is possible to argue that hard-disc systems do have some unique problems of their own. Some engineers, for example, do not listen to the whole of a finished project whilst it is on disc, it being more efficient to listen to the entire project at the time of transfer to a permanent medium. What, then, should happen during this final transfer if one hears something 'wrong' or something that requires improvement—perhaps an unsatisfactory edit, or a track which sounds too loud compared to the previous one? The recording must stop for the correction to be made, and then the transfer must recommence, perhaps from the beginning of the programme.

More words of caution must be added. It is entirely possible to transfer work to hard disc without listening to it, make a few adjustments by selecting isolated excerpts, and then transfer the material for mastering without audition. As a result, a digital glitch, for example, which was recorded on to the original material may be allowed to pass through the post-production chain without being heard.

It would seem that both editing systems have their virtues and drawbacks. In an ideal world, one would use the 3000 system where the work to be carried out is of a known quantity: durations are definitely fixed, running orders are definitely decided, and one has a good idea of the overall sound required. Hard-disc systems come into their own where the material is more diverse, and where changeable creative decisions are required. In addition, if there is enough storage space, a project can be left on disc whilst listening copies are analysed, and speedy corrections can be made before final transfer.

This discussion about hardware may not seem particularly relevant to a chapter dealing with post-production techniques. The critical point is this: the overriding concern of the mastering engineer must be the acknowledgement that he or she will be the last person in the production chain to check that all is present and correct. With analogue mastering, or with the 3000 digital system, one is forced to listen to the material in real time in the same way that most people will listen to the final product. Hard-disc systems, by their very design, make this sequential listening and checking phase harder to implement. Indeed, with the advent of faster than real-time transfer, this crucial element of post-production technique seems set to disappear.

The engineer and client

Although often working alone, it is important for the post-production engineer to be able to discuss lucidly the technical and musical problems that he or she might face. The engineer can adopt a number of roles, at one extreme a dominant role, at the other a submissive one. In the dominant role, it is not unknown for a producer to seek the advice of the mastering engineer before mixing is completed. The 'rushes' can be brought into the mastering studio to be criticized by a 'neutral' set of ears. On the other hand, in a submissive role, the mastering engineer may work entirely 'to order', adding EQ at the whim of the client, even though this client may never have set foot in that room before; or making tiny level changes which will certainly pass unnoticed by the consumer. Some of our best mastering engineers seem to take the former role and are highly respected for it.

We can now look at some of the points of interaction between the engineer and the outside world and examine some of the advanced features included in the term 'post-production'.

Compilation

Compilation takes two forms: either compiling new material (i.e. tracks for inclusion on new albums), or compiling previously released material (e.g. 'Best of . . .' albums). The processes are broadly similar, although each requires a slightly different emphasis.

When dealing with new material, supervision of the post-production session is usually carried out by the producer, the artist, or a member of the record company's A. & R. department. This person should be familiar with the material and also know in what order the tracks are to be placed, how long they are to last, what the maximum running time is to be, and so on. Constructive dialogue between engineer and client is of crucial importance, distinguishing between such often confused terms as 'editing' and 'cutting', or 'fading' and 'editing'.

Important matters for discussion include, for instance: where a fade should start and how long it should last; the length of time to be left between one track and the next; whether a crossfade from one track to another is required, and so on. At times, an engineer may need enormous reserves of patience, while those about him debate the theoretical virtues, or otherwise, of a specific solution. In all such cases, the engineer should suggest adopting a trial-and-error approach. If the timing of a fade, for instance, is unlikely to work, a practical demonstration will be more informative than any discussion.

When remastering previously released material, the engineer will typically be working alone, but should actively encourage the client to find the best source for the material. Rehashes of tracks from old compilations—perhaps taken from CDs—are easy, but these may derive in turn from multi-generation copies. In addition, the client may have to be consulted about the amount of hiss or clicks to be removed from tapes, and advised of the amount of time and expense that might be involved.

In the case of either type of material decisions have to be made about the amount of 'correction' which ought to be made to the individual sound quality of each track. For instance, tracks on an album should be related in level to one another, but this relationship can depend on the relative EQ of each track, since level and EQ are somewhat interdependent. The engineer may have an instruction to alter level but 'not to touch EQ'. Yet, since perceived level depends partially on the balance between bass and treble, to adjust the relative level of tracks without altering their EQ can be a futile exercise. As we have seen, if one track has been heavily compressed and others are not, level matching may be impossible without reducing the overall level of the compressed track, or resorting to some compression on the others.

Music editing

This is again an area where active dialogue is vitally necessary. In electronic editing it can sometimes be difficult for the client to follow on the screen what is happening. A simple explanation of the interface is a good starting-point, showing where the session takes are coming from, or what a join 'looks like'. Similarly a common vocabulary should be defined for such terms as 'in-point' and 'out-point'. Another good communication device is for the engineer to keep the client fully informed as to exactly why he is performing certain procedures, such as recording sections of silence, or what the computer is doing when the 'egg-timer' or 'watch' appears.

With the actual edits themselves, it is up to the engineer to engage in useful dialogue with the client in deciding on the choice of an editing position. At the same time he should always consider, if possible, more options than those suggested. One problem which often occurs is where a splice is audible to the engineer but not to the client (or sometimes vice versa!). The essential point, under these circumstances, is that the engineer must be seen to be doing something of a constructive nature: sometimes a cosmetic change to an edit may produce complete satisfaction!

Computer-aided noise reduction and noise removal

The enormous computing power that desk-top computers now offer has meant that the huge number of calculations needed to perform miracles of audio restoration can be achieved in the studio rather than on main-frame machines. Put simply, noise reduction is achieved by dividing the audio band into many separate frequencies. A 'finger-print' of the offending noise is then taken, where possible, and the computer subtracts only this noise and, furthermore, subtracts it only below a certain user-defined level. Thus, if hiss is the target, it is removed only when it is not masked by other musical material, leaving loud material unscathed. Noise removal, such as declicking, is carried out by the computer intelligently looking at the audio waveform, and deciding where a click occurs. It then synthesizes the audio at this point by looking at material around the click, and redraws the waveform at the click-point, thus eliminating it.

The result of these processes can be nothing short of miraculous, but they can also produce the audio equivalent of making an original Michelangelo painting look like a cheap reproduction. It is all a matter of taste and judgement. The picture might look 'better' without the paint peeling off and the cracks showing, or without the dust of ages obscuring the colour, but there are those who argue that any restoration must by its very nature destroy some of the essence of the original. In the field of 78 rpm disc restoration, the removal of clicks, crackles, and noise undoubtedly makes the resulting material sound very unlike the original. In place of the surface noise there is nothing. Due to psychoacoustical effects, the ear may be 'fooled' into thinking that the presence of extra treble in clicks and scratches constitutes some sort of high-frequency musical content which is removed by the cleaning-up operation. It may be arguable whether the 'clean' rendition of the disc or the unprocessed version is correct. The jury of 78 rpm enthusiasts seems to be evenly divided on the final verdict.

What has this to do with the engineer? The important clue has already been mentioned. Many of the controls on computer noise reduction/

removal systems are user definable. The engineer in consultation with the client can thus set the threshold at which processing will take place. Since many systems are now real-time, the engineer can control the amount of processing whilst listening to the result and make speedy adjustments accordingly. This may explain why some early non-real-time processing was of questionable quality—the vital factor of aural feedback was missing.

Copying

On the face of it, nothing could be easier than copying tapes in the digital domain; especially from and to the same format. One just plugs in the appropriate AES3 (IEC-958 Type I) XLR lead, or SPDIF (IEC-958 Type II) phono-plug and presses 'record'. Indeed, in most cases, this is quite satisfactory. However, it is now becoming commonly accepted that things may be not be quite so simple. The most common problems with digital-to-digital copying are associated with the mechanics of the digital interface which can cause total or partial failure in a myriad of ways, including some which are so subtle that they can easily be overlooked by the unwary. Even transfers between similar data formats, for example SPDIF to SPDIF or AES3 to AES3, may introduce problems. These can be contrasted with those where transfers are made between SPDIF and AES3 equipment which, from the strictly technical point of view, should not be attempted without some sort of interface converter. An added dificulty is that some equipment has AES3 connectors (normal audio XLRs) but uses SPDIF Channel Status conventions. This often causes confusion because the user may be unaware of the possible status conflict.

There are many potential conflict problems between interfaces; too many to enumerate here. From experience, the following seem to be the most common: on some AES3 equipment the CRCC byte is not implemented or is wrong, whilst other systems require this error check byte to be correct before they will receive audio. Indeed this byte is not present on SPDIF transmitters, and is therefore a common cause of incompatibility with AES3 receivers. The Serial Copy Management System copy protection strategy (SCMS) on new consumer equipment using the SPDIF interface supersedes the older system where a 'copy inhibit' bit was provided. Unfortunately, this bit in the SPDIF format maps into the 3-bit emphasis field of AES3. SPDIF receivers may not receive the AES3 data format at all; some may do so, subject only to the copy inhibit bit, and others will implement SCMS and prevent further copies being made from that tape.

In order to function correctly, both transmitter and receiver must be synchronized together. With AES3 and SPDIF formats this is usually carried out by extracting the sync information from the audio signal; however, other methods include connecting a 'wordclock' signal or using a sampling-rate converter which can compensate for the lack of sync between two pieces of equipment. The classic symptom of lack of sync is the presence of regular ticks, usually around one per second or every few seconds— although in the 'worst case' scenario (from the point of view of being aware of the problem) the fault may manifest itself only a few times per hour. One source of poor sync can be a mismatch between AES3 and 500mV SPDIF components.

Finally, we turn to jitter. Put simply, this is the small but finite deviation from the ideal timing of the digital signal waveform. The data bit lengths and transition points may constantly change as a result of poor-quality transmitter circuits, or through the use of low-grade or excessively long cable. Jitter can have a significant effect on audio performance under certain conditions. However, we should first dispel one common myth: it is now generally understood that jitter cannot affect the 'sound' of straight digital-to-digital copies, nor is jitter accumulated by successive generations of copying. Jitter can (but does not always) accumulate if several devices are connected together in series, such as an outboard ADC, digital effects unit, DAT, and monitor DAC and it can have a devastating effect on the sound of a DAC. In extreme cases, jitter can cause momentary unlocking of a receiver, causing ticks and loud thumps.

We can summarize as follows: avoid mixed formats (SPDIF and AES), or use an intelligent interface which can convert both voltage levels and Channel Status data. Take care when determining synchronization strategy and identify a good-quality source of clock. Use good-quality cables, that is with the correct impedance (AES3 is 110 ohm) and low capacitance (less than 50 pF/m). Finally, minimize the use of ancillary equipment unless its behaviour and performance are known to be suitable.

Dither

Dither, or LSB (Least Significant Bit) management, is another area whose importance is just being recognized. As has been stated in most serious discussions on digital audio in recent years, the treatment of the LSB of any audio data is of crucial importance to the overall sound quality, particularly at low levels. The best approach is to preserve the original LSB data intact, but the only way to be certain of doing so is not to pass the data through any signal processing device at all. The manufacturers of most digital editing systems claim that their systems do preserve this data, providing that unity gain is maintained throughout. In practice, this assertion is extremely difficult to validate without substantial technical resources and, even if one went to the bother of doing so, in theory at least, the validation would last only until the next software update. So the industry has little alternative but to trust, and to keep listening.

The main point is that, whenever any operation is performed on a digital signal, be it a gain change or EQ or whatever, there is a strong likelihood that the LSB data of the original will change, and that this change will have an adverse effect on the sound quality. It is obvious that, for the overwhelming majority of post-production work, there is no hope of maintaining 'LSB integrity' throughout. This integrity may, however, be seen as a useful standard for as much programme as possible; fades may have to be corrupted, but the rest of the programme can stay intact by ensuring unity gain and by switching out any processing not actually being used. In other words, the best rule to apply is the same one that applies to analogue technology: the less processing that has to be done, the better.

Where the programme has been subjected to processing and thus the LSB data (at least) has been altered, it is important to ameliorate the effects of this as much as possible. This is facilitated by adding 'dither' noise to the final signal. This is noise whose amplitude should theoretically be half the value of the LSB, though many systems now provide options to vary both the amplitude and shape of this noise. Great care should be taken to determine the optimum setting for these options for any given programme and system. It is important to audition low-level programme when making these decisions, and to do so with the auditioning system referenced to a good master-clock, for reasons described above.

One specialized area of dithering is in the reduction of high bit rates to lower ones. For example, undithered truncation from 20-bit to 16-bit (e.g. a good quality A–D converter to a 16-bit device such as a DAT recorder or computer workstation) gives rise to a grainy, distorted sound on low-level signals. Techniques for re-dithering to achieve a clean conversion from 20-bit to 16-bit have undergone a recent transformation with the application of 'noise-shaping', where the spectral energy of the dither and truncation noise is rearranged to occupy the areas of the audio spectrum in which the ear is least sensitive.

General copying principles

There are a number of general 'rules' in the field of copying, some relevant to analogue copying, some only to digital, but they are worth enumerating as a group:

1. High-quality tape-transports must be used, and must be well maintained and checked. On both digital and analogue machines, heads and tape-paths should be cleaned regularly.
2. Tape stock should be of high quality.
3. Each reel of analogue tape should be individually biased and calibrated.
4. Analogue mastering tapes should have a selection of tones recorded at the

beginning of the first reel. The minimum requirements are: a 1-kHz tone with left/right identification, a high-frequency tone (10–12 kHz), two tones at low frequency (e.g. 50 Hz, 100 Hz), and Dolby tone if applicable. On digital tapes, tones, while not absolutely necessary, do no harm by their presence. A 1-kHz tone with left/right identification plus high- and low-frequency tones can aid the lining up of any post-digital analogue equipment. By convention, CD masters do not carry tones.

5. Lining up tones from analogue tapes should be carried out with scrupulous care, ensuring especially that Dolby tone reads correctly on Dolby meters (or that Dolby SR noise sounds the same as the reference noise). Special care should be taken with setting azimuth, that is the angle at which the replay head sits in relation to the tape passing longitudinally across it. On tone, this can be set on a phase meter, or by looking at a 'lissajous' display on an oscilloscope, or by combining the two channels on to a single meter and adjusting for maximum amplitude. The correct setting must be checked on programme; the tell-tale signs of incorrect setting when listening in mono are, for example, 's' sounds becoming 'sshh', lack of brightness on cymbals, and a general 'clouding-over' of sound.

6. As mentioned above, level alteration should preferably not be carried out when copying. If deemed necessary, care needs to be taken not to overload either analogue or digital equipment—being especially careful with analogue tape machines where an internal elevated level may be used. If level changes are needed on Dolby-encoded analogue tapes, they must be 'de-stretched' before the change is made, and then re-encoded.

7. The use of electrical equipment between tape machines should be kept to a minimum.

8. Except in the most simple of installations, some sort of console should be included to provide analogue monitoring facilities with gain control, gain manipulation, a supply of line-up tones, mono/stereo switching, line-in/line-out switching, and so on.

9. Digital tapes need to be electrically verified on both playback and record machines. In the 1610/30 format, hard-printout verifiers are available which can be adapted for use with some DAT recorders. A verification sheet is a mandatory requirement for U-matic CD masters. Verifying DAT tapes adequately can be difficult, which is one reason why professional read-after-write recorders are essential as most of them include a 'last error' message, or at least a visual indication of error correction. With digital tapes there is no set standard for what is acceptable as far as error-correction is concerned. There should certainly be no concealments or interpolations. CRC rates should not be excessive, if only because experience has shown that a tape with a high CRC count is more likely to give serious errors on playback than one with a low CRC count. A typical 'in-house rule' might be to reject a U-matic tape with more than 500 CRCs/hour or more than 50 CRCs in a single minute.

10. On all formats an aural check should be made at the time of copying. In addition to checking for the correct running order, this will prevent unnoticed digital glitches and mutes, on previously unchecked copies, passing through and beyond the post-production chain. In addition a written record of defects such as clicks or noises which might be mistaken for copying errors should be made.

11. Track titles, track timings, and their timing in relation to the start of programme and/or timecode must be given, as well as an overall total time. Detailed advice on tape presentation will be found in *The Master Tape Book* published by the APRS and The British Record Producers Guild.

12. The minimum requirements for the labelling of tapes and their boxes are:

> Date   Engineer's name   Address of Studio
> Contact telephone number   Name of client company
> Catalogue Number(s)   Name of artist or group
> Track numbers and timings   Total duration
> Indication of line-up tones
> Source of tape (e.g. 'copied from 1610 CD master')
> Description of tape (e.g. 'CD tape master' or 'Copy for radio use')

Analogue tapes should show in addition:

> Speed   EQ   Type of noise reduction (if used)

Digital tapes should show:

> Type of processor   Sampling frequency   Emphasis On/Off
> Verification status (Yes/No)   PQ-encoded (Yes/No)
> Timecode format

The small size of DAT boxes and tapes is no excuse for failing to pass on this information.

Mastering

We have carried out all the work necessary to change the studio tape into a master. What further work is needed to make the tape suitable as a production master? Let us consider the major formats in order.

CD mastering

The current standard for CD mastering tapes is the 1610/30 U-matic format. All factories accept this format. If DAT or other formats are received, they will be copied on to U-matic as a matter of course. SMPTE non-drop-frame timecode is an integral feature of the 1610/30 format and is recorded on to the U-matic's analogue Track 2. It should start at 00.00.00.00 and should be recorded continuously from the beginning of the tape. Programme conventionally starts at 00.02.00.00, but any programme start above 00.01.00.00 seems to be acceptable. At the end of programme, the recording should continue for at least a minute. The longest playing time is 79' 40", but some factories may set a lower limit, and some (off the record!) may accept slightly longer lengths, though this does not conform to 'redbook' standard. A verification sheet must accompany the tape, which should not show any average, hold, or parity errors.

It should hardly need pointing out that the sampling frequency for CDs is 44.1 kHz. The upsurge of 'do-it-yourself' DAT mastering has seen an exponential rise in the number of DAT tapes recorded at 48 kHz presented for CD mastering, and also some with a mixture of sampling rates. The only reason for this must be gross ignorance. Whilst the cost of good-quality sampling rate converters has diminished, the extra processing needed cannot be said to be to anyone's advantage. The CD system can cope with emphasized programme, and also with the unusual situation of the emphasis mode switching between tracks (not within tracks) provided that there is at least a two-second silence preceding a change of mode.

The tape needs to be PQ-encoded, and this can be done either at the factory or at a specialist mastering facility. PQ is shorthand for two of the subcode channels contained on a CD. The P channel designates the start of a track. The Q channel contains such data as the total running time of the disc, the emphasis status, the designated ISRC (International Standard Recording Code) for each track, and also the data bit for enabling the digital output of the domestic CD player. When a tape is mastered, the PQ code is encoded along with the programme content on to the master disc so that, whenever a CD is played, the player can read this information from the disc, telling it exactly where tracks start, whether they have emphasis, and so on. Precise timings (to the nearest SMPTE frame) have to be provided for PQ-ing to take place. This is usually carried out by reading the information from a Sony editor into a specialized computer, the PQ editor, which in turn translates the data into an audio signal which is recorded on to analogue Track 1 of a U-matic tape. The data can also be typed into the PQ editor from a given set of figures. Some hard-disc editors can also collect the data and transfer it to U-matic.

Given that CD players take some time to un-mute when searching for tracks (though not when playing continuously from one track to the next) a negative offset to the start time of each track is deemed desirable. This usually ranges between five to ten SMPTE frames, there being no set standard. If the music is continuous (in live albums, or in opera, for instance) this offset may be reduced in order to minimize the amount of the previous track that is heard when selecting an individual item. The U-matic format may be in its last years as the *de facto* mastering standard. A specialized CD-R format is now becoming acceptable (see Plate 26), especially in the USA, as is Exabyte storage; other optical formats may well be adopted in the future.

Plate 26. The PCM-9000 Master Disc Recorder (Photo: Sony)

Although the 1610/30 format has its idiosyncrasies, it is a pity that the reign of this single world-wide mastering format seems set to wane.

Vinyl and cassette mastering

Provided that the mastering facility has the necessary equipment, almost any professional tape format is acceptable. Whatever format is used, there are a few simple guidelines. The side-break should be indicated and, if possible, there should be a gap in the programme at the side-break point. This is vital and, if the programme (as arranged for CD) is continuous, it may be necessary to record a special master tape with an appropriate fade at the side-break point. Total side durations should be indicated as well as precise track times (related to timecode where possible). It is also useful to give a timing indication of the location of the maximum programme peak level.

Some compromises may have to be made by the mastering engineer in order to achieve safe physical transfer of the material. In the case of vinyl mastering, these include controlling excessive high signal levels at both high and low frequencies, especially if the signal is hard to left or right, or is 'phasey'. Completely out-of-phase bass content may be especially hard to manage. Checking DAT or other digital formats for high error rates is important, as additional costs may be involved if a serious error or 'mute' occurs during transfer.

DCC and MiniDisc mastering

Both these formats normally derive a production tape from existing CD masters, although it is possible to master 'through' the mastering machinery in order to listen for any processing effects which the bit-rate compression techniques introduce. In the case of MD, the CD master is played on to a hard disc along with the PQ information. Any further text is then added, the data compressed by a factor of five, and then recorded back on to U-matic tape. Thus the MD master cannot be played back once it has been copied on to the U-matic.

Digital Compact Cassette differs in that the PQ information has to be adapted to accommodate the side-break. In addition, the text information is prepared on a separate PC. The programme, timing information, and text are then combined, and the result is recorded on to a master DCC.

Conclusion

The aim in this chapter has been to keep a neutral viewpoint when discussing hardware, and only suggest solutions or merely pose questions, when considering specific engineering problems. This is not simply modesty, nor is it accidental. The field of post-production is one where engineers, often left to their own devices, must in the final analysis make their own decisions. This is one of the real pleasures of working in this specialized field for, however invisible this job seems to be, there is great satisfaction in working through an entire project knowing that, with careful work, the skills of many other people will shine the greater, through one's own efforts.

If there are any lessons to be learnt, the most important one must be that, when performing any task, the sheer mental concentration required in constant decision-making and intense listening must be of a very high order, from copying the humblest tape to mastering a future hit album. The post-production engineer must listen constantly for errors, whether entirely man-made or perhaps compounded by the help of a computer. The material must be constantly auditioned, checking that the actual sound itself is correct; listening for level and EQ consistency; correct track location, and so on *ad infinitum*.

The final lesson has not been, perhaps, so neutral in expression. We have many more machines at our disposal than in times gone by. These may be easy to operate, but they are often highly powerful in the way that they can manipulate sound for good and for bad. We may be living in a computer age, but our ears remain firmly analogue, and it is only careful use of our ears that will tell us the truth.

21

Disc cutting

Sean Davies

A disc-recording machine consists of a turntable, a screw shaft (the lead-screw), and a carriage to which may be attached an electromechanical transducer (the cutter head). The leadscrew drives the carriage along a radius of the turntable, and a chisel-shaped tool (the cutting stylus) cuts a groove in the surface of a blank disc placed on the turntable (Plate 27). The turntable normally rotates at a constant speed, and, if the same is true of the leadscrew, then a spiral of constant spacing or pitch will be cut. In practice the leadscrew speed is not constant but is altered to produce a variable-pitch groove, for reasons which will be apparent later.

Plate 27. Modern disc-cutting lathe with video camera attached to microscope for groove examination (Photo: Neumann)

The cutting stylus is made from diamond or artificial sapphire (fused aluminium oxide), and is ground to extremely fine tolerances (Figure 21.1). Up until the early days of microgroove (LP) recording (around 1953) most studios used a slab of specially formulated wax as the recording medium. This has been replaced by a metal-based blank disc with a coating of either cellulose nitrate lacquer or copper into which the groove is cut.

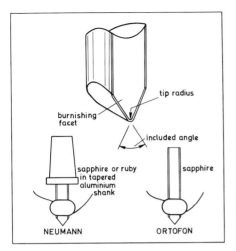

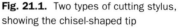

Fig. 21.1. Two types of cutting stylus, showing the chisel-shaped tip

The groove

Information is stored by causing the cutting stylus to move whilst it cuts the groove. For a single-channel (monophonic) signal this movement could be either lateral (Figure 21.2a) or vertical (Figure 21.2b) with respect to the plane of the disc; commercial mono discs always use the lateral system. As the cutter head is an electromechanical transducer, the deflections of the groove are an analogue form of the electrical signal fed to the cutter head, but the conversion is deliberately made non-linear.

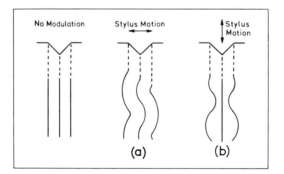

Fig. 21.2. Stylus motion in mono recording could be (a) lateral or (b) vertical

Consider a sine wave of constant frequency and amplitude (Figure 21.3). If this wave is taken to be the motion of a reproducing stylus as it traces a groove, then the maximum or peak velocity of the stylus (V_{max}) occurs as it crosses the centre or zero line. Now $V_{max} = 2fa$, where f is the frequency

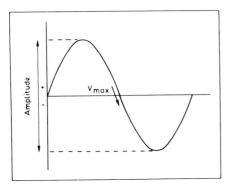

Fig. 21.3. Sine wave: showing that maximum velocity occurs as the signal crosses the zero-amplitude line

and *a* is the amplitude. If we maintain V_{max} constant while *f* is increased, then it is obvious that *a* will decrease. The effect is illustrated in Figure 21.4 for three different frequencies, each with the same V_{max}.

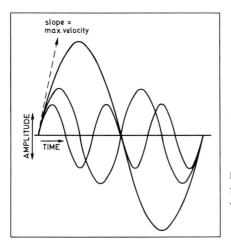

Fig. 21.4. Sine waves for three different frequencies having the same maximum velocity

Conversely, with reducing frequency, *a* must increase. At one extreme the maximum allowable amplitude is governed by: (*a*) the space available between adjacent grooves, and (*b*) the ability of the reproducing stylus to follow the deflections. At the other extreme the minimum allowable amplitude is governed by the noise level of the system. In practice the amplitude of stylus deflections is attenuated during recording for frequencies below 1,000 Hz and boosted for frequencies above. The amount of boost and cut related to frequency is known as the recording characteristic and has been standardized for some years on the RCA New Orthophonic curve, now known variously as RIAA, IEC, or BSI Fine Groove (see Figure 21.5).

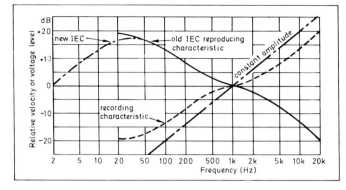

Fig. 21.5. Comparing the standard recording characteristic with the constant-amplitude line, and also showing the IEC reproducing characteristic with and without the more recent bass roll-off recommendation

For correct reproduction of the original signal, the reproducing system must incorporate a network known as the playback equalizer which gives an inverse or mirror image of the recording characteristic. Two points are worth noting: (a) noise inherent in the storage medium (e.g. granular and particle noise in the pressing) is attenuated by the HF section of the playback equalizer, and (b) low-frequency disturbances such as turntable rumble, vibrations, impulses, and induced mains hum are all boosted by the LF section. It is for this reason that the recording characteristic reverts to constant velocity at the extreme LF end.

The recorded level may be expressed in terms of stylus velocity, which can be translated into the output voltage of the pickup. Interaction between the pick-up and disc introduces errors, particularly at high frequencies, but it is here that disc recording has an advantage, in that there exists an absolute method of measuring stylus velocity; that is it is not necessary to play the disc. The method is due to Buchmann and Meyer, and consists in observing the width of the band of light reflected from the groove walls. This width depends on the groove velocity regardless of frequency or disc diameter (but depends on the turntable speed, which is constant). The light used must have parallel rays and be at an angle of 45° to the disc surface, as must the observer (Figure 21.6).

Thus a channel designed to yield a constant-velocity versus frequency cut would show a constant bandwidth. An ideal method for calibrating a system incorporating the RIAA curve is therefore to feed a series of test tones to the cutting amplifier via a precision attenuator which may be set to give the inverse of the RIAA boost at each selected frequency (above 1 kHz). The cut should then show a constant-light bandwidth.

Perhaps the biggest inherited problem of the disc medium is the original

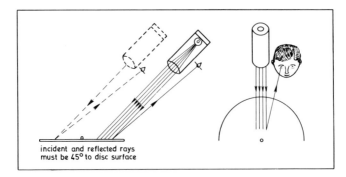

incident and reflected rays
must be 45° to disc surface

Fig. 21.6. Buchmann and Meyer light-bandwidth method of checking recorded velocity

decision to use a constant rotational speed: this means that there is a progressively lower groove speed as the head traverses the disc and, for a given frequency, the wavelength gets shorter. A reduced high-frequency limit and increased harmonic distortion result. Attempts have been made at various times to market constant groove velocity discs but have not succeeded. With compact disc, the freedom offered by a new format has allowed a constant groove speed.

The stereophonic groove

One of the prime requirements of a two-channel stereophonic transmission or storage system is that there should be negligible exchange of information between the respective left and right channels (crosstalk). Although total isolation is not possible in practice, the system should be designed to get as close to this ideal as possible. In an ideal mechanical system, motions acting at 90° to each other would be non-interactive: a cutting stylus could thus carry one channel of information by moving in the plane of the disc (lateral) and the other by moving vertically. Picture a modulation cross placed within a section of the groove (Figure 21.7); by rotating the cross through 45°, the two channels are represented by motions upon the inner and outer groove walls respectively. This system was patented in 1932 by A. D. Blumlein (of the Columbia Graphophone Co. and EMI), and forms the basis of all stereo discs issued today.

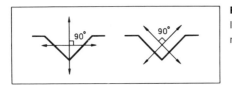

Fig. 21.7. Stereo recording: comparing the lateral/vertical method (left) with the 45/45 method used in practice

An important feature of the 45/45 system is the compatibility achieved with mono (lateral) discs, since lateral stylus movement represents equal in-phase signals on the two channels.

Variable-pitch recording

From early days, disc-cutting lathes were provided with a means of varying the speed of the leadscrew relative to that of the turntable, usually by a precision gear train. The recording engineer decided what pitch to set by consulting a chart showing playing time against pitch. Once set, the pitch was constant for the duration of the side. Since the maximum stylus amplitude depends on the space between adjacent grooves (and the depth of cut) the maximum recording level was determined by the playing time of the programme. It will be clear that, when the stylus amplitude is much less than the maximum allowable (during quiet passages in the music), the groove spacing is unnecessarily wide, leading to a waste of disc surface area (Figure 21.8a). The ideal solution is to adjust the pitch continually so that the prevailing programme amplitude is just accommodated without intercutting (overlapping of grooves).

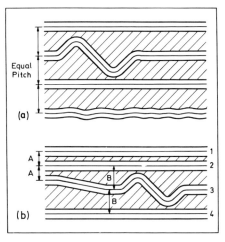

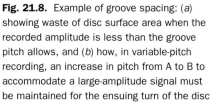

Fig. 21.8. Example of groove spacing: (a) showing waste of disc surface area when the recorded amplitude is less than the groove pitch allows, and (b) how, in variable-pitch recording, an increase in pitch from A to B to accommodate a large-amplitude signal must be maintained for the ensuing turn of the disc

Although such a system was proposed quite early (a patent was taken out by the Parlophone Co. in 1929), it was not until the use of magnetic tape as an intermediate recording medium around 1954 that a working application was possible. The reasons for this will be clear from the following: in Figure 21.8b, the pitch A is known as the basic pitch and allows only a small (approx. 10 μm) space or 'land' between unmodulated grooves. The third turn contains a signal of such an amplitude that the pitch must be increased to a value B in order to preserve the same land between the peak amplitude and the previous groove. Assuming the signal to be symmetrical and no further signals ensuing, the pitch must be maintained at value B in order for the next (fourth) turn to clear the signal. Then, if no further signals occur, the pitch can revert to value A. The change in pitch from A to B implies an acceleration of the leadscrew and hence of the carriage, which latter often has appreciable mass. Now force = mass × acceleration, and so if the new pitch B had to be reached at the same time as the signal arrived at the stylus, infinite force would be demanded of the leadscrew drive motor.

When cutting from analogue tape, there are two playback heads with a tape loop between them. The preview head (position 1 in Figure 21.9) controls the speed of the leadscrew motor: the head at position 2 feeds the audio circuits. The distance d between the two heads is chosen so that the time taken for a signal to traverse the distance at a given tape speed is equal to half a revolution of the disc at the given turntable speed. Alternative tape paths are provided for the various combinations of tape and disc speeds (Plate 28).

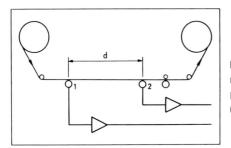

Fig. 21.9. Use of a preview head of a tape machine for variable-pitch recording: the preview head (1) precedes the playback head (2) by a distance d

The two-head system is not practicable when playing a digital tape from one of the rotating drum mechanisms or from most hard-disc units. In this case an analogue output is taken from the player and used to control the pitch system, whilst an additional signal path takes the digital information through a delay unit before D/A conversion to yield the audio signal.

With stereo grooves, the signals are frequently asymmetrical, that is there is a vertical component reaching a maximum in pure vertical motion of the stylus, representing equal anti-phase signals. Such motion could cause the stylus to leave the disc completely on the upward swing. One obvious solution is to have a deeper basic groove. However, we should find ourselves in the same situation as with fixed pitch—having a waste of space at anything other than peak amplitude. Therefore, in addition to varying the groove pitch, we should vary the depth of cut when required by the

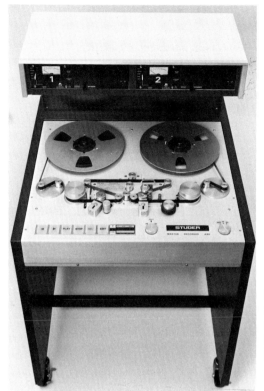

Plate 28. Two-track tape playback unit with separate prelistening heads and choice of tape paths for varigroove tape-to-disc transfer (Photo: Stüder)

phase content of the audio signal. Of course extra depth implicitly requires extra pitch, even before the modulation movements of the stylus are considered, so a complex signal-processing circuit derives the relevant information from the preview head (L–R difference signal) + (right signal for outer groove wall), and the playback head (left signal for inner groove wall) from which the required combination of groove depth and pitch is fed to the cutter-head mounting assembly and the pitch motor.

It is worth noting that, with variable pitch and depth cutting, the space taken up is governed by the programme content, and hence the playing time and maximum recordable level are interrelated.

The cutting head

The cutting head is an electromechanical transducer whose action is best understood by considering the electromechanical system of equivalent units which are set out in Table 21.1.

Figure 21.10 shows a simple moving-coil cutter head and Figure 21.11 its

Table 21.1.

Electrical quantity	Equivalent mechanical quantity
EMF (voltage)	Force
Current	Velocity
Inductance	Mass
Capacitance	Compliance
Resistance	Frictional resistance

equivalent circuit. To obtain a constant velocity-versus-frequency characteristic, the system should be stiffness-controlled (stiffness is the inverse of
compliance), which, by electrical network theory, implies that the system
must operate below its resonant frequency, so the latter should be as high
as possible. This may be achieved by reducing M_1 and M_2 and increasing R_1,
but there are practical limits to the masses involved, and increasing R_1
reduces the overall sensitivity of the system. An alternative approach was
adopted by A. Haddy of the Decca Recording Company in the FFRR head,
which used a very high magnetic flux to obtain high sensitivity (a 25-watt
drive amplifier was sufficient to give full modulation of a 78 rpm disc). The
moving system resonance was around 1 kHz. The variation in R_2 due to
disc diameter was small when cutting a pre-warmed wax blank, but became
severe when cutting lacquer. The addition of a second coil to provide a feedback voltage derived from stylus motion enabled a constant-velocity
response to be obtained irrespective of grades or makes of lacquer. A further
benefit of motion-derived feedback is that the rubber damping, with its
temperature-sensitive drawbacks, may be disposed of, since the feedback
loop provides its own control. The response of such a head with varying
degrees of feedback is shown in Figure 21.12.

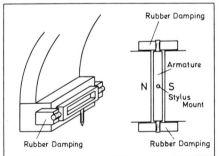

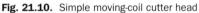

Fig. 21.10. Simple moving-coil cutter head

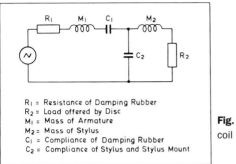

R$_1$ = Resistance of Damping Rubber
R$_2$ = Load offered by Disc
M$_1$ = Mass of Armature
M$_2$ = Mass of Stylus
C$_1$ = Compliance of Damping Rubber
C$_2$ = Compliance of Stylus and Stylus Mount

Fig. 21.11. Equivalent circuit of the moving-coil cutter head

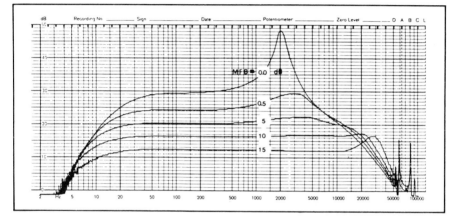

Fig. 21.12. Effect of different amounts of feedback on cutter overall response (courtesy Ortofon)

For stereophonic cutting, two main systems are in use, the Ortofon and the Westrex/Neumann (Figure 21.13). In both types it is important to position the stylus tip at the apex of the triangle of movement. It will be clear that the mass of the moving parts, especially those below the feedback coils, should be kept as low as possible for two reasons: (a) since force = mass × acceleration, the power required at high frequencies is largely determined by the total mass of the moving system, and (b) the above-mentioned parts are outside the feedback control loop, hence non-linear behaviour (e.g. elastic deformations, subsidiary resonances) will not be controlled.

The recording amplifier

The main components of a typical recording amplifier are shown in Figure 21.14. Points to note are: (a) the feedback section must have a very wide

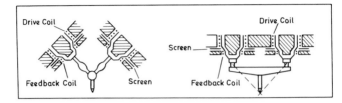

Fig. 21.13. Comparing the Ortofon (right) and Westrex/Neumann types of stereo cutter drive systems

bandwidth (e.g. 2 Hz–150 kHz) in order to avoid phase shifts in the operating range which could cause the feedback to become positive and thus produce instability (in a first-order 6 dB/octave filter the phase shift is 45° at the 3 dB point); (b) the output stage must be capable of delivering sufficient power to the head after the programme has been subjected to the recording characteristic. Since power doubles every 3 dB, there will be considerable demands at high frequencies especially with modern electronic sound sources. A typical amplifier would be rated at 500 W r.m.s.

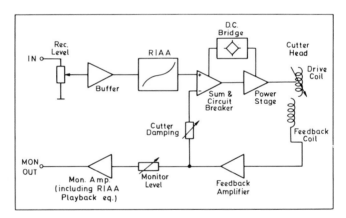

Fig. 21.14. Block diagram of typical recording amplifier

The cutter head cannot stand such a power continuously, so a protection circuit is necessary. This takes the form of a small (c. 200 mV) d.c. potential applied to the drive coil; since copper has a positive temperature coefficient, the resistance of the drive coil is an accurate indication of its temperature, and the voltage drop across the coil is monitored by a bridge circuit. When the imbalance exceeds a pre-set value, a circuit breaker interrupts the drive coil connection. The bridge imbalance may also be used to drive a meter indicating the instantaneous temperature of the coil.

Half-speed cutting

It has long been known that the subjective quality of an audio system is greatly influenced by its transient response, that is its ability to follow a rapidly changing signal. Amongst the benefits of a rapid transient response are: (a) clean high frequencies and clarity of detail, and (b) precise and stable stereo imaging. In disc cutting, transient response is primarily governed by the ability of the cutter head to move the stylus rapidly over a large distance (relative of course to the groove dimensions). From the previously cited relationship $f = m \times a$, and since acceleration $= dv/dt$, it follows that a high-power amplifier with a good power bandwidth (or slew rate) will be required. A typical design has a rate of 60 V/μsec. There is, however, a limit to the amount of power the cutter head can handle before damage occurs.

On the other hand, suppose that the required acceleration rate was halved: this would be equivalent to quadrupling the amplifier power while not endangering the head. By playing the master tape at half its recorded speed, all frequencies are halved, and, if the disc is then cut at 16⅔ r.p.m., a normal spectrum would be heard when playing the disc at 33⅓ r.p.m. Modifications must be made to the equalizing networks in both the tape playback and disc-cutting amplifiers, whilst with analogue tape the wavelength effects at low frequencies must be compensated. Some computer-based digital systems also allow playback at half speed. The undoubted advantages of half-speed cutting are realized only when the master tape contains high-quality transient information, and when sufficient care is taken in the subsequent manufacturing stages.

Direct Metal Mastering (DMM)

During the 1960s a video disc system was developed jointly by Decca in the UK and Telefunken–Decca (Teldec) in Germany, using a vertical cut groove on a disc rotating at 1,500 r.p.m. The tendency of lacquer to relax from its recorded condition, particularly at short wavelengths, rendered it unsuitable as a master medium. Good results were obtained, however, by cutting directly into copper plated on to an austenitic steel substrate. The Teldec video system was marketed in Germany, but, with its restricted playing time of only ten minutes, it failed to secure a sufficient market in competition with the tape-based video systems.

The technology developed for cutting into copper showed interesting features for the audio disc, and a commercial system was offered under licence by Teldec in 1980. Georg Neumann of Berlin then introduced a modified version of the company's VMS 80 lathe and SX 74 cutter head for the new process (the VMS 82 and SX 84)—see Plate 29. The essential features of the system are as follows:

Plate 29. Close-up of disc-cutting lathe employing Direct Metal Mastering on to a copper-coated disc (Photo: Neumann)

The blank disc. An austenitic stainless steel blank 0.8 mm thick is prepared to a high degree of flatness and surface finish. High-purity copper is then plated on to one face of the blank to a thickness of 100 μm. The resulting disc must be cut within a few days as the copper undergoes structural changes which would result in increased noise.

The lathe. Additional power is required in the turntable drive motor, and the removal of the copper swarf requires an air-flow which varies with the depth of cut (hence weight of swarf). Owing to the virtual absence of material flow or relaxation, there is less need to allow extra spacing between adjacent turns of high and low-level modulation, although the effects of creep in the vinyl pressing itself must still be considered.

The cutter head. In the electrical analogy of a simple cutter head (Figure 21.11) the loading of the disc R_L was assumed to be resistive. Whilst this simplification works well enough for a lacquer disc, we have to examine R_L more rigorously for a copper medium.

In the case of copper, C_L assumes a significant value, leading to a resonance at a frequency determined by the combined circuit elements. Two important facts should be noted: (a) for a constant rotational velocity of the disc, Z_L will vary with the position of the stylus on a radius of the disc surface, and (b) the energy required to feed the resonant circuit comes from the turntable motor in rotating the disc. This implies that a recorded 'signal' could occur with no programme input to the head.

In practice such an oscillatory signal has been found useful where the depth of cut changes (as in most stereo material). By suitable design of the head, the oscillatory frequency is placed around 75 kHz; when increasing the depth of cut, a chiselling action occurs which is somewhat similar to that of a pneumatic drill. The stylus has reduced polishing bevels, resembling the sharper profile used in wax recording, and is not heated.

The electronics. The internationally agreed cutting angle of 23° was designed to allow for the lacquer spring-back effect, but this is absent in copper. A physical adjustment of the cutting angle on copper is not feasible for mechanical reasons, so an electrical circuit placed before the drive amplifiers introduces a wave shaping which simulates the correct angle. Increased depth of cut places severe energy demands on the system, so the audio programme is controlled to keep the vertical excursions within preset limits. In other respects the drive electronics are essentially unchanged.

Processing. Since the copper surface is electrically conductive, it does not need to be silvered as lacquer does (see Chapter 22).

Summary comparison between copper and lacquer

Benefits from copper

1. No material relaxation at short wavelengths.
2. Negligible pre/post echo.
3. Considerable cost savings by eliminating silvering.
4. Absence of the noises which originate in the silvering process.
5. Copper blanks may be grown in existing factory plating baths.

Benefits from lacquer

1. Universal acceptability in processing plants.
2. No implicit restrictions on the phase content of the programme. (This may have greatest benefit on coincident microphone recordings where the depth control circuit of a DMM lathe could affect the image.)

Specification of a modern disc-cutting system

Frequency range: 10 Hz–25 kHz.
Dynamic range: 65 dB (with RIAA Curve).
Wow and flutter: 0.02%.
Distortion: variable up to 10%.

The control console

Ideally a master tape should be transferred straight on to disc with only a cutting level control intervening. However, corrections may need to be made either to yield a better finished pressing or because the producer has second thoughts on hearing the tape some time after the mixing session. A typical console layout is shown in Figure 21.15. During cutting, the cutter-head feedback signal, suitably equalized, is fed to the monitoring circuits, and this greatly assists in quality control of the lacquer or copper master (which cannot be played before processing).

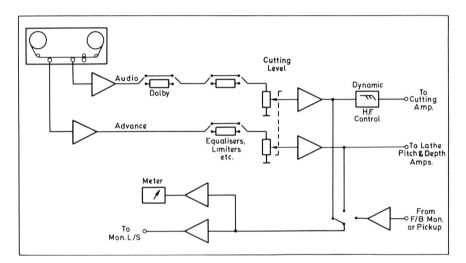

Fig. 21.15. Block diagram of typical cutting chain, showing only one audio and advance channel

Special signal processing

Apart from the familiar filters, equalizers, limiters, etc., the modern disc-cutting console may contain some units not found in the usual studio mixing console. It has been seen that excessive power can damage the cutter head, especially when associated with high-frequency signals. One solution would be to attenuate the HF section of the programme, but this would lead to an audible degradation of the programme quality. The solution adopted is to pass the signal through a low-pass filter, the cut-off frequency of which is normally above the audible range, but a pre-adjustable control circuit allows that frequency to come down very rapidly so as to attenuate a troublesome HF signal to within safe limits. Immediately the dangerous signal has passed, the filter cut-off returns to its supersonic value. The action of such a filter is inaudible, when properly used, and it allows a higher overall level to be cut as well as reducing HF distortion which might arise from pickup tracing difficulties.

Many pickups, especially the cheaper types, have greater difficulty in tracing vertical signals than lateral ones. It follows that it is advisable to restrict the vertical motion of the cutting stylus in high-amplitude passages as long as this does not introduce audible effects. If the two channels of the stereo signal A and B (for left and right) are put through a sum-and-difference network, the resultant two signals will be: (a) the Sum or Middle signal, and (b) the Difference or Sides signal. It is the Difference signal which contains the stereo information, so it is this signal which causes vertical movement of the cutting stylus. If the Difference signal is passed through a high-pass, and the two M and S signals are recombined to obtain A and B again, the resultant groove cut will have a reduced vertical content. The only audible effect would be a narrowing of the stereo image at low frequencies, but since low frequencies are not very directional the effect usually passes unnoticed. A better solution, of course, is to avoid large-amplitude anti-phase signals in the original recording. Certain digital effects units create a pseudo-stereo effect by deliberate phase inversion of the input signal; this causes severe cutting problems and also makes the signal disappear when the recording is played in mono.

The high-pass circuit is variously known as a bass phaser or elliptical equalizer. The turnover frequency (−3 dB point) is sometimes selectable from 40 Hz to as high as 500 Hz, which would be used when cutting a 12-inch disco single with very high level and severe phase problems. The equalizer is rarely used for cutting classical music.

The playback process

The playback pickup cartridge is functionally an inversion of the cutting head, in that it provides an electrical output from a mechanical actuating force. Interactions occur between the moving system and the groove/disc material, and it is desirable to place the resulting pickup resonant frequency above the working range. Another resonance occurs at low frequencies where the compliance of the cartridge assembly combines with the mass of the pickup arm to give a resonant frequency between about 5 and 15 Hz.

A form of distortion known as the *pinch effect* occurs because of the effective narrowing of the groove when the cutting stylus is not at right angles to the tangent of the disc (Figure 21.16). The resulting vertical modulation appears at the output terminals at twice the frequency of the recorded signal. Another form of distortion arises from the finite dimensions of the playback stylus. When the tip radius equals the recorded wavelength, no output is possible: this is known as the *extinction frequency*. As

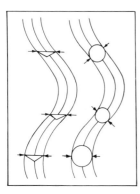

Fig. 21.16. Pinch effect: showing (left) how the cutting stylus inscribes a groove of varying width, and how this causes the replay stylus to ride up and down twice in each cycle

the wavelength of the recorded signal approaches this value, distortion rises rapidly. One solution, used on most good-quality pickups, is to employ a stylus ground to an elliptical (or similar) shape presenting the major axis transverse to the groove (Figure 21.17). Attempts have been made in the past to introduce recorded 'pre-distortion' in anti-phase to the expected playback distortion, but this can work only for a given playback stylus profile and in other circumstances may degrade the quality.

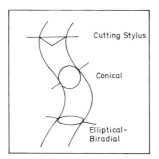

Fig. 21.17. Stylus shapes: showing that an elliptical stylus more nearly resembles the cutter contour, with consequently less distortion on playback

Ideally, the pickup cartridge should traverse a radius of the disc, following the path of the cutting head. A few 'parallel tracking' arms exist but the cartridge is normally mounted on a pivoted arm which results in the stylus following an arc (Figure 21.18). This introduces *'tracking error' distortion*, but careful design of the relevant arm geometry can reduce this to low levels.

Practical points

Many problems in disc rooms arise from tapes being improperly prepared and/or insufficiently documented. Since a disc cannot be stopped and restarted during a cut, there must be no changes during the programme which cannot be corrected while running; these include different azimuths on analogue tapes as a result of different recording machines being used,

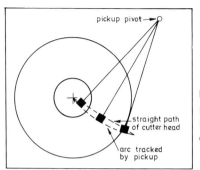

Fig. 21.18. Tracking error occurs with a pivoted pickup arm since it tracks along a curved arc instead of following the straight radial path of the cutter

different Dolby levels, or different recording curves such as NAB and IEC. A frequency run, and a Dolby tone (if used), should be put at the head of at least the first reel in a set. The APRS tape labelling system helps to avoid confusion. The playing time should be clearly stated, and, if the programme has a wide dynamic range, it is most helpful to indicate where the peak level occurs.

When cutting master lacquers, the stylus tip should be cleaned using a piece of pith soaked in acetone before every side. However, do not do this when the swarf suction is on as a fine mist of acetone may be sucked into the swarf tube, where it will dissolve the following swarf leading to a blockage. A stylus should be discarded when the groove walls show marked smudging on accelerations.

When changing makes or batches of lacquer discs, a test cut should be made using different amounts of stylus heating current both at the outside and the inside of the disc; an optimum value will be found for noise. Similarly, the swarf suction should be adjusted to give minimum noise whilst listening to the cutter feedback signal at a very high monitoring level. When using a feedback type cutterhead, the stylus must never be lowered on to a stationary disc with the head connected as this could lead to oscillations which could damage the head.

Perhaps the most difficult feature of disc cutting is variation in the behaviour of the blank discs and cutting styli. It must be remembered that the cutting engineer is expected to produce a mechanical article to tolerances of 1 micron on a surface of the highest polish known to man, and to do this day after day, often against tight schedules. Any variation in the materials used will inevitably cause problems, and it is often difficult to trace the cause of a change in behaviour of a lacquer coating or copper blank: it may be a difference in the stylus, even a change in the humidity of the cutting-room. At such times it is best to telephone another cutting engineer; he may be having the same trouble and possible causes can be discussed and hopefully eliminated.

22 Vinyl disc processing

Jim Hughes (Revised by Robin Allen)

So well established is the practice of disc record manufacture that this chapter nearly became called 'Beyond the Melba Stone'. For the curious, the 'Melba Stone' was laid by Dame Nellie Melba in 1907 during the building of the old Gramophone Company's factory at Hayes in Middlesex. The stone has since been moved and now stands in front of the modern automated vinyl disc and music cassette factory of EMI Music Services (UK), through whose courtesy the following account of vinyl disc processing took shape.

Although the lateral-cut moulded disc is the longest-surviving form of audio software, its deeply rooted manufacturing technology has been continuously updated throughout the years, keeping pace with progressive developments, and today the vinyl disc is a precision moulding made under specialized mass-production conditions.

Manufacture of the vinyl disc may be divided broadly into three main stages:

- Preparing the moulding tool;
- The moulding operation;
- Packaging the record.

Quality assurance is built in at each stage, and the process starts after the programme from a master tape has been cut into a recording blank such as the 'lacquer', which has long been the traditional medium for cutting microgroove records (see previous chapter).

Lacquers, sometimes misnamed 'acetates', consist of plasticized nitrocellulose suitably lubricated and then coated on to a flat aluminium substrate. It is from these that moulding tools are made with the object of producing replicas in the form of vinyl discs, as faithful to the original as commercial practice will allow.

The moulding tool is conventionally referred to as a stamper and takes the form of a nickel negative replica of the lacquer master, from which it is prepared by a series of electroforming operations.

Silvering the lacquer

In order to electroform, it is first necessary to make the lacquer surface electroconductive. Therefore, after embossing an identity code into the lacquer and roughening the centre area to prevent label rupture during moulding, it is cleaned and wetted in an aqueous phosphate surfactant solution. Subsequent processing quality depends upon the effectiveness of this initial cleaning in removing all residual plasticizer from the cut surface before silver is applied.

Silvering is done automatically by rotating the wet lacquer beneath a series of jets angled in such a way that the solutions sprayed from them reach to the bottom of the cut groove. Each of these jets operates in sequence to clean, sensitize, and rinse the surface. Finally, two jets operate simultaneously spraying ammoniacal silver and glucose formaldehyde solutions until a continuous film of metallic silver about 0.1 μm thick has been deposited by chemical reduction.

The nickel master

The surface of the lacquer is now electroconductive and suitable for growing a metal master. To do this, an electroplating bath of nickel sulphamate is used, with nickel pieces as an anode and the silvered lacquer as the cathode. The lacquer is rotated in the electrolyte and first subjected to gentle pre-plating to deposit a thin layer of nickel without distorting the recorded groove. Current density is then raised and plating continued for about 3–4 hours until a nickel master of fine crystal structure and about 400 μm thick has been grown on to the lacquer.

As the nickel is also deposited around the edge of the lacquer locking the two parts together, it has to be trimmed away on a circle-cutting machine before the master is stripped from the lacquer by hand. After separating, the master is washed in solvent spray to remove residual traces of lacquer which may be adhering, and then the silver film, which has now been transferred to the face of the master, is removed chemically before growing a positive. It is possible to play the master using a stirrup stylus (having a V-shaped tip), but normal practice is to examine the surface visually, making sure that all silver has been removed and that the master is in good condition.

The positive

The process of growing a positive from the nickel master is the same in principle as growing a nickel master from the lacquer except that, as the original and the replica are now both metal, the pre-plating technique used with the soft lacquer may be omitted and high current density used throughout. One other essential difference is the need to film the surface of the master so that the two metal parts can be separated after electroforming. Before the master is placed in a plating bath, it is again cleaned and its recorded face passivated by a solution based on potassium dichromate, to provide a separating layer.

After completion, parting is achieved by inserting a small stripping knife at the edge between the interfaces and then, without hesitation, separating in one complete movement to make sure that the recorded surfaces are not damaged by re-contact.

The positive, as its name implies, is the first exact replica of the recorded lacquer, and, like the lacquer, it will have fine 'horns' at the top of the groove thrown up by the cutting stylus. As these are easily damaged, debris from them can cause problems later and the nickel positive provides the first opportunity for their removal. This is done mechanically by working a fine abrasive across the face of the positive for thirty seconds whilst rotating at high speed, then washing away the debris with petroleum spirit.

Several stampers will be grown from a positive, so it is important to make further quality checks before proceeding. Besides a careful visual inspection, the positive is given an audio check with subsequent repair of minor groove blemishes if necessary. The positive is also the starting-point for making 175 mm records with inked or 'painted' labels, which is described later.

The stamper

Last in the generation of metalwork is the moulding tool itself—the stamper—which is electroformed from a positive in much the same way as the positive is grown from the nickel master. Then the two metal parts are held in a vacuum chuck and separated ultrasonically at the filmed interface (see Plate 30), resulting in a negative replica of the lacquer master in the form of a ductile low-stress nickel stamper about 300 μm thick. Another visual quality check is made and a film of flexible PVC is then immediately applied to the front of the stamper, giving protection to the delicate recorded surface during the subsequent finishing processes. This film remains intact until removed in the press just before the record is made.

The next operation is to punch a hole in the exact centre of the stamper, essential if 'swingers' (i.e. off-centre records) are to be avoided at the moulding stage. The stamper is held securely on a vacuum bed and centring is accomplished optically by punching the hole when a rotating image of the concentric groove projected on to a screen passes across the centre of a target.

At this stage the stamper has a mirror-like finish on the front face and a

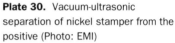

Plate 30. Vacuum-ultrasonic separation of nickel stamper from the positive (Photo: EMI)

matt irregular surface on the back which, if left intact, would impress its pattern through the nickel shell and deform the recorded surface when subjected to the pressures of moulding, resulting in high surface noise and roar. It is therefore necessary to polish the back of the stamper. This is done automatically using four air-driven abrasive heads, each with progressively finer grit to give a consistent finish.

Finally, the stamper, which up to now has existed as a flat disc, is formed to shape in a hydraulic press, and is now ready for fitting into a mould block to provide records of the required profile.

Direct Metal Mastering (DMM)*

The technique of cutting into a copper blank instead of the conventional lacquer (described in the previous chapter) has simplified the methods of preparing a moulding tool as well as providing the end user with very considerable advantages.

As the starting-point for vinyl disc manufacturer, the copper master is already in effect equivalent to a nickel positive in being the metal part from which a stamper can be grown directly.

The flow diagram in Figure 22.1 compares the manufacturing sequences of the lacquer and Direct Metal Mastering systems, showing how silvering, dehorning, and subsequent debris removal are omitted, with an eventual

---

* Trademark of Teldec Schallplatten GmbH, W. Germany.

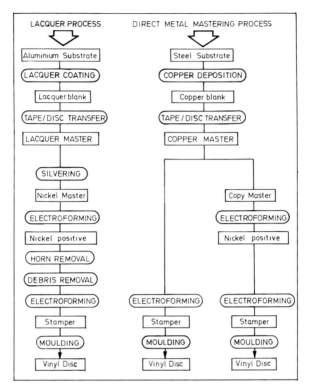

Fig. 22.1. Comparison of the manufacturing flow diagrams for the lacquer and DMM processes

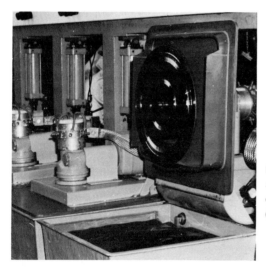

Plate 31. A copper master in position above a plating bath ready for electroforming a nickel stamper (Photo: EMI)

improvement in quality because replication losses inherent in these operations are eliminated.

Once the copper master has been cut, there is a choice of two routes through to the stamper. First, the copper may be put into the plating bath each time it is required to grow a stamper (see Plate 31). Alternatively, where several stampers are needed quickly, it becomes necessary either to cut a number of copper masters or, preferably, to process via nickel positives grown from a copy master. Both systems retain the advantages of direct metal mastering.

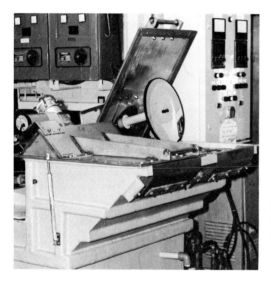

Plate 32. A copper-plated steel disc emerging from the electrolyte ready for passivation (Photo: EMI)

Copper blanks may be prepared on site as required, using a bright stainless steel substrate about 800 µm thick. High surface finish of the flat face to be plated is important, and to achieve this the discs are lapped with diamond slurry, great care being taken to ensure the absence of scratches and other blemishes likely to flaw the plated surface. Cathodic cleaning of the steel surface in an alkali phosphate solution is followed by anodic acid etching of the face to be plated and flash plating with nickel to provide a key for laying down the copper to about 100 µm thickness (Plate 32). This then needs to be dichromate-passivated to prevent oxidation. Two types of plating bath are suitable, either an acid copper or a pyrophosphate copper, and each has certain advantages. The acid copper system tends to have superior levelling and is useful where faster deposition is needed, but the less aggressive pyrophosphate bath can produce blanks with a longer shelf-life before cutting and a better signal-to-noise ratio.

The benefits obtainable from direct metal mastering were stated in the previous chapter on disc cutting, but, looking at them again from the aspect of the vinyl disc manufacturer as well as the consumer, they may be summarized as follows:

- Manufacturing reliability is higher;
- Unlike the lacquer master, it is possible to produce matrices directly from the copper master;
- The DMM process results in significant plating economies;
- Up to 15 per cent more playing time per side;
- Virtual elimination of pre-echo and post-echo;
- Reduction in both rumble and surface disturbances;
- Up to 10 dB improvement in signal-to-noise ratio.

The processes described in preparing the moulding tool, whether from a lacquer or a copper master, are primarily those of electrochemistry, and need controlling to make sure that the resulting metalwork is of correct crystal structure, hardness, and ductility. Besides the checking of the end-products for these properties, frequent tests are made assessing electrolyte concentration, its pH, and the balance of additives. Maintaining solution purity is essential, to ensure the absence of suspended matter and soluble contamination. Therefore, in addition to continuous filtration, the electrolyte is subjected to low current deposition for removal of unwanted cations.

The moulding tool or stamper having been prepared, it is now ready for use to press out the required numbers of vinyl discs. Before this can be done, however, it is necessary to have available the plastic material from which to mould the record.

The record material

The vinyl disc of today is made from rigid PVC based on vinyl chloride/vinyl acetate copolymers, with an average molecular weight of about 47 K and vinyl acetate content in the region of 15 per cent. Some early record materials were formulated on vinylidene chloride copolymers. In some parts of the world, extender resins were incorporated to improve mouldability or reduce costs, whilst at other times there has been extensive application of polystyrene, mainly for 175 mm records. Addition of non-compatible surfactants has also been tried, to obtain an anti-static record. However, this has usually been abandoned, mainly because of cost coupled with a lack of consumer response, or of deterioration resulting from the moisture sensitivity of the moulded groove surface because of the hydrophilic nature and incompatibility of the anti-static agents themselves.

The situation has settled down into two main processing systems founded on granular compound or powder dry blend. The former material is normally prepared by gelling, milling, and dicing after the material has cooled, or alternatively by feeding to a compounding extruder and lace cutting or hot cutting at the die: such material requires to be heated again before moulding the record. Powder blending, on the other hand, has its initial dispersion during high-speed mixing and is subsequently fed to an efficient extruder at the press side, where a second dispersion is obtained and the extrudate presented to the press preheated ready for moulding. This has obvious economic advantages. Whatever system is chosen, dispersion of the raw materials is essential to obtain full efficacy of the stabilizing, lubrication, and pigmenting systems.

Formulation balance is fundamental to success and it is necessary to provide sufficient thermal stabilization to cover all aspects of processing. This, in addition to compounding and moulding, should allow for reprocessing surplus material in the form of flash or rejected records. Earlier practice tended towards over-stabilization through the use of comparatively large amounts of lead-based compounds, having the advantage of long-life processing but the disadvantage of plate-out of non-compatible degradation products on to the surface of the record. Modern technology prefers the use of low-toxicity materials, such as fatty acid alkali metal synergistic stabilizers, added in small amounts but sufficient to provide for necessary material recovery options.

Lubrication is another intrinsic requisite, necessary during compounding or extrusion and release of the disc from the mould, and for better wear performance of the record. To some extent, fatty products liberated from the thermal stabilizer provide a measure of lubrication, but in order to maintain a controlled situation a purpose-designed chemically stable lubricant is added such as a micronized esterified wax derived from lignite.

Pigmentation is a further requirement, and records are by convention black. This was brought about by the addition of a fine-channel carbon black, though dyes have also been used for the purpose, and today furnace blacks are used as being environmentally preferable. Any pigment put into the mix will make its contribution to the steady surface noise character of the record, and this will be directly attributable to the fineness of the pigment and its dispersion. Furthermore, such blacks must be free from iron or other substances which might initiate premature thermal breakdown of the polymer. Where dyes are used for black or other coloured records, they are required to be colour-stable both to heat and light, and to chemical changes within the record compound.

Flow modification of the plastic mass is also desirable to ensure complete filling of the inter-stamper cavity when moulding the record, with consequent avoidance of 'airmarks' or non-fills in the groove. This is usually accomplished by adding a high-molecular-weight, lower-acetate PVC copolymer to the mix. The choice and quantity of this will largely depend upon the type of equipment and processing conditions, but for an effective result the secondary polymer must remain as a separate phase and not be taken into solution during processing.

Control of particle shape and size distribution of the polymers used in airveyed powder blend systems is particularly important, as the presence of excess fines tends to result in a high concentration of additives on the increased surface area presented by the finer polymer, causing problems of plate-out and bloom during the moulding of the record. Quality assurance requirements are embodied in the specifications for polymers to avoid this happening, as well as in the specifications for all other raw materials. Nevertheless, on-site checks still have to be made when polymers are received, particularly to avoid the presence of moisture, which can cause other moulding problems, and to make sure that the material is free of contaminations such as sand and rust particles which would be likely to damage the stampers in the press. In today's declining markets the use of proprietary compounds is more usual for plants producing less than 12–15 million units per year. Before proceeding to mould the disc, the label used to identify the record's content has to be considered.

The record label

The apparent simplicity of paper record labels conceals special technology designed to facilitate processing under automated record-moulding conditions, as well as to guarantee a high standard of commercial presentation. Labels consist of a paper substrate with information printed on the front face, usually by offset lithography. A requirement common to all labels, however pressed, is that the paper should have ample strength to meet the shear forces experienced during moulding, as label failure at this stage (for whatever reason) means a rejected record.

Specialized handling techniques associated with modern vinyl disc production have in turn led to continuous development and standardization of both papers and printing inks. Choice of paper is influenced by the moulding systems used, but additional features which have to be taken into account, apart from strength, are as follows:

- print surface and fabrication, capable of being punched, drilled, or lathe-turned without loose debris which could become trapped in the groove during pressing.
- Predrying at high temperature without curling, excessive strength loss, or discoloration.
- Air permeability: where labels are transferred by suction, air porosity should be low and remain so after drying.

Typical papers consist of a cellulose fibre base, each side coated with chalk-china clay mix in a flexible casein and synthetic latex binder, balanced to minimize curl during drying. Such coatings also have good opacity, and unlike uncoated paper they prevent vinyl bleed into the substrate during pressing, resulting in a moulded label of superior appearance.

Apart from printing well, the inks have to be colour heat-fast and have good release from the mirror-finish nickel shell against which they are impressed during moulding, as any residual ink transfer produces a ghost image on subsequent records in a run and major failure can result in cumulative breakdown of labels.

At the present time, drying of labels is necessary before moulding: one reason for this may be shown by examining the effect of the natural presence of moisture in the paper base, which is likely to be between 5 and 12 per cent, depending upon ambient humidity. If this is not reduced before presenting the label to the press, the moulding temperature of 165°C will cause instant conversion to steam while the label is in intimate contact with the nickel stamper. Steam generated in the closed mould can result in severe groove non-fills near the centre of the record, as well as affecting the label itself by plasticizing the paper coating and ink surfaces. This would make them mouldable, with consequent sticking to the stamper and label delamination on withdrawing the record.

Predrying of labels is done by conveying them (spaced apart on rods through their centre holes) through a circulatory air oven for one hour at 165°C. Air impinging on the labels rotates and disorientates them, balancing out minor grain curl tendencies and dislodging loose paper fibres. Moisture removal at this temperature covers both adsorbed and some molecular water, and, with the paper almost reaching the onset of carbonization, advantage is taken of lower moisture pick-up hystereis when the labels are again exposed to ambient conditions. Oven treatment also results in ink film degradation reducing thermoplasticity, largely through polymerization, oxidation, and distillation of the more volatile binder fractions. After emerging from the oven, the labels are sealed whilst hot into high-density polyethylene bags, ready for use at the press.

An alternative to using paper labels is to print the information directly on to the record just after it has left the mould. Some Continental manufacturers produce 300 mm records in this way, with attractive labels printed in two or three colours. In the UK, direct printing techniques are mainly used for the 175 mm record, which is then often described as having a 'painted label'. This method has an important advantage as it provides a rapid turnround of product where quick response to demand is needed, such as with fast-moving pop records. Delays in waiting for paper labels to be printed, punched, dried, and fed into the mould are avoided, as the label information is processed at the matrix stage early in the production chain.

The method is to etch photographed title copy into the nickel positive using a photoresist, the film of which also protects the recorded area from the etching solutions (Plate 33). Every stamper grown will then be titled in

Plate 33. A nickel positive with photographed title copy etched into its surface ready for growing a 175 mm record stamper (Photo: EMI)

relief, and every record made will come from the mould already titled in recess without a paper label having been used. All that now remains is to colour the land of the label area. This is done as the disc leaves the press, by passing it through transfer rollers coated with a metallic ink to give a brightly coloured label with the design in black (Plate 34).

Plate 34. Immediately after leaving the mould, a 175 mm record with recessed title information passes through transfer rollers coated with metallic ink (Photo: EMI)

Moulding the vinyl disc

With all three components ready—the stampers, the record material, and the labels—the record can now be made. The vinyl disc is made by thermoplastic moulding, which, unlike a thermosetting process, means that the record needs to be cooled in the mould. The method of moulding is much the same whether material is fed to the press in the form of granules or powder blend, but both have to be rendered plastic by heating before presenting to the mould. Powder blend requires further dispersion of additives, however, which is done in a small compounding extruder next to the press.

The general principles of moulding a vinyl disc, which may be classed amongst the most critical mouldings made in any plastics material, can be shown by the example of compression-moulding a 300 mm record. This is done on a microprocessor-controlled press specially designed to withstand continuous working to accurate tolerances, and fitted with two thermally balanced steel mould blocks channelled for rapid steam heating and water cooling. The two stampers used to form the record need to be fitted one on to each block, but before this is done both stampers and block need to be prepared. The reason for this is that, to take advantage of the longer stamper life made possible through modern technology and improved production techniques, it becomes necessary to retard the onset of fretting corrosion in order to obtain high-quality pressings consistently throughout the whole of the run. Corrosion is due to slight movements of the metal interfaces held in contact under heavy stress, resulting in detritus forming behind the stamper which can impress its pattern into the moulded record, thus increasing audio rumble.

With a press working continuously under production conditions, the mould block requires thorough cleaning using a molten wax preparation every time a stamper is changed to remove corrosion by-products and prevent degradation reaching unacceptable limits. Good surface condition of the blocks is maintained by lapping periodically and rubbing down. Abrasives are avoided as the resulting damage provides a nucleus initiating corrosion development. After an anti-fretting agent is applied to the polished back of the stampers, they are clamped to the blocks, surface contact is secured by vacuum, and finally the protective film is removed from the recorded surface.

Dried labels are then taken from their moisture-proof bags and loaded into magazines positioned in front of the extruder nozzle at the press. Sufficient extrudate for a record, plus about 15 per cent extra to allow for flash escape from the mould, is discharged into a preform cup, the lid and base of which are formed by the label magazines. With a label from the magazines adhering to its top and bottom, the preform is moved forward into the mould cavity and positioned centrally on the stamper fitted to the bottom mould block, which by now has reached a temperature of about 165°C (Plate 35). The mould is closed and pressure of about 150 kgf/cm^2 is applied, causing material to fill the mould cavity, with excess leaving as flash. Then the mould is immediately cooled rapidly, the record is carefully

Plate 35. A vinyl preform with two labels positioned centrally on a stamper fitted to a mould block ready to mould a 300 mm record (Photo: EMI)

removed, and the flash is trimmed away. Vinyl discs made in this way, at about 180 an hour, are inserted automatically into bags as soon as they are trimmed to give immediate protection and avoid any handling of the record. The bagged records are positioned horizontally in a box, with a flat separator between every fifth pressing, where they remain until the initial effects of entropy have stabilized. Apart from quality assurance attendant upon the process up to this point, quality control is effected by statistical sampling followed by visual, physical, and audio checks on discs as they are moulded.

The majority of 300 mm discs are made by the compression moulding technique just described. The smaller 175 mm record can also be made by this means, either in single or double moulds, or alternatively it may be injection-moulded; recent developments in injection-moulding machinery have increased the use of this method of manufacture and in 1991 all of the 175 mm disc production at EMI was converted to inked injection moulding.

Whatever method is used for moulding, there is always the need for the recovery and recycling of surplus material. This may exist either in the form of flash or records which have been scrapped for a variety of reasons. Material is generally reused for 175 mm records, but it must be clean and free from contamination. Injection moulded 175 mm discs require a specialized material and so in this case all of the recycled vinyl is reused in 300 mm disc production. Flash can be recovered in its entirety, as can discs with 'painted labels' printed in a compatible vinyl ink, but records with impressed paper labels require the centre to be discarded before recovery.

There remain two types of record which, although neither is suitable for scrap recovery, fall within the broad category of the vinyl disc. The first is the PVC film record, at one time popular as a mailing sampler, which is not moulded but has the groove embossed into the surface of the film with limited and somewhat variable results. The other is the compression-moulded picture disc, consisting of two large-diameter printed labels each encapsulated between PVC film, with an embossed groove and a solid stock core. This is in effect a five-component pressing, but a simpler three-component version may be made by printing a picture on each side of a single sheet of paper and moulding one face in a clear colourless vinyl mix, with the other side embossed into PVC film. All types of record have to be packaged in some way, and a brief survey of this aspect will complete this description of the manufacturing process.

Packaging the record

The primary technical function of the packaging is to protect the contained vinyl disc. At the same time, the packaging has become fundamental and integral to the commercial appeal of the product. Both needs have to be accommodated, and specifications may allow for printing, specialized finishes, or any novelty packaging which may be called for—particularly by the fashionable pop record market—without compromising quality standards. Other aspects to be taken into account are the properties necessary for handling by the disc manufacturer, transit and short-term storage, consumer usage, and long-term storage. Packaging itself assumes different forms according to the type of record being protected, but it falls into two essentially different categories; that which comes into intimate contact with a recorded surface and that which does not.

The bag noted earlier, into which a 300-mm record was inserted at the press, comes into the first category and consists of paper with or without a polyethylene film liner. Important features for automatic handling include air permeability, low electrostatic properties, good slip, close stable dimensional tolerances, a low scratch and damage index (as the material is coming into contact with a record), and freedom from anything being transferred to the disc. Such a bag may be printed and varnished, and it will certainly contain an adhesive to stick either the seams or the film liner. All these substances must be free from migratory agents capable of attacking an enclosed record during storage, and the adhesive bond must remain intact.

Into the second category comes the outer packaging to give further protection, such as jackets and album boxes. Not coming into contact with the actual record, a wider range of durable boards of various types may be employed, but dimensional stability is a prime essential as distortion of such packaging can induce record warp. Similarly, the structural design of jackets must provide correct support to keep records flat by containing the cold flow of the moulding material, either when packed in single jackets or within the structure of a composite pack.

Shipment of discs in bulk is usually done in heavy-duty boxes, having the contents stored vertically with adequate but not excessive side pressure. Packaging and boxes are designed around the product to reduce internal movement and avoid transit damage to both the boxes and their contents.

Stringent packaging requirements laid down by the disc manufacturer are carried forward to benefit the consumer. They are in effect subjected to a practical life-test in the field, the results of which may find their way back to the manufacturer in diverse ways and can eventually modify the specification.

Practical long-term storage includes preventing deterioration of the disc while it is in possession of the consumer, and, in addition to the features mentioned earlier, packaging design has to take into account cold flow properties of the moulded record. The preference is for vertical storage and an evenly distributed sideways pressure at reasonably constant temperatures consistent with normal living conditions.

True long-term storage, however, such as for archival purposes, is not easily predictable and is difficult to design into a commercial product like the vinyl record. With the introduction of new information carriers, the future of the vinyl disc is presently the subject of much discussion, but groove-cut discs in various forms have already been around for well over eighty years, the vinyl disc itself, almost incredibly, for more than forty of those years, and in this respect at least it appears to have the durability for continued existence.

23 Tape duplicating

Gerd Nathan (Revised by John Borwick)

The successful emergence of the analogue compact cassette as a high-fidelity consumer product was largely due to an early recognition of its technical limits, and to a concerted effort by raw-material suppliers and software manufacturers to minimize the effects of these limits as far as possible. Over the last fifteen years we have witnessed a dramatic improvement in the quality of domestic cassette players, cassette tapes, and cassette housings. Cassette players now have better tape transports, resulting in better track alignment and azimuth during playback; cassette tapes have become more tolerant to high-level high frequencies and are less hissy; last not but least, cassette housings are moulded to closer tolerances with consequential improved tape guidance during playback. These are just some of the factors which have placed the analogue cassette 'on the map' as a hi-fi format.

The 1992 launch of the Digital Compact Cassette (DCC) introduced potential improvements in the technical sound quality and user facilities such as text, titles, etc. High-speed duplication of prerecorded DCC cassettes follows the same principles as analogue production lines and will be described at the end of this chapter.

General principles

No manufacturer can survive unless his production process is viable and his prices are acceptable to his potential customers. One way of achieving this goal is to keep non-productive processes such as quality control and administration to an absolute minimum, while still supplying reliable product of adequate quality to the consumer. The successful manufacturer will therefore have a highly reliable, possibly automated, production process, and will use raw materials which are of consistent and adequate, rather than variable and high, quality. In other words, he would rather use cassette tapes and housings which are consistent irrespective of batch or time of delivery than aim for top quality or low price, because not only does variability of raw materials play havoc with automated mass-production machinery, but it will also necessitate the use of extra non-productive personnel for incoming inspection of raw materials and for quality control of the finished product. It is vital to avoid the incidence of random faults in any mass-production process, because no level of quality control short of 100 per cent will prevent faulty product reaching the customer. Within these confines, it is the task of the cassette manufacturer to match the sound of his cassettes as closely as possible to that of the programme material supplied to him.

The programme material

The sound quality of cassettes can only be as good as that of the programme material received by the cassette manufacturer. Unfortunately, he rarely, if ever, has access to original recordings and must therefore rely on the duplicates which are supplied to him. These duplicates represent the starting-point for cassette manufacture, and it cannot be emphasized too strongly that they need to be of the highest quality.

Duplicates are supplied as either 'copy masters' or 'mother tapes'. A copy master is, as its name implies, a 1 : 1 copy of the original recording. A mother tape, on the other hand, is a tape on which the sound has been especially equalized, if necessary, to accommodate the technical limits of the cassette system; it has been fully monitored and is ready to be played on the high-speed playback machine (the 'sender') for copying on to the high-speed record machines (the 'slaves'). A 'QC copy' is a tape identical to the mother tape which has been recorded at the same time but which has not been monitored. It is used either for comparison purposes when the mother tape is not available, or as a replacement mother tape, provided it is first monitored for random faults such as dropouts. The installation of senders and slaves is generally known as a 'high-speed duplicating system', or simply as a 'high-speed duplicator'. A recent development has been a gradual move towards substituting a solid-state memory 'digital bin' for the high-speed tape sender, with advantages in terms of tape wear and mechanical stability. Digital bins are sometimes used for analogue cassette duplication and have an obvious relevance to DCC manufacture, as discussed later.

From Figure 23.1 it will be seen that the mother tape is an essential part of cassette manufacture. However, the preparation of a good mother tape requires equipment which is more usually found in recording studios rather than in factories. For this reason, the starting-point for most factories is the mother tape rather than the copy master or the original. Preparation of the mother tape is dealt with in Chapter 20, but at this point it is important to note that close technical liaison between mother tape and cassette manufacturers is absolutely essential if major disasters are to be avoided.

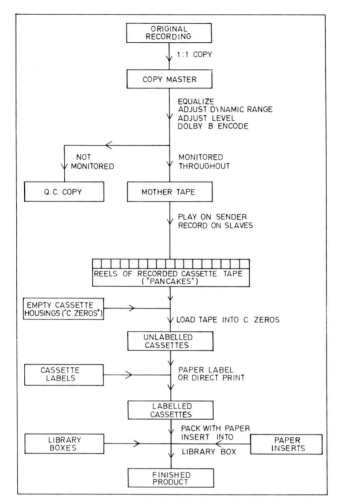

Fig. 23.1. The process stages in pre-recorded cassette manufacture

Liaison between manufacturers of mother tapes and cassettes

The mechanical and electroacoustic properties of the tape used for making mother tapes must be carefully agreed between mother tape and cassette manufacturer. If the tape is known to be reasonably consistent from batch to batch, it is sufficient to specify the particular brand and its type number. Its mechanical properties must be suitable for repeated playings on the high-speed sender and its associated tape reservoir (the loop bin); after repeated playings, the recording must not change in any way (e.g. loss or gain in high frequencies, increase in tape hiss), and it must not shed debris or leave any deposits on the playback heads of the sender. If it does, there is a good chance that random and uncontrollable dropouts of sound will occur on the finished cassette. It goes without saying that the electroacoustic properties of the tape must be very consistent, so that all mother tapes can be played back at identical settings on the high-speed sender.

So much for the tape. There are, however, several technical parameters which are under the control of the mother tape manufacturer and which must be subject to technical liaison and agreement. It is important, for instance, that the recorded tracks on the mother tape should coincide exactly with the gaps of the playback head of the high-speed sender. If they do not, the signal transmitted to the high-speed slaves will not only be too low in level, but will also be accompanied by unnecessary noise. In other words, track alignment between mother tape and the high-speed sender playback head must be very precise (see Figure 23.2 and Plate 36).

Fig. 23.2. Track misalignment

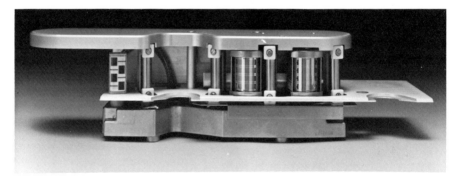

Plate 36. Head block of recorder for making mother tapes for analogue cassette duplication (Photo: Stüder)

Another frequent source of error is an angular deviation between the recording on the mother tape and the gaps of the sender playback head. Under these conditions, the sender playback head will be unable to detect and transmit high-frequency signals from the mother tape to the slaves, and

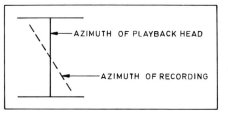

Fig. 23.3. Azimuth error

in consequence the resulting cassettes will sound dull. This error is known as an 'azimuth error' (see Figure 23.3).

Most large-scale production machinery tends to be somewhat inflexible, and the high-speed duplicating system is no exception. Setting and resetting of track alignment, azimuth, frequency response, and gain tend to be long and tedious operations and will, in consequence, lose valuable production time. It is therefore highly desirable that a calibration tape be shared between the mother tape and the cassette manufacturer in order to ensure compatibility between the mother tape recorder and the high-speed sender. Such calibration tapes are best made on the recorder that makes the mother tapes, so that test conditions are as close as possible to production conditions. The use of full-track calibration tapes is not recommended because of fringing errors at low frequencies. The provision of a high-frequency (say 10 kHz) test tone on each mother tape, recorded at the same time as the programme, will give an excellent current check on azimuth compatibility. In these ways, deviations are detected at an early stage and can be rectified with minimum interference to production.

In order to ensure the minimum amount of unwanted noise on the final cassette, it is usual to employ the Dolby B noise reduction system. It works by compressing the dynamic range of the original recording during transfer to the mother tape, thereby achieving a higher signal-to-noise ratio during the quieter parts of the programme. The dynamic range is later restored to that of the original recording by means of expansion on the customer's cassette player, while still retaining the improved signal-to-noise ratio achieved on the quieter parts of the programme. It is, however, a strict condition that the overall compression/expansion (sometimes referred to as 'encoding and decoding') process results in a gain of precisely unity at all frequencies. Unless this condition is met, the sound from the cassette will not be representative of the original recording.

In order to achieve this unity gain at all times, it is highly desirable that each and every mother tape be provided with a test tone recorded at Dolby level, which at the same time provides the cassette manufacturer with a convenient check on the gain setting of his own high-speed equipment.

The use of the Dolby B noise reduction system means that the cassette manufacturer must work to a constant gain, and this in turn means that peak programme levels on the mother tape need to be such as to avoid saturation on the cassette tape. Depending on the cassette tape in use, peak programme levels on the mother tape should lie 2–6 dB above the Dolby reference level.

To summarize, therefore, close liaison between mother tape and cassette manufacturer is essential and agreement must be reached on the mechanical and electroacoustic properties of tape, track alignment, azimuth, Dolby B encoding level, peak programme level, calibration tapes, and the test tones on mother tapes.

The high-speed sender

The sender is basically a tape player which plays a tape over and over again at high speed. In order to do this, the tape must be in the form of an endless loop for which a reservoir must be provided. One version is shown in Plate 37. This tape reservoir is generally known as a 'loop bin' and can be either horizontal or vertical. In either case, the tape passes from the playback head via capstan and tape guides into the bin, and from there out again via more guides and a second capstan, back towards the playback head. The capacity of the loop bin must be great enough to store some 50 minutes of programme, which means a tape length of well over 1800 ft (500 m) for mother tapes recorded at 7½ ips (19 cm/s). The tape width is usually 1 inch (25.4 mm) or ½-inch (12.7 mm).

The speed of the tape across the playback head of the sender is normally 240 ips (6.1 m/s) or 480 ips (12.2 m/s), and at these high speeds it is essential that head-to-tape contact is maintained. This is usually achieved by dual capstans of slightly different diameter, ensuring a constant tension across the playback head. Any intermittent head-to-tape contact is likely to lead to uncontrollable variability of high frequencies on the cassette.

Tape guidance must also be carefully controlled. It can be affected by the tape tensions outside the dual capstans, the positioning of the tape guides, the zenith of the playback head, and, last but not least, the accuracy of slitting of the tape. The effects of poor tape guidance can be, for instance, poor track alignment with consequent loss of signal level; up-and-down movement of the tape across the playback head, resulting in periodic variability of recorded level on the finished cassette; azimuth variation, which can cause high-frequency variability and image shift on the finished cassette; edge damage to the mother tape, which invariably results in its premature rejection for serious mechanical damage.

Wear on the playback head is not normally a problem on the high-speed sender, although periodic inspection is certainly advisable. Grooves worn into the playback head can cause poor head-to-tape contact and can also, in severe cases, adversely affect tape guidance. As with any tape player, fre-

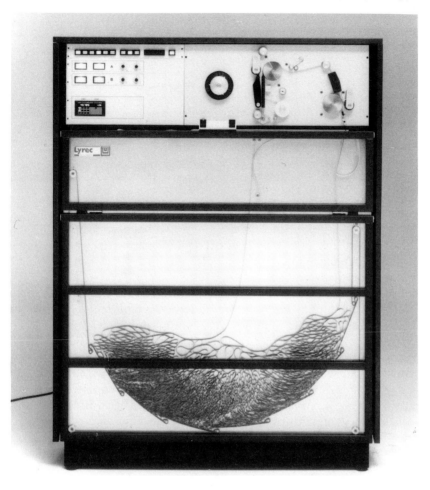

Plate 37. An example of the vertical form of 'loop bin' tape sender (Photo: Lyrec)

quent checks should be made on the gain, frequency response, and azimuth of the high-speed sender, so that these parameters conform to the values as agreed with the mother tape manufacturer. It is always good practice to check the test tones of the mother tape.

Apart from repeatedly transmitting complete programmes to the slaves at high speed, the sender is also activated to start and stop a very low-frequency signal, which is recorded by each slave between the end of one programme and the beginning of the next. The activation is usually achieved by a piece of transparent tape inserted between the end and the beginning of the programme on the mother tape, which, as mentioned before, is in the

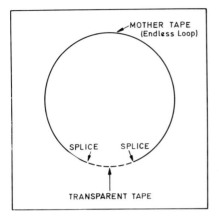

Fig. 23.4. Activation of the cue tone by transparent tape

form of an endless loop (see Figure 23.4). The low-frequency signal is known as a 'cue tone' and serves to locate the inter-programme gaps when the cassette tape is later loaded into cassette housings.

It is also important to keep an eye on environmental conditions. If the humidity in the duplicating room is too low, the build-up of electrostatic charge will lead to erratic running of the tape on the sender and in the bin; if it is too high, the oxide from the tape may start clogging the gaps of the playback head, and this will cause random and uncontrollable dropouts on the finished cassette. It is, of course, desirable that all tape is stored under good environmental conditions, but it is essential that no tape is ever subjected to violent environmental change just before it is used. It should always be stored for a minimum of 24 hours in the environment in which it is to be used.

The cassette tape

The question of tape properties is discussed in Chapter 11, and here it will suffice to list those parameters which are thought to be desirable for cassette tape in particular.

In common with all other raw materials for large-scale manufacture, it is essential that the cassette tape has constant properties, no matter when it was made or how long ago it was stored. These properties may not be the ideal properties, but for mass production it is preferable to have consistency, even if it means a marginal sacrifice in quality. It should, of course, have low basic noise and exhibit low distortion at mid-frequencies, while at the same time being capable of accepting relatively high recorded levels at high frequencies.

Good slitting is very important, because it will not only affect the way the tape transports on the slave but will later also profoundly influence the quality of wind in the finished cassette. Badly slit tape can easily cause cassette jamming. In order to achieve good head-to-tape contact at all times, the recorded side of the tape should have a fair polish, but it should be noted that too high a polish can cause unsatisfactory tape transport in cassette players. Bearing in mind the low tape speed (1⅞ ips, 4.76 cm/s) and low tape tension in a cassette player, the tape should be flexible and show little or no sign of longitudinal or lateral curl. Cleanliness is another factor, the absence of which will lead to uncontrollable random faults such as dropouts, build-up of oxide on tape guides, contamination of capstans, pinch rollers, etc. Tape exhibiting debris or head-clogging should be avoided at all costs.

Cassette tape is usually supplied on reels or on hubs. Reels have the advantages that the tape edges are, at least in theory, protected while the tape is in transit and there is no risk of the tape coil disintegrating as it could do when wound on a hub. It is indeed a sad sight when a hub drops out of the centre of a 3 km coil of cassette tape! A hub, on the other hand, also has great advantages. The tape is less prone to edge damage when being recorded on the slave, and any defective tape is noticed more easily before it is used. Moreover, hubs are much more compact and disposable than reels, and thus save costs on internal and external transport. It is however, particularly important not to subject tape on hubs to rapid environmental changes, because this can cause the wind to fall apart.

Cassette tape should be supplied with a minimum of packing consistent with mechanical safety. It saves costs on packing materials and their subsequent disposal.

The high-speed slave

The slave is a tape recorder which records many miles of cassette tape at high speed. The speed is usually either 60 ips (152.4 cm/s) or 120 ips (304.8 cm/s). The duplication ratio, i.e. the programme time at normal speed divided by the programme time at duplicating speed, varies from one establishment to another, but is generally either 32 : 1 or 64 : 1. Table 23.1 shows how these duplication ratios are achieved in practice. The first figure is in ips, the second in cm/s.

The slave is normally fitted with two two-track record heads, one for each side of the cassette. It is of interest to note that the slave records one side in the same direction as the programme, whereas the other side is recorded in the reverse direction. As with the sender, the tape tension across the record heads is normally controlled by a dual capstan system. The tape tension outside the dual capstan system is critical, particularly on the take-up side, where it controls the quality of wind of the recorded tape. Since the width of cassette tape is only 0.150 inch (3.78 mm) and its overall

Table 23.1. High-speed duplication speeds

Duplication ratios	Mother tape speed: ips (cm/s)	Sender speed: ips (cm/s)	Slave speed: ips (cm/s)	Cassette speed: ips (cm/s)
32 : 1	7½ (19.05)	240 (609.6)	60 (152.4)	1⅞ (4.76)
64 : 1	3¾ (9.5)	240 (609.6)	120 (304.8)	1⅞ (4.76)
64 : 1	7½ (19.05)	480 (1219.2)	120 (304.8)	1⅞ (4.76)

thickness is only of the order of 0.6 mils (15 μm), tape tensions, including instantaneous tensions, must be kept as low as possible (say about 30 g) if tape stretch is to be avoided.

The wavelengths of signals recorded on the cassette tape are very small indeed, because the playing speed of the cassette is low (1⅞ ips, 4.76 cm/s). For a signal frequency of 10 kHz, the wavelength is less than 0.2 mils (5 μm), and this means that the recorded azimuth must be as near perfect as possible. The smallest deviation in azimuth will result in large losses of high frequencies on playback of the cassette tape, and these losses will be compounded by the Dolby decoder on the customer's cassette player.

The Dolby B noise reduction system has been one of the most important contributory factors in establishing the cassette as a 'hi-fi' medium. At the same time, however, it has imposed very severe disciplines on the pre-recorded cassette manufacturer. As mentioned previously, perfect pro-gramme reproduction in the customer's home is achieved only if the overall gain of the combined Dolby B encoding/decoding process is exactly unity at all frequencies within the frequency range over which the Dolby B noise reduction process operates. If it is realized that the encoding process is per-formed on the mother tape, and that the decoding process does not take place until the customer plays the cassette at home, the difficulties of meeting and maintaining the unity gain criterion may be appreciated. Since the Dolby B system operates only over the upper part of the audio fre-quency range, it is of vital importance that the high frequencies of the origi-nal programme material are accurately preserved throughout the entire cassette manufacturing process.

One cause of high-frequency loss is the inability of conventional cassette tapes to accept and retain high frequencies at high levels. In other words, the cassette tape behaves as a limiter for high frequencies, thus introducing non-linearities to the frequency response, which are later accentuated by the customer's Dolby B decoder. One method of overcoming this defect is to use a (generally more expensive) cassette tape specially designed to accept and retain high frequencies at higher levels, such as, for instance, chromium dioxide or pseudo-chrome tape. It is very important that such tapes are recorded to the same characteristic as conventional tapes, i.e. to the 3,180 + 120 µs curve: see Figure 23.5. The use of the 3,180 + 70 µs curve is not recommended, because, for a given recording level, it wastes some of the hard-gained high-frequency headroom of the tape (4.4 dB at 10 kHz). Incidentally, it would also make life more difficult for the customer by introducing a dual playback standard for pre-recorded cassettes.

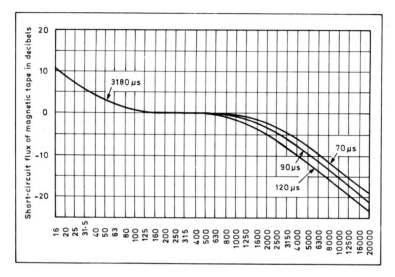

Fig. 23.5. IEC standard playback characteristics, showing the difference between the conventional 120 µs curve used for both ferric and chrome pre-recorded cassettes and the 70 µs curve used for home recording on chrome and metal blank cassettes

A second method of overcoming high-frequency loss due to cassette tape limitation is the installation of the Dolby HX Pro process (see Plate 38). This is designed to increase the high-frequency headroom of cassette tapes by varying, as a function of frequency, the bias (pre-magnetization) current through the record heads of the high-speed slaves. This device therefore enables the cassette manufacturer to enhance the high-frequency performance of conventional cassette tapes, but it requires capital investment as well as subsequent monitoring in order to ensure correct operation. It does have the advantage, however, that its benefits are obtained on any playback machine, since it is a record-stage process only.

High-frequency losses can also be caused by poor adjustment of the high-speed duplicator. In particular, correct azimuth setting of the record heads of the high-speed slaves is absolutely vital and must be checked frequently.

Plate 38. Master tape recorder electronics board with Dolby HX Pro processor unit (Photo: Stüder)

At the same time, gain and frequency response of each slave must be measured and corrected, if necessary. It cannot be emphasized too strongly that unless these requirements are met the Dolby B decoder on the customer's cassette player cannot perform correctly.

It is normal practice to check these parameters by feeding an oscillator to the slave and measuring the output from the recorded tape by means of a test playback head mounted on the slave. While serving as a quick check, this method is not usually sufficiently accurate for setting the slave up precisely. It is better to measure the recorded tape on a real-time reel-to-reel player, which, in turn, should also be checked frequently by an approved calibration tape. A list of suppliers of such approved calibration tapes appear in parts 2 and 3 of Publication 94 of the International Electrotechnical Commission.

Overall performance of the duplicating system should also be checked periodically. This is carried out by playing a calibration tape on the sender, recording the signals on each slave, and assessing the recording on a reel-to-reel player. This is the test method which most closely resembles production conditions, and which also takes into account any deficiencies in cabling between the sender and the slaves. It is a very effective method but somewhat long and tedious, and so it is not particularly popular with engineers or production personnel.

As with all tape transports, correct tape guidance is of paramount importance, and this applies particularly to cassette tape, due to its small size. Up-and-down movement of the tape will cause considerable level changes, which will be compounded by the customer's Dolby decoder. Edge damage to the tape must also be avoided at all costs, because the outer recorded tracks contain the left-hand channel of each programme; if edge damage occurs, the cassette will suffer from intermittent output from the left channel with consequent image shift. Severe edge damage will cause erratic winding of the tape inside the cassette, which, in turn, can cause it to jam.

In view of the vast lengths of new tape which pass over the record heads of slaves, it is vital that frequent checks are made for head wear. The first signs of head wear usually manifest themselves by an inability to record high frequencies at high levels. If frequency response measurements (see above) are made at a fixed recorded level, say x dB below the Dolby reference level of 200 nWb/m, the deviation from flatness at the high-frequency end can be used as a measure of head wear. By the time a record head shows visual signs of wear, it has probably produced many somewhat inferior cassettes.

It was mentioned above that the mother tape, via the sender, starts and stops a low-frequency oscillator between programmes. The signal from this oscillator needs to be recorded on the cassette tape at a fairly high level with a minimum of distortion. The fundamental of the signal is inaudible (it is usually around 5 Hz at cassette playback speed), but the overtones generated by distortion can be a nuisance. In some factories, this cue signal is actually cut from the tape while the cassette tape is being loaded into cassette housings.

Cassette assembly

The machine which spools the recorded cassette tape into cassette housings is known as a 'loader'. Modern loaders are fully automatic in that they accept long lengths of recorded tape plus empty cassette housings (known as 'C-zeros') and combine them into finished but unlabelled cassettes. The loader is fitted with a device which detects the low-frequency signal (the cue tone) that was recorded on the slave between programmes. Detection of the cue tone causes the loader to stop spooling at the right place, so that the leader tape from the C-zero can be spliced accurately to the cassette tape. The cue detector must sense the cue tone reliably while, at the same time, rejecting any low-frequency components which may emanate from the programme. If it does not, more than one programme could be spooled into one housing, or the loader could stop and splice in the middle of a programme.

Loaders must spool cassette tape very fast, while at the same time treating it gently. Any jerking during acceleration or deceleration of the tape could easily cause the tape to become stretched and have disastrous effects on programme quality. All edge damage to the tape must also be avoided.

Cassettes are labelled by one of three processes. The oldest process was rather messy and employed a form of glue. The two processes favoured nowadays are either heat seal or solvent. Heat-sealed labels have a heat-sensitive layer on their back which will stick to the cassette housing when heat is applied to the label. In the solvent process, the surface of the cassette housing is softened, and the label is applied to the softened surface. The solvent process has the disadvantage that fume-extraction apparatus must be installed over the labelling machine, as the solvent is toxic.

Programme information can also be printed directly on to the cassette housing, but the final appearance of the cassette is generally considered to be inferior to its labelled brother. Direct printing requires a good and uncontaminated cassette-housing surface, which must be free from all mould-release agent. This process, however, has the distinct advantage of making the cassette manufacturer totally independent of outside suppliers of printed labels. Moreover, it can effect large cost savings by eliminating label storage and the scrapping of labels surplus to requirements.

Most cassettes are packed into standard library cases, together with their relevant paper inserts. It is obviously important that both the labels and the paper insert should correspond to the programme that has been recorded on the cassette tape. This packing process is usually fully automated, and for this reason it is important that the dimensional characteristics of cassette housing, paper insert, and library case conform to close and agreed tolerances. Non-standard methods of packaging should be discouraged as far as possible, because they usually have to be carried out by hand or require heavy capital investment.

It is highly advisable that the finished product is stored in good conditions: temperature should be moderate to reduce any tendency for print-through between adjacent tape layers and consequent pre- or post-echo. For obvious reasons, the strengths of any magnetic fields in the storage area should be as low as possible.

Quality control

Quality control is a necessary but non-productive, and thus non-profitable, activity. For this reason, the aim should always be to create a highly reliable production process to give a high level of confidence. Preventative maintenance to machinery, regular performance checks, and reliable raw materials all contribute to the establishment of this confidence. Above all, the incidence of random faults should be kept to a minimum at all times. By their very nature, they are difficult to detect and, when detected, are difficult to relate to any particular shortcoming of the production process. Time and money spent on the prevention of random faults are usually an excellent investment. Generic faults, on the other hand, are more easily detected and remedied. They include faults like damage to mother tapes, permanent absence of one channel, or wrong programme.

Direct comparison of the cassette to the mother tape (A/B test) should form the basis of all assessment. If the mother tape is still in the duplicator, the QC copy (see above) may be used instead of the mother tape. If the cassette manufacturer has matched the sound of the cassette exactly to that of the mother tape, he has succeeded in his task.

The principle of A/B testing is a very important one, because it uses the ear as detector in preference to meters and other electronic gadgetry. Bearing in mind that the customer buys a cassette in order to listen to it, it seems only right that quality assessment of the product should reflect that requirement. Meters, oscilloscopes, and other equipment are excellent aids, but the final arbiter of cassette quality must always, ultimately, be the human ear.

The Digital Compact Cassette

Whilst duplication of DCC cassettes follows the same sequence of events as conventional musicassette manufacture, there are important differences reflecting the physical and electromagnetic make-up of the two products.

The DCC cassette has the same length and width dimensions but lacks the thicker front portion of the standard cassette: see Figure 23.6. It has holes for the hubs on the bottom side only, leaving the blank upper side free for a larger label. A metal slider covers all holes and locks the hubs until the cassette is inserted into the player. The tape itself is of standard 3.78 mm (0.150 inch) width but has a video (VHS) type chrome coating on a substrate which is mechanically similar to that of C-90 cassettes.

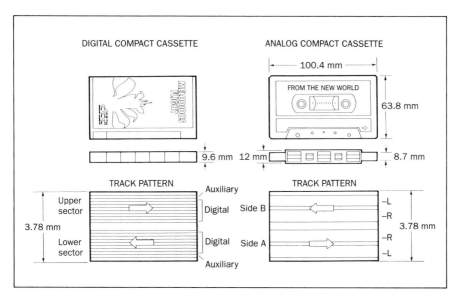

Fig. 23.6. The analogue and digital cassettes compared

The digital signals are recorded with an effective wavelength of only 1 micron, in a multitrack configuration of eight signal tracks and one auxiliary track for each 'side' (tape direction) so that precision is needed in alignment and smoothness of the tape surface.

As mentioned earlier, the high-speed sender for DCC duplication is generally a digital bin. The bits are stored in the same pattern as will be laid down on the slave tracks, using a separate memory for each track. Downloading is a relatively complex operation as the digital signals to be stored comprise not only the digitized audio signals but also sync pulses, timecoder, and text display information. In practice a recorded DCC cassette is normally chosen as the intermediate carrier or 'master cassette'.

The master–slave interconnection is interference-free and may employ twisted pair flat cables or a multiplexed single optical fibre. The slaves are basically similar to the analogue machines running typically at 64 times normal cassette speed. Special thin-film heads are needed, one for each of the 9-track sectors or 'sides', and local clean-air conditions around the slaves. Cassette loading into D-0 cassette shells resembles the production of loaded C-0 analogue cassettes, with provision for the asymmetrical case construction and the metal slider. As the recorded signals are fully digital, quality control can be reduced to automatic electronic monitoring of the digital code-words, following the practices in CD replication. The older style label is replaced by an 'L-card' sealed on to the cassette behind a transparent L-cover. The DCC cassette box is a simpler slide-out box but requires a new type of packaging machine.

Conclusion

No two cassette manufacturing plants operate in the same manner, with the same materials, or with the same machines. The principles involved in the manufacture of good cassettes are, however, universal and include good planning, regular preventive maintenance and performance checks, reliable raw materials, good communications, and, last but not least, good ears and a high level of common sense.

24 Compact disc processing

Gerald Reynolds and Jonathan Halliday

The technology of digital, optically read discs has given rise to a manufacturing process of a new order of complexity. The Compact Disc is a precision moulding carrying detail of truly microscopic size, yet at the same time it is a mass-produced product. Figure 24.1 indicates the main dimensions and features of the disc. As a further indication of the relative complexity of producing CDs rather than LPs, it may be mentioned that the CD tracks are a mere 1.6 µm wide, whereas LP grooves are about 125 µm (see Plate 39).

The coming of high-quality MPEG Video on the familiar 12-cm disc has given new impetus to research by the authors and others to increasing the recording density by a factor of at least four. The resulting pits are then half the size and spaced only 0.8 µm apart radially. Two times existing density

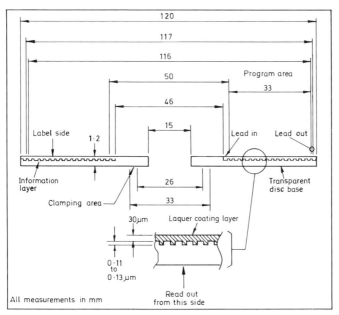

Fig. 24.1. Principal CD dimensions and features

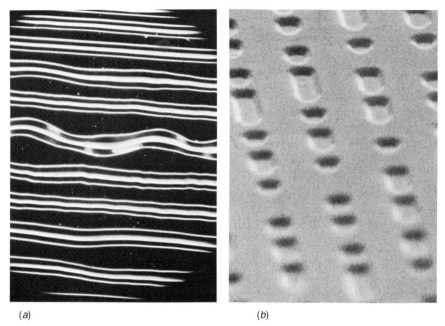

(a)   (b)

Plate 39. (a) detail of LP grooves magnified 60 times; (b) detail of Compact Disc information pits magnified 5,000 times (Photos: Nimbus Technology & Engineering)

has already been proved manufacturable and playable on some CD players. As with all data storage media, optical disc will continue to be refined to carry more information in less space. Mastering and replication equipment will have to continue to improve in performance to meet these new demands.

The process contains more separate stages than LP manufacture, it requires much more stringent standards of cleanliness, and skilled technicians are needed to run it. Above all, the CD mastering process is the key to the whole, and without the understanding that comes from having control of its own mastering system, a pressing plant is poorly placed to judge the quality of the discs it is making and unable to influence it directly.

This chapter describes the various processes which occur, firstly in the mastering system and secondly in the CD pressing plant itself (see Figure 24.2).

Glass master preparation

Whereas an LP is cut by a stylus in a coating of so-called lacquer on a metal substrate (as described in Chapter 21), a CD is etched by the exposure to laser light of a coating of photoresist (a light-sensitive material) on a glass

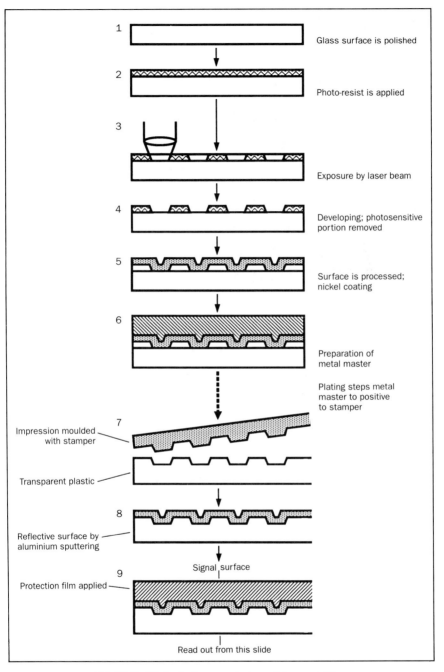

1   Glass surface is polished

2   Photo-resist is applied

3   Exposure by laser beam

4   Developing; photosensitive portion removed

5   Surface is processed; nickel coating

6   Preparation of metal master

Plating steps metal master to positive to stamper

Impression moulded with stamper

7

Transparent plastic

8   Reflective surface by aluminium sputtering

Signal surface

9   Protection film applied

Read out from this slide

Fig. 24.2. Stages in the manufacture of Compact Discs

Plate 40. Glass master preparation line (Photo: Nimbus)

base. This coating (unlike that on an LP lacquer) is normally prepared in the premises where the mastering is done (Plate 40).

The glass base is an exceptionally finely ground and polished disc, which must be prepared to a standard of surface finish considerably in excess of that regarded as good enough for laser-quality optical components, notwithstanding the greater size of the disc. This disc, after scrupulous cleaning, is coated with a layer of photoresist. The equipment used to do this is akin to that used in the semiconductor industry, where similar materials are used (Plate 41). However, the coatings used in semiconductor manufacture are usually about a micron thick and are applied to silicon wafers not more than 80 mm in diameter, whereas for CD the coating is only 0.13 μm thick and the glass disc is typically 240 mm in diameter. Moreover, the coating thickness (which can be measured by ellipsometric methods) is not allowed to vary by more than a few per cent over the central playing area. Suffice it to say that a number of exacting problems have to be solved before arriving at an apparatus adequate for preparing CD master discs under production conditions. The arrival of higher recording densities, up to four times that on current CD Audio discs (see above) will demand even better process control and quality.

Master tape inspection

Prosaically, before proceeding to the actual laser mastering stage it is wise to perform a careful check of the condition of the incoming digital master tape. In some cases, the customer requests that exact PQ editing (the setting of track start and stop times) be done by the laser mastering facility, or he may provide an analogue tape which has first to be transferred to a digital format. Even where, as is preferred, PQ editing has already been done by the customer, or by one of the various independent studios offering this service, the tape still has to be checked for audible playback faults (dropouts) arising at the time of playback, since these are cause for rejection if they occur during laser mastering. It has to be said that the reliability of available digital tape systems has lagged behind that of the CD process itself, and that unrepeatable tape dropouts are a frequent source of rejects even with the most carefully checked tapes. This situation is rapidly improving with the adoption of Exabyte 8-mm tape cassettes as the final input medium to the laser mastering process.

Plate 41. Spin coater for applying primer and photo-resist (Photo: Nimbus)

Audible dropouts which are actually recorded on the tape as a result of some previous step in the editing process are, of course, strictly the responsibility of the customer, but a reputable CD manufacturing organization will make a point of bringing such occurrences to the customer's attention in case he had overlooked the faults and wants to take some corrective action.

Encoding

The pattern of dots and dashes recorded on the disc represents the digital signal which was taken off the master tape, but the format in which this signal is encoded is different from that on the tape. During laser mastering, therefore, the signal on the tape is played back, decoded in the normal way with error correction by the PCM tape processor, and then re-encoded into CD format by the specialized electronics of the CD encoder. Simultaneously, a stream of subsidiary (subcode) data carrying continuous track-timing information derived from the customer's 'PQ' data is fed via the encoder to the laser beam recorder, where it takes its place amongst the audio signals recorded on the disc.

The properties of the CD encoding format are remarkable. The audio data, taken in units ('blocks') of 24 eight-bit bytes representing 6 samples of (two-channel) information, is first expanded to 32 bytes by the addition of 8 error protection bytes, derived from and related to the audio data, in two stages, separated by an extensive interleaving or dispersing of the data in time. The added error protection bytes ensure that, when the disc is eventually played, the decoder can to a large extent detect and correct for erroneously read information by deducing what it should have been. The interleaving, and the reciprocal de-interleaving in the player, has the virtue that erroneous information due to localized faults on the disc is dispersed in time before it reaches the decoding stage, so that the job of correcting it is made easier. The error correction is such that faults up to a certain magnitude are completely corrected and are totally inaudible. Only when this threshold is exceeded is anything untoward heard.

In a later stage of the encoding process, these 32 eight-bit bytes, together with one byte of subcode data, are transformed into the same number of 14-bit words separated by three-bit 'merging' patterns. These words are then fed serially (bit by bit, 4.3 million bits per second) to the laser beam recorder, where they are used to turn the laser light on and off while it is focused on the rotating master disc.

Superficially, the effect of replacing the eight-bit bytes by 14-bit words appears to have been one of increasing the amount of information to be recorded. In actual fact the 4.3 MB/sec data rate is a misleading fiction, because the 14-bit patterns which are used are carefully selected according to certain criteria, one of which is that there are never less than three iden-tical bits in a row. The 'merging' bits are likewise chosen such that this remains true wherever one pattern joins up to the next one. So the highest modulation frequency which is ever actually present on the disc is only about 700 kHz, which is less than it would have been if the eight-bit bytes had been recorded directly. Meanwhile, certain other virtues have been gained, notably that the average mark/space ratio of the recorded signal remains close to unity. This means that the line of pits on the disc presents, in aggregate, a uniform appearance to the optical pickup in the player—hence the performance of the servo which is used to follow this track when playing the disc is more constant than it would otherwise be.

Laser mastering

It is one thing to track a line of pits in the player correctly, but another to generate that line in the first place (Plate 42). The degree of mechanical and electronic stability of the laser beam recorder has to be such as to lay down a spiral track on the glass disc with a pitch of 1.6 µm (and uniform to within a fraction of that amount) while covering the playing area of the disc (radii 23–60 mm). This is done by rotating the disc while the focused beam

Plate 42. Final Optics and Focus Actuator on Laser Beam Recorder in the process of exposing the information pits on the glass master (Photo: Nimbus)

of laser light moves across it. Meanwhile the master tape plays in real time, and the light is interrupted in accordance with the bit-stream coming from the encoder. The disc rotates with a constant linear velocity (1.3 m/s) at the point where the light is focused, which means that the rotational speed and the speed of radial motion are both curious functions of time. Slight variations in the track pitch and linear velocity are allowable, and can be utilized in order to 'squeeze' extra-long playing times on to a CD without the music reaching outer radii on the disc which would be difficult to mould. It is preferred not to use such extreme values, however, because other parameters of the disc then begin to be more critical.

The advent of Exabyte as the replay tape medium has now made it possible to increase recording speeds: 2 × real time is now common and some systems (those made by Nimbus) are able to record at up to 2.8 × real time. Faster replay media will allow 4 × real time recording in the future. Some laser mastering lathes or laser beam recorders (LBRs) are already capable of both these higher speeds but also have sufficient reserves of performance to master at more than 4 times existing densities.

Developing

Next the coated disc, having been exposed to the laser light, is developed in a process basically akin to photographic developing. Those areas which were exposed dissolve away to leave pits in the surface; the intervening areas remain unaffected. The degree of exposure during laser mastering and the extent of development are precisely controlled. Only in this way can the size and shape of the pits be accurately and repeatedly controlled. After rinsing and drying, the developed master is vacuum-coated with nickel to make it electrically conductive. It is then ready for the plating stage.

Plating

The nickel coated glass master is placed in a nickel electroforming bath (electroforming is fast nickel-plating, producing a 0.3–0.4-mm-thick deposit of nickel in 1–2 hours), and a metal master is grown.

This metal master is then separated from the glass master, and after cleaning to remove all traces of non-metallic matter it is passivated and once more placed in the bath to grow a metal positive or mother. The purpose of the passivation is to ensure that the mother can subsequently be separated from the metal master. The metal master is a negative replica of the developed surface of the glass master, so that the mother is once again a positive copy of it.

After separation, the mother is again cleaned and passivated and used to grow a nickel stamper, carrying a negative replica (bumps instead of pits) of the original developed glass master's surface. From the original master several mothers can be grown, each yielding a number of stampers. Each stamper can then be used to mould tens of thousands of discs.

The electroforming technique is largely similar to that used in LP manufacture (see Chapter 22), but with several additional requirements:

1. Extreme cleanliness of the plating solution, all chemicals and water, and a very clean working environment.
2. The stamper must be flat, and its thickness must be uniform to within a few microns over its whole area.
3. The back of the stamper (the electroformed surface) must be prepared to a very smooth finish.

Moulding

Several different processes have been proposed for the mass replication of CDs:

1. The '2P' (photopolymerization) process (used for videodisc)—takes 20–30 seconds—uses an expensive substrate and requires several finishing processes (centring, centre-hole punching, and edge trimming).
2. Compression moulding (Polygram, Hanover)—takes about 10 seconds—also requires centring, centre-hole punching, and edge trimming.
3. Injection moulding (most CD manufacturers)—takes less than 6 seconds—makes a mechanically finished disc.
4. Stamping (DocData prototype)—takes some 2–5 seconds—uses an expensive, difficult-to-make substrate, and requires centring and centre-hole and outside-edge punching.

The material used to make CDs is a special grade of polycarbonate, chosen to combine mechanical and optical properties. PMMA (acrylic resin) in fact has much better optical properties but is sensitive to moisture, and so is used only for balanced, double-sided discs such as videodiscs, while other plastics so far proposed have been unsuitable on grounds such as lack of rigidity or transparency. The purity of the polycarbonate has to be excellent, and all drying and handling of the raw granules must be done in very clean conditions. Optical discs have presented material suppliers and equipment manufacturers with a level of difficulty not encountered elsewhere. Small specks of contamination which would go unnoticed in any other moulded part can render a CD useless.

Whereas most plastic mouldings are complex in shape in order to provide rigidity, the deceptively simple flat disc, which appears so easy to mould, has created a new kind of tightrope for man, machine, mould, and material. The conditions which will produce good discs fall within a very small tolerance. Whatever the method used, the moulding process must accurately reproduce the pits in the surface of the disc while maintaining very low stress in the disc as far out to the edge as possible. To do this, the plastic must be processed at temperatures not far short of those at which it starts to degrade. We have to remember that each CD has on its surface a microstructure of pits as fine as the densest integrated circuits, yet it is twenty times larger in area than the latest VLSIs. Even so, this structure (containing 600 megabytes of information) is mass-produced at the rate of one every 5–6 seconds. Combined with the high capital cost, it is not surprising that fewer companies have engaged in the manufacture of CDs than did in LPs or cassettes.

The importance of stress in the discs is that it causes birefringence; in other words, the light passing through the disc is split into two (polarized) components for which the disc appears to have slightly different thicknesses. The reading laser beam in the player looks at the pits through the thickness of the disc. So the players, especially those using circularly polarized optics, have difficulty in focusing on the pits at all. Such problems due to the disc are aggravated by problems in the player—some players will barely play perfect new discs—which result in difficulties in playing. Unfortunately, the disc manufacturer has to make allowance for the worst players.

Only two of the replication methods listed above have been of commercial importance in manufacturing CDs. One is the compression moulding process used by Polygram. Here the disc is formed very much like a 7-inch single. Hot plastic is injected at the centre of the mould space between two stampers, one with information pits and the other plain. Both stampers are formed at their edges to create a restriction. At a chosen moment, injection ceases and the mould halves move together, compressing the plastic till it extrudes through the restriction to form a flash (excess material). Since the stress is worst at the edge of a moulded disc, trimming off the edge of an oversize disc is an elegant way of overcoming the stress problem. The centre hole is not fully moulded at this stage, and each disc has to be accurately centred and punched later on.

The waste of material, long cycle time, and need for extra processes introduce their own problems, for each stage brings with it the risk of extra rejects. However, this process was the first CD mass-production method to be used in Europe.

The Japanese and all subsequent European manufacturers have instead favoured injection moulding (see Plate 43). Its advantage is that the disc comes from the machine in a fully formed state. Only one, flat stamper is used, and the other half of the mould has a highly polished face. The mould is closed against the stamper and then hot plastic is injected into this cavity very quickly (sometimes in as little as a tenth of a second). Once the plastic

Plate 43. Injection moulding press for compact discs (Photo: Nimbus)

has cooled enough, the centre hole is punched (still within the mould), and the mould then opens for the finished disc to be extracted (Plate 44).

Whichever process is used, the moulding must be performed under class 100 clean air conditions, for the disc is very vulnerable to dust and dirt until it has been metallized. The stamper likewise has to be protected from dirt.

Metallizing

Although the disc as it leaves the moulding machine already carries all the information in the form of pits in the surface, the familiar rainbow colours are only dimly apparent, and a reflective layer must be applied to the information side of the disc before it can be read by a CD player. The usual method of metallizing is vacuum deposition, now almost exclusively by sputtering. Truly continuous vacuum metallizing systems are now very widely used. The batch process has practically disappeared.

In the simplest form of batch process, the discs are loaded on to jigs in a large cylindrical chamber. As soon as the chamber door is closed, large pumps begin to evacuate the space. When a sufficiently high vacuum has been reached, the jigs are moved around heated tungsten filaments which

Plate 44. Robot extracting CD from injection moulding machine—note centre hole and outer edge of disc are already formed (Photo: Nimbus)

have been loaded with high-purity aluminium wire. The aluminium melts and then evaporates, depositing itself on the waiting discs. The whole process takes 20–40 minutes, depending on the equipment used, its cleanliness, and the condition of the discs to be coated. Only a fraction of this time is occupied by the actual evaporation. This process has great risks of contamination of the discs.

In the next step towards a continuous process there are three linked chambers: a load lock, a process chamber, and an unload lock. Jigs carrying discs are placed in the load lock, and when this has been pumped down to a sufficient vacuum a valve opens leading into the process chamber. The jigs now pass one at a time past a sputtering source, from which atoms of aluminium are ejected by a low-pressure gas discharge, and then through another valve into the unload lock. In this way the discs are coated serially. Afterwards, both valves are closed and the coated discs can be unloaded from the unload lock while the next batch is going into the load lock. This is still a batch system, but it wastes less time in loading and unloading. A greater fraction of the total time is spent doing the actual metallizing.

Most of the development effort on truly continuous or 'in-line' metallizing has been concentrated on 'air to air' systems, so called because the discs go direct from normal air into a high vacuum to be processed, one at a time, and again emerge direct into the air. These machines are ideally suited to serve injection-moulding machines which produce discs at a steady rate. In practice, a sizeable buffer is still desirable in case of breakdown of the in-line metallizer and for when it has to be serviced.

The speed of moulding discs has now caught up with that of in-line metallizers, making matched and fully integrated 'monolines' the standard line in use (Plate 45).

It has been found that long 'outgassing' of discs is not necessary, making very compact sputtering machines running at 3 seconds or less a reality. In most of these machines only two discs are within the vacuum chamber (which has a very small volume), one in the load lock and one under the sputtering cathode. In these environmentally conscious times, the cleanliness and speed of this process have enabled it to displace all other methods.

Lacquering and printing

A layer of lacquer is next applied over the metallized layer, so that the information pits are completely sandwiched between the plastic of the disc and the lacquer. This is essential to ensure that the microstructure of the pits and the delicate and easily corroded aluminium layer are protected. Once sealed in, the information layer is safe from any but the most careless handling. The label information is then printed over the top of the lacquer.

These final processes, whilst they have no bearing on the functional performance of the disc, present the first aspect of it to be seen by the buyer, and because of the smooth, shiny appearance of the disc even very small blemishes in the lacquer or print are readily visible. It has been a common experience amongst CD manufacturers that these secondary processes cause almost as much trouble, and as many rejects, as the technically more advanced parts of the mass-production process.

Testing

It is essential to test a wide variety of parameters of the disc, all of which can affect its playability. These include both average error rates and worst-case errors, (Plate 46) stress (birefringence), quality of metallizing, centring, and flatness. Even more important are tests of all the main electronic signals generated by the pits at the output of the laser pickup and its servo circuits. In this way it is possible to infer the correctness of the geometry of the pits. These tests are made on samples at regular intervals during each production run, including a complete computer display of the playing errors present. In this way, any systematic fault or deterioration of the stamper can be traced and suspect discs rejected. All testing of error rates during

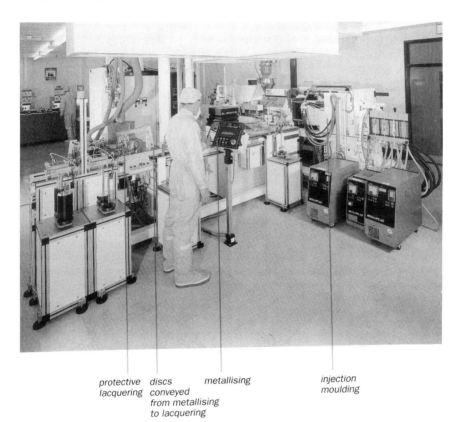

protective discs metallising   injection
lacquering conveyed   moulding
   from metallising
   to lacquering

Plate 45. Latest generation of production line for replicating CDs as a continuous in-line process. Note buffers at various points on the line to allow for maintenance of equipment without lost production (Photo: Nimbus)

manufacture must be directed at giving early warning of levels of error which are well below those which would cause any direct playing problem but which, if left, may reduce the safety margin for individual disc faults or for the effects of dirt and damage in the home.

Automatic inspection equipment can now test in-line for individual disc faults, for example black specks in the plastic or defects in the metallizing. This allows more properties of each disc to be tested to a uniform criterion. However, some types of fault which are easily seen by a trained tester can-

Plate 46. BLER Tester for measuring and printing out both average and peak errors on CDs (Photo: Nimbus)

not always be recognized by a machine. In practice an automatic testing machine is often backed up by skilled human testers who can check on a systematic sampling basis discs from each production run. This can be combined with the full test of disc parameters listed earlier.

The assessment of disc faults has caused some general confusion, especially the use of the 'block error rate' (BLER for short). The CD system standard specifies that the average BLER should be less than 3 per cent, i.e. 220 erroneous data blocks per second, when measured over a ten-second period. This is merely one of many parameters which are specified, and its function is to give an indication of the general quality of the disc. It does not have any direct relation to the audibility of faults on the disc, which are a function of the worst-case errors after de-interleaving rather than of the BLER. A BLER exceeding 3 per cent does not necessarily give rise to any audible fault, nor does a low BLER guarantee that there will not be audible faults, for such faults are largely caused by localized defects which do not show up strongly in the mean BLER. It has always to be remembered that ten seconds is a long time when playing a disc, and that this means BLER is a blunt instrument with which to assess quality.

The basic playability of CDs is influenced primarily by the geometry of the information pits, which dictate the strength of the HF and tracking signals read by the player. The magnitude and consistency of these parameters affect the tolerance of the disc to player problems and handling damage. The dimensional accuracy, reflectivity, and stress level of the disc are the other primary qualities which must be controlled.

Packing

The final stage of manufacture is to bring together the disc, the jewel box, tray, booklet, and inlay card. This can be either a labour-intensive process or a capital-intensive one, depending on the degree of automation used. The jewel box has been criticized as being difficult to open, yet if anyone can invent a better package which retains the advantages of quality, protection of the disc, and the ability to display information on four of its six sides, CD manufacturers and public alike will be delighted.

Allied Media

25 Radio broadcasting

Dave Fisher

In a short space it is very difficult to do justice to so wide a subject as broadcasting, which embraces many engineering and operational disciplines. Therefore I shall try to describe the main differences between broadcasting and the rest of the sound recording industry.

The following differences are generally true throughout broadcasting:

1. Broadcasting can be live. This means that studios, equipment, and operational procedures need to be designed for the possibility of live transmission, even though many programmes are recorded.
2. The absolute technical quality of a programme may take second place to its production 'feel', particularly if it is live. For instance, audience noise (including applause) at a live concert may add more than it detracts from a live transmission.
3. There is a need to generate a feeling of a 'network', in which many individual programmes combine to produce a harmonious whole. This may mean that there is a need for a 'network style' and general agreement about levels of modulation.
4. The technical requirements of the transmission chain, especially that of medium wave, dictate a limit to the frequency response and the dynamic range of the programme; in some circumstances, such as the BBC's External Services, the audience may be listening under the very worst reception conditions, which are completely outside their control. Once again it will be better to ensure that the programme is audible and intelligible rather than that it is flat from d.c. to 20 kHz within 0.5 dB.

Studios for network radio

Radio studios come in almost every size and shape, from talks studios, just big enough for a round-table discussion with half a dozen people, to music studios of concert hall proportions, capable of accommodating a symphony orchestra. Each type of studio will have facilities to suit its needs. For example a talks studio will have an acoustically transparent table and a reverbation time of about 0.3 sec; a drama studio will have live (long RT) and dead (short RT) areas, means of producing 'practical' (spot) effects, like a supply of water to simulate a stream or the sound of someone washing dishes, a set of different stairs (wooden, concrete, carpeted, etc.), effects doors with every conceivable lock, catch, or bolt, and any other props necessary for the type of drama recorded there.

Control rooms

A modern broadcast studio control room (sometimes called a 'cubicle') looks much like that of a modern recording studio, with the addition of record players ('grams'), CD machines, and quarter-inch tape machines.

Grams and CD players

To the broadcaster, discs not only offer a ready and cheap source of programme material, they also allow much quicker changing than tape, since no spooling is necessary. This means that when sources have to be changed in very rapid succession, for example sound effects in drama, discs are preferable to tape. Grams suitable for broadcast use need to be of high technical quality, and must be easy to cue up, so that all or part of a record can be started quickly, without wow or rumble, at a precise cue point. Normally there will also be a fader built into the machine.

The same cueing requirements apply, of course, to compact discs. Professional CD players allow back-cueing, the storage of a large number of cue points, and rapid recueing and starting but are expensive compared to domestic machines. However, when items are to be played from the start of a track or from an index point, a domestic machine may be suitable.

Tape machines

The control rooms of most broadcast studios will have at least two or three quarter-inch tape machines, and a drama or a news studio may have more. Tape machines will be used to play inserts into the programme as well as to record the studio output. The machines will normally have monitoring (headphone, LS, meter—almost invariably a VU meter), and a replay fader so that, if necessary, the levels can be controlled by the tape operator. Music (and sometimes drama) studios will have multitrack machines and mixing desks of the same type as a recording studio. Digital tape machines are now in common use, but the speed and editing convenience of analogue machines will maintain their usefulness for some time to come.

Mixing desks

Channel facilities, routing, and groups will be very similar or identical to those found in a recording studio. The main differences are:

(a) Desk inputs. The circuits from microphone points in the studio will probably terminate on a source jackfield, rather than being hard-wired to a desk channel input (though they may be normalled to channel inputs). This source jackfield will also contain other sources, such as tape machine outputs, grams, and outside sources. An outside source (or OS) is a circuit from a central area in the studio complex where sources external to the studio, such as outside broadcasts (OBs) or other studios, can be routed into the studio to form part of its output. The source jackfield allows flexibility, because the desk can be laid out to suit the programme and unused sources can be removed from the desk.

(*b*) Clean feeds and cue programme. A contributor in a remote studio (for instance, a politician in Birmingham contributing to a news programme originating in London) will need to hear what is going on in the studio. A form of foldback is therefore needed. Generally, however, a simple feed of the studio output will suffice, and is technically simpler to arrange. This feed is known as cue programme. If the contributor is very remote (say if the politician were in America and contributing to a British news programme by satellite) the contributor's delayed voice coming back over cue programme would be very disconcerting (indeed it might be impossible to speak—try attempting to record your voice on tape whilst listening to the machine output on headphones). Furthermore, if the feed from the main studio back to the remote studio must be fed to a loudspeaker rather than headphones, then there is a danger of howlround. The problems of delays over long circuits and of howlround can be greatly reduced, if not always eliminated by the use of a clean feed (in America this is often called 'mix minus').

A clean feed is simply a feed of the desk output but without the source to which it is being fed back. This is rather easier to say than to achieve, because each source requiring a clean feed needs a different mix. A large news or current affairs studio may have to generate up to ten such independent feeds. The normal arrangement is to use one desk group for all the outside sources and then send back to each source a feed of all the other OSs and the non-OS groups. This is often achieved in a separate matrix. For international exchanges, if each broadcasting authority sends the other a clean feed then each can add its own announcements or commentary, whilst sending to the other all 'international sound' such as music or effects. In this way they exchange programmes yet keep their own announcements or commentary.

Where a clean feed is clearly unnecessary, such as with the feed to the local studio headphones or to a reasonably close source, it is normal to send cue programme. This has the advantage that, when the source is faded up by the master studio, people in the remote studio can hear their own output, which is both reassuring and allows cues such as 'And now over to the London Weather Centre' to be given over the air if the programme is live. Furthermore, especially if the source is a remote OB, this can reduce line costs because the feed of cue programme can be obtained off-air from a portable radio receiver.

(c) Visual monitoring. Transmitters not only clip suddenly but can be damaged by being overmodulated. In the early days of broadcasting it was necessary, therefore, to monitor visually the peak level of the signal. Modern transmitters are protected by fast-acting limiters on their inputs, but peak monitoring is still necessary if the balance leaving the studio is not to be changed by a remote limiter. Additionally, the broadcast signal passes through many pieces of equipment between the studio and the transmitter which must not be overloaded.

When the signal for stereo transmission reaches the transmitter, it is coded into M and S form before being modulated on to the RF carrier; for mono transmissions (e.g. medium and long wave) only the M signal is used. There are, therefore, four separate signals—A, B, M, and S—that must be monitored in the studio to ensure that no signal will cause overmodulation. The most convenient way of providing this is by two twin-pointer PPMs, one for A and B with red and green needles, and one for M and S with white and yellow needles. The readings of twin-pointer meters are much easier to interpret at a glance than those of separate meters.

Much useful information can be gleaned from these PPM readings. For instance, for normal stereo material A and B will be approximately equal, and S will normally be 4 to 8 dB less than M. If S is consistently higher than M, then the signal is phase-reversed; if S is zero, then the signal is either mono or very narrow, and so on.

The characteristics of the meter are defined in BS 5428–9: 1979 and IEC 268–10A. The British Standard allows two different scale designs; the one normally used in this country is arbitrarily numbered from 1 to 7 (see Figure 25.1). Zero level or 0 dBu produces a reading of 4, and there are 4 dB between each scale mark. For the marks to be roughly equispaced, the meter must be driven through a logarithmic amplifier (see Figure 25.2); additionally, the drive amplifier must detect the peak level of the input signal and produce a fast rise-time; a slow fall-time makes the meter easier to read.

The standards specify an integration time of 10 ms, and a fallback time of 3 sec. Although a shorter integration time would produce more accurate peak readings, the modulation would be unreasonably low; the chosen value allows very short peaks which should not produce audible distortion to pass. This does, however, mean that some very spiky waveforms may beat even a PPM. Care must therefore be exercised when recording instruments such as clavichords or harpsichords.

The integration time is defined by the CCITT as the duration of a tone-burst which produces, across the integrating capacitor, a voltage which is 80 per cent of the peak voltage of the applied signal; this is produced with a CR time-constant of 2.5 ms. The fallback time is the time taken for the

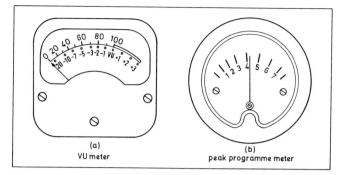

Fig. 25.1. Comparison of VU meter and PPM scales

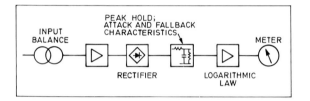

Fig. 25.2. Block diagram of a typical PPM drive amplifier

reading to fall from PPM 7 to PPM 1 when the signal is suddenly removed. The peak level which may be sent to line is +8 dBu, that is PPM 6.

(*d*) LS monitoring. In addition to desk out, the speakers can be switched to a feed of cue prog (that is the output of the destination to which the studio is routed), feeds of each radio network, incoming OSs etc. To make mono monitoring more realistic, the speakers can also be switched to monitor a mono version of the studio output on only one loudspeaker, usually the left one. To check whether or not a source that sounds out of phase really is— without phase-reversing the source because the possible phase reversal may not have been noticed until the source has been put on air—the speakers can also be put out of phase with one another.

(*e*) Line-up tone. To ensure that all levels are set correctly, each source will send line-up tone at a standard level (see later) to its destination before it sends programme. So that tone can be sent whilst the studio is rehearsing, without interrupting the rehearsal, it is normal to be able to switch the line leaving the studio away from the desk output to a feed of standard-level tone (see Figure 25.3). Provided that the loudspeaker and PPM monitoring can be switched between the desk and the line output, this allows rehearsals to continue whilst sending tone.

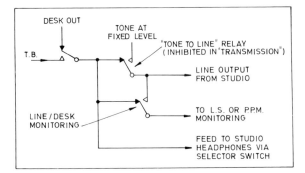

Fig. 25.3. Switching of tone and talkback to line

(f) Foldback. Foldback will be similar to that in a recording studio, but may also be used to feed tape or grams into a studio loudspeaker rather than to a desk input channel. This will help a sound effect to match the acoustic of the rest of the studio action; otherwise it will probably sound too close. An example is making a record sound like background music in a restaurant, or creating a background noise which could not reasonably be produced live in the studio (such as countryside or weather effects) fit behind dialogue.

(g) Ergonomics. The desk will be much easier to use if it has plenty of space to hold a script; the script space is usually a shelf which runs the length of the desk between the operator and the faders. Some broadcasters use faders that fade up when pulled towards the operator, that is they work in the opposite direction to faders on a recording desk. This method has the advantage that the operator's hand can rest on the script tray; this is far more comfortable for the inevitable hands-on style of mixing necessary in broadcasting. It also has the advantage that faders which are accidentally knocked by the script or the operator's sleeve are knocked closed rather than open. Although it may seem back-to-front to someone used to conventional faders, it soon becomes quite natural.

Studio communications

Much useful information can be exchanged between a producer or operator and a studio presenter by hand signals or suitable facial expressions through the studio observation window; looks are almost always more concise than words. Nevertheless, there are some things which can only be put into words, so talkback from the control room to the studio (interrupting the desk output or foldback that is normally on the headphones) is provided.

To provide a fast and secure means of communication, each source is linked to its destination by a telephone circuit called a control line. This control line is established each time a source is routed to a destination, no matter whether the connection is made manually or by a switching system. A studio going on air with, for example, three outside sources will have control lines to each OS, to its destination, and to the Centre Area; in this case five in all. All studio and control room clocks are driven from the same master to ensure exact synchronism.

Green cue lights are used to cue studio action—effects or speech—and are quicker and more concise than talkback. Cue light use can be quite eloquent. Steady for 'Go steady', flicker for 'Go quicker' is an old convention. The studio red lights can usually be switched on locally, as in a recording studio, and also remotely by a continuity suite. When the studio is on air, it is important that some of its facilities are disabled. For instance, it should not be possible to send tone, even accidentally, from an on-air studio; nor should talkback be routed to studio loudspeakers unless all the studio microphones are faded out. These interlocks are provided automatically by putting the studio into Transmission; the opposite condition is Rehearsal, normally indicated by blue lights in and around the studio; these conditions are normally selected from the mixing desk.

Providing that the studio is in rehearsal, it may be convenient to replace the main output with talkback when the talkback key is pressed, as shown in Fig. 25.3. This provides a type of slating, and allows all destinations to hear talkback without the need for a separate circuit. Obviously this facility must be disabled when the studio is in transmission.

Pre-transmission checks

Before going on air, it is important that the continuity suite (which assembles the network from studio and pre-recorded sources) and the studio perform the following checks:

1. Control line

It must be possible to ring and speak in both directions.

2. Routing

Continuity needs to be sure that it is making checks with the correct studio. It can ask the studio to cut its tone and check that the tone arriving in the continuity suite cuts simultaneously; the studio can identify itself and its programme by using rehearsal talkback. Where the audio is sent over a digital link, such as the AES/EBU interface, the source identity can be coded into the bitstream.

3. Level

The studio should send tone to the continuity suite at a known level. In the days when all studios were mono, 0 dBu tone was sent. If it arrived at the continuity at 0 dBu then all was well; if it was more than about 2 dB out then there was a fault which merited investigation. If it was within about 2 dB then correction at the destination was in order. Some broadcasters adopt the same levels in stereo, with 0 dBu on both A and B, which is sensible if M is derived from (A+B) −6dB, because 0 dBu on A and B simultaneously will produce 0 dBu on M. Other broadcasters who derive the M signal from (A+B) −3 dB, send −3 dBu on A and on B, so that the M level will again be 0 dBu wherever it is derived. This has the advantage that any destination, whether stereo or mono, can line up with any source, without needing to know whether it is stereo or mono. So there is no need to distribute the M output of the studio separately; the M output of a stereo studio and the only output of a mono studio will appear identical. If all this seems over-complicated, remember that many radio listeners are still listening on Medium or Long wave, so mono level compatibility is still important.

4. Red lights and buzzers

These are only provided for internal sources such as a studio but not an OB. The buzzer is used from studio to continuity to confirm that the red lights are on, and to indicate the end of the programme.

5. Clocks

The continuity and studio clocks should be in sync; continuity and studio should agree an on-air time and a programme duration.

6. Cues

The studio must check that it is receiving the correct cue programme. In and out cues (words or music) etc. must also be arranged/checked.

Central area

This is often called the control room (the studio control room is then called a cubicle); however, to keep confusion to a minimum I shall call it the central area. The outputs of all the studios are routed to the central area. This is rather like a telephone exchange, providing communications and routing between all technical areas. Routing a source to a destination involves a large number of different circuits (stereo music, control line, cue prog, red lights, buzzer, etc.) and would be time-consuming if each had to be plugged up by hand. Although manual over-plugging is provided for seldom-used sources or for emergencies, remote-controlled switches that switch all these circuits simultaneously are obviously more convenient. Relays, uniselectors, and code bar switches have all been used in the past; modern installations use electric matrices.

The central area also has extensive monitoring facilities, and can examine the signal at every point in its progress through the broadcast chain. In addition, it receives programme from OBs and remote sources, and sends programme to transmitters, other organizations, and remote destinations such as regional studio centres.

Incoming and outgoing circuits

Remote sources may arrive by land line (known as a music line), though an increasing number are on digital links. From an OB site, the music line will go to the nearest telephone exchange. The programme is sent from exchange to exchange, probably on microwave links, until it arrives in the central area of the broadcast centre via circuits known as local ends, where it is equalized and has its level restored. In the Central Area the signal must be equalized (to restore its frequency response due to losses in the local ends and cumulative losses over the other parts of the circuit). Alternatively, the signal could leave the OB site digitally, by microwave or satellite link operated by the broadcaster.

Outgoing circuits may be on land lines, or may be digital and carried on coaxial, fibre optic, copper, or microwave circuits. Outgoing Music Lines are fed via a Line Sending Amplifier, Rep. Coil, and U-links. The line sending amplifier either has variable gain, or a fixed gain of 10 dB followed by a variable attenuator. Programme is sent to line at up to +10 dBr, that is with programme peaks of up to +18 dBu. Programme is sent in this way between buildings, to other organizations or broadcast centres, and to some transmitters.

The use of digital circuits has revolutionized the distribution of broadcast signals. A digital link has many advantages. It is more robust than an analogue land line, the audio quality is almost always superior, there are no problems with the level sent to line or with crosstalk, and other signalling information can be embedded in the bitstream. Circuits for distribution will be permanently rented from the PTT or owned by the broadcaster, as ISDNs are not secure enough (and over a long period of time would not be cost effective) for circuits to transmitters. Systems are available which can be carried 'piggy back' fashion on the digital circuits operated by PTTs (e.g. BT or Mercury).

Before signals are sent to transmitters, they are likely to be processed to reduce their dynamic range, to give the Network a characteristic 'sound', or to aid reception under difficult reception conditions. The processors (e.g. Optimod) have multi-band compressors, whose equalization and compression characteristics can be individually set. Medium and Long Wave are normally processed; whether VHF signals are processed will depend on the network.

ISDN

The public switched telephone system samples conversations at 8 kHz using 8 bits per sample, producing a bit rate of 64 kbit/s. These individual circuits are combined into higher rate trunk circuits by the service providers (e.g. British Telecom). The PTTs can now extend their digital circuits directly to subscribers using the ISDN (Integrated Services Digital Network) standards. There are two rates available at the moment, the primary rate of 2.048 Mbit/s (in Europe), and the basic rate, where the subscriber receives two bearer channels of 64 kbit/s each and one signalling channel of 16 kbit/s making 144 kbit/s in all. Since any data may be sent via the 64 kbit/s channels, they are not limited to telephone quality speech. If high-quality audio can be coded into a small enough bandwidth, it can be sent over the telephone network with no additional loss of quality. The primary rate could be used for permanent circuits, but more importantly, if perceptual coding of the signal is acceptable, the basic rate ISDN, where 128 kbit/s are available for audio, could be used as a 'dial-up' service, though two of these will probably be needed for high quality stereo.

ISDNs are ideal for temporary circuits as they are cheap, require no pre-booking, are available world-wide, and in the case of a breakdown can probably be re-established in the time it takes to redial a telephone number. Though the quality of perceptually coded audio is not so high as that of PCM, the quality is far superior to that of a normal telephone circuit. So, for example, an ISDN could be used for sports commentary. It will be much cheaper than a specially provided analogue circuit, and it may also sound better. A further advantage of the ISDN is that it is duplex, and therefore also provides a reverse circuit back to the OB site for talkback or cue programme.

Continuity suites

In the early days of broadcasting, the signal from a studio was routed directly from the central area to the transmitters. Unfortunately, this led to the problem that there was no one to take overall responsibility for the programme content of the network, and so continuity studios were devised. Each continuity had an announcer who linked contributions from all the sources into an integrated network, and who carried executive authority for the content of the network. The announcer was able to fade out any incoming programme if it was felt to be unsatisfactory for any reason. For some radio networks, like Radio 3 or Radio 4, this is still the major function of the continuity.

A continuity suite consists of a small studio, with a self-drive desk, microphones, grams, CD, and cartridge machines (see Figure 25.4). The control room that goes with the continuity studio has facilities to select outside sources to which it has extensive communications links; pre-recorded programmes can be played in from tape machines.

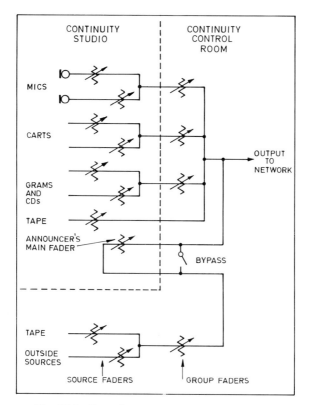

Fig. 25.4. Block diagram of a simple continuity suite

The programme which leaves a studio is routed via the central area to a continuity suite, where it can be monitored and controlled; the continuity and studio exchange pre-transmission checks. About 10 seconds before the start of the programme, the continuity operator will flash the red lights of the studio; the studio will answer with a buzz. When the studio is faded up on the continuity desk, the operator will send a steady red light to the studio.

Since the continuity studio can play records, pre-recorded tapes, cartridges, and compact discs, it is quite capable of originating its own programmes. Therefore many prerecorded music programmes come directly from a continuity. This poses a new problem, in that a continuity cannot rehearse one programme whilst it is on air originating another. There may now be a need, therefore, to switch the network between different continuities. The continuity still remains, however, the last point of operational control within the broadcast chain.

Distribution to transmitters

The output from the continuity suite returns to the central area where it can again be monitored, and is then sent by an extensive system of circuits to the transmitters. The distribution can be by music line, but is more likely to be digital.

The standards needed for distribution networks are not so high as those needed for programme origination. Since VHF transmitters have a bandwidth of 15 kHz, this is sufficient for the circuits distributing programme to them. There is, therefore, a broadcast standard sampling rate of 32 kHz for this application. Furthermore, once the signal has passed through the broadcast chain, it has had its level closely controlled and therefore has a smaller dynamic range than the average commercial classical recording, and will not be further processed before it is radiated from the transmitter. This control of dynamic range has always been necessary, because many people are listening under adverse conditions, e.g. Medium Wave, or high background noise levels (try driving down a motorway at 70 mph listening to wide dynamic range material). Hence the dynamic range available from 16-bit audio may not be necessary, and fewer bits per sample can be used at the distribution stage. In the past the BBC used a 13 bit per sample system; now 14-bit NICAM systems (see next chapter) are in use, as well as the much lower bit rates of perceptual coding. Interestingly, digital distribution is not a new idea; the BBC put its first all-digital distribution system into service in the late 1960s with a system which coded fourteen separate signals (thirteen high quality audio circuits and one Data circuit) and combined them by Time Division Multiplex on to one bearer circuit (either a BT co-axial circuit or an SHF radio link).

Modulation

Before the programme arriving at the transmitter can be radiated from the aerial, it must be modulated on to a radio-frequency carrier.

Amplitude modulation

The simplest form of modulation is AM (amplitude modulation). It is used for the long, medium, and short wavebands. The amplitude of a radio-frequency sine wave (called the carrier) is changed in sympathy with the amplitude of the modulating signal (in this case the audio programme). The result is known as the modulated signal or the envelope (see Figure 25.5). If the peak level of the programme exceeds that which just causes zero amplitude of the modulated envelope, then the demodulated signal in the receiver will be clipped. The use of PPMs for programme control and a fast-acting delay line limiter at the transmitter prevent this happening.

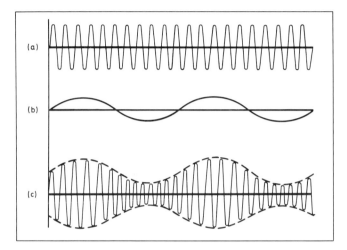

Fig. 25.5. Amplitude modulation: showing (*a*) the unmodulated RF carrier, (*b*) the AF modulating signal, (*c*) the amplitude-modulated signal

If a sine-wave tone is used to amplitude-modulate a carrier, then the output of the modulator will contain three frequency components: the carrier and two sidebands (see Figure 25.6). The sidebands are spaced from the carrier by the frequency of the modulating signal. If, for instance, a 198 kHz carrier is amplitude-modulated by 3 kHz tone, the lower sideband will be 195 kHz and the upper sideband will be 201 kHz. The output from the modulator will therefore contain 195, 198, and 201 kHz. The bandwidth of the modulated signal is therefore twice that of the modulating signal, so audio with a bandwidth of 15 kHz would take up 30 kHz of 'air-space'. In order to fit more channels into the AM broadcast bands, the bandwidth of each broadcast signal is therefore reduced, by international agreement, to about 5 kHz.

Frequency modulation

AM suffers from impulsive interference, because any stray pulse within the bandwidth of the modulated envelope will be demodulated by the receiver

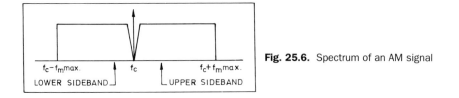

Fig. 25.6. Spectrum of an AM signal

as a click. If the amplitude of the modulating signal is used to change the frequency rather than the amplitude of the RF carrier (Figure 25.7), then most of this interference can be eliminated in the receiver, because the receiver has only to detect the instantaneous frequency of the carrier, and the interference, which tends to change the amplitude of the carrier, can be removed by limiting. The amount by which the frequency of the carrier is changed is called the deviation. In Band II the maximum deviation used is 75 kHz (this corresponds to PPM 6, or +8 dBu).

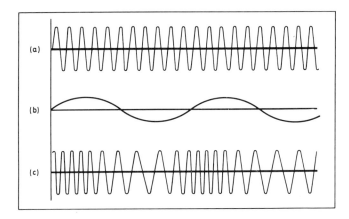

Fig. 25.7. Frequency modulation: showing (a) the unmodulated RF carrier, (b) the AF modulating signal, (c) the modulated signal

If, therefore, a 1 MHz carrier was frequency-modulated by a 3 kHz sine wave to a deviation of 75 kHz, the carrier frequency would rise sinusoidally from 1 MHz to 1.075 MHz, fall sinusoidally to 925 kHz, then return to 1 MHz. Since the modulating frequency is 3 kHz, this whole sequence would be repeated 3,000 times per second.

If an RF carrier is frequency-modulated, an infinite number of sidebands is generated, each separated from the next by the modulating frequency (see Figure 25.8). Clearly this presents a major problem. Luckily, the distortion produced by discarding the more extreme sidebands is small. In practice,

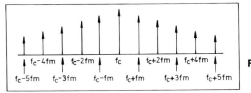

Fig. 25.8. Spectrum of an FM signal

therefore, the bandwidth needed for an FM system (or RF Channel) is twice the sum of the maximum modulating frequency and the maximum deviation, $2 \times (f_m$ max $+ f_d$ max$)$. For a mono signal on band II this is $2 \times (15 + 75) = 180$ kHz.

Zenith GE Pilot Tone system

FM broadcasting on band II (VHF 88 to 108 MHz) started long before stereo broadcasting. The transmission system adopted for stereo had therefore to be compatible with the previously existing mono system. The easiest way of achieving this is to transmit not A and B (the signals corresponding to left and right) but M and S.

The S signal is first amplitude-modulated on to a 38 kHz carrier (see Figure 25.9), with the carrier component of the envelope suppressed (this is called Double Sideband Suppressed Carrier Modulation, or DSBSC). This envelope therefore contains only two sidebands and is contained between 23 and 53 kHz (see Figure 25.10). This signal can therefore be added to the M signal without any overlap of frequencies. In order to demodulate the signal, the receiver must be able to identify the phase of the 38 kHz (suppressed) carrier. Therefore a low-level 19 kHz pilot tone is added, and this composite signal is used to frequency modulate the RF carrier. 90 per cent of the peak deviation is now due to audio information and only 10 per cent to the rest of the transmitted information.

In the receiver, the 19 kHz can be used to re-generate the 38 kHz carrier, reinsert it, demodulate the S signal, and then matrix it with M to produce A and B. However, a useful feature of DSBSC is that its phase changes by 180° when the modulating signal passes through zero. This change of phase means that the 19 kHz pilot tone can be used to identify positive and negative half-cycles of the S signal. A very simple method of decoding is therefore to regenerate 38 kHz from the pilot tone, and use this to switch the composite signal between the left and right outputs of the decoder.

Local radio

Local radio uses many of the methods and techniques of network radio. Since it is on a smaller scale, its programme chain is technically less

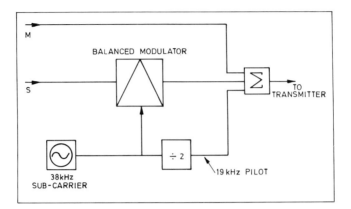

Fig. 25.9. Block diagram of a stereo coder

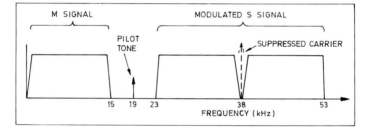

Fig. 25.10. Spectrum of a Zenith GE modulated stereo signal

complex but otherwise similar. Most local radio studios are similar to the continuity suites described above. The studio can be used with its control room for complex programmes or can be self-drive for simpler ones. There are often two studios, each self-drive, either of which can be used with a control room and a news studio. Either studio needs to be able to 'seize' the transmitters so as to go on air. This allows one studio to rehearse whilst the other is on air; at the programme junction when they are to swap, the on-air studio can release the transmitters and the other take them.

A more sophisticated method, often used between network continuities, is for the incoming studio to take the on-air studio as a source, fade it up, and check that the output levels of both studios are identical. If the transmitters are now switched to the incoming studio, there will be no change as far as the listener is concerned, but the incoming studio can either fade out the outgoing studio, or just fade up its own microphones and let the programme presenters have a two-way handover conversation (provided the outgoing studio listens to the correct cue programme).

The future

At the time of writing, Digital Audio Broadcasting (DAB), i.e. radiating digital signals from transmitters, has already been demonstrated and should soon be in regular service. The audio signals are coded using ISO layer II, a slightly modified MUSICAM (Masking pattern Universal Sub-band Integrated Coding And Multiplexing). Six stereo signals are combined into a single multiplex which is radiated in a radio frequency spectrum of 1.5 MHz using a modulation method known as Coded Orthogonal Frequency Division Multiplex (COFDM). This system distributes the bitstream between a very large number of sub-carriers in a way which eliminates the effects of reflections or multi-path distortion. An advantage of this is that all transmitters carrying the same signal can be on the same frequency, leading to significant economy of the RF spectrum. Moreover, satellites could be used with low-power terrestrial transmitters to 'fill-in' areas of poor reception in city centres. The advantages are enormous, particularly for mobile reception.

26 Television

Dave Fisher

The broadcast chain in television is in many ways similar to that in network radio. Of course, pictures add an extra constraint, because in general the pictures and sound must match one another in perspective at least. This is not to say that the pictures or sound must be compromised, but rather that they should fit together harmoniously.

Television principles

Scanning

An image of the scene is focused on to a photo-sensitive pickup device in the camera. It is easy to imagine this as a mosaic-like set of elements (Figure 26.1). Originally cameras used vacuum pickup tubes, but modern cameras use CCD (Charge Coupled Device) sensors. In order to achieve 625-line quality, about 570 elements are needed for each line of the picture. The brightness of each element cannot, therefore, be sent to a monitor simultaneously without a very large number of wires, so they are sent sequentially, using a scanning system which produces a single signal whose voltage represents the brightness of the scene. The picture is scanned from left to right and top to bottom. Each row of elements produces one line of picture signal. When the elements from all lines have been sent, the process starts again at the top. To portray movement without jerkiness it is necessary to send 25 complete sets of elements per second; this is called a picture or frame.

So, for the 625-line system, the scene is scanned horizontally from left to

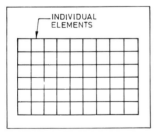

Fig. 26.1. Mosaic-like structure of picture elements

right at high speed (15,625 times per second) and simultaneously from top to bottom at a much slower speed. To reduce the brightness flicker produced by scanning, a system of interlace is used, in which alternate lines are scanned on the first journey down the image and the others are filled in on the next journey (Figure 26.2). Each vertical scan is now called a Field, so in the 625-line system there are 625 lines each frame, and 2 fields per frame. The line frequency is therefore 15.625 kHz, the field frequency is 50 Hz and the frame or picture frequency is 25 Hz. In a monitor an electron beam is used for scanning. It returns quickly from the end of one line or field to the start of the next; this is called flyback.

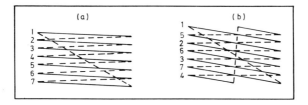

Fig. 26.2. The interlace system: showing (a) a seven-line non-interlaced raster, (b) a seven-line interlaced raster

Synchronization

To ensure that the receiver reassembles the picture in the same order as it was split up by scanning, synchronizing pulses are added at the start of each line and each field. So that a receiver can reliably detect the difference between picture information and sync pulses, picture detail is sent as a positive voltage (black is 0 V and peak white is 0.7 V) and sync information as a negative voltage (−0.3 V), as shown in Figure 26.3.

In the receiver, the electron beam which scans the phosphor in the CRT to reconstruct the picture cannot flyback instantly. If there was picture information whilst flyback was in progress, annoying spurious lines would be displayed. To prevent this, the signal is blanked, i.e. muted for part of each line and field. In the 625-line system, line blanking is 12 μs out of a total line time of 64 μs, leaving 52 μs for the active picture (Figure 26.4); field blanking is 25 lines per field, leaving a total of 575 lines per frame for active picture (Figure 26.5).

Bandwidth

Fine detail in the scene will produce the highest frequency video. The finest detail that can be reproduced will be limited by the bandwidth of the transmission system. The 625-line system has a bandwidth of 5.5 MHz.

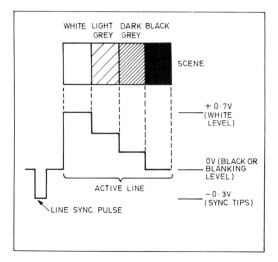

Fig. 26.3. Showing one line of video produced by scanning the scene above

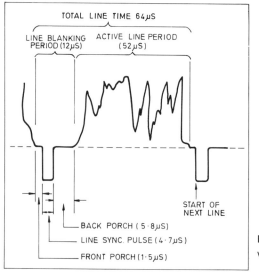

Fig. 26.4. Line timings for a 625-line video signal

Colour

Using a prism it is possible to split white light into the familiar spectrum from red through orange, yellow, green, blue, and indigo to violet. Most visible hues can, however, be analysed into or synthesized from a mixture of

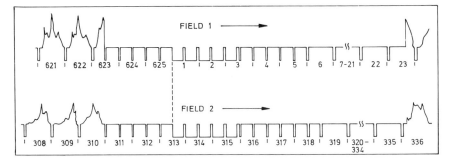

Fig. 26.5. The field-blanking interval

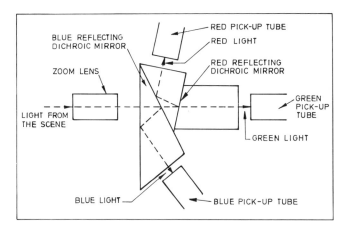

Fig. 26.6. Dichroic block used in the camera to analyse the incident light into its red, green, and blue components

red, green, and blue—the 'primary' colours. In the colour camera, therefore, the light from the scene is split by a dichroic block into three separate images, one red, one green, and one blue (Figure 26.6). Each image is focused on to a different pickup device, so that there are three signals, one red, one green, and one blue. The amplitudes of the R, G, and B signals are adjusted so that they are equal for a neutral scene (one that has only shades of grey). They are 1 volt peak-to-peak, including syncs, for a peak white scene. These three signals are called RGB or GBR.

The three parameters of a colour are hue, luminance, and saturation. Hue is the essential property of a colour which distinguishes it from all other colours, e.g. red and green are different hues. Luminance or brightness is the quantity of light. Luminance is an objective unit (like level in sound); brightness is the subjective sensation produced by light (like loudness in sound). Saturation is the purity or richness of a colour. Highly saturated colours contain only the dominant hue; desaturated colours like pink can be made by adding white light to a saturated colour.

Display tubes

In a colour monitor, the display tube produces a separate electron beam for each of the three primary colours. The electron beams are arranged so that the beam produced by the red input hits only phosphor that glows red, and so on. The inside of the screen is coated with alternate spots or lines of the three phosphors. To prevent any beam hitting the wrong colour phosphor, a perforated metal plate just behind the screen puts all phosphor except the correct one in shadow. This metal plate is called a shadowmask or aperture plate. At normal viewing distances, the eye cannot resolve the separate colours, so the tube can reproduce all the colours which can be synthesized from the three primary colours.

Component systems

Red, green, and blue each have a bandwidth of 5.5 MHz. However because the resolving power of the human eye is less for colour than for brightness, it is possible to modify these signals and reduce the total bandwidth with only a small loss of quality. The overall brightness of a scene is called the luminance, and can easily be generated from R, G, and B, as Y (the luminence) $= 0.3R + 0.59G + 0.11B$. Since this represents the brightness of the scene, it must have full bandwidth, 5.5 MHz.

Colour difference signals can be generated by subtracting the luminance from any of the colour signals; each of these represents the only colouring information and can therefore have a lower bandwidth. In practice, only two colour difference signals are needed, since the R, G, and B can be reconstituted mathematically in a matrix if the luminance is also known; R–Y and B–Y are the colour difference signals used. The international standard CCIR Rec 601 specifies the bandwidth of each colour difference signal as 2.75 MHz. Component systems are widely used within professional installations, but for normal transmission a method of coding is necessary to reduce the total bandwidth to 5.5 MHz.

Coding

Monochrome transmissions have a bandwidth of 5.5 MHz. Hence, if colour signals are to be transmitted with no more RF bandwidth than an equivalent monochrome signal, they must be coded so that a single 5.5 MHz channel carries the information, and meets the following requirements (see Figure 26.7):

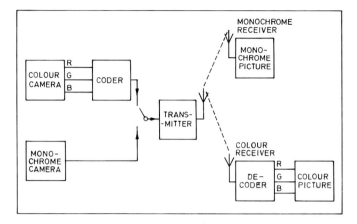

Fig. 26.7. Compatibility and reverse compatibility: a colour transmission must produce a satis-factory picture on a monochrome receiver, and vice versa

1. Compatibility. The colour transmission must produce an acceptable picture on existing monochrome receivers.
2. Reverse compatibility. A monochrome transmission should produce a satisfactory black-and-white picture on a colour receiver without any modification to the receiver.

To achieve compatibility, a monochrome receiver requires the luminance, Y, signal. To achieve reverse compatibility, the colouring information must go to zero for a neutral scene. This is achieved by transmitting colour difference signals R–Y and B–Y. The bandwidth of the colour difference signals for PAL is 1.3 MHz.

R–Y and B–Y are now modulated using Double Sideband Suppressed Carrier Modulation on to sub-carriers of the same frequency, but differing in phase by 90 degrees. In the 625-line PAL system the sub-carrier frequency is 4.43361875 MHz. When the two DSBSC signals are added together, the result is a signal which changes in amplitude and in phase. Its amplitude represents the saturation, and its phase represents the hue of the scene. The resultant chrominance signal is added to the luminance signal to produce the composite signal.

The description so far applies in principle to the NTSC system, although NTSC frequencies are different. Unfortunately phase distortion of the modulated chrominance causes hue errors in the reproduced picture. PAL (Phase Altering Line) is a development of NTSC and reverses the phase of the R–Y sub-carrier on alternate lines so that a signal that has undergone phase distortion will have, after decoding, hue errors which are in opposite directions on alternate lines. For instance, if the distortion causes one line to be a little too blue, the next line will be a little too yellow. Averaging in the receiver will produce a picture that has the correct hue but slightly reduced saturation. This is much less objectionable than hue errors. So that the decoder can regenerate the sub-carrier frequency, a short burst of sub-carrier is transmitted near the start of each line during the Back Porch of the blanking period. The signal is now referred to as Composite Video.

Unfortunately all coding systems introduce some degradation. Cross colour describes the effect of a decoder attempting to reproduce fine luminance detail as though it were colour sub-carrier; the effect, easy to see on fine patterns such as check suits, is a changing colour caste on an area of the picture which should be black and white. Cross luminance is produced when colour sub-carrier is interpreted as luminance, and shows as a crawling dot pattern after large hue changes; the effect is visible on coloured captions or colour bars.

Studios

Television studios, like radio studios, come in many sizes. However, television studios are more likely to be either general-purpose (their use limited only by what will fit into them) or 'News and Current Affairs'. To allow studio equipment, especially cameras, to move smoothly around the studio, the floor is covered in heavy-duty lino and is very flat. Cameras are mounted on pedestals or cranes to give increased mobility.

Microphone booms

A boom is the basic method of dialogue pickup in a television studio. The Fisher boom is the most versatile. A microphone mounted on a boom can follow artistes around the set, and control the perspective (simply by positioning) to suit the action and the pictures (see Chapter 27).

The microphone is usually a cardioid or a stereo pair; M and S pairs are convenient since the width of the stereo image can be easily controlled, they are easy to mount in the cradle, and easier to aim than an XY pair. The 'ideal' position of the microphone should be achieved without the mic being in shot, and without casting shadows into shot. The boom operator therefore needs to be able to see a picture monitor during rehearsals to position the microphone correctly when on air.

Lighting and boom operation are very closely related; a good boom operator needs to understand both. The simplest situation is 'one man to camera'. The keylight, a hard source of light, casts shadows with hard, clearly defined edges; the filler, a soft source of light, casts shadows with a soft, fuzzy edge. When the boom is in the position shown in Figure 26.8, the hard shadow of the microphone cast by the key light is out of shot, on the floor at camera right.

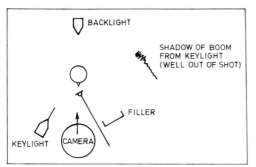

Fig. 26.8. Simple lighting plot for 'one man to camera', using a boom microphone on the same side of the set as the soft filler

Microphone cables

The dimmers used to control the brightness of the studio lights employ SCRs (usually Triacs). They work by switching on the current to the lamp part way into each cycle of the mains; the longer the switch-on is delayed, the dimmer the lamp will be. This method has the advantage that it is very efficient, but the disadvantage that it generates large amounts of interference. To prevent this being audible on microphone circuits (the interference is very wide-band), well-balanced circuits, good desk input balance, and star quad cable are needed.

Star quad cable has four tightly twisted conductors within the screen (Figure 26.9). The object is to ensure that the same amount of interference is induced in each leg of the balanced circuit. Provided this is the case, the desk input will balance out the induced e.m.f. and there will be no resultant interference. The tight twist helps to ensure this. The cable is wired so that diagonally opposite conductors are connected together at both ends of the cable. An interfering field therefore needs to be very close to the cable to induce a different e.m.f. in each leg of the circuit.

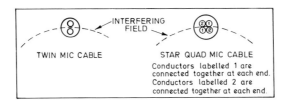

Fig. 26.9. Comparing twin and star quad cables

Radio microphones allow the use of a personal mic without the inconvenience of a trailing cable. A battery-powered transmitter, small enough to fit into the hip pocket, allows any microphone to be used. Frequency modulation is used with a maximum deviation of 75 kHz. There are a number of Radio Mic channels available in the region of 174 MHz, though not all can be used simultaneously; other VHF and UHF frequencies are also in use.

The control room suite

Lighting and vision control room

The camera outputs are fed to the lighting and vision control room, where remote controls allow vision operators to control the black level, optical iris, and fine colour balance of each camera. The outputs of each camera can thus be matched so that when cameras are cut between there is no difference in the exposure of the picture or of its colour balance.

This control room also houses the lighting control desk, which is normally computerized to allow the recall of the large number of lighting cues necessary, particularly in light entertainment.

Production control room

The director is responsible for the production once it is in the studio and, sitting in the PCR, can see the output of each source. These include cameras, VT machines, TK machines (these convert film into television pictures), stills stores, video effects units, electronic caption generators, OBs, and other studio outputs. So that the director can be heard by everyone involved in the programme, whether in the studio, the other control rooms, or at an outside source, there is an open talkback system known as Production Talkback (PTB).

The vision mixer (in Britain a person as well as a piece of equipment; an anomaly avoided in America by calling the equipment a video switcher) can cut between any of the sources available to the studio (Figure 26.10). To be able to superimpose sources, or to wipe between them, requires that they are synchronous with each other and with the studio. To be synchronous, the sync pulses of each source must arrive within 50 ns of each other, and, if the sources are coded, their burst phases must be within 1.3 degrees of each other. Although the sync timing requirement can be met by cutting cables to the correct length (50 ns represents about 10 m of cable), the colour requirement cannot (1.3° of subcarrier represents about 16 cm of cable, and it is not practicable to cut all the cables in a studio to within 16 cm of 'correct'). Some sort of manual or automatic adjustment is therefore necessary before any colour source can be considered synchronous.

Sound control room

The sound supervisor is responsible for all sound aspects of the programme and also mixes it. The sound supervisor is assisted by a tape and grams

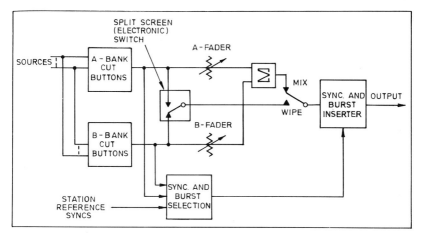

Fig. 26.10. Block diagram of a simple A–B vision mixer

operator who is usually responsible for the whole balance of tape or gram items. TV sound desks are normally larger than radio desks; forty or fifty channels is a common size and 100 channels is not unknown. Otherwise the technical facilities are similar to radio, although more facilities such as FB and clean feeds are generally required. Outputs for public address are also necessary when a studio audience is present. This facility is similar to foldback, available from desk channels or groups, but may incorporate fader backstop switching so that the PA feed can be pre-fade (which has, for instance, the advantage that the PA howlround point does not change if a channel feeding PA is opened further on air than it was in rehearsal), and yet the feed of that channel to PA is automatically cut when the channel (or group) is faded out.

Studio communications

Red lights: indicate transmission, and are switched on locally when recording.

Blue or yellow lights: indicate rehearsal, i.e. the studio is in use (and therefore admission is restricted) but the output is not on air or being recorded.

Buzzers: are used from video tape (VT) and Telecine (TK) to the studio. The advantage of a buzzer is that it requires less concentration on the part of a hard-pressed director than a voice channel would; the disadvantage is that only 'Yes' (one buzz) or 'No' (two buzzes) can be sent.

Production talkback is an 'open' system (i.e. no switch needs to be pressed to energize it). PTB originates from the production desk (director/producer, production secretary, production assistant) and is distributed to everyone involved in the production (camera operators, outside sources, SCR, L & VCR, apparatus room, etc.). Note that the sound supervisor will be listening to PTB on a loudspeaker, and may therefore have difficulty in detecting induction of talkback on to programme sound. For this reason, the studio's destination is often the area responsible for ensuring that there is no such induction. Although PTB is the prerogative of the director, some other operational positions, such as sound supervisor or lighting director, can also speak on it.

Sound talkback (STB) is used by the sound supervisor to direct the sound crew (boom operators, tracking foldback operators, PA operators, etc.) on the studio floor. They, of course, also need to hear the director. Sound talkback therefore normally carries PTB but, when the sound supervisor presses the STB key, the STB distribution is switched away from PTB to the output of the sound supervisor's talkback microphone. A blip of tone is sometimes added to STB whenever the STB key is pressed, to help those listening to STB to identify the different voices. A similar arrangement is available for the lighting director to direct lighting staff (like follow-spot operators) on the studio floor.

Reverse talkback allows an individual to reply to the source of some talkback; for example, camera reverse talkback allows camera operators to reply to the director; sound reverse talkback allows boom operators to reply to the sound supervisor.

Programme sound is a feed of the output of the sound desk (as opposed to studio output, which is fed from after the tone relay). Programme sound will, for instance, allow a camera operator to time a track or a pan to music if it can be mixed with PTB. Boom operators listening to prog sound will be able to hear their own microphone when it is faded up, and will therefore be able to position it more accurately.

Intercoms: talkback channels generally allow one person to speak to a large number of people. Often an individual will want to speak by intercom to another individual: for example the sound supervisor may need to discuss a boom shadow problem with the lighting director.

Control lines: will link every source with its destination; in addition there will be control lines to central areas.

Cue dots: are small black-and white striped rectangles inserted into the top left or top right of a broadcast video signal, by either a Network or Master Control Room, to indicate the proximity of a programme junction. Because they are radiated from transmitters, everyone who watches the transmitted output can see and therefore act upon them. For instance, a remote OB can get cue programme off-air using a receiver and still see the cue dots which will cue them to start their programme. In the BBC, the cue dot appears 30 secs before the start of programme, disappears at 10 secs to go, reappears at 5 secs to go, and disappears again when the source is cut to by Network Control. ITV companies use them to indicate imminent commercial breaks.

On even the simplest programme, all these communication systems will be available (with the exception of cue dots if the programme is not live). Indeed the communications involved in a programme are often more complex than the programme sound.

Videotape recording

Professional VT machines are much more complex, and much larger, than their domestic cousins. They are generally located some way from the studio, under the charge of a specialist operator.

Until the early 1980s all VT machines were analogue and recorded coded signals. However, there are now a large number of formats, some coded, some component, some analogue, and some digital.

Analogue VTR

A coded video signal has a bandwidth that extends from d.c. to 5.5 MHz; unfortunately, using conventional magnetic recording, it is possible to record only about ten octaves. To reduce the number of octaves that it occupies, the video signal is first modulated on to an RF carrier, but this increases the bandwidth. Frequency Modulation is used, because variations in head-to-tape contact cause changes in the level of the replayed signal; these amplitude changes can be removed by clipping.

After modulation, the signal will contain fewer octaves (and therefore be recordable) but contain very high frequencies, so a high head-to-tape speed is needed. The only practicable way of achieving this, whilst keeping the linear speed of the tape reasonable, is by the use of rotating heads. Off-tape jitter must be removed if the replay signal is to be synchronous. VT machines therefore incorporate time-base correctors, which remove the jitter by comparing off-tape syncs and burst with reference syncs and burst, and then switching delays in or out to correct the mistiming. This operation is usually digital.

VT formats

This list is not intended to be exhaustive, as there are now so many formats, but it gives brief details of a representative selection. All these formats use cassettes; the open-reel Quadruplex and C Format machines are now obsolete.

Betacam SP: Originated and mainly manufactured by Sony, this analogue format uses half-inch wide tape in 36- or 110-minute cassettes (the shorter tapes are mechanically the same as domestic Betamax cassettes, but use higher grade tape running at a higher speed). The video is recorded in component form, with one track of luminance adjacent to a track containing time compressed B-Y and R-Y. Dolby C is available on the longitudinal audio tracks, but is not much favoured because of line-up problems especially on multi-generation dubs. The format offers FM audio tracks (like domestic hi-fi machines), but as these tracks can only be recorded at the same time as video, they are not useful for editing. Two digital audio tracks are available, replacing one of the analogue tracks. This machine is the most common broadcast machine at present. Camcorders to this standard are also very common.

M II: Broadly similar performance and features to Betacam, though manufactured and marketed by Panasonic. Programme can be transferred between M II and Betacam using a standard interface (EBU N10).

D 1: This is a relatively expensive digital component format using three-quarter-inch tape with playing times up to 94 minutes. It meets the CCIR Rec 601 standard of 13.5 MHz luminance and 6.75 MHz colour difference sampling rates, with 8-bit quantization. It has four independently editable digital audio channels with 48 kHz sampling and up to 20-bit quantization.

D 2: This is a digital composite format using three-quarter-inch tape with playing times up to 207 minutes. The video signal is sampled at 4-times sub-carrier frequency using 8-bit quantization. It has four independently editable digital audio channels with 48 kHz sampling and up to 20-bit quantization.

D 3: This is a digital composite format using half-inch tape with playing times up to 245 minutes. The video signal is sampled at 4-times sub-carrier frequency using 8-bit quantization. It has four independently editable digital audio channels with 48 kHz sampling and up to 20-bit quantization. Camcorders are available in this format.

D 5: This component machine uses half-inch tape with playing times up to 120 minutes. It has 10-bit video quantization and a widescreen option using 18 MHz sampling with 8-bit quantization. A future option is promised that will record bit rate reduced HDTV. It has four independently editable digital audio channels with 48 kHz sampling and up to 20-bit quantization. Some machines are also able to play D3 tapes.

Digital VTRs using bit rate reduced video

A number of manufacturers produce machines based on 13.5 MHz luminance and 6.75 MHz colour difference sampling rates with subsequent processing to reduce the bit rate. This has the advantage that writing speeds can be lower, with commensurate reductions in machine and tape costs. The degradations produced by these formats will be greater than the previous digital machines, especially in multi-generation use if there is a need to modify the picture between generations, but compare favourably with analogue formats:

Ampex DCT is a component format using three-quarter-inch tape with playing times up to 208 minutes. It has 8-bit video quantization and four independently editable digital audio channels with 48 kHz sampling and up to 20-bit quantization.

Sony Digital Betacam, also available from other manufacturers, is a component format using half-inch tape with playing times up to 124 minutes. It has 10-bit video quantization and four (later eight) independently editable digital audio channels with 48 kHz sampling and up to 20-bit quantization. Some machines are also able to play analogue Betacam tapes.

No doubt even more formats are on the way, and this proliferation makes standardization difficult.

VT editing

VT editing is done by dubbing from one machine to another. If only two machines are available, this only allows pictures to be cut together, although sound can be mixed by off-laying it, playing in the laid-off sound in sync with the original action, and cross-fading from it to the play-in machine whilst recording the result on the record or edit machine. If three machines are available (two play-in and one record), then sound and picture mixes are possible.

Edit points can be located by using SMPTE/EBU timecode (which was originally developed for this purpose). The machines are started by the editing equipment reading timecodes from both machines. At the edit point, the monitoring is switched from the output of the record machine (which is at present in replay) to the output of the play-in machine, thus rehearsing the edit. If it is satisfactory, both tapes must be reset to their original pre-roll positions, and the operation repeated. This time, however, the record machine will be switched automatically into record at the edit point, joining the new material on to the old.

After the VT editing has been completed, multitrack and off-line video cassette tapes can be made for post-dubbing (see Chapter 27), where extensive use is made of hard-disc editors.

Telecine (TK)

A Telecine machine produces a video output from cine film. Many systems are possible, but the best results are obtained from continuous-motion machines.

In an optical projector, a frame of the film is registered in the gate, the frame kept stationary, the shutter opened, and a static image of the frame projected. The shutter is then closed, the film advanced by one frame, and the next frame shown. To reduce the effects of flicker, each frame may be shown more than once. A continuous motion TK machine, however, uses the motion of the film to produce some of the vertical scanning, and has the advantage that the picture is steadier and the wow on Commag or Comopt prints is considerably less than with an intermittent motion machine.

Light from a CRT raster is focused on to the film. The light which passes through the film is split into RGB components and then converted into three electrical signals by photoelectric cells. Alternatively, a CCD sensor and light source may be used. The signal, after processing, is either coded into composite video, or output as component signals. To produce a correctly interlaced output there must be two optical paths (the twin lens machine), the raster must be moved between fields (the Hopping Patch method), or the frame must be scanned in a non-interlaced manner and the signal digitally manipulated to produce two interlaced fields.

Films shot specifically for TV will usually have sep mag sound, that is the sound will be recorded on a separate piece of stock of the same gauge as the picture (for example 16 or 35 mm) coated over its whole width with magnetic oxide. The sep mag sound is run on a separate machine, in sync with and locked to the TK picture mechanism. Film for TV will be shot at 25 frames per second, and run at the same speed; film for the cinema will be shot at 24 frames per second but, using a continuous motion TK machine, will be transmitted at 25 fps, and therefore be about 4 per cent fast.

Central area

There is the same need in television as in radio for a central area to equalize, route, and monitor sources and feed them to the correct destination. For each source in TV there will be video, main sound, at least one control line, cue programme (both sound and video), PTB, and perhaps intercoms, remote controls, buzzers, reverse talkback, red lights, clean feeds, extra sound or vision circuits, and many others. The single word 'source' implies all these circuits. Solid-state matrices are normally used to route all these simultaneously.

Additionally, the TV central area (often called a central apparatus room CAR) needs to generate a reference for the pulses necessary for scanning and coding. There are seven separate signals (mixed syncs, mixed blanking, field drive, line drive, vertical axis switch, burst gate, and colour sub-carrier). Such a set of seven pulses is called a pulse chain. These signals, needed by each source within the studio centre (and often called station syncs or reference syncs), are generated by a sync pulse generator (SPG).

A locking signal (normally a feed of sync pulses with colour burst, called 'black and burst' or 'colour black') can be generated by an SPG in the CAR and distributed to each source, which then locks its own SPG to the reference. If sources were not locked to a central reference, they would not be synchronous at mixing points, and could not be mixed between. Incoming and outgoing circuits to and from the outside world (like OBs, transmitters) will terminate here.

Continuities

As in radio, there is a need to link programmes together into a network. This will be done in a Master Control or Network Control Room, which selects and cues sources in a similar way to radio. The associated continuity studio or presentation area will house an announcer or presenter, who may be in or out of vision, to provide linking and breakdown announcements. Pre-transmission checks with the source will be similar to radio, with the added complication of video and the need to check its synchronism if the source is to be mixed to. Additionally, since a studio that is about to go on air is likely to have its opening titles on VT or TK, and will therefore need to run them some seconds before the on-air time, the studio needs an accurate cue from Network some seconds before Network takes the studio.

Most networks now use some sort of automation to transmit prerecorded programmes. Using bar-code stickers for identification, a robot arm in a large machine picks up video cassettes from separate bins, and inserts them into one of a number of video tape transports. A computer into which the network schedule has been entered can then start the machine at the correct time. Cartridge machines holding hundreds of cassettes are common. Moreover, the machine can compile trails or commercial breaks from cassettes in the bins, whilst other programmes are on the air.

Distribution to transmitters

The video signal may leave the studio centre by microwave link or by coaxial line. The sound will probably be combined with the video signal using a system called Sound in Syncs which has three major advantages:

1. It is cheaper than separate sound and video circuits.
2. It eliminates the possibility of operational errors pairing a video source with the wrong sound source.
3. Being digital it is of better quality over long distances than analogue lines.

The stereo feed to the transmitters is NICAM coded (see later) and then time compressed to allow the bitstream to be inserted into the line synchronizing pulses. Unfortunately, the bandwidth generated by this would be greater than the 5.5 MHz available if a binary system were used.

Therefore, a quaternary system, where each pair of bits is represented by one of four levels, is used. One level represents a digital value of 00, the second 01, the third 10, and the last 11. Compare this with the binary system where each level represents only one bit (either 1 or 0).

Transmitters

At the transmitter, the Sound in Syncs data are removed from the sync pulses, and radiated as NICAM 728. The bitstream is also decoded, converted to mono, and used to feed the analogue FM transmitter. The video is amplitude modulated on a UHF carrier using Vestigial Sideband Modulation; this simply means that only part of the lower sideband is radiated. This saves bandwidth, so allowing more transmitters in a given frequency range. Receivers compensate for the vestigial sideband by their IF response. The mono sound is frequency modulated on a carrier locked to, and 6 MHz higher in frequency than, the vision carrier; the deviation is 50 kHz. The total channel bandwidth, i.e. the frequency difference between adjacent sound or vision carriers is 8 MHz.

NICAM 728

To enable a digital stereo signal to be radiated from transmitters without increasing the channel bandwidth requires reduction of the bit rate, or digital companding. NICAM (Near-Instantaneously Companded Audio Multiplex) achieves this by sampling the original analogue signal at 32 kHz and coding each sample to 14-bit accuracy. The size of each sample is then reduced to 10 bits in a way which depends on the original audio level. After extensive listening tests, it was decided that the signal could be companded in blocks of 32 samples (a period of 1 ms). Each block is coded according to the highest level sample within that block, and each sample in the block has the same coding. Each block starts with a frame alignment word for synchronization, which is followed by five application control bits which allow signalling of information such as whether the bitstream is stereo or twin channel mono. Then there are eleven additional data bits, at present unused, followed by the 64 audio samples (32 left and 32 right). Each sample has one parity bit for error detection protecting the six most significant bits. The final bit rate is 728 kBits per second.

The future

It is likely that widescreen TV will soon be with us. PAL Plus is a compatible standard which allows widescreen transmissions to be received on present receivers with an aspect ratio of 4 : 3 or on new 16 : 9 receivers. A disadvantage is that conventional 4 : 3 receivers display a black band at the top and bottom of the screen. PAL Plus may, however, be a useful stepping stone to high definition television (HDTV).

Recent developments using MPEG–2 coding have produced remarkably low bit rates for digital TV by removing some of the redundancy present in most TV pictures (for instance, large parts of many frames are the same as the frame before or after). Although this coding method produces different degradations to those of conventional analogue systems, the comparisons being made are with 'VHS quality' at 2 Mbits/s, and standard PAL quality at 5 Mbits/s.

HDTV requires very high bandwidths. To double the horizontal and vertical resolution would quadruple the bandwidth; since any future system is likely to be component, this approximately doubles the requirement again.

However, any future video system is likely to be digital. At first sight this would seem to increase the bandwidth by a further factor of ten or so. Advances in bit rate reduction techniques, however, are likely to lead to manageable bit rates. Already contribution quality HDTV pictures are possible at 140 Mbits/s and, using MPEG–2 compression, high definition pictures can be coded at 20 to 30 Mbits/s; future advances should make a digital HDTV service to the home practicable. With five wide-band channels, widescreen HDTV will provide a cinema-like experience in the home. The only problem will be where to put all the equipment.

27 Video

Trevor Webster

It might be supposed that sound for use with pictures is produced in much the same way as sound by itself, for radio or records. Although there are obvious parallels, and some of the same equipment is used, the differences are in fact very considerable. There are basically two ways of recording moving pictures, either of which can be used to originate programmes for subsequent TV broadcasting or videotape distribution. First, they can be recorded directly on to light-sensitive film inside a film camera. Second, they can be picked up by an electronic television camera (a video camera) and fed as an electrical waveform (the video signal) down wires to a videotape recorder. Sometimes these wires are only a few inches long as the recorder is mounted on the back of the camera to form a camcorder.

Two techniques

For many years, the type of camera used (film or video) dictated the way in which the production was organized and therefore the most appropriate sound acquisition technique. This arose from the fact that the film industry developed on a one-shot-at-a-time basis using only one camera, whereas video cameras have their origin in live television where a multi-camera technique is necessary. Clearly the requirements of the first case, where the sounds for only one shot at a time need be considered, are very different from the second where long takes require a whole programme (or whole segment) approach.

The multi-camera technique involves takes of perhaps several minutes. Indeed, in the days when television was predominantly live, a whole 90-minute play would be performed, shot, and transmitted as a single continuous sequence. This is still the pattern with many sporting events, children's programmes, major state occasions, and current affairs programmes.

It is not surprising that the successful techniques which made live television sound possible are still used for multi-camera shoots. The availability of lightweight professional video cameras, however, has revolutionized much of the industry. Situations which would formerly have been accessible only to a very lightweight film camera can now be shot easily using a video camera instead. This may still be used in a filmic manner, however, recording only one shot in each take. On the other hand, it is not difficult to use two of these cameras to produce longer sequences, and this reduces the time required to shoot the programme.

There are other economic considerations too. It has been observed that a single camera unit (a 'film unit') on converting from film to video can reduce its costs for 'stock' (the actual film or tape) by as much as 90 per cent. This powerful motivation has led to the replacement of many film cameras with video cameras.

It is still useful to think of the production of sound with pictures as falling into two sets of techniques, but they will no longer depend on the type of camera being used. Instead, it is the style of shooting which matters. Also the two basic styles may make very different demands on 'post-production'. This chapter deals mainly with the organization of sound for multi-camera shoots, before going on to single-camera arrangements, and describing some aspects of post-production.

Multi-camera video

Live broadcasting has certain disadvantages, including the need to play safe, avoiding anything too likely to go wrong. However, it does have the advantage of producing highly skilled professional operations with very high productivity, and it is largely the tradition of long continuous takes which makes multi-camera sound operations distinct from single-camera work.

Most productions start from a script (or score) which primarily represents the sound element rather than the visual one, and it is generally true that most of the production information is carried in the sound. Not many programmes are worth watching without the sound, whereas in the days when television transmission breakdowns were more frequent it was quite common to continue in sound-only until the vision could be restored. When sound and vision are present together, however, there is little doubt that vision is the dominant sense, and it is actually nonsense to consider the two contributions separately. Experience has shown that only when the sound and pictures work together is a production successful. They need to be regarded as complementary, supporting one another, rather than as radio with added pictures, or as silent film with added sound.

But the organizational needs of the different disciplines—sound, camera work, lighting, etc.—are very different and often difficult to reconcile in a practical situation. The preferred sound coverage can make satisfactory lighting impossible, or vice versa; sound or lighting can make it impossible to shoot; the set design can make everybody's life a misery, and so on. It can be seen that video is a collaborative art, and careful planning of all the elements is essential. The successful sound man will need to learn something of the production problems encountered by lighting directors, cameramen, designers, and directors.

Planning

The type of planning involved varies with the type of production. A one-off drama will have to be planned in considerable detail, with heads of sound, lighting and cameras meeting around the table with the designer, director, and production manager as well as make-up and wardrobe designers. Ground plans and elevation drawings of the studio or location, and of the proposed 'sets', will be studied carefully and perhaps modified as interrelated problems are discussed. Scale models are often made, to show what the set will look like in three dimensions. Considerable negotiation may be needed to formulate a production plan which will work for everybody. All those present (sometimes called the 'realization team') are aware of their individual needs but also of their dependence on each other, and relationships of great trust often form between the members of the team. This explains why the same people are seen to work together time after time.

A major light entertainment production, whether variety or comedy, is planned in a similar way to drama. Other kinds of programmes require a different approach. Current affairs programmes, for example, cannot be planned in such detail because the exact nature of the material is not known until the last minute. In this case, a cover-all plan has to be made which will deal with any situation within certain overall limits. For example, an interview area may be designed which can be used for any interview involving up to, say, eight people. A demonstration area may be used to show objects on a table with a small number of people standing around it. Standard lighting and sound arrangements can be devised which will cope with any situation within those criteria. Detailed requirements are communicated as soon as they become available, sometimes while the programme is actually being made. In some ways this calls for more detailed mental planning than when the precise situation is known in advance. Another example of this situation is in sports coverage. The overall format is predetermined, not least by the rules of the game, but the details of the action have to be dealt with as they arise.

Each type of programme is slightly different—children's, educational, music, the various kinds of outside broadcasts—and all have their separate planning requirements, but the sound supervisor (or audio director) must leave the meeting with a clear idea of how the various problems will be solved. Once a programme has been planned, it is possible to calculate the requirements in terms of staff and equipment.

Staff and equipment

The sound staff on an ordinary programme can vary in number from about three to twelve. All except the most junior will have some special skill in addition to their general expertise. One will perhaps specialize in recording, editing, and playing music and effects, using quarter-inch tape, cart, DAT, samplers, workstations, multitrack recorders, etc. Others will specialize in boom operating, radio microphones, Public Address control, etc.

The equipment used can vary greatly. A wide range of microphones is used, partly for their particular sound quality and partly for their directivity. Unwanted sound is a particular problem in television studios and at many outside locations. Often forty or fifty people have to be on the set. Just the sound of their breathing can be problem. Microphones are therefore as useful for what they exclude as for what they pick up. This also applies with in-vision orchestras, where the layout of the instruments may suit visual requirements better than those of sound. The worst situations can usually be avoided nowadays (like open brass blowing straight into the strings' microphones) because producers understand the importance of good sound, but without directional microphones we would still be in big trouble.

Probably the most useful piece of equipment on the studio floor (from a sound point of view) is still the television microphone boom. It is often underrated by people outside the industry, but is enormously mobile and has the great advantage of instantaneous control by an experienced operator. It can follow an actor who has walked to the wrong place, or a singer who cannot find his floor marks. It can immediately adjust the balance between two contributors or turn its back on some unwanted, unexpected noise. In the hands of a skilled operator, and with a carefully chosen directional microphone, it is a wonderful machine.

New operators can be trained to follow a person who is walking in figures-of-eight talking all the time. A skilled operator can do this with ease, and keep the person 'on mic' the whole time, by co-ordinating five different hand movements so that the microphone can be moved left or right, up or down, and in or out (the boom arm is telescopic). The mic can also be 'panned' and 'tilted' in its cradle. In confined spaces, or out on location, the 'gun mic' and hand-held boom ('fishing rod') are more usual, but their manœuvrability and useful range are comparatively limited.

As well as booms, the full range of microphone stands is used, and microphones are sometimes slung from lighting and scene hoists, attached to the scenery, concealed among 'properties' in the set, or even fitted inside imitation books or other devices. Sometimes they are concealed on the person or, if they are unobtrusive, allowed to show. The small electret capsules have long been considered acceptable 'in shot', except on drama productions, and the new-generation ones are smaller than ever. Often these 'personal' mics are used in combination with a radio transmitter in a pocket or pouch, or hidden in the artist's costume. On many modern radio mic systems the output of the associated receiver can have a quality and reliability approaching those of cabled mics, but there are pitfalls for the unwary. Multi-path concellation, resulting in a momentary loss of signal at the receiver aerial, can have distressing results, and, in some cases, the shielding effects of cameras and other equipment can cause dead spots in certain areas of the studio and enormous variations of RF signal level. These problems can usually be overcome by the use of 'diversity systems', which automatically switch between two receiver aerials (or aerial–receiver combinations) in order to select the best signal from moment to moment. For example, Audio Engineering's well-established Micron system combines the outputs of two receivers if their levels are not more than 3 dB apart. When they differ by more than this, it silently selects the best one. More recent is the development of some quite sophisticated compander systems. The audio is compressed in the transmitter and expanded in the receiver, giving clean audio at much lower RF levels. There is, of course, an eventual cut-off level below which the thing will not work at all, and the sudden transition from beautiful clean sound to complete loss of programme can be disconcerting to say the least.

Where the artist needs to have great mobility, radio mics provide a unique solution. Often they are used in conjunction with radio talkback, which allows the director to talk into the artist's ear-piece by a separate radio system operating in the opposite direction. It is quite common to use twenty or more radio mics at the same time on different artists, with separate radio frequencies and separate pairs of receivers fed from two aerials. Indeed, on some outside broadcasts (such as golf coverage) where large numbers of people are spread over very large areas, the number and variety of radio systems employed is almost beyond belief. The successful operation of such a rig involves careful planning and highly specialized skills.

Television studios

Television studios have a very high capital cost and are almost always designed as general-purpose studios, that is they are not dedicated to any particular type of programme. For this reason they are designed to be acoustically fairly dead, on the basis that it is easier to add reverberation than to take it away. Where reverberation is needed, it is created artificially, using one or more of the many digital devices now available. Indeed, the whole range of special effects devices finds a use in modern television production. Sound desks used in television are often quite large, sometimes having more than eighty channels. The principles are described elsewhere in this volume.

Music has its own special problems. Sometimes a performer is asked to sing and dance at the same time, or to perform in vision a song which was produced for record distribution in a very complex way over a period of several days in a recording studio. If the performance cannot be recreated live for the cameras, it is necessary to pre-record the sound and play it back to the artist in the television studio or location so that he can 'mime' to it. It is sometimes assumed that the original released recording will provide the ideal sound balance for miming, but this is often not the case. In a straightforward song with solo singer and orchestral backing, the cameras will concentrate on the singer, often using close-up shots. In this situation our brains tell us that we should hear more of the singer, and consequently we may consider that the orchestra is too loud. If we switch off the pictures, we hear that the balance is actually correct in sound-only terms. So the balance must be adjusted to match the pictures, and to this end it is sometimes useful to keep the vocal on a separate track so that moment-by-moment adjustments can be made when the shots are seen.

In the case of classical orchestral music, it is the music which dictates the shots. It makes no sense to have a close-up of the violins when the music is featuring the brass section. But even when the pictures are showing the lead instrument or section there is still a feeling that the balance is wrong. The featured instrument sounds too quiet. Over the years, there have been many arguments about whether or not the balance of classical music should be adjusted to take account of this visual effect. There is of course a purist view, that the music should not be changed in any way and that the picture director will have just to make his own arrangements. I favour the opposite view, however, that it is the perceived effect which matters. Television programmes are not primarily aimed at blind people, and to offer a sighted audience something which seems subjectively wrong surely cannot be right. The problem is very complex, however, and involves careful consideration of perspective and reverberation as well as balance. A number of 'spot mics' can be used to increase detail and clarity in the balance, without the need for rapid perspective changes, though one must be careful not to upset the stereo image (more about this later). The move to stereo has certainly helped to produce clarity and detail in an orchestral mix, but only for viewers having the appropriate equipment. A great many people view TV and video material on sets which will not reproduce stereo sound at all, or will provide so narrow an image that it is almost mono.

Communication circuits

In addition to the programme chain, the sound supervisor may have control of a large number of communication circuits (as discussed in Chapter 26).

Some of them provide communication between the various operational groups in the control rooms and studio. These are essential to every production and are used from day to day, usually without much attention. Other facilities can be used in many different ways to give 'talkback', intercom, or telephone communications both within the studio and to remote contributors. An important feature of broadcast television is its ability to take contributions from a number of sources many miles apart, apparently as easily as if they were in the same studio. This relies on the ability to offer adequate communications and the correct programme feed to each one. For example, if six groups of contributors in six locations are having a discussion, each group will need to hear the other five on a loudspeaker (but not themselves, or there would be a great danger of feedback). The special feed to each of these loudspeakers is called (in Britain) a clean feed or (in USA) a mix minus, and all these feeds are provided from a matrix in the sound control room of the master studio. In a similar way, calls from the public telephone system can be put on the air, the remote contributor hearing the whole mix minus himself down the telephone.

Single camera shooting

Many of the sound complexities of multi-camera video disappear when only one camera is used, but other problems arise (as is also discussed in Chapter 28). If a shoot is outside, as most are, the background noise will constantly be changing. Even continuous sounds like traffic and birdsong, which may seem fairly constant at the time of recording, are found to vary considerably in level and quality when different takes are edited together. Also, when speech by an actor with a loud voice is intercut with that of a softer spoken actor, the background sounds may jump up and down alarmingly because different gain settings were used.

To make matters worse, random sounds like a passing aircraft may disappear on one shot only to reappear on the next. This is clearly unacceptable in the finished programme, and steps must be taken both at the shoot and in post-production to avoid such defects. The ideal is to find a quiet location and add the effects later but, when this is not possible, some degree of masking is needed. To this end, it is standard practice to record a 'buzz track' of general sounds at the location, and use this at the dub to smooth out any changes which are revealed by the editing. Obviously this needs to be in stereo for a stereo production.

Stereo may present a further problem, especially when recording on location. This stems from the question of where the viewer perceives himself to be. In the days of mono it was always assumed that the viewer was in the position of the camera. Thus, with the microphone placed close to the camera, more distant actors would actually sound more distant, and the microphone was constantly moving as the shot was changed so that sound and vision perspectives always matched.

In early experiments with stereo TV sound, the same technique was tried using stereo microphones, but the constant swinging of the image proved extremely disturbing. This caused Sound Supervisors to ask the key question, 'Where does the viewer consider himself to be?' The answer to this question defines the sound stage and provides a stereo image which supports the viewer's unconscious sense of orientation. It determines which sound sources should be located to left and right, even when individual shots may tend to contradict this. It appears that, as viewers, we are able to maintain a map of the location and our position in it, though this may change from time to time. Curiously, although we need this map to be supported by the sound, we can at the same time accept views from other angles without losing our sense of place.

In practice, however, the key question is sometimes difficult to answer, and the answer may change many times during a production. In a theatre, the viewer can be safely located somewhere in the middle of the stalls or the front circle. Similarly, with a three-sided set in a television studio, the middle of the theoretical 'fourth wall' is a good starting place. On location, however, the director may be tempted to shoot in all directions, including 180 degree reverse shots, and he may not decide which of these shots to use, or in what order, until the edit!

Given these problems, Sound Supervisors may often be tempted to record all live dialogue in mono, arguing that most viewers will have only a small screen, and very wide stereo would be ludicrous. However, the results from such mono shoots are often disappointing, and panning the dialogue from side to side to match the picture simply causes any coexisting natural effects or location atmosphere (picked up by the same mono microphone) to swing around too. It is generally better to attempt true stereo recording, even when the final choice of shots is not known. It can always be narrowed at the dub or even completely collapsed to mono for a short period if necessary.

Editing

For its first twenty-five years television was mostly live but, since the mid-1960s as videotape recorders became more plentiful, it has become mostly a recorded medium, with the notable exceptions mentioned earlier. However, the ability to record and edit programmes has brought a new problem.

It has become common practice to record a multi-camera sequence several times, and later edit between takes to use only the best bits of each. It is not uncommon for hundreds of edits to be performed, and most of these are usually motivated by the needs of vision, so creating problems with the sound. This is less likely in music shows, where the edits will largely be determined by the music. In drama situations, however, any sound effects or background music which were played in during the recording may cut awkwardly at the edit, and destroy continuity.

For this reason, it is now standard practice to concentrate at the recording stage on getting good clear dialogue and leave the addition of all the effects and music until after the pictures have been edited. They are then added in a post-production process known as dubbing or, in the USA, audio sweetening.

Dubbing

The dubbing of material which was shot on two or more cameras in long sequences is distinct from single-camera dubbing in that whole sections of the original 'live' sound will usually be in a more or less finished state, properly balanced, and with a suitable stereo image. This includes all the live dialogue, and the natural effects—those noises which the actors make as they move about the set. It may indeed include many sounds which are not required, and these must be removed before the production is ready for public viewing. Some of the original sound will have to be treated, and many new sound effects may have to be added in order to create the impression, for example, that two sheets of tile-patterned hardboard and a little steam are actually the corner of a large, busy Turkish Bath.

On the other hand, in the case of a single camera shoot, the Dubbing Mixer will have to construct a properly balanced dialogue track before he can start on the task of enhancing the atmosphere. Often the dialogue will be presented to him on several parallel tracks which may have different background sounds on them, and require different treatment to make them match. This may take a third of his time or even more.

Early systems of dubbing were very crude, using such equipment as was to hand. The edited programme was simply replayed from one videotape machine and re-recorded on to another, the sound being fed via a conventional mixing desk (Figure 27.1). Sounds were added and removed in real time. This was still essentially a 'live' operation and involved an element of operational risk if difficult things were being attempted. There were no synchronous tracks for track laying or pre-mixing in the manner of film dubbing, and all material except the original sound had to be played in entirely by the skill of the operators. A better system was required and there are now two basic approaches. One is based on a workstation, and the other on synchronized tape machines.

Synchronized machines

This system has been used increasingly since 1974. It relies on the use of timecode, an eight-digit code which identifies each individual frame of

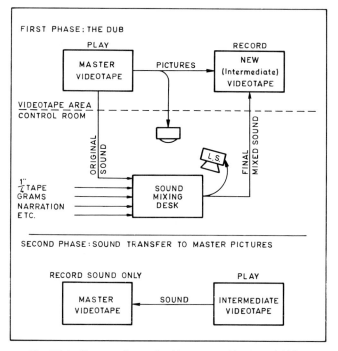

FIRST PHASE : THE DUB

PLAY   RECORD

MASTER VIDEOTAPE — PICTURES → NEW (Intermediate) VIDEOTAPE

VIDEOTAPE AREA
CONTROL ROOM

ORIGINAL SOUND

L.S.

FINAL MIXED SOUND

$\frac{1}{4}''$ TAPE
GRAMS
NARRATION
ETC. → SOUND MIXING DESK

SECOND PHASE : SOUND TRANSFER TO MASTER PICTURES

RECORD SOUND ONLY   PLAY

MASTER VIDEOTAPE ← SOUND — INTERMEDIATE VIDEOTAPE

Fig. 27.1. The two phases in videotape-to-videotape dubbing

picture in a 24-hour period. With 25 frames per second in British television, this represents well over two million separate addresses. Timecode is of course well known and widely used in the recording industry. It originates in a timecode generator (a kind of electronic clock) which gives an audio output (an unpleasant burbling noise). This can be fed down a cable and recorded on tape just like any other audio signal, or it can be fed into a timecode reader which then gives a digital display of the time, updated every twenty-fifth of a second. As a recording on tape, it is sometimes compared with the sprocket holes on film, but of course sprocket holes are all exactly the same, whereas timecode addresses are all different. If two tape machines with recordings of timecode are played into an appropriate interface unit (a synchronizer) it is possible to derive a control signal which will drive one of the machines into sync with the other and keep it there.

The operation begins in the videotape department, after the programme has been edited, and is visually complete. The edited master is replayed and the sound is copied on to two tracks of a multitrack sound recorder (Figure 27.2). Tracks 3 and 4 are used in the illustration. Timecode is copied on to the highest numbered track, in this case track 24. At the same time the pictures are copied on to a domestic or semi-professional videotape machine, along with timecode on one of its audio tracks. Mono sound may be copied on to the other. This will not be of very good quality but may be useful as a guide.

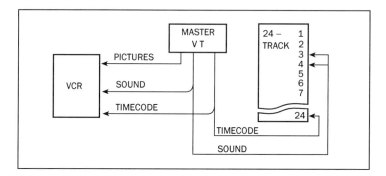

Fig. 27.2. Dubbing phase 1: transfer to multitrack recorder

The master videotape is not needed for the second phase of the operation, which is conducted in a dedicated suite using only the two copies (Figure 27.3). They are timecode locked in sync as described above. The pictures from the video machine are fed to a picture monitor and the stereo sound from the multitrack is fed to two channels of a sound mixing desk. One of the machines, usually the multitrack, is chosen as the master, and is remote controlled from the mixer. The other machine follows it in either

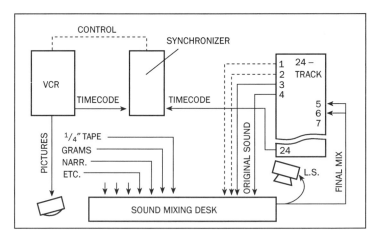

Fig. 27.3. Dubbing phase 2a: the dubbing operation

play or spool modes. Strictly, when in spool, the two machines are not locked in sync. In effect the slave is chasing the master, but within a few seconds of pressing the play button, they fall into sync, and a light indicates this condition to the Dubbing Mixer.

It is now possible to rehearse the first part of the show repeatedly, by simply playing and spooling back, until the results are satisfactory. The final sound is then recorded on to two other tracks of the multitrack (5 and 6 in the illustration), alongside the original sound. In practice, almost every attempt is recorded and, if unsatisfactory, recorded over at the next attempt. The first successful pass is therefore the only take preserved. This recording continues from the beginning of the show until something goes wrong with it. The tapes are then rewound by a few seconds and played. By pressing a balance (comp-check) button, the mixer can compare the level and balance of the last good part of the recording with the level and balance set up on the desk faders for the same section of programme. This ensures that there will be no step (in quality or level) on going into record again. This process of running the tapes back, going into play mode, balancing, and dropping into record is sometimes known as 'rock and roll', and it continues until the whole programme is completely re-recorded.

If parts of the programme are too difficult to get right in a single pass, the Mixer may resort to track-laying (Figure 27.4). Some element of the sound, let us say the music, is recorded on to spare tracks 1 and 2. The original sound is monitored during this process as a guide. After rewinding, the original sound and the music can be monitored while (say) mono narration is recorded on to track 23. All three tracks can then be monitored while some spot effects are recorded on to tracks 7 and 8, and so on. The levels are not

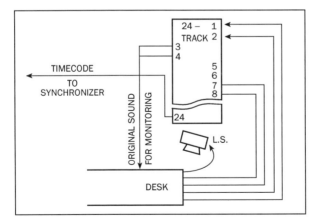

Fig. 27.4. Dubbing phase 2*b*: track laying

critical at this stage, only the timing. When sufficient tracks have been recorded, the Mixer can once again rewind the tape and mix the newly laid tracks with the original to produce the final mix, which will be recorded, as before, on to the final mix tracks.

If a large number of tracks is required, an additional 24-track recorder with a timecode striped tape can be locked to the system using an additional synchronizer. One track will be needed for the timecode, but that still leaves 23 for the audio, and in principle there is no limit to the number of machines which can be locked in. The timecode on these extra machines need not have identical times to the master machine, as an 'offset' can be used. For example, the master picture and sound programme tapes may start at 10 hours, 10 minutes, 10 seconds, 10 frames (i.e. 10 : 10 : 10 : 10), and the extra machine timecode may start at say 14 : 56 : 25 : 19. This problem would be solved by selecting a timecode offset of 04 : 46 : 15 : 09 in the synchronizer. Thereafter the machines would behave exactly as though they had the same timecodes. The same technique can be used for synchronizing quarter-inch tape machines, which may have extra heads to give an additional timecode track (centre track timecode).

The third phase of the operation is carried out back in the videotape area (Figure 27.5) where the multitrack tape is synchronized with the master pictures. The videotape machine is then put into 'record audio only' and the final sound is recorded back on to the master videotape ready for broadcast.

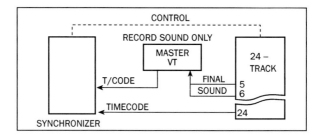

Fig. 27.5. Dubbing phase 3: transfer to master

There are many possible variations on the hardware that can be used for this system. For example, a bank of twin-track tape machines or synchronized DAT machines can be used in place of the multitrack. If digital video machines are used, two of their four digital audio tracks can be used for the original edited sound, and the other two for recording the final mix. This can mean dispensing with the first and third phases of the process completely.

Timecodes

The great technology explosion of recent years has made as great a contribution to video dubbing as to any other sector of the industry. Advanced cueing and mixing systems, using timecodes as triggers, have made very accurate work possible by taking it out of real time. Thus a very difficult operation, where several things have to be done in the space of half a second, can now be programmed into the computer over a period of a minute or two. This actually saves time because many attempts would be needed to achieve an acceptable result in real time. Here is an example. Suppose that an actor in a period piece has ad-libbed a word which is out of period. If this is not noticed at the time, an acceptable alternative word may have to be substituted at the dub. After recording the new word on quarter-inch tape, the following critical operations are necessary:

1. Play the quarter-inch tape of the new word at exactly the right time.
2. Play a quarter-inch tape of background atmosphere to match the original at exactly the right time. (This may be no more than one second long.)
3. Play a quarter-inch tape to simulate any sounds of movement which were under the original word.
4. At precisely the right moment and the right speed, mix from the original sound track to the three quarter-inch tapes.
5. At precisely the right moment (perhaps only six or seven frames later) mix back.
6. Stop all three quarter-inch machines.

If all the levels, equalizations, and reverberation are correct there is a good chance of success, but steps 1 to 5 may need to be accurate to one frame. It is a tall order for human operators, but much easier if those five critical events can be initiated automatically at predetermined timecodes.

Computer-assisted mixing

Computer-assisted sound mixing is useful because some programmes require a very complex mix, and even simple programmes often have one or two short but very difficult sections. Computer assistance is not always fully understood by those who have not had an opportunity to use it. The computer does not actually try to produce a mix without the aid of the Dubbing Mixer. Instead, it carefully notes some or all of the operations which he performs during a mix attempt, and it is capable of repeating them automatically on a subsequent pass of the same material. If, in practice, the first attempt to mix a section of the programme is satisfactory, then the computer need not be used. Also, if the first attempt is completely hopeless, there is little point in using the computer to recreate it. Most of the time, however, the first or second attempt at the mix will be fairly successful—only one or two things may need to be corrected. A further (manual) attempt at the mix may still not be perfect, however, because all the operations have to be performed correctly in the one pass. Frequently, the Dubbing Mixer will correct the previous faults but make a mess of something which he got right the first time. With computer assist, however, the previous mix attempt is repeated exactly by the computer, and the Dubbing Mixer is able to take control of those elements which he needs to change. This is a truly liberating experience because it allows him to concentrate fully on small but difficult elements of the mix. If the mix is still not quite right, the Dubbing Mixer can repeat the process, working either from his new updated computer mix or the old one which he used last time. He can repeat the process as many times as necessary, gradually refining the mix until he is satisfied with it. Only then will he rerun the final computer mix and record the audio on to the final track.

It is possible to store the computer data of a large number of mix attempts, so that they can be replayed and compared before a final choice is made and the final audio mix recorded. In some systems it is possible to combine the best sections of two or more 'data mixes' without even playing the material through. There are two approaches to this. In the first one, certain timed sections are chosen from each mix and the data from those sections is made into a new mix. This allows the Mixer to choose (say) the first thirty seconds from mix 1, the next forty from mix 3, and the rest from mix 2. These can be combined to make mix 4. The second approach is to take some faders from one mix and other faders from another. Thus the rhythm balance from mix 2 might be used with the front-line balance of mix 1. Although the value of these more esoteric techniques is not evident until one attempts an 'impossible' mix, computer-assisted mixing has improved productivity as well as product quality. At the same time, it has reduced the length of many sessions with the spin-off advantage that less-tired directors and Dubbing Mixers are able to make better programme decisions. Another, less desirable result has been the enormous rise in the capital cost of dubbing facilities.

Workstations

Digital audio workstations are now widely used in many branches of the industry. There are many different types ranging from inexpensive low-end versions intended for editing stereo, to high-end models useful in a dubbing situation. They basically work by recording sounds into some form of high-capacity digital store. This may, for example, be a computer hard disc, an optical disc, a magneto-optical disc, or any combination of these and other formats. The individual sounds, whether music, dialogue or effects, are recorded as 'cues' and named and listed in a library. Any cue can be replayed at any specified time-code, generated by an internal clock or supplied externally. In a dubbing situation, the video can be controlled by the workstation and follow its timecode, or the workstation can be made to chase the video recorder's timecode.

The cues can be directed to any one of a number of outputs (or two for stereo) and typically these outputs are represented graphically on a screen as tracks of a multitrack recorder. The required cues are placed against the timecode on these virtual tracks so as to coincide with the appropriate pictures in a kind of synchronous track laying. If one cue is not in quite the right position, it can be slipped in relation to the others (even the others on the same track) without disturbing them. Internal editing and track looping are also provided.

It is possible to set relative replay levels of the various cues on most of these machines, but many operators prefer to use external faders. Some manufacturers now offer digital sound desks which complement their workstations, and offer programmed facilities such as digital equalization as well as computer-assisted mixing.

The future

The history of video sound has been one of innovation, and there is no reason to suppose that this will cease. However, there are some clues as to what the future will bring. In the dubbing theatre, although workstations have achieved dominance in just a few years, the more traditional system, using multitrack machines and conventional sound desks, continues to be employed in many places. Yet, on a cost basis, it seems likely that workstations will gradually take over.

This does not mean the end of other recording formats, of course. In addition to digital video, it is evident that we shall be using a mixture of recording formats for the foreseeable future. Older ones, like quarter-inch tape, are still widely used for acquisition and therefore have to be supported. Synchronized multitracks (either analogue or digital) are still useful for tracklaying alongside workstations, and also for multitrack acquisition. DAT has come of age now that timecode in the subcodes is in common use.

Optical WORM (Write Once Read Many times) formats, including recordable CD continue to be of interest, though running costs have been a problem so far. Yet for many professional applications, CD-R and WORM formats have been overtaken by magneto-optical discs. Like optical WORM discs, these offer high recording density, but with the additional advantage that the recording can be over-written. It will be interesting to see how much of an impact magneto-optical technology has on acquisation equipment.

New formats in recent years have tended to come from research and development for the domestic hi-fi market. Examples are CD and DAT. Now the trend seems to be towards domestic products whose data compression makes them less attractive to professional users, and it appears likely that future spin-off products will come from business computer research. We already use RAM, computer hard discs, magneto-optical discs, and various other digital storage formats. Whatever the future holds, it looks as though 'audio for video' will continue to be one of the most interesting and challenging areas of work in this industry.

28

Film

Graham Hartstone and Tony Spath

This chapter looks at the many aspects of film sound, from recording and mixing through to the finished soundtrack as it is exhibited in the cinema. Almost all high-quality film soundtracks today are mixed for a stereo variable-area optical soundtrack that can reproduce four channels of sound in the cinema, Left, Centre, Right, and Surround (LCRS). By far the most widely used system for this is Dolby Stereo. Therefore this chapter mainly describes the stages used in the production and exhibition of Dolby Stereo soundtracks. Digital soundtracks are now a reality in cinemas, and these are also discussed, although it will be very many years before they reach the world-wide saturation of analogue optical soundtracks on 35-mm film. Compatible digital/analogue prints will therefore be with us for the foreseeable future.

Short history of cinema soundtracks

The photographic or 'optical' soundtrack was the first method of putting sound on film, and it remains the most popular. Several advantages have contributed to its universal acceptance, the foremost being economy. For one thing, the soundtrack is printed photographically on the film at the same time as the picture (Figure 28.1). For another, the soundtrack will have the same life expectancy as the picture.

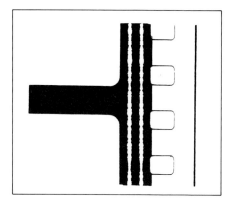

Fig. 28.1. A mono optical soundtrack. Light is directed through a slit and focused on the film soundtrack area. A light sensitive cell on the other side of the film picks up the resulting changes in intensity and produces an output voltage which varies in proportion to these changes. Two identical soundtracks are used to reduce distortion in the event of uneven distribution of light from the slit

By the mid-1930s, the 'talkies' were no longer a novelty but a necessity, and many thousands of cinemas were equipped in a short time to show films with optical soundtracks. This new medium—considered high quality at the time—provided a frequency response in the cinema of about 4 kHz and a dynamic range of around 20–30 dB. In the 1950s, a new magnetic method of putting sound on film was introduced as an alternative to the optical soundtrack. Magnetic sound was a significant step forward, providing much improved fidelity, and offering 'stereophonic' sound. This was not the two-channel Left/Right stereo we know today: Left, Centre, and Right speakers were used behind the screen and a fourth channel, from loudspeakers behind the audience, was used for effects.

By the 1970s, however, the film industry had declined overall, with fewer films and fewer cinemas. The expense of magnetic release prints, their comparatively short life compared with optical prints, and the high cost of maintaining magnetic cinema equipment led to a massive reduction in the number of magnetic releases and cinemas capable of playing them. The situation that prevailed in the mid-1970s was completely changed by the late 1980s. Thanks to new technology and a turnaround in the financial decline of the industry, almost all major titles today (accounting for 80% of the box office) are released with wide-range Dolby Stereo soundtracks.

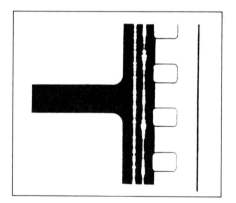

Fig. 28.2. A stereo optical soundtrack. Note the difference in modulation in the two channels of the track

The breakthrough was the development of a practical 35-mm stereo optical release print format (Figure 28.2). In the space allotted to the conventional mono optical soundtrack are two soundtracks which carry not only Left and Right information but also information for the third Centre-screen channel, and a fourth Surround channel for ambient sound and special effects (Figure 28.3). Further, the audio quality was much improved in terms of both dynamic range and frequency response.

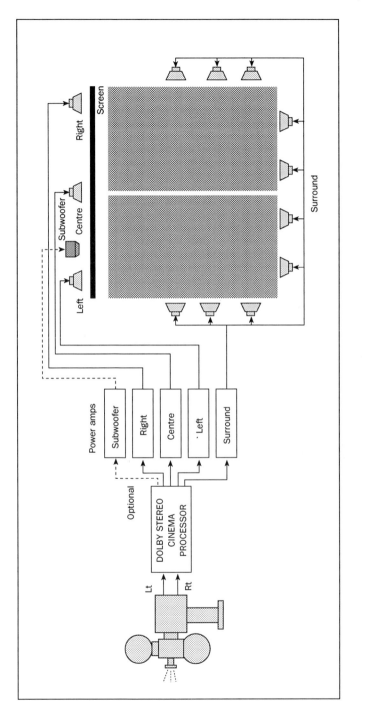

Fig. 28.3. Dolby Stereo cinema installation

Sound in the cinema today

Dolby Stereo

The Dolby Stereo format not only provides 4-channel sound from optical soundtracks, but higher-quality sound as well. Various techniques are applied to improve fidelity both when the soundtrack is recorded and when it is played back (Figure 28.4). These include:

(a) a stereo solar cell and optical preamplifier with slit loss equalization, which together give a response flat to 12 or even 14 kHz;

(b) Dolby noise reduction to lower the hiss and crackle associated with optical soundtracks, and give a dynamic range of 65 to 80 dB, depending on the noise reduction system used;

(c) loudspeaker equalization to adjust the cinema sound system to a standard response curve.

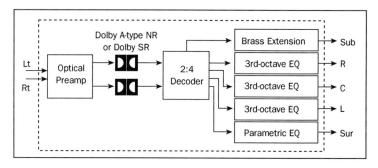

Fig. 28.4. Dolby Stereo cinema processor block diagram

This standard response for Dolby-equipped cinemas has led to a new world-wide playback standard for wide-range stereo prints for both dubbing theatres and cinemas, ISO 2969X (Figure 28.5), which is calibrated with pink noise. By taking account of the absorption at high frequencies by the cinema walls, etc. (the apparent roll-off on the curve), a subjectively flat response is obtained in a large hall.

All this means that these prints can be reproduced in cinemas equipped with Dolby cinema processors, to provide much wider frequency response and much lower distortion than conventional optical soundtracks. A stereo optical release print costs no more to make, and lasts as long as a mono print. Cinema and projector conversion to Dolby Stereo optical are relatively simple (20,000 cinemas world-wide have now converted) and, once the equipment has been installed, very little maintenance is required.

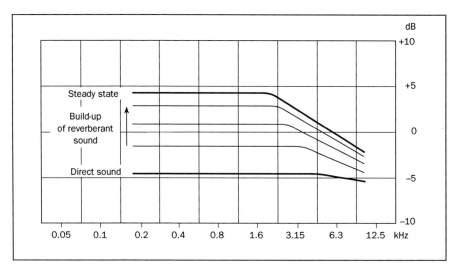

Fig. 28.5. The ISO 2969X equalization characteristic, showing the build-up of steady-state frequency response with pink noise in a reverberant room

Dolby Stereo SR

In 1986, Dolby Laboratories introduced a new professional sound recording process called Dolby SR (spectral recording). Like Dolby noise reduction, it is a mirror-image, encode/decode process to be used both when recording and playing back. Dolby Stereo SR 35-mm prints substitute Dolby SR encoding for Dolby A type. This provides more than twice the noise reduction of Dolby A type, and permits optical soundtracks to capture loud sounds with more accurate frequency response, and lower distortion.

Digital soundtracks in the cinema

Digital audio provides yet another step forward in film sound. The first digital soundtrack format for the cinema to gain wide acceptance was Dolby Stereo Digital, which incorporates a six-channel digital optical soundtrack (set between the film sprocket holes) in addition to a four-channel SR analogue track on the same 35-mm print (Figure 28.6). The prints can be played conventionally in any Dolby Stereo cinema, or the new digital optical track can be reproduced by adding digital readers to the projectors, and a digital decoder which interfaces with the cinema's existing Dolby Stereo processor. The six channels of the digital soundtrack are configured as Left, Centre, Right, Left Surround, Right Surround, and Subwoofer. This is the same loudspeaker format as the Dolby Stereo 70-mm magnetic with stereo surround, but without the expense of a 70-mm print, nor the magnetic stripe process.

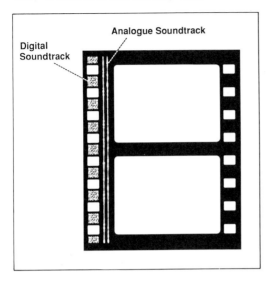

Digital Soundtrack

Analogue Soundtrack

Fig. 28.6. Dolby Stereo digital print

Other Digital Formats have since been released. These include the Matsushita/MCA/Universal DTS (Digital Theatre Sound), a 6-channel system in the same configuration as Dolby Stereo Digital, and Sony's SDDS (Sony Dynamic Digital Sound), which uses five full-range screen channels (Left, Inner Left, Centre, Inner Right, and Right), plus stereo Surrounds, and Subwoofer. DTS uses a digital soundtrack on CD-ROM discs linked to timecode printed optically on the film. SDDS prints two digital tracks on the outer edges of the film. Both systems to date also carry a standard Dolby Stereo optical soundtrack, so one print can be sent to digital and non-digital equipped cinemas. All three systems use bit rate reduction to squeeze the digital data into the restricted space of the chosen soundtrack storage format.

Just like high-quality CDs played on the best home stereo equipment, Dolby Stereo and digital soundtracks are capable of carrying a higher fidelity 'message' than previous formats. Cinemas need to look closely at their amplifier and speaker performance, as the digital soundtrack is capable of extremely wide dynamic range (Figure 28.7). A typical high-quality specification would require each screen speaker to reproduce undistorted signal peaks in excess of 103 dB SPL, when measured at the near-centre of the seating area. Digital soundtracks will reveal any quality defects introduced at the recording and mixing stages more obviously than before. Taking advantage of the new formats has thus required particular care with recording techniques—low background noise, noise- and distortion-free processing, and high-quality recording equipment such as 16-bit digital, or analogue with Dolby SR.

Production techniques for digital soundtracks are largely the same as for

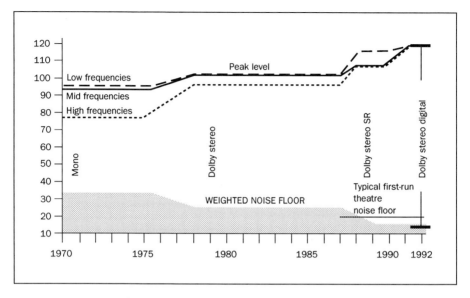

Fig. 28.7. Relative dynamic range: from mono to digital

Dolby Stereo, although SDDS requires more monitoring speakers. The principal difference is in the dynamic range, and digital soundtracks require special care here, as the print has a potentially wider dynamic range than all but the very best equipped cinemas can reproduce. The mixer and director have to be particularly aware of how best to use this. Typically the dialogue level is the reference around which the loud peaks and soft details are judged. Admittedly, the results can vary—the final reproduced soundtrack can be no better than the elements it contains—but at its best it results in not only better-quality sound, but sound which consistently realizes in the cinema itself the director's original intentions.

Multi-channel soundtracks

There are several stages in the production of a multi-channel film soundtrack (see Figure 28.8). Cinema stereo is four-channel (LCRS), but there is only space in the soundtrack area on the film for two tracks. During the early stages of post-production, while LCR and S pre-mixes are being built up from mono or 2-channel elements, the soundtracks are kept discrete, usually as 4-track masters. At the final mix or dub, these four channels are encoded to a 2-track master, for subsequent transfer to optical. Matrix technology is used for the 4-to-2 encoding and for the 2-to-4 decoding in the cinema.

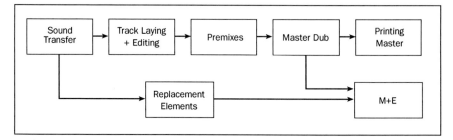

Fig. 28.8. Producing the Dolby Stereo soundtrack

Just as when a sound-only recording is being mixed, the object when mixing music for film is that it should reproduce predictably in its intended listening environment, whilst achieving the artistic aims and intentions of the producer/performers/engineers. Since no matrix can provide the stability and channel separation of a discrete system, it is common practice to listen 'through the matrix' (i.e. linking the matrix encoder and decoder into the monitor chain) while mixing multi-channel elements. This allows the mixing engineer to hear exactly how the matrix will affect his sound, and to adjust it accordingly (Figure 28.9).

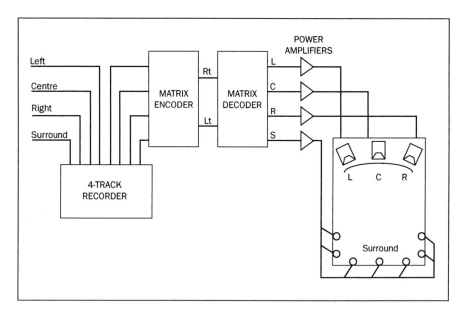

Fig. 28.9. Pre-mixing a stereo film soundtrack

For Dolby Stereo, film studios install a matrix encoder (the DS4E) and a Dolby cinema processor. These are used back to back in the monitoring chain during the pre-mixing stages but, when the final 2-track master is made, the encoder is switched so that the recorded signal passes through it alone, to produce the two encoded tracks, Left total (Lt) and Right total (Rt) (Figure 28.10)

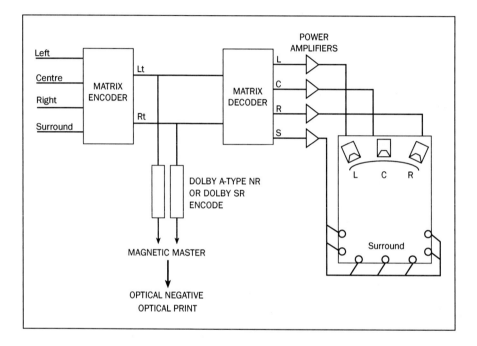

Fig. 28.10. Mastering a stereo film soundtrack

The LCRS monitoring system should be representative of that found in cinemas; and the ISO 2969X curve is used. Unlike in the home situation, the listener in a cinema cannot get up and alter the volume, so a standard-ized relationship between signal level on film and the resulting acoustic level is also important. For Dolby Stereo films, this has been set so that pink noise at Dolby level gives an acoustic SPL of 85 dB(c) from each chan-nel—and Dolby level corresponds to 50% modulation on the optical sound-track; hence signal level on film is linked to acoustic SPL in the cinema.

How the soundtrack is produced

Planning

When planning a film soundtrack, there are many factors to consider. If usable original recordings are important, then it is better to record in a studio sound stage than on location, where there may be noisy background interference. If it is essential to shoot on location, then the sound mixer should be consulted on the choice of site.

For the two stages of post-production (track laying, and mixing), a schedule should be drawn up and stuck to. It is better to work longer hours at the beginning of a project, to avoid getting so far behind that it becomes impossible to catch up later. At all stages it is important to ensure that all recordings, and the presentation of sound material, are suitable for the final release format.

Location recording

All location recording is now carried out on sophisticated portable equipment. Most common is the stereo Nagra using ¼-inch (6.3-mm) tape at 7½ ips (19 cm/s). Synchronization can be either from an FM pulse, or timecode if the Nagra is so equipped. If the transfer bay to be used is suitably equipped, then Dolby SR recordings are advisable. Portable encoders are available.

There is increasing use of DAT for original recording, which often relies purely on an internal crystal for sync. This seems to work adequately over short recordings, but the only way to ensure absolute sync is to use timecode. Having chosen a digital format for acquisition, it is quite likely that the material will be edited on a digital workstation, so the analogue rushes transfers will be used only as a work print. If this is the case, then the original timecode should be recorded on to a spare track on the work print, to make it possible to create an edit decision list in post-production.

The latest addition to field recording options is the Nagra D, which records four digital tracks on open reel ¼-inch tape. This has the unique feature that it provides a full-level recording throughout. The modulation levels are encoded as a 'control track'. The desired levels, as mixed, are faithfully repeated on playback. This control track can be overridden, if necessary, to retrieve a signal that was 'potted out' during recording. The Nagra D can also record timecode. All use of timecode must be clearly documented to avoid confusion due to the variations of frame rate and mains frequency throughout the world.

With the exception of the Nagra D (which records in two pairs) all other production recorders use one or two tracks. These can be used in a variety of ways: Mono, AB Stereo, MS, or two separate Mono pickups (e.g. personal mic and boom). When choosing the format, thought should be given to the end requirements; for example, MS can prove unsuitable for Dolby Stereo release because of the inherent phase shifts. There is a school of thought which considers MS an inadequate system for any stereo drama format because, if the microphone points forward on the same axis as the camera, the correct stereo image for the sides will be maintained, but the middle, and therefore the artists, will go 'off mic' as they move to the edge of frame. If the microphone is made to follow the artist, then the stereo image will be incorrect—a compromise at best. Indeed any form of stereo dialogue is going to attract unwanted attention to reverse cuts during dialogue scenes. Therefore most post-production mixers agree that it is better to have a good clean mono dialogue track, with separate complementary stereo atmospheres.

Accurate documentation is essential, and the relevant information must be relayed to the dubbing mixer. Many hours can be wasted trying to obtain the best mixture of microphone pickups, when a note on the cue sheet would convey the production mixer's intentions. Whenever the original dialogue is unusable or suspect, a wildtrack shot at the time will provide an alternative which will match in performance, mic characteristic, and acoustics. Profanities and blasphemy should also be covered with a wild alternative, as almost all productions will require a censored version for TV or 'in-flight' movies.

When making digital dialogue recordings, it is worth remembering the possibly narrower dynamic range of the end product. With the absence of a perceptible noise floor, it is tempting to make very low-level recordings which allow enormous headroom in case the artist shouts. This extended dynamic range is likely to be too great to transfer successfully on to many analogue recorders and, in any event, the dynamics will have to be restricted at some stage before final release. It is much better to learn the dialogue, and modulate the recording using the same parameters employed for analogue recording. In difficult and unknown circumstances, a safe method is to record one track at an appropriate level, with the same signal routed to a second track say 20 dB lower. If the mixer is caught out by an unexpected shout, then the lower-level track will probably be saved by the extra headroom; again accurate documentation is essential.

Whilst on location, the production mixer should collect useful recordings of atmospheres, crowds, action vehicles, etc. A second recorder is often used for this purpose. All Sound Effects (FX) must be comprehensively logged for the Sound Editor.

Sound transfer

Ideally, new sound transfers should be made for presentation to the dubbing theatre. If this is not possible, a good practice is to make a Dolby SR encoded transfer on to tracks 2 and 3 of the 35-mm tape, with a non-Dolby combined signal on track 1. The combined track may suffer wear and tear during the editing process, while the encoded tracks 2 and 3 will remain in good condition for the final mix. The noise reduction will greatly alleviate the usual problems associated with tape joins, etc. Any problems perceived by the transfer operator should be reported to the mixer immediately.

Sound editing

When track laying for a conventional analogue film, the original sound recording will be split into categories as follows. The usable main dialogue will be laid on AB rolls with overlaps of background sounds, so that the Dubbing Mixer can standardize the dialogue levels, and match the voice qualities with equalization, and acoustic processing. The overlaps in background sounds may need to be extended with matching tracks so that smooth transitions from each camera angle can be achieved. All remaining sync sound is usually compiled into a 'strip track' which may be used as reference.

If a digital workstation is used to prepare tracks, the chosen takes can be automatically conformed into sync using an edit decision list (EDL) which has been derived from the edited picture. A lot of the Dubbing Mixer's work can be carried out by the Sound Editor on a workstation. For example, approximate levels can be set, the backgrounds that needed to be split and extended on film can be smoothed out by careful manipulation in the workstation, and, as all edits are non-destructive, fewer tracks will be used to maintain separation. The sound quality should remain as good as the original recording.

Dialogue replacement

Where the production sound is unusable or unsuitable, the dialogue is replaced by 'post sync' recording. This is commonly called ADR (Automatic Dialogue Replacement), which is something of a misnomer since it automates only the shuttling of the picture (and recorders), the artists' cues, and the record on/off controls. The artists watch their performance in cut sequences of suitable duration. The ADR system will shuttle over each section until a satisfactory take for both sync and performance is recorded. To assist, there are audible and visual cues programmed to the start of each sentence. The original sound is reviewed first, and is always available on headphones as an aid, along with a dialogue script.

Recording can be on almost any medium, the conventional 35 mm, 3 or 4 track, Multitrack, DAT, or on to a magneto-optical disc via a digital workstation. Some workstations offer the facility to fit the new recordings automatically to the original guide track by comparison—a very useful option if not abused. However, it is still advisable to accept only the best sync possible when recording. It is common practice to record a backup on ¼-inch tape or DAT, which kicks into record at each attempt by the artist. If it is decided after the session that a chosen take is not suitable, there is usually a multitude of alternatives on this backup recording. It is very important to ensure that the artist's performance is compatible with the scene. There is a tendency to underplay when in a silent studio. In reality, the scene may have a loud background to overcome, storm, traffic, aircraft, etc. A quick check with the guide track will indicate the level of voice projection necessary.

In general, it is prudent to provide a good full-level recording, leaving all perspective, equalization, and room acoustics until the final mix. There may be ADR from different sources, and almost certainly original tracks, which the Dubbing Mixer must combine into a convincing scene. However, if only part of a scene is to be replaced, care should be taken to match the perspective, voice quality, and pitch. It is often safer to 'post-sync' the whole scene to avoid quality changes. For part scenes or short sections, a wildtrack shot at the location is often the best solution. It should be remembered that, when the original is discarded, *all* the sounds and acoustics of the scene must be recreated.

Footsteps and sound effects

Foley is the commonly used term for all Sound FX recorded in sync after production, named after the effects operator who pioneered it years ago. As well as the actual footsteps and movements of the artists on screen, all other sounds, e.g. doors, keys, fight noises, cutlery, and crockery (everything including the legendary coconut shells for horse's hooves) are recorded using a similar procedure to the ADR. Appropriate attention should be given to the sounds that are most important to the scene.

A Foley theatre will have various surfaces for walking, e.g. road, pavement, solid and hollow wooden floors, sand and gravel troughs etc., and a water tank. There will be a seemingly endless supply of props, from large sections of vehicles to cups and saucers. Any props which are unique to the film or scene, such as musical instruments or firearms, should be made available at the footsteps session. The footsteps artists or Foley walkers are skilled in their art, often with experience in dancing which helps them to assimilate quickly the rhythm of a walk. They usually work in pairs, and bring along suitcases filled with a variety of shoes. All footsteps and FX in the film are recorded separately from the dialogue, so that a 100% international track can be created when all the original English language dialogue is removed. A certain separation must be maintained for subsequent stereo panning, and perspective. Footsteps should approach and continue off screen when an artist enters or leaves frame.

All Sound FX that cannot be recreated in a Foley theatre are obtained either from sound libraries or, if necessary, specially recorded. Unusual action vehicles that may feature in a film will be retained after production for an FX recording session. This is often scheduled at night to eliminate birdsong. Such tracks of action vehicles should be recorded in mono, as any stereo pass is unlikely to fit the action after it has been edited. Crowds and atmospheres, however, should be recorded in stereo. For Dolby Stereo release, a configuration of two widely spaced microphones with little or no programme phase coherency produces the best result.

The dubbing theatre

When all the prepared tracks arrive in the dubbing theatre, the mixer's first priority is to pre-mix the dialogues. Typically he or she will arrange the console so that a selection of sound processors is readily to hand. A compressor will be used to restrict the dynamic range of speech, to ensure that the low sections are not lost when other sounds or music are added. This will also contain the peaks to within the prescribed limits for the final release. If the dialogue suffers from sibilance, a de-esser will be used. This is particularly important if the final track is to be transferred to optical, where sibilants can cause problems if the transfers and printing are not perfect. Noise gates, expanders, and notch filters may be employed to reduce background sounds, and clarify the dialogue but, as all such devices degrade the voice quality to some extent, their use should be sparing.

It is at this stage that any ADR or wildtracks will be blended into a smooth and convincing scene. Telephone effects and other voice treatments will also be applied. Certain elements will be routed to separate tracks in order to allow flexibility in the final mix. Any specific acoustic treatments will be noted so that the same can be applied to footsteps, etc.

When the dialogue pre-mix has been completed, it will be played into the monitor for reference during subsequent pre-mixes. Assuming that all the important dialogue has been given priority, then all the other sounds will be balanced around and under it for maximum dramatic effect, whilst maintaining intelligibility. Each shot should be analysed to establish what part it plays in the narrative. Obviously the most common aspect of the story is the dialogue, but the important feature may be silence, approaching footsteps, specific action, etc. Some cuts progress the action, while others are not intended to be noticed by the viewer. For a series of close-ups during a conversation, the soundtrack should have smooth transitions to avoid drawing attention to the cuts. In scene changes, time lapse, and dramatic shock cuts, the soundtrack can enhance the narrative and clarify the story.

Sound FX pre-mixing

The Sound FX tracks will be pre-mixed as required (Figure 28.11). For a busy action picture it is useful to plan ahead by first studying the cue

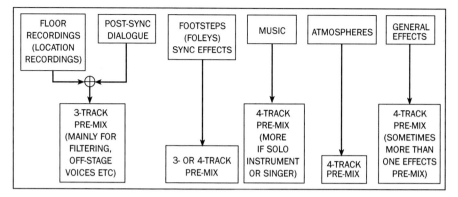

Fig. 28.11. Typical film soundtrack premixes

sheets for each reel, and sorting the laid tracks into groups or categories which can be mixed together. If the tracks are well prepared, they will have been laid for pre-mixing. For example, all the vehicles may be on tracks 1–6, explosions on 7–14, gunshots on 15–20, atmospheres on 21–5. It can be very frustrating for a dubbing mixer to have to pick out birdsong amongst explosions, or a door closing between gunshots. Far simpler to know that tracks 1–6 will contain all the vehicles, etc.

Important 'on screen' Sound FX are pre-mixed first. If the footsteps are to be pre-mixed, care should be taken not to over-pan the principals as their dialogue will almost certainly remain in the centre. Atmosphere or backgrounds, although often left until last, are vital to the soundtrack. They provide the environment or mood of the scene. A well-chosen atmosphere can contain subtle punctuation which will enhance the drama. Atmosphere is also paramount in establishing location changes or time lapses, and forms the common bedrock of sound which allows all the individual sounds from various sources to blend into a realistic soundtrack. Each Sound Effect will be equalized, panned, and played for the required dramatic effect, with frequent reference to the dialogue in order to maintain clarity. As much separation as possible is advisable so that variations of balance and emphasis can be tried in the final mix, particularly where music is to be introduced.

Music

Most music tracks are recorded and mixed in multitrack music studios and transferred to film for dubbing. In effect the music studio supplies the music pre-mix. (This may of course be different in the case of a musical film or if there is a complicated on-screen source effect to create. Here a pre-mix would probably be done in the film dubbing studio.) As films with budgets large enough to afford the recording of special music, rather than relying on library tracks, are now largely being released with Dolby Stereo soundtracks, music studios will install a special studio monitor combination for film soundtrack work. The combination contains the encoding matrix (the SEU4) and the reference Dolby Stereo matrix decoder (in the SDU4), allowing the music engineer to hear exactly how the matrix will affect his sound, and adjust his mix accordingly. The 2-track output of the encoder (Lt, Rt) is hard-wired to the 2-track input of the decoder for music studio use. This configuration is therefore identical to that for pre-mixing in film studios (Figure 28.11). In addition, there is a monitoring section on the SDU4 output: this has a 4-channel monitor level control (most music studios have only a stereo monitor control) and mono and stereo buttons for compatibility checks. Finally there is a pink noise facility for calibrating the acoustic level to 85 dB(c) from each monitor channel, the standard listening level in Dolby Stereo mixing facilities and cinemas alike.

The basic difference between the conventional stereo mixing carried out every day in recording and mixing records, and the mixing of music for Dolby Stereo films, is in the number of monitoring channels. A third speaker must be installed as a centre channel. As the front stereo information is carried on three and not two speakers, this third speaker and its power amplifier should be the same type as used for the left and right channels. In cases where speakers are built in, it is often best to install three separate high-quality speakers and amplifiers on a temporary basis.

At least two further speakers must be used behind the listeners for the surround channel. These do not need to be very high quality. The idea is to present a soundfield, rather than specific point sound location, hence the use of more than one surround loudspeaker. (A good cinema will use surround speakers all around the walls of the back half of the auditorium to create this effect.) The surround channel is band limited, removing extreme high-frequency sound which would otherwise result in the listener hearing a series of point sources rather than a soundfield.

The format on to which the Music is mixed, and the track configuration (LCR, LCRS, LRS, etc.) should be discussed with the studio where the film will finally be mixed. In cases where a solo instrument is particularly important, or where it needs to be panned, this is placed on a separate track, so that the final decision can be taken in the dubbing theatre. Typically the music will ultimately be transferred to 35-mm magnetic film stock for this mix and, if a music studio can mix directly to this, then a tape generation will be saved. Any other formats used should be able to run 'synchronized'.

Provided the music is mixed with the matrix included in the monitoring chain, whatever is heard in the music studio will be pretty much how it will sound in the cinema. In general, the stereo will need to be mixed 'wide' to avoid a build-up of centre channel sound through the matrix. Similarly, some of the stereo generation effects used on synthesizers, chorusing, and digital reverberation will cause some sound to come from Surround. Listening through the matrix allows the engineer to make real-world judgements as to whether these effects are desirable or need controlling. Any other differences will most likely be due to reverberation added by the larger cinema acoustic. This is normally taken into account by the music mixer.

Final mixing

The aim is to start the final mix with all the pre-mixes as close to the final balance as possible (Figure 28.12). The advantage of careful pre-mixing will now become apparent. The director will be seeing his film with all the sound elements for the first time. He should be able to view it in large sections, hopefully whole reels. This gives a far better perspective to the piece, and, with an automated console, the balances can be honed down to suit the action with repeatable accuracy. As this is probably the first time the music is heard with all the sound FX, the reasons for separation in pre-mixing will be appreciated. The internal balance of various sounds when standing on their own is often very different from that required when balancing with music. It may be that no atmospheres are used at all where the music provides the requisite mood and environment.

The final mix will be monitored in the chosen release format, and recorded on some form of multitrack. The Dub Masters or 'Stems' (stereo masters) have the dialogue, FX, and music routed separately. It may be to

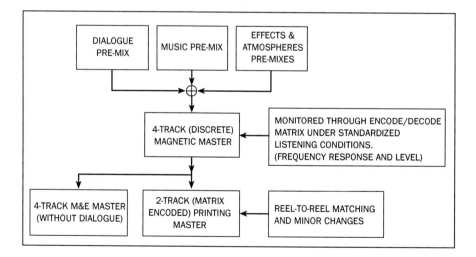

Fig. 28.12. Dolby Stereo final mix

three stereo pairs for TV, or three 6-tracks for cinema release, depending on the transmission or exhibition format. All the delivery requirements in the form of Print Masters will be mixed down from these stems, so the separation allows for re-balancing, equalization, and dynamic processing to suit each format. An international master can also be derived by omitting the dialogue track, and replacing all footsteps and FX which were only on the original recording. Foreign territories add their own language dialogue later.

Equipment

A typical dubbing theatre for feature films will have one or more film projectors, numerous 35-mm replay machines offering up to 6-track play from each, a large automated film-mixing console with noise reduction available for each input, and a variety of sound processors. Recording could be on any multitrack medium, but is most commonly on 35-mm 4- or 6-track recorders—with separate left, centre, right, surround, and bass channels for the three elements, dialogue, FX, and music. As can be seen from Figure 28.10, many soundtrack elements may need to be played back at one time, each requiring numerous channels of noise reduction as well as console inputs.

There is no doubt that, as digital equipment becomes more available, and its operation becomes second nature to talented technicians, all sound acquisition, post-production, and exhibition will be in the digital medium. Digital acquisition and sound editing are now commonplace. Digital assignable mixing consoles are less common, but available. In theory, this means that one person with a digital workstation which incorporates a fully automated digital mixing console could edit and mix an entire action feature soundtrack, one track at a time. However, in practice this would eliminate the infinite variety of creative input that naturally occurs when a well-chosen team works in close harmony.

Optical transfer

Once the film has been mastered as an encoded LtRt 2-track, it is then converted to an optical soundtrack. This transfer is made with a stereo optical recorder on to a photographic sound negative, which is ultimately married to the edited picture negative. The optical recorder (Figure 28.13) consists of a light-tight chamber containing a stereo light valve, and a system of lenses through which the unexposed negative passes. The stereo light valve consists of two pairs of metal ribbons clamped vertically under tension in a strong magnetic field. Audio signals cause these ribbons to vibrate, letting through varying amounts of light from an exposure lamp to expose the soundtrack negative.

The exposed negative is developed and dried before printing on to the

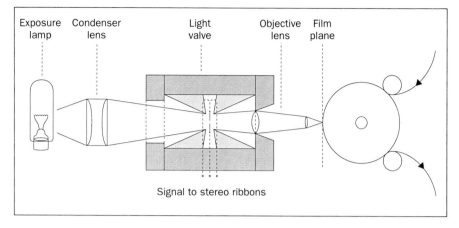

Exposure lamp   Condenser lens   Light valve   Objective lens   Film plane

Signal to stereo ribbons

Fig. 28.13. Principal components of a stereo optical recorder

final print stock, and subsequent developing. Photographic emulsions tend to diffuse an exposed image slightly, with audible distortion on transients and high frequencies as the result. This must be controlled by carefully matching the print density and negative density with the chemical strengths, temperatures, and developing times in the laboratory. In general the parameters for the positive process are kept constant, and matched by varying those for the negative. If these are adhered to, the transfer is basically a one-to-one process.

Multi-channel sound in the home

Nowadays there is considerable potential for producers to extend the earning power of their film productions through video, cable, and broadcasting rights. It is now normal for feature films to be released on video, shown soon after release on cable and pay-TV channels, and, some time later— usually proportional to the box-office success of the film—broadcast on public TV. With this increase in availability of film, and better quality multi-channel soundtracks in the home, the consumer hi-fi industry has turned its attention to the 'Home Cinema' market with multi-channel sound systems for use with video and TV.

The driving force behind this is the same matrix technology as used by the film industry. In the cinema it is called Dolby Stereo; the home equivalent is called Dolby Surround. An LtRt film soundtrack can be transferred to video, just as well as optical. The dynamic range may need to be adjusted—viewers at home do not necessarily need, or want, the wide dynamic range found in the cinema—but, when an LtRt track is transferred to video for broadcast or duplication, the encoded centre and surround information remains embedded in the 2-channel signal.

A Dolby Surround decoder provides matrix decoding facilities similar to those in Dolby Stereo decoders in the cinema, but without the optical pre-amplifiers, professional Dolby noise reduction, one-third octave equalization, etc. In this way the consumer can hear cinema-like multi-channel sound in the home.

Films are widely broadcast, or released on video, with Dolby Surround soundtracks. The encoded tracks are analogue, so they can be recorded or broadcast in conventional 2-channel stereo. The viewer can choose to view them in mono, 2-channel stereo, or 4-channel surround sound. Millions of homes are already equipped with decoders. In addition, Dolby Surround productions are also increasingly being made specifically for television and related video media. These programmes include drama, music, light entertainment, and sport.

What of the future? Widescreen television will certainly go hand in hand with multi-channel sound. A '5.1' channel standard has been recommended in this context by the SMPTE: this would provide Left, Centre, Right, Left-Surround, and Right-Surround wide-band channels, plus an optional Subwoofer channel for low-frequency effects. Dolby Stereo Digital is already using this format in the cinema. The audio coding used for Dolby Stereo Digital, called AC-3, is also the basis of the next generation of multi-channel consumer audio technology, Dolby Surround Digital. To underline the importance of this, AC-3 has been adopted as the standard for future HDTV systems in the USA. Dolby Surround Digital will allow the transfer of Dolby Stereo Digital cinema soundtracks to a new home format. Unlike analogue surround, the AC-3 audio is carried in one single bitstream. The basic monitoring arrangements for the home, like the studio, will require only the addition of AC-3 decoding, extra amplifiers, and loudspeakers.

With so many Dolby Stereo and Surround encoded programmes already in existence, compatibility is an important issue. The AC-3 consumer decoder is therefore able to decode (to analogue) 2-channel LtRt for subsequent surround decoding with a Dolby Surround Pro-Logic decoder, so that the programme will be reproduced as originally intended. On the other hand, some consumers may not have full 5-channel reproduction systems. Here the AC-3 decoder is able to down-mix 5-channel productions to any speaker format less than 5 that the consumer might have.

Conclusion

Mixing sound for multi-channel productions tomorrow will be very similar to mixing for conventional Dolby Stereo or Surround today. It will require a different encoder, the mixing console will require five channels (rather than four) with a master level control, and extra monitoring channels will be needed for the stereo surrounds.

Film production still provides the highest-quality picture and sound, demanding the utmost from sound mixers and soundtrack production techniques alike. It is logical that film will continue to be a principal source for sound-with-picture software, for use inside and outside the cinema, and that current and coming technology will spread the transfer of these high-quality multi-channel soundtracks to the home. From its beginnings in the cinema—where it still continues to flourish—to digital surround in the home, multi-channel sound-for picture will be the standard format in the future, encompassing film, video, and multimedia.

29 Legal rights and sound recordings

Nick Rann

There are a number of contributors involved in the creation of a sound recording, and each of those contributors may acquire a variety of legal rights. Anybody wishing to make, copy, or otherwise exploit sound recordings must ensure that all necessary rights have been obtained from these contributors. In order to explain more about those rights and those who enjoy them, let us look at the process of making a sound recording of pop music.

The principal contributors to a pop record are usually as follows:

1. The songwriter who composes the song to be performed and recorded.
2. The publisher or collection society which licenses the rights in the song composed by the songwriter.
3. The musicians and vocalists whose performances of that song are recorded.
4. The individual producer who directs the administrative, creative, and technical aspects of the recording session.
5. The sound engineer responsible for recording the performances and creating pleasing sounds.
6. The recording studio used to make the recording.
7. The record company which commissions and pays for the recording.

These are four main types of right which the law grants to these contributors namely, copyright, moral rights, performers' rights, and property rights. Copyright, moral rights, and performers' rights are all dealt with under the Copyright, Designs and Patents Act 1988 (the 'Copyright Act'). These three types of right fall into the broad category of rights known as 'intellectual property rights'. They arise in respect of the material captured on a master tape rather than the physical master tape itself. The fourth category, property rights, relates to ownership of the physical master tape.

Copyright generally

Sound recordings and songs are both 'works' which attract copyright protection. Copyright is the collective name given to a bundle of rights granted initially to the 'author' of the copyright work concerned. The 'author' of sound recordings and songs has the exclusive right to use and exploit those recordings and songs in a number of ways. These exclusive rights may be licensed or transferred outright to third parties such as record companies, publishers, and collection societies.

The 'author' of a song is the person who wrote it. However, as we shall see later, the term 'author' in relation to a sound recording is more artificially defined in the Copyright Act. As a result the 'author' of a sound recording may be a number of different people.

Copyright in songs

Looking first at the song to be recorded, the songwriter, as author and first owner of the copyright in his songs, has the exclusive right to copy his songs. By copy, we mean reproducing them in any material form, for example, by making a sound recording of performances of those songs. The songwriter also has the exclusive right to issue copies of his songs to the public. Examples of copies include printed editions and records such as compact discs. He also has the exclusive right to perform the songs in public and to broadcast them or include them on any cable programme service. The songwriter also has the exclusive right to make an 'adaptation' (i.e. an arrangement or transcription) of his songs. Anybody else wishing to do any of these things will need to obtain permission from the songwriter or, as we shall see, a publisher or collection society acting on his behalf.

It is common for songwriters to enter into exclusive songwriting agreements with publishers who thereby acquire the copyright in the songs written by such songwriters. It is the publisher's function to control the licensing and exploitation of these songs and to divide the proceeds of exploitation with the songwriters.

Most songwriters and publishers in the United Kingdom belong to an organization, the full title of which is The Performing Right Society Limited, but which is generally known as the PRS. As a condition of membership, songwriters transfer to the PRS that part of the bundle of rights comprising the copyright in their songs which relates to their public performance and broadcast. The PRS administers these rights on the songwriter and publisher's behalf.

Similarly, many songwriters and publishers belong to the Mechanical Copyright Protection Society Limited. The MCPS, as it is known, administers that part of its members' copyright which relates to the reproduction of their songs in any material form. Examples of this include making master recordings of those songs and manufacturing records reproducing those masters.

It is important to appreciate that the copyright in a song is entirely separate from the copyright in any recording of that song. Because these two different rights often operate in tandem, the distinction between them is easily blurred. Most acts which infringe copyright in a sound recording also infringe copyright in the song which is the subject of that recording. This means that doing a single unauthorized act in relation to a sound recording, such as broadcasting it, may constitute an infringement of the copyrights in both the sound recording *and* the underlying song. Licences are required in respect of *both* copyright works.

Copyright in sound recordings

Under the Copyright Act, the 'author' of a sound recording is defined as 'the person by whom the arrangements necessary for the making of the recording . . . are undertaken'. Although there is no clear case law on the subject at the time of writing, it seems that a number of contributors to the creation of a recording could be considered to be its co-authors. For example, the individual producer, the engineer, the studio, the record company and even perhaps the musicians and vocalists may all play some part in making the necessary arrangements, thus allowing them to claim part authorship of the finished masters. The strength of these claims has yet to be tested in court.

The author of a sound recording is the original owner of the copyright in that recording. The owner of the copyright is granted certain exclusive rights in relation to the sound recording much in the same way as the songwriter is granted exclusive rights in his song. In particular, the copyright owner has the exclusive right to copy the sound recording, to issue copies of the sound recording to the public, to perform or broadcast the sound recording, to include it in a cable programme service or to make an adaptation of it. It follows that anybody else wishing to do any of those things will need permission from the copyright owner or owners.

Performers' rights

The musicians and vocalists (and also actors in the case of spoken word tapes) whose performances are reproduced on a sound recording generally attract so-called 'performers' rights' under the Copyright Act. This means that the performer (and in some cases any record company with whom he has entered into an exclusive recording contract) has the right to prevent others from making and exploiting recordings of his performances. That right is infringed by playing a recording of those performances in public or broadcasting it without the performer's (or his record company's) consent.

Moral rights

Under the Copyright Act the songwriter is also granted another bundle of legal rights known collectively as 'moral rights'. These include the right for the songwriter to be identified as the author of his songs whenever they are published commercially, whenever records embodying recordings of his songs are issued to the public, and whenever his songs are played as part of the soundtrack to a film. Although the songwriter is required to 'assert' this right before he can rely on it, he need only sign a written declaration to that effect to satisfy this requirement.

Another 'moral' right is the right for the songwriter to object to 'derogatory treatment' of his songs. What 'derogatory treatment' means is not entirely clear. However, the Copyright Act provides that for a treatment to be 'derogatory' it must amount to a 'distortion or mutilation' of the songs or be 'otherwise prejudicial to the honour or reputation' of the songwriter concerned. This right is infringed if someone publishes a derogatory treatment of a song, performs it in public, broadcasts it, or sells copies of records reproducing the derogatory treatment to the public.

Whilst it is common for a songwriter to transfer the copyright in his songs to a publisher, the Copyright Act forbids him from transferring his moral rights during his lifetime. This situation creates difficulties when creating and recording parodies of well-known songs for use in TV commercials. The parody may amount to an 'adaptation' of the song, thus infringing the publisher's copyright, *and* a 'derogatory treatment' of the song, thus infringing the songwriter's moral rights. Unless the songwriter has given up or 'waived' his moral rights, permission to broadcast a recording of the parody is required from both the publisher *and* the songwriter. Even after a songwriter's death his moral rights may continue to be exercisable by his nominees or heirs.

How do the various rights identified above affect the process of making a sound recording and manufacturing copies of that recording for retail sale?

Practical implications of legal rights

(*a*) Making a recording

1. MCPS. If a recording features performances of a song which attracts copyright protection then the act of making the recording is an infringement of the copyright in the song concerned.

Does this mean that every time a group goes into the studio to record a cover of a Lennon/McCartney song, for example, it needs a licence to do so from the MCPS even before records of that recording are manufactured? Strictly speaking, the answer is yes. This does not present a problem for the larger record companies with a proven credit record who are accepted on to a licence scheme issued by the MCPS known as the AP1 Agreement. The AP1 Agreement grants these companies the blanket right to make master recordings which feature any songs from the MCPS repertoire.

However, smaller record companies are required by the MCPS to follow fairly strict procedures in order to obtain licences to make recordings and to press records featuring songs from the MCPS repertoire. It is only after this procedure has been properly concluded that the smaller record company obtains the right to manufacture records *or* make the master recording concerned. In practice, many record companies and studios do not put the MCPS procedure into motion until it has been decided to manufacture records of the recording for commercial release. This means that in the period between making the recording and the conclusion of the MCPS licence procedure, the copyright in the song has been infringed by making the recording without a licence.

In recognition of the divergence between practice and strict legal requirement concerning the *making* of sound recordings (as opposed to the subsequent manufacture of copies of the recording concerned) the MCPS and APRS have put together a Code of Practice. This offers studios and mastering facilities who follow the provisions of the Code a form of immunity against copyright infringement proceedings from the MCPS in respect of master records made without prior MCPS clearance. Details and copies of the Code of Practice are available from the MCPS.

2. Adaptations/moral rights. The person making the recording also requires consent from the songwriter and possibly his publisher if the recording embodies an adaptation of the song concerned. The MCPS licence schemes do not grant the right to adapt songs or subject them to 'derogatory treatment'.

3. Sampling. We have seen that when a record company, studio, or group makes a cover recording of an existing song the copyright in the song is infringed. Similarly, so-called 'sampling' or making a recording which includes part of an existing sound recording may also infringe the copyright in that existing recording.

It is not necessary to copy a whole sound recording for the copying to constitute an infringement of the copyright in that recording. Copying is an infringement as long as a substantial part of the recording has been reproduced. What amounts to the reproduction of a substantial part in the context of sampling? At the same of writing, 'sampling' is still a difficult area of law in which there are few decided cases. However, what can be said is that the test is 'qualitative' rather than 'quantitative'. This means that the reproduction of a few crucial and recognizable fragments may be sufficient to constitute an infringement of copyright in the whole recording. This is an area in which expert advice should be sought in each particular circumstance. It has often been said that 'if it is worth copying it is worth protecting'. Contributors such as individual producers, engineers, and musicians should always investigate whether a licence from the owner of an existing sound recording is required before using any 'sample' as part of a recording.

The APRS General Conditions of Hire for recording studios require the studio's clients to take responsibility for clearing all copyright material (including samples) before recording commences.

4. Ownership of copyright in sound recordings. If you are a record company commissioning the making of a recording or if you are a studio which is making a recording on its own behalf, you will wish to ensure that you own the entire copyright in the recording concerned. As was discussed above, copyright ownership may arguably be shared amongst a number of contributors including the record company, individual producer, the studio, the engineer, and possibly even the musicians and vocalists themselves. You will therefore need a *written* assignment (or transfer) of these copyright interests to you if you wish to be able to exploit the recording freely.

The question of copyright ownership is usually addressed in the contracts of engagement signed by individual record producers, the consent forms signed by session players, the recording contracts signed by featured artists, and the contracts of hire between studios and their clients. These contracts almost invariably provide for the entire copyright in the sound recording concerned to be vested in the record company.

If the studio adopts the APRS suggested standard terms and conditions then these will provide for copyright in the sound recording concerned to vest in the studio until the record company has settled its bill! The effectiveness of this provision depends, amongst other things, upon whether the standard terms and conditions have been effectively made part of the agreement between the studio and its client. Even if they have been made part of that agreement, the provision will not of itself affect any share of the copyright in a sound recording which is owned by other contributors to the recording such as producers and artists. The provision should be used as leverage to extract overdue payments from recalcitrant clients rather than as authority for the studio itself to exploit the sound recording concerned. The APRS standard terms and conditions also provide for ownership of the physical master tapes to remain with the studio until the bill has been paid.

It is not common practice to take assignments of copyright from sound engineers although the wording of the Copyright Act arguably gives engineers scope to claim a copyright interest.

Usually people only give up their copyright interest in return for the payment of money or a promise to pay money in the future. In the case of an individual record producer payments usually take the form of fees and/or royalties (and advances against these royalties) on sales of records embodying the recording concerned. Artists' recording contracts with record companies usually provide for featured musicians and vocalists to be remunerated by way of royalties (and advances against those royalties) on record sales. Smaller record companies may offer their artists a share of profits derived from record sales instead of royalties. Session players usually receive a one-off session fee.

5. Performers' rights. Because the musicians and vocalists whose performances are captured on a recording attract performers' rights as discussed above, any record company or studio wishing to make and exploit that recording will need to obtain consent to do so from the performers concerned. These consents are usually given in the record contracts signed by featured artists and in the consent forms signed by session players.

(b) Manufacturing records

1. Copyright in the song. The act of manufacturing records (such as compact discs, vinyl records, and cassettes) which reproduce a master recording is an infringement of the copyright in the song which is reproduced on the recording concerned. This element of the copyright in a song is often referred to as the 'mechanical right'. As almost all songwriters and their publishers place their mechanical rights under the control of the MCPS the following discussion refers to those rights controlled by the MCPS.

Any record company wishing to manufacture records embodying recordings of songs for which the mechanical rights are controlled by the MCPS requires a licence from the MCPS to do so. These licences are known as 'mechanical licences'. A number of mechanical licensing schemes are available from the MCPS. As we have seen, larger record companies with a proven credit record may be accepted on to the AP1 licensing scheme operated by the MCPS. This scheme grants the record company a blanket mechanical licence in respect of all of the songs controlled by the MCPS in the United Kingdom. In return, the record company pays the MCPS 8.5 per cent of the published dealer price on sales of the records concerned. Those larger record companies usually account to the MCPS in arrears on a quarterly basis.

Smaller record companies need to follow the MCPS application procedure for mechanical licences on a song-by-song basis and may be required to pay the mechanical royalty of 8.5 per cent of published dealer price in advance by reference to the number of records they are having manufactured.

As well as granting record companies the right to manufacture and sell records embodying MCPS repertoire, the MCPS licences also grant the right to *make* the recording concerned.

Many record companies subcontract the actual physical manufacture of records to specialist duplication plants. Although the duplicator manufactures to the order of its clients, the duplicator itself infringes the copyright in underlying songs if it duplicates records without either having received clearance direct from the MCPS or having seen evidence of MCPS clearance granted to record company clients. In respect of larger record companies operating under the MCPS AP1 Scheme this is not generally a problem for duplicators, because these companies are granted blanket rights in all MCPS repertoire. However, for smaller record companies and duplicators there can be a problem because, in a fast-moving industry, by the time an MCPS clearance has been obtained, demand for the record concerned may have ceased to exist! In practice, duplicators are faced with the choice of either infringing copyright in the song by manufacturing records without having seen evidence of an MCPS clearance or jeopardizing their clients' chances of success by refusing to manufacture those records until evidence of the MCPS licence is forthcoming. As an attempt to deal with the duplicator's predicament, the MCPS has issued a Code of Conduct which offers duplicators a limited form of immunity from copyright infringement actions by the MCPS if they comply with the procedures set out in the Code before commencing manufacture. At the date of writing, the MCPS Code of Conduct has not met with universal acclaim from duplicators in the United Kingdom.

2. Copyright in the recording. The act of manufacturing records also constitutes an infringement of the rights of the owner of the copyright in the *sound recording*. If a record company is the sole owner of the entire copyright in the recording (having taken an assignment of any residual copyright held by the musicians, the producer, or the studio and engineer) then it has nothing to fear in that respect.

3. Performers' rights. Record companies also need the consent of musicians and vocalists to manufacture records which embody their performances. This requirement should be dealt with in the consent form which musicians and vocalists are asked to sign before the recording session commences. Record companies usually delegate responsibility for having these forms completed to the individual producer engaged to produce a recording.

4. Moral rights. It is worth noting that the MCPS licence schemes do not include the right to manufacture records which reproduce adaptations of copyright songs. Nor do the MCPS licences affect in any way the moral rights enjoyed by songwriters such as the rights to be identified as the author and to object to derogatory treatments. The grant of an MCPS licence, therefore, would not protect a record company or a duplicator from a songwriter claiming infringement of his exclusive right to make adaptations of his song or infringement of his moral rights.

5. Rights clearance—whose responsibility? A record company can control its acquisition of copyright in a recording and its acquisition of the consents from performers which are needed to enable it to freely exploit that recording. It is also in a position to ensure that the recording does not infringe the right to make adaptations of the underlying song or the moral rights granted to the songwriter. By contrast, a duplicator is not in a position to monitor these matters for itself and instead must rely upon the record company's diligence. It is therefore vital that the standard terms and conditions used by a duplicator in fulfilling orders for its record company clients include a warranty from the record company that it has obtained all rights and clearances necessary to enable the duplicator to manufacture the records ordered without infringing the rights of *any* third party. This warranty should be backed up by an indemnity which provides for the record company client to make good any loss suffered by the duplicator as a result of that warranty not having been true. If this simple precaution is taken then a duplicator who is sued by a third party for infringement of copyright, moral rights, or performers' rights has a direct contractual right to claim back any loss suffered as a result (such as an award of damages against the duplicator) from the record company concerned.

(c) Exploitation of records

Even if a record company owns the entire copyright in a sound recording, it nevertheless requires permission to sell records manufactured by it or on its behalf from the copyright owner(s) of the underlying song. These permissions are generally dealt with in the various MCPS licensing schemes, although it is worth checking to see what limitations the MCPS imposes in respect of particular categories of sale such as records sold as premiums and through record clubs. Featured artists and session players usually grant record companies the right to sell records of their performances in their exclusive record contracts and session agreements respectively.

(d) Performance and broadcast

As discussed above, songwriters and publishers usually assign that part of their copyright which comprises the exclusive right to perform and broadcast their songs to the PRS. Anybody wishing to perform or broadcast their songs whether by way of live performance or by playing records which reproduce those songs, requires a licence from the PRS in order to do so. The PRS grants blanket licences in its entire repertoire to many places of public entertainment such as restaurants, shops, and pubs. It also grants blanket licences to large broadcasting organizations such as the BBC and independent television and radio. The substantial revenue which the PRS receives from its licensing activities is for the most part distributed between its songwriter and publisher members in proportion to the level of usage achieved by those members' songs.

As we have seen, record company contracts with artists and individual producers ensure that the record company owns the entire copyright in nearly all sound recordings financed by that record company. The unauthorized public performance and broadcast of a sound recording infringes the record company's copyright in the sound recording. Most record companies are members of an organization called Phonographic Performance Limited (PPL). PPL acquires its members' rights to perform and broadcast the sound recordings owned by them. PPL grants blanket licences allowing places of public entertainment and broadcasters to perform and broadcast sound recordings within PPL's repertoire in much the same way as the PRS grants licences in respect of the underlying songs. This means that radio stations, for example, require a separate licence from PPL (in respect of recordings) and from PRS (in respect of the underlying songs featured on the recordings).

Although record companies are usually the sole owners of the copyright in the sound recordings in their catalogues, not all of the net income collected by PPL from licensing performance and broadcast rights in sound recordings is paid by PPL to its record company members: 20 per cent of net income is paid to featured artists. Similarly, 12.5 per cent of net PPL income is paid to the Musicians' Union, ostensibly on behalf of session players. However, it appears that this situation will soon change. A recent EC Directive (92/100/EEC) requires the British government to implement domestic legislation which will *entitle* performers to share with record companies in the proceeds of the income generated by the performance and broadcast of sound recordings. The Directive requires the new legislation to be in place by 1 July 1994.

(*e*) Legal advice

The above gives a thumbnail sketch of the main legal rights which surround the creation and exploitation of sound recordings in the United Kingdom and the main organizations which control some of those rights on behalf of their members. It is not intended to be a comprehensive guide and should be read in the light of changes to the law and changes in music industry practice which take place after February 1994. It is recommended that specialist legal advice be sought by those who are or wish to be in the business of making and exploiting sound recordings.

Appendices

Appendix I: Units

The SI system of units (Système International d'Unités) is an extension and refinement of the traditional metric system (MKS = metre, kilogramme, second) and is moving towards world-wide acceptance. The main features of SI can be summarized as follows:

1. There are six basic units:

Quantity	Unit	Symbol
length	metre	m
mass	kilogramme	kg
time	second	s
electric current	ampere	A
theremodynamic temperature	kelvin	K
luminous intensity	candela	cd

NB Symbols for units do not take the plural form.

2. Fractions and multiples of units are normally restricted to steps of a thousand. However, the full list of possible fractions and multiples would include the following:

Fraction	Prefix	Symbol	Multiple	Prefix	Symbol
10^{-1}	deci	d	10	deca	da
10^{-2}	centi	c	10^2	hecto	h
10^{-3}	milli	m	10^3	kilo	k
10^{-6}	micro	μ	10^6	mega	M
10^{-9}	nano	n	10^9	giga	G
10^{-12}	pico	p	10^{12}	tera	T

3. Various derived SI units have special names, including the following:

Quantity	Unit	Symbol	Definition
energy	joule	J	$kg\, m^2/s^2$
force	newton	N	$kg\, m/s^2$
power	watt	W	J/s
frequency	hertz	Hz	1/s
electric charge	coulomb	C	A s
electric potential	volt	V	W/A
electric resistance	ohm	Ω	V/A

4. Other derived units include the following:

Quantity	SI unit	Symbol
area	square metre	m²
volume	cubic metre	m³
	(also litre = 1 cubic decimetre)	(l or dm³)
density	kilogramme per cubic metre	kg/m³
velocity	metre per second	m/s
pressure	newton per square metre	N/m²
	(or pascal)	(Pa = N/m²)

Table of conversions

Length

1 thou	= 25.4 μm	1 μm	= 0.04 thou
1 inch	= 25.4 mm	1 mm	= 0.039 inch
1 foot	= 304.8 mm	1 cm	= 0.39 inch
1 yard	= 0.9144 m	1 m	= 39.37 inches
1 mile	= 1.609 km	1 km	= 0.62 miles

Area

1 sq. in.	= 645.2 mm²	1 mm²	= 0.00155 sq. in.
1 sq. ft.	= 0.093 m²	1 m²	= 10.764 sq. ft.
1 sq. yd.	= 0.836 m²		= 1.196 sq. yd.

Volume

1 cu. in.	= 16.387 cm³	1 cm³	= 0.061 cu. in.
1 cu. ft.	= 28.317 litres	1 litre	= 61.023 cu. in.
1 pint	= 0.568 litres		= 0.0353 cu. ft.
1 gallon	= 4.546 litres	1 m³	= 35.315 cu. ft.

Weight

1 oz	= 28.35 g	1 g	= 0.0353 oz
1 lb	= 453.59 g	1 kg	= 35.274 oz
	= 0.4536 kg		= 2.2046 lb

Appendix II: Standards

The following lists show only a selection of the more relevant standards published at the time of writing. Readers are recommended to check on the existence of further standards, or more up-to-date reissues, with the issuing authority.

(a) *British Standards* (British Standards Institution, 2 Park Street, London, W1)

BS 204: 1960   Glossary of terms used in telecommunication (including radio) and electronics

BS 661: 1969   Glossary of acoustical terms

BS 1568: Part 1: 1970   Specification for magnetic tape recording equipment. Part 1. Magnetic tape recording and reproducing systems, dimensions and characteristics

BS 1568: Part 2: 1973   Cassettes for commercial tape records and domestic use, dimensions and characteristics

BS 1568: Part 3: 1976   Eight-track endless-loop magnetic tape cartridge

BS 1928: 1965   Specification for processed disc records and reproducing equipment

BS 2498: 1954   Recommendations for ascertaining and expressing the performance of loudspeakers by objective measurements

BS 2750: 1956   Recommendations for measurement of airborne and impact sound transmission in buildings

BS 3383: 1961   Normal equal-loudness contours for pure tones and normal threshold of hearing under free-field listening conditions

BS 3638: 1963   Method for the measurement of sound absorption coefficients (ISO) in a reverberation room

BS 3860: 1965   Methods for measuring and expressing the performance of audio-frequency amplifiers

BS 4197: 1967   Specification for a precision sound level meter

BS 4297: 1968   Specification for the characteristics and performance of a peak programme meter

BS 4847: 1972   Method for measurement of speed fluctuations in sound recording and reproducing equipment

BS 4852: Part 1: 1972   Methods of defining and measuring the characteristics of disc record playing equipment. Part 1. Disc record players

BS 5428: Part 1: 1977   Methods for specifying and measuring the characteristics of sound system equipment

(b) *German Standards* (Beuth Vertrieb GmBH, 1 Berlin 30, Burggrafenstrasse 4–7)

45510   Magnetic sound recording: terminology (1971)

45511/1   Tape recorder for recording on magnetic tape 6.3 mm (0.25 in) wide: mechanical and electrical specifications (1971)

45511/2   Tape recorder for three- or four-track recording on magnetic tape 12.7 mm (0.5 in) wide: mechanical and electrical specifications (1971)

45511/3   Tape recorder for four-track recording on tape 25.4 mm (1 in.) wide: mechanical and electrical specifications (1971)

45512   Magnetic tapes for sound recording
Sheet 1: Dimensions and mechanical properties to be stated (1968)
Sheet 2: Electroacoustic characteristics (1969)

45513   Sheet 1: DIN test tape for magnetic tapes for 76.2 cm/s tape speed (1968)
Sheet 2: Ditto 38.1 cm/s tape speed (1967)
Sheet 3: Ditto 19.05 cm/s tape speed (1966)
Sheet 4: Ditto 9.5 cm/s tape speed (1968)
Sheet 5: Ditto 4.75 cm/s tape speed (1972)
Sheet 6: Ditto 3.81 mm (0.15 in) wide and 4.75 cm/s tape speed (1972)

45514   Sound recording and reproduction, magnetic tape apparatus: Spools (1961)

45520   Magnetic tape recorders: measurement of the absolute level of the magnetic flux and its frequency response on magnetic tapes (1973)

45521   Measurement of crosstalk in multitrack tape recorders (1963)

45523   Remote control by signals from magnetic tape recorders (1968)

45524   Evaluation of the tape speed of magnetic tape recorders (1968)

45536   Monophonic disc records M.45 (1962)

45537   Monophonic disc records M.33 (1962)

45538   Definitions for disc reproducing equipment (1969)

45539   Record reproducing equipment: directives for measurement, markings, and audio-frequency connections, dimensions of interchangeable pickups, requirements of playback amplifiers (1971)

45541   Frequency test record St.33 and M.33 (1971)

45542   Distortion test record St.33 and St.45 (1969)

45543   Crosstalk record St.33 (1969)

45544   Rumble measurement test record St.33 (1971)

45545   Wow and flutter test records 33 and 45 rpm (1966)

45546   Stereophonic disc records St.45 (1962)

45547   Stereophonic disc records St.33 (1962)

(c) *American (NAB) Standards* (National Association of Broadcasters, 1771 N. Street, NW, Washington, DC 20036)
Disc recordings and reproductions (1964)
Cartridge tape recording and reproducing (1964)
Magnetic tape (reel-to-reel) recordings and reproductions (1965)
Audio cassette recording and reproducing (1973)

(d) *International Electrotechnical Commission (IEC) Recommendations* (1 Rue de Varembe, Geneva, Switzerland)

IEC Publication 50	International electrotechnical vocabulary
IEC Publication 94	Magnetic tape recording and reproducing
IEC Publication 98	1964 Processed disc records and reproducing equipment
IEC Publication 268	Sound system equipment

(e) *International Organization for Standardization (ISO) Recommendations* (1 Rue de Varembe, Geneva, Switzerland)

R131   Expression of the physical and subjective magnitudes of sound or noise

R357   Expression of the power and intensity levels of sound or noise

R532   Procedure for calculating loudness level

Appendix III: Bibliography

General

Bekesy, G. von, *Experiments in Hearing* (New York, 1960)
Davis, D. and C., *Sound System Engineering* (New York, 1974)
Eargle, J., *Handbook of Recording Engineering* (New York, 1992)
Fletcher, H., *Speech and Hearing in Communication* (New York, 1953)
Foster, B., Hollebone, C. and Parsons, A., *The Master Tape Book* (APRS London, 1992)
Gelatt, R., *The Fabulous Phonograph* (London, 1956)
Langford-Smith, F., *Radio Designer's Handbook* (London, 4th edn. 1954)
Olson, H. F., *Music, Physics and Engineering* (New York, 2nd edn. 1967)
Pohlmann, K. C., *Principles of Digital Audio* (Indiana, 1989)
Lord Rayleigh, *Theory of Sound Vols I and II* (London, 1896, republished 1960)
Read, O. and Welch, W., *From Tin-Foil to Stereo* (New York, 1959)
Rumsey, F. J., *Digital Audio Operations* (London, 1991)
Seashore, C. E., *Psychology of Music* (New York, 1938, republished 1967)
Watkinson, J., *The Art of Digital Audio* (London, 1989)
Wood, A., *The Physics of Music* (London, 1947)
Winckel, F., *Music, Sound and Sensation* (New York, 1967)

The studio

Beranek, L. L., *Acoustics* (New York, 1954)
Beranek, L. L., *Music, Acoustics and Architecture* (New York, 1962)
Gilford, C., *Acoustics for Radio and Television Studios* (London, 1972)
Knudsen, V. O., *Architectural Acoustics* (New York, 1952)
Mankowsky, V. S., *Acoustics of Studios and Auditoria* (London, 1971)

The equipment

BBC Monographs (various titles)
Borwick, J., (ed.), *Loudspeaker and Headphone Handbook* (London, 1988)
Borwick, J., *Microphones: Technology and Technique* (London, 1990)
Eargle, J., *The Microphone Handbook* (New York, 1985)
Frayne, J. G. and Wolfe, H., *Elements of Sound Recording* (New York, 1949)
Godfrey, J. W. (ed.), *Studio Engineering for Sound Broadcasting* (London, 1955)
Robertson, A. E., *Microphones* (London, 2nd edn. 1963)
Rumsey, F. J., *MIDI Systems and Control* (London, 1990)

Techniques

Bernhart, J., *Traité de Prise de Son* (Paris, 1949)
Blumlein, A. D., British Patent No. 394325 (1933)

Burroughs, L., *Microphones: Design and Application* (New York, 1974)
Culshaw, J., *Ring Resounding* (London, 1967)
Douglas, A., *Electronic Music Production* (London, 1973)
Eargle, J., *Sound Recording* (New York, 1986)
Franssen, N. V., *Stereophony* (Eindhoven, 1962)
Burrell Hadden, H., *High Quality Sound Production and Reproduction* (London, 1962)
Howe, H. S., *Electronic Music Synthesis* (New York, 1975)
Nisbett, A., *The Technique of the Sound Studio* (London, 1992)
Oringel, R., *Audio Control Handbook* (New York, 4th edn. 1972)
Runsten, R. and Huber, D., *Modern Recording Techniques* (New York, 1986)
Woram, J. M., *Sound Recording Handbook* (New York, 1989)

Manufacturing processes

Guy, P. J., *Disc Recording and Reproduction* (London, 1964)

Allied media

Alkin, G., *Sound Techniques for Video and TV* (London, 1989)
Hilliard, R. L., *Radio Broadcasting* (New York, 2nd edn. 1974)
Johnson, J. S. and Jones, K. K., *Modern Radio Station Practices* (Belmont, California, 1972)
Millerson, G., *The Technique of Television Production* (London, 9th edn. 1972)
Wysotsky, M. Z., *Wide-Screen Cinema and Stereophonic Sound* (London, 1971)

Glossary

Absorption	1. Damping of sound wave on passing through a medium or striking a surface.
	2. The property possessed by materials, objects, or media of absorbing sound energy.
Absorption coefficient	The fraction of the incident sound energy absorbed by a surface or material at a given frequency and under specified conditions. The complement of the sound energy reflection coefficient under those conditions, i.e. it is equal to 1 minus the sound energy reflection coefficient of the surface or material.
a.c.	Abbreviation for alternating current, which periodically reverses its direction, as opposed to d.c. (direct current).
Academy roll-off	Control of the upper frequencies in terms of total response heard by the audience in a cinema, to minimize the effect of unwanted random noise in the system.
Acetate	Alternative term for Lacquer disc.
Acoustics	1. The science of sound.
	2. Of a room or auditorium. Those factors that determine its character with respect to the quality of the received sound.
ADC (analogue-to-digital converter	Circuit whose output is a digital representation of an analogue input.
ADT (Automatic Double Tracking)	Duplication of a voice or instrument with a delay of a few milliseconds to increase the impact or simulate the effect of more performers (see Double-tracking).
Aerial	(American: Antenna.) Wire or system of wires supported at a height above the ground for the purpose of radiating or of collecting electromagnetic waves.
Alignment	The process of positioning tape heads and amplifier pre-sets for optimum tape performance.
Ambience	The combination of reverberation and background noise which characterizes the sound in a given hall or studio.
Ampere (amp)	Practical unit of electric current.
Amplifier	A device in which an input signal controls a local source of power in such a way as to produce an output which bears some desired relationship to, and is generally greater than, the input signal.

Amplitude	Of a simple sinusoidal quantity. The peak value.
Amplitude distortion	That part of non-linearity distortion which is an undesired variation of gain or sensitivity with change of signal level.
Amplitude modulation (AM)	Modulation in which the amplitude of the carrier is the characteristic varied.
Analogue (Analog)	Electronic signal whose waveform resembles that of the original sound (cf. Digital).
Anechoic	Without echo. An anechoic chamber is a chamber or room where walls are lined with a material which completely absorbs sound.
Antenna	(See Aerial.)
Aspect ratio	Proportion of height to width.
Atmosphere microphone	Microphone placed at some distance from the performers to pick up the general ambience.
Attack time	Time taken for a limiter or compressor to produce the necessary gain change.
Attenuation	Reduction in current, voltage, or power along the transmission path of a signal.
Attenuation distortion (or amplitude/frequency distortion)	An undesired variation of gain or sensitivity with frequency.
Audio frequency (AF)	Rate of oscillation corresponding to that of sound audible to the human ear (i.e. within the range from about 20 to 20,000 Hz).
Auto-locate	Tape machine facility giving fast location of chosen points on the tape.
Azimuth	The angle between the gap in a tape head and the longitudinal axis of the tape (should be 90°).
Backing	Accompaniment, as when a group of vocalists record a 'backing track' to which the soloist listens on headphones when recording.
Baffle	General expression for wall, board, or enclosure carrying a loudspeaker. The purpose of the baffle is primarily to separate the front and back radiations from the cone or diaphragm which would otherwise cancel each other.
Balance	Placing of artists, speakers, or other sources of sound in relation to a microphone or microphones, or vice versa (hence 'balance test').
Balanced line	Programme cable in which the twin signal wires are both isolated from earth and are suitably terminated so as to be at equal potential but opposite polarity.

Bandwidth	The interval between the cut-off frequencies or -3 dB points in a response curve, expressed in octaves or as a frequency difference in hertz.
Bel	A scale unit used in the comparison of the magnitudes of powers. The number of bels, expressing the relative magnitudes of two powers, is the logarithm to the base 10 of the ratio of the powers. One bel equals 10 decibels.
Betamax	A ½-inch videocassette format used for PCM digital audio recording.
Biasing	The superposition of a magnetic field on the signal magnetic field during magnetic recording. This additional field may be alternating at a frequency well above the signal frequency range (HF bias). Alternatively, the additional field may be steady (d.c. bias).
Bias trap	Low-pas filter in tape replay circuit designed to attenuate any high-frequency bias present.
Bi-directional	Type of microphone having a figure-of-eight directivity pattern.
Binaural hearing	1. Normal perception of sounds and/or of their directions of arrival with both ears.
	2. By extension, the perception of sound when the two ears are connected to separate electroacoustic transmission channels.
Bit	Contraction of the words 'binary digit' (a '1' or a '0'). A number of bits assembled together, often 4 or 8, is called a 'byte'.
Bit resolution	The number of bits (16-bit, 20-bit, etc.) used for a digital recording: directly related to the dynamic range.
Boom	A mobile carrier for a microphone which incudes a movable arm from which the microphone is suspended.
Break jack	A jack arranged to break the normal circuit when a plug is inserted.
Buchmann and Meyer pattern	The pattern formed by the spread of reflections from a modulated groove when a parallel beam of light is caused to fall normal to the surface of one or the other wall, and when the groove is viewed from the direction of the light source. It is used as a measure of the maximum modulation of either wall of the groove in the calibration of the performance of recorders, and for the measurement of levels on test records.
Bulk eraser	Electromagnet designed to erase a reel of tape in a few seconds.
Bus bar	Common earth or other contact wire.

Cans	Colloquial for headphones.
Capacitance	The magnitude of the capability of an element, or a circuit, to store electric charge. Measured in microfarads (μF).
Capacitor microphone (sometimes called Condenser or Electrostatic)	Type of microphone in which the signal is generated by the variation in capacitance between the diaphragm(s) and a fixed plate.
Capstan (American: Puck)	Drive spindle of tape machine.
Cardioid microphone	Class of microphone having a heart-shaped directivity pattern.
Cartridge	1. Easy-loading magazine of magnetic tape; generally refers to the Eight-Track Stereo format. 2. Disc reproducing head.
Cassette	Easy-loading magazine of magnetic tape; generally refers to the Philips Compact Cassette format.
CCIR	Comité Consultatif International des Radiocommunications: International standards organization.
Chip	American term for swarf (q.v.).
Clapperboard (or slate)	Primitive but efficient system for simultaneously giving an identification to the picture camera and an audible and visual synchronizing point at the start or finish of a filmed section or 'take'.
Clean feed	Version of a programme signal which omits one source (e.g. voice, to allow overdubbing in another language, etc.).
Clipping	Form of distortion due to severe overloading.
Cocktail party effect	The faculty of selecting one stream of information out of a number of voices speaking at the same time.
Coincident	Refers to microphone arrangements in stereophony. Two microphones are said to be coincident if they are placed immediately adjacent to each other so that any differences in the times of arrival of the sound are negligible.
Coloration	Change in frequency response caused by resonance peaks.
Compandor	A combination of a compressor at one point in a communication path for reducing the volume range of signals, followed by an expander at another point for restoring the original volume range. Usually its purpose is to improve the ratio of the signal to the interference entering in the path between the compressor and expander.
Compression moulding	The process of forming a disc by compressing a quantity of suitable plastic in a cavity.

Compressor	Means for reducing the variations in signal amplitude in a transmission system according to a specified law.
Concentric (Finishing groove)	The closed circular groove which succeeds the lead-out groove.
Concert pitch	System of music tuning based on a frequency of A = 440 Hz.
Continuity studio	A small studio from which an announcer, supervising the running of a sequence of programmes, makes opening and closing announcements, and interpolates interlude material when required.
Copy master	1. Reserve or replacement metal negative produced from the positive for use as a master. 2. Identical copy of any master tape: should indicate type of master from which copy was made.
Crossfade	To fade in one channel while fading out another in order to substitute gradually the output of one for that of the other (e.g. to create the impression of a change of scene). Hence 'crossfade' (noun).
Crossover frequency	As applied to a dividing network. That frequency at which equal power is supplied to each of two adjacent frequency channels.
Crosstalk	Form of interference caused by break-through of signals from one circuit or tape track to another.
Cutter head	A recording head with cutting stylus for electromechanical or mechanical recording.
Cycle	Of a periodic quantity. The sequence of changes which takes place during the period of a recurring variable quantity.
Cycle per second (c/s)	Unit of frequency, now generally superseded by hertz.
DAC (digital-to-analogue converter)	Circuit for converting a digital word into the corresponding analogue signal.
Damping	That property of a circuit which tends to cause decay in amplitude of oscillations or reduce resonant peaks.
DASH (digital audio stationary head)	Open-reel formats on ¼-inch and ½-inch digital tape.
dbx	Proprietary noise reduction system.
d.c.	Abbreviation for direct current, which flows in one direction only, as opposed to a.c. (alternating current).
Dead studio	Studio having very little reverberation.
Decibel (dB)	A unit of transmission giving the ratio of two powers. One-tenth of a bel.

De-emphasis	A change in the frequency response of a reproducing system, complementary to pre-emphasis.
Differential amplifier	Device designed to amplify the difference between two signals.
Diffraction	Form of interference by means of which longer-wavelength sounds effectively bend round obstacles.
Digital	Refers to signals which have been converted from the normal 'analogue' form to a series of coded pulses.
Digital interface	A digital input or output conforming to a specified standard.
DIN	Deutscher Industrie Normenausschus: German standards organization.
Direct-cut	Method of recording straight to disc without a tape stage.
Direct disc	Lacquer recording blank which is intended for reproduction without further processing.
Direct injection	Process of recording a guitar or other electronic instrument by feeding the electronic signal direct to tape instead of via a microphone.
Directivity pattern	Graph showing the response of a piece of equipment such as a microphone at all angles in a given plane—sometimes called a polar diagram.
Distortion	The unwanted change in waveform which can occur between two points in a transmission equipment or system.
Dither	Addition of low-level random noise to reduce quantization distortion in digital systems.
Dolby	Noise reduction system named after its inventor, Dr Ray Dolby. Dolby 'A' is used in professional tape mastering; Dolby 'B' and 'C' are simpler systems used for example in domestic cassette recorders.
Doppler effect	The change in the observed frequency of a wave caused by time rate of change in the length of the path between the source and the observer.
Double-tracking	Overdubbing a voice or instrument 'playing along' with a previous track of the same musical line (see also ADT).
Drop-in	Process of inserting a recorded sound by playing up to a chosen point and switching one or more tracks to the record mode.
Dropout	Momentary loss of signal caused by a fault in tape coating, or dust etc.
Dubbing	1. The combining of two or more recordings into a composite recording.

2. The recording so obtained.
Misnomer sometimes used to describe 're-voicing' (in the original or a foreign language) the dialogue spoken by an actor appearing on the screen.

Ducking	Process of automatic compression, e.g. when the announcer's voice signal causes the level of music to be attenuated.
Dummy head stereo	(German: Künstkopf Stereo.) System of recording using microphones placed in the ears of a model head (or of a wearer).
Dynamic range	Of a programme. The range within which its volume fluctuates. (The term is applied to the original sounds and to the electric currents produced by them.)
EBU (European Broadcasting Union)	International body responsible for timecode and digital audio and television development.
Echo	Sound which has been reflected and arrives with such a magnitude and time interval after the direct sound as to be distinguishable as a repetition of it.
Echo chamber	A reverberant room, containing only a microphone and a loudspeaker, through which an output from a studio or hall is passed in order to allow a variable degree of reverberation to be added to the direct output from the same source. The microphone output is combined with the output of the programme source and controlled in volume to give a desired degree of reverberation.
Editing	Process of cutting, rearrangement, and selection of recorded material.
Efficiency	Of mechanical or electrical plant, the ratio (expressed as a percentage) of the output energy in the required form to the total input energy.
Eigentones	(German.) Resonances set up in a room or enclosure at frequencies determined by the physical dimensions.
Electret	Non-conductor which has been given a permanent electrical charge: used in microphones and other transducers.
Electromagnet	Coil of wire, possibly having a core of soft iron, which behaves as a magnet only while a current is passing through it.
Electron	Smallest charge of negative electricity which may exist by itself or as part of an atom. (From the Greek 'elektron' = amber.)
Electronic crossover	Frequency-dividing circuit using split amplifiers rather than passive circuits.

Envelope	Graphical representation of the changing amplitude of a complex wave.
Equalization (EQ)	The process of modifying the amplitude/frequency response in a recording and reproducing system to produce flat overall characteristics, minimize noise, or give an artistic effect.
Erase head	The component in a magnetic recording system that obliterates previous recordings so that the recording medium may be used afresh.
Expander	Means for increasing the variations in signal amplitude in a transmission system according to a specified law.
Farad	Unit of capacitance, which for convenience is subdivided into one million microfarads (µF).
Feedback	The return of a fraction of the output of a circuit to the input. *Note.* Feedback may be either positive or negative, i.e. tending to increase or decrease the output.
Figure-of-eight	Polar response shape of a bi-directional microphone.
Film speed	1. Scale of sensitivity of photographic emulsion. 2. Rate of film travel, related to 24 frames per second. NB For television, in order to avoid stroboscopic effects, the nearest multiple of mains frequency is used. In Europe this is 25 frames per second, which raises the pitch of reproduced sound by a noticeable amount. For films commissioned for television, the speed of 25 frames/sec is adopted.
Filter	Electrical network composed of inductors, capacitors, or resistors, or a combination of these, designed to discriminate between currents of different frequencies.
Flanging	Coarse phasing effect like that obtained by placing a finger on the supply spool of a tape machine (cf. Phasing).
Fletcher and Munson curves	Set of equal-loudness graphs showing frequency dependent behaviour of human hearing.
Flip-flop	Device having two stable states used, for instance, as a binary counter.
Floating	Not connected to any source of potential.
Flutter and wow	Undesired forms of frequency modulation introduced by the recording/reproducing process; for example, by irregular motion of the recording medium. Note. 'Wow' usually refers to the range of fluctuation frequencies between about 0.1 Hz and 10 Hz and is perceived as pitch fluctuations.

	'Flutter' usually refers to fluctuation frequencies above about 10 Hz.
Flutter echo	A rapid multiple echo of even rate.
Flux density	Measure of the concentration of an electric field or magnetic field. (Magnetic flux density is measured in lines per square centimetre, or gauss, or webers per meter of tape width.)
Foldback	Process of feeding microphone or tape signals to headphones or loudspeakers as a cue to artists during recording.
Formant	A band of frequencies in the spectrum of a complex sound which may be associated with a resonance in the mechanism of the production of the sound.
	Note 1. Vowel sounds may possess more than one formant in different parts of the spectrum.
	Note 2. The term may also be used in relation to musical instruments.
Frequency	Of a periodic quantity. The rate of repetition of the cycles. The reciprocal of the period. The unit is the hertz (Hz).
Frequency correction	(See Equalization.)
Frequency modulation (FM)	Modulation of a sine-wave carrier in which the instantaneous frequency of the modulated wave differs from the carrier frequency by an amount proportional to the instantaneous value of the modulating wave.
Fundamental frequency	The highest common factor of a series of harmonically related frequencies in a complex oscillation.
Fuse	Wire or strip of metal connected in an electric circuit so as to act as a protective device by melting, and thus interrupting the circuit, if the current exceeds the maximum safe value.
Gain	1. The ratio of the output load power to the input power.
	2. The ratio of the output and input voltages, or currents, under specified conditions of impedance termination.
	Note. In this case the terms should properly be 'Voltage gain' and 'Current gain' respectively.
Gap alignment	The adjustment of the magnetic gap in relation to the magnetic medium.
	(*a*) Azimuth alignment. The adjustment of the orientation of the magnetic gap in relation to the direction of motion of the magnetic medium.
	(*b*) Lateral alignment. The adjustment of the magnetic gap parallel to the plane of the magnetic medium and normal to its direction of motion.

	(c) Pole face alignment. The rotation of the contact surface in a plane at right angles to the direction of motion of the magnetic medium in order to effect satisfactory contact over the full length of the gap.
Gate	Special amplifier circuit which has zero output unless the input level exceeds a chosen threshold level.
Gramophone record	A processed copy of a disc recording from which sounds may be reproduced by a mechanical or an electromechanical system.
Graphic equalizer	Frequency correction device giving selective control in narrow bands and having slider controls which indicate the approximate response curve chosen.
Groove	In a mechanical or electromechanical recording. The track inscribed in the recording medium by the cutting or embossing stylus.
Guardband	Spacing between tracks on a multitrack tape.
Gun microphone	(American: Rifle microphone.) Type of microphone employing a long tube and being narrowly directional along the axis.
Haas Effect	An effect concerned with the apparent location of the source when the same sound is heard from two or more sources (as in a public address system). Within certain limits of the relative intensities of the separate sounds, and of the time intervals between their arrivals, the sound appears to come from a single source, namely that from which the sounds first arrive even though the later sounds are more intense.
Harmonic	A sinusoidal oscillation having a frequency which is an integral multiple of a fundamental frequency. A harmonic having double the fundamental frequency is called the second harmonic and so on.
Harmonic distortion	A constituent of non-linearity distortion, consisting of the production in the response to a sinusoidal excitation of sinusoidal components whose frequencies are integral multiples of the frequency of the excitation.
Headroom	Amount of increase about the working level which can be tolerated by an amplifier or tape etc. before the onset of overload distortion.
Helmholtz resonator	A resonator consisting of a cavity in a rigid structure communicating by a narrow neck or slit to the outside air. *Note.* The frequency of resonance is determined by the mass of air in the neck resonating in conjunction with the compliance of the air in the cavity.

Hertz	Unit of frequency (= 1 cycle per second).
Hill and dale recording	A mechanical or electromechanical recording in which the modulation is perpendicular to the surface of the recording medium.
Howlround (Howlback)	Instability in a sound reinforcement or other system when feedback is allowed to build up between the output and input.
Hum	Low-frequency noise at the a.c. mains frequency and its harmonics.
Hunting	Fault condition, where the transport mechanism or motor is alternatively reaching synchronous speed and falling back again in rhythmic fashion.
Hybrid transformer	Type of transformer having two secondary windings with minimum crosstalk between them; used to split signal to 'echo send', for example.
Hypercardioid	Class of microphone having a directivity pattern intermediate between cardioid and figure-of-eight.
IEC	International Electrotechnical Commission: international standards organization.
IEC 958	Digital audio interface standard: Type I (AES/EBU) for professional 2-channel; Type II (S/PDIF) for consumer/semi-pro.
Impedance	That property of an element, or a circuit, which restricts the flow of an alternating current. Measured in ohms.
Inductance	The magnitude of the capability of an element, or a circuit, to store magnetic energy when carrying a current. Measured in henrys.
Injection moulding	The process of forming a disc by injecting a liquefied plastic material into a die cavity.
Insulator	Substance or body that offers a very high resistance to the flow of an electric current and may therefore be used to separate two conductors from each other.
Intensity	Of a sound, the objective strength of the sound expressed in terms of the r.m.s. pressure in dynes per square centimetre (or bars)—more recently in newtons per square metre or pascals—or in terms of the power in watts per square metre (cf. Loudness).
Interface	(See Digital interface, IEC 958, MADI and MIDI).
Intermodulation distortion	A constituent of non-linearity distortion consisting of the occurrence, in the response to coexistent sinusoidal excitations, of sinusoidal components (intermodulation products) whose frequencies are sums or differences of the excitation frequencies or of integral multiples of these frequencies.

ISO	International Organization for Standardization.
Jack	A device used generally for terminating the permanent wiring of a circuit, access to which is obtained by the insertion of a plug.
Kilo (k)	Prefix signifying one thousand.
Künstkopf stereo	(See dummy head stereo.)
Lacquer disc	A disc for mechanical or electromechanical recording usually made of metal, glass, or fibre and coated with lacquer compound. It may be coated on one side (single-sided) or both (double-sided).
Land	The uncut surface between adjacent grooves.
Lateral recording	A mechanical or electromechanical recording in which the groove modulation is perpendicular to the motion of the recording medium and parallel to its surface.
Leader	Uncoated tape, usually white, spliced to the beginning of a recording tape.
Lead-in groove	The length of plain groove that starts at the periphery of the record and the pitch of which is greater than normal recording pitch.
Lead-out groove	The length of plain groove which succeeds the recorded surface and the pitch of which is greater than the normal recording pitch.
Level	Intensity of a continuous tone used for test purposes (measured in decibels by comparison with the standard reference level, or zero level, of 0.775 volt r.m.s. which is equivalent to a power of 1 milliwatt in a resistance of 600 ohms); colloquially, intensity of programme output or of noise. Hence 'level test'.
Limiter	Device for automatically limiting the volume during programme peaks so as to prevent accidental overmodulation of a transmitter or overloading of other equipment. (As the volume applied to the input of the limiter increases, the volume at the output increases linearly up to a certain critical point, after which a further increase in input volume produces a much smaller increase in output volume. When the applied volume exceeds the critical value, the device necessarily introduces amplitude distortion, but ought not to introduce excessive non-linear distortion.)
Lissajous figure	Locus of displacement resulting from two signals applied at right angles. The form of ellipse obtained indicates relative phase.

Live	1. Programme broadcast or recorded at the time of its performance to an audience (as distinct from a studio recording).
	2. Studio having a comparatively long reverberation time, and therefore tending to give a brilliant acoustic effect (cf. Dead studio).
	3. Connected to electrically sensitive part of a circuit.
Logarithmic scale	Scale of measurement in which an increase of one unit represents a tenfold increase in the quantity measured.
Loudness	An observer's auditory impression of the strength of a sound.
Loudspeaker	An electroacoustic transducer operating from an electrical system to an acoustical system and designed to radiate sound.
MADI (Multi-channel audio digital interface)	Carries up to 56 channels of digital audio on a single coaxial or fibre optic cable.
Magnetic field	Field of force in the vicinity of a permanent magnet or an electric circuit carrying current.
Magnetic tape	Recording medium in the form of a plastic tape (e.g. cellulose acetate, polyvinyl chloride, polyester), coated or impregnated with magnetizable powders.
Masking	1. The process by which the threshold of hearing of one sound is raised due to the presence of another.
	2. The increase, expressed in decibels, of the threshold of hearing of the masked sound due to the presence of the masking sound.
Master	A recording, in edited or approved form, from which copies can be made.
Matching transformer	A transformer designed for insertion between two circuits having different impedances to reduce the reflection at the junction and increase the power transferred.
Matrix	1. Generic term applied to all processing electroforms.
	2. Circuit designed to mix or separate electrical signals.
Matrix number	Serial number engraved or embossed on the lacquer or subsequently on the metal parts.
Matt backed tape	Type of recording tape with a dulled finish to facilitate proper winding, even on open hubs.
Mega (M)	Prefix signifying one million.
Memory	Device which can be made to store the value of a signal presented to it.
Micro (µ)	Prefix signifying one-millionth part.

Microgroove	A groove of which the unmodulated width at the top is less than 0.076 mm and which is intended to be played with a stylus having a tip radius less than 0.025 mm.
Micron (μm)	One-millionth of a metre.
Microphone	An electroacoustical transducer operating from an acoustical system to an electrical system.
MIDI (musical instrument digital interface)	A method of communication between musical instruments, computers, and audio equipment.
Milli (m)	Prefix signifying one-thousandth part.
Mixer	An apparatus by means of which the outputs of several channels can be faded up and down independently, selected individually, or combined at any desired relative volumes.
Modulation	The process by which the essential characteristics of a signal wave (the modulating wave) are impressed upon another wave (the carrier wave).
Modulation noise	In a recording and reproducing system. That part of the total noise which varies with signal amplitude.
Monaural hearing	The perception of sound by stimulation of a single ear.
Monitor	1. (Verb) To check the technical quality of a transmission.
	2. (Noun) An apparatus for comparing the technical quality of a programme at one point in the transmission chain with that of the same programme at another point and for giving an alarm if there is any significant difference between the two.
Monophonic (mono)	A transmission system in which, at some point, only a single signal exists.
Mother	Electroform produced from the master.
Moving coil	Of a microphone, loudspeaker, etc. depending for its action on the movement of a coil in a magnetic field.
Multiplexer	Circuit in which information from many sources is switched in a defined order to be sent to a single destination.
Multitrack master	A multitrack session tape prepared for mix-down.
Mumetal	An iron alloy used in tape heads and for magnetic screening.
NAB or NARTB	National Association of Radio and Television Broadcasters: American standards organization.
NAB operating level	Equivalent to 0 VU.
Neopilot head	Improvement on the original Piloton system of sync pulse in which two thin tracks are positioned at the cen-

	tre of the tape (where they are more reliable) recorded in opposite phase (push-pull) and so do not reproduce in a full-track scan.
Newton (N)	Unit of force.
Noise	Sound which is undesired by the recipient. Undesired electrical disturbances in a transmission channel or device may also be termed 'noise', in which case the qualification 'electrical' should be included unless it is self-evident.
Noise gate	(See Gate.)
Noise rating curves	An agreed set of empirical curves relating octave-band sound pressure level to the centre frequency of the octave bands, each of which is characterized by a 'noise rating' (NR), which is numerically equal to the sound pressure level at the intersection with the ordinate at 1,000 Hz. The 'noise rating' of a given noise is found by plotting the octave band spectrum on the same diagram and selecting the highest noise rating curve to which the spectrum is tangent.
Noise reduction	Process using gain control devices to improve the signal-to-noise ratio. (See dbx and Dolby.)
Non-linear distortion	That part of the distortion arising in a non-linear system (i.e. a system whose transmission properties are dependent on the instantaneous magnitude of the excitation) which is due to the non-linearity of the system.
Normalled jacks	Sockets on a jackfield having permanently wired interconnections.
Notch filter	Bandpass filter tuned to a very narrow frequency band.
Octave	1. A pitch interval of 2 : 1. 2. The tone whose frequency is twice that of the given tone.
Ohm (Ω)	Practical unit of resistance or impedance.
Ohm's Law	Fundamental generalization describing the flow of direct current in an electrical circuit, by stating that the magnitude of the current is proportional to the potential difference, provided the resistance is constant. The practical unit of potential difference, the volt, has been so chosen that 1 volt is produced across a resistance of 1 ohm when 1 ampere is flowing through it, so that: $$\text{Current (amperes)} = \frac{\text{p.d. (volts)}}{\text{resistance (ohms)}}$$
Omnidirectional (or Non-directional)	Equally sensitive in all directions.

Open circuit	Circuit which is not electrically continuous and through which current cannot therefore flow.
Operational amplifier	Ideal amplifier whose principal properties are infinite gain, bandwidth, and input impedance.
Optical sound track	A narrow band, usually on cinematograph film, which carries a photographic record of sound.
Original master	A fully prepared first-generation tape in final format (i.e. an edited session tape or mix-down of multitrack master).
Oscillator	Apparatus for producing sustained oscillations, usually by means of positive feedback between the output and the input of an amplifying valve or transistor.
Out-takes	Retained non-master material (edited or not edited).
Overtone	A component of a complex wave which may or may not be an integral multiple of the fundamental.
Pad	A network of resistors designed to introduce a fixed loss, or for impedance-matching purposes.
Pan	To shift a sound image as desired between the positions occupied by the loudspeakers in stereo or quadraphonic reproduction.
Pan-pot	(Panoramic potentiometer.) Ganged volume control used in panning.
Parabolic reflector	A light, rigid structure which reflects sounds to a focus at which a microphone is placed.
Parametric equalizer	Frequency correction device which allows both the frequency and the bandwidth of the boost or cut to be selected.
Pascal (Pa)	Unit of pressure = 1 newton per square metre.
Patch	To connect reserve equipment by means of flexible cords and plugs, so that the connections to the normal equipment are automatically broken by break-jacks.
PCM (pulse code modulation)	Widely used technique for digitally encoding audio signals.
Peak Programme Meter (PPM)	An instrument designed to measure the volume of programme in a sound channel in terms of the peaks averaged over a specified period.
Peak value	Of a varying quantity in a specific time interval. The maximum numerical value attained whether positive or negative.
Phantom power	Method of sending d.c. supply to a capacitor microphone by connecting the positive side to both signal wires of a balanced line and the negative to the screen.

Phase distortion	Form of distortion in which wave trains of different audio frequencies travel with different group velocities, owing to the characteristics of the medium (e.g. a land-line).
Phasing	Trick effect obtained by splitting a signal to two tape machines or networks and introducing a time delay in one of them (cf. Flanging).
Pilot tone	A signal wave, usually a single frequency, transmitted over the system to indicate or control its characteristics.
Pink noise	Random noise signal having the same amount of energy in each octave (cf. White noise).
Pitch	1. That attribute of auditory sensation in terms of which sound may be ordered on a scale related primarily to frequency.
	2. Number of grooves per inch.
Plane wave	A wave in which successive wavefronts are parallel planes.
Polar response	A plot of the variation in radiated energy with angle relative to the axis of the radiator. Similarly used for receivers and microphones.
Post sync	Recording of music, effects, or dialogue to synchronize with a previously filmed picture.
Potentiometer (colloquial: pot)	Potential divider or variable attenuator used, for example, to control the volume of a programme.
Pre-echo	The undesired transfer of a recorded signal from one groove to another.
	NB Post-echo can also occur.
Pre-emphasis	A deliberate change in the frequency response of a recording system for the purpose of improvement in signal-to-noise ratio, or the reduction of distortion (see also De-emphasis).
Prefade listening (PFL)	Listening to a programme before it is faded up for transmission or recording; technical facilities provided for this purpose.
Presence	Degree of forwardness in a voice or instrument achieved by boosting in the frequency region 2–8 kHz.
Pressing	Moulding of thermoplastic material produced from the stamper by the application of heat and pressure and subsequent cooling.
Pressure gradient operation	Method of responding to sound signals in which the sound wave has access to both sides of a microphone diaphragm.

Pressure operation	Method of responding to sound signals in which the sound wave has access to only one side of a microphone diaphragm.
Print-through	The undesired transfer of recorded signal from one layer to another of the recording medium when these layers are stored on spools.
Production master	An equalized or otherwise modified copy of the original master for production purposes.
Proximity effect	Increase in low-frequency response which occurs at distances less than about 1 m from pressure-gradient-operated microphones.
Public Address (PA)	Arrangements of microphones, amplifiers, and loudspeakers used to reinforce speech or music over a large audience area.
Pulse code modulation (PCM)	Modulation in accordance with a pulse code.
Q-factor	A measure of the sharpness of resonance.
Quadraphony	System of recording and reproduction using four channels and four loudspeakers in an attempt to recreate a 360° soundfield around the listener.
Quantization	A process in which the range of values of a wave is divided into a finite number of smaller subranges, each of which is represented by an assigned or 'quantized' value within the subrange.
Radio microphone	Type of microphone incorporating a small radio transmitter to give reception at short distances without the need for cables.
RAM (random-access memory)	Memory designed so that the location or 'address' of a given piece of information is independent of the information stored.
Recording head	A transducer whereby the state or configuration of the recording medium is changed in conformity with the signal.
Recovery time	Time taken for a limiter or compressor to return to its quiescent state on removal of the high-level signal.
Rectifier	Device for transforming an alternating current into a direct one.
Reduction	The mixing from a multitrack recording to produce a mono, stereo, or quadraphonic recording as a production master.
Reflection	A return of energy due to the wave striking some discontinuity in its supporting medium.

Register	Device which can store a certain number of bits, usually only temporarily (cf. Memory).
Relay	A device, operated by an electric current, and causing by its operation abrupt changes in an electrical circuit (making or breaking the circuit, changing of the circuit connections, or variation in the circuit characteristics).
Release time	(See Recovery time.)
Reproducing head	A transducer whereby the signal is re-created from a recording.
Resistance	That property of a substance which restricts the flow of electricity through it, associated with conversion of electrical energy into heat. Measured in ohms.
Resonance	A condition resulting from the combination of the reactances of a system, in which a response to a sinusoidal stimulus of constant magnitude reaches a maximum at a particular frequency.
Reverberation	In an enclosure. The persistence of sound due to repeated reflections at the boundaries.
Reverberation time	Of an enclosure, for sound of a given frequency. The period of time required for the sound pressure in the enclosure, initially in a steady state, to decrease, after the source is stopped, to one-millionth of its initial value, i.e. by 60 dB.
Re-voicing	Post-synchronization in the same language as the original but with a different artist.
Ribbon microphone	Type of microphone in which currents are generated by the movements of a metal ribbon suspended in a magnetic field.
Ring modulator	Device which may be used to produce sum and difference frequencies of two signals applied to the input.
Rise time	The interval between the instants at which the instantaneous value of a pulse or of its envelope first reaches specified lower and upper limits, namely 10% and 90% of the peak value unless otherwise stated.
ROM (read-only memory)	Memory having fixed contents which cannot be altered, used to hold microprocessor programs, tables, etc.
Root mean square (r.m.s.)	Of a varying quantity. The square root of the mean value of the squares of the instantaneous values of the quantity. In the case of a periodic variation, the mean is taken over one period.
Rumble	Low-frequency vibration mechanically transmitted to the recording or reproducing turntable and superimposed on the reproduction.

Rushes	First prints (usually made overnight or at speed) from any new material for a film. Usually screened in a preview theatre.
Safety master	Copy of a master recording made for protection purposes.
Sampling frequency (or sampling rate)	Number of times per second that samples are taken of an analogue signal in a DAC (e.g. 44.1 kHz, 48 kHz, etc.).
Scale distortion	Loss of fidelity when the sounds from a large concert hall, for example, are reproduced in a small listening room.
Scroll	Portion of the recorded surface where the groove pitch has been increased to mark the separation of two successive bands of recording.
Sel-sync	The adding of live sound to a spare track to synchronize with recordings on a multitrack tape or film by the temporary use of other tracks of the record head for replay.
Sensitivity	Of an electroacoustic transducer. The ratio of the response to the stimulus under specified conditions. *Note.* This is usually expressed in decibels relative to a reference sensitivity.
Separation	Degree to which individual microphones reject unwanted voices or instruments and give effective control of the desired source.
Session tape	A reel of original recorded material: can include both master material and out-takes.
Signal-to-noise ratio	The ratio of the magnitude of the signal to that of the noise, usually expressed in decibels. *Note.* This ratio is expressed in many different ways, for example, in terms of peak values in the case of impulsive noise and in terms of root-mean-square values in the case of random noise, the signal being assumed sinusoidal (see also Weighted noise).
Sine wave	Waveform of an alternating quantity which varies according to a simple harmonic law, so that the amplitude at any instant is proportional to the sine of the quantity: $2\pi \times$ frequency $\times$ time (the time being reckoned from the instant when the quantity is zero and becoming positive in sign).
Slate	Term used for recording spoken 'take' numbers or cues on tape by analogy with the chalked cues on a film clapperboard.
Slope	1. Steepness of the sloping part of a response curve: usually stated in dB/octave. 2. A plotted slope derived from input and output amplitudes and stated as a ratio (e.g. 1 : 1 a conventional amplifier, 20 : 1 a limiter).

SMPTE (Society of Motion Picture and Television Engineers)	American society responsible for the SMPTE ('simty') video timecode using an eight-digit clock at 30 frames per second.
SMPTE/EBU timecode	European version of SMPTE timecode based on 25 frames per second.
Solenoid	Form of electromagnet permitting remote operation of switches etc.
Sound pressure level (SPL)	The sound pressure level of a sound, in decibels, is equal to twenty times the logarithm to the base 10 of the ratio of the r.m.s. sound pressure to the reference sound pressure. In case of doubt, the reference sound pressure should be stated. In the absence of any statement to the contrary, the reference sound pressure in air is taken to be $2 \times 10^{-5} \mathrm{N/m^2}$ (= 20 μPa).
Sound reinforcement	(See Public Address.)
Splicing tape	Special dry adhesive tape used in butt editing of tape recordings.
Spot effects (Hand effects)	Sound effects created in a studio where the scene of which they form part is taking place.
Stamper	Metal negative, produced by electroforming from the positive or mother and used for the production of pressings.
Standing waves	An interference pattern characterized by stationary nodes and antinodes.
Stereophony	A process designed to produce the illusion of a spatial distribution of sound sources, by the use of two or more channels of information.
Stripe	A narrow band of magnetic material applied as a coating on cinematograph film and which carries the sound record. (Further similar bands are frequently applied to the film for control and other purposes.)
Stylus	The needle, generally diamond or sapphire-tipped, in a cutterhead or pickup cartridge.
Subjective	As judged by the senses: opposite of objective, i.e. measured.
Swarf	(American: chip.) The material removed from the recording blank by the cutting stylus.
Swinger	Record in which the hole is not at the exact centre of the groove spiral.
Sync facility	Feature on some tape machines permitting individual tracks of the record head to be switched to act as replay heads, for example to provide synchronous foldback to artists during overdubbing.

Synthesizer	Device used in electronic music giving flexible control of the pitch, timing, and tonal quality of signals.
Take	Recording of whole or part of a musical item. Thus a long work or one which is difficult to perform might consist of many 'takes' to be edited together.
Talkback	A circuit enabling spoken directions to be given from a studio control cubicle or television control room, or from a production panel to a studio, or other programme source, for the purpose of directing a performance or rehearsal.
Timbre	That subjective quality of a sound which enables a listener to judge that two sounds having the same loudness and pitch are dissimilar.
Timecode	Time reference in hours, minutes, seconds, frames, and bits: used for synchronizing, computer-assisted mixing, and editing.
Time constant	Shorthand method of specifying the values of resistor and capacitor to be used in a frequency correction network by reference to the time taken for the voltage across the capacitor to fall to 37% (approx.) of its original value through the resistor. Equals the product of R and C: stated in microseconds (μs).
Tracing distortion	Non-linear distortion due to the different shapes of the cutting and reproducing styli.
Tracking error	The difference between the curved path followed by a pivoted pickup and the straight radial path of the cutter.
Tracks	Regions of the tape of specified width scanned by the tape heads.
Transducer	A device designed to receive oscillatory energy from one system and to supply related oscillatory energy to another.
Transferring	Copying by re-recording on a different medium.
Transformer	Component having two coils of wire, the primary and secondary, whose length (number of turns) are in a fixed ratio to permit voltages to be stepped up or down and circuit impedances to be matched for maximum power transfer.
Transient	A phenomenon which occurs during the change of a system from one steady state to another.
Transmitter	Equipment for converting the audio-frequency electric currents corresponding to a programme into a modulated carrier wave which can be radiated by an aerial.
Truth table	Convenient method of tabulating the output condition of a gate or system for every combination of inputs.

U-matic	A ¾-inch rotary head videotape format used for storage of digital audio.
Unidirectional	(See Cardioid microphone.)
Variable-area	System of optical recording in which the modulation varies the area through which light is transmitted.
Variable-density	System of optical recording where the width is constant but the transmission factor is varied. This system has largely fallen into disuse with the increased popularity of colour film.
Varigroove	The technique of varying the groove spacing in relation to displacement amplitude of the cutting stylus.
VCA (voltage-controlled amplifier)	Amplifier whose gain is controlled by an external d.c. voltage.
Velocity	Distance travelled in unit time (e.g. velocity of sound in air at 20°C = 344 metres per second; velocity of electro-magnetic waves (light and radio) = 300,000,000 m/s).
Velour effect	Difference in performance of a magnetic tape when it is run in the opposite direction; caused by asymmetrical distribution of the magnetic particles in the coating.
Volt	Practical unit of electrical pressure or of electromotive force, of such a magnitude that if a pressure of one volt is applied across a resistance of one ohm, a current of one ampere will flow (see Ohm's Law).
Volume	Intensity of programme, or of noise, expressed in decibels relative to a standard reference volume or zero volume, according to the readings of a programme meter, the characteristics of which must be specified in order to define the volume accurately (see also Level and VU).
VU (Volume Unit)	A unit for expressing the magnitude of a complex electric wave such as that corresponding to speech or music. The volume in volume units is equal to the number of deci-bels by which the wave differs from a reference volume.
VU meter	A volume indicator the specification of which is given in American Standard 'Volume Measurements of Electrical Speech and Program waves', C16.5-1942.
Watt	Practical unit of electrical power equal to one joule per second. (In a d.c. circuit the number of watts is equal to the product of the volts and amperes; in an a.c. circuit it is equal to the product of the volts and amperes multi-plied by the power factor.)
Waveform	The shape of the graph representing the successive val-ues of a varying quantity.

Wavelength	Of a sinusoidal plane progressive wave. The perpendicular distance between two wavefronts in which the phases differ by one complete period. Symbol λ. *Note.* The wavelength is equal to the wave velocity divided by the frequency.
Weber	Unit of magnetic flux.
Weighted noise	The noise measured within the audio-frequency band using an instrument which has a frequency-selective characteristic.
White noise	Random noise signal having the same energy level at all frequencies (cf. Pink noise).
Wow	(See Flutter.)
Zero level	Standard of reference used when expressing levels. (The zero level generally chosen is one milliwatt, which corresponds to a voltage of 0.775 volt r.m.s. across a resistance of 600 ohms.)

Index